CEMETERY RECORDS

OF

BEDFORD COUNTY

TENNESSEE

REVISED

1985

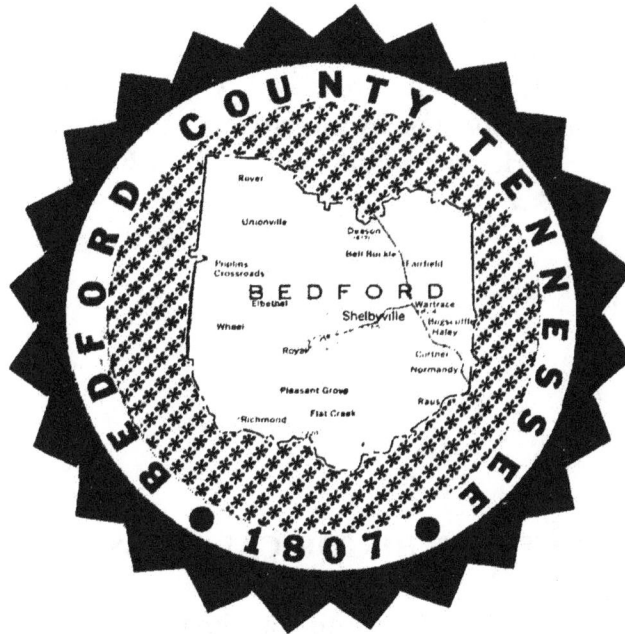

COMPILED

BY

HELEN C. & TIMOTHY R. MARSH
SHELBYVILLE, TENNESSEE

Southern Historical Press, Inc.
Greenville, South Carolina

SOUTHERN HISTORICAL PRESS, INC.
PO BOX 1267
Greenville, South Carolina 29602

ISBN #978-0-89308-723-8

Printed in the United States of America

CONTENTS

ABBREVIATIONS AND EXPLANATIONS

A complete set (14) of Geological Survey Maps, showing all Bedford County, Tennessee, appears in back of this book. The Maps are numbered # 1 thru # 14.

Each cemetery listed in this publications has an assigned number and it will appear on the appropriate Map, showing the exact cemetery location.

A Section Map, made of Willow Mount Cemetery, is located within this book, between pages 255 and 256. It will help to locate graves in each Section of the cemetery.

The symbols *, **, ***, are explained with each cemetery listing.

() & [] inserts by compilers

TM - Temporary Markers

SOR - Soldier of the American Revolution

The compilers accept no responsibility for the absolute accuracy of the material contained in the inserts in this book. Those of a historical nature are well documented. Those of a genealogical nature probably contain an error factor usually found in all first and second hand genealogical records, however every effort has been made to assure the accuracy of the inserted material.

by - Authors

FOREWORD

We are pleased to present this collection of BEDFORD COUNTY, TENNESSEE CEMETERY RECORDS, in hope that it will prove helpful to all who are interested in the final resting place of loved ones, friends and ancestors.

During the past eight years, while in quest of the lost cemeteries in Bedford County, we have been chased by belligerent bulls, dogs and all kinds of animals, there were plenty of times we were unnerved by snakes and rodents, we have waded creeks and muddy branches, crawled through brush, poison ivy, briers and thick and dense vegetation. We have walked many miles, ridden on wagons and tractors, in the constant search for all cemeteries. Many times after much walking and fence climbing, we were distressed to find a few unmarked graves in an unnamed family cemetery, also many times we were exhilarated to find the marked graves of Pioneer Settlers who had contributed much to the growth and development of Bedford County.

Many of the old Family Graveyards have completely disappeared to make way for cultivation, or some other reason. It was amazing to hear over and over again the story of how so many of the old family graveyards were destroyed by tenants or hired hand without the knowledge of the owner, of course, and if the owner did admit to it, well .... "It was probably just an old Indian Graveyard".

It seems the quickest way to deface a cemetery is to put it in pasture. Cattle in a cemetery can do more damage in a few short weeks than years of exposure to the elements and vegetation.

We can only wish that more of the old graves had been marked with inscribed markers. We realize that the lack of finances was in so many cases the reason that commercial markers were not erected but a thoughtful descendant or friend with only a hammer and a chisel by inscribing a few words on a native limestone or slate rock could have contributed so much to this branch of genealogy and history.

We have inspected each and every fieldstone for any visable sign of inscriptions, initials or even dates and when so found, we copied and included in this publication. A number of readers will find that the dates on some of the markers do not correspond with the dates recorded in Family Records, etc. We must remember that many times the markers were erected years after the deceased person was buried and the lapse of time made errors very common, also the stone cutter was subject to human error. Those entries taken from Newspaper Obituary and other records were also subject to error, often names or initials of the deceased and or survivors were listed incorrectly and occasionally the name of the cemetery was listed in error.

The names of many of the family cemeteries is utter confusion in itself, having changed names time and time again down through the years. Quite often the cemetery will bear a name that has no relationship to the persons buried within the graveyard.

We have to the best of our ability, tried to locate and record all the cemeteries in Bedford County. We realize, we have probably missed a few of them.

We are so grateful to so many people for their interest and help in this project. We wish to thank the following people for their great help: Franklin Blanton, who helped in locating and copying many and helped in so many ways, we shall always be grateful to him and his wife Minnie Ellen Blanton. To Jerry Wayne Cook, who furnished us with many cemeteries that he had copied, but no longer exist. To others a Special Thanks, Mary Bass, Wayne Lents, Anderson Joyce, Gladys Farris and Fount Farris, Florence Patterson, and a Special Thanks to our son, Leslie Devons Marsh and our daughter Marsha Markiewicz who helped in so many ways.

It is our earnest desire that this publication may be a significant contribution to a part of BEDFORD COUNTY History and may benefit the present as well as future generations.

Helen Crawford Marsh
Timothy Richard Marsh
Shelbyville, Tennessee
1976 - 1985 Revised

CEMETERY INDEX

MAPS

The following maps are U. S. G. S. Maps with numbered
indicators affixed by the compilers to help in locating
the various cemeteries. They are very detailed maps and
show each house, barn, silo, etc... that was standing
when the area was mapped by T. V. A. They are extremely
accurate, having been produced from aerial photograph.
They were not included in this publication to be used as
a detailed study of the county but rather as a way of
accurately locate the cemeteries. Admittedly they are a
little small for tired old eyes but, in order to utilize
them in this book, it was necessary to reduce them to
8½ x 11 from the original 22 x 27 inches. If a more
detailed study of a particular area is desired, the
original maps in color may be purchased for a nominal fee
from either the Tennessee Valley Authority in Chattanooga,
Tennessee or from the U. S. G. S., Reston, Virginia.

MARSH HISTORICAL PUBLICATIONS
SHELBYVILLE,TENNESSEE

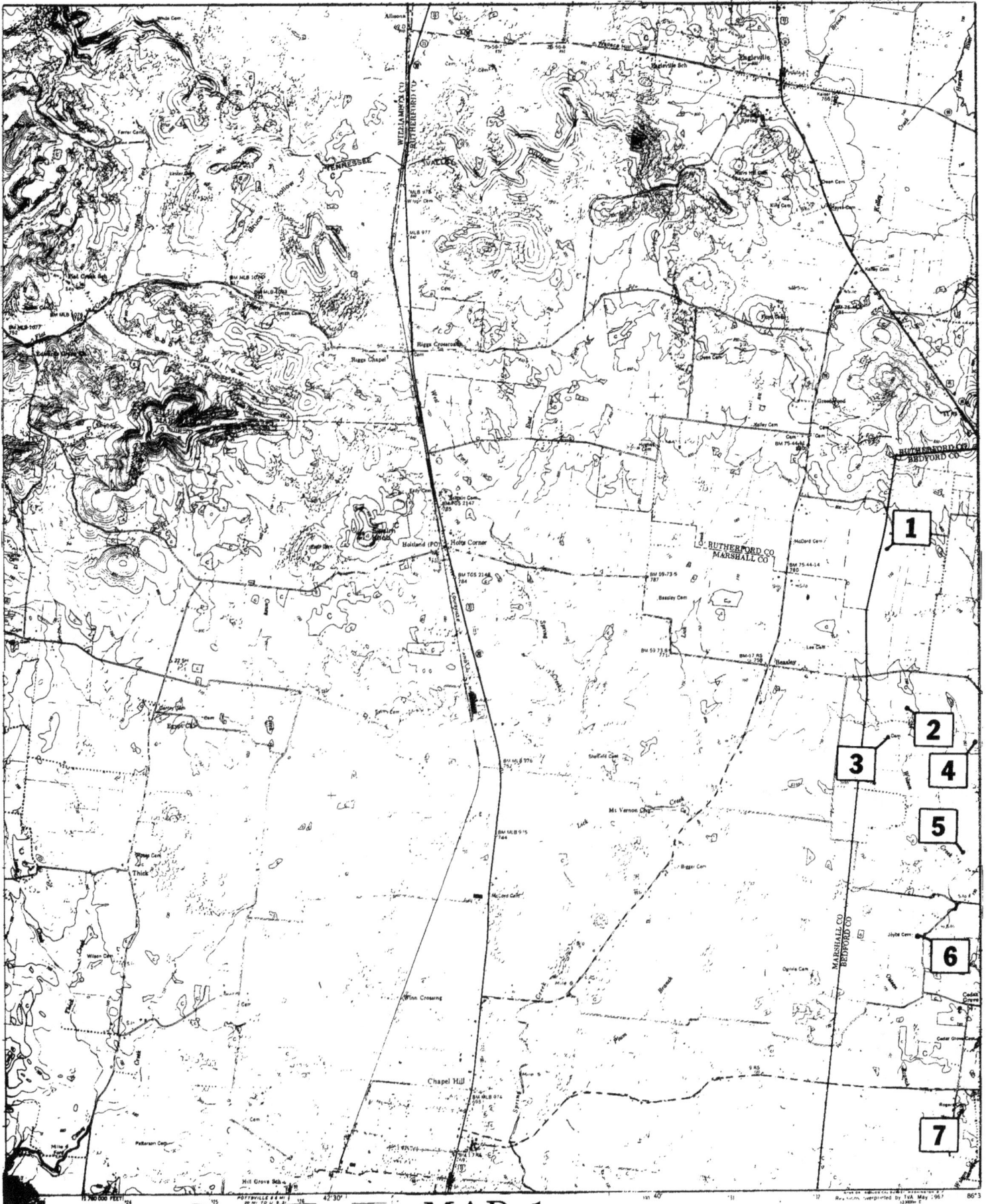

MAP 1

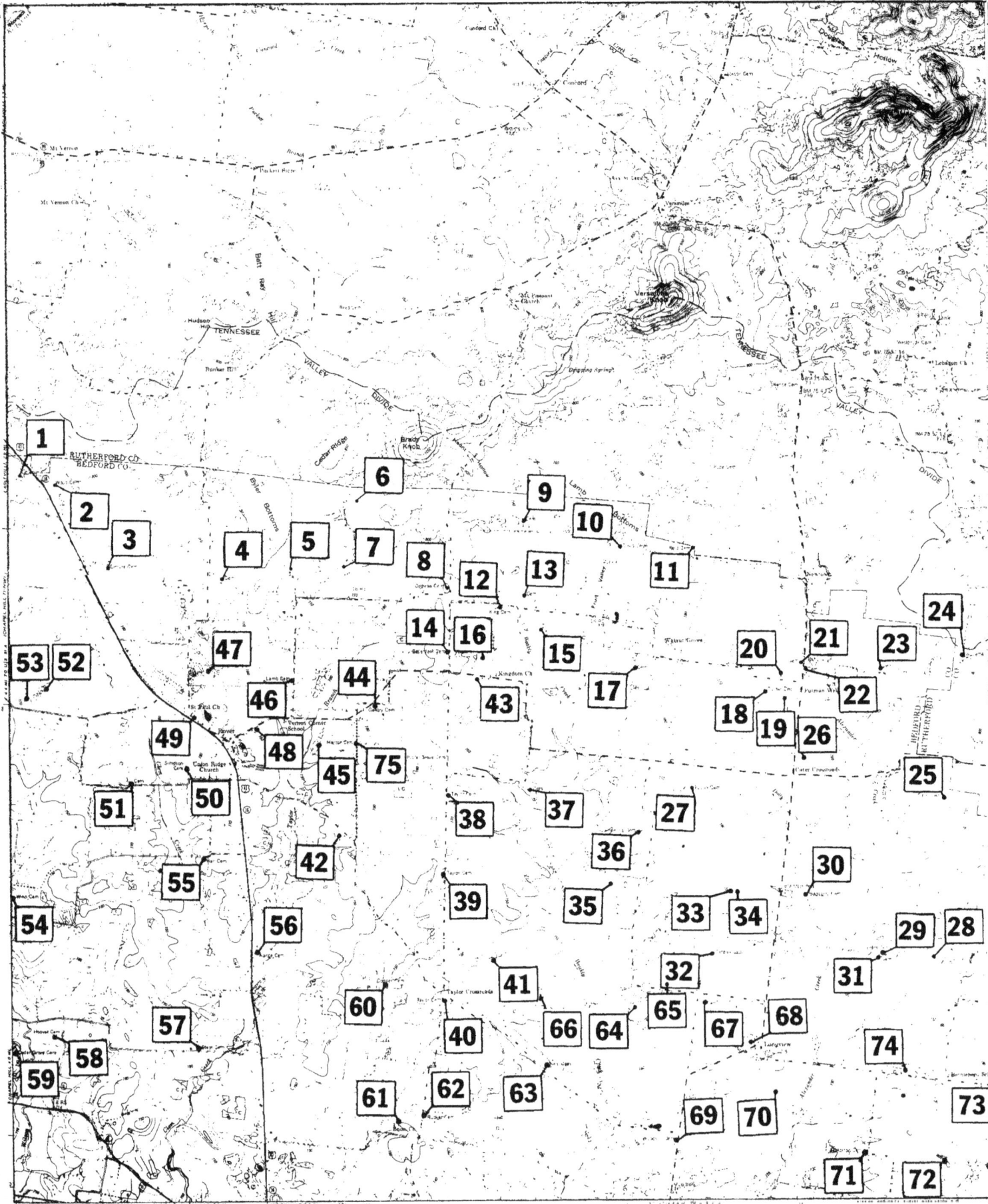

MAP 2

MAP 3

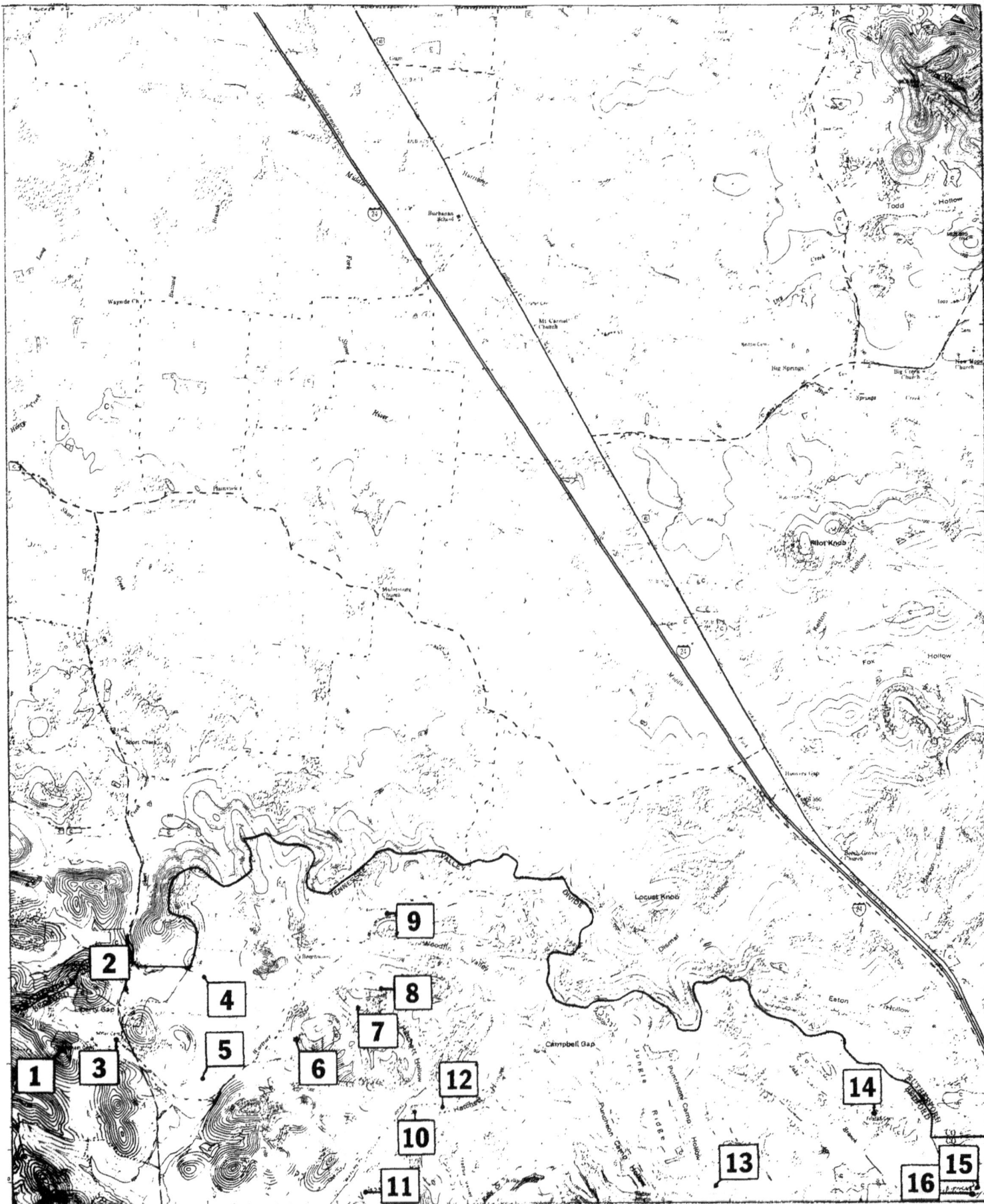

MAP 4

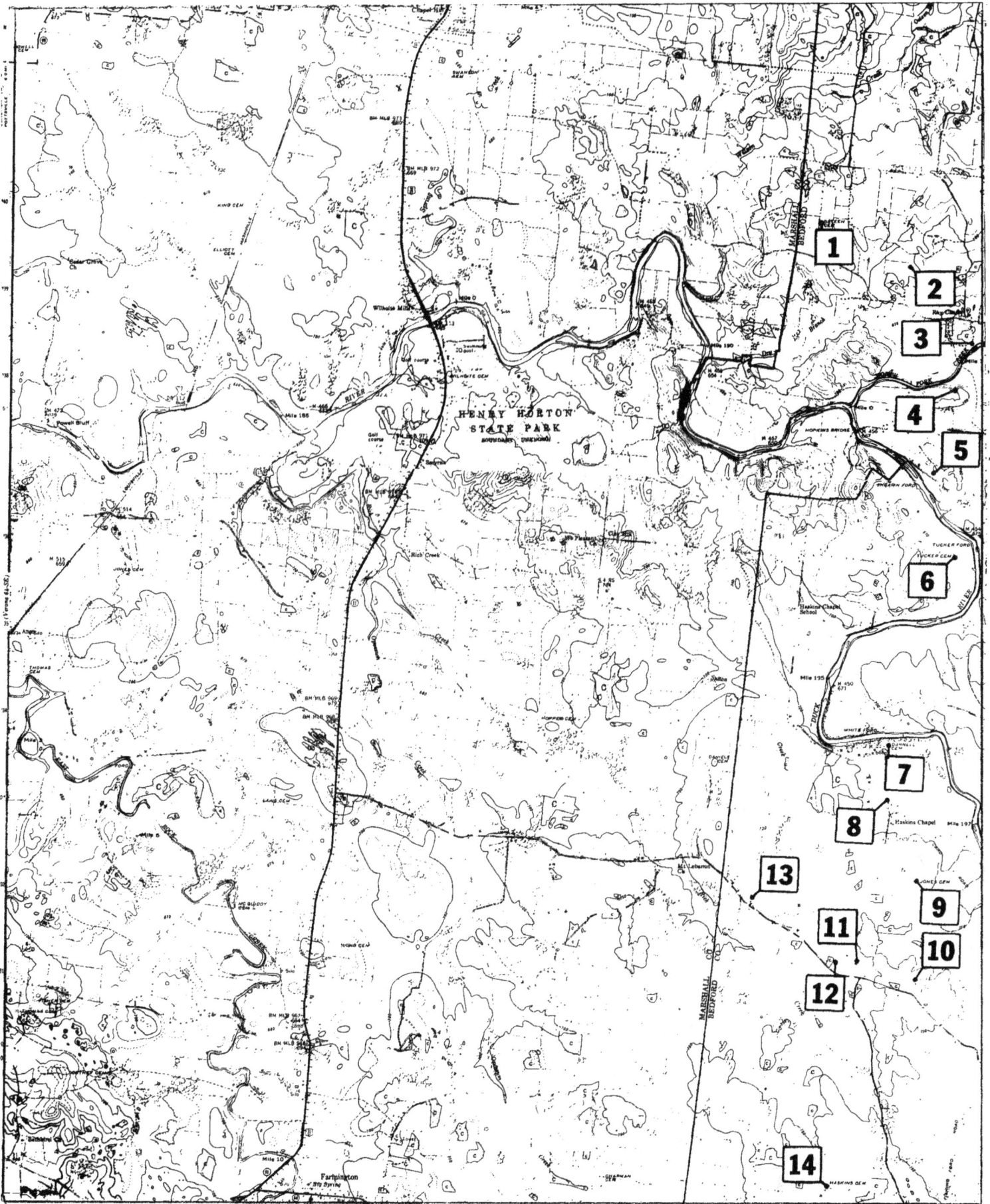

MAP 5

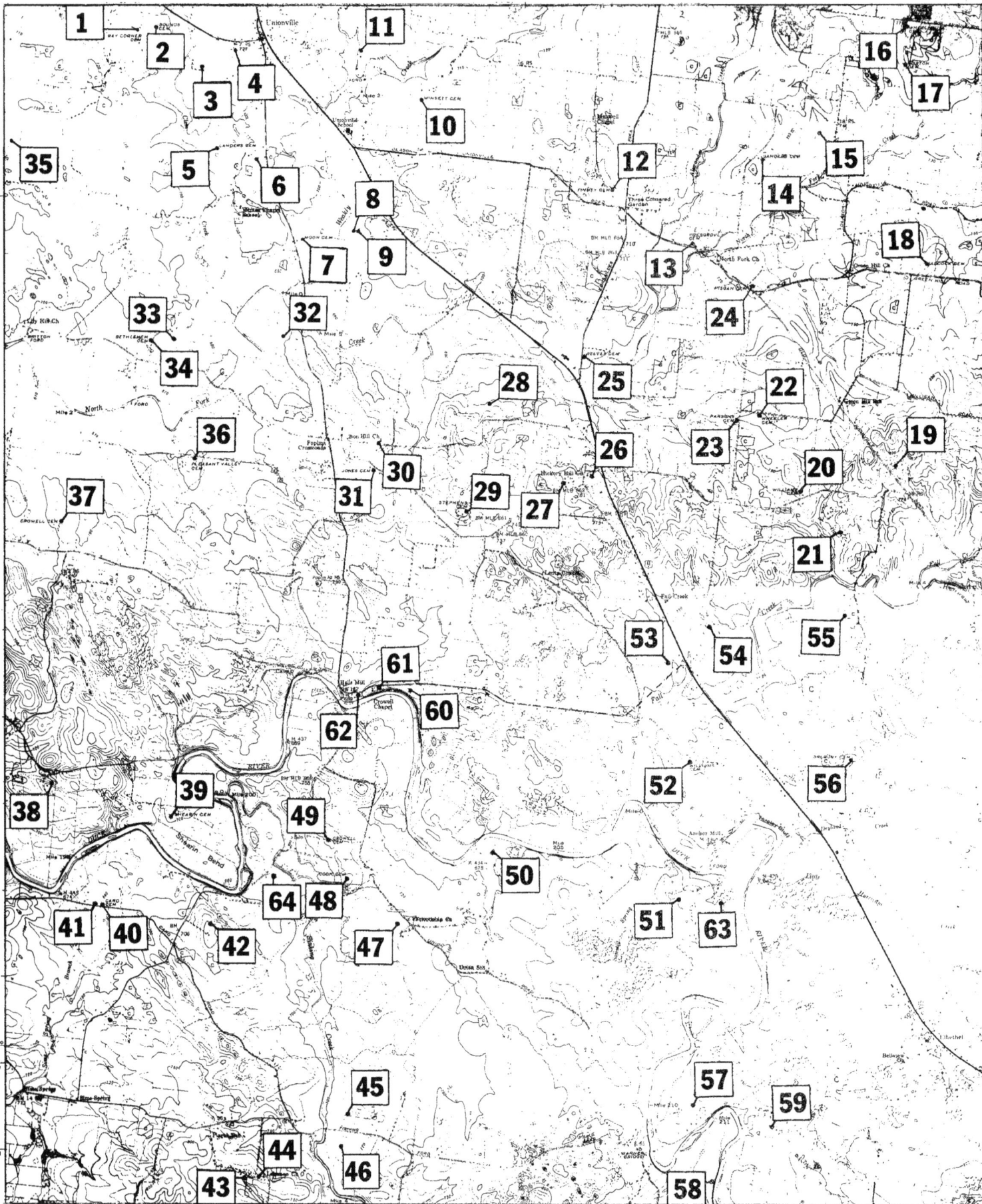

1
2
4
3
11
16
17
35
5
6
10
12
15
14
8
9
7
13
18
32
33
34
24
25
28
22
36
23
19
30
37
31
29
27
26
20
21
53
54
55
61
60
62
52
56
39
49
38
50
64
48
41
40
42
47
51
63
45
57
59
44
46
58

MAP 6

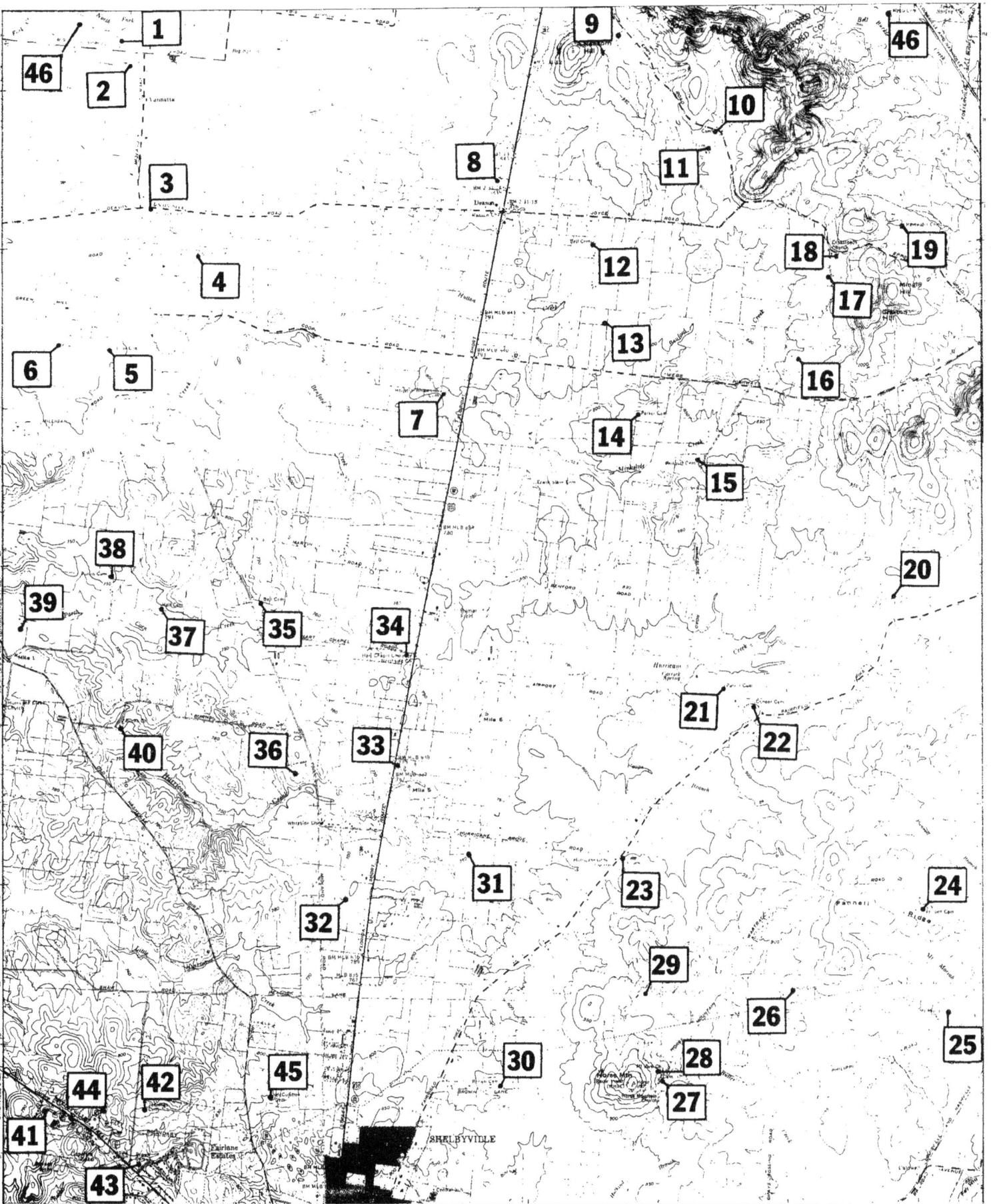

MAP 7

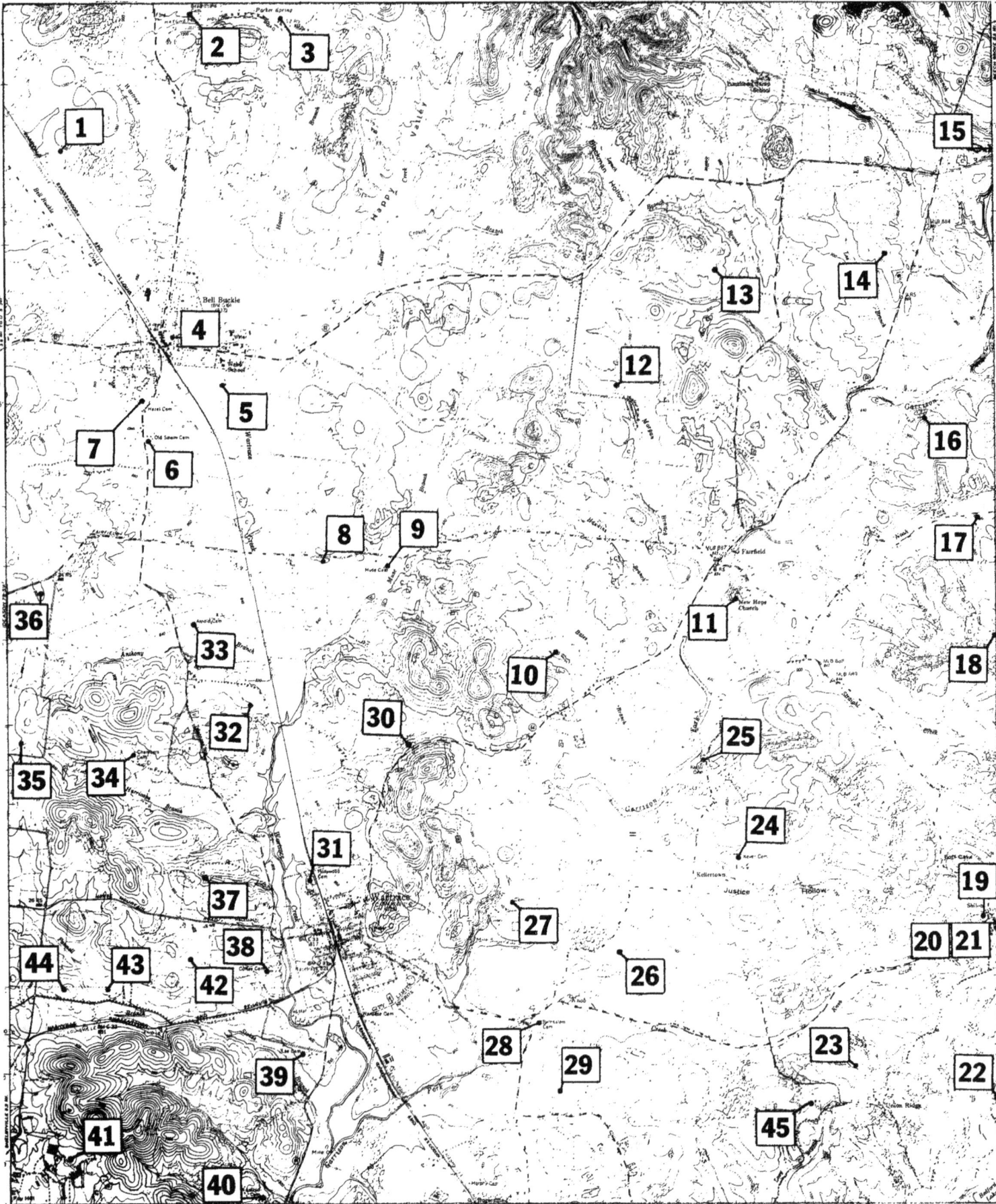

MAP 8

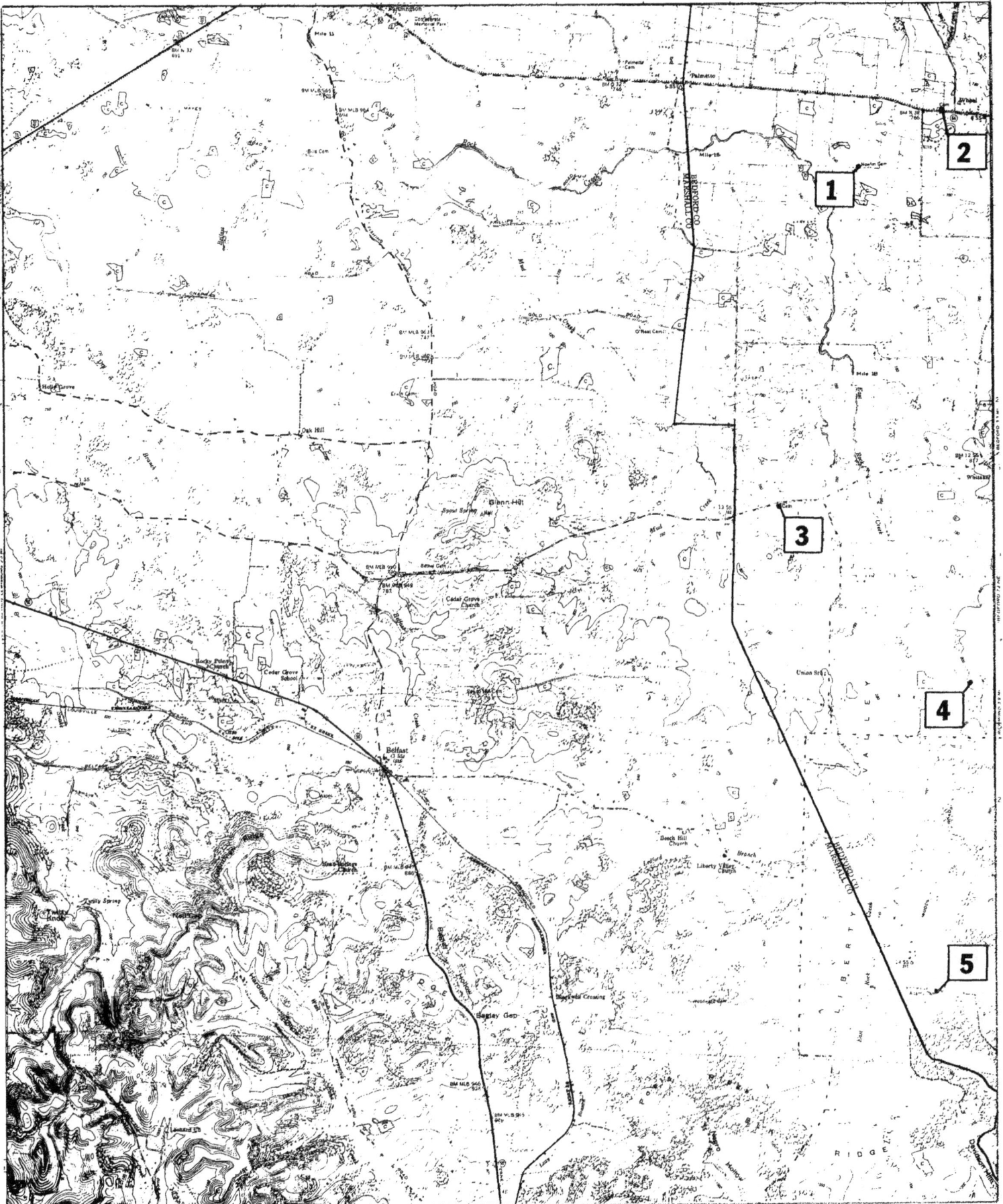

MAP 9

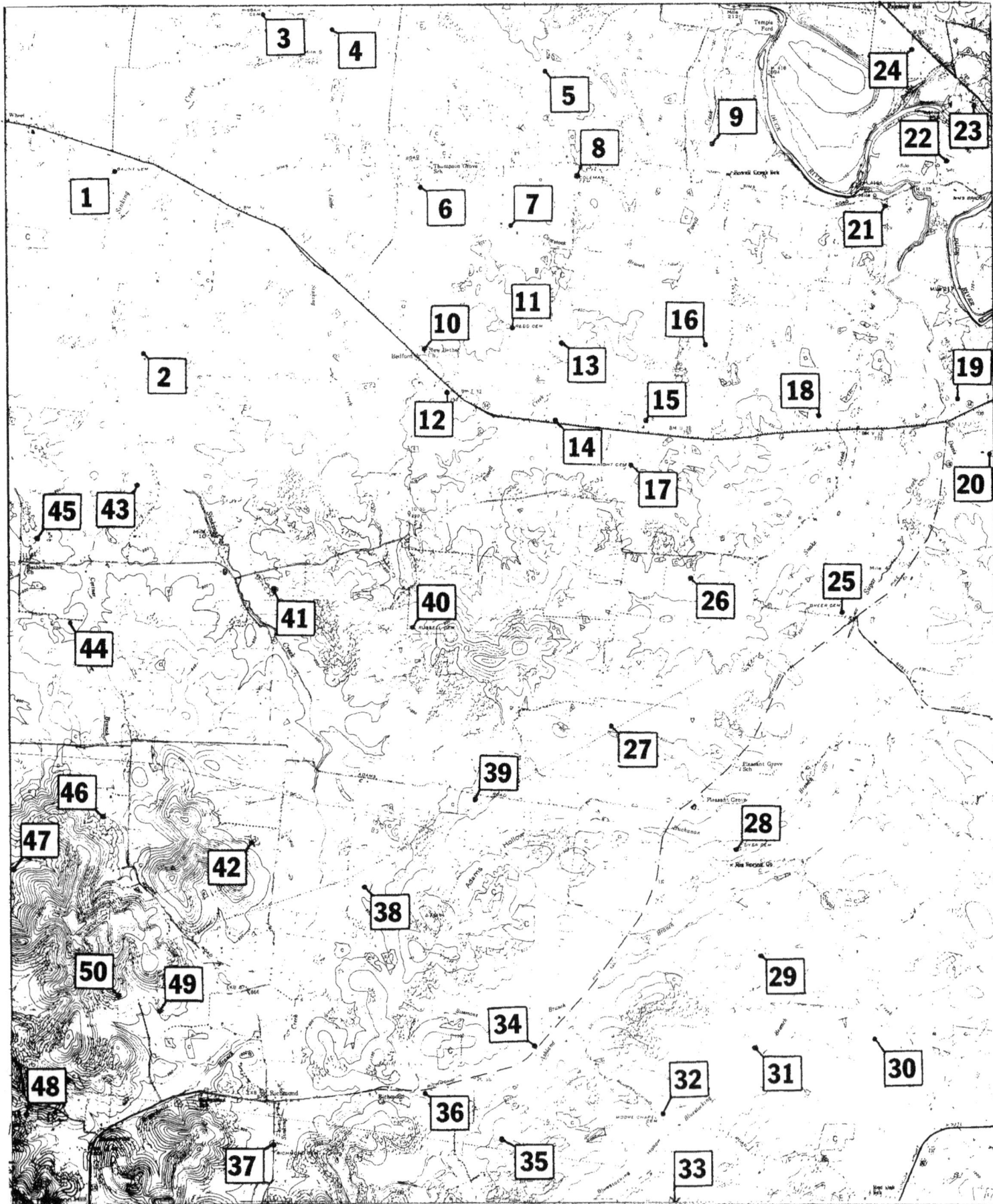

MAP 10

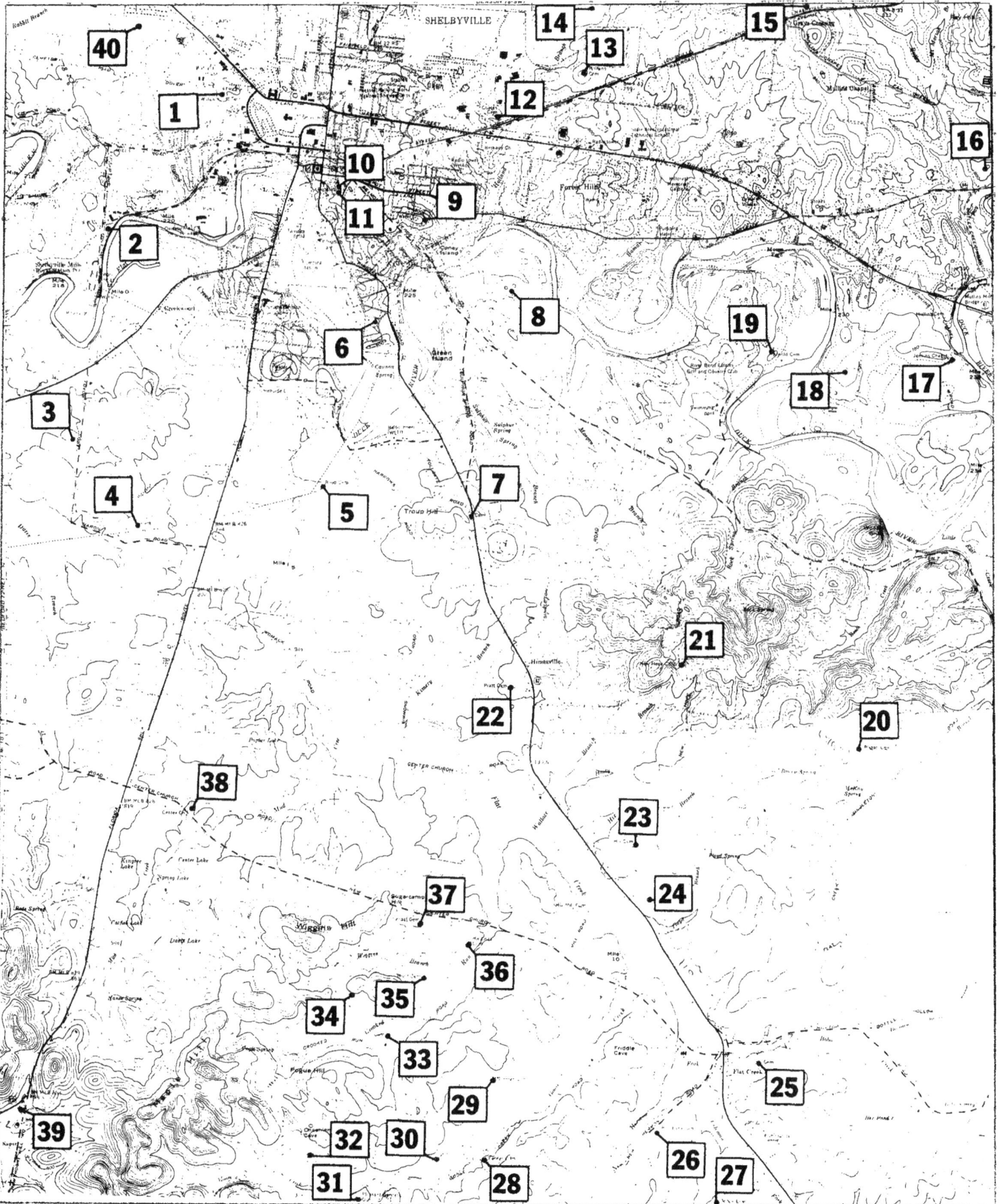

SHELBYVILLE

40

1

14

13

15

12

16

10

9

11

2

8

19

6

18

17

3

7

4

5

21

20

22

23

38

24

37

36

35

34

33

29

32

30

39

31

28

26

27

25

MAP 11

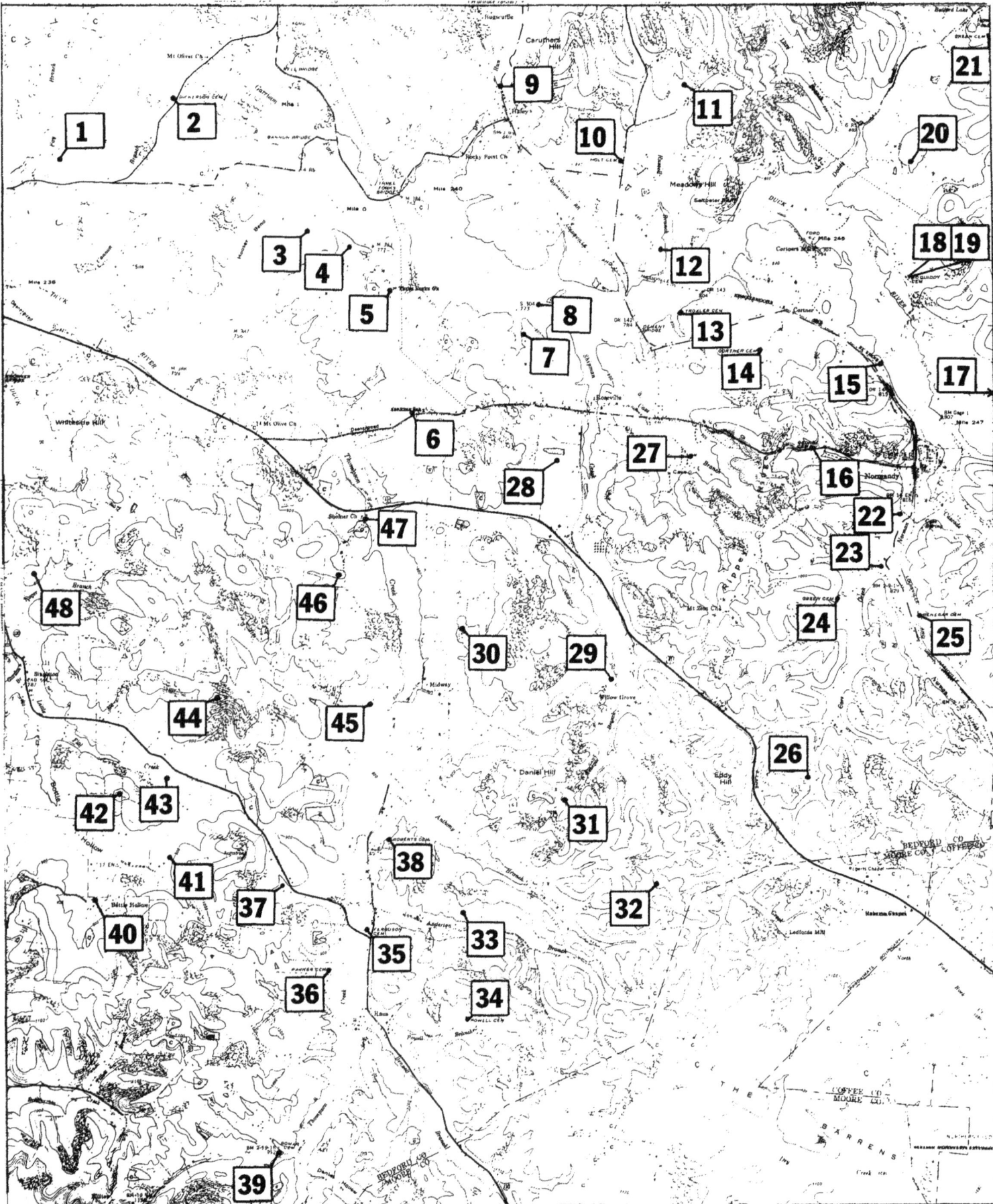

1
2
9
11
21
10
20
3
4
5
12
18 **19**
8
7
13
14
15
17
6
27
28
16
22
23
47
46
48
30
29
24
25
44
45
26
42
43
31
41
38
37
32
40
35
33
36
34
39

MAP 12

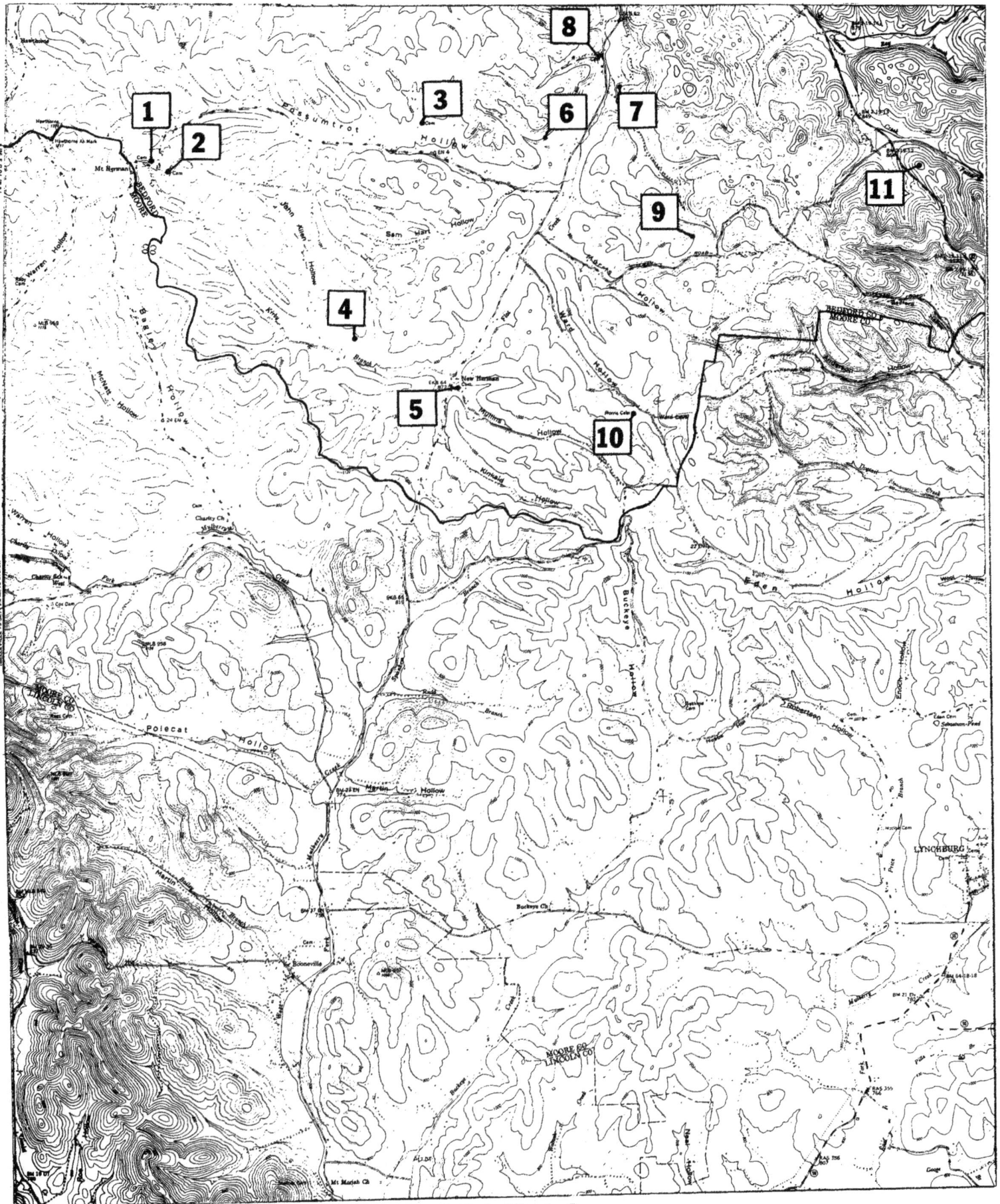

MAP 13

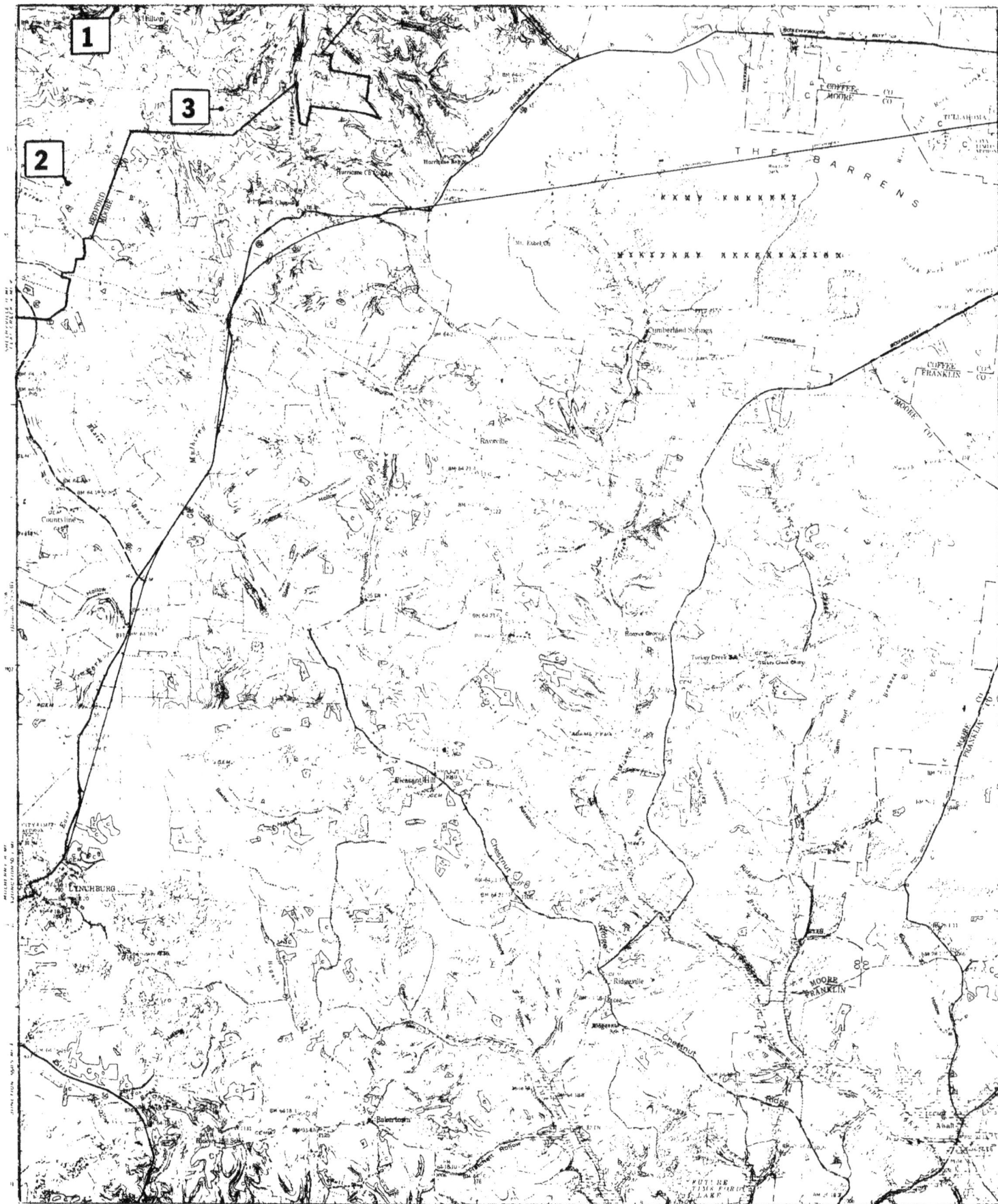

MAP 14

1 GARRETT CEMETERY   Map # 1
Located about 1½ miles West of the Glider-port,
North of Rover, Tn.

Talitha C., wife of
B. G. Drumwright
Dec 22, 1829
Jun 26, 1869
age: 39y, 6m, 4d.

Nancy Garrett
Nov. 9, 1781
Jan 19, 1814
age: 34y, _m, 10d.

Presley J. Drumright
born Mar 16, 1851
departed this life
(broken away)
(childs grave)

1 adult vault beside of
Nancy Garrett, but the
top has been removed.

Presley Jones
Jul 10, 1802
Dec 15, 1867
age: 65y, 5m, 5d.

Doritha C., wife of
Presley Jones
Feb 1, 1808
Jan 17, 1866

2 LITTLE CEMETERY   Map # 1
Located about 2 miles West of Rover, Tn.

Elizabeth McCuistion, dau of
Robert & Charity McCuistion
Jun 22, 1812, died of
Consumption Aug 3, 1834
age: 22y, 7m, 7d.
    by-Thos. McCuistion

Benjamin Little
(no dates)
(In 1850 census: born ca 1815
died after 1850)

Sarah Power
died: 43 years

This Cemetery is very large
and many graves with fieldstones, no inscriptions.

3 JARRELL CEMETERY   Map # 1
Located about 1½ miles West of Rover, Tn.

J. W. Jones
Sep 29, 1837
Jan 28, 1920
&
M. L. Jones
1839
Jul 23, 1895

Mary Sue Jarrell
Aug 3, 1873
Dec 20, 1969
&
Cora W. Jarrell
Jun 10, 1866
Aug 10, 1958
(Sisters)

Ridlie M. Terry
Aug 27, 1909
Dec 6, 1919

Julia F. Medling
Feb 8, 1907
Dec 8, 1920

W. B. Jarrell
May 18, 1889
1974 (TM) &
Roberta K. Jarrell
Jul 18, 1896
Apr 9, 1940

J. M. Rogers
Nov 16, 1873
Jun 20, 1956
&
Thomas Franklin Rogers
Aug 17, 1901
Dec 7, 1918
&
Lula J. Rogers
Apr 18, 1872
Feb 16, 1960

Martha E. Jarrell
1937

Mary B. Jarrell
Feb 20, 1891-Aug 28, 1965

B. F. Jarrell
Oct 27, 1834
Sep 6, 1918
&
Nancy Jarrell
Jun 22, 1840
Mar 3, 1934

Julius S. Jarrell
Feb 21, 1861
Jul 9, 1894
&
Mary E. Jarrell
Jan 2, 1863
Jan 10, 1936

4 THOMASON CEMETERY   Map # 1
Located about 2 miles West of Rover, Tn.

William T. Thomason
Jun 14, 1800
Oct 30, 1859

Mrs. Ona Thomason
Jan 12, 1799
Sep 24, 1873

George W. Thomason
1875-1912

J. S. Thomason
Oct 22, 1836
Aug 21, 1917

Mrs. M. C. Thomason
Oct 16, 1840
Nov 28, 1904

Margaret Jane Thomason
Jan. 11, 1888
July 26, 1911

A. T. Thomason
Feb 22, 1832
Feb 22, 1902

Sandusky, infant son of
A. T. Thomason
(no dates)

Lizzie Sharp
Aug 23, 1840
Jul 3, 1907
&
Floy Sharp
Jan 14, 1874
Feb 26, 1911
&
Clayton Yarbrough
Nov 6, 1900
May 31, 1902

5 GARRETT CEMETERY   Map # 1
Located on Bullock's Farm, West of Rover, Tn.

Mrs. Faney Cheatham
Sep 12, 1788
Mar 11, 1855
NOTE: Her husband is buried
in the Old City Cemetery, in
Shelbyville, Tn.

Dorrington Garrett
Feb 19, 1810
Dec 27, 1856

Nancy C. Garrett, Consort of
Dorrington Garrett
24 Mar 1814
3 Jul 1848
age: 34y, 3m, 9d.

Mary Jane, dau of
Dorrington & Nancy Garrett
Jun 10, 1847
Oct 17, 1847

William Garrett
May 14, 1842
Jun 20, 1861

Few graves with fieldstones,
no inscriptions.

Infant Son of Dorrington &
Nancy Garrett
born Mar 23, 1844 and a corps
the same day.

B. F. Farmer
May 14, 1831
Aug 20, 1879
&
Nancy L. Farmer
Apr 9, 1841
Dec 1, 1923

Nannie F. Bullock
Feb 5, 1863
Jun 3, 1888

6 JOYCE CEMETERY   Map # 1
Located about 2 miles Southwest of Rover, Tn.

James P. Epperson
Jul 23, 1839
Jul 21, 1920
&
Margaret J. Epperson
Jan 6, 1844
Mar 13, 1922

Georgia C. Wallis
Jul 8, 1861
May 14, 1886

Mary J., wife of
John Wallis
Jan 15, 1833
Jan 21, 1885

Wilburn M. Joyce
Mar 13, 1871
Nov 22, 1953
&
Minnie J. Joyce
Dec 23, 1873
Apr 5, 1923

Granny

James R. Haskins
Apr 1, 1807
Jan 13, 1883

J. C. Haskins
Nov 5, 1848
Jul 11, 1914
age: 65y, 8m, 6d.

John T. Epperson
1868-1936
(Dr. John)
&
Nina M. Epperson
1869-1938

B. L. Ezell
Dec 30, 1851
Jun 9, 1926
&
Jemima A. Ezell
Dec 9, 1859
Aug 12, 1925

Orville D. Ezell
1901-1955

Bernice Joyce
Jan 16, 1909
Nov 27, 1966
&
Ruth J. Joyce

"Joyce Sisters"

Elizabeth Haskins
Jan 12, 1808
Aug 14, 1886
age: 78y, 7m, 2d.

Nancy A. Haskins
1856-1942

B. D. Stammer
1878-1923

William M. Epperson
1870-1946
&
Jessie Ann Epperson
1878-1965

Gemima L. Ezell
age: 1m.

W. H. Ezell
1879-1951
&
Fannie Winn Ezell
1881-(no date)

Willie Joyce
1911-1941

Mildred, dau of W. M.
& Minnie Joyce
Jun 11, 1915
Dec 15, 1915

Anderson Joyce
Dec 24, 1820
Nov 17, 1881

Elizabeth A. Joyce
born Nov 28, 1830, professed
faith in Christ, 1838
died Oct 5, 1888

N. C. Joyce
Aug 25, 1865
Jun 4, 1903

Mary A., wife of T. E.
Stammer
Sep 19, 1855
Nov 9, 1894

Bruce Epperson
1900-1971

William R."Dick" Epperson
1908-1968

Willie B., son of W. H.
& F. E. Ezell
Jul 3, 1903
May 19, 1909
age: 5y, 10m, 16d.

James E. Ezell
age: 2m.

Infant son of G. W. &
Macon Joyce
1902

T. J. Joyce
Aug 20, 1847
Apr 14, 1898

Bettie B. Joyce
1856-1936

C. Anderson Joyce
1866-1956

Lena Lois Joyce
1896-1971

Isom S. Joyce
1857-1944

7 ROGERS CEMETERY   Map # 1
Located about ½ mile South of Cedar Grove Church.

Mary Lou Hale
1878-1915

John Wadley
born A. D. 1777
died Mar 17, 1861

Mary, wife of John Wadley
born 1785
died Oct 15, 1862

Susan M. Rogers
May 31, 1833
Sep 19, 1887
age: 54y, 3m, 19d.

J. P. Rogers
Apr 9, 1836
Nov   1864

Mamie C., dau of J. C. &
N. L. Anderson
Feb 5, 1900
Jul 7, 1900

Julia A. Shaw
born Jun 27, 1846, departed
this life in great peace
Oct 7, 1871

Syntha Rogers
Jun 13, 1812
Dec 23, 1884

Thomas M. Rogers
Mar 2, 1813
Jun 7, 1881

Eleanor T. Rogers
Oct 27, 1853
Dec 9, 1871 Age: 18y, 1m, 18d.

George W. Osteen
Feb 27, 1827
Jan 30, 1871

John Stammer
Jun 27, 1827
Jan 10, 1898

Sarah T. Rogers
1864-1908

Susan A. Rogers
1866-1899

M. A., wife of
John Stammer
Jun 4, 1828
Aug 14, 1848

Richard H., son of R. W.
& M. R. Osteen
Oct 10, 1890
Feb 13, 1892

R. W. Rogers
Mar 14, 1843
Mar 19, 1914

Margarett L. Rogers
Jul 15, 1846
Jun 14, 1918

James Bigger
Jan 7, 1798
Apr 24, 1851

Mariah B., wife of
James Bigger
Aug 27, 1802
May 1, 1859

Lettie L., wife of
John Stammer
Jun 12, 1837
Sep 15, 1874

T. A. Rogers
Sep 23, 1845
May 16, 1902
&
Margaret E. Rogers
Jan 17, 1847
Jun 14, 1923

Jesse W. Roberts
1868-1943
&
Mary B. Roberts
1878-1916

J. W. Gentry
Jul 8, 1874
Nov 27, 1902

Bettie Rogers Gentry
1870-1946

W. E. Thomason
Mar 16, 1870
Sep 20, 1891

T. F. Rogers
Jun 27, 1882
Mar 20, 1907

Sarah K., wife of
A. L. Clark
Oct 5, 1859
Nov 24, 1893

Z. T. Rogers
born Aug 18, 1868
married to W. E. Thomason
Aug 31, 1890
died Sep 26, 1891

George Rogers
1893-1974
(Lawrence FH)

Several graves with fieldstones, no inscriptions.

1 POTILLER CEMETERY   Map # 2
Located about 2 miles Northwest of Rover, near Rutherford
County Line.

Richard Henry Potiller,
only child of David Potiller
and Frances, his wife to
whom was born Aug 21, 1829
died Aug 23, 1837, 2 minutes
after 5:00 o'clock A.M. and
emigrated from Va.
aged: 8 yrs & 2 days.

2 WOOD CEMETERY   Map # 2
Located about 2 miles Northwest of Rover, near Rutherford
County Line.

Johnson Wood   and
Jul 24, 1830
Jan 16, 1884

George S. Hemphill, son of
G. K. & S. A. Hemphill
15 Sept 1861
28 Sept 1863

Catharine Hemphill, dau of
G. K. & S. A. Hemphill
Sep 18, 1859
Oct 26, 1859

Lamisa F. Wood   and
Jul 24, 1837
Jul 25, 1907

William J., son of
J. & E. F. McPeak
Jul 23, 1861
Feb 10, 1862 age: 6m & 17d.

Joseph W., son of
J. & E. F. McPeak
Aug 22, 1854
Aug 16, 1855

Susan A. Wood   and
Nov 17, 1830
Jan 5, 1853

Stephen R., son of
J. & E. F. McPeak
Oct 19, 1852
Aug 6, 1853 age: 9m & 17d.

Several graves with fieldstones, no inscriptions.

Stephen J. Wood
born Aug 2, 1866
(no date of death)

3 ELMORE CEMETERY   Map # 2
Located about 1 mile Northwest of Rover, Tn.

James A. B. Smith, son of
James & Levina Smith
Dec 14, 1824
Sep 27, 1832
age: 7y, 9m, 13d.

Robert P. Redmon
1897-1961
(TM)

Woodrow W. Redmond
1913-1946

Edward P. Helton
died Sep __, 1959
age: 75y, & 3m.
(Bratten-Martin FH,
 Nashville, Tenn.)

Era A. Delk
Aug 17, 1897
Jul 22, 1951

H. Frank Delk
Jan 27, 1892
Oct 22, 1932

Mary Ann Anderson
Apr 1, 1811
Mar 11, 1837
age: 21y, 11m, 11d.

Charles H. Redmond
Tennessee
Sgt U. S. Army
W.W.II
Sep 28, 1905
Mar 28, 1959

Bobby Gene Clark
died July 30, 1973
age: 15y, 8m, 4d.
(Bratten-Martin FH,
 Nashville, Tenn.)

Isaih Rowland
1951-1951

Albert Rowland
1935-1935

Alla Beatrice Davis
1931-1936 (Lawrence FH)

Mosalom Powel
Feb 25, 1820
Jul 11, 1850
age: 30y, 1m, 6d.

W. H. "Rooster" Underwood
Apr 3, 1904
Apr 10, 1971
&
Ruth Redmond Underwood
Apr 16, 1908
Feb 21, 1944

Chester E. Hawkins
died Nov 22, 1973
age: 17 days
(Bratten-Martin FH,
 Nashville, Tenn.)

W. D. Lamb
1878-1932

Maude M. Lamb
1871-1908

James M., infant son of
Mosalom & M.E.C. Powel
Dec 6, 1849
Mar 1, 1850
age: 1y, 2m, 25d.

Lum Underwood
Jan 7, 1853
Oct 3, 1935
&
Josie Underwood
Apr 6, 1867
Apr 27, 1933

James C. Nelson
Tennessee
F A U.S.Navy
May 28, 1929
Oct 13, 1954

J. Frank Davis
May 18, 1907
Jun 21, 1967
&
F. Morenie Davis
Jan 2, 1913

James Edward Davis
1935-1935
(Lawrence FH)

Baby Boy Davis
died Dec 5, 1973
(Lawrence FH)

Floyd B. Smith
Jul 22, 1905
Feb 26, 1941
&
Annie F. Smith
Jun 24, 1907
Mar 22, 1963

Grover C. Binkley, Sr.
died Feb 4, 1972
age: 87y, 5m, 12d.
(Buena Vista, Nashville)

Baby Rhinehart
1930-1930

Cathrine Rhinehart
1911-1933

J. H. Elmore
Apr 22, 1829
Jan 21, 1896

N. T. Elmore, wife of
J. H. Elmore
Jan 6, 1834
Mar 21, 1900

Martha E. Elmore
1856-1857

William Elmore
May 22, 1802
Jul 10, 1864
age: 62y, 1m, 18d.
"He was a consistent
member of the Missionary
Baptist Church, 19 yrs. He
leaves his wife Sarah C.
Elmore, 11 children."

Elenora Elmore
Aug 5, 1818
Mar 16, 1858
age: 39y, 6m, 11d.
"She was a consistent
member of the Missionary
Baptist Church, 19 years.
She leaves a Husband, William
Elmore, 11 children."

Maggie Ada Brown
May 20, 1887

Lewis T. Wright
Jul 17, 1857
Apr 6, 1936
&
Emma J. Culley Wright
Jul 25, 1877
Apr 8, 1904
&
Bertie Lee Wright
Oct 1, 1899
Aug 31, 1900

M. R. Davis
1877-
&
Evie Davis
1877-1922

Addie L. Casteel
Feb 26, 1881
Mar 21, 1940
&
Lillian L. Casteel
Nov 10, 1907
Jul 8, 1964

Marvin R. Casteel
Feb 24, 1904
Mar 23, 1907

Charles M. Jackson
1906-1962

W. R. Jackson
Apr 15, 1902
Nov 16, 1969

Nannie L. Jackson
Nov 9, 1874
Jan 26, 1944

Pattie Burton
1872-1958

Infant Son of P. H. &
M. J. Elmore
Sep 13, 1881
Oct 1, 1881

"Father"
D. A. Elmore
Jan 22, 1827
Mar 15, 1900
"Member of Missionary
Baptist Church"
&
"Mother"
E. E. Elmore
Feb 14, 1826
Mar 15, 1900
"Member of C. P. Church"
married Oct 15, 1851

John W. Elmore
1850-1927
&
Sallie S. Elmore
1858-1945

"Mother"
Mary F. Hoofnail
1864-1942

Edgar Elmore
Tennessee
Pvt Co L 131 Inf 33 Div
W.W.I
Aug 30, 1894
May 1, 1953
&
Lula Mae Elmore
Jan 17, 1898
Feb 11, 1975

Many graves are unmarked.

Sallie Beasley
1854-1947

R. H. Beasley
Feb 27, 1861
Aug 19, 1917

Thomas Albert Lamb
Apr 23, 1888
May 15, 1943

Charles Thomas Lamb
aged: 3 years
(no dates)

Naomie V. Hooper
Sep 24, 1856
Mar 19, 1900
"Member of M. E. Church"

Howard Hooper
Jun 3, 1881
Jul 29, 1899

Infant of B. F. &
N. V. Hooper
Jun 16, 1883
died 1883

Maggie Hooper
Jan 14, 1879
Sep 22, 1880

Henry N. Elmore
Feb 20, 1854
Dec 5, 1908

Eva, dau of H. N. &
M. F. Elmore
Jan 24, 1882
Sep 23, 1885

J. T. Elmore
Jul 5, 1875
Aug 29, 1946

Florence M. Elmore
May 24, 1877
May 4, 1947

P. H. Elmore
Aug 12, 1841
May 29, 1916
&
Mary Owen Elmore
Dec 28, 1844
Jun 24, 1931

R. P. Elmore
Aug 3, 1869
Nov 18, 1940

Presley Wright
Jan 29, 1835
Oct 10, 1870
&
Leanna Wright
Jul 5, 1834
Jul 14, 1899

Edmond C. Shearin
1865-1948
&
Annie L. Shearin
1868-1943

James A. Ghee
Jan 21, 1875
Aug 28, 1955
&
Lela B. Ghee
Oct 9, 1885
Oct 21, 1962
&
Pearl B. Ghee
Aug 1, 1880
Oct 20, 1904
&
Oscar Ghee
Oct 12, 1904
Jan 12, 1921

Edna P. Ghee
1909-1952

Lizzie P. Noblett
1918-1956

J. A. Lamb
Dec 26, 1850
Sep 22, 1899
&
Jennie Lamb
Aug 14, 1856
Aug 5, 1922

James W. Elmore
1852-1932
&
Kittie Elmore
1856-1928

James A. Elmore
May 22, 1862
Nov 26, 1913

Thomas L. Pope
1868-1930

Pearl E. Pope
1882-1945

Cora E. Gillespie
Jan 29, 1873
Mar 15, 1951

Robert L. Lynch
1871-1952
&
Cora Lee Lynch
1871-1950

William H. Lynch
Sep 2, 1893
Apr 11, 1962
&
Cora F. Lynch
Aug 11, 1893
Jun 28, 1968

Alfred P. Elmore
Mar 9, 1866
Jul 9, 1940
&
Lou Ida Clardy Elmore
May 17, 1875
Aug 23, 1931

Several graves with
fieldstones, no inscripti

4 WRAY CEMETERY   Map # 2
Located about 1 mile North of Rover, on Bunker Hill Road.

Lucy Wray
Consort of
John Wray
29 Nov 1797
11 Jun 1849

H. M. Bumpus
Mar 5, 1834
May 26, 1891
"A loving husband &
Father dear."

[Was once old Gault place]

Many graves unmarked.

Many graves with field-
stones, no inscriptions.

5 ELMORE CEMETERY   Map # 2
Located about 1 mile North of Rover, Tn.

L. A., wife of
L. C. Elmore
Oct 15, 1846
Aug 24, 1880

Margaret A., Infant dau of
L. C. & L. A. Elmore
Mar 2, 1868
Feb 22, 1869

Mary J. Elmore
Aug 1, 1875
Dec 24, 1876

6 CARLTON CEMETERY   Map # 2
Byler Bottom at Rutherford County Line.

D. C. Carlton
Oct 3, 1828
Jun 13, 1908
&
Martha A. Carlton
Aug 11, 1842
Jan 8, 1926

Maj. Thomas Carlton
Nov 27, 1788
Dec 29, 1863

Nancy Carlton, wife of
Maj. Thomas Carlton
Jun 2, 1787
Aug 20, 1868

7 WARD CEMETERY   Map # 2
Located about 1½ miles North-east of Rover, Tn.
Near Byler Bottom.

Burrell Ward
born -----------
died -----------
(broken away)

Maomy Ward
died Dec 1, 1835
age: 59 yrs.

William Ward, Infant Son of
Burrell & Katharine Ward
Jun 11, 1850
Jan 7, 1851

Infant Son of Burrell &
Katharine Ward
Sep 20, 1846
Jan 28, 1847

8 COTHRON CEMETERY   Map # 2
Located North of Kingdom C. P. Church, near Rover.

Robert Lee Smotherman
Jun 7, 1866
Dec 21, 1938
&
Cassie Carlton Smotherman
May 18, 1872
Feb 4, 1940

Noah W. Looney
1861-1945

Sallie Looney
Dec 15, 1864
Jun 10, 1912

"Brother"
W. Robert Looney
1892-1964
&
"Brother"
Arthur L. Looney
1890-1964

Regina Dunn
1970-1970
(Gowen-Smith)

George W. Myrick
Oct 20, 1963

Margaret S. Vincion
Jan 1, 1960

Bulah L. Dunn
Jun 18, 1947
Jul 3, 1947

Tammy R. Griffy
1958-1974

Thomas E. Leverette
Tennessee
Pvt 6 Infantry 2 Div W.W.I
Feb 9, 1894
Feb 23, 1951

----- Anthony Stem
died Mar 5, 1971
age: 3 yrs.
(Woodfin FH)

Thomas W. Stem
1916-1971
&
Margaret E. Stem
1925-

Mary Jane Pope
Apr 4, 1850
Mar 1, 1930
& Her Daughter:
Lula Pope Heath
Jan 3, 1881
Sep 13, 1936

Esther Pope
1890-1947

Mary R. Pope
1936-1941

Brenda G. Dunn
Sep 26, 1948
May 26, 1949

Wilma Oneida Leverette
Sep 29, 1923
Jan 27, 1928

S. Jessie Cook
1892-1964
&
William C. Cook
1873-1961

Stella Cook
Apr 2, 1918
Mar 31, 1923

Richard Fordham
1975-1975
(Gowen-Smith)

Noah A. Walden
1909-1933

Samuel M. Walden
1876-1967
&
Bertha E. Walden
1886-1973

John C. Sims
1888-1953
&
Mai Farmer Sims
1896-1953

John R. Dunn
Jun 26, 1943
Nov 18, 1950

James E. Leverette
Tennessee
Pfc Army Air Forces, W.W.II
May 1, 1927
May 6, 1972
&
Mayme S. Leverette
1927-
Married Feb 10, 1945

Howard L. Thomas
1920-
&
Christine W. Thomas
1921-
married May 2, 1936

Barbara Thomas
Oct 18, 1938
Oct 30, 1938

Andrew J. Sims
Aug 28, 1860
Aug 27, 1934
&
Emma R. Sims
Jul 29, 1860
Feb 7, 1933

Willie R. Sims
Tennessee
Pfc 104 Inf 26 Div W.W.I
Nov 17, 1890
Feb 18, 1949

Columbus E. Dunn
Jun 20, 1944
Nov 18, 1950

Susie M. Dunn
Feb 19, 1946
Nov 18, 1950

Randy Lee Bush
Jun 1, 1967
Jun 4, 1967

Frances R. Pendergrass
1943-1943

Alvis Wayne Leverette
1938-1973
&
Ethel Bush Leverette
1939-

Earlene P. Leverette
1915-

Albert K. Leverette
1902-1964

Mary C. Leverette
1903-1932

Paul C. Leverette
1926-1932

Alta Mae Leverette
1932-1932

W. Lovvorn
1854-1935

May J. Lovvorn
1848-1935

James A. Lovorn
1890-1975
(Gowen-Smith)

Richard Thomas Lovvorn
Nov 5, 1884
Jan 13, 1926
&
Mary Ella Lovvorn
Mar 25, 1892
Feb 25, 1967
(On TM marker:Mary Ellen Price
                Lovvorn)

Roy Newsom
Jul 14, 1901
Dec 29, 1958
&
Susie Newsom
Apr 29, 1910

Rufus S. Jernigan
1877-1954
&
Maude Lamb Jernigan
1878-1964

Howard M. Jernigan
1900-1960
&
Louise W. Jernigan
---- - ----

Roy C. Jernigan
May 20, 1907
Feb 14, 1972

Willie Columbus Dunn
Tennessee
Pvt 220 Ordance Ham Co
W.W.II
Feb 24, 1915
Feb 7, 1963

Michael Johnson
1957-1957

R. Henry Stephens
Jul 20, 1879
May 2, 1962
&
Susie L. Stephens
Jun 20, 1880
Jan 19, 1965

James Donald Lamb
1958-1958
(Gowen-Smith)

Micky Carol Lamb
1957-1957
(Gowen-Smith)

***Thomas Washington Davis
   22 Feb 1810 (Born)
   (no date)

***Martha Hogan Davis
   8 Jul 1809 (Born)
   (no date)

Willie D. Vincion
1911-1928

Pearl Vincion
1925-1928

W. A. Vincion
1884-1936
&
L. E. Vincion
1888-1945

Huston Lee Adams
1905-1965
&
Nora L. Adams
1892-

Bob Jernigan
Tennessee
Pfc Co M 19 Engineers
W.W.I
Jul 25, 1890
Nov 28, 1958

Grover C. Jernigan
1884-1963
&
Sarah Ann Jernigan
1889-1939

J. H. Jernigan
Jun 22, 1876
Aug 28, 1918
&
Florence Pope Jernigan
Dec 15, 1883
Jun 13, 1918
&
Nettie M. Jernigan
Jun 3, 1904

James H. Adams
1904-1972
(Gowen-Smith)

Theodore "Teddy" R. Trott
Nov 13, 1904
Feb 12, 1973
&
Cassie Jo Trott
Jan 14, 1908
----

*Ella Mae Carlton
 (no dates)

*Gertrude Carlton
 (no dates)

* D. L. Carlton
 (no dates)

*Wayne Carlton
 (no dates)

*Irene Carlton
 (no dates)

*Emma Vincion Carlton
Feb 22, 1887
Oct 1, 1927

*(All family of C.A.Carlton)

C. A. "Kit" Carlton
May 10, 1881
Feb 18, 1961

Raymond Carlton
1921-1964
(Gowen-Smith)

"Brother"
Robert Carlton, Jr.
Jun 13, 1934
Jun 26, 1934
&
"Sister"
Alma Carlton
Jun 30, 1930
Jun 30, 1930

Robert Autho Carlton
Dec 29, 1899
Nov 15, 1963
&
Fannie Mae Hale Carlton
Aug 29, 1906
Dec 17, 1959

Mary K. Jernigan Couser
Mar 13, 1929
Nov 4, 1955

Neil B. King
1847-1930
&
Rebecca L. King
1863-1944

William D. King
1887-1956
&
Charlotte J. King
1876-1952

Jewel Brown Adams
1927-1969
(Gowen-Smith)

Edward Douglas
1941-1970
&
Carlene O. Douglas
1945-

E. P. Douglas
1903-1964
&
Chattie L. Douglas
1905-

Robert L. Stem
1885-1971
&
Mary Lou Stem
1889-1974

J. E. Stem
Jul 8, 1856
Jan 4, 1919
&
Nancy E. Stem
Oct 4, 1858
(no date)

John Wesley Stem
1887-1960
&
Dora Haynes Stem
1893-19

Ralph W. Emerson
Jan 31, 1912

&
Annie Reid Emerson
Dec 25, 1916
Apr 2, 1970

William Robert Douglas
Feb 2, 1907

&
Bertha May Douglas
Dec 23, 1908
May 18, 1971

Willene Douglas
Jan 23, 1938
Sep 7, 1938

Ernest M. Puckett
Jan 28, 1899
Feb 2, 1968

William C., son of
E. M. & O. L. Puckett
Sep 5, 1922
Aug 1, 1924

E. M. Puckett
Mar 28, 1925

Ernest K. Lamb
Alabama
Cook 331 Infantry W.W.I
Jun 16, 1891
Apr 17, 1959

H. P. Smotherman
1823-1902

Walter D. Lamb
Tennessee
Pvt 1 Cl 113 M.G.Bn, 31 Div
Aug 31, 1926

Mrs. Georgia Lamb
(no dates)

Raymond Lamb
(no dates)

Mrs. Lela Lamb
(no dates)

Elisha W. Lamb
Apr 21, 1868
Oct 20, 1950
&
Adell E. Lamb
May 6, 1888
Feb 22, 1968

Robert W. Reid
Jan 2, 1880
(no date)
&
Nash Ralston Reid
Aug 25, 1882
Dec 25, 1956

Ethel Reid
Oct 23, 1903
Sep 25, 1911

Harvey P. Reid
Nov 28, 1846
Feb 25, 1920
&
Rachel Hale Reid
Dec 28, 1854
Dec 16, 1927

John W. Lamb
1867-1930
&
Roxana Lamb
1871-1949

Jesse C. Lamb
May 15, 1817
Jun 4, 1899
&
Nancy V. Lamb
Jun 20, 1820
Oct 15, 1885

Samuel G. Lamb
Sep 4, 1855
Sep 13, 1939

Clarence D. Lamb
1897-1918

George D. Rigsby
Jul 25, 1910

&
Pauline B. Rigsby
Jan 5, 1911

Robert Green, son of
J. G. & T. A. Little
Oct 4, 1904
Aug 31, 1905

Thomas J. Little
May 17, 1898
Oct 11, 1915

John G. Little
Apr 9, 1868
Aug 18, 1925
&
Tennie A. Little
Oct 29, 1874
Mar 11, 1939

Everett E. Davis
Sep 18, 1897
Jul 10, 1969
&
Cassie Mai Davis
Oct 28, 1906
Dec 25, 1945

Marcus K. Rigsby
Sep 3, 1902
Jan 17, 1973
&
Jennie Gannon Rigsby
Jun 18, 1901

Marcus R. Parker, son of
Mr & Mrs Sterling Parker, Sr.
Feb 15, 1951
Jun 17, 1951

Jess A. Gannon
Tennessee
Pfc 127 Inf 32 Div   W.W.I
Oct 22, 1890
Jun 21, 1947

Thomas E. Maxwell
Jan 1934
Aug 1934

Ada F. White, wife of
S. I. White
Jun 13, 1877
Jul 22, 1912

James Ivie Davis
Jan 20, 1890
Feb 16, 1966
&
Maggie Crick Davis
Nov 19, 1893

Joan Davis
1929-1933

William H. Rigsby
1870-1936
&
Sarah P. Rigsby
1880-1937

Evelyn Rigsby
Oct 19, 1930
Jan 30, 1931

Nicholas D. Bellenfant
May 23, 1879
Nov 1, 1957
&
Mattie A. Bellenfant
May 2, 1886
May 2, 1953

Ben W. Bellenfant, Jr.
1942-1942

Dora Lee Bellenfant
1909-1922

Samuel Houston Hale
Feb 15, 1880
Mar 9, 1945
&
Beelie Green Hale
Jul 15, 1884
Jan 11, 1946

Willie M. Epperson
1897-1947
&
Edna M. Epperson
1899-

George Epperson
1916-1937

Alva W. Epperson
Jul 15, 1923
May 14, 1971

Jesse M. Brown
Oct 29, 1905
Jul 29, 1959
&
Mattie M. Brown
Sep 12, 1911

D. E. Ralston
1886-1960
&
Carman Ralston
1895-1945

Joseph E. Crick
1872-1965
&
Permelia E. Crick
1868-1948

Julia A. Crick
Feb 1, 1846
Jan 17, 1939

Fannie Crick
Jan 31, 1900
Sep 9, 1916

James Robert Hale
1883-1960
&
Minnie Ledrew Hale
---- - ----

Jesse Vassar
Tennessee
Cook 156 Depot Brigade W.W.I
Dec 24, 1887
Nov 21, 1950

Theo. Frank Binkley
Jan 30, 1904
May 2, 1968
&
Josephine R. Binkley
Jul 1, 1924

Benjamin Houston Pope
Feb 17, 1942

Patricia Etelene King
1942-1944
(Thompson)

Clarence C. King
1916-1946

William H. King
1883-1951
&
Ethel H. King
1893-1972

Albert M. Pruitt
1895-1943

Gordon Lamb
Oct 4, 1910
Jul 30, 1928

Edward Lamb
Dec 22, 1917
Aug 30, 1922

James L. Vincent
1889-1952
&
Daisie B. Vincent
1897-

Virginia, daughter of
J. L. & D. B. Vincent
Feb 16, 1916
Nov 27, 1921

Will H. Lamb
1876-1951
&
Amanda Lamb
1879-1971
&
Pearl Lamb
1903-1936

Harrison B. Lamb
1910-1950
&
Willie G. Lamb
1913-19(no date)

Arthur G. Lamb
Apr 5, 1881
Jul 21, 1962
&
Pearl Cook Lamb
Oct 28, 1885

S. M. Shrewsbury
1857-1938

Thomas F. Wright
1887-1968
(Lawrence FH)

William H. Haynes
Oct 9, 1887
1974
&
Kitty S. Haynes
Sep 5, 1887

William King, Sr.
Jan 3, 1923
Jul 24, 1965
&
Jewel E. King
Jun 22, 1931
----
married Jul 18, 1947

Ernest Glen Crick
Tennessee
S 2 USNR   W.W.II
Oct 11, 1908
Aug 8, 1969

Sally Mai Crick
1907-1953

Crick
(no dates)

Robert T. Little
1883-1968
&
Elizabeth J. Little
1887-

Thomas S. Stem
Apr 21, 1864
Mar 4, 1945
&
Talitha Stem
Feb 14, 1868
Sep 12, 1934

Thomas R. Stem
Dec 5, 1888
Dec 19, 1918
&
Myrtle J. Stem
Oct 14, 1886
Apr 12, 1958

Alta Mai, infant dau of
T. R. & J. Stem
Oct 7, 1912
Jan 13, 1913

Charles E. Sneed
Feb 21, 1909

&
Blanche F. Sneed
Oct 7, 1917
Dec 7, 1972

Infant King
1963-1963
(Gowen-Smith)

Robert Thomas King
Tennessee
Pfc Co H 3 Army Comp Regt.
W.W.I
Jun 11, 1893
May 10, 1958
&
Algie S. King
1902-1973

William R. Turner
Tennessee
Pvt 1 Conv Center Det W.W.I
Jun 8, 1894
Aug 13, 1966
&
Lottie B. Turner
Jan 17, 1899

Jack Ashworth
Georgia
Pvt 23 Inf Div W.W.I
Dec 4, 1894
Jul 2, 1969

Albert Sandusky, infant of
S. C. & Alta Reid
Jul 19, 1886
Jul 30, 1886
age: 11 days

Susan H., wife of
Samuel C. Reid
Feb 4, 1859
Jun 27, 1880

Walter C. Stem
Dec 4, 1897
Dec 24, 1918
(picture)

Herschel, son of
H. A. & L. M. Martin
Nov 19, 1924
Sep 7, 1926

Judith T. Cothran
1876-1960

J. P. Cothran
Jul 8, 1828
Oct 2, 1888
age: 60y, 2m, 24d.

Mary R., wife of
J. P. Cothran
1836
Jan 28, 1895

John A. H. Cothran
1854-1894
&
Millie J. Cothran
(no dates)
&
Nan Cothran
(no dates)
&
Mary Ellen Cothran
(no dates)
&
Freelon Cothran
(no dates)
&
Eron Cothran
(no dates)

John B. King
1899-1962

Gerald Lee King
1959-1959

John W. Bellenfant
1870-1951
&
Fannie T. Bellenfant
1876-1925

Charlie C. Lamb
1890-1969
&
Mattie Oda Lamb
1893-

Richard Snell Lamb
1892-1950
&
Robbie Singleton Lamb
1896-19

W. H. H. Lamb
Dec 30, 1845
Jul 2, 1931
&
Nannie E. Lamb
Apr 22, 1855
Feb 24, 1935
"Died in faith of Cumber-
land Presbyterian Church."

George R. Lamb
Jan 29, 1895
May 25, 1919
(picture)

John R. Lamb
Jan 26, 1893
Aug 11, 1933
&
Eva T. Lamb
Jun 27, 1893

James Melvin Lamb
Jan 26, 1927
Nov 2, 1950

Drury Webb
Nov 11, 1856
Jun 23, 1944
&
Tula E. Webb
May 13, 1872
Mar 14, 1922

Uel Olen Webb
May 4, 1921
Feb 24, 1924

Ulysses O. Webb
Dec 20, 1888

&
Cora L. Webb
Sep 15, 1893
Mar 15, 1970

Nattie L. Webb
Tennessee
Pfc Co B 113 Machine gun Bn
W.W.I   PH
Feb 13, 1895
Dec 8, 1961
&
Addie E. Webb
Jul 29, 1895
Jul 28, 1958

William Frank Cothran
1896-1951
&
Ethel Ray Cothran
1899-19

Jones Homer Maxwell
Aug 3, 1932
Jun 28, 1974
(Woodfin FH)

Jones Homer, son of
J. E. & Mattie Maxwell
Sep 2, 1896
May 16, 1911
&
Mattie Flora, wife of
J. E. Maxwell
Dec 30, 1871
May 9, 1911

John Edward Maxwell
1870-1944

Jane Ashby Jackson Maxwell
1889-1949

R. H. Lamb
1857-1923

W. D. White
Oct 20, 1884
Feb 21, 1917

R. E. White
Dec 22, 1892
Oct 26, 1914

Fannie H., wife of
W. C. White
Oct 23, 1862
Jan 5, 1914

W. C. White
Dec 29, 1851
Jul 10, 1913

Cornelia E. C., wife of
William C. White
Oct 29, 1856
Jan 14, 1880
age: 23y, 2m, 15d.

J. C., son of
W. C. & Fannie White
Dec 23, 1882
Oct 4, 1909

Bettie C., dau of
W. C. & F. H. White
Jun 8, 1886
Mar 18, 1912

Mary D. White
Jan 11, 1894
Dec 27, 1914

Harold Bumpus
Oct 11, 1934

W. E. Bumpus
Oct 29, 1935

Barry Lynn Alsup
1946

James Wendel Burrus
Aug 8, 1885
Jun 13, 1961

Robert Augustas Burrus
1883-1951

Infant dau of
M. B. & M. J. Cothran
Jan 24, 1901
Jan 28, 1901

Mace B. Cothran
Apr 10, 1874
Dec 9, 1904
&
Mittie J. Cothran
Apr 3, 1879
Dec 6, 1965

Thomas O. Turner
1892-1951
&
Mary S. Turner
1899-19

Gran M. Pope
Apr 6, 1891
(no date)
&
Willie C. Pope
Aug 16, 1895

Minnie M. T. Lamb
1883-1959

Alice Elizabeth Cothran
Sep 25, 1914
Jun 7, 1923

Infant Sons of
J. B. & Alice Cothran
Mar 13, 1924

Fred, Son of
J. B. & Alice Cothran
Sep 23, 1916
May 4, 1921

Clem King
Sep 5, 1895
Jul 1, 1959
&
Mattie Lou King
Apr 14, 1904
Dec 20, 1934

Wallace King
Jan 12, 1928
Jan 16, 1928

Rudolph Lee Potts
Tennessee
Pfc Co M 47 Inf W.W.II
Feb 20, 1927
Apr 11, 1960

Robert Earl Potts
Feb 29, 1924
Sep 18, 1927

Mary E., dau of H. C. &
J. A. Lemmon
Aug 16, 1916-Jul 18, 1917

Grover C. Brannon
1891-1970
&
Rebecca E. Brannon
1894-1948

Joseph Benjamin Cothran
Sep 28, 1881

&
Alice Puckett Cothran
Aug 19, 1883
Dec 20, 1961
married Dec 20, 1908

Macey Pettus Webb
1872-1943
(TM)

Lula, wife of
M. P. Webb
Mar 2, 1880
Jan 20, 1908

Edmond Webb
1823-1908

Mary Jane Webb
1828-1912

Sidney Read
Oct 13, 1870
May 1, 1906

Lou H., wife of
W. T. Gentry
May 12, 1865
Jul 16, 1904

Judith Ann Ralston
Aug 28, 1949
Aug 30, 1965

Infant Dau of
Mr & Mrs G. W. Ralston
Born & Died Nov 11, 1934

Roxie Ann Crick
May 5, 1915
Dec 3, 1961

Alvis M. Stem
Jun 20, 1907
May 9, 1973
&
Gertrude C. Stem
Jul 10, 1910

James F. Stem
Jun 21, 1894

&
Clara H. Stem
Jan 31, 1896

Clara L. Lemmon
1927-1933
&
Zelma J. Lemmon
Oct 12, 1934

Jr., son of
R. L. & Isabell Crick
1933

Thomas E. Crick
1895-
&
Lattis K. Crick
1893-1972

Ellis Crick
1926-1929

W. Thomas Crick
1871-1945
&
Mary F. Crick
1873-1940

J. W. Lovvorn
Feb 22, 1839
(no date)
&
S. E. Lovvorn
Sep 13, 1845
May 15, 1913

E. L. Maxwell
Feb 15, 1841
Mar 8, 1897
&
J. F. Maxwell
Feb 13, 1852
Aug 8, 1904

April Arnold
Oct 11, 1958
Oct 11, 1958
&
Ann Arnold
Mar 6, 1957
Mar 6, 1957
Infant Daughters of
Robert & Hazel Arnold

Johnnie M. Little
May 13, 1916
Dec 4, 1916

Ula T. Little
1891-1922

Paul F. Taylor
May 10, 1911

&
Ethel Stem Taylor
Apr 27, 1917
Nov 16, 1970

George Avery Crick
1941-1941
(Thompson)

A. A. C. (with Crick family)
(no dates)

Marion D. Crick
1883-1917
&
Addie Potts Crick
1891-1968

Effie Mai Webb
May 30, 1893
Feb 24, 1923

Vester E. Davis
1903-1969

Hermon Ralston
1921-1939

Beatrice Cothran Maxwell
1884-1959

Ollie M., dau of
J. R. & J. I. Cothran
May 29, 1889
Feb 23, 1900

Infant Son of
J. R. & J. I. Cothran
Dec 31, 1893
Mar 28, 1894

J. W. Cothran
Jul 2, 1854
Apr 19, 1933
&
Jennie D. Cothran
Nov 6, 1863
Mar 12, 1923

Amasa Authur Cothran
Oct 21, 1883
Jan 8, 1884

Mattie Antonie Cothran
Sep 1, 1887
Jul 14, 1888

A. M., Dau of
F. M. & E. E. Maxwell
Dec 27, 1902
Feb 28, 1903

Milton B. Maxwell, Sr.
1907-1955

Felix M. Maxwell
Apr 16, 1877
Nov 7, 1957
&
Ethel C. Maxwell
Apr 27, 1883
Aug 29, 1966

M. Hale
(no dates)

Nancy Hale
(no dates)

Clara Hale
(no dates)

Harry C. Lemmon
Sep 17, 1885
May 25, 1962
&
Julia Stem Lemmon
May 5, 1890
Jan 14, 1969

William T. Turner
Mar 12, 1864
Jan 26, 1954
&
Rebecca B. Turner
Jan 20, 1872
Jul 17, 1919

Cass Wesley Turner
Feb 13, 1888
Dec 6, 1951
&
Mary Myrtle Turner
Aug 27, 1890
Oct 11, 1932

Agatha Mai Turner
Mar 15, 1919
Jun 30, 1955

Richard H. Stem
Feb 17, 1861
Aug 18, 1946
&
Sarah J. Stem
Aug 28, 1866
Jul 22, 1932

Lorene & Alene, infant
daughters of Roy & Nevada
Pitt
Aug 19, 1929

*** Thomas Washington Davis
born 1808 in North Carolina
died about 1888 or 1889 in
10th District of Bedford
County, Tenn.
Married Feb 28, 1829 in
Rutherford County, Tenn.

Houston Clay, son of
Sam & Esther Carlton
Sep 26, 1935

Sam F. Carlton
1889-1962
(Gowen-Smith)

Franklin D. Carlton
Jul 9, 1933
Oct 11, 1963

Morgan Carlton
Jul 18, 1863
Aug 11, 1939
&
Elizabeth Carlton
Jun 18, 1869
Mar 13, 1942

Fannie Rucker Stem
1890-1923

Willie T.Bailey
(Thelma Puckett)
Nov 1, 1908
Mar 31, 1966

***Martha Hogan Davis
born 1808 in Tennessee
died 1886 in Bedford
County, Tennessee, 10th
District.
(same as on page 6)

R. B."Ben" Lamb
1895-1971
&
Alta M. Lamb
1895-
married Dec 19, 1915

James E. Lovvorn
Feb 2, 1868
May 31, 1956
&
Mary L. Carlton Lovvorn
Jan 18, 1869
Jan 1, 1947

David C. Lovvorn
Jul 9, 1903

&
Lytle Vincion Lovvorn
Oct 3, 1907
Nov 10, 1961

Thomas E. Puckett
Apr 11, 1874
May 8, 1920
&
Thenia W. Puckett
Feb 4, 1876
Nov 14, 1958

Several graves with no
markers.

J. Hoyt Bryant
Dec 30, 1914
Nov 7, 1964
&
Ada C. Bryant
Jan 18, 1912

Debra Y. Upchurch
Infant
1968
(Lawrence FH)

Tracey Binkley
Jun 13, 1973
Jun 14, 1973

David C. Carlton
Sep 12, 1896
Jun 22, 1960

Lucy H. Carlton
Aug 23, 1892
Nov 11, 1955

Jim Bob, son of
Mr & Mrs James R. Carlton
Jan 14, 1943
Feb 8, 1948

Several fieldstones, no
inscriptions.

9 POPE CEMETERY   Map # 2
Located about 1½ miles North of Kingdom C.P. Church, near Rover, Tn.
NOTE: This Cemetery is well kept, and all graves marked.

Infant of
N. M. & Addie Pope
Apr 10, 1915

Infant
(no dates)

Infant
(no dates)

Infant
(no dates)

Infant
(no dates)

Infants (Pope)
Born & Died Apr 4, 1911

"Father"
C. Pope
Dec 15, 1830
Apr 7, 1916
&
"Mother"
T. E. Pope
Nov 2, 1835
(no date)

"Father"
B. F. Pope
Apr 14, 1856
Jun 7, 1919
&
"Mother"
Minnie M. Pope
Dec 23, 1872
Aug 19, 1962

C. T. Pope
Nov 18, 1859
Sep 19, 1924
& wife:
N. J. Pope
Jan 1, 1858
Oct 3, 1942

Ernest Pope
Dec 15, 1884
Jan 13, 1893
age: 8y, & 28d.

May Pope
Sep 10, 1893
Nov 22, 1896

T. M. Pope
Aug 23, 1908
Dec 1, 1915

C. A. Pope
Dec 2, 1880
Nov 17, 1904

Ida Pope
Oct 7, 1888
Feb 24, 1907
age: 18y, 4m, 17d.

Otho Pope
May 18, 1893
Jun 18, 1894
age: 1y, & 1m

Mark Pope
Jan 13, 1905
Feb 16, 1905

M. J. Pope
Jan 27, 1912
Dec 5, 1912

10 DAVIS CEMETERY   Map # 2
Located near Lambs Bottom, Newtown.
NOTE:Several graves, no inscriptions, Davis Family and
Lamb Family said to be buried here.
(continued on next page)

Ones buried in the Davis Cemetery with no markers,
given by Mrs. Gladys Wheeler Farris, Rockvale, Tn.

Samuel T. Davis
born 1831
married Sep 5, 1849
to Susan C. Lowe, born 1832

Bealie Lamb, wife of
Sam Hale
(no dates)

Elisha H. Davis
born 1843
married Oct 19, 1889
to Sally Mosely, had i infant
child.
Elisha H. Davis, son of
Thomas & Martha Hogan Davis.

W. H. (Major) Lamb
(no dates)
&
1st wife: Nancy J. Wade Lamb
2nd wife: Elizabeth Wade Lamb
(Nancy & Elizabeth are sisters)

Jeff Lamb's Father & Mother
(no dates)

Jeff Lamb
(no dates)
&
Clara Lamb
died 1920
&
2 of their children:
Addie & Lem Lamb (no dates)

11 REID CEMETERY   Map # 2
NOTE: ALL GRAVES MOVED TO COTHRAN CEMETERY.

12 KING CEMETERY   Map # 2
Located near Kingdom Cumberland Presbyterian Church, near Rover, Tn.
Fruit Valley Road.

Loudella Lamb
Dec 16, 1881
Sep 7, 1917
age: 35y, 9m, 7d.

John S. Lamb
Jul 21, 1909
Dec 26, 1926
age: 17y, 5m, 5d.

James T. Davis
Apr 21, 1864
Aug 15, 1945

Phebe Ann Davis
Mar 1, 1865
Sep 7, 1938

Robert Lee Davis
Oct 3, 1900
Aug 9, 1906

Bertha May Davis
Mar 10, 1887
Oct 3, 1901

Asa C. Davis
Oct 7, 1888

&
Nancy A. Davis
Feb 9, 1888
May 30, 1960

Mary Lo King
Jul 26, 1871
Sep 26, 1884

Robert R. Boyce
Aug 9, 1877
Jan 26, 1900
age: 22y, 5m, 16d.

Mary E. Boyce Arnold
1875-1915

Mary Jane Boyce
187?-1931

Jessie V. Ray
1923-1947

Joe Dean Ray
1925-1970

Tom Ray
1915-1955

Eddie D. Ray
1913-1928

5 unmarked graves in the
(Stegall Plot)

George H. Davis
1862-1941
&
Mary J. Davis
1863-1942

George W. Davis
Dec 5, 1835
Jan 27, 1914

Elizabeth Lawrence Davis
Sep 6, 1835
Apr 6, 1928

Robert D. King
Nov 13, 1824
Oct 1, 1903

Mrs. Nancy D. King, wife of
R. D. King
May 19, 1828
Apr 29, 1885

Mrs. Amanda Lytle, wife of
R. D. King
Oct 19, 1840
Oct 17, 1927

J. W. Boyce
Jul 27, 1853
Jan 18, 1927

Pauline Rowland
Born & Died Apr 6, 1930

Joseph Newton Coursey
1855-1933
&
Fannie Lawrence Coursey
1855-1930

Minnie M. Wilson
(no dates)

Neal Williams Davis
Feb 2, 1917
Feb 8, 1917

Little Darling
Don't Forget   (Davis Plot)

Neal R. Davis
Sep 13, 1874
1971

Mary Susan Davis
Nov 2, 1875
Mar 19, 1961

Samuel W., son of
N. R. & Mollie Davis
Nov 7, 1915
Mar 27, 1916

R. L. Davis & wife
(no dates)

Nancy M. Stegall
Feb 25, 1870
Apr 22, 1870

John Robert Gentry
died Jul 25, 1947
age: 70y, 3m, 24d.

Minous Newton Boyce
1879-1947
&
Daisy Vaughn Boyce
1888-1968

Robert Francis Boyce
Dec 26, 1910
Oct 7, 1911

Joe G. Holden
1868-1937

Mrs. Joe G. Annie Ray Holden
1866-1952

Clara Mae Dalton
1917-1945

A. J. Ray
1876-1963

Mary E. Ray
1885-1945

Charity Adaline King
                Smotherman
Jan 27, 1832
Dec 6, 1884

Roy Herman Cook
1906-1975

Eva Davis Cook
1878-1908

Lala E. Mathews
Jun 7, 1919

Rollie F. Mathews
Jul 10, 1883
born in Johnson Co., Ark.
died (no date)
&
Nancy D. Davis
Jun 19, 1882
Feb 19, 1971
born in Bedford County, Tenn.

Baby of M. N. &
A. D. Boyce
Sep 1, 1907

Annie D. Boyce
Mar 6, 1880
Sep 7, 1907

Wilson Franklin Boyce
Aug 13, 1912-Oct 22, 1913

John D. Rowland
May 9, 1918
Aug 10, 1950
&
Carmine D. Rowland
Aug 18, 1915

Amanda Caldonia King
Nov 20, 1857
Feb 21, 1930

Samuel Gentry
Feb 24, 1816
Nov 16, 1875
age: 59y, 9m, 8d.

About 30 unmarked graves,
several fieldstones.

Willie G. Windrow
Jan 11, 1902
Sep 13, 1967
&
Beulah R. Windrow
Dec 29, 1910

Ona Vaughn
Jul 15, 1884
Mar 2, 1968

John S. King
May 5, 1868
Jul 15, 1870
&
Minus R. King
May 15, 1854
Apr 19, 1870

Hugh R. Haynes
Apr 22, 1909

&
Pearl R. Haynes
Sep 12, 1905

John Shook King
Sep 1, 1826
Jun 13, 1909
&
Mary E. Gentry King
Jun 14, 1836
Jun 28, 1918

Fannie A. King
Jan 19, 1875
Sep 25, 1904

Tom Garritt Davis, Sr.
Jun 20, 1886
Jul 17, 1950

Leah King Davis
Sep 18, 1888
Sep 28, 1931

Finis E. King
Oct 6, 1866
Sep 29, 1925
&
Mary M. King
Jun 20, 1852
Sep 17, 1928

N. F. Neal
Jan 16, 1859
(not buried here)
&
Nannie King Neal
Aug 26, 1870
Jun 2, 1919

13 HAYNES CEMETERY   Map # 2
Located near Kingdom Cumberland Presbyterian Church, Near Rover, Tn.

Joseph T. Haynes
Jun 1, 1812
Jan 19, 1892

Sarah P., wife of
J. T. Haynes
May 6, 1816
Dec 8, 1898

Henry C. Wade
Jul 18, 1844
Dec 6, 1887

3 or 4 unmarked graves.

William Black
Nov 20, 1768
May 27, 1832
age: 64 yrs.

Infant Son of
T. Black
died Feb 20, 1832

Willie Vernon
Mar 1, 1877
Jun 9, 1879

George W. Crick
Aug 31, 1838
Mar 18, 1875

14 BELLENFANT CEMETERY   Map # 2
Located near Kingdom Cumberland Presbyterian Church, near Rover, Tn.

Absalom S. Bellenfant
Apr 19, 1822
Dec 11, 1907

Mahala J. Bellenfant
May 1, 1844
Jul 12, 1913

Infant Daughter of
A. S. & M. J. Bellenfant
Born & Died-Jun 6, 1864

Absalom D. Bellenfant
Sep 22, 1897
Oct 9, 1897

15 HILL CEMETERY   Map # 2
Located near Kingdom Cumberland Presbyterian Church, near Rover, Tn.

Benjamin Hill
Nov 17, 1795
May --, 1818

Narcisa T. Hill
Oct 19, 1831
Sep 17, 1836

16 UNKNOWN CEMETERY   Map # 2
Located between Kingdom C.P. Church and King Cemetery, near Rover, Tn.

Several fieldstones, no inscriptions.

17 COOK CEMETERY   Map # 2
Located about 1 mile West of Putman Well, at Walnut Grove.

William C. Cook
1854-1944
&
Jane Bell Cook
1853-1921

W. Clarence Cook
1891-1962
&
Nora P. Cook
1895-1922

R. N. King
1857-1910
(Engraved picture)

18 TURNER CEMETERY   Map # 2
Located near Putman Well.

Angeline Cook
1838-1938

Ida Agather, dau of G. W. &
Sallie Turner, born Nov 24,
1901, died Feb 3, 1918

Iray Mae, dau of G. W. &
Sallie Turner, born Jul 30,
1898, died Apr 2, 1900.

Unmarked graves listed on
next page.

George Washington Turner***
born Mar 4, 1862
died Jul 28, 1920

Sallie Tennessee (Cook) Turner***
born Dec 11, 1864
died Jun 9, 1942

William Eadger Turner***
born Aug 20, 1885
died Apr 15, 1945

Arline Holton***
born Sept 17, 1934
died Sept 17, 1934

***Family Records

19 PUTMAN CEMETERY   Map # 2
Located at Putman Well.

This Cemetery has been destroyed.

20 ALLEN CEMETERY   Map # 2
Located at Putman Well.

Martha "Patsey" Ann Allen***
wife of Hugh Allen
(no dates)(no marker)

Only one grave in this Cemetery.

*** Family Records.

21 COOPER CEMETERY (Col.)   Map # 2
Located near Putman Well.

Gladys L. Cooper
Apr 16, 1912
Sep 17, 1948

Nannie Cooper Crawford
Jul 10, 1898
Oct 12, 1959

Ether, Infant Daughter of
T. F. & E. N. Seay
Sep 1, 1907
Dec 15, 1907

Mary Harrison Cooper
Dec 22, 1891
Oct 14, 1956

Ellanora Elmo Seay
Jul 10, 1864
Feb 28, 1937

Howard L. Woods, Jr.
died Nov 27, 1960
(Hellum FH)

J. Arthur Cooper
Dec 1, 1886
May 19, 1967

L. M. Cooper
Apr 24, 1900
Aug 12, 1909

Melissa Murray
died Mar 5, 1972
(Scales FH)

Sherman W. Cooper
Tennessee
Pfc 4967 QM Service Co
W.W.II
May 14, 1917
Apr 13, 1968

22 SMITH CEMETERY   Map # 2
Located near Putman Well.

Arpie W. Robertson, wife of
P. P. Smith
Oct 16, 1861
Jan 13, 1907

P. P. Smith
Jan 20, 1865
Jul 25, 1940

Annie Ralston, wife of
P. P. Smith
Apr 10, 1875
Jul 12, 1918

23 McBRIDE CEMETERY   Map # 2
Located near Putman Well.

Adelaide, wife of
W. L. Chick
Dec 2, 1836
Mar 13, 1905
&
Harriette N. Foster
Mar 28, 1826
Jun 19, 1903

Lorenzo Dow McBride
Dec 15, 1849
Oct 29, 1886

J. T. McBride
Jan 15, 1826
Mar 15, 1886

James T. McBride
Aug 20, 1850
Sep 2, 1856

24 WILLIAMS CEMETERY   Map # 2
Located about 1 mile East of Putman Well, in Rutherford County.

J. B. Reed
d-Nov ------
(fieldstone, illegible)

J. B. Williams
Jul 1, 1847
Apr 1, 1908

Mrs. Jennie Williams
Apr 22, 1850
Mar 30, 1939

W. M. & W. D.
(fieldstone, illegible)

David W. Burton
Aug 3, 1843
Jul 24, 1914

Dora I. Lamb Burton Ralston
Dec 24, 1872
Nov 29, 1945

Capt. Nick Lamb
Co D 24 Tenn Inf C.S.A.
Jul 14, 1831
Fell in Battle at Franklin,
Tenn. Nov 30, 1864
"Erected by Friends, 1906."

James H. Auberry
1872-1950
&
Rockie A. Auberry
1876-1938

C. H. Williams
Jun 6, 1870
May 28, 1900

"Father"
C. H. Lamb
Aug 12, 1835
Feb 10, 1910

"Mother"
N. F. Lamb, wife of
C. H. Lamb
Apr 4, 1845
Nov 27, 1906
age: 51y, 7m, 23d.

Edward W. Lamb
1867-1935
&
Sallie Reed Lamb
1874-1959

George Winfrey
1865-1934
&
Melissa Lamb Winfrey
1863-1925

Several fieldstones,
no inscriptions.

Several graves with no
markers.

25 JONES-HAYNES CEMETERY   Map # 2
Located about 1 mile East of Cater Cross Road.

Ollie Aaron Winfrey
Apr 23, 1895

William David Winfrey
1856-1916
&
C. Tennie Winfrey
1867-1959

Pearl, dau of
J. W. & M. J. Jones
Mar 11, 1894
Aug 9, 1898

Iretta, dau of
J. W. & M. J. Jones
Oct 17, 1902
May 28, 1903

Francis Paul Jones
1889-1967
&
Lois Burris Jones
1899-

Judy Shae Jones
Born & Died Dec 10, 1942

William Anderson Jones
Jan 16, 1885
Jul 25, 1949

Margaret Lee Jones
1934-1934
(TM)

Tabitha E. Haynes
Jan 5, 1865
Dec 30, 1951

W. H. H. Haynes
Feb 11, 1841
Nov 25, 1930

Christenia M., wife of
W. H. H. Haynes
Dec 11, 1835
Nov 11, 1910

Ethel Burris Owen
1889-1924

James Mead Owen
1924-1925

"Mother"
Amanda L. Burris
1859-1937

Iley Erskin Modrall
1908-1910

Robert Pleas Modrall
1884-1926

Gertrude Newman
1906-1921

John Wesley Jones
Jul 13, 1865
Jun 23, 1952
&
Martha Jane Horton Jones
Jul 20, 1860
Jul 4, 1934

Purvis Leone Faulk, wife of
W. A. Jones
Nov 29, 1888
May 16, 1931

Christine, dau of
W. A. & P. L. Jones
Dec 13, 1918
Jun 21, 1931

Willie R., Son of
W. A. & Purvis L. Jones
Nov 19, 1914
Dec 10, 1914

Henry Lee Fann
Jun 23, 1920
Dec 21, 1972
&
Nannie M. Jones Fann
Sep 16, 1918

Herman H. Wheelhouse
Sep 28, 1902
Dec 15, 1924

Lum Wheelhouse
Oct 4, 1863
Feb 4, 1958
& wife:
Nannie Haynes Wheelhouse
Sep 7, 1867
Jan 14, 1923

Lucy Burris Bartlett
Jun 13, 1903
Mar 24, 1925

6 graves with no markers.

Lemuel L. Jones
Feb 12, 1874
Feb 3, 1945

Earle Lee Jones
Sep 12, 1906
Sep 26, 1965
Born in Altona, Ky., passed
away in Mt. View, Calif.,
son of Lucinda & Carroll
Jones. Brother of Roberta
Blaydes, Grace Gourley, Mary
Cauble, & J. Carroll Jones.

"Father"
Joe Brothers
Mar 4, 1886
Apr 1, 1950

"Mother"
Nora Jones, wife of
Joe Brothers
Apr 10, 1887
Sep 7, 1925

Kenneth Austin Smith
Jun 10, 1950
Jun 22, 1972
Son of Kathleen Jones &
Walter Smith
&
Patsy J. Noblitt Smith
Mar 8, 1950
----
married Aug 24, 1968
Daughter of Blanchie &
Doyle Noblitt.

Horace Wheelhouse
Nov 27, 1899
Feb 13, 1902

Clay Wheelhouse
Oct 14, 1896
Jun 28, 1898

Gilbert Wheelhouse
Jun 9, 1894
Jun 7, 1898

William R. Haynes
Mar 1, 1871
married to Ella Spence
May 28, 1902
died Feb 17, 1903

James T. Haynes
Feb 9, 1873
Oct 13, 1907
age: 34y, 8m, 4d.

A. J. White, wife of
L. L. Jones
Oct 24, 1876
Sep 18, 1917

"Our Ma"
Mary Ann Jones
Nov 12, 1840
Sep 12, 1905
age: 65y, & 10m.

F. P. Jones, Sr.
Jan 24, 1844
Sep 25, 1926

S. Macon Brothers
1907-1965
&
Louise Brothers
1911-19

Joseph Marvin Brothers
1913-1970
&
Jessie R. Lamb Brothers
1913-19

Charlie Homer Burris
Jan 8, 1893
Apr 5, 1961
&
Mattie B. Jones Burris
Oct 1, 1899

James Woodson, son of
W. E. & Carrie Mitchell
Apr 17, 1931
Apr 18, 1931

Louise, dau of
W. E. & Carrie Mitchell
May 24, 1924
Jul 10, 1926

Eugene Hollowell
Oct 27, 1861
Nov 2, 1898
age: 37y, & 6d.

Bettie Haynes, wife of
E. P. Hollowell, &
J. S. Westbrooks
Jul 19, 1863
Feb 2, 1942

Clarence Hollowell
Aug 7, 1892
Mar 14, 1899
age: 6y, 8m, 3d.

26 PUTMAN CEMETERY   Map # 2
Located at Cater Cross Roads.

This Cemetery has been destroyed.

27 POPLIN CEMETERY   Map # 2
Located about 1 mile West of Cater Cross Roads.

Dr. Thomas I. Poplin
Mar 12, 1867
Feb 9, 1916

Mattie Poplin Crass
Mar 27, 1877
Mar 26, 1956

Mattie D. Poplin
Jul 10, 1873
Jan 12, 1892

Anna Irene, dau of
Dr. T. I. & Mattie Poplin
Mar 23, 1899
Aug 15, 1899

Albert Sidney, son of
J. W. & Julia A. Nance
Nov 12, 1861
Jul 30, 1868

Julia Ann, wife of
John W. Nance
(dates broken away)

Mattie D. Poplin
Sep 5, 1904
Apr 16, 1907

William Jackson
Born in Prince Edward Co., Va.
May 1, 1802
Jun 9, 1879
age: 77y, 1m, 8d.
&
Drusilla Lytle, wife of
William S. Jackson
Nov 8, 1806
Sep 14, 1871
age: 64y, 10m, 6d.

Amna Jackson, wife of
W. R. Poplin
Apr 3, 1842
May 6, 1920

J. E. Kimmons
Jan 5, 1834
Sep 17, 1887

Drusilla Emily, wife of
J. E. Kimmons
Jan 16, 1840
Sep 7, 1877

28 TAYLOR CEMETERY   Map # 2
Located about 1 mile Northeast of Longview.

John Taylor   and
Apr 1806
died Nov 29, 1844
age: 41y, 7m, 23d.

Jane Taylor
Consort of John Taylor
Born Jul 4, 1814
died Feb 5, 1845
age: 31y, 7m, 1d.

29 JARRETT CEMETERY (Col.)   Map # 2
Located about 1 mile Northeast of Longview.

Richard D. Jarrett   and
1846-1920

Mary A. Jarrett
1850-1924

30 SUDBERRY CEMETERY   Map # 2
Located about 3/4 mile South of Cater Cross Road.

J. H. Sudberry
May 18, 1861
Jul 13, 1934

Mary E., wife of
J. H. Sudberry
Mar 14, 1866
Dec 22, 1914

M. F. Wright
Nov 22, 1881
Feb 22, 1904

Mary E. Wright
Apr 17, 1861
Jun 30, 1902

N. E. Wright
Jun 22, 1867
Nov 12, 1894

Russie Boyce Wheeler
Aug 18, 1883
Apr 17, 1960

E. H. Boyce
died Dec 2, 1924
age: 40 yrs.

Infant Son of
Mr & Mrs J. E. Sudberry
May 26, 1921
May 28, 1921

Samuel Wright
1867-1918

"our Mother"
M. E., wife of
S. A. Wright
Nov 20, 1843
Oct 18, 1907

T. P. Wright
Aug 22, 1838
Jan 6, 1915
& wife:
Susan Wright
Mar 19, 1839
Oct 19, 1917

Gus O. Wright   and
Jan 20, 1879
Jun 20, 1956

Alvice T. Boyce   and
1892-1952

L. M. J.
(fieldstone, no inscription)

_. C. J.
(fieldstone, no inscription)

John Clanton Maxwell
Dec 5, 1920
Jun 10, 1924

Wilma Lee Maxwell
Sep 9, 1925
Sep 10, 1925

Mary A. Faulkner
1856-1893

Infant Son of
J. J. & M. A. Falkner
Born & Died-Dec 7, 1887

Lizzie Wright
Dec 15, 1878
Aug 25, 1949

Gracie E. Boyce
1898-

Tennie B. Maxwell
1869-1918

J. M. Boyce
1862-1923
&
Ellen Boyce
1867-19(no date)

Sarah R. Boyce
Oct 6, 1863
Nov 22, 1905

J. J. Faulkner, Jr.
Aug 15, 1893
Feb 14, 1894

J. J. Faulkner
1849-1915

Bettie H. Faulkner
1864-1936

Homer Boyce
1899-1927

Benjamin F. Boyce
Sep 23, 1857
Dec 28, 1927
&
Nancy Jane Boyce
Sep 24, 1859
Aug 20, 1928

Mary Lee Boyce
Aug 30, 1890
Oct 27, 1963

Several graves with fieldstones, no inscriptions.

Hermon L. Lokey
Aug 9, 1910
Oct 22, 1928

Several graves with no markers.

L. P.
(Foot-marker, headstone
gone)

31 HOSKINS CEMETERY   Map # 2
Located about 1 mile Northeast of Longview.

Infant Dau of
S. B. & Sallie B. Hoskins
Born & Died 1873
&
Infant Son of
S. B. & Sallie B. Hoskins
Born & Died 1870

Sallie B., dau of
S. B. & Sallie B. Hoskins
Apr 10, 1872
Apr 4, 1890
age: 17y, 11m, 24d.

Annah May, dau of
S. B. & Sallie B. Hoskins
Apr 11, 1869
Aug 23, 1890
age: 21y, 4m, 12d.

Sallie B., wife of
S. B. Hoskins
Oct 8, 1838
Aug 9, 1894
age: 55y, 10m, 1d.

Martha L. McCord, wife of
T. N. McCord
Aug 11, 1841
Sep 1, 1874

Mary Hoskins Winn Puckett
Dec 27, 1837
Aug   1862

Sallie Carlton Winn
died Aug 9, 1886
age: 25y, & 9m.

Lizzie Hoskins Winn
died Aug 3, 1885
age: 2y, & 15d.

Nannie D., wife of
Joe F. Butts
May 22, 1861
Jan 16, 1887

Ann M., wife of
S. V. Butts
Jan 28, 1827
Nov 28, 1913

Stephen V. Butts
Born in Brunswick Co., Va.
Mar 30, 1823, and died
Aug 8, 1897, age: 74y, 4m, &
8d.

Nancy A. E. Butts
Apr 22, 1854
Nov 13, 1931

Samuella Gordon, wife of
F. E. Tucker & dau of
S. V. & A. M. Butts
Jan 30, 1865
Dec 6, 1898

Infant dau of
F. E. & Sammie G. Tucker
Born-Dec 5, 1898

Earl Bennett Tucker
Jul 8, 1927
Oct 8, 1930

Mary Ann Tucker
Dec 23, 1930
Dec 17, 1933

Mary Jane, wife of
Louis Tucker & dau of
John & Mary Winston
Sep 2, 1824
Apr 18, 1909

John E. Hoskins
Born in Halifax Co., Va.
Mar 25, 1802
married to Nancy M. North
Feb 3, 1824, died
Mar 24, 1876

William E. Barnes
Sep 27, 1904
Aug 11, 1905

Cranville S. Barnes
Oct 20, 1832
Jan 10, 1917
&
Sarah Hoskins Barnes
May 6, 1834
Dec 22, 1911

Willie D., son of
J. F. & D. A. Butts
Jul 12, 1880
Sep 14, 1882

J. M. North
Dec 12, 1840
May 20, 1894
&
Mary North
Sep 27, 1850
Jul 12, 1933

Marian V. Burton, dau of
R. H. & Ouida Burton
1908-1909

Nancy M. North, wife of
J. E. Hoskins
Born in Prince Edward Co.,
Va. Aug 17, 1800
married Jul 3, 1824
died Oct 19, 1880
(Note: Month of marriage
is different.)

The. N. Hoskins
Mar 16, 1836
died at Eufala, Ala.
Apr 6, 1865

W. W., son of
T. N. & M. L. Hoskins
May 2, 1861
Sep 15, 1862

Several unmarked graves.

32 TARPLEY CEMETERY   Map # 2
Located about 1 mile Northwest of Longview.

Gladys, Infant dau of
J. D. & Tennie Tarpley
Mar 13, 1908
Jul 13, 1908

John D., son of
John & Tennie Tarpley
Jan 5, 1904
Mar 10, 1904

Eddie Hale, son of
W. C. & N. F. Williams
Nov 6, 1896
Nov 21, 1896

Henry B. Webb, Husband of
N. C. Webb
Jun 26, 1863
Oct 21, 1889

Richard Theador Tarpley
Oct 3, 1856
Sep 23, 1866
age: 9y, 11m, 20d.

Mrs. C. C., Consort of
Evan Wallace
May 12, 1798
Sep 6, 1871

Infant dau of
T. J. & N. F. McLain
Born & Died Feb 16, 1885

J. T. McLain
1875-1895

Alice P. McLain
1868-1946

* Dau of Abel & Mary Davis

Edward Tarpley, born
in Charlott Co., Va.
Feb 1794, married
Margaret Davis
Nov 14, 1816
died Dec 25, 1876
age: 82y, & 10m.

Margaret,* wife of
Edward Tarpley, born in
Nash Co., N.C.
May 10, 1794, married
E. Tarpley Nov 14, 1816
died Jun 12, 1875
age: 81y, 1m, 2d.

Minnie, dau of
H. B. & N. E. Webb
born Jul 15, 1883
died (broken & in ground)

Sarah A. R., wife of
Rev. R. R. Jones
Jul 27, 1842
Dec 30, 1867
age: 25y, 5m, 3d.

T. J. McLain
1846-1945
&
Fannie T. McLain
1853-1910

Sarah Damron
Aug 28, 1792
Dec 28, 1885
age: 98y, & 4m.

Utah C. Turner
Born & Died Jan 11, 1865

16

Octa Glenara, dau of
F. M. & O. Atkinson
May 27, 1873
age: 2y, 5m, 28d.

Walter H., son of
F. M. & Octa Atkinson
Born in Bedford Co., Tenn.
Apr 27, 1871
professed faith in Christ
at 12 yrs old, joined
Protestant Methodist Church,
South, died Mar 13, 1891

Octa, Consort of
F. M. Atkinson & dau of
J. D. & A. Webb
Nov 8, 1850
Jan 4, 1874
age: 23y, 1m, 26d.

M. B. Batt
Jun 5, 1856
Jul 9, 1875

G. W. McLain
Dec 16, 1836
married Arminta Batt
Nov 12, 1872
died Feb 11, 1889
age: 52y, _, 26d.

Araminta Batt, wife of
G. W. McLain
Jul 29, 1839
Dec 20, 1894

James H. Tarpley
Born Jun 22, 1820
married Harriet W. Damron
Sep 29, 1847
Died Sec 6, 1855
age: 35y, 5m, _d.

Harriet W., Consort of
James H. Tarpley & dau of
William & Sarah Damron
Born Feb 14, 1825
Died Jun 12, 1881
age: 56y, 3m, 28d.

Lewis Heath Lamb
Born Aug 15, 1828
married Tabitha H. Tarpley
May 11, 1859
Died Oct 19, 1877
age: 49y, 2m, 4d.

Tabitha H., wife of
L. H. Lamb & dau of
Edward & Margaret Tarpley
Born Aug 30, 1828
Died Dec 20, 1890
married May 11, 1859
age: 62y, & 4m.

Edward Davis Lamb, son of
L. H. & T. H. Lamb
Aug 21, 1861
Jan 25, 1864
age: 2y, 5m, 4d.

John A. Webb
Born & Died Oct 19, 1857

Roxaner Webb
Born Oct 30, 1844
age: 4 yrs.

Amanda, wife of
J. D. Webb & dau of
Edward & Margaret Tarpley
Feb 13, 1822
married Dec 21, 1843
Dec 6, 1888
age: 66y, 9m, 23d.

Lucinda J., wife of
John A. Tarpley
May 15, 1834
married Apr 11, 1865
Jun 1, 1871
age: 37y, & 16d.

Fredrick Batte
Feb 8, 1816
Nov 6, 1876
age: 54y, 8m, 28d.

Ephrum Gordon, son of
G. & P. M. Batte
Jul 19, 1872
Aug 20, 1873

Henry Oscar, son of
G. & P. M. Batte
May 28, 1871
Jun 15, 1871

Infant Dau of
G. & M. J. Batte
Nov 1, 1879
Nov 8, 1879

Pheba Matilda Taylor, wife
of G. Batte
Dec 16, 1849
Apr 12, 1877

Margaret Jane Brown, wife
of G. Batte
May 5, 1853
Jan 26, 1880
&
Elizabeth Minter, dau of
G. & M. J. Batte
Born & Died Dec 22, 1878

Infant Dau of
J. T. & S. T. Taylor
Born & Died Jan 21, 1880

Fannie, Infant dau of
T. W. & Pearl Jones
Nov 6, 1903
Nov 28, 1903

A. Sandusky Thomason
Jul 23, 1878
Jun 9, 1879

Mary M., wife of
J. W. Stem
Aug 22, 1824
Aug 11, 1897

M. A. E. Webb, wife of
T. N. B. Turner
Feb 26, 1848
Dec 23, 1921

T. N. B. Turner, son of
M. W. & M. A. Turner
Professed faith in Christ
Sep 27, 1888
Born Sep 8, 1839
Died Aug 8, 1889

John D. Webb
Born in Rutherford Co., Tenn.
Feb 27, 1820
married Amanda Tarpley
Dec 21, 1843
Died Sep 24, 1899
age: 79y, 6m, 28d.

M. A. S.
(fieldstone, no inscription)

Frances E. Tarpley,
Consort of Fredrick Batte
Nov 23, 1818
Jan 26, 1862
age: 48y, 2m, 3d.

Edward Batt
Born Jul 27, 1844
Died (no date)

Mary Rebecca Gannaway, wife
of Edward Batt
Jan   1848
Sep 3, 1876

Infant of
E. & M. R. Batte
(no dates)
&
Infant of
E. & M. R. Batte
died Jan 1870
&
Infant of
E. & M. R. Batte
(no dates)

Sarah J. Snell, wife of
John A. Tarpley
married Jun 10, 1873
Born May 13, 1835
Died Feb 3, 1895
age: 59y, 8m, 20d.

John A. McLain
Jan 23, 1832
Apr 7, 1899
&
Dau: L. L. McLain
Nov 20, 1879
Jul 14, 1900
&
A. L., wife of
J. A. McLain
Oct 10, 1827
Jan 24, 1889

Orlean McLain
Sep 16, 1822
Jan 12, 1911
age: 88y, 3m, 19d.

Jesse Roe, dau of
Frank & Joe Atkinson
Jul 16, 1886
Feb 3, 1887

Frank M. Atkinson
1840-1910

Joe Webb Atkinson
1855-1927

Burt Roy Atkinson
1890-1891

Zela Atkinson
1882-1912

Dan S. Atkinson
Aug 3, 1880
Aug 26, 1962

Ottley L. Williams
Oct 13, 1883
Jul 5, 1922

J. A. Tarpley
May 8, 1826
Feb 25, 1915

Lucinda J. Wallace, wife
of J. A. Tarpley
May 15, 1834
married Apr 11, 1865
Died Jun 1, 1871
age: 37y, & 16d.

India(Indianna) Jackson,
wife of J. A. Tarpley
May 19, 1835
married Oct 10, 1855
Died Mar 18, 1864

Richard T., son of
J. A. & L. J. Tarpley
Oct 3, 1856
Sep 23, 1866

Infant son of John A. &
Sarah J. Tarpley
Born & Died May 18, 1874

J. A. Tarpley
Son
Richard T. Tarpley
Infant Son
1874

L. A. McLain
Apr 21, 1861
Jul 10, 1863
&
W. L. McLain
Sep 13, 1856
Oct 8, 1861
&
G. W. McLain
Dec 19, 1874
Oct 4, 1877
"Children of John A. McLain"
NOTE: Also 4 unmarked
children graves in McLain's
plat.

17

J. A. McLain
Nov 30, 1802
Oct 2, 1895
age: 92y, & 10m.

Richard N. McLain
Sep 16, 1841
Apr 5, 1873

B. F. McLain
Apr 1, 1881
Aug 16, 1911

B. A. McLain
Oct 7, 1832
Sep 1, 1913
&
Sue E. McLain
Aug 17, 1839
Mar 14, 1922

33 JONES CEMETERY   Map # 2
Located 1 mile South of Cater Cross Roads.

12 graves with fieldstones, no inscriptions.

34 SMOTHERMAN CEMETERY   Map # 2
Located 1 mile South of Cater Cross Roads.
This Cemetery joins the above Jones Cemetery.

W. L. Smotherman
1873-1935

J. P. Smotherman
(no dates)

About 2 unmarked graves.

35 JACKSON CEMETERY   Map # 2
Located about 1½ miles Northwest of Longview.

John Jackson
Apr 4, 1789
Dec 9, 1866
age: 77y, 8m, 5d.

John L. Jackson
Sep 30, 1819
Oct 1, 1848
age: 30 yrs.

Jamima Allison, dau of
John Jackson
Nov 4, 1833
May 6, 1850
age: 16y, 6m, 2d.

Rebecker Jackson, wife of
John Jackson, & dau of
James Lytle of North
Carolina.
Born Jun 15, 1801
Died Aug 6, 1875
age: 74y, 1m, 21d.

Mark L. Jackson
Nov 14, 1830
Sep 8, 1847
age: 16y, 9m, 24d.

"Our Mother"
Nancy J., wife of
D. C. Jackson, & dau of
Stephen & Mary Wood
Born Jul 24, 1838
Died Jul 21, 1884

Rebecca V. Garrett
Mar 14, 1841
Mar 26, 1864
age: 23y, & 12d.

James Little Jackson, son
of Jas L. & Mary C. Jackson
Aug 21, 1853
May 3, 1863
age: 9y, 8m, 13d.

Martha D., dau of
James L. & Mary Jackson
Dec 23, 1863
Sep 20, 1894

James L. Jackson
Jun 28, 1824
Nov 13, 1896

Rebecca Stacy Ann Rucker
Apr 19, 1856
Oct 2, 1857

Angeline Francis Jackson,
dau of John & Delphy
                    Landrum
May 13, 1827
Dec 27, 1851
age: 24y, 7m, 14d.

Mary Charlotte, wife of
James L. Jackson, & dau of
Hardy & Jane Pope
Nov 8, 1836
Mar 20, 1875
age: 30y, 4m, 12d.

36 KIMMONS CEMETERY   Map # 2
Located about 1½ miles Southeast of Kingdom C.P.Church.

Mattie Garrett, wife of
J. W. Kimmins
Oct 30, 1872
May 2, 1909

Estelle Kimmins
1868-1941

Frances Elizabeth, dau of
J. T. & M. E. Shearin
Jun 9, 1923
Nov 3, 1924

John F. Kimmons
Apr 29, 1872
Aug 22, 1963
&
Claudia M. Kimmons
Sep 2, 1883

Julia A. Kimmins
Jan 14, 1875
Jun 5, 1901

Iris Estelle Kimmins
Oct 14, 1908
Jun 5, 1911

Mattie Kimmins
1917-1921

Anna Florence Rucker
Oct 26, 1877
Aug 6, 1917

J. Will Kimmins
Mar 10, 1870
Jan 8, 1953
&
Sallie G. Kimmins
Apr 5, 1875
Jul 11, 1970

37 GARRETT CEMETERY   Map # 2
Located about 1 mile South of Kingdom C.P.Church.

Fain Stevens Garrett
1882-1883

Infant dau of
Robert & Martha Garrett
Apr 21, 1884

Lizzie Garrett Johnson
1877-1958

Robert Cannon Garrett
1844-1938

Martha Jackson Garrett
1843-1893

William Thomas Garrett
Feb 28, 1869
Jan 25, 1925

Rebecca Lee Garrett
1874-1892

38 TAYLOR CEMETERY   Map # 2
Located about 1½ miles North of Taylors Cross Road.

Margaret J. Taylor
Apr 8, 1866
Sep 5, 1934

Infant Son of
N. R. & Mary A. Taylor
Apr 3, 1885
Apr 11, 1885

C. A. Taylor
1861-1927
& wife:
Annie E., & dau of
Lemuel & Poly Manier
Sep 20, 1860
married Sep 20, 1884
died Aug 19, 1885
&
Evvea E., wife of
C. A. Taylor, & dau of
Lemuel & Poly Manier
Oct 1, 1862
married Mar 7, 1886
died Sep 15, 1904

Nathaniel R. Taylor
Nov 18, 1852
Dec 16, 1911

Mary A., wife of
N. R. Taylor, Jr., & dau of
Jas L. & Mary A. Jackson
Apr 24, 1855
Sep 30, 1886
age: 31y, 5m, 6d.

C. P. Taylor
Jan 11, 1825
Oct 9, 1909
&
Elizabeth K. Taylor
May 3, 1827
Nov 20, 1885

Mary A., wife of
C. P. Taylor
Oct 4, 1837
Jun 9, 1907

Infant Son of
N. R. & Mary A. Taylor
Born & Died Sep 7, 1886

Mary Lena, dau of
N. R. & Mary A. Taylor
Apr 2, 1880
Apr 18, 1907

Emma, dau of C. A. &
Evie Elizabeth Taylor
Aug 10, 1888
May 15, 1921

Della K., wife of
W. L. Chick
Oct 17, 1869
Feb 8, 1907

Myrtle Vance, dau of
S. J. & M. E. Taylor
Dec 3, 1893
May 29, 1915

Infant Son of
S. J. & M. E. Taylor
Born & Died Nov 21, 1899

Sidney Harrison, son of
N. R. & Mary A. Taylor
Aug 16, 1883
May 9, 1884
age: 8m, & 23d.

Evie Sue, dau of
C. A. & Evie Elizabeth
Taylor
Jun 20, 1901
Feb 27, 1923

Clare Taylor Barnett
Mar 15, 1859
Nov 23, 1927

M. E., wife of
S. J. Taylor, & dau of
D. C. & Nancy Jackson
Jun 1, 1863
Jun 14, 1901

Herbert, son of
S. J. & M. E. Taylor
Aug 29, 1891
Jul 16, 1892

39 TAYLOR CEMETERY   Map # 2
Located about 1 mile North of Taylor Cross Roads.

Eld. T. J. Taylor
Dec 29, 1838
Aug 11, 1918

Cornelia Taylor
Apr 7, 1838
May 3, 1893
age: 55y, & 26d.

W. D. Farmer
Sep 30, 1868
Jan 5, 1917

Nelia Farmer
May 1, 1872
Sep 17, 1907

40 TAYLOR CEMETERY   Map # 2
Located at Taylor Cross Roads.

James P. Taylor
Oct 31, 1821
Jan 9, 1880

Margaret A., wife of
J. P. Taylor
May 10, 1829
Apr 25, 1895

Dr. William A. Lytle
Jul 12, 1872
Apr 12, 1909

Mary L. Lytle
Feb 9, 1879
Mar 1, 1956

C. N. Taylor
Dec 1, 1850
Mar 24, 1933

William V., son of
James P. & M. A. Taylor
May 10, 1853
May 8, 1880

Jemima Rogers
1837-1926

Hugh M. Elmore
Sep 28, 1864
Sep 15, 1907
&
Flora L. Elmore
Oct 21, 1870
Jan 23, 1950

Mary O. Taylor
Apr 18, 1860
Jun 4, 1888

Capt. Jas. K. P. Lytle
Feb 25, 1838
Jul 18, 1879

Mary A. E., wife of
J. K. P. Lytle
Feb 5, 1848
Oct 5, 1886
age: 38y, & 8m.

Emma F. Taylor
May 29, 1859
Jan 6, 1937

Adda A. E., dau of
J. K. P. & M. A. E. Lytle
Sep 19, 1876
Feb 3, 1878
age: 1y, 4m, 14d.

Harvey W. Lytle
Sep 20, 1840
Jul 29, 1896
&
Millie A. Lytle
Sep 30, 1844
Oct 1, 1903

41 HASKINS CEMETERY   Map # 2
Located near Taylor Cross Roads,
½ mile North of Coopertown

C. F. Haskins   and
May 5, 1823
Feb 6, 1909

E. L. Haskins, wife of
C. F. Haskins
Jan 7, 1839
Nov 4, 1891

[James & Mary (Harris) Lawrence
buried here in unmarked graves
after 1880. They married in 1834.
This was once Harris land. Some of
Harris family may be buried here.
From Records of Gladys Farris]

Allie B. Rogers, dau of
W. T. & S. F. Rogers
Mar 23, 1899
Aug 22, 1900

Lizzie, dau of
R. M. & M. E. Potts
Nov 10, 1874
Jul 25, 1876

William E. Beasley
1881-1884

Jim Ed Collins
Tennessee
Pvt 57 Pioneer Inf
Oct 18, 1918

T. F. Bullock
Mar 9, 1821
Nov 25, 1908

Amy King Bullock
Nov 30, 1821
May 6, 1890

Martha Tennessee Bullock
Jul 5, 1856
Nov 26, 1912

Thomas R. Dishmon
1932

Myrtle Lorene, dau of
H. S. & A. K. Crick
Sep 11, 1919
Sep 10, 1921

W. N. Crick
1870-1934

Madge Crick Graham
1879-1954

W. D. Graham
1878-1954

Thomas Warren Bullock
1940-1940

E. E. Bullock
Nov 9, 1882
Apr 30, 1910

John P. Bullock
1894-1934

McKame W. McLain, son of
John McLain
Born May 3, 18_7
Died ___ __, 182_
(Illegible)

Several unmarked graves.

H. Lawson Maxwell
1861-1936

Mrs. H. Lawson Maxwell
(no dates)

Nora May Maxwell
1873-1960
(Gowen-Smith)

Foster L. Hooker
May 12, 1838
Sep 30, 1881
&
Lavina K. Hooker
Oct 27, 1840
Nov 16, 1907

Lola M. Bullock   and
1884-1902
&
Amy K. Bullock   and
1890-1890

Sopha A. Crick
Mar 11, 1875
Jun 21, 1901

Dallas Crick   and
Dec 23, 1843
May 5, 1919

Roy Wade Crick
Mar 20, 1906
May 18, 1906

Henry Stem Crick
Apr 23, 1881
Dec 24, 1921

Amy Rogers Crick
Jun 24, 1886
Dec 12, 1929

Herbert Cooper
1906-
&
Beatrice C. Cooper
1909-1970

Thomas F. Bullock
1925-1942

B. I. Phillips
May 12, 1794
Sep 3, 1858

Nancy L. Phillips
Jan 2, 1799
Dec 28, 1885

Homer Mangrum
(no dates)

J. A. Maxwell
1853-1930

Nelia N., wife of
J. A. Maxwell
Aug 13, 1857
Jul 29, 1894
age: 36y, 11m, 15d.

Esther E., dau of
F. L. & L. K. Hooker
Mar 28, 1878
Sep 5, 1879

J. W. Maxwell
Dec 15, 1817
Jul 31, 1898

Benj F. Bullock   and
1879-1915
&
Minnie F. Bullock   and
1879-1915
&
Fannie E. Bullock
1867-1898

M. E. Crick***
Mar 18, 1851
Jan 7, 1926

Thomas F. Crick
1872-1948
&
Della (King) Crick***
1878-1950

Geneva Ruth, dau of
Mr & Mrs W. N. Crick
Jun 4, 1901
Oct 26, 1924

Vivian Ann Cooper
Jan 23, 1948
Jan 26, 1948

Thomas C. Creswell
Tennessee
Sea U.S.Navy
Jun 6, 1878
Apr 8, 1961

Sarah J. Phillips
Nov 18, 1828
Apr 3, 1830

W. C. Mangrum***(W.Cleveland)
(no dates)

J. C. Mangrum***(Jake C.)
(no dates)

Hattie Mangrum
(no dates)

N. C. Maxwell
Apr --, ----
Apr 25, 1879
(broken)

N. J. Maxwell
Feb 5, 1828
Apr 10, 1894

William D. Collins
1865-1920
&
Callie Hooker Collins
1868-1920

Mahalie F. Maxwell
Apr 13, 1818
Feb 13, 1899

Fannie May Bullock
1898-1898
&
Thelma G. Bullock
1907-1907

*** Family Records.
*** 5 Infants "Crick"
(no dates)

Martha Jane, dau of
Mansfield Whitehead
Apr 20, 1835
Oct 31, 1839
age: 4y, 6m, 1d.

Lurline, child of
B. O. & L. A. Crick
Jun 26, 1918
Nov 2, 1929

Oscar Crick
1878-1946
&
Lillie A. Crick
1881-1954

Brenda Gayle Bullock
Jan 31, 1953

John Wayne Bullock
Jun 24, 1950

Beverly Ann Bullock
Oct 11, 1947

Henrietta Sudberry
Jan 16, 1900
May 13, 1924

*** Family Records.

43 HENDRIX CEMETERY — Map # 2
Located near Kingdom C.P.Church.

William W., son of
_. _. & S. J. Hendrix
Born Sep 1855
Died __ 18, 1856

About 4 or 5 graves,
with fieldstones,
no inscriptions.

44 GENTRY CEMETERY — Map # 2
Located near Rover, Tn.

Samuel H. Gentry
Dec 5, 1869
Mar 5, 1870
&
Leander Gentry
Apr 4, 1873
Apr 12, 1873

J. P. Gentry
Dec 15, 1843
Nov 29, 1911
&
Mintory Gentry
Jan 27, 1848
Dec 2, 1930

Mary M. Lamb
Mar 13, 1866
Sep 25, 1917

Several graves marked with
fieldstones, no inscriptions.

J. S. Lamb
May 1, 1890
Dec 17, 1918

Emma J. Lamb
Nov 9, 1920
Mar 19, 1921

45 BYLER-MARCHANT CEMETERY — Map # 2
Located about ½ mile East of Rover, Tn.

In Memory of
Nancy Ann Marchant, wife of
W. B. Marchant, who was
Born 26 April 1821 &
Departed this life
April 5, 1845.

In Memory of
John H. Marchant
Born Jan 27, 1845
Died Aug 7, 1845

In Memory of
Median Byler, wife of
John Byler
Born Jun 3, 1799
Died May 10, 1845

"Our Little Sister"
Litha Cumi Gentry
Born Oct 1, 1879
Died Sep 3, 1886

46 LAMB CEMETERY — Map # 2
Located about ½ mile Northeast of Rover, Tn.

Eldridge W. Lamb
Sep 23, 1868
Mar 21, 1943
&
Laura Alton Lamb
Jun 20, 1898
Dec 6, 1904
&
Laura G. Owen Lamb
Nov 24, 1875
Feb 9, 1948

Julia Lamb, wife of
W. S. Sanders
Oct 8, 1885
May 11, 1903

John W. Lamb
1861-1935
&
Eliza J. Lamb
1863-1946

Mary A., dau of
W. T. Morrison
Dec 18, 1889
Oct 20, 1890

Willis H. Lamb
Dec 10, 1839
Nov 20, 1909
& wife:
Sarah E. Lamb
Mar 12, 1841
Jul 20, 1912

Infant Son of
J. W. & E. J. Lamb
Aug 31, 1899

George W. Taylor
Feb 28, 1868
Apr 11, 1918
&
Nannie E. Taylor
Nov 28, 1872
May 9, 1940

Cora May Lamb
May 10, 1890
Aug 2, 1905

47 JOHNSON CEMETERY — Map # 2
Located about ½ mile North of Rover, Tenn., on
Bunker Hill Road.

J. T. Johnson, Consort of
W. T. Johnson
Mar 17, 1849
Jul 15, 1877
age: 28y, 3m, 29d.

W. T. Johnson, Sr.
Dec 25, 1835
May 21, 1918
age: 82y, 4m, 25d.

Herbert Lytle, son of
W. T. & Lizzie L. Johnson
May 26, 1902
Nov 13, 1906
age: 4y, 5m, 18d.

48 BYLER CEMETERY — Map # 2
Located at Rover, Tenn.

Nancy Byler, Consort of
Abraham Byler, Esq.
Apr 11, 1775
Nov 3, 1842
age: 68 yrs.

Mrs. Eliza L. Jones
Apr 15, 1822
Sep 26, 1873

Abraham Byler
(Marker with no inscription,
footmarker is there)

W. T. Vernon
Born Dec 14, 1826, married
to S. A. Battle Feb 6, 1879,
died Jan 2, 1912
Age: 86y & 19d.
"An Old Confederate Veteran"

Infant Dau of
J. P. Smith
Born & Died Oct 26, 1841

Samantha Ann Vernon
Born Nov 17, 1840, married
to W. T. Vernon Feb 6, 1879,
died May 14, 1922
age: 81y, 5m, 27d.

Infant Dau of
J. P. Smith
Born & Died Aug 2, 1842

Many unmarked graves.

Located in the Church Yard, Rover.
(Markers now gone.)

Allen Wade***
Jun 24, 1814
Jun 17, 1887

Rebecca Wade***
Sep 14, 1814
Sep 23, 1887

*** Record by
Franklin Blanton
Rover, Tn.

50 SIMPSON CEMETERY   Map # 2
Located at Rover, Tennessee

G. W. Williams
Jan 25, 1849
Jul 11, 1924
&
Luranie Williams
Nov 16, 1852
Jan 3, 1923

A. S. Weaver
Oct 14, 1809
Feb 26, 1848
&
Emely Little Weaver
Sep 19, 1816
married Oct 2, 1834
died Jun 17, 1889

"Brother"
Charlie Boyce
Nov 10, 1898
Sep 8, 1915
&
"Sister"
R. Ophelia Boyce
Jan 28, 1911
Jul 1, 1912

George W. Gentry
Jan 11, 1885

&
Tempie Lou Gentry
Nov 6, 1883
Aug 17, 1966
(picture of both)

Rev. Samuel J. Gentry
Jan 4, 1861
Feb 25, 1927

Sarah T., wife of
S. J. Gentry
Aug 31, 1862
Nov 15, 1891

James R. Clay
Sep 5, 1888
Sep 29, 1936

Charlie E. Clay
Jul 24, 1884
Mar 10, 1896

Elizabeth Fulmore
died Feb 27, 1906
(no age given)

James M. Fulmer
Dec 19, 1826
Jun 12, 1828

W. C. Cook
Apr 4, 1811
Jan 1, 1882

Elizabeth Cook
1814-Sep 5, 1880

Jennie May Boyce
Aug 12, 1900
Feb 15, 1940

Joe Boyce
Sep 1, 1868
Oct 14, 1938
&
Ella Boyce
Jan 30, 1871
Jul 10, 1937

Evander W. Boyce
Apr 2, 1866
Dec 17, 1944
&
Alda Sue Boyce
May 10, 1877
Jul 5, 1951

Rev. William H. Gentry
1872-1949
&
Lillie Perry Gentry
1888-1965

Mark E. Morton
Dec 27, 1898
Oct 7, 1899
&
Mary L. Phillips, wife of
Jerry Morton
Dec 11, 1869
Sep 22, 1899

Eliza A. Elrod(y)
Feb 11, 182_
Oct 11, 1870

James H. Clay
Apr 3, 1849
Jun 1, 1912

Amanda Jackson Clay
Oct 18, 1854
Jun 13, 1946

Sabra Fulmer
Jan 8, 1811
Aug 12, 1823

John C. Fulmer
Nov 1, 1812
Aug 15, 1815

Thomas W. Lamb
Oct 6, 1873
Mar 12, 1955
&
Lillie M. Lamb
Dec 21, 1894

May Lamb, wife of
T. W. Lamb
Dec 12, 1870
Feb 18, 1913

Rubie Maude Boyce
Dec 14, 1906
Jun 28, 1921

Ira M. Boyce
Aug 19, 1896
Jun 22, 1897
&
Infant Baby Boyce
died Mar 28, 1905

Felix Gentry
Sep 8, 1862
Dec 23, 1945
&
Nick Gentry
Jun 4, 1866
Apr 9, 1942

W. T. Phillips
1866-1940

May Bell P. Thaxton
1893-1969

William H. Phillips
Dec 27, 1834
Apr 22, 1914
&
Amanda Phillips
Mar 15, 1843
Jan 11, 1928

Lula Macon Clay
Jan 18, 1879
Apr 26, 1899

T. Mayfield Farmer
1873-1959

Mary Clay Farmer
1876-1942

Nancy R. Fulmer
Oct 1, 1816
Sep 30, 1824

P. L. T. (fieldstone, no
inscription)

"Mother"
Lena Chick
1871-1952

Margaret Chick
(no dates)

Emma Chick
Jul 4, 1875
Dec 24, 1875

W. L. Chick
1846-1917
&
Sarah Faris Chick
1840-1876

James Boyce, Jr.
(no dates)
&
Maggie Virginia Boyce
(no dates)
"Children"

James W. Boyce
Mar 17, 1895

&
Bessie H. Boyce
May 9, 1894
Apr 23, 1952

"Mother"
Willie Raby, wife of
Rev. S. J. Gentry
Oct 31, 1892
Dec 18, 1938
&
"Son"
W. Elon Gentry
Born Jan 17, 1914
killed in Italy
Sep 16, 1944

Mastin Clay
Who was born in Dinwiddie
Co., Va., Feb 14, 1800
died Feb 24, 1873
age: 73y, & 10d.

Sallie, wife of
Mastin Clay
Mar 24, 1822
Apr 9, 1908

----------,departed this
life Sept the ---------- .

(fieldstone, illegible &
next to fieldstone P.L.T.)

Lula Macon Shearin
Feb 2, 1905
Feb 3, 1905

Infant Dau of
W. O. & M. Shearin
Born & Died Jan 25, 1908

William Oliver Shearin
Mar 2, 1867
Jul 8, 1923
(picture)

Manie Clay Shearin
Jan 13, 1874
Apr 15, 1932

Richard E. Williams
Jul 20, 1931
Jul 24, 1931

Joey Lynn Boyce
Born & Died Jul 23, 1961

John William Boyce
Jun 1, 1905
Dec 3, 1962
&
Wilma G. Boyce
Aug 23, 1905

Georgia Blanton, wife of
Fred Simpson
Nov 30, 1899
Mar 8, 1931

Benjamin T. Simpson
Tennessee
Pvt 314 Inf, W.W.II
Feb 19, 1925
Jul 12, 1944

Robert E. B. Floyd
(no dates)

Maggie Taylor Floyd
(no dates)

"Father"
R. E. B. Floyd
Jul 30, 1846
Oct 25, 1936
&
"Mother"
W. C. Floyd
Nov 30, 1842
Nov 7, 1899

Nathan S. Sanders
1861-1935

Mary E. Reed, wife of
R. L. Sanders
Dec 27, 1888
Apr 1, 1922

Randolph L. Sanders
1888-1952

Gertrude, wife of
J. B. Taylor
1885-1918

M. B. Gentry
May 10, 1838
married to L. F. Arnold
Jan 19, 1859
died Apr 11, 1904

Lumiza F., wife of
M. B. Gentry
Nov 8, 1842
May 4, 1917

"Mother"
Martha T. Gentry
May 9, 1859
Mar 8, 1911

Mandy S. Wright
1880-1959

Hazel V. Gentry
Jun 19, 1927
Mar 24, 1928

Herman B. Gentry
Jul 3, 1931
Jul 10, 1933

Allie Cole, wife of
R. C. Knott
died 1883
(no age given)

Lillian Cooper, wife of
E. H. Boyd
1875-1927

William Floyd
May 19, 1812
Jan 26, 1889
&
Julia G. Floyd
Aug 4, 1813
Jun 12, 1894
&
John W. Chambers
Nov 17, 1839
Mar 12, 1888
&
Rebecca E. Chambers
Nov 2, 1849
Feb 14, 1887

Henry Taylor Floyd
Jul 31, 1876
May 25, 1919

Fannie Fulmer
Oct 4, 1840
Jan 2, 1910

Bobby E. Sanders
Tennessee
A3c 388 Tactical Hosp. A.F.
Apr 14, 1936
Apr 12, 1955

James B. Taylor
1883-1940
&
Fannie Powers Taylor
1882-1975(TM)

Clark
(no dates

George D. Gentry
Jun 29, 1941
Jan 29, 1942

Grace Dorris Gentry
Jun 12, 1902
Nov 23, 1921

"Father"
Braly B. Gentry
Aug 22, 1897
Aug 4, 1949
&
"Mother"
Allie N. Gentry
Aug 11, 1898

Kristy Lynn Stevenson
Born & Died May 26, 1957

W. G. Purvis
May 21, 1871
Jul 23, 1949

William McKinley Gentry
Jul 21, 1902

&
Lena Bell Gentry
Mar 28, 1912

W. T. Blanton
1854-1937

Lula Cooper, wife of
W. T. Blanton
Nov 19, 1861
Mar 6, 1920

George W. Fisher
1828-1907
&
Louisa J. Fisher
1830-1903
(Old Stone:Lizy Fisher,
died July 21, 1903)

Thomas H., Consort of
Lettetia Spence
Aug 1, 1840
Nov 20, 1878

Effie Sanders, wife of
J. E. Parker
Dec 30, 1898
Jul 2, 1915

Arch Prater
died 1928
(Gowen-Smith)

Parlee Prater
died 1927
(Gowen-Smith)

Thomas Lee Taylor
1870-1951
&
Bettie Irene Taylor
1887-19

Clark
(no dates

George William Ryan
Sep 13, 1921
Jul 7, 1926

James Edwin Ryan
Sep 1, 1925
Jul 3, 1926

Donald E. Ryan
May 4, 1933
Jun 1, 1934

James T. Ryan
Jul 8, 1898
Jun 29, 1966

Pearlie Mai Ryan
Aug 29, 1904
Dec 21, 1951

Thomas N. Adcock
Tennessee
Tec 4 39 Signal Const. Bn
W. W. II
May 30, 1925
Nov 24, 1952

May Blanton
1898-1920

Virgil D. Blanton
1858-1943
&
Willie W. Blanton
1869-1940

Ella Blanton
Jun 30, 1880
Nov 13, 1928

James W. Simpson
1856-1934
&
Kitty K. Simpson
1868-1951

John W. Simpson
Jul 14, 1812
Oct 31, 1869

M. W., wife of
John W. Simpson
May 6, 1830
Aug 15, 1909

"Our Grandmother"
Rebecca Simpson
Oct 1786
Apr 1867

John T. Wilson
1850-1932

Mary D. Wilson
1850-1934

Annie D. Wilson
1887-1929

John Bell Taylor
1922-1922

Edd M. Street
Nov 15, 1897
Nov 11, 1965
&
Jessie L. Street
Mar 27, 1902
Nov 14, 1973

H. C. "Tom" Yarbrough
Feb 2, 1863
Jul 16, 1928
&
Mary Thomason Yarbrough
Mar 31, 1873
Aug 15, 1947

Benjamin T. Yarbrough
Tennessee
Pfc U.S.Marine Corps
W. W. I
Nov 6, 1895
Jul 7, 1969
&
Elma C. Yarbrough
Jul 10, 1892
Dec 22, 1968

William P. Yarbrough
Aug 20, 1902
May 21, 1967
&
Selma R. Yarbrough
Dec 4, 1904

Edward Ghee
1881-1958
&
Emma Eva Ghee
1882-1928

John W. Ghee
Mar 23, 1848
Apr 10, 1907
&
Martha E. Ghee
Dec 12, 1850
Mar 20, 1938

Fannie Mai Ghee
Apr 1904
Jun 1905

W. H. "Bill" Simpson
Dec 31, 1925
Sep 23, 1966
Tennessee
S1, U.S.N.R.
W. W. II
&
Millie H. Simpson
Oct 5, 1921

James M. Thomason
1861-(no date)
&
Bettie Stegall Thomason
1861-1936

Albert C. Hudson   and
May 28, 1903
Dec 13, 1960

W. Cullen Taylor
Oct 11, 1879
May 28, 1957
&
Emma D. Taylor
Sep 8, 1884
Jun 18, 1972

Virginia T. Taylor
1857-1937

F. L. Taylor
Jul 18, 1838
Jul 19, 1900

A. Fonzie White
1886-1940
&
Mary B. White
1890-1927

Marvin P. Wood
Mar 15, 1883
Aug 23, 1969
&
Mary B. Wood
Apr 6, 1895

J. W. Winn
Mar 4, 1842
Dec 5, 1917
&
Mrs. R. Winn
Jul 29, 1841
Aug 5, 1918

John L. Jackson
Jun 4, 1846
married to Susan E. Chick
Nov 22, 1867
died Feb 13, 1909

Sue Chick, wife of
J. L. Jackson
1851-1919

W. M. Tucker
Feb 19, 1838
Jun 14, 1921
&
M. J. Tucker
Sep 21, 1845
Feb 18, 1918

John W. Tucker
1866-1950

Martha F. Sims
Oct 28, 1837
Nov 6, 1913

Edd. M. Clay
Oct 22, 1881
Jan 25, 1966
&
Alta S. Clay
Oct 4, 1884
Nov 26, 1973

Jennie Newsom Hudson
Dec 12, 1904
Jun 5, 1960

Irvin B. Jackson
1904-1944
&
Virginia Jackson
1910-19

Thomas J. Taylor
Sep 23, 1894
Nov 12, 1896

Annie G. Taylor
Aug 17, 1892
Sep 13, 1892

Infant Son of
T. L. & B. I. Taylor
Aug 13, 1906
Aug 14, 1906

H. Maynard Crick
Jun 9, 1885
Dec 26, 1970
&
Lillie F. Crick
Jul 11, 1891

William G. Davis
1869-1961
&
Amanda E. Davis
1871-1952

Clara Mai, dau of
W. E. & Z. L. Smotherman
Aug 11, 1918
Oct 30, 1921

B. I. Simpson
May 29, 1856
Sep 22, 1932

Edna K., wife of
B. I. Simpson
Apr 5, 1861
Jul 20, 1943

Eris K. Simpson
Oct 17, 1900
May 3, 1923

A. C. Lamb
Dec 7, 1831
Sep 9, 1904

Robert W. Simpson
Dec 9, 1887
Jan 1, 1965
&
Cora H. Simpson
Feb 11, 1892

Annie B. Pugh
Apr 11, 1889
Oct 23, 1918

J. L. H.
(fieldstone, no inscription)

Grady Holton
Nov 14, 1911
Apr 25, 1933

Finous M. Sudberry
Apr 5, 1888
Nov 19, 1971
&
M. Adelade Sudberry
Oct 24, 1889
Dec 4, 1941

J. E. Newsom
1874-1935

Mary Amanda Newsom
1875-1953
(Lawrence FH)

John E. Bumpus
1870-1940
&
Addie S. Bumpus
1869-1948

Martin Bumpus
Mar 15, 1893
Oct 7, 1915

Mrs. Mary E. Maupin
1876-1960
(Gowen-Smith)

Alonza C. Heath
Oct 22, 1896
Jul 15, 1964
&
Mary E. Heath
Jun 23, 1890
(no date)

Thomas E. Simpson
1890-1973
&
Elizabeth B. Simpson
1892-

Margaret Simpson
Sep 20, 1917

John R. Phillips
1867-1955
&
Mary B. Phillips
1877-1945
&
Raymond Phillips
1908

Holland G. Davis
1880-1955
&
Naomi E. Davis
1881-1943

Edward Clary Davis
Sep 4, 1903
Jul 18, 1904

Ben Ragsdale
May 13, 1900

Emma J. Ragsdale
Jan 1, 1884
Oct 22, 1954

Lee M. Hudson
Feb 26, 1880
Nov 21, 1967
&
Mary B. Hudson
Mar 28, 1882
Nov 11, 1966

Jessie Puckett Hudson
1909-1975
(Lawrence FH)

William S. Sanders
1882-1973
&
Lizzie B. Sanders
1879-1954

P. R. Sanders
1910

Infant Sanders
1911

Hattie Sanders
1885-1919

Robert Lee Leverette
Jul 4, 1896
Nov 8, 1932
&
Serena Bell Leverette
Jan 11, 1899

Robert C. Leverette
Mar 6, 1856
Apr 4, 1930
&
Sarah E. Leverette
Jun 8, 1866
May 5, 1929

E. C. Lester
1882-1937

Mance Mangrum
1885-1957
(Lawrence FH)

Lillie Mangrum
1889-1972
(Lawrence FH)

Romus Robinson
1889-1948
&
Annie Robinson
1896-19

N. L.
(fieldstone)

Robert T. Smotherman
Oct 30, 1886
Jul 26, 1967
&
Ellen Ghee Smotherman
Jan 27, 1887
Nov 21, 1957

Ben R. Smotherman   and
Aug 29, 1909

Charles L. McCracken
Georgia
Cpl Army Air Forces
W. W. II
Jan 29, 1918
May 22, 1967

Richard N. Davis
Nov 8, 1851
Mar 24, 1924
&
Martha S. Davis
Aug 15, 1852
Oct 7, 1938

Esther D. Drumright
Nov 9, 1894
Jun 14, 1971

J. H. Arnold
Feb 22, 1848
Sep 18, 1905
&
Susan J. Arnold
Feb 27, 1855
Dec 13, 1900

Grady, son of
J. H. & S. J. Arnold
Aug 31, 1894
Feb 16, 1899

Mary Arnold
Jun 8, 1828
Sep 15, 1905

C. B. Armstrong
Jun 17, 1881
Jun 4, 1919
&
M. B. Armstrong
May 31, 1876
(no date)

Tom Freeman
Sep 28, 1868
Aug 15, 1930

Ma----- Freeman
(fieldstone)

Mary R. Freeman
Jan 27, 1878
Jul 10, 1949

James Don Freeman
Sep 10, 1942
Nov 20, 1972

Kate Lee Vaughn
Nov 8, 1888
Apr 3, 1951

Willie Hammond
age: 6y, 7m, 2d.
(no dates)

Martha Ellen Smotherman
Apr 1, 1925
Sep 14, 1927

Lou Ada Smotherman
Jun 8, 1910

James Thomas Taylor
Jul 25, 1870
May 11, 1948
&
Susie Lue Taylor
Mar 20, 1876
Dec 15, 1964

Allie Pear, dau of
J. T. & S. L. Taylor
Jan 10, 1898
Oct 22, 1899

John Hollin Taylor, son of
J. T. & S. L. Taylor
Aug 16, 1899
Feb 8, 1916

Mary Glen, dau of
J. T. & Susie Taylor
Feb 11, 1910
Aug 19, 1917

Murray J. Osmundson
Dec 11, 1903
Dec 21, 1954
&
Owene Lamb Osmundson
Feb 2, 1908
Oct 6, 1964

Clarence Rowland
Jun 7, 1906
Aug 18, 1963
&
Lena Mae Rowland
Nov 9, 1908

Viola Bell, wife of
B. H. Forester
age: 24y, 2m, 6d.
(no dates)

Issaic E. Wright
1875-1947
&
Emma Wright
1869-1951

Mary E.(Emma) Wright
Dec 2, 1872
Feb 14, 1961

Mrs. Margaret Wright
Mar 22, 1842
Oct 18, 1925
age: 83y, 6m, 26d.

Isac Wright
Co A 24 Tenn Inf
C.S.A.

Bettie Louise Bolden
Feb 14, 1945
May 12, 1946

Rhonda Gail Blanton
Dec 18, 1951
Jul 15, 1957

Bobby C. Smotherman
Dec 31, 1936
Dec 13, 1940

J. Clinty Boyce
Feb 20, 1880
Jul 1, 1914

Phoebe A. Boyce
Dec 2, 1880
Mar 10, 1911

Elma R. Loyd
1933-1934

W. J. Loyd
1866-1941
&
Rebecca Loyd
1873-1965

Lonnie W. Lamb
Sep 17, 1900
Jan 26, 1914

Thomas D. Lamb
Jun 17, 1856
Nov 13, 1925
&
Deanie Pearson Lamb
Oct 27, 1876
Feb 16, 1974

Leroy Holton
1948-1954
(Lawrence FH)

Eva M. Holton
1939-1939
(fieldstone)

Alonza Birt Loyd
Jul 28, 1896
Nov 13, 1947

William Richard Loyd
(no dates)

Walter Freeman
Jul 2, 1882
Jul 2, 1940
&
Nancy J. Freeman
Oct 30, 1885
Jun 4, 1962

Thos. E. Freeman
Dec --, ----
Jul 28, 1937
(fieldstone)

William T. Freeman
Tennessee
S1 U.S.N.R. W.W.II
Jun 23, 1920
Jul 11, 1966

Fred Wiley Bolden
Mar 25, 1946
Apr 10, 1946

Bonnie Sue Bolden
Dec 14, 1949
Dec 15, 1949

Claude Sanders
Jun 1, 1931
Jun 4, 1931

Clyde Sanders
Jun 1, 1931
Jun 2, 1931

Eugene C. Sanders
Apr 7, 1885

&
Mahallie P. Sanders
Oct 13, 1889
Dec 7, 1969

Ellen Ruth Sanders
Jul 5, 1933
Dec 23, 1933

Sam B. Blanton, Jr.
Tennessee
Cpl Btry B 756 FA Bn
Nov 9, 1924
Feb 10, 1958

Sam B. Blanton
1893-19
&
Ruth Elmore Blanton
1893-1942

F. W. Elmore
Aug 22, 1859
Jul 5, 1925

Salome Hester, wife of
W. F. Elmore
Jan 8, 1867
Sep 29, 1933

John Bolin
1889-1970
&
Della Bolin
1890-1952

Tina Marie Kyle
1970-1970
(Lawrence FH)

Hugh G. Elmore
Jul 20, 1908

&
B. Pearl Elmore
Sep 14, 1894
Apr 25, 1970

Evalee Thomas Elmore, wife
of Hugh Elmore
Apr 27, 1913
Mar 8, 1933

Pamela F. Graham
Sep 16, 1964
Sep 17, 1964

Gilbert R. Brown
Tennessee
Staff Sgt 392 AAF
Bomb Group W.W.II
Dec 30, 1919
May 29, 1944

Nannie E. Sanders
Mar 26, 1919
Jul 28, 1936

Sam L. Ghee
Aug 6, 1889
Oct 9, 1970
&
Susie L. Ghee
May 11, 1896

Sammie Lee Ghee
Aug 20, 1926
Aug 8, 1943

Raymond H. McCulloch
1894-1967
&
Dovie Taylor McCulloch
1890-1936

James W. Slaughter
Jul 15, 1862
Oct 21, 1931
& wife:
Sallie A. Tucker Slaughter
May 29, 1874
Aug 27, 1945

Nellie Marie Elmore
Apr 13, 1932
Feb 6, 1949

Sarah C. Elmore
Dec 25, 1925
Aug 30, 1926

Arthur H. Elmore
Jan 8, 1899
Sep 5, 1966
&
Gertie M. Elmore
Nov 8, 1906

Will M. Gregg
1891-1960
&
Mary D. Gregg
1901-

W. M. Pope
Mar 8, 1864
Aug 5, 1930

Mrs. L. J. Pope
Aug 13, 1872
(no date)

James "Ronnie" Gregg
1957-1973

Dorothy Jean Brown
1930-1933

Fred Elrod Brown
Tennessee
Pvt U.S.Army W.W.II
Sep 1, 1916
Dec 3, 1968

Thompson Brown
1884-1948
&
Beulah E. Brown
1885-1970

William L. Cooper
Tennessee
Pvt 165 Infantry W.W.I
Oct 23, 1887
Aug 24, 1970
&
Jewell S. Cooper
Aug 9, 1909

James T. Shearin
Tennessee
Cpl Btry B 318 Fld Arty
W. W. I
Jun 5, 1891
Dec 4, 1967
&
M. E. Taylor Shearin
Nov 18, 1893
Jan 17, 1974

James Thomas Shearin, Jr.
Dec 23, 1921
Jan 29, 1931

F. Blanton Smotherman
Mar 1, 1912

&
Eliza Myrtle Smotherman
Oct 2, 1912

Elmer Jordan Smotherman
Apr 6, 1913
May 29, 1930
&
John Hugh Smotherman
May 3, 1915
Apr 14, 1930

John W. Smotherman
Apr 19, 1877
Aug 24, 1941
&
Mary E. Smotherman
Nov 18, 1886
Oct 6, 1959

Robert Earl Puckett
Sep 3, 1920
Nov 3, 1920

Charles C. Puckett
Nov 10, 1876
Dec 9, 1929

William L. Gentry
1871-1970
&
Etta Gentry
1872-1928

R. M. "Jack" Gentry
Jun 1, 1897
Jan 21, 1961
&
Algie N. Gentry
Oct 8, 1903
Mar 8, 1971

Nora Thomason Smith
Jun 24, 1863
Mar 19, 1952

E. Robert Brown
Feb 14, 1907
Jan 16, 1969
&
Jessie D. Brown
Jun 7, 1910

J. Worth Brown
1882-1946
&
S. Tennie Brown
1885-1968

Tom Ed Taylor
1893-1974
(Lawrence FH)

Alva Taylor
1880-
&
Minnie S. Taylor
1887-

Polly, wife of
Leon Taylor
Mar 27, 1901
Dec 16, 1925

A. Evelyn, Baby of
Fred & Luella Taylor
1926-1927

James M. Read
1902-1959
&
Alla D. Read
1903-

Howard Lamb
Jul 7, 1903

&
Effie Lamb
Oct 18, 1903

Charles T. Floyd
1874-1946
&
Emma F. Floyd
1883-19(75)(TM)

T. C. Gentry
Dec 10, 1846
Dec 11, 1928
&
Mary R. Gentry
Jan 7, 1852
Jan 5, 1926

Willie E. Lamb
1885-1973
&
Henry H. Lamb
1887-1939

Sarah Lamb
(no dates)

Rev. J. D. Smith
Apr 12, 1847
Apr 21, 1931

Russell Chick
Sep 20, 1920

&
Patricia Ann Chick
Jul 26, 1934
Aug 23, 1966

B. T. Chick
1879-1945
&
Myrtle Chick
1894-19

John D. Cooper
1908-1972
(Lawrence FH)

John E. Sanders
May 19, 1879
Jul 31, 1962
&
Fammie A. Sanders
Jun 24, 1887
Apr 28, 1948

Ira Hix Taylor
Apr 19, 1896
Dec 22, 1971
&
Beulah F. Taylor
Dec 14, 1896

Robert F. Sanders
Feb 18, 1901

&
Maude W. Sanders
Oct 10, 1901

Melody Dawn Smith
Oct 4, 1963
Jan 24, 1972

Mary Ann Hargrove
Feb 12, 1950
Feb 14, 1973

Danny Moss
1973
(Watson FH)

James D. Elmore
Dec 17, 1913
Aug 25, 1963
&
Sarah L. Elmore
Dec 5, 1918

Thomas P. Tucker
Feb 24, 1870
Jan 30, 1961
&
Nanalou E. Tucker
Nov 2, 1872
Oct 11, 1958

Johnie Coleman
Nov 7, 1953
Jun 13, 1961

Charlie R. Dishmon
Jul 27, 1907

&
Annie Mai Dishmon
Sep 27, 1905
Feb 14, 1972

Jasper L. Dishmon
1905-1944

"Sisters"
Mary E. Heath
Nov 18, 1887

&
Jimmie C. Heath
Feb 25, 1899
Jan 30, 1961

Jim Edd Ghee
Oct 17, 1909
Feb 15, 1967
&
Nannie Mai Ghee
May 22, 1907

Odell Gentry
Jul 26, 1921

&
Nell Gentry
Jan 23, 1925

Timothy Dwight Lamb
Born & Died Oct 9, 1972

William Pruitt
Aug 15, 1894

&
Omega Y. Pruitt
Aug 21, 1899
Dec 11, 1971

Fred L. Abernathy
Alabama
Pvt Provost Guard Co
W. W. I
May 5, 1895
Aug 2, 1960
&
Emma Lee J. Abernathy
Aug 6, 1901
Oct 20, 1969

Jesse S. Shearin
Jul 24, 1895
Oct 28, 1971
&
Nettie Read Shearin
Jan 8, 1897
Jan 16, 1972

Willie G. Shearin
Jul 20, 1901

&
Lillian E. Shearin
Jan 26, 1909

Samuel C. Pugh
Dec 18, 1920

&
Malindor D. Pugh
Nov 5, 1933

Basil Dewitt Read
1892-1947
&
Ruth Heath Read
1896-19

Emily Fay Crick
Oct 21, 1960
Oct 22, 1960

James Donald Giles
Oct 31, 1942
Mar 1, 1946

Fred M. Crick
Nov 21, 1916
Jan 11, 1947

Edgar W. Crick
1880-1963
&
Emma L. Crick
1885-1967

Lytle C. Loyd
1906-
&
Alta Mae Loyd
1907-

Arthur Lee Dalton
Sep 15, 1903
Nov 18, 1967
&
Allie Mai Dalton
Apr 12, 1907

J. Forrest Boyce
Jun 30, 1913
Oct 31, 1973
&
Aline C. Boyce
Nov 19, 1910

John Thomas Beasley
Oct 19, 1899
Dec 6, 1949

Thomas Kenneth Lorance
Sep 9, 1951
Oct 26, 1951

Timothy Lee Cook
Sep 10, 1961
Mar 19, 1962

Kathy Jean Sanders
Born & Died Aug 30, 1954

Jeffrey Bert Green
Born & Died Feb 12, 1956

W. Howard Read   and
1892-1957

Millard Earl Monday
Pfc U.S.Army
W.W.II
Jul 4, 1922
Dec 14, 1967

Willie S. Knois
Tennessee
Pfc Hq Btry 74 AAA
Gp CAC   W.W.II
Dec 20, 1917
Oct 9, 1956

W. D. Knois
Apr 30, 1874
May 11, 1939
&
Alta M. Knois
Jan 2, 1889
Jul 27, 1969

Jimmy Lath Hogan
Sep   1897
Nov 22, 1973

Lath Hogan
Feb 14, 1865
May 25, 1939

Telitha Hogan
Apr 11, 1859
Nov 13, 1947

Eugene Lamb
Jun 24, 1907

&
Christine Lamb
Sep 15, 1909

Elizabeth Rowland Brannon
Apr 5, 1940
Jun 4, 1971

John Marvin Boyce
Mar 14, 1907
Oct 16, 1974
&
Evelyn Rusher Boyce
Jan 13, 1912
----
married Nov 15, 1926

Albert M. Boyce
"Shorty"
May 27, 1939
Aug 19, 1973

Peggy Joyce Leverette
May 26, 1952
Nov 26, 1958

Herman Leverette
Jun 30, 1921

&
Ruby S. Leverette
Feb 3, 1923

Florence J. Read
1893-1974

John H. Tucker
1908-

Maggie B. Tucker
1912-1956

George A. Tucker
Aug 31, 1880
Nov 4, 1960
&
Beckie G. Tucker
Mar 1, 1883
Dec 6, 1971

Robert L. Tucker
Mar 28, 1884
May 22, 1972
&
Addie G. Tucker
Sep 28, 1889

James I. Edmondson
Aug 15, 1900
May 22, 1965

Michael R. Edmondson
Sep 30, 1957
Sep 8, 1968
(picture)

Walter S. Taylor
1875-1958
&
Martha Lamb Taylor
1880-1966

Carroll E. Blanton
Jul 18, 1892
Sep 17, 1964
&
Myrtle B. Blanton
Dec 11, 1893
----
married Dec 22, 1912

Thomas H. Crick, Jr.
May 8, 1935

&
Annie D. Crick
Aug 1, 1940
Sep 18, 1962

W. Richard Sanders
Apr 16, 1912

&
Katherine S. Sanders
Mar 8, 1913
Nov 12, 1963

John Scott Sharp
Mar 29, 1973
Apr 24, 1973

Kathy Jean Sudberry
Sep 30, 1955

Karran Ann Sudberry
Oct 9, 1954

Hubert L. Freeman
Mar 17, 1905

&
Esther Tucker Freeman
Jun 9, 1907
Aug 26, 1973

Childress W. Read
Jun 4, 1881
Oct 24, 1957
&
Ora Taylor Read
Jun 2, 1883

Lucille Joyce Watts
1918-1973

Robert B. Knois
1914-1965
&
Jennie L. Knois
1913-1974
married Sep 8, 1934

Thomas Wilkie Knois
Jan 4, 1958
Jul 30, 1958

Archie Tucker
May 2, 1898

&
Ethel Tucker
Feb 19, 1902

J. Willis Taylor
May 15, 1905

&
Opal W. Taylor
Oct 27, 1912

Dennis W. Taylor
Sep 7, 1912
Dec 9, 1963
&
Ethel W. Taylor
Dec 3, 1918

Tommie Lee Haynes
Jun 4, 1908

&
Alta Pugh Haynes
Jun 16, 1909
Oct 21, 1964

Several graves with fieldstones, no inscriptions.

William P. Elmore
Tennessee
Pvt 374 MP Escort Gd Co
W. W. II
Nov 3, 1899
Mar 15, 1952

Granville S. Elmore
Aug 28, 1875
Apr 7, 1951
&
Jemima T. Elmore
Aug 20, 1895
Mar 23, 1954

James William Holton
Tennessee
Cpl Co C 844 Eng AVN Bn
Jan 21, 1932
Jan 8, 1955

James H. Griggs
Dec 24, 1935
May 13, 1973
&
Bobbie L. Griggs
Feb 1, 1938

Robert L. Holton
Oct 27, 1909
Apr 11, 1961
&
Mary G. Holton
Feb 15, 1910

Willie D. Holton
Oct 24, 1904
Sep 30, 1969

Larry Eugene Smotherman
Mar 24, 1950
Aug 8, 1966

Brenda Lewis
Jan 10, 1955
Jul 22, 1964

Willie B. Sudberry
Jul 29, 1885
Oct 2, 1969
&
Minnie Cole Sudberry
Sep 16, 1888
Jan 6, 1973

O. H. Lorance
May 15, 1881
Nov 24, 1959
&
Fannie E. Lorance
Dec 21, 1889
Dec 13, 1966

Many unmarked graves.

Humphrey H. Boyce
Sep 23, 1875
Dec 9, 1966
&
Harriet S. Boyce
Feb 7, 1869
Dec 20, 1960

Mary A. Boyce, wife of
Carl Boyce
1897-1950

John H. Wright
Oct 14, 1908
May 14, 1966
&
M. Adelaide Wright
Feb 23, 1913

Oscar Ervin Wright
1900-1962
&
Emma Pearl Wright
1905-1953

J. P. Walls
May 11, 1892
Jul 25, 1963
&
Belle Noe Walls
Aug 20, 1882
Jul 5, 1961

John C. Pittman
Feb 14, 1884
Jun 17, 1967
&
Freda F. Pittman
Jan 23, 1892
Jan 19, 1974

Ruby Marie Pittman
May 30, 1916
Mar 20, 1970

W. Tom Floyd
Oct 31, 1898

&
Verna J. Floyd
Dec 25, 1908

Lowry C. Floyd
Jan 11, 1906
Mar 31, 1966
&
Mary F. Floyd
Jul 22, 1905

Webb Pugh
1887-1969
&
Alta Pugh
1890-

51 SMOTHERMAN CEMETERY   Map # 2
Located about ½ mile Southwest of Rover, Tn.

Carrie J. Terry
1893-1968
&
Bertha E. Terry
1889-1966

Tenie Terry
Feb 11, 1869
Mar 14, 1917

Solon Landers Terry
Tennessee
Pvt 383 Inf W.W.I
Jul 7, 1896
Apr 23, 1960

William Lee Terry
May 17, 1866
Jan 30, 1946

D. D. Smotherman
Co A 24 Tenn Inf
C.S.A.
Feb 23, 1844
May 23, 1906

George Terry
Born & Died Sep 16, 1904

Jeffie Terry
1923-1939

Martha Jane Smotherman
Jan 31, 1848
Sep 4, 1923
age: 75y, 7m, 4d.

Emma Winn Anderson
Aug 28, 1875
Sep 18, 1954

Della K. Smotherman
May 18, 1876
Jun 22, 1911

Amanda Holsterd
1838-1912

52 MAXWELL CEMETERY   Map # 2
Located about 1 mile West of Rover, Tenn.,
on Beasley Road.

Sallie J. Joyce
Jun 7, 1868
Jan 14, 1908

Several unmarked graves.

George W. Faris
Nov 9, 1833
Jun 5, 1881

Several fieldstones, no
inscriptions.

Eliza Ann Faris
1835-1910

Mary H. Maxwell, Consort
of John W. Maxwell, Born
Apr 18, 1817, Died Apr 25,
1850. age: 33y & 7d.
"Daughter of J. & R.
Prentice, leaving a husband
and two daughters.

53 BROWN-LITTLE CEMETERY   Map # 2
Located West of Rover, Tenn.

J. Henry Brown
May 27, 1872
Aug 7, 1896

Several unmarked graves.
Several fieldstones, no
inscriptions.

No Marker:***
Jake Brown, Brother of
Henry Brown
age: 18 yrs.
(no dates)

Algie P. Brown, dau of
W. F. & T. A. Sanders
Oct 24, 1874
Oct 18, 1900

No Marker: ***
Jim Brown
(no dates)

Nancy Evelin, 3rd daughter
of William & Lucy C. Little***
Jul 21, 1846
Jun 7, 1848
age: 1y, 10m, 17d.

***Lucy Caroline Little.

No Marker: ***
Dollie Brown, Sister of
Jim Brown
age: 2 yrs. (no dates)

Emma Catharine, 6th dau of
William & Lucy C. Little
Mar 7, 1855
Jul 10, 1855
age: 4m & 3d.

***Records given by
Mr & Mrs W.H.Bullock
and
Mr & Mrs Billy Fulton

54 WINN CEMETERY   Map # 2
Located about 1 mile North of Cedar Grove, on Bullock Farm.

Lizza E. Winn   and
Jun 2, 1838
Oct 24, 1919

L. Z. Winn   and
Mar 18, 1848
Apr 15, 1928

Lillie M. Winn
Jul 21, 1874
Oct 15, 1876

Several unmarked graves.
Several fieldstones, no
inscriptions.

55 HALL CEMETERY   Map # 2
Located about 1 mile South of Rover, Tenn.

Annia Lee, dau of
John L. & Julia A. Hall
Mar 2, 1865
Jun 14, 1868

Julia A. Hall
Dec 18, 1837
Nov 11, 1896

Several graves with fieldstones, no inscriptions.

56 NANCE CEMETERY   Map # 2
Located about 1½ miles South of Rover, Tenn.

James W. Nance   and
1829-1910

Catherine Snell Nance
1830-(no date)

J. W. S.(John W. Snell)
1832-1907
(footmarker)

James Snell
Born --- 23, 1819
Died Nov --, 1854
(stone is in pieces)

Curtis I Snell
Born Sep 1811
Died Jul 1, 1854
age: 42y, & 10m

John W. Hester
Feb 8, 1827
Nov 24, 1910

Frank Besley Scales   and
Dec 6, 1867
Mar 17, 1935

Joella, dau of
J. W. & M. N. Hester
Apr 17, 1860
Oct 1, 1883

Mary N., wife of
J. W. Hester
Jun 18, 1828
May 19, 1883

Anna Nance Scales
Sep 23, 1869
Nov 6, 1944

Sallie J., dau of   and
J. W. & M. N. Hester
Dec 1, 1856
Feb 5, 1860

Alfred Ransom
Born Mar 1803
Died July 1869

Gurney A. Lemons   and
Mar 30, 1904

Joseph E., son of
J. W. & M. N. Hester
Jan 15, 1859
Jul 28, 1860

Mrs. Sarah Jane, wife of
the late Alfred Ransom
May 17, 1808
Sep 23, 1875

Sarah Scales Lemons
Mar 21, 1907
Feb 15, 1957

57 STEM CEMETERY   Map # 2
Located about 1 mile East of Cedar Grove Church.

Mary Ruth Kendall
Dec 19, 1908
Oct 25, 1910

Mary Francis Stem, dau of
A. S. & E. A. Stem
Aug 17, 1863
Married _. H. Faris
Aug 28, 1884
Died May 2, 1889
age: 25y, 8m, 15d.

T. A. H. Floyd
1856-1924

Algie Stem Floyd
1860-1936

J. R. Stem
Nov 25, 1822
Mar 21, 1878

Susan S., wife of
J. R. Stem
Aug 23, 1830
Nov 30, 1898

George W. Wadley
Nov 8, 1813
Feb 15, 1852
"He professed faith in Christ
Aug 6, 1835."

Partheny C. Wadley
Apr 13, 1819
Nov 17, 1852

J. L. Stem
1847-1933

"Our Mother"
L. E. Batte
Dec 19, 1833
May 6, 1916

A. E. Atkinson
Jan 23, 1817
Mar 3, 1895

Jane, Second wife of
A. E. Atkinson
Mar 21, 1825
Dec 20, 1910

S. J. Birdwell
Feb 1829
Feb 1910

Agnes Floyd Capley
1878-1916

Alvis Floyd
Aug 9, 1881
May 13, 1902

Frances, Infant dau of
T. A. & A. L. Floyd
Jun 11, 1877
Aug 27, 1877

Ann, Consort of
J. R. Stem & dau of
B. & _. Sprouse
Mar 5, 1827
Jan 2, 1854
(in ground & broken)

Charlie Atkinson
Nov 2, 1872
Mar 7, 1881   .

Edwin Batte
Aug 23, 1808
Apr 20, 1881
age: 72y, 8m, 28d.

Asa Stem
Died Sep 3rd, 1864
age: abt 74 yrs.

William Richard Sims
Sep 16, 1857
Oct 1, 1909
& wife:
Mary E. Stem Sims
Feb 12, 1865
Oct 27, 1919

D. L. Batte
Mar 18, 1895
Jan 18, 1916

A. S. Stem
Feb 1826
Jan 1912

Martha A., wife of
A. S. Stem & dau of
J. & S. Hoover
Jan 21, 1844
Jul 14, 1885
age: 41y, 5m, 7d.

Rev. W. N. Stem
Sep 4, 1858
Jan 18, 1882

Marena T., dau of
J. W. & M. F. Maxwell
Jun 24, 1851
Sep 20, 1869

Mary Ann Atkinson
Jul 30, 1875
Nov 26, 1876

Mary Lula, wife of
W. H. Mitchell
Jul 31, 1869
Apr 22, 1920

Nancy Stem
Born Sep 14, 1788
Died Jan 5, 1870

Thomas LeClaire Sanders
May 3, 1913
Oct 27, 1913

Richard S. Sanders
Dec 6, 1914
Jul 13, 1918

Eugene E. Batte
Jan 5, 1861
Aug 4, 1929
&
Elizabeth B. Batte
Jun 3, 1863
Jul 1, 1956

Elizabeth A., wife of
A. S. Stem & dau of
M. & M. Birdwell
Jun 15, 1830
Feb 2, 1879
age: 48y, 7m, 17d.

Margaret A., Consort of
J. W. Stem
Feb 12, 1828
Jun 17, 1859
age: 31y, 4m, 5d.
"She professed faith in
Christ in 1849."

James Washington Stem
Feb 15, 1821
Mar 12, 1871

"Our Mother"
Elizabeth C., wife of
A. E. Atkinson
Feb 3, 1818
Nov 2, 1867

Several graves with fieldstones, no inscriptions.

58 HOOVER CEMETERY   Map # 2
Located near Cedar Grove

James Hoover
Jul 20, 1814
Mar 4, 1894

Soloma D., dau of J. W. &
J. R. Winn
Dec 3, 1878-Aug 4, 1892

Mrs. M. J. Hoover
Jun 4, 1844
Sep 15, 1926

Mary Jane, wife of
R. W. Hoover
Jul 12, 1844
Sep 11, 1899

James S. Hughson
1857-1896

"Our Mother"
Alice D., wife of
J. W. Tucker
Jan 10, 1863-Jun 12, 1897

30

Sacred to the Memory of
Philip Sprouse, who lived
upward of 54 years &
died Feb 28, 1860

Wiley Perry
Born in 1800
Died Aug 5, 1868

Mary Paralee Rucker, dau of
Philip & Sarah Sprouse
Jan 18, 1832
Nov 8, 1849
age: 17y, 9m, 21d.

Lettitia Perry
Nov 9, 1805
Jul 31, 1867

Albert Gallitan Rucker,
son of Ellet P. & Mary P.
Rucker & grand Son of Philip
& Sarah Sprouse
Oct 8, 1848
Oct 17, 1853

Several unmarked graves.
Fieldstones, no inscriptions.

Mrs. Mary Moore
Died July 27, 1848
aged: 72y, 5m, 27d.

Jimmie Lynn, wife of
W. H. Harris
Nov 16, 1850
May 5, 1881

60 CEDAR GROVE CEMETERY   Map # 2
Located just South of Cedar Grove Church.
This Cemetery is sometimes known as the Osteen Cemetery.

John Edward O'Steen
1879-1959
&
Susanna Reid O'Steen
1879-1947

Paul Newton O'Steen
1909-1944
"Killed in action in France"

Infant Son of
Virgil & Gladys Beasley
Nov 18, 1947

Rev. Willie R. Ralston
Jun 22, 1907
Nov 6, 1969
&
Dola M. Ralston
Sep 6, 1901
Dec 26, 1969

A. Monroe Ralston
Oct 3, 1879
Jan 29, 1943
&
Fannie T. Ralston
Oct 6, 1884
Jan 16, 1967

Jim N. Beasley
May 18, 1876
Jul 26, 1962
&
Charlotte A. Beasley
May 6, 1885

Elbert M. Marlin
Sep 13, 1864
Mar 15, 1937
&
Ella Lee Marlin
Nov 8, 1869
May 3, 1952

T. Kelton Marlin
Sep 6, 1910
Nov 11, 1968
&
Mildred C. Marlin
May 27, 1912

Julia Maud Beasley
May 29, 1905
Jul 6, 1906

Bettie Jane Dowell
Born & Died Jan 23, 1935

Roscoe Charles Keller
May 2, 1913
Apr 18, 1973
&
Margaret O'Steen Keller
Feb 11, 1915

Samuel T. Chrisman
1877-1953
&
Nancy E. Chrisman
1872-1945

Haywood R. Vaughan
1902-1966
&
Ellen C. Vaughan
1903-

Mary Frances Ralston
May 14, 1943

Monroe M. Ralston
Tennessee
Tech Sgt 4152 A.A.F. Base
Unit , W. W. II
Jun 17, 1916
Apr 29, 1947
(picture)

R. C. Marlin
1890-1957

James H. "Bub" Marlin
1921-1952

Bessie Mai Evans
1923-1950

Mary H. Calvert
1931-1933

R. M. Marlin
1855-(no date)
&
Arcenia Marlin
1854-1924

W. A. Marlin
Nov 12, 1877
Oct 10, 1910

Ben S. Redman Osteen
1853-1917
&
Sarah Frances Osteen
1857-1910

Janet Ruth Orr
Mar 23, 1939
May 23, 1966

Donna Yvette Wood
Oct 24, 1956
Jan 6, 1957

J. Frank Hoover
1877-1950
&
Sammie S. Hoover
1887-19

F. Oscar Hoover
Jul 15, 1870
Dec 17, 1957
&
Anna S. Hoover
Dec 4, 1870
Sep 4, 1956

Annie J. Ralston
Born & Died Nov 20, 1918

T. W. Smotherman
Oct 18, 1888
Jul 26, 1971
&
Ora B. Smotherman
Jan 17, 1884
Feb 3, 1965

Annie Lou Smotherman
Sep 5, 1920
Jun 5, 1949

Lester Lee Smotherman
1911-1970
(Lawrence FH)

J. Hollis Johnson
1871-1940
&
Lora A. Johnson
1882-1966

J. W. Lish
Feb 5, 1873
Sep 11, 1915

Clarence L. Cooper
Sep 1, 1889
Jan 12, 1965
&
Mary M. Cooper
Jan 14, 1890

Charles T. Orr
Nov 17, 1909
Mar 12, 1960
&
Nannie Belle Orr
Sep 28, 1912

Harvey R. Jones
Oct 29, 1882
Feb 13, 1953
&
Annie Maud Jones
Jan 2, 1886

Infant Son of
John T. & Barbara Taylor
Aug 6, 1949

Ike L. Davis
Apr 5, 1910
Sep 11, 1944
&
Matilda M. Davis
Dec 7, 1910

William T. Clay
1884-1935
&
Mattie M. Clay
1883-1971

Gordon B. Clay
1916-1961
&
Imogene Clay
1917-

W. L. Cooper
Mar 27, 1852
Mar 5, 1916
age: 64y, 1m, 8d.

M. J. Cooper
Jan 30, 1857
Aug 23, 1920

Willie J. Walls
1891-19
&
Julia Annie Walls
1877-1948

J. W. Walls
(no dates)

Mary Walls
(no dates)

M. K. Beasley
Feb 5, 1850
Feb 6, 1923

William R. Beasley
Mar 15, 1853
Aug 10, 1914

Emmett W. Beasley
Apr 24, 1878
Jan 14, 1962
&
Bettie L. Beasley
Apr 10, 1887
Aug 5, 1943

Leslie Charles Beasley
Minister of The
Evangelical United Breathren
Church
1907-1965

W. H. Osteen
Oct 29, 1847
Aug 31, 1934
&
Sarah Allison Osteen
Jan 21, 1854
Mar 27, 1916

M. P. Osteen
Nov 9, 1821
Jul 29, 1902
&
W. J. Osteen
Mar 11, 1819
Feb 24, 1907

Rev. Edward Osteen, a faith-
ful and successful Minister
of Christ and Member of the
Methodist Ep. Church, South.
Sep 1, 1801
Jan 3, 1869

Elizabeth Osteen, Consort of
Rev. Edward Osteen
Born 1791
Died May 16, 1863

*** David Osteen, Rev. Soldier,
buried here, no marker.
(Family Records)

N. Haggard Dowell
Aug 8, 1906
Jan 25, 1971
&
Sue B. Dowell
Jul 23, 1908

Charlie Clark
1870-1942

Emma Clark
1872-1937

J. H. Clark
Oct 21, 1846
(no date)
&
E. V. Clark
Feb 22, 1843
May 24, 1903

M. E. Clark
Nov 7, 1873
Dec 2, 1874
&
V. D. Clark
Jun 28, 1886
Oct 30, 1889

W. T. Kelton
1867-1948
&
Amanda Kelton
1860-1938

Herbert, son of
E. F. & H. C. Osteen
May 17, 1907
Jun 11, 1907

S. A. Garret
Aug 7, 1831
Jun 10, 1863
age: 31y, 10m, 3d.

Milton H. Horn
Born 1843
Died Jun 10, 1902

Isaac Phillips
Jun 16, 1773
Oct 17, 1835

John L. Farris
1862-1946
&
B. G. Farris
1873-1943

Maude S. Crowell
Feb 28, 1883
Oct 5, 1952

Leslie Edwin Cooper
Jun 15, 1915
Jun 17, 1915

Oscar L. Cooper
1883-1941
&
Maggie M. Cooper
1881-1915

Robert E. Cooper
1915-1917

Dennis Cooper
1922-1922

John Edwin Crowell
1911-1965

John Whitwell White
Mar 25, 1892
Sep 22, 1964
&
Evelyn Stammer White
Sep 7, 1905
Dec 3, 1965

Nannie M. Knox
Dec 24, 1851
Jul 5, 1899

Nancy Stallings, wife of
J. N. Stallings
Apr 1826
May 23, 1856

E. F. Osteen
1867-1938

Charlotte Phillips
Born 1771
Died Jan 19, 1836

T. E. Stammer
Oct 14, 1853
Jan 18, 1915

Thomas Guy Stammer
May 30, 1886
Feb 8, 1901

Ewing Marlin
1880-1907

James W. Marlin
Sep 10, 1832
Sep 17, 1908
&
Anna E. Marlin
Apr 12, 1855
Jan 1922

John W. Mincy
1872-1938
&
Nancy M. Mincy
1878-1952

Lucile Sears
1911-1950

James R. Stammer
Jan 1, 1862
Jan 12, 1901

Isham Stammer
Died Mar 13, 1904
age: 75y, 4m, 4d.

Elizabeth Ann Stammer
Aug 20, 1833
Apr 23, 1900

W. S. Stammer
1865-1950
&
Rebecca Stammer
1875-1930

Mary Ruth Stammer
Mar 1, 1833
Jan 9, 1858

Several old fieldstones,
no inscriptions.

60 COOPER CEMETERY   Map # 2
Located near Taylor Cross Roads, Southeast of Rover, Tn.

Walter Dillard
Feb 17, 1888
Mar 28, 1915

Edna C. Dillard
Sep 16, 1892
Jun 16, 1911
age: 18y & 9m.

Abel Litel
Oct 10, 1804
Dec 20, 1841
age: 37y, 2m, 10d.

Bright Cooper
Oct 12, 1886-Oct 22, 1886

Van Dillard
1844-1895
& wife:
Jerusha Dillard
1850-1933

Albert Cooper
Aug 16, 1868
Dec 15, 1902

William Litle
8 Dec 1802
Aug 2, 1842
age: 39y, 5m, 24d.

Several fieldstones, no inscriptions.

A. M. Cooper
Jan 10, 1824
Sep 16, 1911

Elizabeth, wife of
A. M. Cooper
Aug 25, 1827
Apr 18, 1909

Mrs Dillie Litle
Jun 2, 1809
Apr 24, 1893
age: 83y, 10m, 22d.

George William Cooper
Nov 4, 1854
Jan 29, 1932
&
Annie Neal Cooper
Aug 27, 1857
Aug 12, 1942

Job Cooper
Oct 20, 1824
Apr 15, 1855
&
Alsey Cooper
Aug 27, 1832
Nov 7, 1854

John P. Moon
Jun 7, 1804
Nov 8, 1842

Barbra P.------
dau of --------

(broken away)

William Rucker
Jul 8, 1803
Apr 25, 1850
age: 46y, 9m, 17d.

Sarah J. Rucker, dau of
G. Low & wife of
W. J. Rucker
Nov 19, 1829
Jan 19, 1859
age: 29y, & 2m.

Louisa G. Rucker
May 22, 1821
Jul 6, 1855
age: 34y, 1m, 11d.

Mattie Florence, wife of
R. A. Davis, & dau of
J. W. & Rebecca Rucker
Oct 2, 1860
Nov 17, 1883

Emmet H. Rucker
Sep 13, 1870
Nov 11, 1881

Nancy C. Cooper, wife of
John Cooper, & dau of
Robert Love of East
Tennessee
Died Apr 7, 1816
Born Apr 12, 1783
age: 33 yrs.

Ellen M. Whitaker, dau of
William & Hester Collins, &
Consort of J. G. Whitaker
Oct 16, 1831
Jun 4, 1858

Susan Marchant
Sep 27, 1809
Aug 24, 1858
(Vault)

James C. Marchant, son of
Wilie & Susan Marchant
May 24, 1835
Sep 18, 1836

W. S. Taylor   and
May 8, 1804
Sep 14, 1887
"Joined the Primitive Baptist
Church, Enon in 1828."

George W. Taylor   and
1846-1925

Joel Kimmins
Died Oct 22, 1835
age: 38y, 9m, 10d.

Elliotte Rucker
Died Nov 29, 1841
age: abt. 62 yrs.

Nancy Rucker, dau of
Elliotte Rucker
Died Aug 19, 1838
age: 32y, 3m, 9d.

Jesse Rucker
Dec 23, 1810
May 30, 1846
age: 35y, 5m, 7d.

Stacy Rucker
Died Dec 18, 1866
age: abt. 84 yrs.

Elliotte P. Rucker
Feb 4, 1825
Jan 16, 1852
age: 26y, 11m, 12d.

Jno. W. Rucker
Aug 7, 1823
Nov 7, 1898

Nancy J. Rucker
Jun 15, 1858
Aug 7, 1918

James L. Short
Died Mar 31, 1831
age: 43y, & 11m.

Margaret Short
Died Aug 8, 1827
age: 36y, & 8m.

Henry G. Soaps
Died Sept 1852
age: 23y, 4m, 13d.

Mrs. Milley Putman, wife of
Joseph Putman
1774-Oct 1, 1834
age: 60 yrs.

Willie F., son of
J. & A. M. Hooper
Died Jan 12, 1868
age: 28 days

Nancy, wife of
W. S. Taylor
May 25, 1806
May 29, 1888, "Joined the
Enon Church in 1831."

Manerva J. Taylor
1851-1935

Violet Adaline, Consort of
W. H. Low, who was born
Jan 19, 1830 & died
Apr 14, 1850

Caleb Cox
Aug 6, 1789
Jul 29, 1837
age: 47y, 11m, 23d.

J. G. Harrison
Oct 7, 1827
Mar 16, 1885
age: 58y, 5m, 9d.

Jemima M. Harrison, wife of
J. G. Harrison
May 18, 1832
Jul 3, 1887

Infant Dau of
J. G. & T. B. Harrison
Born & Died Jul 27, 1886

Joel G. Harrison, Son of
J. G. & J. M. Harrison
Aug 3, 1854
Nov 6, 1891
age: 37y, 8m, 3d.

Priscilla Dollar, wife of
Ruben Dollar, dau of
Daniel Putman
Aug 25, 1810
May 30, 1835
age: 24y, & 9m, 4d.

Jelitha Putman
1824-July 1833
age: 91 yrs.

Haney Putman
Died Oct 11, 1825
age: 16 yrs.

William B. Taylor
Mar 16, 1846
Jul 23, 1846

Almira W. Taylor
Jul 12, 1835
Oct 18, 1835

J. W. Taylor
1861-1936
&
Elizabeth K. Taylor
1866-1945

W. S. Taylor, Jr.
Jan 15, 1835
Oct 31, 1898

William L. Taylor
1890-1890

Capt. Joe A. Taylor
Nov 7, 1830
May 1, 1908

Elizabeth Wood
Born Oct 7, 1804
Died Nov 25, 1884
age: 80y, 1m, 18d.

Virginia C. Cooper
Oct 7, 1865
Jul 27, 1897

W. R. Poplin
Sep 25, 1845
Apr 2, 1879
age: 34y, 7m, 7d.

Sacred to the Memory of
inestimable departed ----
-----------excellence &
virtur, Dr. J. M. Davis,
whose remaines are here
deposited, who departed
this life the 27th day of
January in the year of our
Lord 1838. Age: 35 yrs.

David Fain
Jul 26, 1781
Feb 8, 1831
age: 49y, 6m, 10d.

Katharine Fain
Feb 20, 1776
May 2, 1859
age: 83y, 2m, 13d.

Fain
(no dates)

William Dollar
Died Jan 27, 1831
age: 52 yrs.

Francis M. Ray
Sep 9, 1834
Jan 25, 1879

Emaline R. Taylor
Mar 12, 1806
Jan 24, 1852
age: 45y, 10m, 12d.

Jonas Sutton
1873-1875

Margaret J., wife of
J. W. Nichols
May 20, 1833
Mar 1, 1902

W. H. Jackson
Aug 18, 1840
Feb 7, 1883

E. Elizabeth Jackson
Jun 13, 1845
Dec 17, 1913

Kittie B. Taylor
May 30, 1850
Feb 10, 1903

[This Church & Graveyard is located on a TN Land Grant #2459 issued
to Captain John Byler in 1810]

J. C. Taylor
Dec 25, 1835
May 7, 1911

Mary E., wife of
J. C. Taylor
Aug 27, 1836
Nov 15, 1896

Amanda C. Henly
Born Oct 9, 1835
married to William H. Henly
Sep 13, 1853
Died Jan 4, 1890
age: 64y, 2m, 25d.

Many unmarked graves.
Many fieldstones, no inscriptions.

No Marker:***
William Poplin
Born in Montgomery Co.,
North Carolina abt 1789
and Died abt 1880.

Susan R. Taylor
Jan 13, 1842
Aug 19, 1917

Mary Taylor Sutton
1837-1932

Lillian S. West
1871-1963

J. J. Henly
Sep 25, 1855
May 24, 1908

No marker:***
Alfred Poplin
Born 1819
Died abt 1900

James Eron, son of
J. W. & Lizzie Taylor
Oct 25, 1892
Dec 9, 1892

"Heath Twins"
Nellie Heath
Apr 11, 1902
Jul 13, 1902
&
Nettie Heath
Apr 11, 1902
Jun 11, 1902

T. L. Heath
Feb 4, 1858
Dec 23, 1907

Nancy R. Heath
Apr 7, 1860
Jan 21, 1918

No Marker:***
James P. King   married to
1820-abt 1850

N. S. Heath, dau of
J. C. & Mary Taylor
Born May 4, 1863,
age: 39y, 11m, 13d.
married to S. K. Heath
Dec 4, 1884 and
Died Apr 21, 1902

S. K. Heath
Feb 4, 1860
Jan 15, 1928

Pearl Heath
Jun 18, 1893
Jun 18, 1898

Mary S. Heath, wife of
Jarrell Burrow
Sep 25, 1853
Dec 8, 1933

No Marker:***
Mary Ann Jordon King
1817-died ?

62 RUCKER CEMETERY   Map # 2
Located near Enon Church, Northeast of Unionville, Tenn.

William J., son of
Johnson & Lamira Wood
Jul 22, 1857
Apr 1, 1943
    & wife:
Nannie L., dau of
Jordan & Drucilla Rucker
Jul 2, 1861
Jun 26, 1930
married Sep 20, 1882

Jordan Rucker
Jan 22, 1814
Feb 23, 1891
age: 77y, 1m, 1d.

Drucillar R., wife of
Jordan Rucker
Feb 26, 1826
May 18, 1897
age: 71y, 2m, 23d.

James P. Rogers
Dec 11, 1864
Sep 19, 1931
age: 66y, 9m, 8d.

Mrs. Lou A. Rogers
Jan 3, 1865
Feb 22, 1906

Elmer D. Wood
Nov 6, 1894
Feb 20, 1953

Infant Son of
W. J. & N. L. Wood
Born & Died Nov 6, 1894

Rucker, Son of
W. J. & N. L. Wood
Sep 22, 1899
Oct 4, 1899

J. J. "Johnie", Son of
W. J. & N. L. Wood
Feb 6, 1884
May 22, 1901

William H., son of
C. & J. E. Jones
Nov 15, 1873
Jan 26, 1874.

1 unmarked grave.

John W. Jackson
Nov 26, 1869
Aug 8, 1952
&
Ella W. Jackson
Dec 24, 1871
Apr 10, 1914

Jemime E., wife of
C. Jones, & dau of
Jordan & D. Rucker
Aug 19, 1851
Jan 17, 1879

Mary E., dau of
C. & J. E. Jones
Apr 22, 1877
Sep 2, 1893

63 NEAL CEMETERY   Map # 2
Located about 1 mile Southeast of Taylor Cross Road.

N. F. Neal
Died Apr 13, 1874
aged: 82y, 4m, 9d.
"He was a Soldier of the
War of 1812."

Elizabeth Carrie Neal
Jan 30, 1854
May 11, 1913

64 TARPLEY CEMETERY   Map # 2
Located about 3/4 mile West of Longview.

Thomas D. Tarpley   and Wife:
Jul 26, 1817
Aug 2, 1904

Casander, wife of
E. D. Jones
Feb 13, 1846
Mar 26, 1878

Nancy P. Tarpley   and Wife:
Dec 29, 1821
Mar 24, 1904

Edward Henry, son of
T. D. & Amanda Tarpley
Aug 9, 1855
Dec 9, 1855
age: 4m.

Amanday Tarpley
Jan 5, 1823
Sep 25, 1855

Benjamin Franklin, son of
T. D. & Amanda Tarpley
Oct 3, 1847
Feb 10, 1856
age: 8y, 4m, 7d.

Annie E. Ott
Born Nov 23, 1845
married G. W. Tarpley
Nov 22, 1866
Died May 19, 1880
Age: 34y, 5m, 26d.

65 NORVELL CEMETERY   Map # 2
Located about ½ mile Northwest of Longview.

Arch. Norvell
died 1921

Nealy Ann Smotherman
1830-1870

[Some of the Lile family may
be buried here. Information
by John Kimmins]

66 HARRIS CEMETERY   Map # 2
Located about ½ mile east of Taylors Cross Roads.

This was on or adjoining lands of John T., John S., Esther
and Simpson Harris. No markers.

67 BATT CEMETERY   Map # 2
Located near Longview.

Henry Batt
Jan 15, 1778
Feb 17, 1832

C. L. Batt
Nov 3, 1827
Mar 16, 1855
age: 27y, 4m, 3d.

Samuel G. MacGowan
Aug 10, 1815
Apr 15, 1853
age: 37y, 8m, 5d.

Marian D. Ozment
Nov 21, 1817
Mar 21, 1818
age: 4m.

68 HARRIS CEMETERY   Map # 2
Located at Longview.

This Cemetery has been destroyed.

69 WOODSON CEMETERY   Map # 2
Located about 1 mile Southwest of Longview.

Thomas M. Woodson
Jan 14, 1858
Aug 3, 1925

2 graves, unmarked.

Mary J., wife of
T. M. Woodson
Feb 2, 1853
Oct 10, 1906

James T. Woodson
Nov 20, 1853
Oct 25, 1909

Mollie S. Woodson
Dec 25, 1853
Apr 5, 1932

Willie Tom D., son of
H. N. & L. P. Sudberry
Jul 1, 1904
Jun 18, 1905

70 COOPER CEMETERY   Map # 2
Located at Longview.

John B. Cooper
1831-1915

Rebecca F. Cooper
1838-1927

Anderson Landers
Jul 3, 1807
Apr 8, 1876
age: 68y, 9m, 5d.

2 unmarked graves in
Cooper's plat.
Many unmarked graves, with and
without fieldstones, no inscriptions.

Part of Cemetery for the
Harris Family.

71 MORTON CEMETERY   Map # 2
Located about ½ mile Southeast of Longview.

Rufus Morton, Sr.
Died Dec 1, 1960 ·
(TM)(no age given)

George W. Morton
1840-1930

Jacob Morton
Feb 17, 1787
Sep 4, 1855

"Our Mother"
Anna Morton
Apr 27, 1796
Jul 16, 1869

Herbert, son of
B. P. & S. E. Crowell
Mar 12, 1909
Aug 12, 1909

"Mother"
Annie Guy Lanier
Oct 28, 1913
Oct 13, 1968

Nannie Jarrett
Aug 28, 1869
Mar 10, 1889
age: 19y, 6m, 12d.

Emily A. Neal
Aug 10, 1829
Dec 3, 1902

Mary D., dau of P. B. &
S. E. Crowell
Jan 26, 1908
Jun 20, 1908

Felix Morton, son of
Nancy Morton, Born in
Bedford County, Tenn.
Feb 1, 1827, & died
Mar 22, 1853
age: 26y, 1m, 21d.

E. A. Morton
Sep 12, 1842
Aug 19, 1907

E. A. Whitworth
Feb 22, 1822
Aug 24, 1868

Nancy A. Whitworth
Dec 26, 1824
Mar 6, 1893

Emmett Morton
Oct 14, 1869
Nov 14, 1938

Jewett Morton
1915-1961
(Gowen-Smith)

"Uncle"
James Lafayette Neal
Oct 30, 1865
May 23, 1953

Martha A. Whitworth
Apr 6, 1846
May 11, 1889

Norris J. Morton Crowell
Jun 17, 1905
Jun 30, 1906

Repsia Crowell, dau of
J. J. & S. E. Morton
Sep 4, 1882
Jun 12, 1909

John Jacob Morton
Jun 16, 1884
Dec 11, 1908

Mark J. Morton
Sep   1864
Oct 13, 1903

Laura F., wife of
R. H. Morton
Mar 3, 1877
Nov 18, 1905

Rufus Lytle, son of
Mr & Mrs R. H. Morton
Aug 18, 1907
May 28, 1908

Several graves unmarked.

James O. Baird
Sep 29, 1882
(no date)
&
Dora E. Baird
Nov 16, 1882
Jun 20, 1943

James L. Morton, M.D.
May 3, 1880
May 31, 1940
"He was a friend to Mankind"

Q. E. Morton, Sr.
Sep 24, 1835
Oct 21, 1922

Nancy M., wife of
Q. E. Morton
Feb 10, 1839
Sep 3, 1896

Several fieldstones, no
inscriptions.

72 CLARK CEMETERY   Map # 2
Located about 1½ miles Southeast of Longview.

John B. Morton
1887-1944
&
Elnora Morton
1879-

Emmett Lee Price
Feb 15, 1882
Jun 29, 1955

Mary A. Burge, wife of
E. L. Price
1889-1922

James A. Robertson
Dec 8, 1868
Nov 13, 1951

Fannie W. Robertson
Feb 22, 1878
Jul 10, 1909

Emma Alice Robertson
Jul 15, 1887
Mar 31, 1966

Mary Kathrine Robertson
Nov 16, 1916
Sep 15, 1966

Damsel Clark
died 1903
(TM)

Thomas J. Clark
Died 1911
(TM)

Cora Clark
Died 1929
(TM)

James B. Clark
Died 1936
(TM)

3 Clarks
(no other information)

Annie Rebecca Clark
Jan 10, 1909
Feb 5, 1939

William H. Falkner
Co F
3 Tenn Inf.

Lela Burge
Jul 1, 1894
Mar 21, 1969

Andrew Burge
1859-1927
&
Ludie Burge
1867-1962

Angie Faulkner
1856-1901

E. T. Robertson
Sep 5, 1838
Mar 31, 1890

Emley L. Robertson
Mar 7, 1845
Aug 4, 1895

William T. Robertson
May 2, 1884
Aug 5, 1885

George O. Robertson
Apr 13, 1897
Oct 31, 1898

Charlie B. Robertson
May 27, 1905
Nov 18, 1908

Lydia Ann Smith
Feb 10, 1953

Calvin Baxter Smith
1955-1955
(Cothron-Thompson)

Joe Floyd Smith
1969-1969
(Gowen-Smith)

James W. Suggs
Feb 25, 1897
Jan 9, 1970

Georgia Trott Faulkner
1898-1921

Infant Douglas
1966-1966
(Gowen-Smith)

James R. Stem
1899-1970
&
Gladys K. Stem
1901-19

James A. Stem
Nov 26, 1919
Mar 25, 1920

John Wesley Stem
Tennessee
Pvt Btry C 386 FA Bn W.W.II
Jan 21, 1921
Oct 31, 1957

L. Chester Turner
Oct 27, 1860
Apr 15, 1881

M. Hutton Turner
Jul 20, 1850
Feb 20, 1871

Robert W. Turner
Nov 5, 1837
Sep 5, 1865

Monroe W. Turner
Jan 2, 1816
Sep 16, 1879

Mary A. Clark Turner
1817-Feb 3, 1871

J. E. Williams
Jul 3, 1853
Jul   1936
&
N. M. Williams
Mar 18, 1856
Jun 12, 1928

Annie Mai Harris
Oct 1, 1904
May 9, 1948

George B. Trott
1865-1931
&
Kittie T. Trott
1864-1950

Zebedee Jackson Bogle
May 29, 1875
Oct 29, 1961

John W. Trott
1874-1958
&
Rebecca J. Trott
1875-1935

Leslie Trott
1916-1925

Rutha Trott
Jan 23, 1911
Jun 1, 1911

Mich'l Trott
Co M
5 Tenn Cav.

Charity M. Trott
1844-1894

Tennie Robertson Dalton
Sep 24, 1874
Jan 23, 1941

Alvin Thomas Smith
Tennessee
Pvt U.S.Army, W.W.I
Mar 20, 1890
Feb 12, 1968
&
Lula H. Smith
Aug 29, 1896
Dec 29, 1971

Martha J. Smith
1867-1953

Albert B. Smith
Tennessee
Pvt U.S.Army
Jun 8, 1903
Dec 24, 1943

Infant Son of
C. P. & L. R. Lovvorn
Oct 1924

Lula R. Lovvorn
Oct 1, 1899
Nov 22, 1928

J. R.
(fieldstone, no insc.)

Neal S. Bogle
1849-1921

J. Frank Smith
May 1, 1896
Apr 30, 1970
&
Mary D. Smith
Jun 14, 1896

Miss Katie Smith
1881-1962
(Gowen-Smith)

Martha K. Womack
Jun 3, 1861
May 16, 1925

Robert F. Tucker
Jun 5, 1933
Apr 3, 1934

John H. Taylor
Mar   1842
Jan 10, 1883
    & wife:
Mary E. Faulkner Taylor
Mar   1845
Sep 10, 1885

Joe F. Smith
1868-1944
&
Lou M. Smith
1872-1900

William Caleb Smith
Nov 13, 1893
Apr 4, 1967
&
Euda Powell Smith
May 4, 1894

Alice Jones Boatright
Jun 8, 1874
Jul 9, 1947

Walter L. Taylor
1868-1948

Edna Delitha Taylor
Mar 28, 1878
Mar 30, 1966

V. T., dau of
F. B. & S. J. Price
May 13, 1843
professed faith in Christ
in 1860, & died
Apr 11, 18_5
(part of year gone)

Alice Puckett
1861-1944

James W. Jones
Feb 19, 1868
Aug 3, 1952
&
Lurana A. Jones
Mar 14, 1878
Nov 9, 1960

Charlie C. Tucker
Apr 1, 1898
Apr 6, 1968
&
Luenett T. Tucker
Aug 30, 1902

Mrs. Lemmer May Tucker
1869-1954
(Gowen-Smith)

John Minus Tucker
May 22, 1897
Aug 4, 1928

H. Selmer Jones
1918-1940

Valter R. Jones
1901-1927

Frank A. Jones
Aug 9, 1916
Jul 25, 1954

Many graves marked with
fieldstones, no inscript-
ions.

#73 TARPLEY CEMETERY   Map # 2
Located near Bethleham School, East of Longview.

This Cemetery has been destroyed.

#74 TUCKER CEMETERY   Map # 2
Located near Longview.

Katie, wife of
J. M. Tucker
Feb 28, 1861
Mar 19, 1906

#75 MORTON CEMETERY (Col.)   Map # 2
Located about 1 mile East of Rover, Tenn.

Jessie Perry, Sr.
Died Feb 14, 1973
(no age given,
Scales & Son FH)

Will M. Lanier
Apr 22, 1882
Aug 7, 1956
&
Ellen Lanier
May 9, 1884
Mar 3, 1970

T. H. Morton
Apr 9, 1855
(no date)
&
Matilda Morton
May   1856
Sep   1925

3 or 4 unmarked graves.

Sanford Perry
May 29, 1884
Dec 9, 1903

Sanford Perry
Died Mar 23, 1965
(TM)

Irene Morton
Feb 11, 1886
Feb 27, 1926

"Father"
E. Dowin Lanier
Sep 19, 1908
Nov 18, 1962

#1 DAVIS CEMETERY   Map # 3
Located about 2 miles North of Blankenship Church.

John Franklin Eley
Jan 3, 1878
Dec 11, 1897
age: 19y, 11m, 22d.

Rebecca J. Davis
Aug 1, 1856
May 13, 1917

Elizabeth Williams, wife of
N. C. Crick
May 30, 1815
Apr 15, 1902

Robert Mathew Davis
Dec 5, 1854
Nov 10, 1935

Alfred W. Davis
Apr 19, 1860
Aug 26, 1882

B. N. Davis   and wife:
Jan 30, 1817
Mar 12, 1891

William Barton Davis
Jan 6, 1866-Dec 27, 1945

Sarah E. Davis
Jun 30, 1862
Oct 12, 1886

Louisa M. Williams Davis
Nov 12, 1830
Mar 15, 1907

No Markers***
Robert Williams   and wife:
Born 1773
Died 1856

No Marker:***
Mary Williams
Born 1790
Died (no date)

No Marker:***
Mary Williams who married:
Died July 7, 1889

Josiah Eley
Born 1809

No Marker:***
Howell Williams
Died 1899

***Family Records of Mrs Frank Harper.

Edgar Howell Davis
Aug 16, 1895
Jul 17, 1969

Mary Gladys Ward
May 5, 1899
Dec 4, 1917

G. Y. Ward
Sep 19, 1892
Dec 3, 1894

Burl Ward
Aug 31, 1855
Jun 22, 1920
& wife:

Emma Davis Ward
Jun 30, 1862
Feb 26, 1940

John M. Ward
Jan 7, 1886
Feb 3, 1950

James T. Davis
(TM-James Thomas)
1868-1952
&

Mary E. Ward
Oct 7, 1858
Aug 8, 1901

James R., son of
J. W. & W. P. Ward
Nov 18, 1922
Dec 28, 1930

Margaret, dau of
J. W. & W. P. Ward
Oct 29, 1918
Jun 22, 1922

Inez Davis
1872-1960

Alma Rebecca, dau of
J. T. & Inez Davis
Jun 7, 1900
Dec 21, 1901

Susie Mai Ward
May 31, 1914
Jun 1, 1914

James Patterson Spence
Died Nov 21, 1966
age: 1 day

3 graves with
fieldstones.

2 WEBB CEMETERY   Map # 3
Located about 2 miles Northeast of Longview.

John A. Webb
Apr 14, 1805
Nov 30, 1872

Ann E. T. Webb
Aug 8, 1821
Aug 30, 1882

John R., son of
John A. & A. T. Webb
Born & Died Feb 22, 1839

Many unmarked graves.
Many graves with field-
stones, no inscriptions

3 McLEAN CEMETERY (Col.)   Map # 3
Located about 2 miles Northeast of Longview.

Dee N. McLean
1868-1954
(Bradberry-Massey FH)

Several unmarked graves.

4 BARNES CEMETERY   Map # 3
Located near Blankenship Church.

W. W. Blankenship
Mar 19, 1861
Jun 19, 1911

Marthie Susie Barnes
              Blankenship
Oct 7, 1864
Mar 29, 1947

D. W. Barnes
Mar 25, 1839
Jun 29, 1912

Virginia W. Barnes
Jul 11, 1841
married D. W. Barnes
Sep 24, 1862
Died Feb 26, 1904

Thomas F. Barnes
Nov 3, 1830
Mar 23, 1906

Sioda Barnes
Mar 11, 1836
Oct 6, 1899

Johnnie E. Barnes
Sep 27, 1878
Jan 23, 1879

Mark J. Barnes
May 15, 1896
Nov 5, 1899

Daniel W. Harrison
Jan 9, 1892-Sep 23, 1904

1 grave with fieldstone, no inscription.

5 COOPER CEMETERY (Col.)   Map # 3
Located about 1 mile North of Blankenship Church.

Rosanna Cooper Smith
Dec 18, 1848
Sep 8, 1912

Malinda Cooper
Mar 15, 1820
Oct 19, 1908

May Cooper
Jan 24, 1845
Nov 25, 1919

6 BLANKENSHIP CEMETERY   Map # 3
Located about 1 mile Northeast of Blankenship Church.

G. W. Faulkner
1857-1925

Lillie Faulkner
1869-1959

Stephen Butts Smith
Mar 27, 1898
Mar 24, 1973

Sallie Payton Smith
Aug 24, 1895
Jan 4, 1972

Infant Smith
1956-1956
(Gowen)

Ida T. Smith
1870-1912

James F. Smith
1870-1934

A. D. E.
(no dates)

Ida Wheelhouse
1885-1971

E. D.
(no dates)

Lester E. Wheelhouse
1874-1875

Mary C., dau of
J. A. & A. T. Webb
Nov 22, 1844
Jul 16, 1847

Cassie Wheelhouse
1875-1960

Strother Key
Born in Abermàel Co., Va.
1787-1842

Beulah A. Wheelhouse
1878-1896

Many unmarked graves.

Payton Hill Wheelhouse
1833-1908

M. C. K.
(footmarker, headstone gone)

Johnie D. Wheelhouse
1882-1884

Ann, wife of
Payton Wheelhouse
1847-1937

T. A. Smith
(no dates)

Sarah G. Wheelhouse
1880-1882

7 WOODFIN CEMETERY   Map # 3
Located about 3 miles North of Deason, Tenn.

Gracie May Underwood
Sep 1, 1904
Jul 8, 1905

Lester Lee Lynch
Jan 9, 1906
May 16, 1908

Selma B. Lynch
Mar 31, 1904
Nov 19, 1906

Mrs. Ruby L. Mullins
Mar 3, 1917
Dec 22, 1961
(Woodfin FH)

Lutishey B. Manning
Mar 17, 1864
Jul 25, 1918

Ruby F. Mullins
Mar 3, 1911
Dec 22, 1961

Edward Thomas Swafford
Jul 6, 1875
Jun 9, 1968
(Woodfin FH)

Miss Jane Woodfin
Apr 22, 1803
Mar 31, 1826

Nicholas Woodfin (SOR)
Aug 2, 1759
Dec 21, 1832

Mrs. Hannah Woodfin
Relict of N. Woodfin
Died Aug 8, 1845
age: 80 yrs.

John Naylor
Died Feb 10, 1855
age: 68 yrs.

Thomas M., son of
J. H. & E. Woodfin
Nov 12, 1865
Mar 29, 1882

Robert D. Woodfin
Dec 27, 1858
Nov 26, 1889

Tennie Agee
Jul 4, 1865
Nov 27, 1909

Eld. H. F. Agee
Sep 10, 1840
Nov 18, 1907

M. P. Agee
May 29, 1837
Oct 3, 1911

Rev. L. D. Agee
1870-1930

Ruth, wife of
L. D. Agee
Sep 6, 1874
Jun 7, 1905

Sallie H. Agee
Feb 26, 1881
Jun 13, 1915

Williw E., dau of
L. B. & S. L. Agee
Mar 3, 1890
Sep 9, 1892

Samuel Woodfin
1791-Apr 29, 1863
age: 72 yrs.

Mariah, wife of
Samuel Woodfin
Dec 9, 1796
Mar 8, 1863
age: 66y, 2m, 29d.

Oliver B., son of
__ash & _____ Woodfin
Apr 2, 1817
May 6, 1818

Nicholas B. Woodfin
Jan 26, 1861
Oct 20, 1868

James H. Woodfin
Sep 19, 1819
Aug 21, 1876

Mrs. Eveline Haile Woodfin
Nov 18, 1823
Mar 28, 1910

Thomas Walter, son of
T. L. & M. A. Elam
Jan 14, 1887
Feb 5, 1887

Robert T., son of
T. L. & M. A. Elam
Dec 24, 1887
Aug 6, 1888

W. E. Wilkerson
Mar 25, 1871
(not here)
&
Lavinia Kilzer Wilkerson
Aug 20, 1865
Jul 2, 1928

J. Leslie Wilkerson
Nov 27, 1890
Mar 7, 1967

Samuel Robert Wilkerson
1868-1950
&
Tennie Kilzer Wilkerson
1869-1937

Andrew J. Rigney
Aug 11, 1883
Dec 27, 1939
&
Myrtis S. Rigney
Mar 7, 1897

Nancy J. Rigney
1849-1916

Rebecca A., wife of
G. N. Edwards
Born in North Carolina
Oct 21, 182_
(broken and gone)

Millard T., son of
G. N. & R. A. Edwards
Oct 1, 1856
Sep 24, 1857

Samuel H. Thomas
1830-1909
& wife:
Rebecca Thomas
1855-(no date)

John Thomas Woodruff
1880-1948
&
Bettye Carter Woodruff
1880-(no date)

Charley D. Carter
Aug 26, 1887
May 23, 1973

Mary Elizabeth, wife of
J. D. Roulstone
1834-Aug 7, 1904

William D. Williams
Feb 7, 1885
Oct 24, 1918

Leatha Jones Williams
(no dates)

Wavie G., Infant dau of
W. D. & Leatha Williams
Oct 3, 1918
Oct 19, 1918

David S. Williams
Aug 9, 1837
May 25, 1916

W. M. Williams
Jul 24, 1856
May 23, 1931

Lucy Williams
Nov 12, 1912
Jan 10, 1913

Mary Lee, dau of
W. M. & Stacy Williams
Mar 14, 1882
Jul 23, 1921

Maria L. Thomas
Jun 22, 1835
Dec 16, 1884

Farrer Brothers
(no dates)

Vina Thomas Brothers
(no dates)

"Father"
Ellis P. Thomas
Sep 30, 1875
Jul 13, 1931
&
"Mother"
Beulah Mae Thomas
Dec 5, 1882
Sep 21, 1942
&
"Son"
M. LaDell Thomas
Jul 20, 1911
Sep 12, 1943

Mary L. Lewis
1877-1935

Joseph P. Hale
Dec 14, 1828
Nov 27, 1904
&
Elizabeth C. Hale
Sep 11, 1834
(no date)

Harley Hale
1883-1900

William Lewis Fulton
1903-1935

Hattie Epps Fulton
1884-1947

William Fulton
1879-1964

Joan N. Gilmore, dau of
J. B. & Ona Gilmore
1943

Robert Lee Gilmore
Apr 3, 1868
Jul 18, 1921

Nora Faulk Gilmore
Apr 20, 1886
Jun 29, 1956

J. H. Gilmore
1894-1935

John B. Gilmore
(no dates)

Leander Edwards Gilmore
Sep 17, 1907
Mar 5, 1952
&
Ollie Rigney Gilmore
Oct 9, 1909

J. M. Edwards
Oct 12, 1845
Apr 8, 1928

Mattie A., wife of
J. M. Edwards
Jul 23, 1850
Jun 29, 1886

Thomas Davidson Gilmore
1882-1953
&
Belle Marlin Gilmore
1887-1956

John D. Gilmore
Apr 6, 1841
Apr 24, 1914
&
Mary Luvenia Gilmore
Jan 8, 1844
Nov 19, 1923

Horace P. Edwards
Sep 13, 1890
Oct 25, 1966
&
Martha L. Edwards
Dec 3, 1894

Rosa B. Edwards
Oct 6, 1885
Mar 3, 1970

Andrew H. Edwards
1852-1896
&
Nannie J. Edwards
1857-19(no date)

Blanche A., dau of
A. H. & N. J. Edwards
Nov 28, 1885
Oct 12, 1886

Pauline Williams
(no dates)

Charles C. Bingham
Jun 9, 1858
Sep 24, 1911

Martha Bingham
1857-1942

James H. Gilmore
Jun 11, 1861
Jul 10, 1926
&
Mattie A. Gilmore
Jan 11, 1871
Apr 27, 1954

J. W. G.
(in Gilmore Section)

Charlie
(in Gilmore Section)

Kitty Neely
(no dates)

Florence, dau of
J. M. & M. A. Edwards
Feb 20, 1880
Feb 21, 1880

Mary E. Neelie Edwards
Nov 1853
Jun 1941

Lester Arnold Edwards
1897-1950

Thomas James Edwards
Jul 6, 1872
Sep 13, 1953
&
Susie Margaret Edwards
Dec 20, 1872
Jun 3, 1949

Nannie, dau of
E. H. & M. E. Hale***
***(Ellis H. & Mary E. Hale)
Jul 30, 1856
Aug 26, 1890

Miss S. J. Hale***
***(Sarah J. Hale)
Jun 4, 1844
Aug 3, 1890

Mal, wife of
John W. Hale
Dec 4, 1828
Jun 22, 1901

E. J. H. Hale
Feb 5, 1856
Jan 12, 1882

Bettie Hale
Mar 1, 1861
May 18, 1880

Margaret Lin_ow, wife of
James A. Elam
Jan 7, 1835
Feb 27, 1907

David Lee Vaughn
Mar 15, 1896
Aug 2, 1900
&
Douglas Vaughn
Born & Died
May 30, 1898

Edwin E. Edwards
Aug 25, 1870
Dec 21, 1960
&
Sarah J. Edwards
Aug 27, 1888
Nov 15, 1963

Leander H. Edwards
1842-1897
&
Eudora E. Edwards
1842-1929

Elleanora, dau of
L. H. & M. E. Edwards
Sep 2, 1887
Oct 12, 1888

"Sister"
Annie Edwards Lewis
1872-1950

Sarah N. Edwards
Dec 13, 1898
Feb 24, 1973

Roleigh Overton Edwards
1903-1934

Roberta Powell Taylor
Feb 16, 1922
Dec 24, 1949

Mary O. Powell, dau of
Jordan & Emma Powell
Oct 16, 1931

Eunice Powell Lane
Mar 7, 1924
Jun 12, 1953

Anita Louise Lane
Jan 7, 1953

Maude Newby
(no dates)

Emmit Fulton
(no dates)

Claude Fulton
(no dates)

Josephine Fulton
(no dates)

Will Fulton
(no dates)

"Unknown Traveler"
(no dates)

Sarah Fulton
(no dates)

Florence Fulton
(no dates)

John B. Lewis
Apr 12, 1899
Apr 12, 1970
&
Eudora G. Lewis
Jul 9, 1904

Wilma Jean Lewis
Aug 29, 1928

George M. Edwards
1869-1958
&
Florence W. Edwards
1876-1958

Infant Daughter of
B. G. & Ora Bingham
Born & Died
Aug 12, 1909

Infant Son of
J. W. & M. E. Edwards
Apr 27, 1874
Jun 27, 1874

Wade M. Edwards
Tennessee
Pvt Co B 60 Pioneer Inf
W. W. I
Aug 31, 1896-Jul 29, 1959

John W. Edwards
Apr 20, 1848
Feb 8, 1917

Mary Elizabeth Miller,
wife of John W. Edwards
Mar 20, 1851
Nov 16, 1913

Lissie Pearl, dau of
J. W. & M. E. Edwards
Nov. 3, 1872
Oct 4, 1908

Marvin Wade Edwards
Jul 13, 1934
Aug 4, 1934

George N. Edwards
Apr 6, 1823
Nov 18, 1903
    &
Dobartha A. Edwards
May 16, 1833
Feb 1, 1908

W. M. Oakley
Aug 11, 1845
Feb 3, 1918

Fannie C. Oakley
Nov 24, 1849
Jun 10, 1891

J. L. Oakley
Mar 3, 1858
Jun 26, 1887

A. E. O.
(fieldstone)

N. H. O.
(fieldstone)

Malissa Edwards McElroy
Dec 15, 1851
May 19, 1915

No Marker:**
Floyd Kenneth Williams, son
of E. K. & Maybell Williams
(no dates)

No Marker:**
Sam Gilmore
1875-1919??

No Marker: **
James B. Gilmore
Dec 2, 1913
Jul 21, 1974

Porter Edwards
Aug 4, 1879
Dec 14, 1963

Robert T. Edwards
Sep 14, 1860
Dec 1, 1926

Alice G. Edwards
Jan 7, 1868
Jan 28, 1913

Nannie Gilmore Edwards
Sep 13, 1868
Nov 15, 1956

Thula Edwards
Feb 9, 1874
Nov 17, 1919

William M. Edwards
Nov 21, 1849
Aug 17, 1892

Ada J., wife of
W. S. McLain
Sep 16, 1877
Aug 13, 1901

W. W. Newby
Nov 23, 1856
Jan 7, 1929

Martha Janie Edwards Newby
wife of W. W. Newby
Jan 16, 1856
Jan 9, 1914

Tomie P. Newby
May 3, 1880
Aug 5, 1902
age: 22y, 3m, 2d.

James Frank Newby, Jr.
Jul 24, 1909
Mar 8, 1910

No marker: **
Margaret, wife of
W. M. Williams
(no dates)

No marker:**
Willie Lewis Oakley
(no dates)

No Marker:**
Morgan Houston Swafford
Died 1919

No Marker:**
Bessie Lewis Swafford
Died 1927

Lievenia P. Vaughan
Jan 2, 1803
Oct 17, 1876

Lievenia C. Vaughan
Apr 18, 1842
Apr 27, 1862

Martha J. Johnson
1822-1855

Mrs. M. J. Hale
1850-1928

E. H. Hale***
(Ellis H. Hale)
Jan 5, 1850
Aug 16, 1903

Eula J. Hale
Jul 18, 1877
Feb 11, 1900
age: 22y, 6m, 22d.

2 Adult graves, marked with
fieldstones, no inscriptions.
(These could possibly be:
E. H.Hale, Sr. & wife:Mary E.
Hale, they were living in
1850.)

W. A. Edwards
Jul 26, 1867
Feb 7, 1916

Margaret Clay Edwards
1865-1936

Infant Daughter of
Thomas & Martha J. Edwards
Apr 1, 1860
Apr 3, 1860

Thomas Edwards
Oct 31, 1809
Jul 11, 1899

Martha J. Vaughan, wife of
Thomas Edwards
Jan 16, 1824
Oct 12, 1906

No Marker:**
Kate E. Neely
1874-1961
"Kitty"

No Marker:**
E. Tom Swafford
Died June 9, 1968

**Records given at May 1975
Decoration Day.

Willis Vaughan
Feb 14, 1788
Dec 23, 1861

Benjamin F. Holden
Apr 15, 1856
Dec 6, 1873

S. B. G.
(no dates)

Virginia A. Crutchfield
Mar 1, 1924
Jul 21, 1925

Infant Son of
Ethel & W. T. Tucker
1911-1911

Infant Daughter of
Ethel & W. T. Tucker
1911-1911

W. T. Tucker
1870-1953
   & wife:
Mattie Ethel Tucker
1873-1921

Frank O. Tucker
1906-1908

David Kenneth Wiser, son
of Kenneth W. & Edwina Cates
Wiser
May 26, 1954
May 13, 1973
(picture)

Davison Gilmore Lewis
1913-1973
(Woodfin FH)

No Marker:***
Lenciel Andrew Edwards
   "Stripling"
Born Jan 19, 1783
Died May 6, 1864
   and Wife:
Mary Woodfin Edwards
Born Apr 3, 1790
Died Oct 1867
"They came from Buncombe
County, North Carolina to
Rutherford County, Tenn.
about 1810."

*** Family Records of
Edwards Family.

41

8 GUY CEMETERY   Map # 3
Located about 2 miles North of Deason, Tenn.

Maj. William Guy
Departed this life
Apr 15, 1847
age: 59y & 6m.

Dr. Preston Frazier
Died Dec 31, 1865
age: 65 yrs.

NOTE:--This Cemetery was destroyed
several years ago, we
restored this Cemetery along
with the help of Mr. Karl

[See addendum]

Edwards, on Dec 1975.
Many stones has not been
found.-Editors.

9 McELROY CEMETERY   Map # 3
Located about 1½ mile North of Deason, at Coop Road.

Melissa C. Smith, wife of
Thomas S. Kitrell
Aug 3, 1887
Jul 14, 1910

Henry M. Horton
1862-1940
& wife:
Victoria Smith Horton
1866-1929

Harbert Gilmore
Mar 5, 1839
Jul 31, 1911
&
Martha N. Gilmore
Mar 26, 1841
Jul 15, 1919

J. L. McElroy
1846-1918

Willie Marlin Spence McElroy
Jun 5, 1904
Jun 11, 1972

Sara E. McElroy
Jan 30, 1896
Jun 7, 1896
age: 4m & 7d.

John L. Spence
1872-1950
&
Malissia Jane Spence
1870-1929

W. N. Bryant
Mar 16, 1831
Jan 19, 1911

Margret Ann Bryant
Nov 21, 1836
Nov 8, 1904

Roy Smotherman
1904-
&
Myrtle Smotherman
1905-1971

Infant Son of
S. H. & B. Horton
Born & Died
Jan 18, 1898

Harriet McElroy, wife of
G. W. Horton
Aug 11, 1843
Apr 29, 1893

J. Evan Horton
May 5, 1896
Mar 1, 1917

Infant of
Mr & Mrs C. N. Haynes
Born & Died
Dec 4, 1890

Robert McElroy
Sep 16, 1888
Sep 19, 1870
&
Sadie C. McElroy
May 19, 1897
Apr 13, 1957

Willie Bryant
Died Oct 5, 1970
age: 76 yrs.
(Woodfin FH)

Sarah Myrtle Gillcoat,
wife of William N. Bryant
May 10, 1902
Jan 26, 1925

Harb G. Bryant
May 29, 1882
Apr 17, 1907

Hattie E. Bryant
Mar 9, 1875
Aug 21, 1907

Horace M. Watkins
Nov 27, 1878
Aug 4, 1957
&
Kate M. Watkins
Sep 10, 1883

Mrs. Malissie J. Spence
May 16, 1870
Jan 5, 1929

Fount D. Brothers
Jan 10, 1884
Aug 6, 1969
&
Hattie H. Brothers
Jun 12, 1887

Ann Eliza, wife of
Robert E. Epps
Nov 9, 1857
Mar 26, 1881

Mary Jane, wife of
W. C. Alexander
Sep 18, 1838
Jul 4, 1880

Infant Son of
A. N. & Jimmie Miller
1914

Lilly Dean, dau of
John M. & Tempy D. Bryant
Mar 27, 1897

John M. Bryant
1865-1940
&
Tempie H. Bryant
1870-1964

Maggie C. Bryant
Nov 3, 1872
Nov 9, 1958

Sam M. Bryant
Jun 11, 1877
Mar 15, 1944
&
Mary F. Bryant
Jun 5, 1880
Dec 28, 1921

Shelia Ann Watkins
Aug 27, 1947
Sep 20, 1947

Mary E. McElroy
1865-1933
(TM-Miss Mary E. McElroy)

Samuel L. McElroy
Dec 27, 1830
Aug 31, 1916
& wife:
Harriet Weaver McElroy
Oct 11, 1835
Jun 1, 1907

A. M. McElroy
Aug 15, 1811
Feb 23, 1881
age: 69y, 5m, 8d.
&
Mary A. McElroy
Jan 10, 1815
Jun 8, 1855
age: 40y, 4m, 29d.

Samuel A. McElroy
1848-1927
&
Sallie Oden McElroy
1853-1936

Oden M. McElroy
Jan 18, 1881
Apr 7, 1898
age: 17y, 2m, 19d.

Sallie Bryant, wife of
R. H. Lovvorn
Jan 20, 1880
Feb 5, 1908

Sammie G. Bryant
Nov 21, 1908
Apr 14, 1940

Gurttie M. Bryant
Mar 28, 1912
May 8, 1912

Jason Randall Neese
1973-1973
(Gowen-Smith)

Several fieldstones, no
inscriptions.

1 BINGHAM CEMETERY   Map # 4
Located at Liberty Gap, in the Northeast part of County.

William Bingham
Born in N.C. 1775, Emigrated
to Tennessee 1816, and
Died July 19, 1843
age: 68 yrs.

Jane, wife of William
Bingham, Born in N. C. 1784,
and Emigrated to Tennessee
1816 and Died Sept 6, 1856.
age: 72 yrs.

Wife of Timethy Parker, Our
Mother, Ann S. Parker,
Borned 1808, Died 1838
"Blessed are the dead which
die in the Lord."

NOTE:This Cemetery is on
one of the highest peaks
in Bedford County, copied
by: Leslie D. Marsh and
Jimmy Knight.

2 BIGHAM CEMETERY   Map # 4
Located at Liberty Gap, North of Bell Buckle, Tenn.

Elihu Bigham	Mary L. Bigham	[Family says Samuel Bigham
Died Aug 28, 1873	Jul 21, 1805	here]
age: 73y, 8m, 14d.	Apr 21, 1887	Only two graves.

3 MILLER CEMETERY   Map # 4
Located at Liberty Gap, North of Bell Buckle, Tenn.

Robert Black Bigham
Jul 4, 1828
Jul 14, 1900

Isaac J. Miller
Oct 3, 1800
Jul 17, 1855

R. B. Fields
Dec 3, 1873
Jan 23, 1874

Elizabeth Naron
Died Jun 7, 1884
age: 70 yrs.

Mary J. Bigham
Oct 6, 1833
Feb 11, 1882
age: 48y, 4m, 5d.

Mary Miller, wife of
Isaac J. Miller
May 22, 1805
May 17, 1849

Several unmarked graves.

4 CLARK CEMETERY   Map # 4
Located near Liberty Gap, North of Bell Buckle, Tenn.

John M. McClure
May 2, 1775
Feb 5, 1848

In Memory of
Anthony Clark, who died
July 14, 1827,
age: 78 yrs.
(Epitaph unreadable)
(A Revolutionary Soldier)

James Clark, Consort of
Jane Clark
Born Sept 23, 1782
Died Jan 30, 1842
age: 59y, 4m, 7d.

Cicero J. Clark
Aug 1, 1831
Feb 12, 1847

Phoebe McClure
--- --, 1785
Jun 15, 1819

Eliza C. Baley
died Dec 13, 1821
age: 8 days.

Mary M. Clark, Consort of
Robert Clark
Died Oct 3, 1856
age: 64 yrs.

Paralee M. McClure
Oct 15, 1823
Jun 14, 1849

About 35 fieldstones, no
inscriptions.

Marker gone:***
James H. Curry
Born Aug 16, 1847
Died Feb 18, 1859

*** Family Records of
Mrs. Ralph A. Bigham.

No Marker***
Abraham Cooper
Born-?
married Miss ---- Browning
about 1775 in Virginia, His
wife died in Carter County, Tenn.,
He came to Bedford County after
1812, from Smith County, Tenn.
Died-? (A Rev. Soldier)

***Cooper Family Records.

[William Cooper died here
before 1837]

5 HATCHETT CEMETERY   Map # 4
Located near Liberty Gap, North of Bell Buckle, Tenn.

Emily Hatchett
Jun 18, 1812
Jul 25, 1911

W. C. Hatchett
Mar 26, 1837
Mar 20, 1858
(beside this grave is another
adult grave with the marker
broken. Inscription gone)

Juda Hatchett
Jul 19, 1847
Jun 10, 1858

F. E. Hatchett
Feb   1852
Oct 15, 1855

Thomas Hatchett
Sep 26, 1806
Feb 6, 1858

Albert Hatchett
May 22, 1849
May 30, 1849

John Hatchett
Jun 24, 1846
Oct 14, 1846

Nathan Chaffin
Born Aug 1, 1789
married Dec 26, 1811
Died Oct 28, 1858

Died Apr 7, 18--
(illegible)

Many unmarked graves.

6 UNKNOWN CEMETERY   Map # 4
Located near Beechwood, North of Bell Buckle, Tenn.

10-12 graves with fieldstones, no inscriptions.

7 STINNETT CEMETERY   Map # 4
Located in Stinnett Hollow, North of Bell Buckle, Tenn.

continued on next page.

W. E. Stinnett
Born 1820
Died Nov 29, 1885

Parlee, wife of
W. E. Stinnett
Nov 13, 1823
Oct 9, 1883
age: 60 yrs.

8 JERNIGAN CEMETERY   Map # 4
Located in Stinnett Hollow, North of Bell Buckle, Tenn.

Walter Jernigan ***
(no dates)

J. W. Jernigan, Child of
Monroe Jernigan***
(no dates)

*** Copied by Charlie Adcock.

9 HOOVER CEMETERY   Map # 4
Located about 2 miles Northeast of Liberty Gap.

Maggie E., dau of
W. D. & Lizzie Allison
Nov 26, 1879
Jun 29, 1880

Laura Hoover
Born Jun 9, 1855
married Aug 2, 1881
Died Dec 2, 1883

10 LYNCH CEMETERY   Map # 4
Located in Hatchett Hollow, North of Bell Buckle, Tenn.

Mattie Linch Vaughn
Dec 26, 1889
Jun 28, 1972
dau of
John & Amma L. Vaughn

William Alton Frizzell
Dec 7, 1885
Dec 25, 1893

Mary Marrow Frizzell
(no dates on stone, but had
just been buried, 1974-Eds.)

No marker:***
Robert, son of
Iota Linch
(no dates)

John Vaughn
Feb 24, 1863
Apr 26, 1898

Lillard, son of
Mr & Mrs Sim Lynch
Sep 3, 1885
Sep 22, 1886

No marker:
W. W. Dearing & wife ***
Eliza Austin Dearing
(no dates)
No marker:***
Mary Edna "Mollie" Lynch
(no dates)

*** Family Records of
Charlie Adcock.

Amma Linch Vaughn
Mar 26, 1858
Sep 16, 1925

John R. Frizzell
Nov 14, 1860
Jan 18, 1950

Nannie Gray Lynch Frizzell
Sep 22, 1855
Apr 4, 1941

No marker:***
Queenie Josephine Linch
Born Nov 24, 1869
Died Dec 3, 1871

Lewis Linch
Jan 9, 1828
Jan 15, 1910
&
Mary Ann Matilda Linch
Aug 30, 1830
May 8, 1879

No marker:***
Elizabeth Frances Linch
"Betty", dau of John Thomas
& Paralee Lynch
Born Jul 13, 1873
Died Mar 6, 1876

No marker:***
Children of Sewell &
Mattie Linch: Nettie &
Baby Boy (no dates)

11 LYNCH-FRIZZELL CEMETERY   Map # 4
Located on Hatchett Hollow Road, North of Bell Buckle, Tenn.

James Frizzell   and
Died Jan 28, 1873
age: 74 yrs

Rachel Frizzell   and
Died Jan 28, 1873
age: 60 yrs.

Rebecca Frizzell
(no dates)

5 Graves with Rock Slab
markers, no insc.

2 Adult pyramid type, very
old graves, no insc.

6 or more graves with
fieldstones, no insc.

(Rev. Soldier Nathan Frizzell could be buried here, Eds)

12 KELLY CEMETERY   Map # 4
Located on Hatchett Hollow Road, North of Bell Buckle, Tenn.

Joe. P. Kelly
Apr 15, 1814
Jan 13, 1881
age: 66y, 8m, 28d.

Several graves with fieldstones, no inscriptions.

Several unmarked graves.

13 STEPHENSON CEMETERY   Map # 4
Located on Puncheon Camp Hollow Road, Northeast of Bell Buckle, Tenn.

S. J. Anderson
Oct 12, 1871
Jun 1, 1951

Laura E., wife of
S. J. Anderson
Feb 24, 1872
Oct 15, 1905

Infant Daughter of
Newton & N. C. Manley
(no dates)

Hattie, Daughter of
Newton & N. C. Manley
Born Jun 1867
Died Aug 1867

14 FRIZZELL CEMETERY   Map # 4
Located near Beech Grove, Tenn.

J. R. Frizzell
Oct 17, 1838
Nov 18, 1912

Lorene Frizzell
Jul 11, 1904
Apr 28, 1920

Infant of W. J. &
N. C. Nesbitt
Born & Died Nov 27, 1891

John Jakes
Mar 5, 1814
Apr 13, 1893

Nancy, wife of
John Jakes & dau of
William & Catharine Eoff
Dec 19, 1821
Jan 15, 1892

Owen M. Bell
Feb 16, 1904
Oct 26, 1907

Mary L. Bell
Oct 20, 1896
Aug 24, 1897

J. I. C. Jakes, dau of
B. H. & L. Jakes
Apr 16, 1889
May 31, 1889

Ernest, Infant of
A. & Malinda Jakes
Apr 17, 1900
Jul 4, 1900

Robert Eaton
Mar 11, 1856
Jan 4, 1913
&
Nannie Eaton
Jun 15, 1860
(no date)

Infant Daughter of
J. J. & N. G. Crosslin
Stillborn Sep 1, 1905

Robie Allen, Dau of
J. J. & N. G. Crosslin
Dec 24, 1906
Jan 25, 1907

Abbie M. Frizzell
1853-1931

J. C. Jakes
Oct 2, 1884
Feb 11, 1899

Mary N., wife of
Lee Hoover
Jan 27, 1880
Jun 26, 1908

This is a very large Cemetery.
Many unmarked graves.
Fieldstones, no inscriptions.

Willie Carmack, son of
J. W. & Effie Crosslin
Jan 20, 1911
Mar 7, 1911

Pauline, dau of
J. W. & E. L. Crosslin
Aug 25, 1902
Nov 20, 1904

Abram McMahan
May 15, 1840
Jun 6, 1910
& wife:
M. J. Jakes McMahan
Apr 30, 1842
Jun 20, 1928

15 BIVINS CEMETERY   Map # 4
Located near Beech Grove, Tenn.

William Stephens
Dec 1, 1805
Joined the Baptist Church
in 1828
Died Oct 28, 1854

William L. Stephens
Jun 1, 1839
Nov 2, 1860

Jemima Stone
(fieldstone, no dates)

Many old Rock Markers,
no inscriptions.

Mary C., dau of
J. P. & M. S. A. Stephenson
Sep 15, 1865
Mar 14, 1873

George A., son of
J. P. & M. S. A. Stephenson
May 21, 1860
May 5, 1871

Rebecca C., dau of
William & Rachel Keele
Oct 10, 1847
Nov 17, 1865

Tobitha, wife of
G. A. Shelton
Aug 15, 1836
Dec 13, 1861

G. Jakes
1899
(fieldstone)

3 graves with fieldstones,
marked with "K" (no dates)
(These graves are with the
Keele graves.)

Eulice A., Son of
J. R. & N. A. Eaton
Jul 13, 1889
Sep 19, 1890

M. E. Keele
(no dates)

Lutie E. Keel
(no dates)

William Keele*
Jan 17, 1781
Feb 17, 1861

*Newspaper

16 ROBINSON CEMETERY (Col)   Map # 4
Located beside the Bivins Cemetery, near Beech Grove, Tenn.

John Murray
Died Dec 2, 1973
(Scales-Sims FH)

------- Robinson
Died Dec 15, 195_
age: 66 yrs.
(Manchester FH)

Tommie Robinson
1909-1958
&
Emma C. Robinson
1919-

Oia Robinson
Died Jun 23, 1970
age: 65y, 6m, 29d.
(TM)

Henry Robinson
Tennessee
Pvt 42 Co 158
Depot Brigade
W. W. I
May 15, 1890
Aug 28, 1958

I. M.
(Information gone)

Several unmarked graves.

1 OSTEEN CEMETERY   Map # 5
Located about 1 mile Northwest of Rays Chapel.

Sallie Osteen Ray
Dec 18, 1885
Jul 26, 1913
(picture)

James F. Osteen
Sep 27, 1881
Jul 28, 1906

James W. Osteen
Feb 28, 1845
Nov 19, 1919
&
Sarah E. Osteen
Aug 31, 1851
Jan 27, 1936

Cleo B. Osteen
Dec 10, 1891
Jun 21, 1899

Enlis C. Osteen
Feb 8, 1889
Jul 1, 1900

Clary Ann Osteen
Nov 21, 1871
Jan 18, 1951

John Lelon, son of
W. F. & P. E. Osteen
Sep 19, 1905-Jun 30, 1907

Elgin L. Cooper   and   Mary E. Cooper   2 or 3 unmarked graves.
1865-1929   1868-1940

2 WHEELER CEMETERY   Map # 5
Located about ½ mile Northwest of Rays Chapel, in the 11th District,

Benjamin Franklin Lish
1890-1949

Earnest Fred Lish
1885-1944

Mary Etta Lish
1878-1907

Wiley J. Hopkins
Apr 17, 1826
Jul 11, 1897

Elizabeth, wife of
W. J. Hopkins
May 1833
Dec 30, 1902

Lena May, dau of
S. M. & F. J. Hopkins
Mar 9, 1899
May 13, 1899

Fannie Josephine Hopkins
Jul 28, 1866
Mar 22, 1899

Paul Watson, son of
R. L. & A. F. Lish
Apr 26, 1905
Jun 19, 1906

R. L. Lish
1868-1939
&
Ada F. Lish
1868-1935

John S. Simmons
Feb 29, 1876
Nov 16, 1910

Hallie L. Simmons
May 11, 1869
Feb 3, 1912

Thomas F. Simmons
Jul 15, 1834
Mar 15, 1905
&
Sallie H. Simmons
Jul 3, 1841
Jul 25, 1902

B. L. Cooper
1863-1908
&
Fannie Cooper
1866-1936

Bettie Cooper, wife of
G. B. Cooper
Dec 25, 1862
Dec 7, 1902

Rev. D. A. Lish
1846-1901
&
Betty Johnson Lish
1848-1923

David Watson Lish
1881-1899

Sarah E. Lish
1870-1895

Sallie Tucker
1874-1953

Newton Tucker
Jan 26, 1906
Feb 28, 1906

Walter Wheeler
Nov 22, 1883
Sep 3, 1899

Lutishie E. Wheeler
Oct 22, 1877
Jul 14, 1901

W. E. "Lish" Wheeler
Nov 3, 1889
Nov 1, 1971

Rufus T. Wheeler
Apr 23, 1850
Jan 26, 1923
&
Martha I. Wheeler
Apr 20, 1848
Mar 3, 1923

John R. Locke
1848-1911
&
Mary J. Locke
1863-1940

Thomas W. Locke
Tennessee
Pvt U.S.Army   W.W.I
Jul 1, 1889
Dec 9, 1963
&
Emma Cooper Locke
Nov 2, 1892

James B. Lynch
May 14, 1890
Jul 14, 1940

Barbara J. Lynch
1940-1970

Fred M. Lynch
Jan 19, 1936
Aug 24, 1938

Rev. James R. Adams
Dec 5, 1864
May 6, 1909

Alice, wife of
J. R. Adams
Feb 15, 1866
Aug 12, 1907

Etta V., wife of
J. R. Adams
May 25, 1864
Jul 12, 1891

A. C., son of
J. R. & E. V. Adams
Sep 6, 1884
May 24, 1903

Nathaniel L. Wheeler
Tennessee
Cpl U.S.Army, W.W.I
Feb 19, 1887
Aug 6, 1968
&
Rose A. Wheeler
Sep 25, 1896
----
married Oct 17, 1920

Dora Nadine, dau of
I. C. & M. R. Wortham
Mar 3, 1915
Sep 4, 1915

Ivan C. Wortham
Jan 16, 1889
Jun 4, 1967
&
Mary Ruth Wortham
Dec 25, 1892
----
married Jun 7, 1914

J. R. Hopkins
1849-1929

Delia Anne Hopkins
Jul 22, 1851
Mar 29, 1899

Nancy E. Hopkins
Mar 13, 1870
Mar 25, 1915

W. M. Fisher
Jul 31, 1852
May 31, 1908

Cheryl Lynn Lynch
1974-1974
London FH)

William E. Rollins (Edward)
Tennessee
Pvt U.S.Army W.W.II
Mar 14, 1919-May 14, 1956

W. D. Wheeler
Mar 12, 1836
Jun 18, 1913

Martha L., wife of
W. D. Wheeler
Aug 21, 1840
Apr 26, 1887

Mary Ann Wheeler
Nov 17, 1862
Apr 3, 1945

J. N. Dickens
Aug 19, 1836
Oct 27, 1898

Sarah G., wife of
J. N. Dickens
Died Jul 29, 1908
age: 66y, 10m, 8d.

Nannie L. Dickens
1870-1911

W. M. Blackburn
Apr 14, 1830
Apr 1, 1902
&
H. M. Blackburn
Oct 11, 1836
Apr 1, 1902

Jerry Lee Smith
1946

Jas White
Co I
2 Tenn Mtd
Inf.

Amanda Jane White
May 17, 1851
Mar 20, 1934

W. T. Allen Hopkins
Feb 6, 1904
Nov 11, 1907

Essy T. Hopkins
Feb 18, 1908
Jun 11, 1908

George L. Hopkins
Apr 4, 1909
Aug 6, 1909

John Blackburn
1857-1938
&
Anna Blackburn
1861-1954

Glen Edward Rollins
1952
age: 7 days
(Lawrence FH)

E. L. Lynch
1887-1962
(Lawrence FH)
&
M. E. Lynch
1899-

Infant (Lynch)
(no dates)

Sarah F. Rogers
1854-1933
&
W. T. Rogers
1867-1947
&
Martha A. Rogers
1875-1945

Walter Marion "Palen" Little
1894-1974
&
Fannie Wheeler Little
1908-

Samuel A. Lynch
Mar 27, 1884
Mar 27, 1911

Margaret Elnorn Lynch
May 1, 1875
May 21, 1908

William Joshua Osteen
Sep 8, 1877
Dec 21, 1952

Mary Gladis O'Steen
Oct 2, 1904
Dec 26, 1908

Pearl Harber
Oct 30, 1885
Jan 12, 1960

Marion W. Little
Aug 13, 1946

Rufus L. Calahan (Lee)
Feb 7, 1888
Apr 4, 1965
&
Clara D. Calahan
Apr 11, 1892
Feb 1, 1972

Aubrey Harber
May 24, 1893
May 10, 1926

W. H. Harber
Oct 28, 1860
Jul 10, 1931

Tennessee L., wife of
W. H. Harber
Oct 10, 1862
Jun 14, 1911
"A loving wife, a Mother
dear."

Jim B. Wheeler
1845-1921
&
Martha J. Wheeler
1853-1927

John Watson Wheeler
Jan 6, 1869
Sep 30, 1942
&
Martha Osteen Wheeler
Aug 16, 1877
May 3, 1959

Sallie Ann Wheeler,
wife of W. M. Little
Jan 22, 1901
Jun 14, 1925

3 or 4 unmarked graves.

3 YOES CEMETERY   Map # 5
Located near Rays Chapel.

Newton Dickens
  Co B
2nd Tenn Mtd. Inf.

M. E. Yoes
May 29, 1848
Feb 8, 1890

Many graves with fieldstones,
no inscriptions.

A. J. Dickens
  Co A
5th Tenn Cav.

Mollie, dau of
J. S. & M. E. Yoes
Mar 17, 1872
Dec 19, 1894

Corp'l George T. Yoes
  Co F
1 Ala & Tenn
Vidette Cav.

Edgar, Infant Son of
J. S. & Nora E. Yoes
Born & Died
Jul 27, 1894

Sophia E. Yoes
Mar 17, 1846
May 8, 1890

1 Adult Wheeler grave,
(no marker)
1 Child grave(no marker)

4 RAY CEMETERY   Map # 5
Located near Rays Chapel.

There are no markers with inscriptions.

No Marker:***
"Uncle Dock" Ray
Died about 1920
Marlin Cleveland Ray
  "Dock"
Born Nov 18, 1848
Died Feb 12, 1934

No marker:***
Sharp Ray
Died 1830

No marker:***
Thomas Mc. Shearin
Born May 29, 1859
Died about 1867

No marker:***
Robert Ray
Born 1795
Died 1852

No marker:***
Mary "Polly" Ray
Born 1810
Died Jun 7, 1902

*** Records of Mrs. Mary Crowell.

5 SHEARIN CEMETERY   Map # 5
Located on Shearin Ford of Duck River.

William Shearin
Jul 16, 1826
Nov 16, 1914

Sarah, wife of
William Shearin
Oct 10, 1830
Feb 1, 1892

*** Records of Mrs. Mary
            Crowell.

Sallie J., wife of
James F. Ray, & dau of
J. W. & Mary R. Shearin
Feb 10, 1854
Nov 17, 1879
age: 25y, 9m, 7d.

No marker:***
Infant Son of O. G. &
Lommie Shearin
Born & Died 1919.

Blanch, dau of
James F. & Sallie J. Ray
Oct 2, 1878
Aug 6, 1879
&
Infant dau of
James F. & Sallie J. Ray
Born & Died
Oct 22, 1879

No marker:***
Eliza Potts Shearin
Born 1868
Died 1905/6

No marker:***
Sarah Shearin
Born 1905/6
Died: age 6 months.

6 TUCKER-HOPKINS CEMETERY   Map # 5
Located at Tucker's Ford on Duck River.

W. W. Hopkins
Nov 15, 1817
Feb 16, 1887

Rebecca Hopkins
Feb 17, 1817
Jan 16, 1890

Eli H. Hopkins
Oct 3, 1811
Jul 31, 1841
&
M. J. Meek Hopkins
Dec 4, 1817
Mar 28, 1893

No marker:***
Mattie Cleek
Died 1899

James M. Lentz
Feb 14, 1829
Dec 23, 1902
&
Elizabeth Lentz
Apr 15, 1838
Jan 22, 1914

Mary Lue Lentz Shearin
Apr 21, 1872
Jan 24, 1918

No marker:***
William Tucker
Died before April 5, 1847.

No marker:***
Mattie Cleek's little Sister
age about 4 or 5 yrs, died
before Mattie Cleek.

" Sister "
Rosie Lee Shearin
Jun 21, 1913
Nov 2, 1917

Samuel J. Lentz
Jun 17, 1864
Jan 18, 1923

1 Very Old Grave, said to
be Tucker.

No marker:***
Granny Tucker died before
April 5, 1847, she was the
wife of William Tucker.

No marker:***
Mrs. ------ Moses
Died about 1900

Allen Morris
Died Apr 13, 1862
age: about 56 yrs.
&
Margrete Morris
Born Oct 15, 1812
Died Mar 11, 1886

Allen R. Morris
Nov 27, 1872
Apr 28, 1873

No marker:***
William Hammill
Died May or June 1852.

*** Records from
Mrs. Mary Crowell.

7 DARNELL CEMETERY   Map # 5
Located about ½ mile North of Haskins Chapel.

John F. Darnell
Jul 15, 1828
Sep 17, 1895
age: 67y, 2m, 2d.

Nancy Ann, wife of
John F. Darnell
Apr 21, 1831
Dec 13, 1885
age: 54y, 7m, 22d.

Johnnie S. Batten
1902-1902

About 4 other graves with
fieldstones, no inscriptions

8 GLASSCOCK CEMETERY   Map # 5
Located at Haskins Chapel.

David Milton Birdwell
Jan 9, 1840
Jan 16, 1863

Martha K., wife of
H. H. Hopper
Oct 23, 1833
Mar 10, 1867

William G. Glasscock
1834-1917
&
Louann F. Glasscock
1849-1876

Infant Dau of
W. G. & L. F. Glasscock
(no dates)

Milton Birdwell   and
Died Mar 23, 1863
(no age given)

Several unmarked graves.

Mary Ransom
(no dates)

9 JONES CEMETERY   Map # 5
Located near Haskins Chapel.

------------ (could be Jimmie
Bell)
Died Feb --, 1924
(fieldstone)

Lonzo Bell
Born Oct 13, ----
Died (illegible)

William Lonzo, son of
Lonzo & Jimmie Bell
Jul 31, 1921
Mar 4, 1922

Marvin Lee Jones
1948-1951
(Thompson)

M. A. J.
Aug 21, 1882
Apr 8, 1925
(fieldstone)

Robert A. Jones
Died Jan 12, 1955
age: 5m.

C. E. Jones
1863-1932

Thomas E. Jones
Feb 6, 1924
Feb 7, 1924

Simeon Jones
1822-1896
&
Lucinda Jones
1825-1899

Jessie Paul, son of
I. A. & Beula Jones
May 11, 1917
Jan 15, 1919

W. J. Jones
May 15, 1852
Nov 11, 1924
(fieldstone)

T. G. Jones
1860-1903
(fieldstone)

Dora Jones
(no dates, fieldstone)

Frances Darnell, Infant of
Isaac & Lula Darnell
Feb 28, 1926
Dec 17, 1926

Edwin Darnell, son of
Isaac & Lula Darnell
Jun 26, 1928
Mar 17, 1930

Susan Vianie, wife of
W. J. Jones
Aug 2, 1866
May 29, 1915
(fieldstone)

Emmett H. Jones
Apr 4, 1877
Aug 3, 1955
&
Nannie L. Jones
Jul 13, 1888
Nov 28, 1948

Marie Darnell
Jun 23, 1940
Feb 16, 1941
Infant of Isaac & Lula
Jones (TM-Gladys Marie)

Several fieldstones, and
Several Wooden Slabs.

10 DARNELL CEMETERY   Map # 5
Located about 1 mile South of Haskins Chapel.

Allen Darnell
  Co E
10 Tenn Inf.

Copied by Jerry Wayne Cook.

Joel Darnell
  Co E
10 Tenn Inf.

There are many graves marked
only with fieldstones.

W. T. Lynch
  Sgt Co E
10th Tenn Inf

James V. Cozart
1874-1961

Julia Florence Cozart
Oct 7, 1874
Jul 19, 1943

11 HILL CEMETERY   Map # 5
Located about 1 mile South of Haskins Chapel.

This Cemetery was located in field on Haskins Chapel Road,
near where Fishingford Road crosses, in 18th District.
          No markers .

No marker***
Washington Hill
     &   wife.
(no dates)

No marker***
Doc Hill
     &
Nannie Hill, wife of
Doc Hill (no dates)

*** Records of
Jerry Wayne Cook.

12 ZION BAPTIST CHURCH CEMETERY   Map # 5
          (BELL CEMETERY)
Located about 1 mile South of Haskins Chapel.

Thomas Sherman Bell   and
Jan 26, 1865
Jul 27, 1925

Amanda F., wife of
J. M. Helton
Mar 19, 1867
Sep 30, 1907

Flownie Bell   and
Dec 4, 1879
Feb 23, 1915

Margaret D. Coldwell
Oct 7, 1862
Nov 25, 1918

Maude Ethel Bell
Mar 3, 1905
Nov 25, 1919

1 Adult grave beside of
Margaret D. Coldwell,
marked with Wooden Slab,
(no inscription)

William R. Bell
Apr 11, 1874
Dec 4, 1918

Many, many graves with
fieldstones, no insc.

13 STALLINGS CEMETERY   Map # 5
Located about 1 mile Southwest of Haskins Chapel.

D. S. Stallings
Jan 30, 1839
Jun 2, 1921
     &
Georgia A. Stallings
Mar 20, 1846
(no date)
     &
Denita C. Stallings
Jul 16, 1841
May 18, 1864

Margaret B. Claxton, wife of
T. M. Oneal
Mar 2, 1871
May 8, 1900
age: 29y, 2m, 6d.

T. M. Oneal
Mar 8, 1869
Jul 3, 1900
age: 31y, 3m, 25d.

James J. Claxton
1839-1924

Everline D., wife of
J. J. Claxton
Aug 29, 1849
Sep 6, 1899
age: 50y, & 12d.

Laura Claxton
1858-1926

Marium, wife of
Joel Stallings
Nov 23, 1820
Apr 20, 1854

JOHN T. STALLINGS* |1792-1864| a
native of Johnston Co., N.C. brd.
here with other members of family

*by Jack & Thomas Stallings
     (Several unmarked graves)

14 HASKINS CEMETERY   Map # 5
Located about 1 mile Northwest of Wheel, Tenn.

Bill Moblet
(no dates)

Jack Ernest Plebst
(TM-1905-Sep 23, 1969)
     &
Dixie Winona Plebst
May 31, 1911
Apr 30, 1963

Jno. Britt Snelling
Mar 11, 1878
Feb 24, 1953

P. H. Snelling
May 6, 1874
Jan 18, 1923

R. C. Benjamin
Oct 11, 1872
Apr 15, 1949

Ann Haskins Benjamin
Mar 17, 1887
Nov 30, 1960

Robert L. Benjamin
1906-1940

Infant Haynes
1946-1946
(Thompson)

Roy A. Vaughn
1938-1938

Roy T. Butler
1908-1960
     &
Sadie E. Butler
1911-

Lester Butler
1909-1911

Josie Butler Bell
1888-1964

Billie B. Baker
1893-1956
(Lawrence FH)

Thomas D. Canady
Sep 23, 1907

     &
Dora Mae Canady
Jul 23, 1909
Jul 2, 1962

Mabel L. Canady
1931-1932

Bessie Canady
1938-1938

Chas. Kennedy
  Co C
5th Tenn. Cav.

James Canady
1865-1936
&
Nancy Canady
1867-1944

Maude Haskins Davis
1880-1959
(McFarland-Thompson)

J. B. Dalton
1882-1945
&
Nora E. Dalton
1892-

Walter Hay
1886-1965

Sarah Rachel Goodman
1954-1954
(Gowen)

Sarah A. Sikes
Jul 23, 1833
May 18, 1899

I. W. Clark
Co F
1st Ala. Cav.

Benjamin B. Clark
Jul 1857
Aug 1857

James Riley Helton
1851-1946
(Thompson)

Samuel H. Helton
Sep 6, 1919
Dec 14, 1919

Betty Mae Helton
1902-1949
(Thompson)

Grace Mae Thomas
1911-1954
(Thompson)

McKinley A. Haskins
1895-1961

Amy Murphree Haskins
1919-1964
(Gowen-Smith)

William T. Haskins
Tennessee
Pfc Co B 318 field Sig Bn
W. W. I
Feb 2, 1887
Jan 27, 1960

Margaret Elma Haskins
Mar 2, 1894
Nov 11, 1958

George A. Haskins
1852-1933
&
Mary M. Haskins
1855-1938

Benjamin A. Haskins
1851-1910

Martha White Haskins
1870-1936

Joseph F. Haskins
Sep 17, 1839
Mar 2, 1905
& wife:
Amandy V. Haskins
May 12, 1837
Oct 21, 1912

Bryom Haskins
1869-1942

Jim Helton
1863-1937

James Marvin Helton
1916-1960

Mary F. Brown
Apr 18, 1922
Oct 17, 1922

S. M. Perryman
Feb 19, 1886

Samuel M. Perryman
Jun 16, 1829
Apr 1891
Co E 10th Tenn Inf.
&
Nancy C. Perryman
May 2, 1852
Sep 5, 1914

Bennie Perryman
1887-1889

William McGuire
Co C
5th Tenn Cav.

Absalom Perryman
Co E
10th Tenn Inf.

Beulah Haskins Jones
1895-1923

Ethel Estelle Jones
1915-1930

Albert C. Hopkins
1892-1971
(Howell)

Mary H. Hopkins
1887-1969
(Howell)

Fred L. Helton
Tennessee
Pfc U.S.Army   W.W.II
Jun 27, 1914
Apr 25, 1968

John H. Brown
1882-1945
&
Minnie A. Brown
1898-

Several graves, no markers.

B. A. Haskins
Jan 1811
Dec 5, 1890

Priscilla, wife of
B. A. Haskins
Feb 8, 1819
Mar 5, 1893
age: 74y, & 25d.

J. P. Haskins
Apr 4, 1846
Jan 16, 1895
Co C 4th Tenn Mt'd Inf

H. D. Glasscock
Apr 9, 1840
Jul 3, 1917
& wife:
Sarah E. Glasscock
Dec 9, 1841
Feb 7, 1899

Roy Taylor Clifford
1951-1951
(Thompson)

Frances Haskins
1925-1927

Roy D., son of
C. F. & S. F. Haskins
1905-1906

Edward Lee Rice
Born & Died Nov 1, 1945
(TM)

Edgar Wright
Apr 30, 1918
Sep 2, 1918

Margrette Bell
Aug 7, 1909
Oct 4, 1935

J. T., son of
J. H. & M. A. Brown
Aug 19, 1918
Aug 31, 1922

1 RAY CORNER CEMETERY (Col)   Map # 6
Located about 1 mile West of Unionville, Tenn.

Earnest Johnson
Tennessee
Pvt 37 Co 158 Depot Brig
W. W. I
Dec 2, 1889
Mar 19, 1969

Samuel Crowell
Mar 10, 1870
Apr 5, 1871

Willie L. Biggers   and
Feb 12, 1907

Many unmarked graves.

Joe Lewis Johnson
Jul 1, 1938
Jul 18, 1960

Dolars Johnson
Jul 19, 1928
Mar 28, 1932

Nina V. Freeman
1898-Dec 21, 1966

Myrtis L. Biggers
Jun 25, 1909
Aug 4, 1966

Effie Lentz
1910-1974
(TM)

Carlene Fishback
Nov 22, 1952
(Scales & Sons)

George W. Biggers
1874-1945
&
Vinnie G. Biggers
1876-1926

Sam Johnson
Sep 18, 1858
Sep 2, 1890

G. R. Ray
Aug 29, 1873
Jul 16, 1917

Cynthia Ray
Jan 23, 1880
Apr 22, 1959

Katherine L. Biggers
May 22, 1930
May 10, 1955

Fannie B. Taylor
1859-1938

N. R. Taylor
1895-1945

"Father"
George W. Bounds   and
Sep 25, 1818
Mar. 7, 1892

Herbert T. Scott
1884-1946

Alice E. Scott
1887-1963

Mary E. Berryhill
Feb 3, 1917
Sep 23, 1967

Marcus F. Batte
Jul 18, 1884
Sep 2, 1944
&
Alta E. Batte
Oct 30, 1887
Mar 24, 1973

Benjamin S. Batte
May 8, 1859
Nov 13, 1935
&
Lucy J. Batte
Jun 9, 1859
Jan 12, 1936

William E. Batte
1882-1946
&
Clara H. Batte
1889-1968

Clyde Faris Allen
Nov 30, 1915
Jul 14, 1916

Ernest B. Allen
1943

Rev. Warren B. Josselyn
Nov 3, 1889
Feb 20, 1920

2 BOUNDS CEMETERY   Map # 6
Located about 1 mile West of Unionville, Tenn.

John Bounds
1858-1939
&
Lizzie Bounds
1861-1930

"Mother"
Mary A. Bounds   and
Sep 24, 1822
Feb 23, 1905

3 ALLISON CEMETERY   Map # 6
Located about ½ mile South of Unionville, Tenn.
This Cemetery has been destroyed.

*** [Robert Allison, native of
Scotland, emigrated to Granville
Co., NC, then to Bedford Co., TN,
died June 6, 1832, age 84 years,
8 months, & 29 days. Death notice
from National Banner. Family
Records say died at age 96 years.]

No Marker:***
William Allison
Jun 19, 1777
Aug 26, 1852
married Dec 3, 1808 to
Charity Patton Upshaw in
Williamson County, Tenn.

4 UNIONVILLE CEMETERY   Map # 6
Located in Unionville, Tennessee
          (Methodist Church)

Rev. C. I. Kelley
1861-1947

Orney B. Watson Kelley
1888-

Isham L. Kelley·
Aug 3, 1902
Dec 8, 1963

J. Kirk Middleton
1881-1939
&
F. Louie Middleton
1886-1974

J. Redmon Walls
1877-1947
&
Sulie F. Walls
1883-1962

W. T. Lamb
Oct 27, 1890
Nov 30, 1933

Mary E. Allen
1871-1914

Walter T. Allen
1883-1941

Sallie K. Allen
1897-1940

Jesse B. Allen
1879-1950
&
Mattie Allen
1882-1962

Lenelle, dau of
B. H. & Clata Thompson
May 4, 1907
Jun 6, 1909

"Sister"
Annie Bounds   and
Jul 3, 1860
Apr 23, 1878

No Marker***
Robert Allison
Born 1734
Died
married to
Sarah Ogilvie Allison

James R. Faris
Apr 12, 1891
Oct 29, 1960
&
Rothwell S. Faris
Apr 2, 1892

Willie N. Maxwell
Dec 31, 1890
Mar 16, 1963
&
Edna L. Maxwell
Oct 27, 1895
Jan 16, 1943

Joe W. Evans
Jan 15, 1887

&
Lou Allie Evans
Mar 17, 1893
Jan 16, 1963

Chas. Earnest Neal
Dec 5, 1879
Jan 17, 1920
&
Lela Joyce Neal
Dec 12, 1879
(no date)

Irene Neal
Sep 10, 1901
May 14, 1926

Roy C. Moore, son of
C. C. & M. J. Moore
Apr 10, 1892
Sep 5, 1912

Annis, dau of
Ben Holms & Clatie
                    Thompson
May 3, 1912
Jan 20, 1913

"Brother"
James C. Bounds
Sep 23, 1854
Mar 23, 1876

*** Records of
Mrs. L. Fount Farris.

Shelia Diann Wade
1950-1951
(Gowen)

Lucille Powell Wade
1918-1945

F. Z. King
Aug 1, 1899
Oct 23, 1939
&
Clatie E. King
Sep 27, 1904

Charlie Shearin
1869-19(no date)
&
Cassie B. Shearin
1885-1923

Wash Shearin
1914-1937
&
Zella B. Shearin
1917-1941

J. N. Smith
Jan 15, 1892
Apr 26, 1918

Mary Elizabeth Moore
Oct 20, 1918
Jul 7, 1928

Lewis Franklin Moore
Aug 10, 1897
Jan 3, 1961
&
Ada Bell C. Moore
Sep 17, 1891

Francis M. Eley
Oct 23, 1857
Mar 11, 1922

Harriett C., wife of
F. M. Eley
Apr 4, 1842
Dec 24, 1920

Joe R. Crowell
1891-1935
&
Lela M. Crowell
1892-1923
&
Lola M. Crowell
1892-

J. M. Crowell
Nov 5, 1847
Aug 27, 1913
&
Susan A. Crowell
Sep 19, 1856
Apr 27, 1902

Emmett M. Eads
Aug 20, 1897
Aug 13, 1963
&
Elizabeth M. Eads
Mar 18, 1888

Frank Blanton
1855-1936
&
Fannie Blanton
1862-1932

Ann Murphy
1904-1940

Jack Murphy
1926-1932

Elvira McFadden
May 20, 1833
May 13, 1900

Lillie Kirby Hatcher
1860-1954

"Father"
H. R. Freeman
Dec 25, 1835
Aug 7, 1917

Lucy Blanton Manier
Died Aug 13, 1926
age: 84 yrs.

Alex Hatcher
1830-1912

Mrs. Nasmi Hatcher
Jul 31, 1829
Mar 26, 1893
age: 63y, 7m, 26d.

Arabella T. Adams
Died 1910
(no age given)

F. H. Moore
Sep 3, 1844
Dec 14, 1917

E. H. Moore
Oct 24, 1848
Mar 15, 1924

William Franklin Hoover
1906-1953
&
Allie Pearl Hoover

Edwin H. Crowell
1885-1931
&
Sallie B. Crowell
1887-1969

Robert A. Moon
Aug 9, 1891
Aug 13, 1973
&
Doshia Clay Moon
Oct 28, 1891
Oct 23, 1970

Allen Vincent
(no dates)
&
Netta Vincent
(no dates)

Marion A. Vincent
1888-1958
Lou Ida T. Vincent
1892-1969

Neal Vincent
1914-1938

Marie Vincent
1927-1945

Andrew J. Vincent
1860-1939
&
Parilee B. Vincent
1861-1939

H. C. Blanton
1893-1918

J. B. Blanton
1911-1911

E. Blanton
1823-1900

Lucy F. Blanton
1825-1905

J. R. Blanton
1852-1918

Annie V. Blanton
1857-1930

William E. Blanton
Nov 19, 1887
May 12, 1973

James L. "Fate" Cooper
Aug 3, 1898
Oct 10, 1974
&
Lula T. Cooper
Sep 12, 1900
----
married Oct 15, 1924

James Elvin Cooper
Aug 1, 1925
Jul 14, 1928

William T. Tucker
1901-1970

Ernest Thomas Haynes
Jan 18, 1926

Thomas L. Crowell
Jul 16, 1875
Apr 16, 1906

Margaret Jane Crowell
Aug 28, 1873
Jul 16, 1956

Thomas L. Crowell
1905-1966
&
Aileen R. Crowell
1915-

William A. Eley
Jul 18, 1884
Feb 28, 1961
&
Evie W. Eley
May 31, 1889

Don Bright Eley
Jul 22, 1919
Sep 30, 1919

Roy Bryan Cooper
1896-
&
Mary Beatrice Cooper
1910-1970

Robert J. Cooper
1856-1936
& wife:
Joe M. Bigger Cooper
1864-1947

Sarah Ogilvie Hatcher
May 3, 1845
Dec 9, 1904

J. William Hatcher
Jul 9, 1857
Sep 9, 1943

R. O. Blanton
1884-
&
Helen M. Blanton
1888-1941
&
Lilly B. Blanton
1906-

May Belle Faris
1879-1912
&
Emry E. Faris
1877-1953
&
Edna E. Faris
1878-1929

Clarence E. Faris
1903-1946

Paul Clinton Wortham
Oct 21, 1916
Apr 19, 1972
&
Glendon Carpenter Wortham

Robert L. Carpenter
1970-1970
(Howell)

Mark Edwin Carpenter
1967-1967
(Gowen)

Ollie B. Anderson
1897-1919
&
Salomie E. Anderson
1891-1918

James C. Anderson
1866-1943

Leoatie Anderson
1871-1931

Elizabeth, dau of
Mr & Mrs J. C. McGowan
Jan 28, 1917
Nov 14, 1919

Dulane, dau of
Euless & Virginia Smith
1942

Paulyne Cooper Clanton
1929-1953

Winfield Scott
Feb 25, 1838
Sep 4, 1902

Lillie D., wife of
H. T. Scott
Aug 15, 1883
Oct 8, 1913

Emily Scott Brown
1854-1943

Elizabeth Bigger
Feb 28, 1838
Nov 9, 1909

Martha J., dau of
Rev. W. W. & A. E. Graves
Apr 5, 1883
Sep 10, 1900

Capt. William Crisp Blanton
Co F 23 Regt. Tenn Inf
C.S.A.
Dec 27, 1817
Oct 24, 1887

Elizabeth Tilford Blanton
Aug 6, 1820
May 2, 1898

Leigh Grady Thompson
Oct 15, 1904

&
Susie Moon Thompson
Nov 9, 1886
Sep 22, 1966

Lester L. Evans
Jan 28, 1878
Mar 29, 1949

Maude C. Evans
Jan 6, 1884

Freddy C. Jones
1901-

Susan Stallings
Jun 12, 1821
Feb 18, 1907

Kate Elizabeth Call
Nov 15, 1905
Dec 20, 1907

William T. Call
1865-1943

Alice O. Call
1867-1959

Richard Lee Call
1903-1922

William B. Call
1899-1939

John C. Wilson
Sep 25, 1812
Dec 12, 1885

Mrs. Mary, wife of
John C. Wilson
Apr 12, 1815
Mar 8, 1878

Rena F., wife of
W. B. Wilson
Aug 16, 1855
Apr 10, 1888

Richard Franklin, son of
W. B. & Rena Wilson
May 30, 1882
Jan 22, 1884

Lee G. Faris
Dec 23, 1880
married Maggie Cromer
May 27, 1903
Died Mar 16, 1904

"A Soldier of The War of 1812"
Merideth Blanton
Born in Cumberland Co., Va.
Jun 19, 1792
Departed this life
Jul 5, 1879
age: 87y & 16d.

Nancy, wife of
Merideth Blanton
Mar 7, 1797
Nov 14, 1885
age: 94y, 8m, 7d.

Famie Kate Klien
1863-1938

Jesse Covington
Apr 15, 1831
Feb 26, 1907

Elizabeth Covington
1837-1911

"Mother"
Lou Vicia Covington Stem
1853-1933

Benjamin F. Covington
1895-1931

Fannie Covington Burton
1891-1918

John A. Covington
1855-1936

Alice Covington
1865-1936

Garrett Christopher Covington
Mar 15, 1885
Oct 6, 1970

Mishie Martin Covington
Aug 27, 1882

J. W. Allen
Nov 19, 1859
Jun 22, 1921

Sarah M. Allen
Feb 8, 1859
Oct 14, 1924

Edgar Lee Allen
1882-1952

Arvle C. Allen
Sep 9, 1894
May 26, 1970
&
Jennie W. Allen
Sep 5, 1898

Adda Anderson
Sep 31, 1867
Aug 1, 1868

Benjamin Blanton
May 16, 1802
Nov 23, 1885

Martha, Consort of
Benj. Blanton
Jun 3, 1807
Proffessed faith in Christ
in 1832 and Died
Jan 24, 1869

Dr. G. L. Landis
Mar 15, 1847
Feb 21, 1930
&
Cassie Landis
Sep 12, 1854
Jul 6, 1906

Virginia Allison, wife of
Dr. G. L. Landis
1865-1928

Florence Landis
Jul 1, 1878
Nov 3, 1970

Ruth Landis
Mar 3, 1900
Apr 25, 1900

Lizzie M. Faris
Jun 25, 1882
Dec 22, 1901

Allen Stallings
1856-1924

Bettie Stallings
1865-1929

Willie Sanders
1906-1944
"Killed in action in
Germany."

Faine Sanders
1898-1918

William P. Sanders
1873-1924
&
Annie C. Sanders
1874-1947

R. B. Landis
Mar 14, 1844
Oct 12, 1882
&
Nannie E. Landis
Jun 15, 1848
Sep 16, 1916

"Wilson" (Landis plat)
(no dates, on reverse side
of marker: R. B. L.)

Dora, dau of
F. S. & Sarah Landers
Sep 8, 1873
Sep 24, 1875
age: 2y, & 16d.

Joseph T. Blanton
Feb 20, 1828
May 23, 1904

Julia A. Jones
1853-1948

William T. Clary
1859-1933
&
Laura K. Clary
1866-1924

Annie May Clary
1886-1911

Leslie F. Clary
1891-1891

Clarence G. Clary
Tennessee
Pfc U.S.Army W.W.I
Sep 20, 1892
Sep 8, 1971

Eliza Ann Clary
Apr 1, 1825
Jun 15, 1875

Mrs. Alla Delphia Clary
Oct 12, 1802
Jun 7, 1884

Mary E. Jackson
Jun 7, 1885
Mar 13, 1970

George Rufus Ezell
Aug 7, 1889
May 14, 1973

Margie I. Ezell
Nov 30, 1889
Sep 25, 1963

James B.(Ezell plat)
1878-1953

Elizabeth E. Lanier
Apr 16, 1883
Jun 13, 1971

George Gentry White
1874-1953
&
Nannie Ezell White
1880-1944

"Father"
E. F. Kirk
Apr 4, 1809
Nov 22, 1883
&
"Mother"
S. J. Kirk
May 17, 1817
Aug 21, 1877

Ransom, son of
C. B. & A. K. Neal
Apr 12, 1896
Nov 16, 1897

W. L. Faris
Jun 17, 1854
Dec 27, 1927
&
Amanda R. Faris
Aug 3, 1855
Aug 24, 1927

Julian L. Faris
1879-1931
&
Bera Stammer Faris
1885-1950

Richard H. Stem
Feb 11, 1822
Apr 10, 1891
age: 69y & 2m
"Not lost but gone
before wife."

G. Nowlin Brown
1893-1963
&
Addie Landis Brown
1889-1956

William E. Faris
Sep 7, 1889
Dec 13, 1962
&
Sue L. Faris
Nov 23, 1884
Jul 2, 1970

Earl Landis
1911-1943
"He gave his life for
his Country."

Barry Earl Landis
Sep 4, 1949
Sep 10, 1949

Dean McLain Landis
1887-1924

Bryant E. Landis
1881-1955

Josephine Hopper Landis
1890-19

Alvis Landis
1914-1925

Landis Cathey
1937
Infant

George B. Landis, Sr.
Aug 30, 1877
Sep 12, 1960

G. B. Landis, Jr.
1927-1930

Sibyl Delene Osteen
Apr 25, 1920
Sep 28, 1931

Jeanne Marie Murrah
1960-1964

Charles N. Neal
Nov 7, 1849
Mar 23, 1918
&
Algie K. Neal
Jan 20, 1861
Apr 23, 1949

Herman Kliem
Nov 29, 1891
Aug 24, 1961
&
Nola G. Kliem
Apr 1, 1904

Burchette E. Kliem
1872-1955

Lucy E. Kliem
Feb 17, 1888
Mar 11, 1911

Fred Kliem
1862-1916

"Mother"
Ann Kliem
Died Sep 8, 1896
(no age given)

C. G. Kliem
1882-1935

Homer K. Scott
Jul 4, 1875
Jan 30, 1961

Minnie H. Scott
Sep 22, 1881
Jul 20, 1927

Estella Paschal
1887-1956

Ben Holmes Thompson
Jan 29, 1878
Jun 7, 1962
&
Clatie Ann Thompson
Feb 7, 1878
Aug 22, 1958
married May 22, 1898

G. B. Cooper
Mar 11, 1861
Feb 21, 1949
&
Mrs. G. B. Cooper
Aug 23, 1879
Apr 6, 1940

Clarence I. Collins
Tennessee
Pvt U.S.Army   W.W.I
Dec 2, 1893
Mar 13, 1970
&
Ona Haynes Collins
Apr 19, 1897
Jan 31, 1968

Albert F. Knott
1819-1879
&
Malinda A. Knott
1832-1919

Charlie Rufus, son of
Albert & Malinda Knott
Apr 17, 1871
Jun 19, 1907

Virginia T. Knott
Oct 18, 1858
Sep 10, 1862

Matilda Dickens Fisher
1880-1944

Willis F. Burden
1875-1969
&
Clary Dickens Burden
1876-1936

Eston Foster Burden
Oct 28, 1903
Jan 21, 1946

Zechariah Cleek
1848-1927
&
Mary Ann Cleek
1849-1934

Rufus B. Osteen
Tennessee
Pvt 1Cl 113 M. G. Bn   30 Div
May 27, 1940

James D. Jeffress
1841-1923
&
Frances A. Jeffress
1846-1934

Thomas E. Jeffress
1874-1942
&
Sarah Etta Jeffress
1875-1957

Douglas C. Jeffress
Feb 27, 1887

&
Maggie O. Jeffress
Apr 25, 1889
Jul 24, 1970
married Mar 10, 1910

Howard Clif Osteen
Tennessee
Pvt 105 Trench Mortar Btry
W. W. I
Nov 4, 1894
Aug 1, 1959
&
Eva Faris Osteen
Dec 12, 1891
Sep 12, 1969

W. Crockett Stem   and
1867-1954

Dr. John W. Clary
Jul 28, 1821
Jun 26, 1888

Mattie Clary, wife of
Dr. J. W. Clary
1839-1919

Infant
Jaycee B. Dickens
1931

Jason Landis Dickens
Apr 28, 1890
May 17, 1963
&
Emma Lee Reid Dickens
Feb 14, 1890

Lou D. Dickens
1871-1948

Malcom A. Dickens
Nov 25, 1873
Apr 2, 1918
(picture)

Jason B. Dickens
Oct 13, 1852
Aug 8, 1932
&
Virginia F. Dickens
Nov 21, 1852
Jan 27, 1927

"Father"
R. S. Mincy
May 20, 1832
Mar 22, 1922
&
"Mother"
S. C. Mincy
Aug 14, 1848
Mar 18, 1939

Elisha C. Reid
Sep 23, 1844
Apr 24, 1921
&
Mary C. Reid
Jan 6, 1857
Jun 26, 1925

Arthur Reid
1896-1928

R. Crawford Reid
1888-1954
&
Margaret Eads Reid
1891-19

William O. Eads
Nov 5, 1886
Sep 22 1968
&
Alta R. Reid Eads
Apr 19, 1886

Judie V. Stem
1868-1927

Ernest Grady Purvis
May 3, 1895
Jun 22, 1962
Tennessee
Pfc Co D 6 Engineers
W. W. I
&
Martha Stem Purvis
Mar 27, 1899

Earl N. Potts
Oct 4, 1886
Mar 18, 1965
&
Henrietta E. Potts
Apr 2, 1889
Oct 23, 1945

J. L. Eley
1877-1931

Mary Frances Eley
Jun 6, 1890
Feb 10, 1969

Harry W. Faris
Aug 28, 1936
Aug 29, 1936

No marker:***
Sophie P. Blanton
wife of James Albert Knott
Born Aug 21, 1846
Died Jul 9, 1884

Willie Orbun Stem
1894-1935
& wife:
Argie C. Anthony Stem
(no dates)

J. Pruett Wood
Dec 7, 1891
Mar 22, 1964
&
Georgia W. Wood
Dec 9, 1900

Wiley Fredrick Moore
Jun 1, 1877
Apr 22, 1933
&
Mary Lytle Moore
Oct 6, 1877
Aug 13, 1965

Herbert E. Harlan, Sr.
1896-1930

John Lee Taylor
1893-1972

Ben Comer Neal
1888-1944

Bula Taylor Neal
1887-1926

*** Records of Mrs. Joe
Neeley.

Thomas Frank Woosley
1873-1943
&
Annie Belle Woosley
1874-1953

Cooper Fisher
Aug 25, 1889
Jul 20, 1930

Ona Fisher
Feb 15, 1900
Oct 14, 1927

Joe P. Fisher
Jun 7, 1858
Apr 15, 1928

Susanah Fisher
Mar 6, 1862
Apr 18, 1948

William F. Neal
1851-1928
&
Ollie Faris Neal
1885-1970

Charles Randy Neal
Aug 11, 1952-Jun 26, 1972
(color picture)

No marker:***
James Albert Knott
Born 1843 & Died 1876

Thomas L. Dillard
1881-1947
&
Lillie B. Dillard
1882-1931

Thomas J. Biggers
Nov 13, 1854
Dec 19, 1930

William H. Wade
Nov 27, 1873
Apr 22, 1946
&
Florence F. Wade
Nov 14, 1881
Apr 4, 1946

John R. Corbitt
1866-1948
&
Susie Corbitt
1869-(no date)

Edna W. Corbitt
1904-1945
(Gowen-Smith)

No marker:***
Minnie Hayes Blanton,
daughter of Hiram H. and
Sallie Bronson Blanton
Died young, about 5 yrs.
Died early in 1880's.

5 LANDIS CEMETERY   Map # 6
Located about 1 mile South of Unionville, Tenn.

Sacred to the Memory of
Rev. John W. Stamps, who was
born April 3rd 1822. Embraced
Religion July 24, 1843.
Became a Candidate for the
Ministry Oct 12, 1844, was
licensed to preach April 13th.
1846. Ordained April 10, 1848.
Died Dec 8, 1849.
age: 27y, 8m, 5d.

Kimbrough Allison
Jan 1, 1794
Jan 18, 1869

Sallie Allison
Jan 3, 1804
Nov 19, 1879

Bryant Landis
May 5, 1815
Jan 10, 1888
&
Margaret Ogilvie Landis
Sep 14, 1811
married to B. Landis
Feb 19, 1831
died Dec 17, 1886
&
Briant E. Landis
Oct 25, 1851
Aug 27, 1881

R. C. Ogilvie
Born 2 June 1828
married to E. J. Foster
Sep 7, 1847
Died 22 Aug 1852
age: 24y, 2m, 20d.

Mrs. Sarah Ann, wife of
Dr. T. D. Whitaker
Apr 29, 1834
Mar 3, 1874

James Hervey, Infant Son of
Dr. T. D. & S. A. Whitaker
Feb 24, 1870
Apr 16, 1870
age: 1m & 22d.

Margaret A. Hendon, consort
of J. R. Hendon and
daughter of A. & Nancy
Wilson
Oct 18, 1842
Feb 15, 1863
age: 20y, 10m, 27d.

Katharine Orlenia Smith
Nov 2, 1853
Aug 10, 1857

Sallie J. Allison
(her marker is in ground &
against Iron-fence)

William Ogilvie, who was
born June 4th 1767 and
died June 26th 1847
age: 80y, & 22d.

Nancy Ogilvie
Apr 12, 1789
Jun 20, 1858
age: 69y, 2m, 8d.

William Allison
Aug 3, 1858
Jul 13, 1881
&
Sallie J. Allison
Jul 15, 1847
Nov 9, 1887
&
Emma Allison
May 15, 1856
Aug 6, 1876
&
Elvira, wife of
R. S. Allison
Aug 24, 1826
Jun 4, 1903

Richard S. Allison
Aug 10, 1825
Apr 23, 1869

(This Cemetery is very bad
condition, but has Iron fence.)

William P. Ogilvie
May 9, 1825
Jan 7, 1842
age: 16y, 7m, 28d.

Elizabeth Jane Ogilvie
Apr 2, 1835
Jun 16, 1848

Martha J., Consort of
J. R. Wilson and daughter
of Adison & Susan Adams
Jan 13, 1841
Feb 1, 1871
age: 30y & 18d.

Joseph D. Landis
Nov 22, 1854
Feb 9, 1858

Horace B. Landis
Aug 25, 1856
Aug 22, 1860

Yeola Landis
May 24, 1882
Aug 17, 1882

Eliza Jane Williams
Jul 10, 1852
May 2, 1903

Located about 1 mile South of Unionville, Tenn.,
near Landis Cemetery.

There is only 1 grave with fieldstone, no inscription.

[Christopher C. Covington buried here in unmarked grave, born ca 1821, died after 1880, son of Luvicy & Jesse Covington]

Located about 1½ miles South of Unionville, Tenn.

Zollie B. Neese
Jun 11, 1920
Jun 12, 1920

William Clark
Co C
4th Tenn Mtd Inf.

W. H. Clark
Apr 27, 1831
Jan 15, 1888

Robert A. Moon, Jr.
Jan 10, 1924
Apr 10, 1924

Martin E. Vincent
Jan 21, 1859
Jan 4, 1925

William Claudius, son of
M. E. & M. J. Vincent
Nov 1, 1888
Nov 30, 1895

Thomas D. Mincy
1856-1932

Sybil L. Thompson
Jan 19, 1909
Apr 1, 1919

P. B. Moon
May 4, 1835
Jul 13, 1902

Sarah Ann, wife of
P. B. Moon
May 9, 1834
Sep 20, 1894

William Bell Moon
1860-1943
&
Martha P. Moon
1864-1945

Dr. John Robert Moon
1853-1934

Mattie Dryden Moon, wife
of Dr. J. R. Moon
1858-1935

Francis L. Moon
Mar 9, 1898
Sep 20, 1899

Several unmarked graves.

Located about ½ mile Southeast of Unionville School.

W. G. White
1853-1928
(picture)

Tabitha White
Jul 25, 1851
Apr 7, 1935

Bettie Lee White
Nov 28, 1889
Nov 11, 1903

Eva May, Infant dau of
W. G. & M. T. White
Dec 17, 1883
Jul 23, 1884

Mary Catherine, Infant dau
of W. G. & M. T. White
Aug 17, 1882
Aug 28, 1883

W. Roy Moore
Nov 2, 1893
Apr 17, 1962
&
Modena J. Moore
Dec 31, 1895

Roy Moore, Jr.
Jul 9, 1925
Jan 2, 1926

W. T. B. Moore
Nov 18, 1843
Feb 3, 1921

Sarah E., wife of
W. T. B. Moore
Jun 18, 1848
Mar 22, 1889

James Ogilvie Moore
Apr 17, 1874
Nov 29, 1880
age: 6y, 7m, 12d.

Infant Daughter of
W. T. B. & S. E. Moore
Born & Died same day
(no dates)

"Mother"
Mary Artimiss Moore
Apr 29, 1857
Sep 10, 1935

Harold Moore
Tennessee
Pfc 1419 A.A.F.Base Unit
W. W. II
Dec 13, 1918
Jan 10, 1946

Horace W. Moore
Sep 2, 1885
May 19, 1970
&
Florence W. Moore
May 10, 1881

Herbert, Son of
H. W. & E. F. Moore
Jun 13, 1907
Jun 16, 1908

Paty J. Moore
Tennessee
Pvt 315 Inf 79 Inf Div
W. W. II
Jan 30, 1923
Nov 20, 1944

Paul T. Moore
Mar 20, 1920

&
Ruth B. Moore
Nov 23, 1931
----
married Jul 2, 1949

Garrett W. Moore
Tennessee
S Sgt 3860 Air Base Gp A.F.
Korea
Oct 17, 1931-Apr 10, 1965

Teddy Wayne Burris
Sep 14, 1953
Sep 16, 1953

Infant Daughter of
J. K. & Ann Lou Allison
Oct 8, 1913

Virginia Mae Fulton
Aug 22, 1925
Apr 29, 1960

John Eric Moore
1970-1971
(Lawrence FH)

John Ralph Moore, Sr.
Tennessee
Pvt U.S.Army W.W.I
Nov 2, 1893
Feb 17, 1966

Myrtle May Moore
Apr 18, 1896
Sep 23, 1939

Frank, son of
J. R. & M. M. Moore
Jul 2, 1921
Aug 20, 1922

Located about ½ mile Southeast of Unionville School.

In Memory of
William Locke, who departed
This life May 22nd 1823.
age: 44y, 9m, 6d.

William H. Locke
Feb 23, 1819
Sep 27, 1837
age: 18y, 7m, 4d.

Mrs. Martha Mayfield
Apr 15, 1787
Mar 9, 1871
age: 83y, 10m, 22d.

Infant Son of
James & Jane Ogilvie
Born & Died Aug 6, 1847

Emily M. Lock
Oct 23, 1840
Jun 5, 1841

M. P. Lock
Jun 19, 1815
Oct 24, 1853
age: 38y, 1m, 5d.

Martha A. Poplin, Consort of
Dr. G. L. Poplin
whose remains are here
deposited. Who was born
May the 30, 1832 A.D. &
departed this life
Nov 21, 1849. age: 17y, 5m, &
21 d.

Many unmarked graves.

10 WINSETT CEMETERY   Map # 6
Located about ½ mile Northeast of Unionville School.

John E. Winsett
Sep 24, 1858
Sep 7, 1863
&
Martha A. Winsett
Jul 9, 1842
Dec 25, 1860

Elijah D. Winsett
Mar 1, 1813
Jul 17, 1865

A. M. Winsett
Aug 10, 1837
Aug 8, 1878
age: 40y, 11m, 28d.

John M. Neely
May 30, 1838
Jan 21, 1921

Mary E., wife of
J. M. Neely
Oct 13, 1839
Jul 5, 1903

L. E. Winsett
Oct 3, 1841
Dec 1, 1883
age: 42y, 1m, 28d.

Lurana J. Winsett Jones
Mar 6, 1821
Sep 9, 1908
age: 87y, 5m, 18d.

Hugh J. Neely
Apr 13, 1876
Jul 5, 1904

E. E. Winsett
Mar 22, 1866
Aug 14, 1866

Ann Kelley
Died Sep 17, 1875
age: 74 yrs.

J. H. H.(foot marker)
(Headstone broken away)
Feb 12, 1853
Feb 24, 1926

Edna Winsett
Feb 20, 1861
Jul 13, 1866

11 ALLISON CEMETERY   Map # 6
Located near Unionville, Tennessee.

Mrs. E. A. Clary, wife of
Dr. J. W. Clary
Nov 23, 1834
May 13, 1859
age: 24y, 5m, 20d.

Infant Dau of
J. M. & N. J. Moore
Born Feb 21, A.D.

(broken away)

Mary J., dau of
J. M. & N. J. Moore
Dec 13, 1856
Apr 19, 1858
age: 1y, 4m, 6d.

Several graves with fieldstones, no inscription.

Alla Jane, dau of
J. W. & E. A. Clary
Jan 1, 1857
Jun 3, 1858

Earnest L. Parker
May 20, 1867
Sep 30, 1867
age: 4m & 10d.

Tabitha, wife of
T. N. McCord
Nov 25, 1839
Jun 6, 1863

Harvey P. Allison
Oct 11, 1841
Jan 13, 1862
age: 20y, 3m, 2d.

Robt. Allison
Jun 12, 1816
Mar 27, 1891

Edwin M. Frost
Jan 4, 1833
Sep 15, 1855
age: 22y, 8m, 11d.

Robert Allison
Feb 3, 1780
May 24, 1842
age: 62y, 3m, 21d.

Elizabeth Allison
Mar 28, 1791
Jun 23, 1851

Colmon Allison
Sep 15, 1806
Sep 17, 1827

Mary Allison
Apr 12, 1816
Nov 21, 1868
age: 52y, 7m, 9d.

Nancy Steed***
Apr 22, 1795
Nov 19, 1854
age: 59y, 6m, 27d.

***From Frost Records:
Nancy Steed was wife of
Abner Steed, also wife of
Clary, Frost & Brown. Abner
Steed buried elsewhere
between 1862-65.

"My Husband"
Jos. R. Brown***
Died Jan 22, 1875
age: 63y, 8m, 12d.

***From Frost Records:
Jos. R. Brown was the
Husband of Mary Ann Clary
Brown.

Several unmarked graves.

12 FINNEY CEMETERY   Map # 6
Located at Three-Corner Garden.

Lee Reed
1863-1939
&
Ella Reed
1867-1933

Margaret Elizabeth Finney
wife of Kinion Carlton
May 29, 1833
Feb 26, 1908
age: 74y, 8m, 27d.

Rebecca A. Finney Rucker
Nov 25, 1837
Dec 9, 1914

Martha A. Finney
Jan 11, 1841
Mar 25, 1899
&
Mary Ophilia Finney
Mar 25, 1848
Feb 10, 1897
"Two loving Sisters who were
inseparable in life."

James Finney
Jan 31, 1796
Aug 17, 1870

Alice, wife of
James Finney
Apr 26, 1806
Jun 27, 1871

Willis Carson
Sep 22, 1817
Sep 5, 1882
age: 64y, 11m, 13d.
&
Zilpha A. Carson
Aug 3, 1828
Mar 6, 1894
age: 65y, 5m, 5d.

J. M. Carson
1848-(no date)

Mary E. Carson
Apr 8, 1850
Aug 5, 1926

William F. Carson
Dec 19, 1855
Apr 24, 1937

Alice L. Carson
Aug 29, 1858
Sep 18, 1939

Section out-side Walled Cemetery:***

In Memory of
Delpha & John A. Rushing
who departed this life
Jan 20, 1854, Delpha in the
12th year of her age & John A.
in the 2nd year of his age.

***Section copied by Dick
Poplin.

Asa Rushing, Consort of
Sarah J. Rushing, who
departed this life Oct 24th
1837. Age:27y, 3m, 12d.

Ann Gilley, departed this life
Feb 4, 1834 in the 27th year
of her age.

Elizabeth Rushing, Consort
of Abel Rushing, who departed this life Sept. the 7th
1838. Age: 23y, 2m, 10d.

A. A. Rushing, son of
Abel Rushing, departed this
life on the 23rd of Oct. 1838.
age: 2 months.

To the Memory of
Tallitha Landers, wife of
Obriant Landers & dau of
John & Sarah Rushing, who
departed this life in the
22nd year of her age,
Oct 29, 1837.

13 PRESSGROVE CEMETERY   Map # 6
Located about ½ mile Southeast of Three-Corner Garden.

Manor S. Sudberry
Oct 23, 1897

&
Annie E. Sudberry
Jan 7, 1895
May 12, 1973

Clarence E. Adcock
Jul 14, 1919
Sep 6, 1962
&
Clara H. Adcock
Jan 28, 1918
Nov 19, 1974
married Dec 15, 1940

Walter E. Adcock
Sep 2, 1887
Jun 3, 1967
&
Mary L. Adcock
Oct 27, 1888
Jan 15, 1962

Thomas Kellie Adcock
Jan 12, 1912
Aug 1, 1936

John Winchester Phelps
Jun 15, 1899
Jun 10, 1960

Estelle D. Phelps
1896-1947

William G. "Bill" Haynes
Aug 10, 1881
Dec 12, 1961
&
Florence Malissa Haynes
Aug 30, 1881
Oct 13, 1960

Ernest R. Threet
Sep 22, 1898
Jan 25, 1964
&
Pearl V. Threet
Feb 10, 1903

Jas. Herbert Threet
1941-1942

"Father"
Durward Jackson
1896-1974
&
"Mother"
Tommie L. Jackson
1899-1970

Sheila Moore
May 23, 1944

Lillard J. Batey
May 20, 1910
Oct 30, 1966

M. A. Brown Adcock Batey
Sep 19, 1911

Nellie G. Clardy
1893-1935

Thomas H. Brown
Jul 28, 1889
May 20, 1958
&
Emma E. Brown
Mar 17, 1886
Sep 18, 1973

Thomas Kennard Brown
Apr 2, 1909
May 17, 1929

Alvin Calvin Brown
Nov 16, 1893
Apr 11, 1963
&
Josie Lee Brown
Jul 17, 1894

Richard Franklin Brown
Jan 27, 1934
Dec 11, 1934

R. F. Threet
Jul 31, 1864
Jun 7, 1928
married Jul 31, 1889

Agnes Threet
1868-1943

Joe Benford Barber
1894-1971
&
Jennie B. Barber
1896-

Travis E. Brown
Sep 1, 1914
Jun 5, 1963
&
Carolyn C. Brown
Nov 2, 1916
----
married Jun 15, 1935

Robert L. Woodson
Apr 15, 1889
Sep 15, 1965
&
Salina M. Woodson
Jul 26, 1902

Mildred, Infant dau of
Mr & Mrs W. B. Molder
Mar 13, 1941

W. D. Molder
1862-1939
&
Ina Molder
1867-1922

Gertrude Molder
1888-1923

Infant Son of
Mr & Mrs J. H. Molder
1926

Judy Carol Sanders
1943-1943
(Thompson)

Walter B. Molder
Jun 9, 1900
Aug 31, 1958
&
Margaret E. Molder
Apr 8, 1905
Jun 8, 1973

Kenneth Robert Molder
Aug 1, 1970
Aug 2, 1970

George W. Rogers
Feb 17, 1893
Jan 20, 1964
&
Etta B. Rogers
Sep 28, 1888

John Thomas Hester
1887-1972
&
Lou Fannie H. Hester
1884-1964

Ollie Dean Hester
1885-1958
(Gowen-Smith)

Nannie Hester
1857-1940

Samuel Otha Hester
Mar 14, 1909
Aug 27, 1960

Albert Lee Hester
Aug 1, 1923
Sep 23, 1963
&
Clara Sue Hester
Jul 5, 1925
----
married Jun 7, 1942

John Elvis Clardy
Jul 17, 1918
Jan 9, 1972
&
Bonnie Mai Clardy
Jul 7, 1926

James Alvis Clardy
Jul 17, 1918
Feb 16, 1971
&
Lucille S. Clardy
Aug 28, 1923

Marvin C. Threet
1925-1926

Nellie Westbrooks
Nov 29, 1883
Dec 28, 1958

D. A. Mincy
Sep 25, 1862
Dec 9, 1930

Joe Crowder
Sep 9, 1869
Jan 30, 1942

Tennie Crowder
Apr 25, 1879
Dec 12, 1923

Larry R. Lamb
1940-1965

C. May Sudberry Lamb
1939-

Cathy Jane Haynes
Mar 4, 1953
Mar 5, 1953

Jno. William Smith
1878-1948
&
Mary Bell Smith
1894-19

Doyle G. Sudberry
1930-1932

Mona C. Sudberry
1933-1936

Larry Gilbert Sudberry
Nov 18, 1934
Jan 31, 1936

Lannie Donald Sudberry
Jan 22, 1945
Sep 21, 1953

Henry N. Sudberry
Nov 13, 1870
Sep 29, 1964
&
Lou Paralee Sudberry
Feb 18, 1868
May 29, 1949

Earnest A. Rich (Rev.)
Sep 20, 1900
Jun 26, 1967
&
Birdie Rich
Sep 9, 1901
Jan 20, 1961

Robert T. Moore
Nov 11, 1886
Feb 12, 1964
&
Jemima H. Moore
Mar 9, 1886

Mary Ann, wife of Gabe Capley
Mar 11, 1837
Apr 26, 1866

James H. Wilkinson
Dec 3, 1892
Mar 1, 1954
&
Gertrude Wilkinson
Feb 14, 1897
Dec 16, 1973
married May 30, 1936

Riley J. Wheeler
1875-1954
&
Margaret E. Wheeler
1875-1940

E. A. J. Mathews
1854-1927
&
Mattie Mathews
1877-1927

Mary Frances Brown
Feb 27, 1914
Mar 26, 1927

William E. Brown
1888-1946
&
Elizabeth M. Brown
1889-19

E. L. Haney
(wooden Slab-no dates)

Sandy Nevada Sanders
Mar 6, 1964
Mar 8, 1964

N. M. Wheeler
Sep 25, 1815
Mar 5, 1894

Rhody, wife of N. M. Wheeler
Mar 14, 1841
Jun 7, 1907

Mary Wheeler
Oct 16, 1814
Oct 13, 1877

Zilpha Wheeler
Mar 6, 1838
Oct 10, 1904

James Eulus Holden
Oct 2, 1884
Apr 2, 1956
&
Annie H. Gregg Holden
Sep 3, 1891
Oct 25, 1963

Della D. Holden
May 7, 1894
Apr 4, 1972

John W. Holden
Nov 10, 1858
Jun 20, 1933

Lou R. Holden
Feb 13, 1860
Apr 18, 1932

Miness Pressgrove
1850-1935
&
Tennie Pressgrove
1853-1925

Sam L. Pressgrove
1876-1937

Thomas Pressgrove
1839-1924
& wife:
Julia Ann Pressgrove
1845-1926

Willie Houston Blanton
Jul 6, 1894
Dec 2, 1971
&
Mattie Ethlyn Blanton
Nov 8, 1884
Apr 25, 1956

Ewing Pressgrove
Aug 19, 1879
Oct 3, 1960
&
Mary C. Pressgrove
Jun 29, 1884
Feb 8, 1964

Flora E., dau of
Thomas & Julia Pressgrove
Aug 26, 1866
Mar 21, 1904

John Pressgrove
Mar 17, 1817
Sep 1, 1886
&
Mary Pressgrove
Nov 21, 1817
Mar 29, 1852
&
Harriet Pressgrove
Mar 23, 1823
Jul 9, 1899

James F. Wilson
Dec 22, 1833
Aug 7, 1862
age: 28y, 7m, 16d.

Rufus M. Wheeler
Oct 4, 1889
Sep 15, 1971
&
Nannie C. Wheeler
Jul 15, 1891

Sherry Ann Wheeler
June 5, 1961

James R. Wheeler
Mar 6, 1926
Sep 20, 1931

Bettie Florence, wife of
O. J. Sanders
1890-1922

Pink Clardy
1869-1930
&
Luella Clardy
1874-1950

Ava Myrtle Clardy
Jul 26, 1891
Nov 26, 1961

Ann Burton Clardy
Apr 26, 1853
Feb 6, 1927

B. F. Burton
1848-1925
&
Fannie Wheeler Burton
1847-1933

Darling Wheeler
Aug 11, 1851
Feb 7, 1940

Chloe T. Wheeler, wife of
D. Wheeler
Dec 30, 1855
Jun 21, 1916

Andrew Cartwright Potts
May 10, 1905
Dec 23, 1973

Robbie Lee Potts
Feb 12, 1907
Nov 5, 1942

Albert Lee Potts
Oct 9, 1925
Nov 17, 1927

Marcus L. Potts
Jan 2, 1857
Jun 26, 1927

Caldonia Potts
Mar 13, 1859
Jan 19, 1887

Nancy Elizabeth Mincy
Feb 20, 1856
Jan 12, 1923

J. L. Potts
Feb 21, 1851
Mar 9, 1924
&
Parthenia Potts
Aug 2, 1852
Jan 30, 1923

J. Henry Sanders
Jan 2, 1855
Apr 15, 1933
&
Malissia J. Sanders
Mar 28, 1859
Mar 25, 1927

Mattie Lou, dau of
O. J. Sanders
1922-1922

Emily Short
Aug 11, 1835
Mar 14, 1901

Elizabeth Short
Sep 20, 1800
Jul 15, 1899

Meardy B. Short
Aug 6, 1839
Dec 14, 1894

James Short
Jun 6, 1841
May 20, 1863

Peyton S. Vinson
Dec 22, 1822
Jun 23, 1867
age: 44y, 6m, 2d.

Annie L., wife of
P. S. Vinson
Jun 6, 1830
Jan 17, 1899
age: 69y, 7m, 8d.

Mary Johnson Taylor
1852-1936

Thomas Levi Johnson
Mar 2, 1844
Aug 18, 1871
age: 27y, 5m, 16d.

J. Thomas Johnson
Oct 6, 1871
Jun 23, 1955
&
Margaret M. Johnson
Feb 19, 1890

John F. Price
1877-1952
&
Bertha M. Price
1887-19

Spencer A. Clardy
1877-1953
&
Orlena J. Clardy
1874-1957

J. M. Clardy
Sep 19, 1845
Mar 30, 1893
&
Temperance Clardy
Feb 4, 1840
Nov 22, 1911

Lem Clardy
1867-1951
&
Pearl Clardy
1872-1936

Sidney Jeffress
1874-1933

John Wheeler
1835-1895

Bettie Wheeler
1847-1924

Ella Wheeler
1880-1946

George A. Earnhart
Jun 6, 1880
Aug 10, 1964

Maudie W. Wheeler
May 20, 1894
Jun 2, 1944

Talitha Ann Wheeler Sanders
Sep 1, 1856
Dec 16, 1932

William Franklin Sanders
Aug 6, 1850
Jun 18, 1932

Oscar L. Wheeler
Jan 3, 1892
Jun 24, 1955

Martha J."Mattie" Wheeler
1883-1944

Annie Sanders Hamilton
Oct 23, 1905
Dec 5, 1931

Lottie C. Landers
Jan 21, 1875
Feb 16, 1943
&
Eunice A. Landers
Dec 13, 1882
May 23, 1966

Infant Sons of
Marvin & Doris Hasty
1932-1933

Benjamin Franklin Potts
Nov 8, 1878
Oct 8, 1896

Mary Mahala Potts
Dec 3, 1875
Oct 10, 1891

George Alven, son of
J. L. & M. P. Potts
Aug 27, 1889
Jun 15, 1890

Johnie P. Gregory
Sep 3, 1911
Oct 16, 1974
&
Sybil R. Gregory
Feb 14, 1912
----
married Nov 5, 1932

Mike Wheeler
1844-1916
&
Surmantha Wheeler
1849-1933

Ollie Lee Harris
1890-1942
"Husband of Mattie Tolbert
Harris"

Mattie Tolbert Harris
1891-1962
"Wife of Ollie Lee Harris"

Buford Lee Harris
Tennessee
Pvt Btry B 202 Coast Arty
W. W. II
Sep 30, 1912
Jan 18, 1972

Albert P. Sanders
Sep 11, 1878
May 1, 1925
&
Carrie E. Sanders
Mar 15, 1885
Jan 21, 1964

Thomas J. Wheeler
Nov 15, 1874
Jan 27, 1963
&
Fannie E. Wheeler
Apr 13, 1874
Sep 28, 1951

Arthur W. Wheeler
Tennessee
Pvt Co C 779 Tank Bn W.W.II
May 19, 1909
Aug 5, 1964

Fannie A., wife of
W. F. Hooker & oldest dau of
Jessie & Perliner Wheeler
Aug 22, 1849
Jan 7, 1887

William B., son of
Robert & B. F. Blankenship
Mar 19, 1861
Oct 9, 1890

Albert J. Wheeler
Oct 19, 1870
Jan 29, 1888

J. P. Wheeler
Feb 5, 1877
Oct 17, 1915

John G. Robinson
Nov 3, 1876
Jun 11, 1949

Cora Robinson
(no dates)

Bessie Porter
(no dates)

John A. Norvell
May 23, 1910

&
Vena Bell Norvell
Feb 25, 1910

Richard Joe Lentz
Jun 4, 1883
Mar 8, 1963
&
Eliza W. Lentz
Oct 12, 1882
Jul 28, 1962

William Nat. Wheeler
1864-1941
&
Dora M. Wheeler
1860-1946

John J. Rucker
Mar 11, 1855
Apr 1, 1903

L. Josephine Rucker
Mar 21, 1859
Mar 11, 1920
age: 60y, 11m, 20d.

Jasper Marion Haynes
Jun 19, 1928
May 30, 1948

Margaret Ann Haynes
Jul 28, 1925
Oct 15, 1926

Cooper C. Haynes
1886-1971
&
Annie C. Haynes
1889-1951

Fannie Burton W. Morris
1885-1963

R. C. Collins
Dec 8, 1873
Jul 25, 1926

Laura Frances, wife of
R. C. Collins
Nov 16, 1865
Jun 25, 1930

Alex A. Flippo
Jul 12, 1897
May 5, 1970
&
Rosa Zelar Flippo
Dec 7, 1897
-----------mrd- 1916

John W. Norvell
Oct 19, 1868
Apr 19, 1935
&
Tennie Elizabeth Norvell
Mar 31, 1870
Jan 3, 1963

Ernest B. Hargrove
Sep 13, 1903
Feb 4, 1973
&
May D. Hargrove
Dec 3, 1909

Oscar J. Sanders
1884-1958

Walter N. Sanders
Sep 8, 1891
Oct 12, 1965

Clarence H. Sanders
Apr 15, 1899
Dec 22, 1966

Joseph M. Hooker
Oct 26, 1875
Mar 7, 1950
&
Ella J. Hooker
Jun 29, 1870
Oct 19, 1932

Marvin P., son of
J. M. & Ella Hooker
Oct 25, 1898
Sep 16, 1903

George J. Sanders
Oct 30, 1885
Jan 31, 1961

Maggie Pressgrove Sanders
Mar 18, 1882
Jun 10, 1936

R. L. "Bob" Chambless
May 7, 1904
Jul 7, 1973
&
Mary Lee Chambless
Mar 7, 1903

Milton O. Chambless
1927-1946
(picture)

Mary A. Chambless
1929-1946
(picture)

James Clyde, son of
R. L. Chambless
(no dates)

R. Lee Sudberry
Dec 8, 1883
Aug 25, 1971
&
Bettie C. Sudberry
Oct 18, 1881
Sep 25, 1963

Jessie H. Wright
1911-1948
&
Ruby E. Wright
1914-

Tennie S. Rowland
Jun 30, 1866
Sep 10, 1934

James Ruel Jacobs
Sep 9, 1911
Nov 9, 1926

W. L. Gregory
1884-1934

Ruthie E. Gregory
1884-1951

Bernice A. Gregory
1905-1936

William Lewis Gregory
Jan 30, 1930
Oct 25, 1930

J. M. Pressgrove
Sep 28, 1845
Dec 22, 1902
&
Mat Pressgrove
Jan 4, 1855
Aug 3, 1941

Nat L. Sanders
May 18, 1920
Mar 14, 1971

Buford Wayne Sanders
1912-1974
(Gowen-Smith)

J. Herman Adcock
Jun 26, 1914
Oct 3, 1967
&
Agnes E. Adcock
May 26, 1913

L. A. "Buster" Potts
May 22, 1881
Jul 17, 1938
&
Cora Moore Potts Crosslin
Mar 23, 1889
Jun 28, 1973

Alleene, dau of
L. A. & C. A. Potts
Jan 24, 1914
Jul 21, 1915
age: 1y, 5m, 27d.

M. B. Damren
Nov 13, 1836
Mar 22, 1915

Marzee, wife of
M. B. Damren
Apr 10, 1845
May 21, 1908

Reva M. Collins
Dec 16, 1928
Feb 12, 1934

Elizabeth A. Collins
1933-1934

Melonie Beth, dau of
Charles M. & Dot E. Collins
June 28, 1957

John T. Jacobs   and
1881-1962

Burnice P., son of
A. & S. Vincent
Mar 6, 1889
Oct 29, 1889

Sallie A., wife of
A. A. Vincent
Dec 24, 1851
Aug 22, 1891

A. A. Vincent
Feb 13, 1855
Apr 13, 1927
&
Bettie Vincent
Aug 27, 1856
(no date)

J. W. Potts
Apr 9, 1853
May 16, 1939

Sarah J., wife of
J. W. Potts
Oct 25, 1853
Apr 30, 1915

Lou Ada, dau of
J. W. & S. J. Potts
Feb 8, 1881
Mar 15, 1903

Thomas H. Haynes
Feb 15, 1876
Jul 31, 1963
&
Minnie B. Haynes
Nov 2, 1879
Dec 11, 1905

Mattie M. Wheeler, dau of
J. M. & M. J. Orr
Dec 24, 1888
Aug 29, 1910

Alla Wheelhouse, wife of
Thomas H. Haynes
(no dates)

Annie B. Wheeler
1917
&
Albert Wheeler
1919
&
Clara Wheeler
1924

D. H. Wheeler
Jan 26, 1868
Dec 18, 1938

Oscar B., son of
O. B. & Lizzie Sudberry
Aug 27, 1910
Jul 25, 1912

Pet H. Rowland
1892-1974
(Gowen-Smith)

Lela Myrtle Jacobs
1883-1963

William E. Woodson
Dec 7, 1879
May 31, 1958
&
Alvie E. Woodson
Aug 30, 1881
Apr 13, 1975

H. H. Haynes
Oct 18, 1821
Aug 24, 1905

Mary V. Haynes
May 7, 1832
Nov 20, 1902

Fannie Haynes
Feb 20, 1854
Apr 17, 1918

James A. Vincent
1866-1934
&
Kate E. Vincent
1878-1967

Joe R. Vincent
Nov 5, 1895
May 25, 1971

Margaret Jane Haney
Jan 12, 1938
Mar 4, 1938

Solon D. Wheeler
1886-1954
(Lawrence FH)

Infant dau of
W. E. & Alvin Woodson
Feb 14, 1909

Willie Elmer, son of
W. N. & E. D. Wheeler
Jul 22, 1898
Jun 4, 1911

John M. Wheeler
Michigan
Corp 433 Motor Truck Co.
Q.M.C.
Nov 9, 1940

Maude Wheeler Thomas
1901-1968

Jessie C. Wheeler
Sep 29, 1840
Nov 21, 1911
&
Louisa T. Wheeler
Feb 28, 1841
Feb 22, 1912

Oscar B. Sudberry
Feb 26, 1878
Mar 11, 1955
&
Lizzie J. Sudberry
Dec 13, 1878
Feb 17, 1961

George W. Blackburn
Sep 5, 1839
Apr 26, 1923
&
Sarah P. Blackburn
Mar 5, 1850
Apr 25, 1935

Elisha J. Wheeler
1878-1939
&
Nannie J. Wheeler
1884-1927

Johnnie L. Wheeler
Tennessee
Tec 5 SVC Co 744 TK T Bn
W. W. II
Aug 20, 1909
Jan 22, 1972

J. W. Wheeler
1873-1932

Joseph W. Wheeler
Aug 2, 1911
Apr 15, 1971

William C. Wheeler
Nov 19, 1869
Jul 24, 1951

Ann Wheeler Harris
Feb 18, 1871
Aug 9, 1960

Frank B. McClain
Apr 1, 1885
Jun 22, 1966
&
Emma W. McClain
Feb 15, 1894

Johnny Wilkinson
1970-1970
(TM)

Several unmarked graves.

"Mother"
Mattie B. Turner
Nov 7, 1893
Mar 18, 1970
&
"Son"
Mitchell D. Turner
Mar 20, 1930

Edwin Morgan Jacobs
Apr 5, 1943
Mar 23, 1964

Marie Lamb
1940-1940
(Gowen-Smith)

Rosie Mae Simmons
Mar 11, 1914
Nov 24, 1949

Thomas C. Orr
1875-1944
&
Lizzie Blanton Orr
1874-1964

J. A. Hale
1879-1934

Ruby Nell Spence
May 4, 1945
May 20, 1945

Lincoln Burks, Jr.
May 7, 1947
May 31, 1947

Rachel May Burks
Feb 14, 1952
Feb 14, 1952

Juanita Cawthron
1925-1970
(Gowen-Smith)

Willie N. Pressgrove
Jun 25, 1889
Aug 25, 1973
&
Annie V. Pressgrove
May 13, 1884
Nov 6, 1970

Levie May Pressgrove
May 4, 1914
Oct 19, 1915

William J. Potts
1893-1958

Donnie Eva Potts
1893-1922

Madison H. Potts
1914-1939

J. Regen Harrison
1889-
&
Era B. Harrison
1892-

Mrs. Siota Harrison
1857-1940

Larking Jasper Cawthron
Nov 4, 1886
Feb 4, 1962
&
Leaner H. Atnip Cawthron
Jan 11, 1892
Mar 1934

Betty Cawthron
Jul 14, 1936
Feb 7, 1963

Lizzie Cawthron
1911-1944
(TM)

Vernie Clanton   and
Sep 22, 1910

Robert T. Adcock
1889-1958
&
Virginia R. Adcock
1894-1972

Jannie Maud, wife of
R. T. Adcock
Oct 20, 1897
Jun 24, 1919
(picture)

Thomas J. Adcock
Mar 16, 1860
Jan 27, 1941
&
Lucy Elizabeth Adcock
Jan 23, 1859
Jan 11, 1939

Arch C. Adcock
1885-1968
&
Guynnie D. Adcock
1884-1961

Infant Son of
Mr & Mrs R. H. Adcock
Mar 4, 1940

Andrew Allen Adcock
Feb 27, 1950
Nov 4, 1967

Infant Son of
A. G. & Mattie Adcock
Jul 16, 1947

Johnnie S. Chambless
Jan 19, 1900
Dec 1, 1974
&
Alice L. Chambless
Jun 6, 1903

Mary Bell Clanton
Oct 23, 1912
Dec 6, 1974

14 SANDERS CEMETERY   Map # 6
Located about 1 mile North of North Fork Church.

William S. Chambless
1870-1912
&
Tennie T. Chambless
1875-1970

Nancy Chambless
Apr 4, 1848
Dec 28, 1933

G. A. Chambless (C)
Dec 31, 1847
Aug 8, 1891

Hulda, wife of
S. S. Sanders
Jun 28, 1843
Mar 4, 1901

Mollie, wife of
N. S. Sanders
Feb 2, 1865
May 5, 1893

Eva Belle, dau of
N. S. Sanders
Aug 5, 1885
Oct 12, 1885

Joe E., son of
N. S. & E. C. Sanders
Nov 10, 1896
Apr 10, 1899

John W. Sanders
1853-1931
&
Nancy A. Sanders
1851-1921

R. C. Thompson
1873-1919

Fannie Lee Thompson
1904-1908

Stephen S. Sanders
Jul 1, 1825
Jun 19, 1910
age: 84y, 11m, 18d.

Elizabeth Sanders
Jun 22, 1825
Oct 8, 1897
age: 62y, 3m, 16d.

Calvin Brown   and
1858-1932

Willie Clarence Sanders
Oct 30, 1898
Nov 11, 1920
(on wooden slab)

May, dau of R. C. Sanders
Sep 30, 1890
May 9, 1903

Colie, son of R. C. Sanders
Oct 14, 1894
Oct 3, 1901

R. C. Sanders
Sep 8, 1867
Jan 14, 1901

Sallie Brown
1861-1933

Infant Son of
T. H. & Emma Brown
May 1, 1908
&
Infant Daughter of
T. H. & Emma Brown
Nov 2, 1917

David Payton Sanders
Apr 10, 1916
Jun 9, 1917

Fannie Lee Sanders
Jul 10, 1902
Jun 27, 1904

Martha Sanders
May 3, 1864
Jan 8, 1865

Infant
Born & Died
Sep 10, 1887

Dessie May Sanders
Sep 3, 1897
Sep 7, 1897
&
Bessie D. Sanders
Sep 3, 1897
Sep 4, 1897

Minnie Lee Sanders
Apr 11, 1882
May 24, 1900

Dealie Ada, dau of
H. A. & E. A. Sanders
Sep 24, 1896
Dec 1, 1911
age: 15y, 2m, 7d.

Bennie S. Sanders
Oct 3, 1880
Oct 17, 1881

Several graves with fieldstones, no inscriptions.

Emma Dean, dau of
H. A. & E. A. Sanders
Aug 21, 1886
Feb 3, 1908
age: 21y, 5m, 12d.

H. A. Sanders
Mar 31, 1859
Apr 19, 1917
age: 58y & 19d.

Emma Ann Sanders
Dec 13, 1862
Sep 24, 1916
age: 53y, 9m, 11d.

William Harvey Earl, son of
W. F. Sanders
Jul 9, 1880
Sep 10, 1881

Pearl Sanders
Feb 19, 1904
Jan 19, 1921

Lenard B., son of
G. W. & R. M. Sanders
Dec 1, 1911
Nov 14, 1912
age: 11m & 14d.

Ruby S., dau of
S. L. & M. D. Sanders
Oct 25, 1914
Nov 17, 1914

Sherry Jean Sanders
1950-1950
(Thompson)

Child Grave
(marker gone)

15 WILLIAMS CEMETERY   Map # 6
Located about 1 mile Northeast of North Fork Church.

Jimmie E., son of
W. T. & Emma Williams
Sep 2, 1904
Jul 16, 1905

Copied by Franklin Blanton

Several unmarked graves.

16 WHEELHOUSE CEMETERY   Map # 6
Located about 1 mile North of Green Hill Church.

Sam M. Neal***
1877-1959
&
Mattie W. Neal***
1881-1919

J. T. Neal***
(no dates)

S. K. Neal***
(no dates)

Patsy S.***
(fieldstone)

Emett Alrous Cook***
Nov 12, 1893
May 18, 1894
age: 6m & 6d.

Many unmarked graves.

Samuel Mitchell Neal
Jun 19, 1877
Sep 25, 1959
son of James & Mary Palmer
                Neal.
        &
Mattie Wheelhouse Neal
Aug 29, 1881
Jan 23, 1919
dau of Joshua Thomas &
Roberta Frances Turner
        Wheelhouse.

Lila***
(no information)

Isaac***
(no information)

"Mother"
Robertie Wheelhouse***
1847-1927

Ollie B.,***dau of
R. W. & Amanda Burris
Apr 16, 1887
May 29, 1903

Ennice P.,***Dau of
R. W. & Amanda Burris
May 17, 1901
Oct 13, 1904

Many fieldstones, no insc.

James Thomas Neal
Apr 1, 1917
Nov 15, 1918
son of Sam & Mattie Wheelhouse
        Neal.

Samuel Keithly Neal
Sep 1, 1913
Dec 8, 1918
son of Sam & Mattie
    Wheelhouse Neal.

J. T. Wheelhouse***
Dec 26, 1824
Married to Parthena Primrose
Dec 25, 1847
Died Sep 10, 1904

Parthena,*** wife of
J. T. Wheelhouse
Oct 22, 1826
Jul 12, 1871

Cass Buchanon Cook***
1857-1908

Clamenza Aneteh, wife of
C. B. Cook
Jan 8, 1866
Aug 31, 1894
age: 28y, 7m, 23d.

Laura Wheelhouse Cook***
1876-1960

Patsy S.
Amanda Virginia "Patsy"
        Smith, dau of
Levi G. W. & Roberta Frances
Turner Smith
Born Oct 4, 1869
Died Mar 16, 1890
Half Sister to Mrs Evie
Wheelhouse Eley.

Emma G. Sanders***
Jan 1, 1871
Jun 16, 1918

Mrs. Mary E. Puckett***
1848-1948
(Thompson)

Manda Francis Wheelhouse***
Sep 12, 1856
Feb 17, 1922

Willie B. "Dock" Cook***
Jul 30, 1888
Jul 31, 1973

*** Family Records are
furnished by Mrs Edward
Harper, Unionville, Tn.
(see below)

Lila Wheelhouse
Apr 7, 1886
Dec 10, 1886
dau of J. T. & Roberta
Turner Wheelhouse

Isaac Wheelhouse
Oct 21, 1883
Feb 28, 1885
son of J. T. & Roberta
Turner Wheelhouse.

Roberta Frances Turner
                    Wheelhouse
Oct 28, 1847
May 11, 1927
dau of Monroe W. & Mary Ann
Clark Turner.

Armanda Frances Vincent, 1st
wife of William Thomas
                    Wheelhouse
Sep 12, 1856
Feb 17, 1922

Emett Alrous Cook, son of
Cass Buchanan & Clemenza
Anetah Wheelhouse Cook
Nov 12, 1893
May 18, 1894

No marker***
Annie Louise Williams
twin dau of William & Ollie
   Neal Williams
Born Oct 15, 1922
Died   1923

No marker:***
"Baby Neal, child of
Wayne & 1st wife, Mary
          Lizzie Neal
(no dates)

No Marker:***
William Thomas Wheelhouse
son of J. T. & Roberts T.
                    Wheelhouse
Born Aug 17, 1856
Died Aug 23, 1931

Joshua Thomas Wheelhouse
Dec 26, 1824 in Va.
son of Dennis & Mary Ann
Browder Wheelhouse
married to Parthena Primrose
Dec 25, 1847 & Died at home
near Wheelhouse Cemetery on
Sep 10, 1904.

Ollie Blanche, dau of
R. W. & Amanda Burris
  (Bible Record:)
Apr 16, 1887
May 20, 1902

Clamenza Aneteh, 1st wife of
Cass Buchanan Cook and dau
of Joshua Thomas & Parthena
Primrose Wheelhouse.
Jan 8, 1866
Aug 31, 1894
age: 28y, 7m, 23d.

Willie Bogle, son of Cass B.
& Clemenza Anetah W. Cook,
known as "Dock".
Jul 30, 1888
Jul 31, 1973

No marker:***
Edna Wheelhouse, twin dau of
J. T. & Roberta T.Wheelhouse
& twin sister to Mrs Evie
Wheelhouse Eley of Unionville,
Tenn.
Born May 31, 1889
Died Aug 29, 1898

Parthena Primrose, wife of
Joshua Thomas Wheelhouse
Oct 22, 1826
Jul 12, 1871
dau of William & Mary
Elizabeth Culberhouse
          Primrose.

Eunice Primrose, dau of
R. W. & Amanda Burris
(Robert Weakley & Amanda
   Louisa Wheelhouse Burris)
May 17, 1901-Oct 13, 1904

Cass Buchanan Cook
Born Jun 5, 1857
Died Mar 15, 1908

Laura Wheelhouse Cook, 2nd
wife of Cass Buchanan Cook,
& dau of Joshua Thomas &
Roberta Frances Turner
Smith Wheelhouse.
Born Mar 23, 1876
Died May 12, 1960

No marker:***
Beta Wheelhouse
dau of J. T. & Roberta T.
                    Wheelhouse
Born Sep 20, 1879
Died Oct 27, 1891

Several unmarked graves.

Emma G.Puckett Sanders
Jan 11, 1871
Jun 16, 1918, dau of
James Allen & Mary
Elizabeth Wheelhouse
                    Puckett.

Mrs. Mary Elizabeth
                    Puckett
Oct 23, 1848
Nov 20, 1948, dau of
Joshua Thomas & Parthenia
Primrose Wheelhouse

No Marker:***
James Allen Puckett
Died Aug 3, 1879
(no age), husband of
Mrs. Mary E. Puckett.

Fieldstone with P. W.***
(now gone)
Parthenia Wheelhouse
dau of Joshua Thomas &
Parthenia Primrose
                    Wheelhouse.
Born Jul 11, 1870
Died (no date)

Fieldstone with S.W.***
(now gone)
Miss Sally Wheelhouse
Sister to Joshua Thomas &
Died 1899, left a Will.

#17 BURTON CEMETERY   Map #6
Located about 1½ miles North of Green Hill Church.

W. S. Brame
May 4, 1819
Jul 9, 1890

Louisa M., wife of
Thomas C. Rankin
Jan 25, 1810
Apr 14, 1875

Several fieldstones, No
inscriptions.

#18 ADCOCK-GREEN CEMETERY   Map #6
Located about ½ mile East of Green Hill Church.

Charlie Ivie Knott
May 5, 1892
Jul 19, 1918
"Killed in France"

Thomas Landers, husband of
Elizabeth R. Landers
Died May 5, 1879
age: 66y, 6m, 14d.
"He lived a Christian over
   48 years."

"Sarah", S. M. Green's wife
Born 1845
"Our Mother"
Boys   Girls
Joe C. G.   E. J. G.
D. W. G.   M. E. G.
T. T. G.   A. J. G.
W. H. G.   H. S. G.
J. W. G.
(no death date)

"My Mother"
Malissie F. Knott
(no dates)

Elizabeth, wife of
Thomas Landers
Born Mar 15, 1815
Died Sep 21, 1886
age: 71y, 7m, 16d.
"Lived a faithful member of
the C. P. Church for 53 yrs."

Fred Clanton
Died Jan 25, 1905
age: 9 months
     &
Alice J. Clanton
Jul 22, 1878
Dec 14, 1904

Infant of Walter & Mary
          Adcock
Apr 3, 1910

J. R. Adcock
1848-1925
     & wife:
Caroline Adcock
1862-1924

Flora Clanton
Died Jan 23, 1917
aged: 45 yrs.
     &
Clifford Clanton
Died Apr 19, 1914
age: 9 yrs.
     &
Sarah Clanton
Died Dec 30, 1912
age: 4 yrs.

J. L. Turner
1823-1900
     &
M. A. Turner
1830-1912

W. A. Landers
Jun 7, 1837
Jan 23, 1905
     & wife:
Jane Landers
Aug 24, 1834
Oct 19, 1890

William H., son of
S. M. & Sarah Green
(no dates)

Jas W. Green
1884-1925

Sam'l M. Green
Feb 17, 1835
Jun 30, 1919
&
Rebecca E., 2nd wife of
S. M. Green
Born Jan 19, 1850
Died (no date)
M. L. G. & A. C. G.
"her children"

George Hill
1900-
&
Ida G. Hill (TM-Gertrude)
1902-1952

Many unmarked graves.

G. F. Clanton
Apr 28, 1842
Nov 20, 1901
&
Sarah C. Clanton
Oct 1, 1846
Oct 26, 1900

"Mother"
Mrs. Elizabeth Green
1814-(no date)(After 1850)
& "Daughter"
M. A. Green (Mariah,1850)
1830-(no date)(after 1850)

George C. Hill
Dec 24, 1938
Jan 4, 1939

Richard Nichols
1908-1955
(Gowen)

William Nichols
1946-1946
(Thompson)

Martha M. Gregory Purvis
Jan 8, 1837
Sep 4, 1909

Laura Henretta Frizzell
(TM-Mrs. Laura Nichols)
Jun 13, 1880
Nov 10, 1948

Many fieldstones, no insc.

Samuel M. Adcock
Jan 21, 1899
Nov 20, 1900

James Gregory
Born Aug --, 1807
Died Sep 4, 1897
age: 90y, 1m, 22d.

Mary Minerva Gregory
Nov 2, 1814
Nov 14, 1902

Thomas Nickles
1905-1935

Richard Hill, Jr.
1942-1945

19 TERRY CEMETERY   Map # 6
Located about 1½ Miles South of Green Hill Church.

William J. Terry
May 9, 1839
May 23, 1871

Elizabeth N. Terry
Apr 5, 1811
Aug 30, 1867

Copied by Franklin Blanton.

20 WILLIAMS CEMETERY   Map # 6
Located about 1½ miles East of Hickory Hill.

Charles F. Williams
Feb 5, 1855
Aug 14, 1926

"Wife & Mother"
Eva W. Coons, wife of
J. M. Coons
Died Aug 14, 1899
age: 33y, 7m, 28d.

Mattie M. Williams
wife of R. A. Rushing
Jul 11, 1870
Apr 23, 1899

"Wife & Mother"
Margret E. Gregory
Born Nov 21, 1853
married Charles F. Williams
Oct 1, 1879
Died Aug 16, 1904
age: 50y, 8m, 25d.

Tune, son of
M. M. & S. A. Williams
Aug 16, 1876
May 2, 1877

M. M. Williams   and
Apr 15, 1827
married to S. A. Tune
Dec 9, 1853
Died Jan 19, 1899

John P. Purvis
Aug 6, 1863
Apr 26, 1893

Dooly Pate, Husband of
M. J. Pate
Apr 6, 1860
Mar 4, 1884

Fred, son of
Dooly & M. J. Pate
Feb 4, 1883
Feb 4, 1884

S. A. Tune, wife of
Nov 25, 1834
Apr 21, 1903

Rev. John T. Williams
Feb 2, 1861
Sep 29, 1887

Marilda J. Williams Pate,
wife of James W. Bivins
Aug 29, 1859
Apr 22, 1886

Edward P., son of
Dooly & M. J. Pate
May 10, 1881
Jan 1, 1882

21 LOYD CEMETERY   Map # 6
Located about 2 miles East of Hickory Hill Church.

William J. Loyd
Jul 16, 1829
Aug 14, 1907
(marker now gone)

Roda Shelton Loyd
(no dates-marker now gone)

Joel N. Stallings
Oct 18, 1858
Feb 7, 1892

A. E. Murphy
Oct 11, 1834
Nov 5, 1862

22 WHEELER CEMETERY   Map # 6
Located about 1 mile Southwest of Green Hill Church.

Charley Wheeler
Aug 29, 1880
Dec 25, 1899
age: 19y, 3m, 26d.

Joseph R., husband of
Mary E. Burton
May 4, 1850
Dec 18, 1884

W. N. Wheeler, son of
G. H. & L. P. Wheeler
Born Aug 29, 1855
married to Anna L. Floyd
Mar 18, 1879, Died
Oct 2, 1888
age: 36y, 1m, 6d.

Henry R., son of
Joseph R. & Mary E. Burton
Jun 21, 1872-Nov 9, 1881

Anna L., dau of
W. W. & M. A. Floyd
Born Mar 3, 1858
Married to W. N. Wheeler
Mar 18, 1879, Died
Nov 3, 1894
age: 36y, & 8m.

Infant of
J. W. Burton
1947-1947 (TM)

T. M. Taylor
Jul 28, 1850
May 11, 1915

Mary E. Taylor
Sep 6, 1849
Apr 25, 1937

L. P. Fisher
Dec 12, 1844
Jul 14, 1892   68y & 4m.

Maggie P. Wheeler
1891-1970
&
Henry Thomas Wheeler
1879-1946
&
Jennie B. Wheeler
1883-1908

Charles N. Capley
1868-1917
&
Lula E. Capley
1871-1911

Joseph F. Stem
1877-1962
(Gowen-Smith)

Thomas C. Fisher   and
Aug 19, 1847
Oct 31, 1918
(picture)

J. D. Wheeler
May 18, 1848
Sep 30, 1925
&
Rebecca A., wife of
J. D. Wheeler
May 26, 1847
Jul 23, 1895

Thomas Wheeler
1866-1928
&
Mary Wheeler
1878-1969
&
Lucile Wheeler
1920-1930

Sarah J. Fisher
Apr 18, 1851
Oct 25, 1928

Oscar Wheeler   and
1872-1947

C. H. Wheeler
Mar 15, 1824
married to L. P. Fisher
Dec 12, 1844 & Died
Jul 14, 1892
age: 68y & 4m.

Mrs. L. P., wife of
C. H. Wheeler
Feb 3, 1826
Aug 12, 1900
age: 74y, 6m, 9d.

Arthur Fisher
1881-1944
&
Dora S. Fisher
1881-(Dora S. Fisher Mize,
died Dec 27, 1971 and buried
at Kadiz, Ohio, age: 90 yrs.
Family Records by Mrs. Henry
Sadler)

Ellen Wheeler
1876-1971

William N. Landers
Sep 9, 1842
May 17, 1913
&
Phebe A. Landers
Dec 24, 1852
Jul 16, 1925

John H. Fisher
1868-1950
&
Mary J. Fisher
1873-1911

Norris Wheeler
Oct 3, 1900
Feb 16, 1928
&
Mayme Wheeler
Aug 4, 1901
Aug 19, 1923

23 PARSONS CEMETERY   Map # 6
Located about 1 mile Southwest of Green Hill Church.

Clem Nance
Dec 28, 1840
Dec 28, 1924

Ola Parsons Gentry
Jan 1, 1886
Dec 9, 1949

Sallie A., wife of
P. C. Haynes
Jun 17, 1888
Jan 16, 1916

M. F. Parsons
Feb 3, 1850
Jul 17, 1924
&
Viannie Parsons
Feb 17, 1855
Mar 9, 1938

Walter G. Parsons
1875-1938

Lila Parsons Hill
Jan 13, 1890
Mar 7, 1936

W. T. Nance
Jul 2, 1835
Apr 28, 1919
&
Eliza Nance
Feb 24, 1848
May 24, 1918

Sarah O. Wheeler
Dec 8, 1808
Jul 23, 1892
age: 83y, 7m, 15d.

Henry A. Noblitt
Feb 23, 1892
Dec 9, 1974
&
Susan C. Noblitt
Dec 12, 1897

Infant Son of
J. C. & M. A. Parsons
Jun 21, 1894

John C. Parsons
Feb 20, 1861
Apr 5, 1927
&
Mary E. Parsons
Aug 30, 1864
May 29, 1937

Caleb A.(Allison) Parsons
Mar 21, 1883
Jan 4, 1967
&
Tiny C. Parsons
Jul 2, 1886

T. F. Carlton
Mar 7, 1853
Sep 4, 1924

Albert C. Parsons
1855-1930

Evelyn & Jordan, Infant Dau
and Son of A. C. & Ida Parsons
(no dates)

Jane M. Nash, dau of
Robert & Elizabeth Alison
Mar 28, 1811
Dec 25, 1885
age: 74y, 8m, 27d.

Clair Hoyte Parsons
Dec 17, 1902
Mar 19, 1952

William J. Parsons
May 23, 1848
Oct 10, 1866
age: 18y, 4m, 13d.

G. W. Parsons, Esq.
Apr 19, 1821
Nov 5, 1903
&
Elizabeth Ann Allison, wife
of George W. Parsons
Apr 12, 1825
Jan 24, 1903

G. Newt Parsons
1865-1954
&
Gertrude Parsons
1872-1951

E. A. A. P.
(no dates)

Land
(no information)

Parks
(no information)

Infant Son of
J. T. & A. L. Wade
(no dates)

J. T. Wade
Oct 9, 1834
Aug 24, 1879

Hattie N. Eads, wife of
V. S. Parsons
Nov 3, 1855
Jun 17, 1890

Minnie May Parsons
Aug 18, 1878
Sep 20, 1887

Volney L. Parsons
Sep 7, 1880
Mar 27, 1881

Ada Eunice Parsons
May 29, 1877
Sep 17, 1877

William D. Barbour
Oct 29, 1842
Oct 6, 1908
&
Bettie F. Barbour
Feb 16, 1845
(no date)

Sallie Barbour, wife of
G. N. Parsons
Sep 18, 1869
Sep 19, 1907
&
Bessie, dau of
G. N. & S. B. Parsons
Nov 12, 1889
Aug 18, 1907

R. E. Winstead
Nov 9, 1869
Jul 12, 1916

Buena Parsons Foster
1868-1950

Bettie, dau of
N. B. & Louesa Parsons
May 6, 1852
Mar 15, 1873
age: 20y, 10m, 9d

Rebecca Rice Maddox,
nee Parsons
Jul 24, 1885
married to James N. Maddox
Jan 14, 1904
Died Feb 5, 1905

John W. Parsons
Jan 3, 1824
Mar 14, 1900

Rutha C., wife of
J. W. Parsons
Aug 12, 1818
Jun 20, 1881

John S. Parsons
1854-1924
&
Clemie H. Parsons
1872-1957

"Father"
George T., son of
N. B. & Louise Parsons
Aug 29, 1857
Jan 30, 1901
age: 43y, 5m, 1d.

Jordan, son of
N. B. & Louise Parsons
Feb 6, 1877
Dec 2, 1902
age: 25y, 9m, 25d.

Mary E. Parsons
May 21, 1856
Dec 10, 1873

Edna Parsons
Mar 18, 1891
Nov 1, 1906

Gilbert Lee, son of
C. C. & R. C. Tribble
Jan 20, 1905
Jul 10, 1905

Knott (no information)

Newton B. Parsons
Oct 22, 1826
Jan 26, 1906
&
Louisa Parsons
May 3, 1832
Jun 29, 1914

Nannie L. Parsons
Dec 29, 1869
Apr 18, 1915

N. H. Parsons
1858-1946
&
Laura Parsons
1863-1945

Gertrude, dau of
H. H. & Winnie Holden
Sep 22, 1908

Winnie D. Parsons Holden
Feb 17, 1891
Apr 13, 1914

Marye Winsett Parsons
Jan 15, 1874
Mar 31, 1973

Robert Parsons
Jan 19, 1850
Feb 20, 1939

W. C. Parsons
1853-1919
&
N. A. Parsons
1857-1926

Charley T., son of
W. C. & N. A. Parsons
Nov 30, 1876
Jan 5, 1877

Cad Crunk Tribble
Jul 28, 1879
Sep 17, 1950
&
Ruth Parsons Tribble
Sep 13, 1880
May 30, 1965

24 PISGAH CEMETERY   Map # 6
Located near North Fork Church.

Louise Harris
Aug 12, 1921
Feb 1, 1924

Bettie E. Harris
Feb 14, 1838
Jul 14, 1905

W. C. Harris
Jul 5, 1883
Sep 27, 1897

Matilda F. Mathews
Jul 10, 1850
Feb 23, 1906

"A Loving Husband"
G. T. Tucker
Mar 22, 1829
Apr 3, 1891

Several unmarked graves.

John Sanders, Jr.
1797-Oct 7, 1841

Mary, wife of
John Sanders, Jr.
1795-Jan 30, 1840

S. A. Proctor
Sep 30, 1843
May 15, 1911

S. E. M., dau of
J. C. & M. Barber
Nov 5, 1877
Nov 11, 1879

"Our Mother",
Matilda, wife of
G. T. Tucker
Jun 27, 1827
Sep 5, 1886

John Sanders, Sr.
1772-1831

Elizabeth L., dau of
John & S. Claxton
Sep 15, 1832
Apr 11, 1853

John Kimbro Claxton
Jul 16, 1829
Oct 3, 1830

Cannon L. Claxton
Dec 10, 1850
Oct 27, 1920

John Claxton*
Jan 12, 1804
Aug 10, 1869

Lizzie Mai Neal
aged: 2 (no dates)

Nancy A., dau of
G. T. & M. Tucker
Aug 2, 1860
Aug 7, 1860

Thomas J., son of
G. T. & M. Tucker
Apr 1, 1854
Jan 26, 1857

Sophia Jane, wife of
J. Holden & dau of
J. & S. Claxton
Sep 24, 1825
Jan 7, 1872

Willie T., son of
G. T. & S. J. Tucker
Jul 9, 1888
Apr 3, 1890

* See addendum

25 REEVES-WHEELER CEMETERY   Map # 6
Located 1 mile South of Three Corner Garden.

Felix J. Winsett
1845-1909
&
Annie A. Winsett
1850-1920

William Talbot Nowland
Sep 3, 1900
Jan 25, 1901

Polly, dau of
J. W. & Willie Reeves
Jan 17, 1900
Oct 29, 1900

Mary A. Dozier
Feb 23, 1833
Apr 21, 1909

Little E. L., son of
E. L. & Ella Dozier
Aug 31, 1906

Bert, son of
E. L. & Ella Dozier
May 17, 1899
Oct 15, 1900

E. L. Dozier
1860-1942

Elizabeth, wife of
Absolem Reeves
Jul 20, 1803
Jul 18, 1882

Absalom Reaves
Jul 12, 1802
Feb 5, 1879

Salie C., dau of
Jesse & Elizabeth Covington
Nov 27, 1857
Jan 29, 1874
age: 29y, 2m, 2d.

Aaron Gambill
Jun 6, 1835
Feb 8, 1902
&
Nancy E., wife of
Aaron Gambill
Jun 5, 1830
Nov 12, 1876
&
Solomon Gambill
Jan 9, 1870
Oct 29, 1891

Jas. Edward Call
Aug 8, 1858
Nov 9, 1884
age: 26y, 3m, 1d.

Harry Allott, son of
Edgar & Mattie Winsett
Mar 22, 1896
Nov 18, 1900

Nathan Wheeler
1783-Nov 12, 1842

Permelia Wheeler
1779-Jun 25, 1837

Luvicy, wife of
Jesse Covington, Sr.
Oct 22, 1801
Nov 18, 1866
age: 65y & 26d.

R. C. Jennings
Jul 30, 1789
Sep 2, 1875

Mary Eglintine Graham
                    Jennings
Nov 28, 1849
Sep 17, 1873
          &
Emmitt Cross Jennings
Sep 19, 1847
Nov 20, 1912

Emily Mariah Jennings
Aug 19, 1809
Jan 23, 1869

Joseph Carol Green
Jul 3, 1832
Aug 3, 1905

Ann P., wife of
J. C. Green & dau of
Nathan Wheeler
Aug 19, 1840
Aug 25, 1890

R. F. Norman
Jun 14, 1828
married Dec 9, 1847
died Oct 20, 1857

E. C. Norman
Apr 5, 1827
Married Dec 9, 1847
Jan 10, 1895
"A Tender Mother &
    faithful Friend."

Ephrim R. Dryden
Jan 4, 1842
Feb 1, 1911

Elizabeth Norman Dryden
Dec 11, 1848
Sep 17, 1936

Mary Eunice Dryden
Jul 15, 1886
Oct 31, 1911

Mrs. Luvicy Casander
                    Murray
Oct 25, 1833
married Oct 25, 1851, in
the 21st year of her age,
on her birthday & Died
May 18, 1857

Many unmarked graves.

26 HICKORY HILL CHURCH CEMETERY   Map # 6
Located at the Hickory Hill Methodist Church.

Rev. W. Cooksey
1830-1868

Henry L. Brown
Dec 13, 1824
married Feb 13, 1847
died Feb 9, 1904
          &
Mary M. Tilford Brown
Sep 3, 1830
Dec 8, 1906

Mary E. Goodrum, wife of
W. H. Lock(old marker)
Jun 1, 1840
Apr 6, 1898
age: 57y, 10m, 5d.

Della Tabitha, dau of
William H. & Mary E. Locke
Jan 11, 1873
Oct 5, 1875

Andrew Johnson, son of
William H. & Mary E. Locke
Jan 18, 1879
Oct 26, 1882

Hartwell Freeman
Jan 1, 1798
Jan 8, 1871
age: 73y & 8d.
          & wife:
Nancy W. Freeman
Feb 8, 1801
Dec 30, 1902
age: 101y, 10m, 22d.
          & Dau:
Miss Celia Ann Freeman
Feb 29, 1824
Aug 8, 1901
age: 77y, 5m, 9d.

Lucy Ann Tillford Harris
Aug 17, 1822
married Hiram Harris
May 5, 1844 & died
Jul 19, 1894

W. E. Turner
Jun 24, 1882
Sep 26, 1883

Malissa Turner
Aug 13, 1865
Jun 24, 1873

William H. Lock
Nov 13, 1836
Aug 20, 1905
          &
Mary E. Lock
Jun 1, 1840
Apr 6, 1898

James Turrentine Rowland
May 14, 1870
Mar 1, 1901

Nancy T. Harris
1840-1895
          &
Melissa E. Harris
1834-1898

John H. Haynes
1829-1901

Caroline Haynes
1824-1890

Many unmarked graves.

Marlin C. Stephens
Jul 19, 1846
Feb 27, 1922
   & wife:
Amanda E. Stephens
Jul 6, 1851
Feb 13, 1925

Ella Stephens Winn
Mar 7, 1872
Mar 1, 1898

Maria E., wife of
J. M. Thompson & dau of
J. T. & M.A.Brittain
Feb 17, 1849
Apr 15, 1884

John F., son of
J. M. & M. E. Thompson
Jul 9, 1870
Jan 13, 1877

Nannie Williams Green
1851-1920

William Thomas Haynes
1848-1876

Mary H. Fisher
1854-(no date)

Ada M. Davis
Born & Died
    1887

William S. Knott
Feb 1, 1813
Feb 29, 1868

S. L. M., dau of
M. C. & M. E. Stephens
May 9, 1881
Jun 25, 1882

Hattie Tennessee, dau of
M. C. & M. E. Stephens
Jun 17, 1876
Aug 25, 1886

Carrie Prewett, dau of
M. C. & M. E. Stephens
Jun 31, 1883
Sep 10, 1886

Mary Jane, wife of
W. T. Rowland
Died Jul 2, 1876
age: 27y, 3m, 22d.

James Turrentine Williams
May 26, 1854
Apr 14, 1888

Martha G. A., wife of
M. F. Williams
Sep 2, 1828-Aug 28, 1869
age: 40y, 11m, 26d.

Michael F. Williams
Oct 12, 1820
Feb 18, 1900

Martha A., wife of
W. S. Knott
Jan 19, 1818
Mar 17, 1890

27 WILLIAMS CEMETERY   Map # 6
Located at Hickory Hill, near Hickory Hill Methodist Church.

(Wm.C.) Knox stone in
large hole, and partly
covered.

E. C. Williams
Sep 9, 1831
married William C. Knox
Sep 23, 1855 & died
Mar 17, 1893

W. T. Williams
Aug 29, 1852
Nov 24, 1874
          &
Casander Williams   and
Aug 1, 1856
Jul 14, 1866
"Children of D. & S. T. Williams."

Sophronia Williams
Nov 21, 1834
Jun 23, 1915

S. D. Williams
Aug 1, 1836
Mar 12, 1908

Joseph Williams
Apr 23, 1845
Oct 9, 1880

Ellen T. Williams   and
Jan 19, 1849
died in infancy

Mary Greenville Thompson
Jun 24, 1880
Nov 23, 1882

W. J. Collins, son of
William & Hester Collins
Oct 25, 1835
Jul 21, 1866

"Mother"
Almedia J. Collins
Oct 6, 1837
May 28, 1888

Nancy A. Williams
Dec 28, 1840
died in infancy

Joseph Williams
Oct 10, 1782
May 13, 1876

Charity, wife of
Joseph Williams
Oct 5, 1796
Nov 1, 1878

Thomas, son of
Joseph & Charity Williams
Oct 22, 1827
Jun 29, 1836

28 POTTS CEMETERY   Map # 6
Located about 1 mile Northwest of Hickory Hill Methodist Church.

Abnor Cartwright Potts
Dec 30, 1811
Mar 30, 1897
          &
Mary Franklin Jackson Potts
Dec 26, 1815
May 2, 1898
(These two were moved to the
Zion Hill Church Cemetery)

Bell Damons Potts***, 2nd
wife of Marcus Potts
(no dates)

Ernest Potts,*** Infant son of
Elisha & Flora Marbury Potts
(no dates)

Ruthie Isabel,*** dau of
Darling & Chloe Potts Wheeler
Born 6 Feb 1873
Died   Sep 1885

*** Family Record of
    Mrs. Gladys Wheeler Farris.

Infant dau*** of
Riley J. & Margaret Green
Wheeler
Born & Died 7 July 1895

Infant Son*** of
Riley J. & Margaret Green
Wheeler
Born & Died
20 June 1898

29 STEPHENS CEMETERY   Map # 6
Located about 1 mile Southeast of Poplin Cross Roads.

Robert Thomas King
Sep 1, 1897
Feb 3, 1899

(large stone)
no inscription.

Henry Stephens
Sep 21, 1818
Oct 22, 1886
& wife:
Nancy Stephens
Sep 21, 1818
Jan 14, 1908

"Brother"
Thomas V. Stephens
Nov 9, 1862
Aug 17, 1930

Several unmarked graves.

"Sister"
Sallie M. Stephens
Jul 20, 1856
Jan 28, 1928

30 ZION HILL CHURCH CEMETERY   Map # 6
Located near Poplin Cross Roads, at the M. E. Church.

Infant of
C. T. & S. A. McKee
(no dates)

Cheryl E. Cunningham
1947-1948
(Thompson)

Charlie T. McKee
1874-1924

Sallie Ann McKee
Oct 5, 1870
Apr 19, 1943

Katherine, dau of
D. R. & Z. B. McGowan
Feb 16, 1915
Jun 26, 1917

S. D. Shearin, Jr.
1916-1922

Ethel Blanie Reed
Oct 9, 1903
Apr 4, 1904

William Searcy Reed
1878-1952
          &
Pearl Reed
1881-19

Jennie Oneal, wife of
J. C. Potts
Feb 18, 1860
Aug 5, 1910

Marion Potts
1889-1944

George M. Locke
1876-1945
          &
Naomi T. Locke
1878-19 (no date)

Chesley Williams
1872-1937
          &
Femmie Williams
1862-1945

Uda Webb
Jan 17, 1911
Sep 6, 1911

J. B. Potts
1862-1940

Marvin D. McGowan
Jan 7, 1889
Jun 9, 1973
          &
Willie R. McGowan
Mar 10, 1897
----
married Dec 16, 1915

Cooper McGowan
1866-1945
          &
Susanna McGowan
1868-1947

Robert W. McGowan
Sep 7, 1891
Dec 28, 1927
(picture)

William P. "Tuss" McGowan
Jan 4, 1898
Nov 19, 1971

William Leslie Blackburn
Aug 25, 1902
Oct 19, 1958
&
Nell C. Blackburn
Jan 20, 1904
----
married Nov 15, 1924

Sarah J., wife of
E. P. Blackburn
Jul 24, 1851
Aug 14, 1914

Mary Vincent Claxton
Sep 1, 1868
Apr 23, 1956

George R. Reed
Jan 15, 1849
Sep 11, 1929

Frances Reed
Apr 2, 1853
Oct 12, 1918

several unmarked graves.

"Father"
William C. McGowan
Jan 8, 1869
Oct 29, 1900
&
"Son"
Ed Cooper McGowan
Nov 29, 1892
May 3, 1927

Lula Blackburn
1881-19

Clarence Elisha Blackburn
Aug 9, 1897
Nov 16, 1899

Robert Keathley Blackburn
Aug 2, 1906
Oct 28, 1906

Alonza Marbury Blackburn
Jan 27, 1901
Jan 11, 1927

Grover C. Smotherman
1885-1947
&
Blanie E. Smotherman
1884-19

Zora Lee Smotherman
Nov 10, 1909
Oct 6, 1918

Bettie McGowan Purvis
1871-1947

James H. Locke, Jr.
1917-1919

William C. "Cap" Blackburn
Jan 21, 1874
Nov 28, 1948
&
Ida May M. Blackburn
Jul 1, 1875
Feb 26, 1943

Elijah P. Blackburn
Apr 21, 1842
Oct 27, 1898

Burl A. Uselton
Feb 4, 1897
Jul 24, 1967
&
Hattie R. Uselton
Nov 16, 1894
1973 (TM)

Hurbert Uselton
1925-1934

H. C. Clark
Jun 19, 1842
May 11, 1913

William Locke
1848-1933
&
Sallie Locke
1855-1942

Charly Swanson Locke
Jul 3, 1897
Oct 19, 1900

Elisha H. Potts
1859-1926
&
Flora E. Potts
1861-1921

R. M. Potts
Sep 13, 1845
Apr 20, 1928
&
Mary E. Potts
Oct 30, 1848
Mar 7, 1909

Eleanor E. Keener
Dec 24, 1828
Aug 5, 1912

Lenora Maxwell, wife of
H. C. Clark
Feb 6, 1853
Mar 5, 1909

31 JONES CEMETERY   Map # 6
Located near Poplin Cross Roads.

Jimmie, Infant Son of
Alec & Flora Fry
Jan 28, 1951

John E. Presgrove
1877-1959
&
Laura E. Presgrove
1879-1951

Albert Haynes
1866-1937
&
Annie T. Haynes
1868-1943

Roy H. Haynes
Jun 22, 1900
Feb 10, 1972
&
Carrie Pylant Haynes
Jul 26, 1901
Dec 15, 1970

"Mother"
Isabella Mincy
Apr 16, 1836
Feb 3, 1898
&
"Daughter"
Louisa Ann Mincy
Jan 6, 1853
Jan 6, 1879

Charlie L. Blankenship
Aug 24, 1886
Jul 7, 1970

Flora Jones Blankenship
Jul 1, 1879
Nov 27, 1945

Cora Lee Thompson
1876-1945

Robert H. Haynes
Aug 4, 1950
Aug 4, 1950

Elizabeth D. Haynes
May 2, 1926
May 3, 1926

Hobert B. Haynes
Oct 16, 1896
May 25, 1899

James Leslie, son of
Robert A. & Minerva J. Locke
May 8, 1894
Jul 28, 1894

Ulass Grant Mincy
Jun 24, 1870
Nov 26, 1944

Several unmarked graves.

Walter R. Jones
1876-1948
&
Mary W. Jones
1883-19

Philander Houston Jones
Feb 28, 1884
May 10, 1963
&
Fern Norton Jones
Aug 4, 1896

James B. Jones
Jul 21, 1838
Aug 28, 1909
&
Ruth E. Jones
Apr 17, 1849
Mar 11, 1905

Grover Goodrum, son of
Robert A. & Minerva J. Locke
May 25, 1892
Aug 25, 1892

J. C. Claxton
1831-1909

Mary E., wife of J.C.Claxton
1841-1926

William B. Jones
1864-1930
&
Judgie E. Jones
1871-1975

J. Tom Fleming
1910-1957
&
Ruth H. Fleming
1899-

Houston B. Haynes
1868-1939
&
Dean Jones Haynes
1872-1954

J. S. Jones
Jun 28, 1838
Jan 21, 1916

Annie E., wife of
J. C. Claxton
Sep 16, 1836
Sep 16, 1890

William C. Moore
1972-1972
(Gowen-Smith)

Graves with fieldstones,
no inscriptions.

32 CLARK CEMETERY   Map # 6
Located 1 mile North of Poplin Cross Roads.

John S. Clark	Elizabeth Clark
Nov 10, 1812	Mar 21, 1805
Dec 12, 1874	Nov 21, 1878

2 or 3 unmarked graves.

33 MOON CEMETERY   Map # 6
Located 1½ miles South of Unionville, Tenn.

SEE ADDENDUM

Page 327

34 BETHLEHAM CEMETERY   Map # 6
Located 1 mile North West of Poplin Cross Roads.
"Land donated by Nancy Wilson"

N. A., wife of
J. M. Parsons
Nov 29, 1820
Oct 5, 1883
age: 62y, 10m, 6d.

"Father"
Cooper W. Haynes
Oct 5, 1865
Aug 14, 1957
&
"Mother"
Martin W. Haynes
Oct 5, 1858
Mar 9, 1956
married 71 yrs.

Tolley D. Haynes
Tennessee
Pvt MG Co 50 Inf W.W.I
Jan 10, 1890
Jun 27, 1957

Salomie J., wife of
H. R. Freeman
Died Nov 27, 1878
age: 32y, 11m, 10d.

R. F. Landis
Jul 19, 1849
Nov 27, 1899
   & wife:
M. E. Landis
May 12, 1850
Jan 13, 1912

W. A. Landis
1874-1947

Annie E. Eads
1852-1930

William Wortham
1852-1921
&
Louisa A. Wortham
1870-1927

Annie H. Wortham
1890-1972
(Lawrence)

Carrie Alice, dau of
T. H. & A. E. Wortham
Nov 1, 1876
Aug 20, 1896

T. H. Wortham
Apr 15, 1825
Mar 26, 1889

Thomas H. Wortham
1873-1952 (TM)

Sarah A. B., dau of
B. F. & N. A. Duggan
Nov 11, 1841
Sep 22, 1854

Algesena Antonette, eldest
dau of B. F. & N. A. Duggan
Nov 17, 1839
Jul 1, 1859
age: 19y, 7m, 13d.

William W. Eads
Oct 31, 1841
Jun 8, 1925
   &
Dora B. Eads
Sep 7, 1860
Jan 13, 1907

Robert Warren Wortham
Sep 27, 1894
Jul 1, 1972
   &
Lillie May Wortham
Nov 20, 1890
Apr 4, 1973

Robert A. Wortham
1857-1925
&
Ida M. Wortham
1865-1938

Chas. D. Wortham
1902-1946

James C. Wortham
Aug 6, 1818
Dec 5, 1912
   & wife:
Elizabeth Wortham
Mar 30, 1829
Dec 23, 1886

Laura V. Wortham
Nov 27, 1855
Mar 1, 1925

B. F. Duggan M.D.D.D.
Jan 22, 1821
Mar 1, 1898

Nancy A., consort of
B. F. Duggan
Oct 23, 1806
Jun 24, 1888

Jane S., wife of
Dr. B. F. Duggan
Oct 1, 1845
Jul 19, 1926

Benjamin D. Thompson
1851-1911
&
Ella Laura Thompson
1858-1941

"Father"
M. F. Thompson
Mar 3, 1822
Jul 22, 1896
&
"Mother"
E. C. Thompson
Nov 9, 1818
Jun 13, 1908

William E. Thompson
Nov 28, 1848
Oct 16, 1939
&
Nancy I. Thompson
Apr 2, 1852
Oct 3, 1938

William Collins
Apr 18, 1806
Sep 7, 1884
age: 78y, 5m, 11d.
&
Hester Collins
Feb 21, 1809
Jun 17, 1887

Rev. George Jones
Born July 17, 1897 and
Died April 1879 in his
82nd year, was a Minister
of the Gospel in the Methodist Protestant Church
50 years.

Baby, Infant Son of
W. O. & Alta B. Eads
Born & Died July 1911

Baby, Infant Son of
W. O. & Dora B. Eads
Born & Died June 1900

No marker:***
Clara Wortham, dau of
Tom & Annie B. Wortham
(no dates)

Mrs. Pearl Wortham
1879-1959
(McFarlin FH)

No marker***
Ned Wortham & wife:
Martha Favors Wortham and a
son: William Oscar Wortham.
(no dates)

No marker:***
Tina Wortham
(no dates)

Louiza W. Shaw
Aug 1, 1851
Aug 25, 1868

No marker:***
Mary Wortham, neice of Ned
Wortham(no dates)

No marker:***
Neda Wortham
(no dates)

Nancy Wilson
Died May 22, 1849
age: 65y, 4m, 15d.

No marker:***
Annie Bet Wortham, wife
Tom Wortham, who was a
brother to Ned Wortham.
(no dates)

*** Records from
    Mrs. Ruby Lee.

---

35 WILLSON CEMETERY   Map # 6
Located about 2 miles Southwest of Unionville, Tenn.

Rachel, wife of
J. H. Thomas
Jul 10, 1849
Sep 16, 1889

William Willson
Oct 20, 1806
Nov 11, 1895

Nancy Willson
Mar 28, 1814
Jun 12, 1886

1 grave with fieldstone,
no inscription.

---

36 PLEASANT VALLEY CEMETERY   Map # 6
Located about 1 mile West of Poplin Cross Roads.

Joe H. Simmons
Jun 17, 1874
Jul 16, 1930
&
Nannie E. Simmons
Aug 25, 1871
Sep 24, 1932

William C. Simmons
Feb 7, 1882
Nov 19, 1953
&
Cassie Locke Simmons
Dec 7, 1890
Aug 26, 1965

William Orr
1814-1905

Edward Riddle
1914-1941
(Bills-McGaugh)

Edmond S. Wortham
Aug 27, 1828
Mar 10, 1912
&
Elizabeth J. Wortham
May 4, 1842
May 6, 1917

Infant Daughter of
E. S. & E. J. Wortham
(no dates)

Laura M., wife of
J. M. Wortham
Jan 3, 1870
May 7, 1891

Samuel E. Wortham
1874-1940
&
Edna M. Wortham
1882-1956

Abraham C. Claxton
Oct 23, 1888
Aug 28, 1966
&
Margaret E. Claxton
Mar 6, 1880
Mar 11, 1955

Cassie C. McKee
1874-1902

Neese Infant
(no dates)

A. E.(Anderson Ewing) Neese
Jun 28, 1888
Sep 27, 1957
&
A. Neese
Aug 12, 1887
Aug 14, 1972

Robert F. McGowan
1865-1932
&
Elizabeth McGowan
1870-1932

Allie E. McGowan
Apr 15, 1901
Dec 22, 1901

Betty Florence Russell
Mar 21, 1926

Infant Daughter of
J. P. & S. W. Fisher
Born Oct 1, 1896
age: 18 days.

J. R. Orr
Mar 2, 1838
Sep 30, 1908

James A. Crowell
1850-1909
&
Alice Orr Crowell
1850-1894

Thomas Franklin Crowell
May 21, 1876
Apr 6, 1911

Sallie Crowell
1867-1938

Frank O. Harrison
Jan 9, 1898
Feb 8, 1964
&
Gladys W. Harrison
Dec 4, 1906

Josie Pearl Vandagriff
Oct 22, 1896
Oct 17, 1971

Luna Cleo Osteen
Jan 12, 1898
Oct 22, 1900

Ruth L. Osteen
Died Aug 7, 1911
age: 3 months.

Pauline Molder
1911-1912

Jasper Washington Molder
Nov 6, 1832
Feb 11, 1920
&
Tribble Molder
Sep 11, 1854
Aug 22, 1934

James C. Wortham
1860-1936
&
Annie J. Wortham
1868-1956

Horace, son of
J.C. & Lula Wortham
Dec 8, 1912
May 26, 1913

Thomas Infant
(no dates)

Cooper Infant
(no dates)

George L. Wortham
1875-1936
&
Dora J. Wortham
1881-1967

Franklin Cooper Locke
Aug 12, 1869
Dec 11, 1934
&
Mary Wortham Locke
Apr 2, 1872
Jul 4, 1920

George W. Molder
1878-1944
&
Melisa S. Molder
1886-1957

Molder Infant
(no dates)

Molder Infant
(no dates)

Molder Infant
(no dates)

Rebecca W. Shaw
Apr 22, 1878
Mar 1, 1900

Corbin Burdett Shaw
Jul 9, 1898
Aug 31, 1899

John Rufus Shaw
Oct 23, 1878
Dec 17, 1949
&
Nancy Jane Shaw
Oct 11, 1884
Apr 23, 1956

William Sanford Shaw
1834-1890
&
Susan M. Shaw
1852-1948

Rev. W. M. Shaw
Jul 5, 1806
Nov 6, 1886

Mahala, wife of
Rev. W. M. Shaw
Jan 15, 1809
Jul 3, 1885

Matilda S., wife of
A. M. Shaw
Apr 9, 1844
Nov 18, 1906

J. W. Anderson
Jun 4, 1851
Jul 22, 1921
&
Sallie Anderson
Mar 18, 1866
Mar 15, 1929

Lucinda Anderson
Born in Orange Co., N.C.,
Jan 15, 1809 & died
Nov 11, 1891

John W. Orr
Dec 1, 1876
Oct 2, 1936

Fannie Orr
1882-1918

J. H. Potts
1844-1915

Martha T. Potts
1859-1913

R. A. Potts
1888-1907

John T. Glasscock
Nov 20, 1889
Oct 25, 1945
&
Mattie H. Glasscock
Aug 29, 1892
May 4, 1947

J. R. Orr
Mar 2, 1838
Sep 30, 1908

Mary L., wife of
J. R. Orr & dau of Rev. W.M.
& Mahaly Shaw
Oct 9, 1836
Feb 10, 1906

Martha Hanie Shaw
Aug 31, 1859
Feb 10, 1890

W. L. Smith
Dec 20, 1831
Dec 29, 1904

Belinda I., wife of
W. L. Smith
May 19, 1828
May 9, 1884

Mary Clair Smith
Mar 4, 1898
Dec 5, 1899

Luther Kester Smith
1863-1958

Samuel T. Shaw
1877-1940
&
Minnie B. Shaw
1882-1959

Jakie Blackburn
1847-1921
&
Lucinda Blackburn
1857-1909

Thomas Blackburn
1889-1938

James E. Blackburn
Dec 13, 1914
age: 3 days

Euless G. Blackburn
May 13, 1885
May 18, 1951
&
I. V. Marlin (Moulder)
May 6, 1895
Mar 16, 1972

Martha L. Collins
1843-1923

Maggie W. Orr Darnell
Oct 8, 1886
Oct 10, 1972

William M. Claiborne
Dec 30, 1897
Jul 15, 1964
&
Ruth M. Claiborne
May 11, 1906

Harriet M. Jones
Sep 9, 1842
Jun 25, 1884

Smith Infant
(no dates)

Martha Elizabeth, wife of
J. H. Potts
Born Jul 10, 1858
Died-(dates gone)

Alton D. Scales
1938-1940

Mary A. Culberhouse
Apr 12, 1815
Apr 12, 1899

Dora K. Rogers
1879-1907

John C. Wilson
1849-1901

Sarah E. Wilson
1850-1895

Larkin B. Orr
Jun 1, 1808
Jan 6, 1892

Martha C. Orr
Feb 15, 1815
Nov 15, 1890

Joseph M. Orr
May 1, 1841
Jul 7, 1890
&
Margaret J. Orr
Aug 27, 1846
Dec 20, 1919

John T. Fisher
Jan 22, 1834
Mar 22, 1911
&
Nancy Fisher
Mar 1, 1839
Jul 23, 1909

David H., son of
J. T. & Nancy Fisher
Feb 7, 1863
Jan 23, 1892

Robert J. Fisher
Nov 6, 1874
Jan 6, 1919

Samuel J. Molder
Dec 16, 1866
Feb 24, 1940
&
Sallie Mai Molder
Sep 6, 1874
Apr 9, 1952

Annie Yoes, dau of
S. J. & S. M. Molder
Jun 11, 1896
Nov 22, 1915

William Faires Osteen
Dec 9, 1896
Sep 15, 1900

Alice Orr Osteen
1868-1953
(Lawrence)

Jno. Ewell Orr
1866-1940
&
Margaret J. Orr
1871-1927

Mary E. Orr
Feb 20, 1904
Oct 15, 1904

James Orbane Orr
Aug 6, 1895
Oct 4, 1896

R. Mitchell Orr
Jul 16, 1907
Oct 10, 1971
&
Adrien J. Orr
Aug 21, 1908
----
married Dec 23, 1933

James A. Orr
Apr 6, 1886
Nov 6, 1953

Rozzie Lee Orr
1885-1937

James A., son of
J. A. & R. L. Orr
Oct 5, 1912
Jan 12, 1913

Ervin A., Infant of
Mr & Mrs E. C. Russell
Born & Died Oct 6, 1916

Nora Ethel, dau of
M. E. & M. J. Crowell
Jan 15, 1897
Jan 4, 1898

Archie T. Smith
Nov 2, 1888
Apr 7, 1972
&
Permelia C. Smith
Dec 19, 1900
Jun 21, 1971
married Dec 3, 1916

George T. Yoes
Aug 17, 1895
Jan 3, 1963
&
Mary Lee Yoes
Feb 8, 1910

Aaron Doyle Haskins
Jul 9, 1928
Jul 2, 1930

John Charles Haskins
Born & Died Jan 29, 1927

Florence Haston Grissom
Apr 7, 1878
Dec 28, 1950

Several unmarked graves.

Lon C. Rollins
Sep 1, 1891
Oct 23, 1954
&
Pearl H. Rollins
May 6, 1897

Kimera D. Grissom, Sr.
Apr 1, 1911
Sep 21, 1970
&
Hazel S. Grissom
Jan 25, 1912
Mar 24, 1970
married Sep 14, 1935

Lester K. Grissom
Aug 20, 1903
Apr 22, 1974
&
Carrie C. Grissom
Apr 3, 1908
----
married Jul 20, 1924

37 CROWELL CEMETERY   Map # 6
Located about 3 miles Northwest of Halls Mill.

Infant Son of
D. A. & Ethel Crowell
(no dates)

Mike Crowell
Jul 14, 1826
Jan 24, 1906
&
Sarah R. Crowell
Feb 18, 1833
Feb 18, 1907

John A. Crowell
1941-1941

William Crowell
Apr 3, 1811
May 5, 1885
&
Jane Crowell
May 5, 1815
Dec 4, 1884

John C. Crowell
1855-1909
&
Annie Crowell
1861-1929

Many unmarked graves.

No Marker:***
Benjamin Crowell
Born Oct 12, 1812
Died abt 1863

No marker:***
Margaret Anderson Crowell
Born abt 1817
Died Sept 1855

Ben F. Crowell, Sr.
1858-1941
&
Mary L. Crowell
1876-1922

Richard M. Crowell
Aug 1, 1900
Nov 15, 1974
&
Ida Mae V. Crowell
Mar 4, 1902

Mary Louise, dau of
R. M. & May Crowell
Mar 10, 1925
Oct 27, 1925

B. S. Crowell
Jan 25, 1890
Jun 19, 1911

Birder J. Crowell
Jan 11, 1883
Mar 11, 1883

Garrett White Crowell
May 6, 1896
Aug 5, 1900

George L., son of
W. A. & Ellen Crowell
Oct 26, 1879
May 15, 1885

*** Records of
      Jerry Wayne Cook.

Thomas M. Crowell
1892-1967
&
Flossie H. Crowell
1903-(no date)

Infant Son of
S. W. & A. C. Crowell
Born Dec 23, 1897
age: 1 day

Infant of
S. W. & A. C. Crowell
Born & Died Dec 22, 1905

Lizzie R., dau of
S. W. & A. C. Crowell
Dec 2, 1901
Apr 8, 1915

W. H. Claxton
Oct 28, 1840
Mar 21, 1874

Joseph Anderson
May 10, 1805
Aug 10, 1873
age: 68y, & 3m.

Capt. William Anderson
Dec 25, 1803
Feb 1, 1847

Jennie, wife of
Capt. William Anderson
Aug 10, 1813
Jan 13, 1849

Joshua Crowell
Apr 13, 1852
Aug 14, 1893
&
Alice L. Crowell
May 25, 1856
Nov 20, 1897

Carter Parsons
Jul 8, 1894
Jul 6, 1896

Nancy A., wife of
E. H. McGowan
Jul 22, 1844
Aug 30, 1885

Mary E., wife of
Joshua Crowell
Dec 20, 1834
Jun 3, 1863
age: 28y, 5m, 14d.

William Jefferson, son of
J. M. & M. J. Orr
Feb 21, 1873
May 4, 1873

Infant Son of
J. M. & M. J. Orr
Jan 31, 1872

38 LENTZ CEMETERY   Map # 6
Located near Shearin Bend on Duck River.

Freddie Lentz
Jan 26, 1879
Dec 6, 1900   Only one grave.

39 SHEARIN CEMETERY   Map # 6
Located at Shearin's Bend of Duck River.

"Our Brother"
William M. Ray
Feb 7, 1826
Apr 23, 1902

Edgar Crowell
Nov 9, 1885
Mar 27, 1907

Annie May, dau of
G. H. & Madora Shearin
Jul 19, 1890
Jul 31, 1890

Abbie Dell, dau of
A. J. & L. C. Shearin
Apr 26, 1876-Nov 15, 1879

D. A. Crowell
Feb 9, 1856
Oct 11, 1890

Sarah, wife of
D. A. Crowell
Apr 30, 1862
Feb 24, 1898

Howard Crowell
Feb 9, 1890
Oct 4, 1906

Jennie Smith
Aug 17, 1860
Apr 19, 1884

John M., son of
George & M. E. Smith
May 7, 1858
Jun 5, 1884

Nancy Smith
Nov 12, 1812
Aug 21, 1839
age: 26y, 9m, 9d.

No Markers:***
Thomas Shearin
Died March 1849

No marker:***
Thomas Stweart Shearin
Born Apr 27, 1855
Died between 1860-1870

No marker:***
William F. Shearin
Born Dec 12, 1857
Died between 1860-1870

No marker:***
Infant Son of
Daniel & Beular Crowell
Born & Died 1907

No marker:***
Sallie May Crowell
Born Mar 22, 1895
Died Feb 21, 1898

Georgetta, dau of
George & M. E. Smith
Jan 7, 1862
Jan 5, 1863

W. T. Ledbetter
Dec 15, 1843
Jan 18, 1852
age: 8y, 1m, 3d.

No marker:***
Sarah Mayfield Shearin
Died 1824 or 1825

No marker:***
Virginia Ann Russell
Born May 15, 1835
Died June 6, 1888

No marker:***
E. A. Russell
Born 1843
Died Feb 9, 1895

No marker:***
Infant Son of
Daniel & Beular Crowell
Born & Died 1905

No marker:***
William Everett Crowell
Born Feb 23, 1899
Died Oct 26, 1899

George R., son of
George & M. E. Smith
Jun 18, 1872
Sep 17, 1872

Maria Robinson, consort of
James Robinson
Born Feb 14, 1814 & Died
Nov 25, 1887
"Who left an affectionate
husband and four children to
mourn her loss."

No marker:***
Thomas Shearin, Jr.
Born Jun 17, 1820
Died July 1865

No marker:***
Andrew Jackson Shearin
Born Dec 16, 1828
Died Dec 27, 1906

No marker:***
Beular Crowell
Born----------
Died Oct 3, 1913

No marker:***
Infant Son of
Ben F. & Kate Crowell
Born & Died Mar 22, 1902

*** Records of Mrs. Herman (Mary) Crowell.

Albert Oscar, son of
George & M. E. Smith
Feb 1, 1876
Jan 18, 1879

Many unmarked graves.

No marker:***
Sallie Tucker Shearin
Born 1804
Died between 1870-1880

No Marker:***
Sallie Shearin
Died between 1824-1849

No marker:***
William Thomas Shearin
Born May 25, 1859
Died between 1890-1900

No marker:***
Abbie "Aby" Dell Shearin
Born Apr 26, 1876
Died Nov 18, 1879

No marker:***
Sarah Brittain
Born 1868
Died 1870-1880

No marker:***
Infant Son of James M. &
Willie F. Brittain
Born & Died 1866

40 CARD CEMETERY   Map # 6
Located about 1½ miles Southeast of Haskins Chapel.

William H. Card
Jul 6, 1823
Nov 29, 1851
age: 28y, 4m, 23d.

Samuel H. Card
Born in Smith Co., Tenn.
Oct 4, 1800
May 10, 1891
age: 90y, 7m, 6d.

Joseph N. Card
Jan 24, 1822
Jun 18, 1854

Margaret S. Card
Born in Georgia
Oct 16, 1800
Jul 6, 1885
age: 84y, 8m, 20d.

Isaac C. Campbell
Mar 8, 1836
Mar 9, 1918

James M. Card
Dec 10, 1826
Jun 2, 1848
age: 21y, 5m, 22d.

William Card
Born on Chesapeake Bay, Md.
Apr 10, 1770
died Jan 19, 1840
age: 69y, 9m, 8d.

Sarah M. Campbell
Nov 30, 1834
Jun 24, 1916

Samuel T. Card
Apr 1, 1831
Jun 4, 1858
age: 27y, 2m, 3d.

Allen Stanley Musgraves
Dec 24, 1823
Sep 19, 1851
age: 27y, 8m, 26d.

Several graves with
fieldstones, no insc.

$ 41 HARRIS CEMETERY   Map # 6
Located across the fence from Card Cemetery, 1½ miles Southeast
of Haskins Chapel.

Nancy T. Harris
Jan 1831
Oct 1888

Ruth C. Harris
Apr 14, 1837
Aug 29, 1927

Ann H. Anderson
Apr 6, 1833
Jun 10, 1917

J. R. N. Harris
Mar 14, 1878
Nov 10, 1878

Several unmarked graves.

Nannie Anderson
Feb 5, 1860
Jul 25, 1920

James Lawson Harris
Jan 19, 1839
Mar 1, 1928
&
Nancy Jane Harris
May 9, 1849
Apr 24, 1919

James Harris*
1797-1879

Mary L. Harris
1805-1897

* Son of John & Ruth Harris

42 LUCAS CEMETERY   Map # 6
Located on the South side of Shearin Bend of Duck River.

Copied by Jerry Wayne Cook.

Samuel H. Lucas	John Z. T. Lucas	P. A. Lucas
Dec 9, 1841	Feb 2, 1849	(no dates)
Dec 21, 1854	Oct 1, 1851	
age: 13y, & 12d.	age: 2y, 7m, 29d.	

43 STORY CEMETERY (Col)   Map # 6
Located near Mt. Lebanon Church, near the rear.

Major Story
Co H
15 U.S.C.I.   Copied by Jerry Wayne Cook

44 MT. LEBANON CHURCH CEMETERY   Map # 6
Located at the Mt. Lebanon Church.

Melba Frances Wright***
(block marker)
***Melba Frances Wright
  Mar 26, 1923
  Jun ---, 1923

Infant Wright
(block marker-no dates)

Roy Avery Wright
Tennessee
Cpl 738 Tank Bn W.W.II
Aug 27, 1924
May 5, 1965

Martha Jane Wright
Sep 4, 1855
Nov 26, 1916

Isham Tranton
1850-1910

Tonya Renee Vaughn
Sep 16, 1971
Jun 17, 1972
(colored picture)

James A. Lucas
Jan 8, 1836
May 6, 1910

Joseph A. Lucas
Oct 22, 1837
Nov 24, 1922

Sarah Margrett Lucas
Feb 2, 1845
Dec 18, 1923

John D. Lucas
Dec 13, 1813
Apr 7, 1896
  &
Martha C. Lucas
May 10, 1816
Feb 20, 1895

Herman S. Neeley
Oct 15, 1898
Apr 2, 1918

Pauline Stevens
1920-1968
(Howell-Thompson)

Infant Boyce, dau of Jean &
Wayne Boyce
Sep 29, 1969

Coy Rayburn Boyce
Jan 27, 1954
May 20, 1974

Herschel Boyce
Apr 18, 1916
Dec 14, 1973
  &
Myrtle L. Boyce
Jun 24, 1919
----
married Dec 14, 1939

Charles Glenn Boyce
Jan 6, 1942
Jan 6, 1942

Milton Bryan Boyce
Dec 1942
Feb 7, 194-

Robert Carl Rogers
Feb 7, 1943
Mar 3, 1943

L. Fred White
Feb 9, 1916

  &
Christa Lee White
Sep 10, 1919
Jul 18, 1965

Miss Lizzie Clay
1890-1950
(Thompson)

William L. Neeley
Sep 5, 1903

  &
Georgia S. Neeley
Jun 8, 1903

Ola Louise Neeley
Aug 12, 1910
Nov 11, 1958

James Perryman
Jun 16, 1878
Jun 4, 1907

Absalom Perryman
Jul 6, 1846
Feb 21, 1917
  &
Elizabeth Perryman
Oct 7, 1846
(no date)

Gracie Myrtle Perryman
Oct 25, 1909
Oct 6, 1910

C. Melvin Perryman
Jul 27, 1940
Nov 23, 1966
  &
Wanda C. Perryman
Nov 21, 1943

Daisy Dean White
1904-1947

Clifford J. Burraham
1940-1941
(Thompson)

Ernest Burrahm
Dec 21, 1891

  &
Etta Burrahm
Mar 4, 1874
Apr 12, 1965

Mary Ruth Burrahm
Nov 16, 1917
Feb 19, 1924

Hubert S. Neeley
Nov 2, 1918

  &
Nell Gates Neeley
Sep 20, 1921
----
married Jun 17, 1939

Birdie Perryman
Apr 24, 1884
Mar 23, 1914

Infant dau of
G. W. & R. A. Perryman
Oct 11, 1917

Louise Luna
Jul 4, 1910
Jan 16, 1918

Rena Ann Perryman
1886-1927

S. J. Perryman
1919-1919

Edd L. Perryman
Apr 12, 1899
Apr 29, 1956
  &
Aline S. Perryman
Mar 3; 1913

Edward Perryman
May 31, 1937

Barbara Perryman
Jul 25, 1936

Avery Perryman
Aug 24, 1942
Oct 28, 1942

Michael O. Perryman
1955-1955
(Cothron-Thompson)

Emmett M. Gates
Feb 1, 1884
Nov 11, 1969
  &
Lora Bell Gates
May 25, 1898
----
married Jun 18, 1916

Raymond Lester Neeley
Mar 19, 1923

Quiley F. Crowell
Jul 12, 1875
May 29, 1898

John S. Neeley
Mar 12, 1875
May 11, 1931
&
Daisy D. Neeley
Aug 12, 1883
Nov 15, 1926
&
Tennie K. Neeley
May 30, 1875
Oct 19, 1899

J. M. Neely
Born Jun 18, 1865
age: 20 years

N. H. Neely
Jun 29, 1869
Apr 9, 1881

Minnie E. Naron
1914-1932

William J. Dryden
Sep 30, 1856
May 2, 1931

Lucinda E., wife of
W. J. Dryden
Jun 23, 1857
Aug 6, 1926

Dryden Grave
(no dates)

Dryden Grave
(no dates)

Rev. U. G. Paschal
1870-1915
&
M. E. Paschal
1870-1955

In Paschal Plat:
Pauline (Paschal)
1913-1915

Charles (Paschal)
1900-1900

Paul (Paschal)
1896-1898

James D. (Paschal)
1903-1918

James W. Neeley
Aug 22, 1843
Sep 13, 1926
&
Mary E. Stephenson Neeley
Feb 28, 1852
Feb 18, 1936

A. A. Stephenson
1871-1948
(Thompson)

Joseph Newton Neeley
Jun 13, 1841
1906

Margaret R., wife of
J. Neeley
Mar 2, 1837
May 30, 1903

Earnest A., son of
W. T. & L. N. Pickle
Died 1897

Richard Capley
1831-1914
&
Nancy Almedia Capley
1835-1918

Willie Mae Cook
Feb 12, 1888
Sep 2, 1971

Bal D. Capley
1866-1935

Alice M. Endsley
Apr 4, 1888
May 9, 1935

In Dryden Plat are these
graves:

E. B. D.   B. B. D.
(no dates)   (no dates)

L. E. D.   E. O. D.
(no dates   (no dates)

J. N. D.   Infant
(no dates)   (no dates)

Christopher C. Damron
1873-1944
&
Susie Paschal Damron
1873-1936

M. R.
(foot marker)

J. H.
(foot marker)

E. B.
(footmarker)

W. Gee Baxter
Born in Bedford Co., Tenn.
Jun 26, 1868 & died in
Bedford Co., Tenn.
Aug 14, 1887
Age: 19y, 1m, 19d.

Rev. John W. Crowell
Nov 19, 1867
Feb 22, 1894   and
Died in College at
McLemoresville, West Tenn.
"Father"

For PASCHAL see addendum
page 331.

Daniel Spencer Stephenson
Aug 26, 1848
Aug 4, 1930
&
Theana Prudence Stallings
Stephenson
Aug 3, 1851
Jun 16, 1900

Alec Stephenson
1882-1900

H. Clyde Stephenson
Jun 25, 1893
Nov 28, 1965

"Mother"
T. P. Stephenson
1851-1900

Joseph H., son of
Thana & Daniel Stephenson
May 26, 1874
Aug 14, 1880

William A., son of
Thana & Daniel Stephenson
Oct 1, 1878
Oct 2, 1878

Oliver "Boss" N. Neeley
Jan 3, 1884
Jan 3, 1969
&
Emma M. Neeley
Feb 20, 1865
Aug 6, 1937

Mary Jane Neeley O'Steen
Jan 5, 1882
Apr   1910

Joseph Hiram Neeley
Tennessee
Teamster 156 Depot Brig
W. W. I
Feb 15, 1896
Feb 6, 1969
&
Ruth Raschal Neeley
May 26, 1901

H. Spencer Neeley
Jan 25, 1872
Oct 15, 1962
&
Alice L. Neeley
Apr 3, 1882
Aug 7, 1969

Haley Williams, wife of
H. S. Neeley
Oct 21, 1877
Nov 26, 1906

"Mother"
Margaret E. Crowell
Jun 7, 1841
Feb 10, 1921

Mary A. Capley, wife of
W. H. Jones
Jan 27, 1836
Apr 17, 1905

Nancy C., wife of
J. N. Dryden
Aug 26, 1834
Dec 7, 1892
"A Tender Mother & a
faithful Sister."

D. O. Dryden
Oct 2, 1866
Aug 1, 1891

Bettie Lentz
1856-1930

Nora Nelson
Died Apr 28, 1942
(Gowen)

John Wesley Paschal
Jun 30, 1833
Nov 19, 1925
&
Fanny Jane Paschal
Nov 6, 1839
(no date)

W. H. Stephenson
Jul 31, 1806
Feb 27, 1887
age: 80y, 6m, 24d.
"He was converted & joined
the M.E. Church when only
16 yrs of age. His last
words were:"I am Happy."

Elenor Stephenson
Mar 18, 1808
converted & joined the M.E.
Church at the age of 13 yrs.
Died Apr 20, 1889
age: 81y, 1m, 2d.

Zilpha Curtis
1876-1899

John K. Gentry
Sep 12, 1904

&
Harriet Morey Gentry
Apr 22, 1908

&
Edith Gentry
1905-1921

L. M. J. Williams
Apr 6, 1858
Sep 2, 1918

Denny Elley (Eley)
1898-1959

Edna Carroll Hyatt
1886-1962
(Gowen-Smith)

John F. Grogan
Aug 11, 1897

&
Katie C. Grogan
Mar 19, 1892
Oct 29, 1968

Charley Crowell
Mar 1, 1840
May 18, 1916

Mary Crowell
Nov 22, 1837
Aug 8, 1923

W. R. Crowell
Aug 11, 1872
Dec 30, 1906

James S. Crowell
1866-1947
&
Fannie C. Crowell
1868-1951

W. M. Neeley
1873-1958
&
Minnie J. Neeley
1878-1930

Louise Neeley
Dec 31, 1916
Jun 25, 192_

Mrs Viola Cook Joyce
1900-1954
(Thompson)

"Father"
J. M. Cook
Oct 20, 1868
Jan 14, 1949
&
"Mother"
Tennie Cook
1866
Mar 11, 1926

Jimmy Neeley
Apr 2, 1866
(no date)
&
Jennie L. Neeley
Feb 5, 1864
Jan 15, 1931

William T. Neeley
1875-1942
&
Della Neeley
1878-1943

Ben O. Cook
Aug 1, 1902
Jul 7, 1932

Robert Lee Grogan
1948-1949
(Thompson)

Thomas D. Harrison
Aug 14, 1879
Dec 15, 1955
&
Cora Harrison
May 7, 1886
Jun 30, 1950

E. P. Harrison
Feb 9, 1840
Nov 13, 1926
&
Eliza I. Harrison
Oct 15, 1843
(no date)

Lena P. Harris, wife of
C. E. Crowell
Mar 14, 1897
Aug 25, 1918

Little James, Infant Son of
Robert & Annie Watson
1922

W. T. "Tommy" Glasscock
Oct 9, 1918
Feb 19, 1971

W. L. Glasscock
Mar 23, 1900
Apr 7, 1924

Gurtie, wife of
W. L. Glasscock
Mar 21, 1900
Nov 30, 1921

James Marcus Trott
Sep 20, 1872
Nov 7, 1944
&
Tinnie Viola Trott
Sep 17, 1900
Jun 17, 1954

James Leslie, son of
James & Tinnie Trott
(no dates)

Helen H. White
Nov 1, 1914
Jan 19, 1936

Albert O. Joyce
Pvt U.S.Army
Apr 7, 1895
Jun 13, 1974

Gean R. Cook
Apr 19, 1887
Feb 6, 1957
&
Alta B. Cook
Jul 6, 1902

Minnie E. Naron
1914-1938

Many unmarked graves.

(con't)

Jesse W. Lentz
Nov 29, 1918

&
Beatrice L. Lentz
Feb 20, 1918
Jun 30, 1974

Gene Lentz
1937-1938

Berry Lentz
Jan 21, 1846
Nov 3, 1918

Jesse Huel Cook
Aug 29, 1897
Oct 30, 1974
&
Ethel I. Neeley Cook
Jun 12, 1897
----
married May 10, 1914

"Daughter"
Aline Ozell Cook
Nov 30, 1925
Sep 25, 1927

"Son"
Leonard Harold Cook
Jan 14, 1918
Feb 12, 1920

Joan Cook
1943-1943
(TM)

James M. Lentz
Dec 5, 1856
Jul 19, 1923
&
Mary C. Lentz
Oct 7, 1858
Mar 8, 1924

Samuel J. Lentz
Sep 8, 1826
Aug 16, 1910
& wife:
Louisa Ann Lentz Springer
Jul 6, 1831
Apr 28, 1916

Judge L. Lawson Cook
Jul 1, 1872
May 16, 1945
&
Nancy L. Jane Cook
Jan 11, 1878
Nov 17, 1931

William W. Cook
1858-1943
&
Nannie L. Cook
1865-1942

William T. Cook
1882-1968
(Howell-Thompson)

James S. F. Stephenson
Oct 27, 1865
Jul 26, 1866

Nancy L. Stephenson
Jun 8, 1867
Dec 7, 1887

Homer Shearin
Dec 24, 1909
Feb 2, 1930

Gladis C. Shearin
Jan 2, 1907
Mar 17, 1907

Johnie Earl Shearin
1921-1922

Infant Son of
Johnie & Lilly Shearin
Dec 10, 1913
Dec 25, 1913

Johnnie C. Shearin
Nov 21, 1885
Jan 5, 1962

Lillie Neeley Shearin
1884-1926

Lula L. Shearin
Jan 27, 1895
Mar 3, 1963

Newton Cannon Shearin
Sep 10, 1838
Jan 28, 1892
age: 53y, 4m, 18d.
&
Martha J. Shearin
Dec 25, 1845
Oct 5, 1913

R. S. Shearin
Feb 15, 1917
Jun 27, 1938

Richard A. Neeley
Jun 10, 1876
Dec 6, 1946
&
Ellie Lentz Neeley
Jan 16, 1880
May 17, 1940

Robert L. Lentz
1868-1942
&
Willie E. Lentz
1886-1948

Parker Lentz
1911-1926

Hiram B. Cook
Aug 1, 1873
Mar 15, 1961
&
Tennie C. Cook
May 1, 1878
Apr 22, 1967

People who are known to be buried in Mt. Lebanan Cemetery,
at Mt. Lebanan Methodist Church, 18th District. These do not
have markers:*** Copy by Jerry Wayne Cook.

Alma Frances Wright***
(block marker)
Mar 26, 1923
May 17, 1923

Mellia Frances Wright***
Mar 26, 1923
Jun 6, 1923
"Twins of Roy P. & Annie Bell
Cook Wright. Mellia may have
a stone but illegible, records
are from their mother's records.

Queenie Brame Clay***
(no dates)

Will Clay***
Feb 27, 1910
age: 19 yrs.

Mary Berlin Clay***
1903

Ford Clay***
1902

Clay***
(no dates)

Nora Elizabeth Stephenson**
May 5, 1872
Jul 14, 1948

Pauline Paschal**
Aug 13, 1913
Oct 11, 1915

John Carroll***, born in N.C.,
died about 1896. His grave is
in the same row as that of
Edna Height Lentz, near the
center of the Cemetery.

Isabella Causey Carroll***
died about 1903-4, wife of
John Carroll.

Jonnie Cook***
Feb 10, 189_
Jul 31, 1898

Mary Cook***
Oct 30, 1883
Nov 6, 1883

Infant *** of
Gus & Mary Clay
(no dates)

Clay***
(no dates)

** by Mrs. Joe Neeley
No markers**

Fred Damron**
Born & Died Jan 1900
buried by J.C.J.Paschal

James Daniel Paschal**
May 14, 1903
Nov 21, 1918 buried by
Rev. Paschal.

Christiana A. Molder Green
Nicholas "Addie" ***
Born abt 1842
Died after Nov. 1890

Chester Morton Neese***
Mar 6, 1931
Mar 11, 1931

Lester Lee Neese***
Mar 6, 1931
Mar 6, 1931

Gustave A. Clay***
1831-1907

----- Clay***
(no dates)

Infant Clay***
Infant of Gus & Mary Clay
(no dates)

Infant Clay*** of
Gus & Mary Clay
(no dates)

Paul Paschal**
Oct 24, 1896
Jun 15, 1898

Edith May Paschal,** sister
of Mrs. Joe Neeley,
Jul 26, 1905
Sep 22, 1921

Cecil Earl Neeley***
died Jan 27, 1942
age: 22y, 7m, 18d.

Cecil Franklin Grogan***
Jan 18, 1923
Feb 10, 1923

Martha Stephenson Neeley***
Mar 11, 1859
May 18, 1895

Bennie Coble Ray***
May 28, 1913
Jun 4, 1913

Josephine Grogan***
1941-1941

Merle Burrahm***
Feb 1899
May 1899

Andrew Jackson Burrahm***
Dec 7, 1872
Dec 22, 1898

Melba Frances Wright***
Mar 26, 1923-Jun --, 1923

Charles McKabe Paschal**
Jan 25, 1900
May 16, 1900

45 MOLDER CEMETERY   Map # 6
Located about ½ mile Northeast of Mt. Lebanan Church.

Jacob Molder
Born Jan 21, 1806
and hanged by bushwackers
near this spot during the
Civil War.

Susan Capley Molder
Born abt 1803 and
died July or August 1888, wife
of Jacob Molder.

Copied by Jerry Wayne Cook.

46 HARRISON CEMETERY   Map # 6
Located about ½ mile Northeast of Mt. Lebanan Church.

No trace of this Cemetery is visible now, but at one time was
very large. Information about this Cemetery comes from Mrs.
Eva Mae Wright.

No marker:***
Mahulda J. Harrison
Born 1832
Died Mar 28, 1897, sister
to E. P. Harrison

No marker:***
Mary Paschal Harrison, wife of
Doc. Harrison
(no dates)

No marker:***
A Colored Man, who drowned
in Sinking Creek, is buried
here. (no dates)

No marker:***
Parents of E.P.(Elisha P.)
Harrison
(no dates)

Many graves were here.

No marker:***
Elley Harrison, dau of
Doc. Harrison
(no dates)

*** by Jerry Wayne Cook.

47 LENTZ-WILLIAMS CEMETERY   Map # 6
Located about 1½ miles South of Halls Mills.

The Lentz-Williams Cemetery, at the Old Samuel J. Lentz
homesite in the 18th Civil District, east of Sinking Creek.
Only 4 graves and they are marked by fieldstones, no insc.
                by Jerry Wayne Cook

No Marker:***
Mary Caroline Lentz Williams
Born Jan 23, 1854
Died May 10, 1878
dau of Samuel J. Lentz.

No marker:***
Ella Williams
Born Mar 10, 1873
Died Nov 13, 1878
dau of Tom & Mary Caroline
Lentz Williams

No marker:***
A Baby of Tom & Mary Caroline
Lentz Williams
(no dates)

*** by Jerry Wayne Cook.

No marker:***
Samuel B. Lentz
Born Oct 16, 1878
Died prior to 1880
son of James Monroe &
Mary C.(Capley) Lentz.

48 COOK CEMETERY   Map # 6
Located about 1½ miles South of Halls Mill.

Supplied by Jerry Wayne Cook.

William Cook
Tennessee
Pvt 2 Regt West Tenn Mtd
     Gunmen
1798-1854
"Seminole War Soldier"

Nancy (Lentz) Cook
1807-1896

Mattie E., dau of
M. E. & W. I. Cook
Sep 20, 1883
Aug 6, 1888

Infant Daughter of
M. E. & W. I. Cook
Born & Died Dec 22, 1889

Sam Franklin Cook
1870-1947

***unmarked graves by
   Jerry Wayne Cook.

No marker:***
Ozroll Lawwell
(no dates)

No marker:***
Charlie Cook
Born Mar 19, 1892
Died   1892

No marker:***
Thomas Newton Cook
Born abt 1862
Died 1913-4

No marker:***
Sarah E. Patterson Cook
Born May abt 1836
Died   1912

No marker:***
Hattie E. Cook
Born Feb 2, 1896
Died (no date)

Lucy Jane Cook**
Born abt 1840
Died before 1850

Andrew Jackson Cook, Sr.
Oct 15, 1835
(no date)

"Uncle"
T. L. Lawell
1872-1955

Henrietta Lawell
1876-1932

Henry Lawell
1833-1914

W. I. Cook
1860-1923

Margarette, wife of
W. I. Cook
Jun 5, 1864
Sep 3, 1907

Infant Daughter of
Mr & Mrs F. E. Patterson
(no dates)

No marker:***
Hugh Lawson White Cook
Born abt 1843
Died Sep 23, 1871

No marker:***
Luther Cook
(no dates)

No marker:***
Jessie Thomas Neeley
Dec 12, 1927
Dec 12, 1927

No marker:***
Henry Oscar Cook
Sep 10, 1899
Died before 1904

No marker:***
Bessie Dean Cook
Aug 19, 1897
Aug 4, 1901

Newton Cannon Cook**
Died before 1850

Mary E. Stephenson
Jun 11, 1888
Jun 11, 1950

W. H. Lawwell
May 1, 1878
Nov 3, 1921

Octtia Lawwell
Mar 4, 1882
(no date)

Frank Patterson
1836-1864

Sarah Patterson
1839-1900

"Father"
William H. Patterson
May 28, 1861
Jun 17, 1925

"Mother"
Lucie A. Patterson
Jun 21, 1862
Feb 13, 1910

Allar H. Patterson
Mar 22, 1884
Nov 22, 1901

No marker:***
Author Lawwell
Dec 10, 1902
Jun 20, 1903

NOTE:*** An arm of
Andrew Jackson Cook, Sr.,
buried beside him in abt
1896-1897.

No marker:***
Nancy Lee Clark Cook
1864-Nov 16, 1904

Lucy Lawwell**
Born abt 1871
Died (no date)

"Mother"
Nellie Tucker
Aug 28, 1871
Jun 4, 1919

"Father"
William Lawwell
Nov 30, 1842
Sep 4, 1905

"Mother"
Frances Lawwell
Nov 12, 1852
Sep 28, 1914

Mattie C., wife of
C. F. Patterson
Apr 22, 1886
Sep 5, 1905

Leonard Hershel Cook
Oct 22, 1919
Mar 17, 1972

Mattie E. Patterson
Dec 2, 1889
Oct 3, 1907

No marker:***
Mary Mattie Lee Cook
Born abt 1881
Died (no date)

No marker:***
Thomas Jefferson Cook
Mar 20, 1830
Feb 28, 1911

No marker:***
Manerva Jane (Aaron) Cook
Born abt 1837
Died (no date)

No marker:***
Infant of Louis J. Lawell
Born abt 1913

NOTE: ** It is not proven but it is believed that these
         are also buried here- Jerry Wayne Cook.

William Henry Harrison Cook
Oct 31, 1842
Died before 1850

49 CROWELL CEMETERY   Map # 6
Located about 1 mile South of Halls Mill.

Everete Crowell
Jul 22, 1886
Jul 24, 1888

Lizzie M. Crowell
Nov 6, 1882
Sep 27, 1885

No marker:***
James L. Crosslin
Born & Died May 24, 1948

No marker:***
Walter Eugene Crowell
Apr 4, 1889
Jan 10, 1939

No marker:***
Willie Washington Crowell
Jan 31, 1880
Feb 12, 1881

Infant Son (Crowell)
Born & Died Feb 27, 1885

Infant Daughter (Crowell)
Born & Died Feb 12, 1889

***Unmarked graves- by
     Jerry Wayne Cook

No marker:***
James Crowell
(no dates)

No marker:***
Dora Vilet Crowell
Mar 18, 1886
Aug 20, 189_

No marker:***
Mary Crowell
Born abt 1862
Died before 1880

Robert H. Crowell
1850-1932
     &
Martha A. Crowell
1861-1939

6 markers
(no inscriptions)

No marker:***
Thomas Crowell
(no dates)

No marker:***
Elizabeth Leota Crowell
Feb 17, 1881
Nov 3, 18__

No marker:***
Jennie Liggett
Oct 3, 1881
Sep 28, 1882

Samuel Crowell
1810-May 7, 1887
"A Devout Member of the
Lutheran Church for more
than 50 years."
     & wife:
Mary Crowell
Aug 9, 1816
Feb 7, 1858
     & 2nd wife:
Mary E. Crowell
Nov 3, 1831
Apr 26, 1904

No marker:***
Nannie Liggett
Apr 13, 1885
Apr 26, 1885

50 COLLIER-JONES CEMETERY   Map # 6
Located 1½ miles Southeast of Halls Mill, South of Duck River.

NOTE: There is only one marker, with several fieldstones.

Lula, dau of
N. M. & R. R. Collier
Mar 10, 1873
Apr 30, 1873

***People who are known to be buried in this Cemetery- by Jerry Wayne Cook

No marker:***
Monroe Jones
drowned in Duck River while

No marker:***
"Sis" Jones
Died abt 1890

No marker:***
Frances Delk has 2 children
buried here(uncertain of
these two)

No marker:***
Larry Jones
Born qbt 1816
Died abt 1896
(Mr. J. C. Paschal helped
dig his grave)

No marker:***
Nancy Jones
Born abt 1822
Died abt 1892
wife of Larry Jones

No marker:***
Child of Cooper & Eliza
Kimmons Jones (uncertain of
this one)

51 LANDERS CEMETERY   Map # 6
Located at Anchor Mill.

Annie Landers Warner
Nov 18, 1866
May 6, 1914

Bettie A., wife of
H. W. Landers
Died Feb 16, 1907
age: 60y, 5m, 13d.

Clarence C. Landers
Aug 13, 1901
Nov 20, 1904
age: 3y, 3m, 7d

5 or 6 unmarked graves.

52 WILLIAMS CEMETERY   Map # 6
Located about 2 miles Southeast of Hickory Hill Church.

James Harris
Feb 10, 1777
Nov 3, 1863
Tennessee
Pvt 3 Regt, West Tenn Mil
     War of 1812
     &
Ann Harris
Oct 29, 1780
Aug   1869

Eunice W. Williams   and
1882-1938
     &
Eulus Williams
1887-1953

Sam Knox Williams
Jul 1, 1862
Jul 19, 1894
     &
Margaret H. Williams Osburn
1862-1949

Ellen J. Collins
Dec 29, 1866
Dec 27, 1948

Grace T. Williams
1879-1905

David Williams
May 7, 1815
Sep 28, 1887
     &
Mrs. S. T. Williams
Dec 1, 1816
Oct 4, 1910

Norma Williams
Mar 19, 1879
Nov 2, 1936

Emma Williams
Sep 26, 1874
Jan 25, 1910

Louvenia Williams
Sep 6, 1839
Feb 25, 1900
     &
Mary Jenkins Williams
Aug 2, 1859
Jul 14, 1889

Jas. H. William
Oct 25, 1850
May 16, 1901

Caldonia Dozier, wife of
James Williams
1853-1941

53 OSBORN CEMETERY   Map # 6
Located about 1½ miles Southeast of Hickory Hill Church.
(Back of Bobo's Sale barn)

William C. Osborn
Jul 10, 1812
Mar 28, 1883   Copied by Franklin Blanton
age: 70y, 8m, 18d.   Only one grave.

54 JONES CEMETERY   Map # 6
Located about 1½ miles Southeast of Hickory Hill Church.

Rosannah Claxton   B. Jones   S. E. Claxton   Many fieldstones, no insc.
Born 1811   Died Oct 22, 1844   (Emaline Claxton
Died after 1880   (fieldstone)   Born 1843   Many unmarked graves.
(no marker)   Died after 1880) Fieldstone

55 WHITMAN-GREGORY CEMETERY   Map # 6
Located about 2 miles Southeast of Hickory Hill Church, on
Hurricane Creek.

George W. Gregory   "My Wife"   Sallie V. Whitman   Susan P. Whitman, wife of
Mar 8, 1816   Mary V. Gregory   Feb 8, 1839   Dr. D. W. Terry
Dec 16, 1890   Nov 18, 1836   Sep 9, 1885   1841-1879
"Sergeant, Company G, Sep 11, 1893   age: 46y, 7m, 1d.
45th Tenn.   Edward P. Whitman
Regt., C.S.A.   Several unmarked graves. Many fieldstones, no insc. 1832-1844

56 GREAGORY CEMETERY   Map # 6
Located about 2 miles Northwest of El Bethel, on Green Hill Road.

J. T. Greagory   Calvin D. Williams   "Brother"   T. J. Little
Dec 14, 1843   1883-1969   George R. Holden   Co A.
(no date)   &   Jun 27, 1901   4th Tenn Mtd Inf
&   Zora E. Williams   Jun 25, 1902   Jun 17, 1842
Susan Greagory   1888-1941   &   Dec 29, 1894
Sep 23, 1846   "Sister"
Mar 10, 1924   Infant Son of Bob Gordon Infant of Mr & Mrs J. W.
                      Born & Died Nov 25, 1936 Holden
                      (Thompson)   May 12, 1901

NOTE: The South Section of this Cemetery is Colored Cemetery.

57 WARNER CEMETERY   Map # 6
Located on the East side of Warner's Bridge.

Mary A. Dixon, dau of John Warner *   Richard Warner   Huldah B. Warner
Hilliard & Eliza Dixon Jan 11, 1783   Born July 27, 18_8 [1818] Jul 3, 1848
Nov 16, 1837   May 11, 1834   Died Sept 28, 1835   Aug 20, 1851
Jan 10, 1843   "Leaving a wife & 4 children
                       to mourn his loss."   Cpl S. J. Warner   Perdy V. Warner
William Dixon, son of   Co K   Nov 30, 1851
John & Eunice Warner   Eunice, Consort of John 1st Tenn Inf   Jan 27, 1852
Born Dec 1, 1815   Warner & dau of William & Mexican War
Died --- 27, 1842   Mary Dixon
                       Apr 5, 1792
  * Second Sheriff of Oct 2, 1852   Many unmarked graves.
    Bedford County, TN. "Leaving two Sons & two Daus
                       to mourn her loss."   This Cemetery is in bad condition.

58 STREETER CEMETERY (Col.)   Map # 6
In the Bend of Duck River, South of Warner's Bridge.

Emlie Hanna Streeter   Many unmarked graves.
(no dates)   Fieldstones, no inscriptions.

59 STREATER CEMETERY   Map # 6
Located about 3 miles West of Shelbyville, on Fishingford Road.

John Streater
Who was born in Wake Co.,
N. C., Sept 22, 1805 &
Died Aug 20, 1852

Nancy Streater
Born in Wake Co., N.C.,
About 1803 and Died
Sept 10, 1876

2 graves with fieldstones,
no inscriptions.

Susan A. Streater
Born at Hilliandston, N.C.
Dec 12, 1821 and
Died Oct 14, 1880

Many unmarked graves.

Dorothy B. Fonville
Born Apr 18, 1783, the
wife of Asa Fonville, who
died July 9, 1830

60 CROWELL CEMETERY (Col.)   Map # 6
Located about ½ mile East of Halls Mill.

George Thompson
Died Jan 7, 1922
(no age given)

Shine Harris
Apr 15, 1947

Henry Thompson
1845-1917

Jane Thompson
1857-1892

Arthur Harris
Died Jul 8, 192_
age: 58 yrs.
(TM)

Minerva Jane Thompson
Feb 14, 1837
Sep 23, 1896
age: 71y, & 3m.

M. C. Robertson
1898-1957
(Welton)

Mai Eller Brown
190_-1959
(Bradberry-Massey)

------- Harris
Died Aug 27, 1936
(TM)

Many unmarked graves.

Lucy Parsons
Oct 19, 1841
Apr 9, 1895

Mitchell Thompson
1845-1917

Acklen Leonard Johnson
1903-1952

Lillie Gipson
Mar 10, 1910
Feb 1, 1911

Mrs. Lucinda Harris
Died Nov 30, 1953
age: 86y, 4m, 29d.

Anderson Warner
Aug 8, 1840
(no date)
&
Dinah Warner
Feb 25, 1850
Jul 20, 1913

Clifford C. Crowell
1892-1973
(TM)

Harry H. Thompson
Sep 20, 1861
Apr 14, 1910

Esther Bailey
1903-1963 (TM)

61 CROWELL CHAPEL CEMETERY (NEW)   Map # 6
Located at the Crowell Chapel Lutheran Church, Halls Mill.
Church built 1880 and Dedicated 1881.

Benton Crowell
Aug 14, 1899
Dec 23, 1917
"Apprentice Seaman at
Norfolk, Va."

Joshua Crowell
Jan 23, 1814
Jun 3, 1883

Ervin Crowell
1889-1961
&
Blanche Crowell
1893-19

Dorithy Evelyn Crowell
Jul 14, 1920
Oct 31, 1920

Amanda T. Crowell
Oct 9, 1857
Nov 30, 1930

William R. Crowell
Oct 24, 1892
Apr 22, 1920

W. H. Claxton
Nov 2, 1852
Nov 30, 1921
&
Margaret Claxton
May 8, 1860
Nov 25, 1925

Benjamine S. Parsons
Feb 3, 1831
Dec 2, 1917

Jane Parsons
Jan 8, 1839
Mar 5, 1911
age: 72y, 1m, 25d.

Emmitt A. Crowell
Jul 14, 1881
May 12, 1971
&
Sallie A. Crowell
Apr 18, 1888
Nov 19, 1956
&
Dewey P. Crowell
Apr 18, 1915
Jun 15, 1916

Samuel Kembro Moulder
Sep 25, 1845
Dec 26, 1936
&
Roseanna Moulder
May 13, 1849
Mar 12, 1933

George W. Claxton
Apr 17, 1858
Nov 21, 1952
&
Isabelle Claxton
Nov 3, 1869
Jul 28, 1924

James Edward Boyce
Jun 13, 1939
Jan 10, 1942

Infant Brian Taylor Osteen
Sep 6, 1950

E. O. Crowell
Apr 19, 1883
Mar 20, 1920

William A. Crowell
1850-1944
&
Martha E. Crowell
1856-1926

Earl Crowell
Apr 5, 1905
Mar 25, 1927

Willie Elmore Burrahm
1888-1942
&
Beula Etta Burrahm
1892-1969

Mary Jane Burrahm
1932-1933
age: 13 mo.

William H. Claxton
Sep 5, 1890
Killed in France
May 1, 1919

John R. Lentz
Oct 29, 1882
Jan 14, 1961
&
Virginia C. Lentz
Sep 6, 1887

J. Harlin Crowell
May 13, 1892
Jul 11, 1966

Elizabeth Cooper Crowell
May 23, 1890
Feb 8, 1945

G. Alvin Loyd
May 20, 1916

&
E. Earlene Loyd
May 30, 1920
Feb 18, 1975
married Apr 18, 1936

Evelyn Jaunita Loyd
Born & Died
Aug 27, 1940

Genoa A. Claxton
Jan 5, 1861
Nov 16, 1920
&
Arena E. Claxton
Oct 27, 1853
Feb 8, 1951

R. S. Wright
Mar 14, 1880
Jan 13, 1928

Clement H. Wright
1846-1936

Edgar Crowell
Dec 26, 1908
Dec 19, 1969

Daniel Crowell
1883-1941
&
Mary Crowell
1892-1938

Ruth Crowell
1920-1923

N. E. Shearin
1865-1940
&
Lomie Shearin
1868-1964

R. M. Shearin
Dec 9, 1906
Nov 21, 1922

Sarah S. Shearin
1868-1964
(Same as Lomie Shearin)

L. C. Shearin
Apr 12, 1840
Dec 17, 1921

Charles P. Parsons
1896-1967
&
Mina M. Parsons
1902-

Edison T. Molder
1923-1973
(Daves-Culberson)

"Father"
Thomas Evans Moulder
Nov 19, 1894
Jun 26, 1968

"Mother"
Ora Sanders Moulder
Sep 1, 1895
Mar 25, 1970

Rever Moulder
Apr 1, 1934
Aug 6, 1936
&
Martha Moulder
Feb 22, 1930
Apr 14, 1934

Cooper Stephenson
1882-1935

Lizzie Stephenson
1861-1935

D. H.
(no dates)

George Fisher
(no dates)
&
Elizabeth Fisher
(no dates)

Robert H. Claxton
Dec 20, 1886
May 18, 1921
&
Emma N. Claxton
Jun 25, 1885
Nov 11, 1966

Jacob Henry Moulder
Apr 13, 1887
Jul 5, 1962
&
Maggie Vera Moulder
Jan 11, 1882
Dec 4, 1953

W. Kimbro Moulder
Sep 17, 1907
May 12, 1971
&
Mable N. Moulder
Jun 19, 1915

Henry Floyd Moulder
1910-1974

Major J. Moulder
1887-1962
&
Tempie A. Moulder
1882-1962

Claude P. Crowell
Oct 26, 1907
Mar 23, 1968
&
Myra H. Crowell
Sep 17, 1910

Edgar G. Reeves
Apr 2, 1879
Jun 6, 1922

George W. Parsons
1858-1925
&
Sallie C. Parsons
1859-1929

Robert Taylor Parsons
Sep 17, 1886
Feb 15, 1974
&
Mary Etta Parsons
Sep 1, 1892

Salomie A. Parsons
Oct 6, 1893

Lealon Parsons
Jul 28, 1910
Aug 22, 1932

William J. Smith
Jun 24, 1871
Sep 15, 1947
&
Lula Locke Smith
Feb 14, 1879
Dec 26, 1970
&
Hanie E. Smith
Jul 4, 1903
Sep 19, 1950

William A. Neeley
Jul 4, 1855
Aug 25, 1931
&
Permelia F. Neeley
Jan 8, 1853
Nov 19, 1932

John Charles
Mar 25, 1865
Nov 1, 193-4
&
Alice Charles
May 31, 1864
(no date)

Zannie Charles
Nov 29, 1888
Sep 27, 1933

Willie Fisher
1864-19(no date)
&
Lettie Fisher
1871-1940

Eugene Clanton
1913-1941
&
Virginia Clanton
1911-19

James Alford Edwards
Sep 15, 1889
Apr 15, 1927
age: 38y & 6m.

Zolie Lee Crabtree
Mar 18, 1926
Dec 8, 1968
&
Virginia M. Crabtree
May 12, 1929

Henry Bell Crowell
Jan 21, 1876
Apr 12, 1920
&
Tribble Ann Crowell
May 1, 1894
Oct 18, 1972

Jasper M. Crowell
Jun 9, 1912
Dec 12, 1954
&
Mary Y. Crowell
Mar 6, 1920
Sep 10, 1951

William Hall
1872-1936
&
Martha Hall
1873-1940

Edd Hall
May 11, 1898
Mar 11, 1971

Hattie H. Hall
1866-1941

Robbie Crowell Warren
Feb 6, 1924
Nov 8, 1961

Joe Stephenson
Nov 13, 1893
Dec 5, 1967
&
Rowena Stephenson
Feb 5, 1901
Apr 10, 1972

Pearl C. Bell
1896-1973
(Thompson)

E. H. Bell
1894-1945
(Thompson)

B. F. Lentz
Jan 3, 1839
Nov 14, 1924
&
Nanzy J. Lentz
May 29, 1845
Apr 30, 1940

Benjamin C. Lentz
Sep 24, 1874
Feb 10, 1954

Beulah Lentz
Jul 22, 1871
Dec 22, 1960

Philey Crowell
Jul 19, 1880
Feb 23, 1930
&
Annie Crowell
Jan 17, 1891
Jul 23, 1973

Richard T. Boyce
Jun 11, 1956
Aug 4, 1974
(color picture)

Joe Christopher Baker
Sep 12, 1877
Mar 19, 1950
&
Sarah Jane Baker
Jan 25, 1882
May 7, 1922

Andrew C.(Cooper) Card
1875-1947

T. C. (no dates)

"Brother"
Roy Dunn
Jun 1, 1929
Feb 2, 1930
&
"Sister"
Emma Jane Dunn
Jul 2, 1931
Nov 14, 1931

Ellen C. Carlton
1874-1946

Harrison T. Clark
1885-1968
&
Fannie Mae Clark
1900-1964

Will B. Cook
Apr 13, 1903

&
Ruby S. Cook
Apr 27, 1911
Feb 28, 1967

W. B. Cook
Feb 24, 1935
Aug 26, 1961
(picture)

John H. Lentz
Dec 31, 1861
Nov 20, 1937
&
Tennie L. Lentz
Aug 28, 1868
Apr 9, 1953
married Feb 20, 1887

Preston Locke
1873-1940
&
Nancy Locke
1879-1957

William R. Turrentine
1888-1951
&
Lillie D. Turrentine
1893-1972

Albert Temple
1876-19(no date)
&
Lucy E. Temple
1881-1931
&
Minnie Temple
1885-19(no date)

Hoyl Elrod
Nov 21, 1885
Apr 6, 1959
&
Grace Elrod
Jun 23, 1887
Dec 10, 1972

J. M. "Bud" Elrod
1857-1937
&
Ellen Elrod
1863-1938

Charlie L. Gassaway
Dec 19, 1901
Apr 4, 1925
&
Herbert S. Dunn
Dec 25, 1903
Feb 5, 1961
&
Lizzie S. Dunn
Jun 7, 1906

Frank W. Scales
Jun 2, 1895
Jan 27, 1974
&
Lorene F. Scales
Apr 24, 1904

Cecil L. Scales
1936-1945

J. W. Dunn
Mar 20, 1901

&
V. Allie Dunn
Aug 17, 1896
Nov 10, 1965

Ell T. Dunn
1870-1928
&
Emma Dunn
1876-1959

J. W. "Bud" Ray
1852-1936
&
Fannie Ray
1855-1930

John Albert Claxton
1864-1940
&
Susan Jane Claxton
1864-1937

William Neal Crowell
Feb 3, 1875
Oct 21, 1968
&
Effie W. Crowell
Jul 31, 1879
Sep 19, 1961

Luna Crowell
Jul 23, 1885
Dec 9, 1970

Grady Shearin
1891-1937

Lomie L. Shearin
1898-1975

Robert H. Shearin
Feb 24, 1861
Oct 4, 1948

B. F. Shearin "Book"
1872-1954

William J. Paschal
Feb 1, 1868
Jun 20, 1926

Pearl Stephenson
Jan 30, 1895
Sep 5, 1929

William H. Stephenson
Corp Co C 4 Tenn Mtd Inf.

John O'Steen
1851-1933
&
Nannie O'Steen
1873-1933

Comer L. Claxton
Feb 11, 1915
Apr 13, 1974
&
Kathleen M. Claxton
Jun 3, 1914
----
married Dec 16, 1934

Infant Son of Mr & Mrs
Commer Claxton
Sep 28, 1937
Oct 3, 1937
age: 5 days

Peter S. Scales
1869-1935
&
Nannie J. Scales
1867-1938

Mack Crick
1897-1974
&
Kate Crick
1894-1938

John Thomas Paschal
Jun 28, 1872
Mar 22, 1958
&
Sallie Ann Paschal
Dec 25, 1871
Oct 24, 1950

Clarence L. Paschal
Jun 26, 1916
Feb 11, 1941
(Navy picture)

James Thomas Goin
Jul 12, 1940
Aug 23, 1941

Annie Nadean Goin
May 8, 1916

Pvt John E. Crowell
Jul 27, 1920
Lost his life in the line
of duty for his Country in
Belgium
Dec 17, 1944
(picture)

Samuel Stephenson   and
1857-1944

Elijah B. Dickens
Dec 24, 1873
May 22, 1940

Saloma C. Dickens
Dec 24, 1878
Oct 3, 1927

Vaden W. Dickens
Feb 10, 1911
Jul 11, 1948

Mattie P. Dickens
1913-1938

Ernest Lee Brown
1947-1947

Infant Mary Brown
1955-1955

J. D. Robertson
Jan 15, 1896
Feb 14, 1935
&
Fannie M. Robertson
Feb 13, 1900

(picture of both)

Mattie Bell Lentz Robertson
Nov 1, 1897
Dec 4, 1929
age: 32y, 1m, 3d.

John K. Lawell
1880-1943
&
Martha Ann Lawell
1887-(1971-TM)

Charlie Price
May 10, 1888
Aug 7, 1943
&
Hattie Price
Dec 24, 1891
Sep 7, 1967

Mrs. Susie Neese
1874-1946
(Thompson)

Andy J. Neese
Feb 2, 1886
May 4, 1957
"erected by R. B.,Jr. &
W. H. George"

Frank P. Lentz
Nov 21, 1904
Mar 15, 1932

Thomas C. Franks
Jun 4, 1908

&
Mabel C. Franks
Feb 13, 1897
Jan 6, 1967

Sallie Stephenson
1884-1958

J. Ollie Robertson
Jan 16, 1900

&
Lettie M. Robertson
Oct 8, 1898
Sep 20, 1957

Elsie G. Robertson
Mar 23, 1907
Apr 5, 1964
&
Strick Parsons
May 12, 1918

&
Martha V. Parsons
Jul 5, 1920
----
married Aug 23, 1943

W. Everette Parsons
Jan 28, 1913

James E. Parsons
Oct 11, 1938
Jan 31, 1960

Sherry Denise Grissom
Aug 27, 1965
Jan 25, 1970

William P. Glasscock
Feb 22, 1900

&
Zelma S. Glasscock
Feb 28, 1905
Dec 6, 1972

Royal Tommie Edde
Aug 11, 1902
Nov 30, 1959
&
Nancy Lizzie Edde
Apr 22, 1901

Oscar J. Parsons
Aug 10, 1889
Nov 26, 1974
&
Bonnie O. Parsons
Feb 23, 1890
----
married Mar 27, 1910

Torris C. Parsons
Tennessee
S/Sgt 41 Armd Inf
2 Armd Div W.W.II
Jan 5, 1915
Apr 7, 1945

Several unmarked graves.

Willie P. Barlow
Mar 2, 1912
Jan 25, 1972
&
Ruby N. Barlow
Sep 6, 1925

W. H. "Willie" Adcock
Aug 6, 1895
Mar 22, 1959

Robert G. Charles
Sep 27, 1900
Jan 26, 1964
&
Ora C. Charles
Mar 16, 1904

Sarah Jane Charles
Feb 15, 1942

Joseph Marvin Crowell
1887-1973
&
Maud Patterson Crowell
1890-1963

Donna Kay Houston
Jun 25, 1964
Jun 26, 1964

Michael Crowell
Jan 3, 1867
Dec 28, 1947
&
Martha Crowell
Nov 11, 1871
Jul 25, 1940

Rosa Ann Crowell
Oct 11, 1903
Dec 26, 1973

E. Clifton Russell
Oct 2, 1891
Sep 14, 1946
&
Susie C. Russell
Dec 11, 1892

Infant Daughter of
W. L. & Tabitha Pewitt
Sep 23, 1959

Susan Camille Crowell
Oct 19, 1958
Oct 22, 1958

Infant J. B. Brumitt
1965-1965
(Gowen-Smith)

62 CROWELL CHAPEL CEMETERY (OLD)   Map # 6
Located at Halls Mill, near the Crowell's Chapel Lutheran Church.

John Thompson, son of
Thomas & Margaret Thompson
Born in Orange Co., N.C.,
March 16, 1777, emigrated
with his father in 1784 &
settled on the Cumberland
River near Nashville, Tenn.,
moved to Duck River in 1806
& settled at what is well
known as Thompson Ford,
Bedford Co., until the time
of his death. Departed this
life for a better home on the
5th Oct 1857.
age: 80y, 6m, 9d.

Mary, wife of
John Thompson
Jan 18, 1784
Jul 6, 1862

James Paschal
Jun 2, 1795
Jun 22, 1855
&
Elizabeth Paschal
Feb 5, 1801
Aug 6, 1873

William Jones, son of
Equiller & Rebecca Jones
Aug 16, 1821
Mar 13, 1837

Jacob M. Parsons
Aug 29, 1819
Jan 28, 1884

Lucinda Parsons
Aug 9, 1820
Aug 19, 1857

R. C. Parsons
Jan 12, 1863
Sep 23, 1910

Edmond S., son of
R. C. & H. F. Parsons
Dec 7, 1886
Sep 8, 1887

Mary J. Anderson
Dec 21, 1854
Apr 27, 1908

B. F. Capley
Jan 15, 1827
Jan 30, 1900
age: 73y, & 15d.

Medaline Capley
May 30, 1831
Jul 8, 1910

G. W. Parsons
Dec 27, 1787
Nov 16, 1842
age: 54y, 10m, 19d.

Samuel Crowell, Sr.
Born in N. C.,
Jul 12, 1786
Jun 24, 1865, died at his
Residence in Bedford Co., at
the age of 79 yrs, for more
than half a century a member
of Church of Christ.

Catharine, wife of
Samuel Crowell
Feb 11, 1788
Jul 2, 1854
age: 66y, 4m, 12d.

Zora Dean Osteen
Apr 10, 1899
Jun 30, 1902

Mich'l Fisher
Pa Mil
Rev. War
May 20, 1766
Dec 18, 1833

Sarah Fisher, consort of
Jacob Fisher
Born July 28, 1791 & died
Jan 5, 1815
age: 24y, 5m, 8d.

Margret Parsons
Jul 23, 1793
Apr 26, 1854
age: 60y, 9m, 3d.

J. J. Lentz
Mar 13, 1842
Jun 6, 1886

Laura T., dau of
Jno. J. & Martha F. Lentz
Aug 31, 1865
Sep 2, 1872

Volentine F. Lents
Nov 7, 1810
Oct 28, 1866
age: 55y, 11m, 21d.

Sarah E., dau of
N. F. & C. Lents
Sep 25, 1860
Apr 22, 1885
age: 25y, 6m, 27d.

N. C. Thompson
Dec 25, 1819
Mar 29, 1899
age: 79y, 3m, 4d.
&
Mary E., dau of B. C. &
S. F. Green
Born Mar 26, 1844, married
to N. C. Thompson
Mar 14, 1866 & died
Mar 9, 1887
age: 42y, 11m, 13d.

Sarah Snell, Died Jan 23, 1849. aged: 101 years & 5 months."Her maiden name was Thompson, born in Duplin Co., N. Carolina the 14 day of August 1747, according to her birth as was written in a Prayer Book she brought to this Country, & kept till her death."

Sarah J., wife of
J. W. Molder
Mar 19, 1838
Jun 20, 1874
age: 36y, 3m, 1d.
(she has two markers, below)
Sarah Jane Molder
Mar 19, 1838
Jun 20, 1874

Thomas C. --------
Born Apr --, ---9
Died --- --, 1847
"Leaving --------
--- William C.---
(illegible)

Annie Edwards Capley
1885-1913

Martha, wife of
John Smith
Jul 16, 1805
Aug 8, 1892

Malcom D. Smith
Jul 23, 1836
Aug 16, 1913

Margaret, wife of
M. D. Smith
Jan 20, 1829
Jun 20, 1898

Tom S. Prince
Jan 24, 1898
(TM --- 1975)
&
Flora E. Prince
Aug 11, 1895
Oct 8, 1967

Lucy Prince
Jan 11, 1862
Jan 28, 1929

NOTE:People who are known to be buried in the Crowell Chapel Cemetery but who do not have stones. *** by Jerry Wayne Cook.

Hulda Capley***, wife of
John Reed
Born abt 1826
Died 1850/1860

Child,** of John & Hulda Reed. (no dates)

John F. Thompson
Nov 24, 1813
Aug 21, 1883

Rutha F. Thompson
Jan 10, 1813
Jan 24, 1899

Margaret J. Haynes
Oct 27, 1856
Aug 1, 1886

Mary R. Claxton
Jun 11, 1864
Jun 21, 1906

Palstine Claxton
Born Dec 2, 1856
Died Mar 6, 1881
(Wooden-slab)

Felix Turrentine
1811-1895
&
Martha A. Turrentine
1822-1882

John V. Hall
Mar 31, 1841
Mar 29, 1915

Ella F., wife of
John V. Hall
Nov 24, 1854
Oct 23, 1890

Sammie B., son of
Jno V. & Ella F. Hall
Jun 21, 1882
May 7, 1884

Hazzard Scales
1901
3 months

Margaret Jane Prince
Died Nov 16, 1922
age: 84 yrs.

Lenard E. Prince
Apr 16, ----
--- -- ----
(broken away)

Hollis Prince
Mar 11, 1888
Apr 4, 1926

Infant Son*** of
H. P. & J. E. Prince.
(no dates)

Mary Ann Capley Crowell*** wife of Samuel Crowell
Born abt 1821, died Spring of 1905, buried near the grave of Benjamin Franklin Capley.

Harriet Paschal** wife to
Tom Berlin
Born 1827 & Died (no date)
(Harriet & Jennie are sisters)

William N. Parsons
1856-1950
&
Tennie V. Parsons
1861-1887

John H. Holden
Jan 9, 1884
Oct 1, 1967
&
Ella H. Holden
Apr 8, 1887
Jan 13, 1972

Claud C. Reeves
Jan 20, 1913
Mar 15, 1913

Major Samuel Turrentine
1769-1824
&
Alexander Turrentine
1772-1808
&
James Turrentine
1774-1848
"Three Brothers from North Carolina who settled on this land in 1807 & donated this Plot for a Community Cemetery." Erected by the Turrentine Family Association. 1952

Infant Son of
J. A. & A. N. Edwards
Oct 7, 1916

Lucy C. Lentz
Jan 4, 1880
Aug 15, 1906

Ora Lentz
Sep 20, 1888
Dec 5, 1901

Infant dau of
John R. & Lucy C. Lentz
Aug 5, 1906

B. E. Capley
Sep 10, 1869
Aug 14, 1902

Elmer, dau of
B. E. & D. J. Capley
Jul 1, 1897
Apr 6, 1902

Peter Capley***
Born abt 1760
Died Oct 21, 1852

The Wife,*** of Peter Capley
Died before 1829.

John Crowell***
Mar 6, 1825
Aug 28, 1855

Jennie Paschal** wife to
Tom Berlin, Born 1830 & Died
(no date)

Newton Franklin Card
Jan 5, 1837
Oct 17, 1901

Ritha F. Card
1850-1923

Martha A., wife of
William H. Smith
May 18, 1831
Apr 11, 1886

B. J. Dryden
Apr 16, 1842
Jun 6, 1918
&
M. J. Capley
Apr 15, 1844
Jun 4, 1918

Felix, son of
D. A. & M. F. Turrentine
Nov 7, 1884
Aug 19, 1887

D. A. Turrentine
Feb 14, 1847
Jun 17, 1917

Mary F. Turrentine
Oct 21, 1850
Jun 28, 1950

W. R. Lentz
Nov 18, 1865
Sep 6, 1915
&
Isa Lentz
Oct 26, 1868
Feb 10, 1896
&
Lizzie Lentz
Nov 17, 1864
Feb 29, 1908

Effie A., dau of
W. R. & Isa Lentz
Jan 24, 1888
Aug 12, 1892

Argie, dau of
B. E. & D. J. Capley
Oct 3, 1899
Apr 4, 1902

Benjamin Newton Franklin
Lentz***
Oct 1, 1834
Mar 15, 1914

Catharine Capley,*** 2nd wife of B.N.F. Lentz
Born abt 1834 & Died Jan 1910. She is buried not far from her two sisters who died in 1918.

NOTE: The birth date of Major Samuel Turrentine should be 1763-NOT 1769.-by Jerry Wayne Cook.

** by Mrs. Joe Neeley

63 LENTZ CEMETERY   Map # 6

Located near Anchor Mill, on the South side of Duck River.
(Copied by Jerry Wayne Lentz)

Benjamin Lentz	James S. F. Stephenson***	Stephenson Baby***	*** by Mrs Herman Crowell
Feb 2, 1800	Oct 27, 1865	(no dates-no marker)	
Oct 5, 1875/8	Jul 26, 1866		
	(no marker)		

64 LOWELL CEMETERY   Map # 6

Located about 1 mile South of the mouth of Sinking Creek.
(Copied by Jerry Wayne Lentz)

John K. Lowell   Mary Sampson Lowell
Born abt 1799   Born abt 1813
Died in 1853   Died (no date), wife of
           John K. Lowell

1 SMITH CEMETERY   Map # 7

Located about ½ mile North of Vannatta

Several fieldstones, no inscriptions.
Several unmarked graves.

2 COOPER CEMETERY   Map # 7

Located at Vannatta Community.

John B. Hall	Caleb Lindsey Cooper	Adelaide R., dau of John &	John L. Cooper
May 19, 1878	Oct 25, 1825	Fannie G. Cooper & wife of	Nov 20, 1807
Jan 16, 1958	Feb 3, 1914	Joseph S. Malone, Born in	May 13, 1895
&		Bedford County, Tenn.	
Sarah Jane Hall	Sabella H. Smith, wife of	Sep 16, 1838 and Died in	Fannie G. Cooper, consort
Aug 16, 1882	Caleb L. Cooper	Philadelphia, Pa.,	of John L. Cooper
Nov 23, 1964	Feb 20, 1836	Dec 24, 1876	Jun 28, 1813
	Feb 15, 1903		Mar 25, 1874
Tempie E. Cooper		Robert Browning Cooper	
Sep 9, 1850		Dec 27, 1856	
Aug 30, 1935		Dec 23, 1912	

3 SPRINGER CEMETERY   Map # 7

Located about 1 mile South of Vannatta.

------ Springer   Several graves with fieldstones, no inscriptions.
    C.S.A.
(marker now gone)   Many unmarked graves.

4 STEELE CEMETERY   Map # 7

Located about 1½ miles South of Vannatta Community.

Joseph Steele	Dorcas Wilson Steele	Wilson Steele	Jane Steele Knott
Died July 4, 1846 in his	Died Nov 7, 1835	Died Aug 25, 1835	Died Aug 9, 1857 in her
78th year. "More than 40	age: 66 yrs.	age: 41 yrs.	60th year.
years a member & officer			
in the Presbyterian Church."		Marinda Steele	
		Died June 6, 1864 in her	
	NOTE: All stones are down.	69th year.	

5 STEELE CEMETERY   Map # 7

Located about 1½ miles South of Vannatta Community.

Elizabeth F., dau of	Jas. C. Steele	William L. Steele	Kitty Steele Hutton
P. C. & Elizabeth Steele	Apr 1, 1835	Jan 19, 1828	Feb 6, 1852
Oct 22, 1833	Aug 12, 1848	Jun 25, 1848	Dec 7, 1932
Jun 24, 1906		"Served his Country 12 months	
		in the War with Mexico."	Edmund Cooper Steele
John W. Steele, M.D.	Caleb L. Steele		Jul 16, 1853
Sep 12, 1830	Sep 16, 1859	Mrs. Katharine Steele, consort	Jun 29, 1854
Feb 7, 1911	Nov 27, 1938	of C. D. Steele	
		Mar 1807-Aug 10, 1857	

Price C. Steele, Sr.
Died July 2, 1880
age: 80y, 1m, 2d.

Henrietta S., wife of
Price C. Steele, Sr.
Aug 14, 1820
May 9, 1898

Elizabeth B. Steele, Consort
of P. C. Steele
Oct 21, 1804
Dec 11, 1842
age: 38y, 2m, 7d.

Several unmarked graves.

John Davis
Jun 7, 1794
Nov 6, 1868
age: 74y, 4m, 29d.

Zara, dau of P. C. & Eliza F.
Steele
Aug 14, 1883-Sep 4, 1886

Catharine Davis, wife of
John Davis
Dec 8, 1784
Oct 11, 1863
age: 78y, 10m, 3d.

6 UNKNOWN CEMETERY   Map # 7
Located about 2 miles South of Vannatta Community.

2 very old rock-slab markers, no inscriptions.
Several unmarked graves.

7 HOUSTON-WHITWORTH CEMETERY   Map # 7
Located about 1½ miles South of Deason, Tenn.

Robert Lee Taylor III
1968-1968
(Gowen-Smith)

Colonel Bean
Jan 11, 1886
(no date)
&
Annis Bean
Aug 26, 1887
Jul 16, 1953
&
May Bean
Jul 2, 1912

Fred Pope
May 17, 1891
(no date)
&
Mary Earl Pope
May 13, 1896
Sep 8, 1956

Willie Mai Pope
Feb 24, 1890
Jan 25, 1972

John H. Ward
1839-1907
& wife:
Tabitha Ward
1846-1928

Mattie Ward
(no dates)

Charlie Ward
(no dates)

Henrietta Ward
(no dates)

George L. Moulder
Feb 7, 1871
Jan 2, 1958
&
Kate W. Moulder
Oct 6, 1864
Oct 27, 1950

Catherine Painter, wife of
Guy Faulk
Jul 31, 1921
Jul 2, 1951

Elroy Pope
Jun 20, 1900

&
Lacy H. Pope
Dec 6, 1898
May 11, 1966

W. S. Pope
Dec 12, 1866
Jan 12, 1934

Mary J. Pope
1866-1948

John Cas Pope
1872-1936
&
Mary Adams Pope
1868-(no date)

Lottie Bell, dau of
J. C. & M. A. Pope
Oct 21, 1894
Mar 1, 1911

Robert J. Neil
1881-1946
&
Annie W. Neil
1885-(no date)

W. G. Murphree
Feb 8, 1880
Jun 6, 1955

Clara P. Murphree
Jan 15, 1888
Feb 13, 1961

L. N. Murphree
Jul 6, 1858
Jan 18, 1933

Sarah E. Murphree
May 18, 1857
Sep 21, 1920

Albert Lee Fann
Dec 22, 1944
Jul 24, 1963

Jess Williard Fann
1916-1966

Charlie B. Taylor
Dec 26, 1880
1969 (TM)
&
Lena P. Taylor
Oct 28, 1883
Jul 13, 1959

David Russell Haynes
1941-1942
age: 7m & 3d.

Herbert, son of
Grace Naron Jackson
1919-1920

Jim Crutchfield
1882-1975

Nora, wife of
J. J. Crutchfield
May 31, 1874
Nov 7, 1932

G. W. Martin, Jr.
Apr 27, 1863
Sep 2, 1919

Molly Martin
Oct 9, 1868
Apr 2, 1942

George Michael Gibbs
1968-1968
(Gowen-Smith)

Ozella Thorneberry
Nov 2, 1910
Jun 21, 1915
age: 4y, 7m, 19d.

Ludie Thorneberry
Jul 7, 1908
Jul 13, 1914
age: 6y, & 6d.

Thomas E. Moulder
Nov 19, 1894

&
Martha R. Moulder
Feb 14, 1889
Oct 21, 1966

Annie May, dau of
Sam W. & Hattie Lamb
Jan 30, 1910
Oct 29, 1918

W. T. Lamb
Jan 20, 1816
Aug 28, 1907
"Killed by lightning."

Sam W. Lamb
Jun 11, 1886
Oct 20, 1918

Hattie L. Arnold
1881-1967

Willie Mat Pope
Feb 24, 1890
Jan 25, 1972

Laura B. Pope
Aug 30, 1876
Jul 11, 1953

Nick Pope
Oct 12, 1839
Dec 6, 1913

S. R. Pope
Jun 7, 1849
Jul 11, 1907

Minnie B. Arnold
Nov 10, 1879
Sep 2, 1919

Mattie M. Coop Jackson
Sep 16, 1881
Oct 4, 1970

Ruth May, dau of
Maggie & W. W. Faulk
Sep 8, 1904
Jun 19, 1909

Willie May Faulk
Oct 18, 1891
(no date)
&
Stammer E. Faulk
May 25, 1890
Jan 11, 1959

William C. Faulk
Oct 27, 1939
Nov 9, 1939
&
James M. Faulk
Jul 24, 1938
Jul 24, 1938

J. Faulk
(Baby-no dates)

Riley S. Tribble
1876-1951
&
Florence F. Tribble
1881-1932

Clarence S. Tribble
Jul 30, 1903
May 3, 1966

Frank Tribble
Nov 9, 1908
Nov 24, 1908

Horace L. Thompson
1881-1943

Nettie Thompson
1890-1936

Alonzo P. Thompson
1856-1922

Maggie B. Thompson
1858-1937

Edward Thompson
1896-1927

Nannie Mae Fowlkes
(no dates)

Linda Fay Joyce
3 mos & 16da.
1944

Willie G. Gregory
Oct 6, 1928
Dec 25, 1930

Claud T. Beene
1871-(no date)
&
Lula O. Beene
1873-1937

John W. Orr
1869-1936
& wife:
Emma B. Smith Orr
1870-1936
&
Bertram Steel Orr
1902-1931

John H. Orr
Aug 10, 1839
Jan 16, 1912
&
Belle W. Orr
Aug 24, 1850
Feb 25, 1912

S. B. Faulk
1859-1937
&
Susan Faulk
1861-1939

J. W. Green
Jun 16, 1903
Dec 9, 1930

Genoa Green
1880-1939

Annie Roane, wife of
Thomas J. Roan
Died Apr 14, 1853
age: 18y, 4m, 14d.
"Also Infant Daughter"

Hattie, wife of
E. M. Whittworth
age: 34 years
Nov 8, 1874
also their infant dau
Minnie Lee & Lillie May.

Thomas Bell Whittworth
1829-Jun 28, 1852
age: 22y, 1m, 3d.

Sallie Lee, dau of
E. L. & S. E. Whittworth
Apr 15, 1874
age: 4m & 27d.

C. N. Harris
Jul 30, 1839
Mar 25, 1915

Julia Harris
1842-1924

Samuel F. Harris
1876-1934

W. H. Harris
1884-1957
&
Myrtle Harris
1887-1955

B. M. Harris
1879-1915

Edna J. Harris
Feb 19, 1880
Jul 31, 1969

Joe Baxter Harris
Tennessee
Pvt 120 Inftry W.W.II
Oct 23, 1906
Jul 30, 1952

B. F. Whitworth
Died Oct 27, 1876
age: 62y, 9m, 6d.

Minerva L., wife of
B. F. Whitworth
Apr 30, 1819
May 7, 1900

J. P. Wallis
1857-1940

Fannie Wallis
1862-1946

Syd Houston
1849-1921

Maggie Blankenship Alexander
Oct 20, 1859
Jul 12, 1955

S.
(no dates)

L. S.
(no dates)

S. S.
(no dates)

S.
(no dates)

Hugh P., son of
James M. & R. A. Brooks
Died Jul 10, 1867
age: 5m.

S. R. Crutchfield
Jun 27, 1852
Nov 24, 1930

Susan Crutchfield
Dec 18, 1862
Jan 16, 1948

Samuel Foster
1878-1943

Martha Foster
1880-1946

Walter A. Featherston
1886-1946
&
Myrtle J. Featherston
1886-(no date)

Robert Cecil Ray, Sr.
Mar 17, 1924
Sep 23, 1970
&
Sarah Jane Ray
Oct 11, 1926

John G. Worke
Born in Iredell Co., N.C.,
Sep 14, 1805
Died in Rutherford Co., Tenn.,
Feb 15, 1863
age: 57y, 5m, 1d.

Robert S. Worke
Born in Statesville, N.C.,
Sep 19, 1812 & Died
Oct 12, 1857

Nell Clifford
1942-1943
&
Betty Lou Clifford
1935-1935

Willie R. Alexander
1891-1927

William Avery Alexander
Jul 26, 1927
Nov 7, 1928

John Phillip Shearin
1964-1964
(Gowen-Smith)

Bernice Phillips Shearin
1903-1953
(Thompson)

George W. Phillips
Jun 3, 1871
Apr 1, 1950

Ella Phillips
1869-1939

Rev. Thomas M. Henley
1869-1930

Jennie S. Henley
1865-1951

James W. Henley
1875-1958
&
Algie E. Henley
1877-1936
&
Rebecca C. Henley
1874-1960

Thomas Henry Smith
Jan 15, 1854
Mar 3, 1936
&
Ida Clifford Smith
Jul 24, 1871
Mar 7, 1967

Sallie M. Smith
Sep 21, 1904
Jul 19, 1965

Eva Jane Smith
Jan 16, 1913
Jun 21, 1937

A. S. (Smith)
(no dates)

M. S. (Smith)
(no dates)

Mary, wife of
Robert Worke
Born in Lancaster Co., Pa.,
Sep 14, 1785 & Died in
Bedford Co., Tenn.,
Jul 25, 1853

Samuel Guy Thompson
1823-1909
"Asleep by his Aunt
Annie Guy"
NOTE: there is a fieldstone
next to this grave, but no
inscription of Ann Guy, who
was born 1775 in N. C., &
died after 1850.

Benjamin F., son of
B. F. & M. L. Whitworth
Jun 3, 1851
Jul 5, 1852
Stone by-Hummel & Cardone,
        Piqua, O.

Ricie C. Record
1937-1972
(Gowen-Smith)

Nathan A. Jackson
1895-1964
(Howell-Thompson)

Jack Sanders
Born & Died
Sep 15, 1933

Elma Sue Sanders
Oct 8, 1938
Jun 8, 1939

Winston Wood Gill
Apr 20, 1884
Sep 29, 1958

Mary Sue Gill
Mar 11, 1888
Jan 30, 1969

W. D. Record
1895-1951
(Howell)

James D. Harris
1880-1953

Caldonia Fulton Harris
1872-1961

William M. Hutton, M.D.
Nov 15, 1821
Aug 16, 1886

George D. Hutton
May 18, 1819
May 3, 1886
     &
H. Davidson Hutton
Feb 10, 1858
Aug 28, 1863

Mrs. Jess Gamble
1896-1936

Helon Frances Gambill
1918-1925

Myrtle Gamble
Oct 15, 1937
Feb 17, 1938

Hon. John P. Steele
May 15, 1811
Dec 31, 1877
age: 66y, 7m, 16d.

Mrs. Martha Steele
Died Mar 11, 1882
age: 72y, 2m, 18d.

Martha T., dau of
B. F. & M. L. Whitworth
May 15, 1842
Sep 21, 1842

Henry Thos.
     Co C
4th Tenn Inf

Infant Curtis
1967-1967
(Gowen-Smith)

Samuel R. Harris
1869-1942

Sallie F. Harris
1880-1953

Shelia Ann Harris
1951-1951

Sarah Frances Johnson
1922-1968
(Gowen-Smith)

Euless Prince
Sep 3, 1889
Jun 19, 1972
     &
Mary B. Prince
Feb 6, 1894

Maude Lee Harris
Apr 27, 1903
Apr 17, 1919

Floyer W. Leverette
1905-1965
(Gowen)

Kattie Connell Fulton
1855-1895
"Mother & 3 Infants"

John William Connell
Sep 9, 1807
Oct 28, 1878
age: 71y, 1m, 19d.

Ruth, wife of
R. S. Miller
Sep 8, 1836
Jan 4, 1884

Martha Reaves
Aug 12, 1831
Jul 25, 1899

Sidney F. Gamble
1941-1941

Sarah McRee
Feb 10, 1786
Nov 9, 1843
age: 57y, 8m, 29d.

Dr. Thomas W. Wood
Jun 3, 1835
Sep 21, 1930

Edgar M. Joyce
Sep 21, 1898
Jan 31, 1973
     &
Annie Mai Joyce
May 7, 1899
Nov 18, 1966

Margaret Holden
Oct 7, 1921
Nov 25, 1957

Charles F. Fulton
1885-1934

Lula A. Smith
Feb 9, 1901
Oct 11, 1971

L. S.
(no dates-could be same
   as above)

Viola Smith Moulder
1898-1973
(Howell)

Hugh Gibbs
1909-1941

B. H. Gambill
Tennessee
S1 U.S.N.R.   W.W.II
Apr 23, 1923
Aug 5, 1965

Pinkey S. Leverette
1882-1937
(Howell-Thompson)

Tennie Leverette
1873-1926 (TM)

Will Edward --------(gone)
1873-1955
(Thompson)

Corp Alfred Sutton
     Co M
5 Tenn Cav.

Eula May Sutton
Nov 16, 1910
Oct 27, 1911

John H. Sutton
1883-1937

Mary Joe Record
Apr 5, 1955
Jul 13, 1955

Charlie T. Sullivan
Feb 24, 1885
Jun 14, 1966
     &
Mary O. Sullivan
Dec 17, 1888
Mar 22, 1961

William C. Sullivan
Tennessee
Pfc 143 Inf 36 Inf Div
     W. W. II
Nov 9, 1914
Nov 9, 1944

Dr. James P. Temple
1856-1944
     &
Nannie G. Temple
1861-1935
     & Son:
John G. Temple
1882-1944

Charles T. Sullivan, Jr.
May 11, 1923
Apr 6, 1968
     &
Louise H. Sullivan
Feb 12, 1923

Gustav Adolph Peel
Jan 31, 1877
Mar 18, 1947

Fannie Sanders
1895-1959

Rollie Reese Faulkner
Aug 18, 1888
Jul 12, 1969
     &
Annie Tucker Faulkner
Nov 23, 1885

Margaret M. Hutton
Aug 19, 1793
Oct 30, 1855

Samuel F. Hutton
Aug 3, 1826
Nov 4, 1852

Josiah M. Hutton
Apr 8, 1834
Aug 30, 1862
age: 28y, 4m, 22d.

Bryan I. Gambill
Nov 14, 1896
Dec 4, 1961
     &
Pearl B. Gambill
Jan 30, 1900

Marietta M. Heath
Oct 30, 1888

Mamie (no last Name)
1897-1921

John W. Mash
Jul 18, 1855
Jan 22, 1933

Florence Mash
Nov 10, 1860
Aug 25, 1926

Thomas E. Mash
Mar 9, 1883
Apr 5, 1962

Robert Work Houston
1839-1925
&
Blanche Venable Houston
1849-1926

James S. Houston
1845-1919

Corinne, dau of
Robert W. & Blanche V.
Houston
1868-1951

C. P. Houston
Jun 3, 1810
Feb 1, 1902

Jane M., wife of
C. P. Houston, Sr.
May 23, 1815
Jun 18, 1887

H. J. M. Houston
May 23, 1815
Jun 18, 1887
(Same as above)(2nd marker)

William Preston Featherstone
1908-1947
&
Mattie Lou Featherstone
1908-19
&
Sam Eugene Featherstone
1933-1951

Loretta Lynn Smith
May 31, 1965
May 25, 1973
dau of Howard H. &
Agnes S. Smith.

Many unmarked graves.

L. Fate McCarty
Nov 27, 1869
Nov 28, 1958

Emma Faulk McCarty
May 18, 1880
Oct 20, 1918

Noble Faulk
1858-1934
&
Nannie Faulk
1856-1940

Thomas A. Coop
1880-1948
&
James T. Coop
1921-1955

M. R. C. (Coop plot)

Robert W., Jr., son of
Robert W. & Blanche V.
Houston
1867-1938

Claude Venable Houston
Dec 31, 1865
Jun 7, 1917

Dr. William Houston
who died Mar 9, 1844 in the
68th year of his age.

Mrs. Sarah Houston, Consort
of Dr. William Houston
Died 1st April 1851, in the
66th year of her age.

William Houston
Died Mar 28, 1853
age: 33y & 9m.

Ollie Freeman Smith
Oct 23, 1902
Jun 5, 1970
&
Lettie Jane George Smith
Jan 18, 1904

Thomas A. Smith
Oct 27, 1929
Aug 9, 1931

Several fieldstones, no insc.

S. Eakin Chambers
Mar 28, 1890
Feb 4, 1960
&
Winnie F. Chambers
Aug 20, 1894
Apr 10, 1959

Nannie Brown
1853-1928

Morgan Anderson, son of
W. G. & Ann E. Sharp
Sep 15, 1865
Oct 16, 1867

Ann Eliza, Consort of
W. G. P. Sharp
Jan 4, 1845
Apr 14, 1865
&
Virginia Florence, dau of
W. G. P. & Eliza Sharp
Mar 11, 1864
Jul 13, 1866
&
Morgan, son of
W. G. P. & Eliza Sharp
(no dates)

Martin Phifer Erwin
Died May 11th, at 9:20 P.M.
1882. age: 28y, 11m, 1d.
"He was a devoted Husband
and loving Father."

Thomas C. Loyd
1876-1939
&
Maggie E. Loyd
1873-1936

Alonzo Loyd
1903-1919

Fred D. Loyd
Jul 31, 1906
Nov 25, 1959
&
Stella S. Loyd
Jul 26, 1907

Alice T. Eady
Mar 10, 1864
Sep 25, 1958

A. H. Eady
1863-1939

Oscar L. Dodd
Aug 12, 1901
Oct 20, 1965
&
Georgia E. Dodd
Nov 27, 1913
Sep 17, 1973

Morgan Smith
Jul 4, 1797
Nov 20, 1875

Mary Mabel, dau of
J. H. & T. W. Webb
Died Dec 29, 1868
age: 1y, 11m, 23d.

I. B. (Isaac Baisye) Webb,
husband of F. E. (Frances
Eleanor Smith) Webb
May 10, 1818
Jun 4, 1855

Mrs. F. E. Norman
Dec 16, 1824
Oct 21, 1914

John T. Hardison
Dec 9, 1878
Dec 18, 1946
&
Lula W. Hardison
Sep 5, 1884
Jun 16, 1955

Lesley H. Hardison
Oct 13, 1888
Oct 29, 1907

James H. Hardison
Jun 12, 1859
Aug 13, 1908
&
Lillie H. Hardison
Jul 18, 1860
May 11, 1962

Raymond V. Burris
May 26, 1906
Dec 17, 1963
&
Lillie L. Burris
Feb 18, 1901
Oct 20, 1965

Infant Son of
Mr & Mrs Raymond Burris
May 28, 1932

(Colored Section of Houston-Whitworth Cemetery)

Donald Loyd
Died Apr 4, 1974
(Scales & Son)

Judy Bowman
Born Oct 6, 1903
Died (no date)

Bettie Turtine
1902-1936

Mr. Famie Turrentine
1882-1960
(Welton)

Louella B. Davis
1917-1974
(Welton)

John Kizer
died Feb 17, 1960
(no age given)

Mr Jim Buckingham
1883-Mar 15, 1950

Several unmarked graves.

Several fieldstones, no
inscriptions.

92

Richard O., son of
W. K. & S. A. Ransom
Jan 31, 1860
Aug 3, 1883

John S., son of
W. K. & S. A. Ransom
May 2, 1845
Aug 13, 1850

Laura Addie, dau of
W. K. & S. A. Ransom
May 2, 1855
Nov 2, 1885

J. A., son of
W. K. & S. A. Ransom
Dec 27, 1853
Oct 5, 1887

M. Ransom, son of
W. K. & S. A. Ransom
Jul 15, 1851
Jul 25, 1861

Charlie W., son of
N. S. & L. A. Jenkins
Nov 19, 1877
Aug 9, 1878

Charlie F., son of
W. K. & S. A. Ransom
Feb 28, 1857
Apr 10, 1881

James W. Ransom, son of
W. K. & S. A. Ransom
Jun 4, 1849
Jun 27, 1854

W. K. Ransom
Aug 18, 1812
(no date)
&
Sarah Ann Ransom
Aug 31, 1821
Jan 23, 1892

M. E. Ransom, dau of
W. K. & S. A. Ransom
Mar 11, 1842
Jan 4, 1844

Benjamin M., son of
W. K. & S. A. Ransom
Jan 18, 1841
Apr 4, 1862
"Died at Corinth in the
Confederate Army."

There are about 4 graves within a Rock Wall.
          No markers.

No markers remain in this Cemetery.

Cemetery markers are now gone.

NOTE: The following is a Copy of some of the markers, copied
          earlier by Charlie Adcock.

David Jones Wheeler
Born Dec 25, 1820
Died Nov(Mar) 26, 1864
married Sept. 1844

Elizabeth Caroline Rushing
Born Jun 15, 1827
Died Apr 12, 1859
"Dau of Rev. John &
  Sarah Keele Rushing."

Thomas Wheeler
Born ----
Died abt 1856/7

(Martha Miller & her brother
Nathaniel Miller, Orphans of
Joseph Miller & Wife,(a Beasley)).by-Charlie Adcock.

Martha Miller, wife of
Thomas Wheeler
Born ----
Died 1851

Robert C. Hoover
Jan 3, 1853
married to Dollie Bell
Oct 22, 1879
Died Sep 27, 1884

Fannie Bell, wife of
R. A. Hoover
Born Oct 7, 1846
Obeyed the Gospel
August 1866
married Oct 3, 1867
Died Jan 12, 1888

Our Little Archie,
age: 2y, 1m, 4d.
child of R. A. & M. F.
Hoover (no dates)

S. Haynie Bell, wife of
L. B. Bell
Feb 5, 1843
Oct 20, 1889
&
Bessie, dau of
L. D. & S. H. Bell
Dec 21, 1887
Sep 16, 1888

Willie C. Hoover
Nov 5, 1874
Aug 11, 1888

G. W. Bell
Mar 28, 1813
Sep 26, 1888
&
Eveline Bell
Jan 22, 1822
Feb 20, 1905
married Jan 20, 1841

J. C., son of
J. C. & E. B. McQuiddy
Feb 4, 1886
Mar 19, 1886

W. J. Bell, son of
G. W. & E. Bell
Oct 26, 1857
Jul 6, 1863

Sofronia Ann, wife of
J. E. Word
Jun 29, 1848
Jun 29, 1876

Charlie Smith, son of
J. E. & S. A. Word
May 14, 1876
Jul 7, 1876

13 OGILVIE CEMETERY   Map # 7
Located about 1 mile Southeast of Deason Tenn.

James Ogilvie
Oct 25, 1805
May 24, 1862

Jane C. Ogilvie, wife of
James Ogilvie
Mar 22, 1811
Jan 11, 1885

only these 2 graves.

14 PARKER CEMETERY   Map # 7
Located on Mink Slide Road at Webb Lane.

Walter E. Womack
Jun 6, 1921
Sep 10, 1927

Clara N., wife of
J. P. Jarman & dau of
J. & M. A. Parker
Aug 23, 1858
May 22, 1884

Lee Parker
1869-1946
(Thompson)

Many Old fieldstones, no
        inscriptions.

Many unmarked graves.

15 PHILPOTT CEMETERY   Map # 7
Located on Mink Slide Road.

Copied by Franklin Blanton

Tagya, wife of
W. A. Philpott
1842-1876

16 BIGHAM CEMETERY   Map # 7
Located about 3/4 mile South of Cross Road Church, near Webb Lane.

W. E. Bigham
Feb 14, 1852
May 18, 1852

Signs of other graves, but
no markers.

17 DIAL CEMETERY   Map # 7
Located near Cross Road Church.
All signs of this Cemetery has been destroyed, no markers of
                any make remain.

No Marker:
Jeremiah Dial, A Revolutionary Soldier,
Born 1758 in Dublin, Ireland
married Nancy Anna McDaniel
Died Sep 22, 1834
age: 76 years.

Several graves at one time.

18 CROSSROADS CHURCH CEMETERY   Map # 7
Located about 2½ miles East of Deason, Tenn.

James Falk
1854-1899
&
Sallie B. Falk
1854-1900

Emmett Falk
1875-1899

William S. Mashe
1847-1937
&
Henrietta Mashe
1858-1919

Mashe
(no other info)

Florence Adcock
1886-1917

Robert Winston Hill
1932-1933

A. J. N.(Naron)
(fieldstone-no dates)

N. (Naron)
(fieldstone-no dates)

N. (Naron)
fieldstone-no dates)

Sophia Lee Parker
Oct 6, 1873
Feb 24, 1895

Andrew C. Hoover
1855-1934
&
Mary M. Hoover
1857-1945

John W. Hoover
1881-1969
(Hoover FH)

M. C. Anderson, wife of
G. W. Anderson
Jul 17, 1839
Jul 29, 1883
age: 44y, & 12d.

Mary B., wife of
E. H. McCulloch
Jul 7, 1862
Aug 3, 1885

Maggie Falk
Nov 23, 1861
Jan 27, 1890
"Member of Christs Church
 over 9 years"

Mary F., wife of
J. H. Falk
Jan 20, 1833
Oct 22, 1890
"Member of Christ Church
 39 years"

Susie E. Neal
Born Jun 1, 1865
married to J. E. Clifford
Jan 13, 1889 &
Died May 29, 1901

William C. Loyd
Oct 10, 1872
Sep 17, 1917

Aaron Williams
Died Apr 16, 1891
age: 83 yrs.

Laura Falk
Dec 29, 1869
Jan 19, 1890
"Member of Christ Church
 over --(gone) years."

Infant Smith
1954-1954
(Gowen)

William Calut Murphy
May 26, 1870
Jan 19, 1884

Ella Captoller Murphy
Jun 15, 1859
Mar 23, 1910

Georgie Ella Murphy
Dec 7, 1887
May 1, 1912

Walter J. Murphy
1894-1942
(Thompson)

Annie M. Murphy
1888-1968
(Howell-Thompson)

Mrs. G. C. Keller
Jul 13, 1886
Jul 11, 1921
(Nannie M. Murphy, wife of
Grover Cleave Keller)

No marker:***
Grover Cleave Keller
Born Oct 22, 1885
married Nannie M. Murphy
Feb 10, 1906
Died (no date)

***by-Charlie Adcock

T. N. Coop
Oct 27, 1850
Jan 23, 1921
&
Mattie R. Coop
Jul 22, 1854
Feb 27, 1884
&
Walter W. Coop
Oct 24, 1875
Aug 13, 1904

Deallie Mai Faulk
1914-1915
"Dau of Cleve & Iry Faulk"

Glenda Gail Price
Died Dec 20, 1957
age: 4 yrs.

L. B., dau of
D. & N. C. Bowlin
Apr 15, 1872
Aug 3, 1874
age: 2y, 3m, 18d.

M. B.(could be Bowlin, as is
near Bowlin plot)

Davie, Infant Son of
H. & H. E. Coop
Died Jul 28, 1862
age: 3y, 5m, 2d.

Horatio A. Coop
Apr 22, 1814
Jan 7, 1890
&
H. E. Coop
Jan 11, 1818
Dec 7, 1896

NOTE:Following the above
graves are 5 graves, marked
only with fieldstones. One
is the grave of a Revolutionary Soldier, Horatio Coop and
buried there beside him is
his wife. Horatio Coop, Born
1756 and Died 1843. He was a
Pvt Wgn Maryland Militia &
Virginia. Nat. No. S3193.
(The above two are buried
in the South-east section
of the Walled-in Cemetery)

------ Stephen McCarty
Died Dec 14, 1948
age: 2m.

Charles Butner
(no dates)

J. D., son of
D. & N. C. Bowlin
Apr 22, 1863
Jul 22, 1864
age: 1y & 3m.

John A., Son of
H. A. & H. E. Coop
Died Aug 15, 1874
age: 29y, 11m, 13d.

James H. Coop
Dec 27, 1841
Aug 16, 1927
&
Susan S. Coop
Mar 31, 1841
Jul 31, 1908

Sam Dean Coop
May 29, 1875
Apr 20, 1933

Volney Parson Coop
Dec 12, 1901
May 1, 1903

Mattie R., dau of
A. J. & Rebecca Bingham
Born Jul 22, 1854
married to T. N. Coop
Dec 24, 1874 &
Died Feb 27, 1884
age: 29y, 5m, 5d.
"May God bless her two little
Boys, Walter & Tommie & her
two little girls, Georgie &
Lillie."

Joseph Faulk
1853-1913

Sara R. Faulk
1851-1920
"Given in memory of
Joseph & Sarah Faulk, by
Aline Faulk Ballard"

Milly Ann Whitworth
Consort of Jacob Whitworth
Died Sep 10, 1859
age: 42 yrs.

Jesse Albert Threet
Mar 6, 1884
Jan 19, 1919

Ann E., dau of
H. A. & H. Coop
Born May 29, 1843
married to R. S. Anthony
Feb 20, 1868 &
Died Apr 29, 1875
age: 31y, & 11m.
"May God bless her little
Boys, Willie & Oscar."

Emma Bell, dau of
James H. & Susan S. Coop
Jun 7, 1883
Aug 1, 1883

Ella Lee, dau of
W. & Susan Coop
Jun 6, 1873
Jul 8, 1879

Walter W. Coop
Wagoner 1 Tenn Inf
Sp. Am. War
Oct 24, 1874
Aug 13, 1904

#19 RAINWATERS CEMETERY   Map #7
Located about ½ mile Northeast of Cross Roads Church.

"Husband"
John Rainwaters
Born 1808
Died Apr 23, 1888

Polly Rainwaters
Jan 1, 1818
Nov 6, 1895

Bettie Adcock
1822-1915

5 or 6 graves, marked with
fieldstones, no inscription.

#20 SUTTON CEMETERY   Map #7
Located about 5 miles from Shelbyville on Fairfield Pike.

Evaline Sutton
Mar 20, 1840
Jun 14, 1876
age: 36y, 2m, 24d.

Arabella, wife of
Boney Sutton
Born Aug 11, 1839
Died Nov 13, 1886
age: 47y, 3m, 2d.
"Our dear Mother with 9
children, with 7 of them lies
south of her dead & not forgotten in glory. Professed

her hope in glory August 10,
1872 & lived a faithful member until her death."

No other markers were
found.

[Part of old John Sutton
place]

21 PARKER CEMETERY   Map # 7
Located about 1 mile Northeast of Hurricane Grove Church.

W. C. Parker
married M. A. Terry
Born Nov 1834
Died Feb 24, 1905

Timmothy Parker
Apr 10, 1804
Oct 25, 1888
age: 84y, 6m, 15d.

Tommy, son of
J. T. & S. J. Parker
Born & Died Jul 9, 1882

Columbus Parker
Mar 28, 1849
Jan 19, 1903
&
Mary E. Parker
Jan 20, 1851
Aug 18, 1909

Ella, dau of
J. T. & S. J. Parker
Oct 17, 1883
Jan 15, 1887

Gideon M. Still
1867-1946
&
Eliza A. Still
1875-(no date)

(James) Thomas Parker***
1864-1943

Laura C. Parker
1870-1938

Margaret L.(Lutie) Parker***
Jul 9, 1863
Oct 14, 1906

No Marker:***
Florence Parker
Died 1937
dau of E. W. & Martha Parker

Several unmarked graves.

Pheba Clementine (Parker)***
Apr 8, 1866
Dec 23, 1872
age: 6y, 8m, 5d.

Nehemiah Parker
Jan 20, 1806
Feb 7, 1876
age: 70y & 17d.

Harrett J., wife of
Nehemiah Parker
May 10, 1831
Jun 14, 1903

*** by Mr. Wynn Parker.

22 COOPER CEMETERY   Map # 7
Located about 1 mile Northeast of Hurricane Grove Church.

Charles Cooper
Apr   1786
Sep 9, 1823

Sarah Cooper
Feb 17, 1787
Apr 2, 1858

Mary C., wife of
W. J. Cooper, who died
Aug 28, 1847
age: 24y, 4m, 14d.

1 unmarked grave.

23 HURRICANE GROVE CHURCH CEMETERY   Map # 7
Located on Fairfield Pike at Hurricane Grove Church.

John S. Arnold
Arizona
Pfc 20 Engineers W.W.I
Oct 7, 1887
Apr 12, 1952

Samuel B. Arnold
Mar 5, 1855
Aug 5, 1926

Joshua C. Yell, son of
J. B. & R. A. Yell
Mar 20, 1870
Apr 20, 1892

Annie R. Jordan
1861-1941

Albert W. Jordan
South Carolina
Pvt 317 Field Arty 81 Div
W. W. I
Feb 20, 1895
Feb 21, 1947

Albert Luther, son of
Mr & Mrs Alex Watkins
Feb 1, 1935
Aug 27, 1935

John Alex Pendergrass
1914-1972

S. S. Arnold
Jul 20, 1824
married Elizabeth Medearis
Oct 12, 1847 & Died
Mar 31, 1901
& wife:
Elizabeth Arnold
Dec 3, 1825
Apr 9, 1897

Novela, dau of
J. C. & Hallie Yell
age: 3m.
(no dates)

Grover Cleveland Jordan
Pvt Bat. D 318 F.A.-A.E.F.
Oct 3, 1892
Jun 15, 1953

Dr. J. M. Jordan
1873-1941

Isom B. Pendergrass
1878-1953
(McFarlin-Thompson)

Maggie Pendergrass
1887-1936
(Thompson)

Several unmarked graves.

"Mother"
Mary F. Williams
Feb 2, 1846
May 21, 1907
&
"Son"
John H. Williams
Aug 20, 1877
Apr 7, 1907

Eddie B. McAdams
Sep 16, 1881
Jan 11, 1887
age: 5y, 3m, 25d.

Nannie B. McAdams
dau of Joshua & Rebecca Yell
Jul 28, 1854
Jan 23, 1883

Jack M. Pendergrass
1876-1968
(Howell-Thompson)

John Pendergrass
1951-1951 (TM)

Jennie Pendergrass
1907-1940
(Thompson)

J. F. Williams
Aug 6, 1887
May 4, 1944

Lula L. Williams
May 1, 1885
Oct 3, 1959

P. W. Norman
May 2, 1818
Nov 18, 1895

Adah A. Yell, dau of
J. B. & R. A. Yell
Feb 29, 1872
May 6, 1892

Frank Pendergrass
1940-1941
(Thompson)

Mary Pendergrass
1916-1941
(Thompson)

Charlie McCoy, son of
Ira & Hattie Pendergrass
May 7, 1939
Apr 8, 1941

Rev. C. W. Phillips
Feb 26, 1826
Mar 14, 1894

Eliza Jane, Consort of
C. W. Phillips
Dec 3, 1826
Jun 11, 1896

Samuel Phillips
Jan 1, 1787
Jan 12, 1864

Anna, wife of
Samuel Phillips
Jan 2, 1793
Jan 30, 1863

Lettie, wife of
J. P. West
Dec 31, 1868
Jun 27, 1904

Frank Hoover
Feb 15, 1889
Feb 20, 1905

Ethel S. Proby
Sep 28, 1885
Jan 31, 1904

Nora Lee Jarman
Aug 10, 1881
Feb 29, 1884

James Y. West
Dec 8, 1831
Jul 5, 1902

James C., son of
J. P. & A. Jarman
Nov 16, 1892
Sep 18, 1899

Lena Proby
Feb 22, 1877
Oct 15, 1880

Samuel W., son of
J. S. & S. J. Grider
Aug 23, 1878
Oct 14, 1878

T. C., wife of
J. Y. West
Born Sep 26, 1834
Died (no date)

Lettie, dau of
J. P. & A. Jarman
Apr 7, 1900
Apr 19, 1900

Bertha Proby
Jan 23, 1890
Apr 25, 1914

John Spencer Norvell
1844-1876

Annie J., dau of
J. Y. & A. S. West
Jul 16, 1872
Aug 25, 1872

Carrie Lee McGee
Oct 4, 1880
Jan 9, 1902
"Member of M.E.Church, S."

Rufus Y. Proby
Aug 10, 1852
Apr 19, 1914

William, son of
H. T. & P. E. Moore
May 5, 1874
May 12, 1874

Archie West
Apr 16, 1869
Jun 20, 1880

Isaac West
Nov 9, 1788
Apr 27, 1851
age: 62y, 3m, 18d.

Axie McGee Snelling
1875-1903

James G., son of
H. T. & P. E. Moore
Feb 4, 1878
Mar 21, 1878

J. W. Brown
Dec 4, 1854
Apr 3, 1877

Sarah D. West, Consort of
Isaac West
1793-Apr 21, 1865

Flavius J. Bomar, son of
William & Elizabeth N. Bomar
Sep 21, 1846
Sep 27, 1847

Izzabell, wife of
G. S. George
Nov 1, 1822
Jul 29, 1904

Annie Jane, Consort of
J. Y. West, & dau of
J. J. & Sallie Phillips
Feb 12, 1837
Aug 11, 1872
age: 34y, 5m, 29d.

Nancy A. Cobbs
Died Jul 28, 1849
age: 28y, 7m, 9d.

Flavius Josephus Bomar
Sep 17, 1870
Feb 1, 1871

Nancey E. Brown
Nov 28, 1829
Mar 1, 1869

William V. Roberson
Feb 11, 1851
May 13, 1870
age: 19y, 2m, 27d.

Francis Moore Shriver
Born in Rowan Co., N.C.,
Nov 7, 1795 & Died
Oct 23, 1878
&
Abraham S. T. Shriver
Born in Rowan Co., N.C.,
Sep 14, 1790 & Died
Feb 13, 1875
"He came to Tenn. 1800."

Louisa J. Holt
Jul 15, 1825
Jun 5, 1876

Nannie C., wife of
J. C. Morton
Dec 19, 1848
Oct 13, 1872

Tabitha, wife of
Morgan Smith
Aug 15, 1800
Aug 14, 1882
"Our Grand Mama."

John Moore
1760-Jan 6, 1842
age: 82 yrs.
(A Revolutionary Soldier)

Col. John A. Moore
Sep 28, 1798
Jul 11, 1868

Jacob S. Shriver
Aug 9, 1818
May 22, 1881
age: 61y, 9m, 13d.

Eleanor G., Consort of
John Moore
1760-Dec 9, 1851
age: 91 yrs.

Nancy Yell Moore
Jul 13, 1803
Mar 27, 1883

Infant Son of
Tom & Ola Stokes
1918

Erected by Rev. J. B. Stevenson
To the Memory of his Sainted
wife, Eleanor G., dau of A. &
T. Shriver.
Born Nov 4, 1821
Died Mar 16, 1866

Thomas M. Shriver
Jun 2, 1831
May 5, 1866
age: 34y & 11m.

Fountain Jones George
Sep 13, 1862
Feb 18, 1865

Archie S., son of
T. F. & F. Carrick
Dec 2, 1876
Nov 13, 1877

J. A. Bryan
Sep 23, 1826
(no date)

Frances W. Daniel
Died Jul 9, 1848
age: 45 yrs.

Rev. Anderson Sharp
Jan 19, 1808
Aug 20, 1863
age: 55y, 7m, 1d.

Nicy Sharp
May 9, 1809
Sep 12, 1879

William Sharp
Sep 6, 1786
Jul 26, 1848

Isabella Sharp
Feb 28, 1790
Jan 5, 1826

Many unmarked graves.

Theodocia C. Clagett, dau of
William G. & Theodocia Clagett
Mar 28, 1838
Aug 12, 1852

John D. Sharp
Jun 6, 1835
Oct 10, 1852

Many graves with field-
stones, no inscriptions.

See Addendum

26 AULT CEMETERY   Map # 7
Located about 1 mile Northwest of Phillipi Church.

Margaret Ault Jul 28, 1793 Dec 7, 1875	Mary Ault Jan 6, 1811 Jul 22, 1898	Martha Ault Sep 14, 1819 Dec 23, 1877	Esther Ault Apr 28, 1822 Apr 12, 1867

2 graves unmarked.

27 HORSE MOUNTAIN CHURCH CEMETERY (OLD) Map # 7
Located on the Horse Mountain Road at Horse Mountain Church.

Elijah Bomar* 1782-(no date - died ca 1860) Frances Bomar, Consort of Elijah Bomar Oct 12, 1788 May 24, 1852	Cornelius H., son of B. B. & C. F. Bomar Mar 4, 1846 Sep 23, 1862 * Native of Halifax Co., VA	Lieut. William McGuire and 1 Art Regt Cont'l Troops Born Mar 12, 1748 Died 1834 married 1777 (A Rev. Sol.) Many unmarked graves.	Mary Shirley McGuire Born Feb 17, 1762 Died 1845

28 MT. VIEW CEMETERY   Map # 7
Located on the Horse Mountain Road at Horse Mountain Church.

George Avery Arnold Jul 23, 1927 Jul 1, 1969 (beside this grave is a new grave, unmarked, 1975)	James H. Phillips Jan 21, 1891 Aug 25, 1961 & Ethel J. Phillips Sep 22, 1894 1974	Ernest Robinson 1866-1943 Daisy Robinson Alsup 1878-1950	Enoch S. Bingham May 30, 1883 Sep 4, 1956 & Cleta A. Bingham Apr 12, 1887 Feb 27, 1969
Newt Johnson 1867-1937 & Emma Johnson 1870-1943	Frances Arnold 1912-1957	George T. Bledsoe Oct 26, 1886 Oct 27, 1960 & Bettie P. Bledsoe Aug 26, 1891 ------------	Archie L. Hardison Feb 6, 1894 ------------ & Nim P. Hardison Jun 10, 1883 Feb 5, 1964
Ina May Robinson Harden 1898-1918	Estell Arnold 1918-1924		
Thos. Farris Arnold 1920-1942	"Father" H. A. Arnold Sep 12, 1850 Apr 10, 1915 &	Fred Bledsoe Aug 14, 1913 Jul 4, 1974 & Margaret Bledsoe Nov 18, 1927 ------------	John Thomas McCreery, Jr. Jan 19, 1908 Feb 7, 1974 & Elizabeth Jones McCreery Nov 27, 1907 ------------
Clyde Arnold 1922-1938	"Mother" M. E. Arnold Jan 10, 1854 Apr 10, 1915		
Ada Mash Hurt Jan 28, 1884 Dec 26, 1953		married Nov 6, 1965	
Jona Mash 1869-1958	George L. Bragg Oct 25, 1878 Apr 22, 1957 &	Baby J. T. Bledsoe Dec 21, 1947	Mary Alice Pruitt Aug 16, 1888 Aug 6, 1959
Willie Hurt Morgan 1909-1929	Lora Lee Bragg Nov 29, 1880 May 30, 1940	James W. Pruitt 1885-1950 & Dannie B. Pruitt 1888-1965	W. J. Pruitt Oct 10, 1851 Feb 9, 1915 &
James Luther Martin Apr 12, 1860 May 11, 1931	Martha L. Bragg Jun 26, 1916 Mar 26, 1917	John T. Pruitt May 6, 1878 Aug 21, 1969	S. A. Pruitt Dec 19, 1853 Aug 6, 1938
Thomas J. Stokes, Jr. Jun 22, 1910 ------------ "Son of Thomas J. Stokes & Viola E. Bomar" & Mary Cassie Stokes Dec 3, 1916 ------------ "Daughter of James W. Pruitt & Dannie B. Phillips."	G. F., wife of B. B. Bomar Apr 18, 1815 May 9, 1889 Horton Hurt Jan 6, 1911 Mar 18, 1925 Fannie McGee , 1st wife of J. W. Hurt Mar 12, 1874 Jul 5, 1905	Jessie B. Pruitt, wife of J. T. Pruitt 1878-1950 James E. Jones 1873-1948 Estella B. Jones 1886-1956 J. W. Hurt Jul 8, 1870 Apr 7, 1940	Alton Ray Robinson Jun 7, 1913 Nov 5, 1933 Cleaver Stokes 1855-1922

William McGee
(no dates)
Given in Memory by
Grandsons: Carney & Earl
Hurt

Mary C. Bomar, wife of
William McGee
1851-1909

C. S. George
Feb 18, 1864
Oct 31, 1931

Bettie, wife of
C. S. George & dau of
W. J. & S. A. Pruitt
Apr 17, 1872
Jan 24, 1898

Lena S. Burkhalter
Aug 27, 1872
May 25, 1907

Frances E. Shriver
Nov 14, 1869
Dec 28, 1905

Lily A., dau of
B. B. & Amy Shriver
Aug 13, 1880
Jul 24, 1904

Elijah T. Bomar
Mar 18, 1835
May 19, 1886
age: 51y, 2m, 1d.

Jennie A., wife of
E. T. Bomar
Jan 29, 1841
Mar 17, 1893

Elijah "Dave" Bomar
Mar 21, 1894
Jan 31, 1943

John Robert Bomar
Mar 20, 1856
Apr 29, 1935

Elizabeth "Lizzie" Blessing
Jun 17, 1892
Feb 4, 1957

S. K. Phillips
Apr 9, 1876
Jan 16, 1905

Dee C. Phillips
Apr 21, 1873
Sep 5, 1927
&
Blanche P. Phillips
Dec 28, 1882
Jun 15, 1966

Donley C. Phillips
Tennessee
Cpl 51 TC Sq AAF W.W.II
Aug 17, 1916
Aug 14, 1966

Dennis P. Phillips
Oct 3, 1910
Sep 18, 1939

Dennis V. Phillips
May 1, 1879
Apr 25, 1939

S. E. Phillips
Dec 10, 1859
Aug 15, 1929

Cassie E., wife of
S. E. Phillips
Oct 18, 1868
Apr 10, 1900

Kitty B., wife of
S. E. Phillips
Feb 29, 1870
Mar 22, 1910

Georgia A., wife of
S. E. Phillips
Dec 23, 1878
Nov 28, 1916

Samuel E. Phillips
Oct 25, 1903
Oct 31, 1903

Allen H., son of
S. E. & G. A. Phillips
Oct 25, 1914
Sep 4, 1918

B. B. Shriver
"Bud"
1841-1915

E. W., son of
R. & Margret Bomar
Jul 17, 1860
Jan 9, 1888

B. Bomar
Mar 14, 1829
Jun 13, 1909
&
Margaret Bomar
Jul 24, 1825
May 6, 1902

Don C. Shriver
Mar 31, 1817
Jul 13, 1893
&
Susan McGuire Shriver
Nov 10, 1816
Apr 9, 1905

Infants of
D. C. & Blanch Phillips
1910

Marvin M., son of
D. C. & Blanch Phillips
1925-1927

E. M. B. Norvell   and
Feb 7, 1813
Jun 18, 1892

Richard Pruitt
1903-1920

Nannie Pruitt
1878-1908

Lizzie Beattrace Bomar
Aug 1, 1908
Jun 17, 1910

J. B. Bomar
Jan 1, 1840
Jun 14, 1895
& wife:
Sallie Bomar
Nov 14, 1847
Jan 19, 1908

Mary Shriver, wife of
H. H. Rittenberry
Nov 19, 1871
Sep 10, 1906

R. G. Purdie
Jan 30, 1856
Oct 31, 1911
&
Laura B. Purdie
May 9, 1862
Jun 27, 1931

Allen N. Hatley
1856-1889
&
Carrie Newby Hatley
1866-1947

Thomas Walter, Infant of
R. G. & L. B. Purdie
Born & Died --- 4, 1889

William Marian Chitwood
Jan 11, 1856
Jul 29, 1883

Kate Chitwood Arnold
1862-1945

Robert A. Arnold
Dec 24, 1832
Oct 11, 1907
"Son of James H. & Louisa H.
Arnold." Given by Great
Grand Daughter Lois Arnold
Claxton.

Ellen A., wife of
J. B. Stevenson & dau of
D. C. & Susan Shriver
Aug 14, 1845
Apr 8, 1876

Mary B. Gibson
1907-1929

Lettie M. Bomar, wife of
J. W. Nobles
1898-1923

Jerusha Norvell
Aug 10, 1822
Sep 22, 1893

J. B. Bomar
Mar 6, 1825
Jan 6, 1897

Francis C. Bomar
Nov 12, 1827
Apr 9, 1902

B. B. Bomar
Dec 3, 1812
Jul 12, 1893

G. F., wife of
B. B. Bomar
(for dates see page 98)

M. B. Ayers
Jun 15, 1858
Oct 27, 1906

Sallie T. Ayers
Sep 28, 1861
May 16, 1924

Joe W. Ayers
Feb 6, 1895
Oct 25, 1961
&
Kathleen P. Ayers
May 30, 1897
Jul 7, 1973

Ava Ayer George
(no dates)

J. W. George
1820-1886
&
Eliza A. George
1842-1898

William H. George
1869-1943
&
Sallie B. George
1885-1966

Clarrie George
Oct 15, 1902
Oct 29, 1902

R. C. George
1938-1941

Tabitha Petway, wife of
Arch Y. Phillips & dau of
D. C. & Susan Shriver
Mar 1, 1852
Apr 2, 1881
age: 29y, 1m, 1d.

M. D. Bomar
May 5, 1872
Oct 24, 1919

Kythe C. Bomar
1880-1944

Baby Stokes
(no dates)

"Mother"
Nannie Pruitt Farris
Apr 28, 1913
Feb 4, 1975

S. C. Phelps
Oct 15, 1840
Oct 27, 1906

J. W. H.
(Child-no dates)

29 ARNOLD CEMETERY   Map # 7
Located about ½ mile North of Horse Mountain.

Elijah Arnold
Born Oct 6, 1795
Jul 29, 1869
age: 73y, 9m, 23d.

(Elijah Arnold's wife: Sarah,
 Born 1795 in N. C.,
 living in 1850. Elijah was
 born in N. C.)

Only 1 grave remain in this
Cemetery.

30 BROWN CEMETERY   Map # 7
Located Northeast of Shelbyville, on Fairfield Pike.

John H., son of
L. J. & A. A. Parker
Aug 29, 1852
Jun 11, 1853
age: 9m & 11d.

"Mother"
Mrs. N. C. Hill
Mar 8, 1834
Apr 8, 1884

"Our Mother"
Sarah K. Brown
Jul 15, 1815
Jun 2, 1873

Mollie T. Brown, wife of
S. L. Brown
Sep 23, 1842
Dec 6, 1888

"Our Father"
Henry Brown
Nov 10, 1800
Jun 29, 1873

Benjamin Brown
beloved husband of
Elizabeth Jane Brown, who
died May 29, 1857
age: abt 83 yrs.

Dr. Alfred S. Brown
Jan 22, 1847
Jul 3, 1876

"Our Mother"
Lucy F. Arnold
Jun 9, 1853
Sep 13, 1889

Many unmarked graves.

31 McADAMS CEMETERY   Map # 7
Located on Hurricane Grove Road.

E. F. M.
(fieldstone-no dates)

Amos McAdams
Sept 1st 1786
Aug 31, 1847
aged: 61 yrs.

Nancy Elizabeth, dau of
W. W. & Patia Ann Arnold
Oct 18, 1848
Dec 18, 1848

J. A. McAdams
  Co B
4th U.S. Cav.

John A. McAdams
Aug 10, 1816
Mar 6, 1875

Several fieldstones, no insc.

Several unmarked graves.

Elizabeth T. McAdams
May 30, 1826
May 12, 1880

32 DAMRON CEMETERY   Map # 7
Located about ½ mile South of Whiteside Road, on Murfreesboro Hwy.

No Marker:***
Peyton Henry Coats
Born 1802 & Died after 1850
& wife:Elizabeth Richardson,
Born 1807 & Died after 1850,
& 2nd wife: Sarah, who was a
Sister to 1st wife.

J. P. Damron   and
Apr 4, 1856
Jul 22, 1913

Julia E. Damron
Dec 25, 1856
Mar 10, 1886

Maybe 2 other unmarked
                        graves.

***by- Mr John Lane.

33 UNKNOWN CEMETERY   Map # 7
Located about ½ mile South of Shelbyville Airport, on Hwy.

1 unmarked grave.

34 HART CHAPEL CEMETERY   Map # 7
Located near the Shelbyville Airport, North of Shelbyville.

Mrs. Virginia Hart
Sep 3, 1827
Jun 8, 1863
age: 35y, 9m, 5d.
"We three, Father & two sons
do agree to meet you three
Mother & two daus in Heaven."
        AMRY   5849

T. H. H.
(Foot marker)

Corea Bell, Youngest dau of
John & Virginia Hart
Sep 17, 1858
Apr 19, 1863
age: 4y, 7m, 2d.

Catherine, oldest dau of
John & Virginia Hart
Jun 18, 1849
Apr 14, 1863
age: 13y, 9m, 26d.

Lillian C. Hart Overbey
May 31, 1866
Jul 8, 1893

Lucretia, wife of
Berry D. Holt
Mar   1823
May 16, 1863

Nathaniel B. Hart
Dec 24, 1824
Mar 7, 1880

John Hart
Born 1829
Died (After 1850 census)

Narcissa, wife of
John Hart
May 11, 1835
May --, 1888

James W., son of J.H.&
A.P. Hart
Feb 11, 1879-Aug 11, 1879

Catharine G., Consort of
Thomas Hart
Born in Wilksborough, North
Carolina, Mar 20, 1828, &
professed religion 1848,
Died Jun 24, 1862

***by Mrs. R.L.Patterson.

24 graves inside Wall of
Hart Plot.

Mort Lambert
Mar 10, 1885
Oct 15, 1953

Robert Lambert
1894-1952
(Gowen)

Jim B. Lambert
Died Mar 27, 1957
age: 77 yrs.

Mollie Burks Prince
1862-1954

James G. Reed
1881-1929

Ella Reed
1888-1936

Dwight J. Nelson
1946-1946 (TM)

Gene Ray Nelson
1948-1948 (TM)

W. J. McAnally
Dec 27, 1872
Feb 17, 1920

W. M. Halmontaller
1874-1935

Walter W. Halmontaler
1881-1921

Archie D. Halmontaller
1833-1913
&
Bettie Halmontaller
1843-1921

William H. Whiteside
Dec 8, 1840
Mar 25, 1923

Sallie Whiteside
1848-1914

Horace E. Sudberry
1879-1956
&
Bettie M. Sudberry
1877-1938

Roy E. Sudberry
Aug 3, 1902
Nov 7, 1919

T. H. C.   # 40
W. G. Heart
Feb 8, 1830
Aug 3, 1858
age: 28y, 5m, 5d.

Sarah Jane, wife of
W. G. Hart
Dec 25, 1838
Nov 4, 1878
"Member of C.P.Church."

George W. Overcast
1882-1950
&
Mary P. Overcast
1896-1930

David Overcast
May 16, 1924

Mary B. Overcast
Oct 30, 1921
Nov 19, 1922

Frank, son of
F. H. & C. Naron
Jun 15, 1905
Oct 17, 1908

Infant Son of
F. H. & C. Naron
Died Mar 9, 1902

Sallie Damron
Feb 22, 1865
Nov 21, 1927

Minnie May Ray
1880-1919

"Father"
F. M. Tucker
Dec 16, 1846
Feb 3, 1914
&
"Mother"
L. S. Tucker
Apr 3, 1843
May 22, 1922

Granville T. Tucker
1875-1942

Ada Tucker
Apr 25, 1880
Apr 29, 1959

Fannie Pearl Tucker
Jun 6, 1923
Dec 3, 1928

"Mother"
Malinda Painter
Jul 1823
Mar 5, 1907

Rachel Painter
1784-Jun 5, 1889

Jane Painter
Oct 30, 1847
Nov 17, 1885

No marker:***
James Hart
Born 1790
Died (after 1850 census)

Sarah Hart, Consort of
James Hart
Born in Orange C., N.C.,
Aug 15, 1786
Aug 3, 1860
age: 73y, 11m, 19d.

John W. Coats
Apr 7, 1859
Aug 22, 1938

Alice Coats
Feb 18, 1874
Mar 22, 1937

Baby of
Fred & Novella Coats
Jul 18, 1921

Rufus D., Infant of
R. H. & K. A. Reed
Born & Died Nov 11, 1926

George Overcast
1871-1943
&
Dollie Overcast
1884-19

Thelma C. Overcast
Jun 16, 1908
Sep 20, 1925

Mary M. Overcast
Aug 8, 1887
Apr 10, 1917

Walter Rufus Overcast
Apr 26, 1881
Sep 23, 1957

J. P. Reed
1832-1907
& wife:
Amanda Reed
1843-1912

James W. Harmon
Apr 12, 1843
May 5, 1912
&
Margarette Henley Harmon
May 30, 1851
(no date)

Harvy T. Painter
Mar 28, 1870
Jul 17, 1896
age: 26y, 3m, 19d.

L. F. Parker
Mar 10, 1860
Jul 5, 1880

Joseph L. Majors
Nov 14, 1832
Jun 26, 1860

William Shipley
1875-1938
&
Fannie Shipley
1875-1940

Burnes L. Shipley
1906-1919

Mrs. Cordie Neil
1868-1952 (TM)

John W. Neal
Mar 1, 1874
May 23, 1904

Caleb Neal
Feb 19, 1902
Nov 28, 1913

James H. Hart
Feb 11, 1847
Apr 22, 1902
&
America P. Hart
Mar 18, 1848
Jul 17, 1913

Anna Anthony Hanson
Oct 24, 1868
Jul 1, 1911

Infant Daughter of
Mr & Mrs Ed Delk
May 30, 1916
Jul 27, 1916

Golda Mai Thompson Everett
1886-1934

J. T. Bond
Jan 30, 1856
Feb 24, 1914

Clarence L. Sutton
1881-1940
&
Matilda F. Sutton
1883-19(no date, newspaper
          has date as 1961)

Lurley Florence Sutton
Jun 6, 1923
Dec 3, 1928

Mary Sutton
1946-1946 (TM)

Donald Lee Sutton
1947-1947 (TM)

Newsom Parker
May 22, 1868
Jun 20, 1903

Mattie Arnold Parker
1876-1945

John D. Parker
Tennessee
Pvt Co K 60 Pioneer Inf
W. W. I
Jan 3, 1897
Oct 29, 1968

David Whiteside
1785-1860
&
Louisa Whiteside
1812-1884

Joe Whiteside
1842-1912

Mary E. Whiteside
Jan 19, 1843
Jun 12, 1876

Tabitha H. Houston, wife of
R. W. Houston
Apr 4, 1840
Aug 2, 1861
"Member of the M.E.Church."

Anna Cora, Infant Dau of
R. W. & Tabitha Houston
Jul 25, 1861
Sep   1862

Rufus C. Overcast
Jan 1, 1853
Feb 16, 1898

Infant dau of
R. C. & S. R. Overcast
Dec 16, 1889
Dec 24, 1889

Cora B., dau of
R. C. & S. R. Overcast
Sep 8, 1893
Dec 12, 1895

Infant son of
R. C. & S. R. Overcast
Mar 22, 1897
Mar 23, 1897

Lewis Overcast
Nov 29, 1884
Apr 17, 1886

Arthur Overcast
Jun 28, 1883
Feb 28, 1901

Several unmarked graves.

R. F. Tindle
Co A
4th Tenn Mt'd Inf.

Sarahan Lane, Consort of
Harden C. Lane
Jan 25, 1829
May 7, 1862

Elizabeth Lain (could be Lane)
Jul 6, 1804
Mar 21, 1903

James M. Overcast
1846-1911

Susan Overcast
1841-1892

Jos. Nicolas
Co C
5th Tenn Cav

P. M. Overcast
May 3, 1884
Jul 6, 1901

L. C. Overcast
Jan 9, 1882
Sep 23, 1899

Infant Son of
Mr & Mrs P. M. Overcast
(no dates)

W. B. Overcast
Dec 4, 1839
Jan 19, 1922
&
Amanda Overcast
1844-1896

Wiley H. Overcast
1850-1930
&
Sallie L. Overcast
1851-1933

Burton Overcast
Feb 1, 1875
Mar 31, 1901

John D. Parker
May 30, 1834
Aug 15, 1895

S. E., wife of
J. D. Parker
Apr 23, 1840
Jul 14, 1872

James, son of
J. D. & S. E. Parker
May 27, 1865
Feb 15, 1868

Infant Son of
J. D. & S. E. Parker
(no dates)

C.J.(Crawford J.)Overcast***
Co C (Born-1847)
4th Tenn Mt'd Inf

F.C.(Franklin C.)Overcast***
Co A (Born-1843)
5th Tenn Cav

*** 1850 Census.

Little Tom, Infant son of
L. H. & Mattie Halmontaller
Jul 19, 1889
Jun 12, 1891

Clarence Halmontaller
May 21, 1895
Dec 27, 1918

Annie M. Tune
May 13, 1895
Apr 30, 1916

C. T. Philpott
Jun 23, 1813
Oct 4, 1896.
& wife:
Rebecca R. Hix Philpott
Oct 14, 1816
Aug 14, 1905

Joseph Jones
Apr 12, 1831
Sep 20, 1881
age: 50y & 5m.

Mary Bethna, wife of
W. F. McAdams
Sep 26, 1832
Aug 11, 1856

James R. McAdams
Feb 9, 1843
Jul 4, 1863

Rebecca Hooker
Nov 19, 1817
Aug 8, 1903

Annie Hooker
Aug 31, 1819
Jul 3, 1887

W. J. Swan
Jan 20, 1842
Dec 1, 1919

Nannie Swan
Jul 31, 1847
May 1, 1911

Martha Ann Henley
Mar 13, 1847
Mar 17, 1862

Mary Olive Henley
May 31, 1858
Jul 22, 1872

Thomas H. Tune
Apr 18, 1813
Oct 17, 1888

Mary Jane Haggard, wife of
Thomas Tune
Apr 10, 1832
Jul 12, 1885

Mary Lee, dau of
R. J. & F. R. Tune
Jan 19, 1878
Nov 20, 1882

35 BELL CEMETERY   Map # 7
Located about 1 mile West of Hart Chapel, Midland Dirt Road.

Samuel Bell
Jul 21, 1810
Converted Sep 29, 1839
Died Sep 10, 1847

Elizabeth M. Bell
Dec 9, 1813
Professed Religion Oct 1829
Died Jul 12, 1859

1 Child grave
(no inscription)

36 TUNE CEMETERY   Map # 7
Located about ½ mile North of Whiteside Church, on Midland Road.

John Tune
Born in Halifax Co., Va.
Mar 29, 1791 &
Died in Bedford Co., Tenn.
May 17, 1880

Mary Tune, wife of
John Tune
Apr 25, 1797
Jul 19, 1852

James C. Tune, son of
John & Mary Tune
Feb 18, 1820
Jun 19, 1855

Eva C. Tune, dau of
John & Mary Tune
Sep 8, 1839
Aug 3, 1884

Joe Eaton, son of

Born 8th ---, 1855
age: 1y & 27d.
(Broken)

Malinda C. Tune, dau of
John & Mary Tune
May 9, 1833
Jul 20, 1852

Charles, son of
John & Mary Tune
Sep 2, 1826
Jul 20, 1852

Enoch Williams
Mar 9, 1797
Mar 3, 1873

William Williams
Sep 8, 1790
Jan 21, 1859

Elizabeth Williams
Nov 4, 1798
Jun 15, 1875

Charles, Infant son of
W. T. & _____ Tune
Born -------
Died -------
(illegible)

37 HALL CEMETERY   Map # 7
Located about 2 miles West of Hart Chapel.

John A. Hall
Oct 12, 1810
Feb 28, 1865

Elizabeth M., wife of
C. H. North
Jul 9, 1859
Jun 14, 1878

5 graves with fieldstones,
no inscriptions.

38 PURVIS CEMETERY   Map # 7
Located about 2 miles West of Hart Chapel.

"His wife: M. M. Purvis &
May 15, 1827
May 25, 1870

M. E. Purvis   and
Nov 11, 1851
Oct --, 1861

J. F. Purvis   and
Apr 8, 1854
Oct   1857

I. J. Purvis
Jan 15, 1859
Aug 12, 1876

3 or 4 graves with fieldstones, no inscriptions.

39 ORR CEMETERY   Map # 7
Located on Hurricane Creek at Parch Corn Branch.

Mary Jane, wife of
W. H. Orr
Mar 1, 1842
Aug 13, 1865

About 25 other graves with
fieldstones, no inscriptions.

40 BURNS CEMETERY   Map # 7
Located on Hurricane Creek at Burns Chapel.

A. J. Goodrum
Born May 5, 1813
professed faith in God
Oct. 1833, married to
Matilda Cooper
Jan 2, 1834 &
Died Sep 15, 1878
age: 65y, 4m, 10d.

Matilda Cooper,
Born Jul 30, 1816
Died Apr 8, 1882.
married to A. J. Goodrum
Jan 2, 1834

W. J. Goodrum
Born Jun 26, 1852
married to Ella Sims
Dec 1, 1880 &
Died May 21, 1888
age: 35y, 10m, 26d.

J. W. McAnally
Sep 20, 1830
Jan 28, 1908

Margret J. McAnally
Oct 2, 1847
Nov 20, 1924

Charley Lafayett, son of
Dr. J. L. & M. A. Goodrum
Nov 26, 1879
Aug 22, 1882

James Arthur, son of
Dr. J. L. & M. A. Goodrum
Oct 20, 1873
Apr 4, 1885
age: 11y, 5m, 14d.

Marilyn Sullivan
1942-1942 (TM)

Maynard Ingle, son of
T. M. & N. L. Wheeler
Mar 1, 1910
Jul 4, 1910

Wilma Ruth Walls
(no dates)

John T. Gambill
1872-1949

M. R. Gambill
Jun 17, 1881
Jul 27, 1911

Annie Lou Gambill
Apr 14, 1909-Jan 26, 1912

Samuel A. Swoape
May 9, 1836
Mar 5, 1905

Edward W. Hall
1874-1942
&
Annie B. Hall
1880-1963

P. F. Cartwright
Feb 20, 1840
May 7, 1909

Z. A. Cartwright
Aug 15, 1844
May 16, 1920

Infant dau of
J. T. & E. L. Cartwright
Born & Died Aug 1899

Jessie Lee, dau of
J. T. & E. L. Cartwright
Sep 24, 1900
Oct 2, 1900

Carl F. Cartwright
Mar 27, 1908
May 21, 1909

William Carroll Orr
Feb 13, 1829
Nov 21, 1898
& wife:
Temperance Miller Orr
May 15, 1830
May 14, 1876
married 1854

John Fain Orr
Oct 30, 1854
Nov 22, 1854

Jacob T. Cartwright
Apr 30, 1868
Mar 3, 1949

Ella L. Nees, wife of
J. T. Cartwright
Jul 30, 1872
Oct 9, 1900

Nancy Ann Cartwright,
wife of J. T. Gambill
Oct 5, 1872
May 3, 1901

Infant of J.T. &
N. A. Gambill
(no dates

"Father"
S. P. McAnally
1869-1911
&
"Mother"
A.L.(Annie Laura) McAnally
1867-1953

W. M. McAnally
Aug 9, 1896
May 8, 1940

J. D. McAnally
May 4, 1901
Jul 23, 1931

Esther Clanton
1899-1941

Annie Blanch Clanton
Dec 13, 1918
Apr 24, 1934

Jacob Clanton
1938-1939

Infant Son of
Mr & Mrs J. M. Clanton
1933

Eva Clanton
1903-1926

Lorene Clanton
1926-1926

James, Infant Son of
C. B. & Montie Clanton
17 days
(no dates)

Charlie B. Clanton
1909-1936

Frank Clanton
1866-1940
&
Annie Clanton
1871-1944

Deary Clanton
Nov 1, 1916
Oct 8, 1932

Clarence, son of
C. S. & Mary Barbour
Aug 30, 1892
Apr 13, 1908

Ollie, dau of
C. S. & Mary Barbour
Jun 9, 1882
May 17, 1915

Charles S. Barber
Aug 10, 1856
Sep 9, 1917
&
Mary E. Barber
Feb 10, 1858
Jun 1, 1930

Peggy J. Barber
Jan 27, 1948

Mary Elizabeth Moran
1927-1952
(Thompson)

J. T. Whittemore
Mar 31, 1876
Nov 6, 1949
& wife:
Sarah Williams Whittemore
Jan 15, 1886
Feb 13, 1958

David A. Williams
1866-1943
&
Mary L. Williams
1874-1948

J. Elroy Robinson
Aug 25, 1887
Jun 29, 1937
&
Octia G. Robinson
Apr 18, 1892

Elizabeth Robinson
Jan 9, 1925
Feb 28, 1925

Matt M. Clanton
1876-1949
&
Fannie N. Clanton
1885-1948

G. W. Gregory
Feb 17, 1840
Oct 15, 1915
&
Sarah C. Gregory
Jun 20, 1850
May 6, 1925

James Gregory
1916

Bob H. Gregory
1854-1948
&
Tennie G. Gregory
1855-1942

Arthur Jetson, son of
R. H. & M. T. Gregory
Mar 8, 1886
Jul 31, 1889

E. Pressley Gregory
Jun 29, 1871
Jul 28, 1953
&
Elizabeth P. Gregory
Oct 27, 1868
Jun 9, 1952

Christine Gregory
Jun 1933
Oct 1933

William B. Barber
Oct 25, 1942

Allen D. Cartwright
Aug 7, 1888
Apr 28, 1968
&
Vollie L. Cartwright
Feb 14, 1889
Jun 26, 1966

Harry A. Cartwright
Nov 24, 1908
Jan 17, 1927

Sarah M. Spears, wife of
W. S. Swan
May 30, 1811
Apr 8, 1896

M. G. Phillips
Feb 4, 1836
Mar 28, 1920
age: 84y, 1m, 24d.

John A. Loyd
Jan 21, 1858
Jun 16, 1930
&
Mary J. Phillips Loyd
Sep 24, 1858
Sep 14, 1938

Arthur P. Puckett
Aug 26, 1828
Sep 17, 1917
&
Mattie E. Puckett
Mar 15, 1848
Apr 19, 1938

Willie Ann Puckett
Oct 1, 1872
Dec 23, 1960

Louisa C. Tribble
Jul 14, 1829
Apr 20, 1914

Cam R. Tribble
1848-1933
&
Nannie O. Tribble
1848-1929

Joseph M. Burnett
Jul 17, 1806
Aug 17, 1886
age: 80y & 1m.

James C. Burnett
Mar 22, 1829
Sep 12, 1885
age: 56y, 5m, 20d.

Harvey W. Burnett
Jul 15, 1841
Feb 22, 1875
age: 33y, 7m, 7d.

Charity, wife of
Joseph Burnett
Jul 5, 1808
Nov 17, 1893
age: 85y, 4m, 12d.

William T. Philpott, Sr.
Nov 23, 1885
Jan 20, 1971
&
Mary D. Philpott
Jul 27, 1895

Bascom J., son of
P. H. & F. L. Tribble
Mar 13, 1878
May 30, 1898

J. Summerfield Swan
Dec 26, 1876
Sep 4, 1912

Burrel Henley
1861-1923

Samuel H. Chambers
1855-1930
&
Mollie H. Chambers
1865-1942

Mary Lee Swan, wife of
J. F. Swan
Sep 15, 1878
Jul 20, 1900

John Arch McAnally
Sgt U.S.Army W.W.I
Jun 6, 1894
Jul 2, 1966

Infant Son of
Thomas W. & Mary J. Tillman
May 19, 1891

Louisa Hall Turner
May 21, 1818
Jan 29, 1909

Allen Brown
1868-1927
&
Roda Ann Brown
1857-1921

Luke E. Jones
Dec 20, 1850
Dec 21, 1910

Sarah J. Jones
Mar 20, 1848
Dec 6, 1914

Jasper B. Snell
Oct 12, 1875
Jul 19, 1906

R. W. Coats
Jan 1, 1829
Feb 24, 1914

Mary Frances, wife of
R. W. Coats
Jul 21, 1837
Apr 6, 1896

Bascom Johnston
1844-1928
&
Margaret H. Johnston
1843-1923

John C. Landers
1870-1947
&
Hattie M. Landers
1874-1938

William F. Neil
Oct 15, 1845
Nov 24, 1902

Charity A. Neil
1849-1939

James V. Neil
1875-1939

William D. Robinson
Sep 2, 1867
Apr 20, 1939

Tennie Johnson
1856-1936

Robert Byron Chunn
Apr 21, 1897
Dec 18, 1906
&
Eliza Irene Chunn
Jun 20, 1900
Jan 4, 1903

George W. Vannatta
Nov 1, 1846
May 7, 1918

Frances J. Swain, wife of
G. W. Vannatta
Oct 9, 1846
Mar 28, 1931

James Vannatta
Feb 9, 1811
Jun 28, 1888
age: 77y, 4m, 19d.

Jerusha, wife of
James Vannatta
Apr 3, 1818
Sep 5, 1907

"Dear Jack"
J. J. Vannatta, son of
G. W. & F. J. Vannatta
Jun 20, 1880
Nov 6, 1897

Eliza F., wife of
F. L. Jacobs & dau of
J. & J. Vannatta
Jun 23, 1853
Sep 23, 1879

James Clardy
Feb 15, 1782
Feb 7, 1866
age: 83y, 11m, 22d.

John Caswell Barber
1851-1939
&
Mary Jane Barber
1858-1941

Mitchel North Barber
Dec 7, 1909
Jun 3, 1915

W. R. Cartwright
1865-1925

Annie Cartwright
1873-1929

Raymond T. Cartwright
1892-1930

Samuel B. Mallard
May 21, 1850
Jun 16, 1927

Fannie H. Mallard
May 15, 1848
May 3, 1922

Mary V. Mallard
Dec 5, 1929
Nov 13, 1932

"Son"
James A. Cunningham
Oct 8, 1934
Jul 13, 1935
&
"Daughter"
Mary L. Cunningham
May 10, 1936
Nov 25, 1936
&
"Daughter"
Alta M. Cunningham
Mar 22, 1939
Nov 27, 1940

J. H. Henley
Apr 25, 1835
Dec 31, 1916
& wife:
Jane Clardy Henley
Mar 11, 1839
Jul 24, 1879
& wife:
Caroline Muse Henley
Nov 13, 1842
Feb 19, 1922

Peter E. Clardy
Aug 11, 1810
Jul 3, 1880

Catherine, wife of
P. E. Clardy
Dec 8, 1814
Apr 12, 1885

Francis Clardy, wife of
James Clardy
Mar 17, 1787
Jul 3, 1862
age: 75y, 3m, 16d.

William Coleman Jordan
Mar 16, 1868
Dec 10, 1927
&
Mary Etta Neil Jordan
Aug 31, 1871
Jan 19, 1959

Susie Green
1894
&
Hattie Green
1896
"Infants of D. W. &
Anna Green"

James P. Burnett
Feb 27, 1874
Jun 18, 1911
age: 37y, 3m, 21d.

Infant Son of
J. T. & K. G. Green
Born & Died Mar 15, 1902

Sophronia A. Harris
1832-1913

Mattie E., wife of
S. G. Gregory
Aug 29, 1878
Aug 17, 1905

Cecil A. Smith
1901-1941
&
Blanche C. Smith
1904-1969

Howard S. Smith
1927-1928

Guy A. Parsons, son of
J. W. & Belle Parsons
Sep 20, 1899
Jan 4, 1913

S. D. Green
Jun 10, 1836
Jul 17, 1907
age: 71y.

Harriett A., wife of
S. D. Green
Jun 14, 1843
Feb 1, 1880
age: 36y, 7m, 17d.

W. J. Green
Jul 14, 1865
Nov 27, 1915

Emma Stephens Duncan
1873-1947

Joe H. Threet
Aug 8, 1860
May 4, 1935
&
Mattie E. Threet
Feb 23, 1871
Mar 25, 1958

Audrey Louise Robinson
Nov 19, 1933
age: 1 day

(name gone) _____
Died 1958
(Thompson)

NOTE: The above grave is
      next to the following:
George Newton Thomas
1881-1956
(Cathron-Thompson)

F. A. Thomas
Dec 30, 1839
Feb 6, 1914
&
J. M. Thomas
May 9, 1840
Mar 27, 1928

Franklin L. Knott
Jan 11, 1841
Dec 20, 1885

M. J., wife of
F. L. Knott
Oct 5, 1839
Jan 11, 1875
age: 35y, 9m, 6d.

Fannie K. Knott
Jul 17, 1877
Aug 7, 1877

Dau of
F. L. & S. J. Knott
Born & Died Oct 15, 1880

Henry R. Knott
Dec 7, 1882
May 6, 1883

Willie Orr Knott
Sep 14, 1884
Oct 7, 1896

(name gone)
1874-1948 (TM)

William T. Jones
Jun 18, 1868
Jun 7, 1942
&
Laura M. Jones
Feb 17, 1873
(no date)

Alfred H. Hall
Apr 21, 1910
Apr 6, 1912

Robert N. Presgrove
Aug 3, 1898
Oct 21, 1898

John B. Robertson
Co B
1 Ala Cav
Aug 31, 1848
Feb 11, 1924

John G. Chambers
Sep 4, 1817
Aug 27, 1882
age: 64y, 11m, 23d.

Angeline Chambers
Dec 15, 1825
Aug 6, 1911
age: 85 yrs.

R. N. Chambers
1853-1926

Rachel Skidmore
Dec 27, 1788
Jul 6, 1868
age: 79y, 6m, 20d.

John Skidmore
Mar 27, 1826
Sep 5, 1855
age: 29y, 5m, 8d.

Allie Skidmore
1833-1915

Elizabeth H. Skidmore
Sep 5, 1820
Apr 3, 1891
age: 70y, 6m, 28d.

Isabella Skidmore
Apr 5, 1823
Jul 27, 1885
age: 62y, 3m, 22d.

James Haley
Virginia
Pvt Va. Militia
Revolutionary War
1757-1841

Edward Taylor Haley
Tennessee
Pvt 2 Regt West Tenn Militia
    War of 1812
1779-1858

Martha E. Mallard, Consort
of Eldridge T. Mallard
Born Aug 2, 1849
Professed Faith in Christ
August 1866
Died Aug 5, 1870
age: 21y & 3d.

William Alfred, Infant Son of
Eldridge T. & Martha E.
Mallard
Dec 28, 1869
Mar 21, 1870
age: 2m & 23d.

Infant Son of Eldridge T. &
Martha E. Mallard
(no dates)

J. W. Loyd
Jun 2, 1857
Jan 24, 1922

Eliza Ann Loyd
Nov 21, 1856
Jan 6, 1921

Jacob M. Clanton
Jan 4, 1901
Nov 11, 1973
&
Eva A. Clanton
Dec 20, 1898
Apr 8, 1975

Lillie May, dau of
J. H. & L. C. Rice
Jul 13, 1869
Oct 11, 1875
age: 6y, 2m, 26d.

Clarence E. Cunningham
Jun 12, 1878
Jan 22, 1926
&
Mary Sudberry Cunningham
Sep 27, 1882
Sep 18, 1963

Zelma A. Cunningham
Mar 31, 1903
Jun 12, 1905

Susan Jane Cunningham
1930

John M. Barber
Apr 12, 1820
Mar 23, 1912

Walter G. Glenn
Sep 23, 1881
Apr 10, 1900

Sarah C. Glenn
Jan 8, 1842
Mar 12, 1894

Thomas Gregory
1849-1930
&
Elizabeth Mallard Gregory
1851-1907

Minnie Myrtle, dau of
E. T. & Susan E. Mallard
Apr 13, 1882
Jul 28, 1883

E. T. Mallard
Aug 13, 1843
Oct 15, 1914

Susan E. Mallard
1848-1923

John Wood
Nov 4, 1795
Sep 25, 1854

Elizabeth Wood
Feb 27, 1805
Aug 18, 1883

J. B. Robinson
Feb 26, 1837
Feb 13, 1920
&
E. J. Robinson
Nov 5, 1848
Jul 7, 1906

J. T. Clardy
Jun 3, 1837
Jul 27, 1921

Martha F., wife of
J. T. Clardy & dau of
John & Penelopy Morgan Orr
Born Oct 9, 1835
married Dec 9, 1860
Died Feb 21, 1901

"Our Only Child"
John R., son of
J. T. & Martha F. Clardey
Apr 12, 1863
May 4, 1903

Mary E. Wallace
1866-1940

George W. Sudberry
Sep 1, 1855
Jun 29, 1939
&
Susan W. Sudberry
Nov 26, 1859
Apr 8, 1936

William F. Sudberry
Mar 4, 1885
Nov 14, 1906

Emmette L. Jordan
Mar 27, 1882
Aug 30, 1891

Mary Ann Chunn
Born Apr 1, 1851
Professed Faith
Aug 16, 1866
Died Jul 13, 1869
age: 18y, 3m, 12d.

Minnie T. Chunn
Jul 24, 1872
Sep 26, 1878

Robert W. Eley
Mar 11, 1852
May 18, 1906
&
Mary Losson Eley
Sep 4, 1850
Jan 21, 1876

Thomas Wood
Jul 28, 1829
Jul 31, 1853

Margaret Wood
Dec 4, 1838
Sep 14, 1844

John C. Wood
Dec 4, 1838
Jan 27, 1862

Juliette R. Pate
Feb 1, 1859
Feb 21, 1885

Nancie E., wife of
S. B. Mallard
Mar 12, 1855-Nov 1, 1875

Joe Burgie, dau of
J. H. & Mattie Threet
Jan 30, 1899
Dec 7, 1903
age: 4y, 10m, 7d.

William Buford Threet
Aug 11, 1889
Aug 15, 1974

Dorsey Burge
Apr 25, 1848
Jun 6, 1875

Lantha Clardy, wife of
Dorsey Burge
Mar 7, 1850
Aug 18, 1874

Louella Burge
Feb 15, 1873
Mar 15, 1874

"Father & Husband"
W. J. Chunn
Aug 31, 1821
Jul 30, 1897

Martha S. Chunn
Aug 30, 1823
Jul 21, 1905

William A. Jordan
Mar 3, 1841
Jul 23, 1893

M. Tabitha Barber
1868-1934
&
Annie Grace Barber
1898-1914
&
Sarah Fay Barber
1889-1891

W. T. Barber
Apr 11, 1808
Oct 28, 1882

Sarah Barber, wife of
W. T. Barber
Apr 7, 1811
Oct 9, 1883

John N. Barber
Aug 9, 1849
Sep 2, 1866

Margaret E. Barber
Dec 24, 1845
Jun 4, 1864

Susan L., wife of
N. W. Haley
Dec 12, 1834
Jun 12, 1903

Mollie, wife of
G. T. Parsons
Sep 10, 1861
Dec 2, 1883

Sarah J. Gwin
Mar 2, 1832-Aug 13, 1862

Addie R., dau of
J. W. & E. A. Loyd
May 18, 1883
Feb 21, 1890
age: 5y, 9m, 3d.

Raymond, son of
J. W. & E. A. Loyd
Oct 30, 1891
Feb 17, 1915

Mary L. P. Vannoy
Jan 18, 1829
Nov 3, 1870

Henretta Vannoy
Sep 3, 1855
Oct 11, 1877

Andrew Vannoy
Nov 30, 1783
Jan 25, 1869

Jane Vannoy
Jul 24, 1796
Feb 5, 1872
age: 75y, 6m, 12d.

James A. Vannoy
Jan 7, 1847
Nov 22, 1869

Frances J. Vannoy
Mar 8, 1847
Jul 27, 1863

Matilda A. Vannoy
Dec 13, 1850
Aug 27, 1868

NOTE: The following 4 are
on the same stone:
Jeremiah B. Booth
Apr 8, 1812
Nov 24, 1871
    & wife:
Elizabeth J. Booth
Nov 9, 1821
Sep 10, 1897
    &
William S. Watkins
Jun 17, 1848
Feb 1, 1871
    &
Jennie Lee Booth
Aug 8, 1865
Jun 1, 1875

Elizabeth McChristian
Apr 11, 1884
Apr 23, 1902

Elizabeth Hodges
Died 11 June 1850
age: 84 yrs.

John Wesley Feezor
Oct 25, 1844
Jan 2, 1852

Mary Jane Moore
1856-1926

Louisa F. Vannoy
Feb 20, 1862
May 25, 1862

Thomas J. Vannoy
Jul 1, 1857
Apr 2, 1862

Mary L. Anderson, wife of
Thomas Tune
Aug 26, 1820
Jul 1, 1862

Travis Eli Tune
Oct 4, 1841
Jun 6, 1859

    McAdams
(fieldstone-no dates)

    McAdams
(fieldstone-no date)

Infant McAdams
Born 6 Feb 1820
Died 19)ct 1820
(fieldstone)

Francis Virginia, wife of
J. S. Neeley
Nov 24, 1878
Feb 2, 1918

Infant Son of
J. S. & Francis V. Neeley
Feb 18, 1905
Feb 18, 1905

William B. Brown
Feb 26, 1814
Mar 1, 1892
age: 78y & 6d.

Charlott A. Wood, wife of
W. B. Brown
Dec 26, 1821
Jun 15, 1861

James T., son of
W. B. & C. A. Brown
Mar 25, 1850
Aug 19, 1 52

Mary Evaline B., dau of
W. B. & C. W. Brown
May 22, 1858
Sep 30, 1874

William S. Sutton
Mar 14, 1858
Aug 27, 1903
    &
Sarah Ivy Sutton
Apr 19, 1859
(no date)

James F. Sutton
Sep 17, 1889
May 13, 1903

Infant Baby (Sutton)
Born & Died
Aug 1, 1901

William H. Henley
Jul 16, 1897
(no date)
    &
Mattie C. Henley
Mar 18, 1897
Sep 4, 1963

No marker:***
Frances(Wynn) Miles is buried
near the graves of the
Vannoy & Vannatta graves.
No dates.

*** by- Mr John Lane.

John W., son of
Andrew & Rebecca A.L.Vannoy
Dec 21, 1852
Dec 25, 1852
age: 5 days

Elisha Collins, son of
C. T. & R. R. Philpott
Born Oct 14, 1866
age: 13 yrs.

Kittie Jane Philpott
Jun 16, 1897
Nov 10, 1898

James M. Philpott
1859-1938
    &
Louisa J. Philpott
1860-1902

James Kolk Philpott
Feb 12, 1890
Aug 15, 1909

Walter Allen Philpott
Sep 18, 1948
Sep 19, 1948

James R.(Riggs) Philpott
Jun 3, 1915
Jun 14, 1955

Frances E. Nowlin
Nov 24, 1881
Sep 15, 1886

Huldah A. Nowlin
Nov 6, 1883
Nov 19, 1885

John T. Nowlin
1835-1912
    &
Margaret E. Nowlin
1854-(no date)

Many unmarked graves.

many fieldstones, no
    inscriptions.

41 STEWART CEMETERY   Map # 7
Located behind the Fairlane Foods Store, near Josten's.

John Lane, son of John Lane
(A Commissioner who laid
 off Original Lots in Shelbyville, B ----, D abt 1847),
Buried here or McCuiston Cem.
(by- Mr John Lane)

Grayson H. Stewart
Born (broken out) 1808
Died Jan 1, 1860
age: 52 yrs.

This Cemetery is believed
to have been a Community
Cemetery, it is very large &
all Commercial markers have
been destroyed.

Many fieldstones, no insc.
Many unmarked graves.

42 JENNINGS CEMETERY   Map # 7
Located North of the Fairlane Estates.

Garrett Phillips
Apr 14, 1815
Mar 18, 1875

Charlotte, wife of
Garrett Phillips
Jun 1, 1816
Dec 13, 1889

Mary S., dau of
Garrett & Charlotte Phillips
Sep 7, 1842
Nov 21, 1869

Samuel T. Jennings
Mar 19, 1841
Jan 24, 1907
&
Louvicie Phillips Jennings
Apr 1, 1845
Jun 22, 1917

Infant Son of
P. G. & Minnie M. Jennings
Born Aug 21, 1898

Emma J. Stewart, wife of
R. H. Jennings
Jan 5, 1872
Apr 28, 1901
age: 29y, 3m, 23d.

"Mother"
Annie Marks Orr
1865-1914

T. C. A. Marks
Aug 8, 1864
Oct 1, 1891

Julia L., wife of
W. G. Rutledge
Mar 15, 1855
Jan 16, 1876
age: 20y & 10m.

Julia L., dau of
W. G. & J. L. Rutledge
Jan 11, 1876
Jul 16, 1876

Several unmarked graves.

43 BROWN CEMETERY   Map # 7
Located within the City Limits, at Fairlane Estates.

Ulysses S. Brown
1873-1951
&
Mary E. Brown
1881-1948

John F. Brown
Jun 13, 1829
Jul 31, 1896
age: 67y, 1m, 18d.
&
E. M. Brown
Oct 5, 1849
May 15, 1904
age: 54y, 7m, 10d.

S. S. Brown, Jr.
May 1, 1884
Jun 23, 1888

Nina Brown Victory
1912-1962

S. S. Brown
1852-1921
& wife:
E. A. Brown
1863-(no sign of grave)

Mary Brown Snell
1881-1964
(Gowen-Smith)

Infant son of
S. S. & E. A. Brown
Jan 8, 1887
Jan 30, 1887

Thomas J. Brown
Jan 5, 1816
Jan 11, 1885
age: 69y & 6d.

Elizabeth Jane, wife of
Thomas J. Brown
Mar 7, 1816
Jan 31, 1888
age: 71y, 10m, 11d.

Infant Son of
S. S. & E. A. Brown
Dec 8, 1887
Dec 14, 1887

George W. Brown
1877-1949

G. W. Brown
Aug 5, 1841
Jan 25, 1915
& wife:
Margaret Jane Temple Brown
May 31, 1845
Dec 15, 1891

Emily Elizabeth, 2nd wife
of G. W. Brown
Jun 15, 1860
Oct 6, 1933

James L. Brown
1906-1934

Mary E. Brown
1883-(no date)

44 PHILLIPS CEMETERY   Map # 7
Located West of the Fairlane Estates, City. ·
(This Cemetery has been destroyed and no signs remain)

No Marker:***
Mathew James Phillips
Born Jun 29, 1828
Died Nov 29, 1908
married to Amanda Robinson
Jan 10, 1855

*** by Mrs. Carlyle Langley,

No Marker:***
Amanda Robinson, wife of
Mathew James Phillips
Born-(no date)
Died Oct 11, 1900

(Information taken from
Phillips Family Bible Record.)

No Marker:***
Adolphus J. Phillips
Born Jan 28, 1857
Died Nov 2, 1870

No marker:***
Tennessee Phillips
Born Apr 15, 1870
Died Mar 30, 1898

No marker:***.
Mary M. Phillips
Born Mar 23, 1864
Died May 23, 1901

45 McCUISTON CEMETERY   Map # 7
Located about 1 mile North on Nashville Dirt Road.

Sarah McCuiston, dau of
Benjamin & Sarah McCuiston
Feb 2, 1816
Jan 18, 1836
age: 19y, 11m, 16d.

Ann McCuiston
Died Sep 30, 1819
age: 2 yrs.

Sarah McCuiston, dau of
Thomas & Ann McCuiston
Jan 17, 1766
Sep 1821

Benjamin F. McCuiston, son of
Benjamin & Sarah McCuiston
Jan 9, 1814
Aug 29, 1841
age: 27y, 7m, 20d.

Benjamin McCuiston
Aug 8, 1772
Nov 4, 1842
age: 70y, 2m, 26d.

Thomas McCuiston, son of
Samuel McCuiston
Born 1808 & departed this life
Dec 11, 1829
age: 21 yrs.

Ann M. McCuiston, dau of
Benjamin & Sarah McCuiston
Nov 5, 1811
Jan 28, 1813

Frances E., dau of
J. C. Whitworth
Jul 13, 1833
Oct 21, 1834

Susan G. Chunn, dau of
Sarah McCuiston
Nov 19, 1803
Jan 19, 1822

Jasper Newton Williams,
Aug 3, 1835
May 21, 1839, "Grandson of
Jacob & Cynthia Whitworth"

	On One Side:	and	On Reverse Side:
		Sacred to the Memory of	

On One Side:		and Sacred to the Memory of	On Reverse Side:
James McCuiston	Sarah Behol	Thomas McCuiston	Ann Moody
Thomas McCuiston	Ann Moody	Dec 17, 1731	May 17, 1732
Robert	Elizabeth McWhorter	Dec 9, 1783	Sep 30, 1819
Joshua McCuiston	Mary Elizabeth O'Neal	"Son of James McCuiston &	"Wife of Thomas McCuiston
Noah Wesley McCuiston	Elizabeth Jordan	Sarah Behol"	& Dau of Thomas Moody &
Charleen McCuiston	Floyd Garwood		Jean McCuiston"
Robert Jordan Garwood	Theresa Testman		

46 WEBB CEMETERY   Map # 7
Located about 3 miles Northwest of Bell Buckle, Tenn.

Benjamin Webb	Elizabeth Whiteside Webb,	Benjamin Franklin Webb	Anderson Miller Webb
Born June 16, 1792	dau of John & Mary Reeves	Jan 28, 1825	Jul 19, 1827
married Elizabeth W. Reeves	Born July 21, 1796	Oct 8, 1889	Jun 7, 1870
Sept 26, 1821, An Elder in	married to Benjamin Webb	aged: 64 yrs.	
the C. P. Church 60 years.	Sept 26, 1821. Professed	"A Brave & faithful Officer	
Served his Country in the	Religion & joined the C. P.	in C.S.Army."	
Indian Wars of 1812 and 1818.	Church Sept 1832 &		
Died June 18, 1884	Died Jan 9, 1858.		
aged: 92 yrs & 2 days.			

1 DAVIS CEMETERY   Map # 8
This Cemetery is located about 1½ miles Northwest of Bell Buckle, Tennessee.

Elnathan Davis	Rebeca Davis, wife of	Mary E. Davis	Copied by John A. Joyce
Born 1794	Elnathan Davis	Born Aug 9, 1822	
married Jan 15, 1817	Born 1797	Died Feb 1864	
Died Aug 4, 1856	Died Nov 12, 1884	married Feb 20, 1851	
		(to Elnathan Davis, II) by Eds.	

2 BEACHBOARD CEMETERY   Map # 8
Located about 2 miles North of Bell Buckle, Tenn.

Rebecca Creecy	J. R. Arnold	R. W. Beachboard	Dr. Jones Beachboard
1813-1848	Feb 20, 1854	Aug 29, 1819	Jul 27, 1854
age: 35 yrs.	(no date)	Sep 15, 1876	Nov 26, 1898
	& wife:	& wife:	&
John Nelson	Susan E. Beachboard	Elizabeth Arnold	Lula Beachboard
1776-1858	Nov 22, 1860	Feb 11, 1834	Died May 18, 1907
age: 82 yrs.	Sep 6, 1917	Jul 12, 1906	(no age given)
Susan Nelson	Mary Ruth, dau of	Leslie Beachboard	Robert N. Beachboard
1775-1857	J. R. & S. E. Arnold	Jun 24, 1905	Jan 23, 1886
age: 82 yrs.	Feb 12, 1893	Jun 6, 1906	Nov 21, 1911
	Nov 28, 1917		
		About 10 graves unmarked.	

3 MANLEY CEMETERY   Map # 8
Located on Hatchett Hollow Road, North of Bell Buckle, Tenn.

Reuben Manley	------- Manley	James H. Brandon, son of	John Temple Brooks
Oct 14, 1782	Jan 17, 1783	H.--(broken)	Died Sep 1, 1859
Oct 7, 1854	Jul 25, 1827	Co. F --- Tenn Regt.	age: 28 yrs.
		Died --- 30, 1862	
Martha Manley		age: 19 yrs.	
Nov 23, 1801			Many unmarked graves.
Feb 1, 1858			

Annie Peacock
Dec 25, 1852
married J. M. Freeman
Dec 25, 1872
Died Sep 18, 1882

NOTE: Beside the above grave,
1 adult, 3 Infant graves, &
1 adult grave, unmarked. Ed.

"Our Son"
Born & Died March 1882
J. M. & A. F. Freeman

"Our Son"
Born & Died June 1875
J. M. & A. F. Freeman

Burrell Featherstun
Born of Jessee & Catherine
Featherstun, in Buncombe Co.,
N. C., Oct 7, 1791 &
Died May 27, 1868
&
Henrietta Featherstun,
Consort of Burrell Featherstun
& Born of Robt. & Mary Smith
Mar 5, 1793
Mar 30, 1868

Virginia W. Featherstun, dau
of Burrell & Henrietta
           Featherstun
25th Dec 1813
7th Feb 1831
age: 17y, 1m, 12d.

John W. Peacock, son of
Thomas J. & Mary S. Peacock
Who was Born 1st Feb 1840
aged: 4y, 5m, 9d.

Infant Son of Thomas J. &
Mary S. Peacock
Died 28th Aug 1840
age: 1m.

Henrietta S. Lamb
Oct 12, 1847
Dec 28, 1933

Virginia Belle Lamb
Nov 21, 1870
Aug 5, 1889

Several fieldstones, no insc.

Henritta S. Peacock, dau of
Thomas J. & Mary S. Peacock
Who died 7th Feb 1840
age: 2y, 5m, 14d.

Sophia C. Peacock
Died Aug 26th 1843
age: 2m & 23d.

Sadie Cooper, dau of
W. J. & S. R. Hoover
Born & Died Feb 7, 1881

James Hervey, Infant son of
W. H. & Hettie V. Klyce
Jun 9, 1887
Jan 16, 1888

"Father"
William J. Peacock
Dec 15, 1810
May 6, 1881
     &
"Mother"
Katherine Thorne Peacock
Jan 11, 1822
Nov 23, 1902

Many unmarked graves.

Mrs. Mary S. Peacock, late
Consort of Thomas J.
Peacock & Dau of Burrell
Featherstun & Henrietta
Featherstun, who departed
this life Jul 5th 1848
age: 31y, 5m, 2d.

S. E., Infant dau of
W. J. & S. E. Peacock
May 8, 1840
Jul 26, 1840

Sophia E. Peacock, late
Consort of William Peacock
& dau of Burrell & Henrietta
Featherstun
Sep 10, 1815
May 24, 1840

"Father"
George W. Ivey
1833-1863
     &
"Mother"
Mary E. Ivey
1837-1908

Here lies Mary Norvell,
She died the 14th of
February 1813, in the 78
or 79 year of her age.

Margret Norvell
Jun 25, 1808
Nov 5, 1818

Several unmarked graves.

abt 9 visable graves, no insc.

Nancy M. Yell
May 21, 1837
Died of Typhoid fever
Jul 16, 1854
age: 17y & 15d.

Dr. Willis Pruett
Apr 16, 1826
Mar 20, 1858

"Mother"
Arsena E. Pruett
Nov 29, 1823
Jun 19, 1882
age: 58y 6m, 21d.

Eugene Avery, son of
Dr. Willis & Arsena E.Pruett
Feb 19, 1857
Apr 14, 1857

Susan G. Cooper, Consort of
W. F. Cooper
Sep 12, 1817
Jul 5, 1851
age: 33y, 9m, 23d.

William Knott
Mar 4, 1774
Feb 28, 1828

Elizabeth Knott
Sep 21, 1784
Oct 21, 1854

Hugh McCrory
Dec 25, 1819
May 12, 1848

Eliza McCrory
Died Feb 28, 1859
age: 34y & 10m.

Sallie P. Sparkman, dau of
Hue & Martha McCrory
Aug 7, 1846
Jul 27, 1872

Ann McCrory
Died Jan 22, 1864
age: 73y, 3m, 11d.

John McCrory
Died Oct 15, 1874
age: 86y, 8m, 7d.

Sarah Ann Warner, Consort of
Richard Warner & dau of
John & Elizabeth Sutton
Died 13th of Mar 1825
age: 27y, 3m, 21d.

Arraminta, dau of
Richard & Sarah Ann Warner
Died Jul 3, 1824
age: 3y, 1m, 10d.

W. & B.
(Rock Slab, no dates)

A. J. L.
(Rock Slab, no dates)

I. L. Sparkman, son of
Newborn & Lidia Sparkman
Jun 21, 1841
Sep 19, 1876

Leander Sherman Johnson, son
of D. H. & Lucy Johnson
Apr 19, 1834
Jul 25, 1850

Mary R., dau of
John & Elizabeth Sutton
Apr 5, 1819
Jul 28, 1826

Henrietta S., dau of
Richard & Sarah Ann Warner
Died 11th of Sept 1827
age: 8y, 11m, 6d.

Elizabeth Sutton, Consort
of John Sutton
Died 24th of Oct 1829
age: 50y, 8m, 3d.

Robert P., son of
R. D. & Matilda Rankin
Dec 3, 1858
Apr 6, 1863

Amos White & Margaret Albria,
Infant Son & Dau of
R. D. & M. Rankin
Feb 24, 1855
Jan (deep in ground)

Maggie Berry, dau of
W. R. & N. A. Muse
Apr 4, 1872
Mar 12, 1880

"Our Babies", was Born
Dec 6, 1868
Died Apr 30, & May 26, 1869
W. R. & N. A. Muse

Mary Reeves Thomas
Dec 28, 1803
Aug 18, 1885

Little Albert, son of
D. G. & Laura T. Rankin
Jun 7, 1877
Apr 21, 1882

Sadie Hollins, dau of
W. T. & Sallie Rankin
Feb 3, 1885
Nov 17, 1885

Sallie Hollins Hare
  "Mama"
Jun 11, 1855
Sep 4, 1946

William B. Sutton, son of
John & Elizabeth Harris
Sutton
Jul 12, 1824
married Catherine Suttle
Jul 10, 1860 & Elizabeth
Alexander, Nov 17, 1885
Died Aug 12, 1888

William Thomas, Sr.
Jan 31, 1807
Mar 29, 1861

Jane McCrory Thomas
May 28, 1816
Oct 1, 1882

Infant dau of
W. & Jane Thomas
(no dates)

Infant Son of
W. & Jane Thomas
(no dates)

William Thomas, Jr.
Feb 6, 1860
Dec 24, 1861

James Scruggs
May 13, 1809
Dec 29, 1879
age: 70y, 7m, 16d.

M. B., son of James
& Jane Scruggs
Dec 19, 1844
Jul 10, 1846
age: 1y, 6m, 21d.

Malinda Linch
Mar 1, 1809
May 28, 1875

Granville H. Frazer
Jan 27, 1803
Feb 23, 1868
age: 65y & 27d.

Jane T. Frazer
Mar 13, 1807
Aug 7, 1833
"The youngest dau of
  Hugh & Jane Frazer."

W. R. Fields
Jan 8, 1845
Feb 16, 1921

Sue Fields
Oct 18, 1845
Jan 16, 1927

B. G. Fields, Jr.
1855-1880

B. G. Fields, Sr.
1822-1878

Mrs. B. G. Fields
1823-1915

Orville Henslee
Jan 22, 1822
Dec 17, 1910

J. L., son of
R. A. & J. L. Wright
Jan 13, 1884
Jul 28, 1884

R. D. Rankin
Mar 1, 1811
Jan 29, 1899
   &
Matilda Rankin
Nov 1, 1817
Jun 1, 1900

Edward Fanning Mitchell,
Infant Son of Samuel &
Sarah Jane Mitchell
Nov 3, 1834
Feb 16, 1836

Caroline M. M. Davis, dau of
John & Caroline Davis
Jul 28, 1822
Jul 2, 1856
age: 34 yrs.

William Norvell
Apr 20, 1768
Jun 26, 1833

Colbert P. Harrison, son of
Thos. D. & Emily M. Harrison
Jul 29, 1851
Jul 3, 1852
age: 11m & 4d.

Elisha M. Hopper
24 Dec 1811
 9 Jan 1843

John Taylor
Apr 14, 1778
Jun 8, 1856
Age: 78y, 1m, 22d.

Joseph Taylor
Died Jan 8, 1883
age: 57 yrs.

Sallie Taylor
Mar 18, 1831
Sep 14, 1901

Salie D. Taylor
Mar 25, 1845
Mar 28, 1874

Elvirah Taylor
Jun 8, 1823
Feb 23, 1894

Thursey Taylor
Aug 4, 1829
Jan 30, 1895

Ellenor Taylor
Oct 26, 1832
Feb 23, 1895

Joanah, wife of
T. A. Ragsdale
Jun 24, 1825
Jul 12, 1893

Charlie Skeen
1881-1886

D. H. Skeen
1823-1886

Elvira Frazor
1900

Tommie J., Jr., son of
Thomas J. & M. A. Ogilvie
Died Dec 6, 1883
age: 1y, 10m, 8d.

Josiah H. Maupin
was born Aug 16, 1827
and died Nov 14, 1867

Susan F. Maupin
Jul 3, 1841
Oct 29, 1864

Annie Fugitt, wife of
S. M. Lynch
Apr 10, 1848
married Jan 28, 1878
Died Jan 27, 1883

Sally Campbell Lad Majors,
dau of Robert H. & Sarah C.
Majors
Born (Broken away)
Died (Broken away)

Mary E., dau of
James & Jane Scruggs
Born Jan 18, ----(gone)
Died May 9, 1840

John H. Vaughn
May 18, 1825
Mar 23, 1898
   &
Mary J. Vaughn
Dec 26, 1834
Feb 26, 1920

Kate Alford
1865-1943

Hensley Orville
Nov 7, 1844
Dec 19, 1890
   &
Mary E. Orville
Oct 18, 1847
Feb 9, 1895

B. F. Smalling
Nov 24, 1824
Dec 3, 1903

Ann Fisher, wife of
B. F. Smalling
Jan 13, 1831
Feb 16, 1891
age: 60y, 1m, 3d.

Bettie A. Smalling
Nov 1, 1859
Aug 18, 1912

Ben F. Smalling
1856-1917

James M. Smalling
1852-1926

Merriel Asenith, wife of
C. W. Smalling , born
Oct 20, 1859 in Napa Co.,
Cal., Died Jan 31, 1886
age: 27y, 1m, 11d.

Lebinda B. Linch
Dec 12, 1824
Mar 11, 1914
"Member of C. P. Church".
   &
Tennessee R. Linch
Aug 1, 1853
Jul 30, 1873

Gray Linch
Apr 13, 1788
Oct 22, 1872

Hassie May, dau of
J. B. & M. F. Howland
Died Nov 18, 1880
age: 1m & 4d.

Maggie M., wife of
B. F. Ransom & dau of
A. D. & Jane M. Fugitt
Apr 5, 1846
Feb 2, 1882

Robert H. M. , Infant son
of Thos. D. & Emily M.
Harrison
Sep 9, 1848
Jul 9, 1849
age: 10m.

Dody, son of
T. J. & Cassie Peacock
Died Sep 4, 1872
age: 17 Y 25d.

Nehemiah Suggs
Jan 14, 1809
Nov 10, 1867
age: 58y, 9m, 26d.

Launny, Consort of
N. Suggs
Jun 22, 1811
Apr 30, 1857

Louise "Lou" Johnson Gilmore
Apr 10, 1857
Apr 12, 1881

William Prestridge Johnson
Apr 28, 1833
Apr 30, 1895

Nancy J. Johnson
Jul 22, 1839
Mar 19, 1907

Joshua P. Johnson
Jan 4, 1881
Apr 11, 1901

Charles E. Sutton
1833-1915
&
Ann E. Sutton
1844-1913

Sallie S. Sutton
May 21, 1869
Jul 8, 1885

Ellis W.(William) Sutton
Jul 1, 1837
May 13, 1884
&
Sallie B., dau of
A. D. & Jane Fugitt
Jun 16, 1840
Dec 13, 1882

Ada Ella, dau of
E. W. & S. B. Sutton
age: 1m & 16d.
(no dates)

Martin Hancock
Aug 27, 1798
May 6, 1886

Mary Blair, wife of
Martin Hancock
Jun 21, 1803
Sep 21, 1884

B. M. L.
(foot marker)

William Linch
May 13, 1811
Jan 19, 1874

Susannah C., Consort of
William Linch
Jun 18, 1823
Sep 23, 1849

Infant Son of
William Susannah C. Linch
Sep 20, 1849
Sep 20, 1849

Nancy T., dau of
William & Susannah C. Linch
Jan 29, 1842
Sep 23, 1849

W. F. Cooper
Apr 17, 1818
Mar 4, 1862

"Father"
M. S. Gilmore
Apr 24, 1845
Aug 6, 1917
age: 72y, 3m, 13d.
&
"Mother"
Mattie J. Gilmore
Feb 13, 1851
Mar 25, 1896
age: 45y, 1m, 12d.

W. E. B. Epps
Feb 23, 1825
Jan 8, 1892
&
M. A. Epps
Aug 31, 1828
May 2, 1904
&
D. S. Epps
Jun 30, 1857
Jun 15, 1878

John A. Smith
Oct 27, 1855
Sep 3, 1934

Mattie W. Smith
Dec 28, 1862
Mar 21, 1914
(her maiden name: Chambers)

Nannie J. Frazer, wife of
James F. Anthony
Born Sep 10, 1851
Died near Nashville
Aug 19, 1886

Mattie Ida, dau of
James F. & Nannie J. Anthony
Feb 2, 1884
Jun 21, 1884

Lizzie, dau of James F. &
Nannie J. Anthony
Sep 17, 1877
Dec 5, 1877

M. E. L. (Vault)
(no dates)

G. C. Fugitt
Born Aug 10, 1838
Was a Member of 2nd Tenn.
Regt. C.S.A. & was killed
at the Battle of Shilo
Apr 6, 1862

Ada E. Fugitt, dau of
A. D. & Jane M. Fugitt
Jun 3, 1856
Oct 31, 1876

John N. Fugitt
Born Jan 30, 1842
was a member of 2nd Tenn.
Regt. C.S.A. &
Died Dec 8, 1863

James William, son of
G. H. & F. M. Johnson
Jan 16, 1861
Jan 21, 1879

John Thomas
Nov 17, 1816
Aug 28, 1878

Sarah H. Thomas
Dec 21, 1822
Sep 18, 1892

"Brother"
Clayton A. Thomas
Aug 10, 1849
Aug 25, 1911

John McCrory Thomas
Oct 12, 1855
Sep 25, 1868

Sue G. Thomas
Sep 4, 1852
Sep 25, 1882

Charlie Sutton, wife of
A. C. Frizzell
Oct 2, 1852
Jun 8, 1890

Jessee Frizzell, son of
Arch C. & Charlie E. Frizzell
Apr 29, 1880
Jan 20, 1883

Dr. Charles Finley Sutton
Born in Prince William Co., Va.,
May 24, 1803
Jul 30, 1872
age: 69y, 2m, 6d.

Matt. Sutton, son of
Charles F. & Francis H. Sutton
May 27, 1833
Aug 11, 1833

Q. T. Sutton, son of
John & Loues Sutton
May 26, 1836
Oct 12, 1857

Mrs. M. A. Conn
Died Dec 3, 1889
age: 83 yrs.

Jesse B. Gordon
1841-1892
&
Vandalyn E. Gordon
1850-1917
"Erected by Son:T.M.Gordon."

Reuben Gordon
(no dates- in 1850 census,
        he was 38 yrs)
&
Mary Gordon
(no dates)
"erected in their memory
byGreat- Granddaughter,
Eula Gordon."

Mrs. Bettie S. M. Kelly,
wife of A. J. Kelly
Born Oct 4, 1849
joined the Baptist Church
in 1866, married Jan 30,1873
Died Jan 11, 1881.

John H. Wilson
Mar 6, 1836
Feb 2, 1871

Rebecca A., wife of
John H. Wilson
Dec 2, 1840
Oct 5, 1894

Mary Lee, wife of
Alexander Lee
Apr 28, 1805
Mar 10, 1870

A. Arnold
Mar 25, 1844
Dec 14, 1909
& wife:
Mary J. Mullins Arnold
Apr 25, 1851
(no date)

"Father"
Hollis Watson
Sep 14, 1822
Jul 24, 1899
&
"Mother"
Mrs. Adeline Watson
Sep 11, 1835
Jun 9, 1906

Mary T. Lowe Babb
Dec 3, 1879
Sep 23, 1913

A. B. Newsom, son of
M. M. & M. B. Newsom
Died Jul 5, 1878
age: 16y, 8m, 21d.

"Daughter"
Florence M. Newsom
Died Nov 11, 1859
age: 9m & 4d.

Dr. G. A. Conn
Died Dec 15, 1867, in
his 66 year.

Pauline C. Mayhew, wife of
Rev. C. C. Mayhew of
Tennessee Conn.
Nov 13, 1833
Jun 18, 1873

"Father"
William A. Powell
Aug 22, 1858
Jan 15, 1922

"Mother"
Fannie Powell
Dec 15, 1867
Mar 17, 1932

Atlas Powell, son of
William A. & Fannie Powell
Jun 24, 1908
May 11, 1909

Brince Powell, son of
William A. & Fannie Powell
Apr 23, 1900
Jul 5, 1913

Jerusha Coffey, dau of
Rice & Sarah Coffey
Who was born May 4th 1792
Died Mar 10, 1810
"She was the first buried
in this Cemetery."

Elvira Coffey, dau of
Rice & Sarah Coffey
May 14, 1794
Jul 20, 1849

Sarah Coffey, Consort of
Rice Coffey
Jun 22, 1770
Sep 3, 1840

Nancy E. Coffey, Consort of
A. H. Coffey
Aug 24, 1810
Oct 29, 1841

N. B. Coffey, son of
A. H. & N. E. Coffey
Born Sept 28, 1829 in
Bedford Co., Tenn &
Died Feb 13, 1856 in
Jackson Co., Ala.

Elizabeth Campbell, Consort
of James Campbell, who was
born 1740 & Died Sep 30, 1839

R. (Rock Slab, no dates)

-. R. (Rocl Slab, no dates)

William W. Miller
Mar 1, 1807
joined the Baptist Church
in 1849 &
Died Jul 14, 1855

No Marker:*
Robert Doak Blair
Born Feb 4, 1818
Died Jun 7, 1881

Williamson Haggard
Jul 6, 1813
Oct 18, 1883
age: 71y, 4m, 16d.

Frankie A., wife of
Williamson Haggard
Died May 28, 1890
age: 67 yrs.

Lu A. Chambers, Consort of
J. N. Chambers
Oct 16, 1837
Sep 11, 1866
age: 28y, 10m, 25d.

Smith Bowlin, M.D.
and Grandchildren
Ernest Wright & Jesse Wright
(no dates)

"Father"
James R. Bowlin
Mar 9, 1849
Oct 31, 1889
&
"Son"
Eddie A. Bowlin
Jan 10, 1887
Feb 24, 1939

Townzin Fugitt
Aug 12, 1774
May 2, 1872
&
Jane Fugitt
Apr 3, 1784
Mar 18, 1837
NOTE: She has 2 markers.
Jane Fugitt, wife of
Towzin Fugitt
Apr 3, 1784, married
Mar 11, 1801, joined the
Baptist Church, 1815, &
Died Mar 18, 1837.

Sacred to the Memory of
Robert Majors, was Born 14th
Mar, 1761, & departed this
life Apr 29, 1847. age: 86y,
1m, 15d."Was a Soldier in
the Revolutionary Army, was
a Member of the Methodist
Church 62 years, and died
as he lived a Christian."

Sacred to the Memory of
Huldah Majors, Consort of
Robert Majors, who was born
Oct 1st 1764, and departed
this life the 24th of Jan
1845.

Mrs. Mary Hoffer
Born 24 Dec 1811
Died 9 Jan 1843

No marker:*
Melville Blair, son of
Born Dec 21, 1854
Died Dec 22, 1883

Robert M. Lowe
Sep 6, 1854
Jul 15, 1878

J. R. Lowe
Nov 28, 1876
Dec 26, 1877

Sallie Ann, wife of
Sam W. Lowe
Died Oct 24, 1890
(no age given)

W. H. McCarver
1840-1927

Ellen R., wife of
W. H. McCarver
1847-1912

Pinckney E., son of
W. H. & E. C. McCarver
May 24, 1876
Jun 29, 1878

Matilda L., dau of
W. H. & E. C. McCarver
Jan 15, 1872
Jul 3, 1878

Maggie N., dau of
W. H. & E. C. McCarver
Sep 27, 1873
Jul 17, 1878

Lucy Bonner McCarver
Jan 7, 1880
Dec 13, 1900

Sacred to the Memory of
John Peacock
Born Jan 1, 1762
Died Apr 9, 1823, who left
a wife and 15 children to
lament the loss of an affectionate Husband, a kind and
indulgent Father. Giving in
his last illness full evidence of his faith in the Redeemer.

Mrs. Mary Peacock, wife of
Thomas A. Peacock, formerly
of the County of -------,
State of Georgia, Died May 12,
1830. aged: 48y, 3m, --d.

Cathrine J. Peacock, dau of
Thomas & Mary Peacock
Died May 16, 1824
age: 14y, 5m, 7d.

No marker:(Newspaper)
Mr Thomas Dennis
Died Jan 1888
(Paper-Jan 26, 1888)

No marker:**
Martin David Payne
(no dates)

No marker:**
Clara Jane Mason Payne
(no dates)

Janie Adel Hancock
Oct 7, 1875
Sep 26, 1877

Mary Elizabeth Mullins
1846-1915

J. C. Payne
Sep 19, 1839
Aug 4, 1912
&
Sarah V. Payne
Feb 1, 1840
Oct 18, 1905

James Payne
Aug 9, 1875
Jun 28, 1902

W. W. Payne
Jan 25, 1820
May 10, 1904
&
Nancy P. Payne
Aug 5, 1818
Mar 19, 1888

Clara Belle Payne
Sep 12, 1873
Feb 6, 1882

Ezekiel Driver
Jan 20, 1868
Feb 27, 1940
&
Sarah Bell Driver
Oct 12, 1870
Jan 27, 1926

Sacred to the Memory of
Mrs. Ann Peacock, Consort
of the late John Peacock,
who was born 18th Sept 1782
and departed this life 21st
Nov. 1844. Aged: 62 yrs,
9 mos & 6 da. The deceased
was a Member of the Pres-
byterian Church for a number of years.

Adam A. Peacock, son of
Thomas & Mary Peacock
Died Dec 1, 1826
age: 12y, 9m, 5d.

James Peacock, son of
Thomas & Mary Peacock
Died Apr 2, 1824
age: 16y, 6m, 22d.

Many unmarked graves.
Many fieldstones, no
inscriptions.

No marker:**
Mary Ann Payne
(no dates)

No marker:**
Leahr Bell Payne
(no dates)

No marker:**
Sallie Payne
(no dates)

No marker:**
Claudia Bomar Payne
(no dates)

No marker:**
Mary Ellen Payne
(no dates)

No marker:****
Elizabeth Cleveland Coffey
wife of James Coffey and
Mother of Rice Coffey and
Sister of Benjamin Cleveland.
1727-1827. (Col. Benjamin
Cleveland of Wilkes Co., N.C.,
& of King's Mountain.)

[Salem Meeting House, an
early Methodist Church was
located here]

* by Miss Merle Jacobs
** by Mrs. George W. Parker
*** by Mrs. Bertha Henslee
**** by Miss Mary Bass
***** by Mrs Walter Parrish

No marker:**
Ruth Payne
(no dates)

No marker:**
Nancy Butner
(no dates)

No marker:**
John Thomas Faulk
(no dates)

No marker:**
Vencie Nelson Faulk
(no dates)

No marker:*****
Sacred to the Memory of
Jane Allen Fugitt, Consort of
James Scruggs Who was born
1812? Died 1898?. Jane is
buried next to her
husband James Scruggs. A
marker was requested in the
James Scrugg's Will. The
wishes of the Will were never
carried out. Her marker is
a rock, no inscription.

No marker:***
Henry Green
Born abt 1846
Died Jan or Feb 1903
age: abt 57 yrs.

No marker:***
Bettie Sharp Green
Died abt 1874
age: abt 26-28 yrs.

No marker:***
Maggie Thomas Pearson
Born Nov 28, 1873
Died (no dates)

No marker:*****
Sacred to the Memory of
Elizabeth S. Fugitt, Consort
of William W. Miller, who
died in 1855, was then married
to Isaac Young. She was Born
1810? & Died 1895?. A marker
was requested in the Elizabeth Young Will. The wishes
of the Will were never carried
out. Elizabeth is buried next
to her niece and namesake
Bettie S. Miller Scruggs Kelly
Bettie S.M.S.Kelly has a marker)

No marker:***
"Mother"
Clara E. Henslee Pearson
Born Oct 2, 1847
Died (no date)
&
"Daughter"
Maud Hunter Pearson
Born Dec 22, 1869
Died (no date)

No marker:***
Beulah Franklin Pearson
Born Sep 23, 1877
Died (no date)

No marker:*****
Arch Kelly
Born Jan 30, 1853
Died Jan 30, 1885
married to Bettie S. Miller
Scruggs.
(Rock for a marker)

NOTE: Old Salem Cemetery
continued on page
131.

7 HAZEL CEMETERY   Map # 8
Located in Bell Buckle, Tennessee

Arthur J. Stacy, Sr.
Pvt U.S.Army
Feb 12, 1923
Aug 20, 1974

Will J. McCarty
Aug 1, 1878
Apr 18, 1956
&
Lillie F. McCarty
Jul 20, 1881

Lonnie McCarty
1921-1969
(Gowen-Smith)

Webb Guy
1894-1964
(Hoover)

Willie E. Harris
Mar 20, 1886
Jun 21, 1961

Jane McCarty Murphree
1873-1959

Oscar S. Cobb
Mar 7, 1889
Feb 18, 1958

Kenneth R. Carter, Jr.
1969-1969
(Gowen-Smith)

Frank Dye
Jun 23, 1918
Mar 16, 1973
&
Margie Ruth Dye
Dec 8, 1924

John H. Nelson
1889-1963
&
Lillie C. Nelson
1896-19

Debra Kim Earls
Nov 7, 1959

George W. Faulk
Feb 12, 1910

&
Mildred L. Faulk
Aug 6, 1910
Jan 11, 1964

Claud Mooneyham
1883-1955
&
Mary D. Mooneyham
1890-19

Calvin R. Carter
Jan 22, 1908
Apr 4, 1955
&
Sarah E. Carter
Sep 10, 1914

John M. Adams
Mar 15, 1909
May 14, 1972
&
Eunice E. Adams
Feb 16, 1908
----
married Oct 6, 1933

John William Price
Aug 28, 1902
Feb 24, 1967

Oliver Lee Stephens
1914-1967
(Gowen-Smith)

Walter L. Brown
1887-1967
(Howell-Thompson)

Lula Green
Jan 11, 1877
Dec 28, 1968

Chesley N. Barclay
Dec 9, 1901
Apr 27, 1955
&
Catheran B. Barclay
Oct 2, 1910

John Robert Alford
Jan 15, 1891
Nov 30, 1956

W. S. Delbridge
Aug 11, 1885
May 19, 1956

Alice C. Delbridge
Jan 24, 1889
Dec 1, 1958

Lucille Delbridge
Mar 30, 1910

George W. Delbridge
Feb 14, 1914
Apr 3, 1973

James M. Thompson
Tennessee
Pfc Co K 4 Inf W.W.I
Feb 14, 1911
Sep 10, 1967
&
Willie Mae Thompson
1912-

Ronald Ray
1962-1963
(Hoover)

William C. Richardson
U. S. Army
Sep 11, 1889
Mar 30, 1967

Jimmie E. Walters
Apr 16, 1881
Feb 29, 1960

Elie M. Shelton
Nov 1, 1882
Feb 4, 1963
&
Ora Harper Shelton
Aug 14, 1891
(no date)

J. R. Delbridge
Oct 6, 1881
Mar 7, 1953
&
Mary F. Delbridge
Oct 30, 1887
Oct 8, 1954

Mary Bell Williams
Sep 10, 1896
Oct 28, 1935

Leslie F. Crosslin
1896-1967
(Gowen-Smith)

Doris Jean Richardson
age: 1y, 1m, 13d.
(no dates)

Robert Harrell
Apr 1874
    19(no date)
&
Elizabeth Harrell
Apr 1879
    1940

J. F. Knox
1846-1933
"Was Confederate Soldier,
joined the Army 1861, be-
longed to 4th Tenn. Calv.
fought under Gen. Forrest,
Parolled 1865."

Mary Ruth Knox
Dec 16, 1857
Jun 18, 1936

James Frank Knox
Nov 5, 1896
Apr 7, 1897

Myrtle Ruth Knox
Mar 27, 1883
Jun 16, 1899

John Wyatt Acuff
1835-1908
    & wife:
Eva Lillard Acuff
1845-(no date)
    & Dau:
Mary Louise Wyatt Acuff
1868-(no date)
    &
Minerva Acuff Cox
1840-1897

Clayton H. Bush
Dec 29, 1904
Apr 28, 1966
&
Pauline G. Bush
Dec 8, 1907

Sallie M.(Mae) Brymer
Jul 3, 1903
Jun 22, 1974
&
Rebecca C. Brymer
Jun 23, 1871
Apr 16, 1973

Ashton A. Pruett
1884-1955
&
Alice H. Pruett
1887-19

James A. Bryant
Oct 22, 1895
Jan 23, 1968
&
Louise Liggett Bryant
Mar 16, 1894
Aug 14, 1973

O. T. French, Sr.
1892-1940
&
Daisy French
1883-1940

Jennie E. Hatchett
1858-1947

Ernest J. Hatchett
Jan 11, 1882
Jan 5, 1962
&
Mary W. Hatchett
Oct 30, 1884
Jan 10, 1953

Annie E. Hatchett
1904-1928

"Father"
John L. Espy
1860-1940

"Mother"
Malinda E. Espy
1863-1938

"Sister"
Maud F. Espy
1886-1937

John Luther Espy
Dec 14, 1892
Nov 24, 1966

Mary Celester Espy
Nov 27, 1887
(no date)

Samuel F., son of
J. L. & M. E. Espy
Nov 29, 1895
Mar 27, 1897

R. K. Crawford
Oct 13, 1883
Jan 1, 1914

Leland T. McCarty
Jan 16, 1915
Jul 8, 1964

Kennerd H. Hatchett
Aug 11, 1916

&
Minnie Lee Hatchett
Apr 18, 1918

G. W. Anderson
Jan 15, 1822
Aug 8, 1902
&
Mrs. N. E. Anderson
May 20, 1822
Jul 26, 1904

Frank W. Richards
Jul 7, 1882
Mar 13, 1953
&
Addie A. Richards
Sep 6, 1887
Jan 4, 1974

Burr James Mitchell
1917-1968
&
Pauline D. Mitchell
1917-
married Nov 9, 1940

William C. Sanderson
1885-1960
&
Rachel L. Sanderson
---- - ----

E. Leland Sanderson
S/Sgt U.S.Army Air Corps
Apr 28, 1917, killed in
action Jan 20, 1945

Martha M. Henry
1875-1947

William Riley Hill
Nov 2, 1890
Jun 16, 1966
&
Eathel P. Hill
Dec 9, 1889
(no date)

Charles Edward Hill
Tennessee
Cpl U.S.Army, Korea
Nov 15, 1929
Feb 9, 1973

Josiah Parker
Aug 22, 1855
Apr 21, 1929
&
Ida T. Parker
Jun 2, 1871
Sep 12, 1951

W. P. Crawford
Jan 25, 1857
Oct 4, 1921

Lula Ridley Crawford
Dec 9, 1860
Aug 28, 1923

Tony R. Spence
Jan 1, 1886
May 12, 1968
&
Alma H. Spence
Oct 7, 1893

Arthur W. Crosslin
Jun 18, 1908
Apr 17, 1972
&
Rosie Lee Crosslin
Sep 18, 1910

Glen Avery Carter
Feb 20, 1949
Feb 24, 1949

James L. Campbell
Jan 28, 1894
Mar 23, 1970
&
Evelyn S. Campbell
Aug 10, 1893
Feb 10, 1967

Nina Norris
1890-1942

Otho Lisenby
1864-1942

Ansel Melton
Dec 3, 1832
May 31, 1904
&
Sarah J. Melton
Died Jun 9, 1890
age: 59 yrs.

Charles A. Henry
1874-1911

Robert C. Melton
Apr 16, 1858
May 11, 1904

J. B. Melton
Apr 23, 1860
Mar 11, 1894

Sallie M. Joyce
1869-1942

E. Luke Winnett
Feb 11, 1864
Feb 26, 1918

William Henry Winnett
Oct 21, 1857
Jun 9, 1899

G. Mitchell, son of
J. N. & M. Z. McDonald
Oct 8, 1871
Jan 1, 1891

Bartlette Ewing Thomas
1851-1910

Lizzie Crawford Thomas
1860-1919

Thomas Wayne McCarty
Sep 17, 1967
Dec 6, 1967

Ellen D. Muse
1867-1914

Margie Howard
1887-1901

Milton F. Hime
1862-1918
&
Elizabeth Hime
1880-1942

L. J. Whitaker
Dec 16, 1841
Dec 15, 1900

Lucius John Whitaker
Aug 7, 1872
May 10, 1878
age: 5y, 9m, 3d.

Alice
(in Whitaker plot & deep
in ground)

Jesse Culley
Oct 23, 1874
Oct 16, 1889
&
Eliza Beachboard, wife of
A. D. Culley
Sep 10, 1852
Aug 18, 1900

James C. Loyd
1857-(no date)
& wife:
Betherana Loyd
1858-1922

Robert H. Loyd
1883-1930

Jessie J. Loyd
1889-1933

Col. William Washington
                Anderson
Ga. Line, Co 116 Reg.
1819-1895
&
Jane Cauble Anderson
1829-1904

Willie Mason Anderson
1866-1947

Carl H. Slater
1889-1965

Eva May Kay
1870-1938

George W. Gibson
1852-1909
& wife:
Amaryllis Kay Gibson
1859-1932

Willy Muse Cooke
Sep 16, 1879
Apr 11, 1927

Nannie Rankin Muse
Jul 8, 1839
Jul 30, 1921

W. R. Muse
1841-1909

Henry Walker Smith
1915-1954
&
Alline Spence Smith
1916-

Ernest D. Spence
Jun 2, 1893
May 1, 1973
&
Ruby I. Spence
Aug 22, 1893

Jennie McKee, wife of
W. D. Lee, Sr.
1850-1927

Turner Boyce, Infant son of
Rev. H. R. & L. E. Schramm
Nov 21, 1889
Jan 31, 1890

P. A. Arnold
Aug 10, 1855
Jul 20, 1920
&
Nancy J. Arnold
Oct 7, 1855
(no date)

Mechanic Jim Arnold
of Co. D., 167 inft
Born Nov 8, 1891
Died in France
Jun 12, 1918
buried Jun 5, 1921

Sarah Thomas Bartlett
Aug 29, 1897
Jul 1, 1899

Thomas Franklin Garner
1864-1917

Elizabeth Anderson Garner
1848-1897

William M. Garner
1880-1920

Dr. W. A. Moon
1860-1935

John F. Brandon
Aug 12, 1822
Nov 2, 1892

Hattie M., wife of
J. S. Brandon
Dec 9, 1867
May 18, 1897

Nancy Marie Arnold
Sep 15, 1926
May 6, 1950

Infant Dau of
Leona & Emmett Arnold
Sep 21, 1925
Sep 24, 1925

Emmett Richard Arnold
May 4, 1897
(no date)
&
Leona Lillian Arnold
Jul 24, 1897
Dec 12, 1972

Ernest Richard Arnold
Jun 9, 1915
Aug   1916

Walter E. Murray
1897-1961

Mable M. Jernigan
1895-1928

Roy Newt Napper
Aug 18, 1898

&
Mattie Butner Napper
Mar 23, 1900
Feb 20, 1975

Jessey Walton Murray
Oct 30, 1860
Jun 22, 1927
&
Leona F. Murray
Mar 1, 1875
Aug 9, 1939

Andrew J. Dearing
1885-1926

Ida Mashe Dearing
1888-1971
(Moores FH)

Faris Sears Dearing
Jul 17, 1908
Dec 20, 1912

Leon Francis Dearing
Tennessee
Landsman for Carpenters
Mate-U.S.Navy
Aug 2, 1935

Mary Katherine Beachboard
1846-1919

Ben Beachboard
Feb 9, 1881
Mar 19, 1912

Robert L. Beachboard
Aug 18, 1886
Oct 3, 1957

John P. Hoover
Apr 6, 1827
Jan 31, 1904
&
Lawson Hoover
Dec 10, 1845
Nov 14, 1878
&
Sarah D. Hoover
Mar 15, 1851
Feb 15, 1900
&
James B. Hoover
Nov 4, 1856
Jun 30, 1899

James Richard Harrell
Mar 13, 1946
Jan 1, 1972

Ricky M. Parker
Oct 24, 1950
Dec 27, 1971

Martha Lynch Parker
1954-1974
(Gowen-Smith)

Jackie Majors
1936-1962
(Gowen-Smith)

Thomas A. Huff
1859-1928

Rev. William Huff
Born in Botetourt Co., Va.
Dec 21, 1825
Oct 27, 1898

Martha E., wife of
Rev. William Huff
May 20, 1838
Aug 26, 1923

Della May, dau of
Rev. Wm. & M. E. Huff
Oct 25, 1870
Sep 2, 1886

William T. Lynch
1869-1943
&
Tommie D. Lynch
1893-1941

Jane Skeen
1830-1902

M. L. Skeen
1850-1911

Ida Ivie Skeen
1852-1935

William Alonzo Dennis
Jul 13, 1922
Jul 14, 1922

Ida Myrtle Dennis
Nov 20, 1894
Aug 12, 1896

Robert Wilson Dennis
Sep 12, 1858
Dec 29, 1940

Mary Elizabeth Dennis
Sep 6, 1865
Apr 17, 1957

Robert Dennis
Nov 25, 1829
Aug 27, 1888
&
Nancy Jane Dennis
Dec 11, 1830
Sep 26, 1901

John R. Dennis
Jan 7, 1890

&
Olive Ruth Dennis
May 15, 1894
Oct 12, 1966

J. T. Dennis
1862-1938
& wife:
Mary F. Dennis
Jul 15, 1868
Jan 21, 1888

John Henry Dennis
Jan 10, 1870
Sep 20, 1930

William E. Blackburn
1860-1939
&
Jessie C. Blackburn
1863-1936

J. N. Chambers
Dec 31, 1833
Feb 16, 1908
&
Mrs. J. N. Chambers
Feb 22, 1848
Feb 21, 1908

John J. Crosslin
Jun 25, 1882
Feb 2, 1954
&
Nannie Gray Crosslin
Jan 12, 1887
Jun 23, 1941

"Father"
Marvin White
1899-1933
&
"Mother"
Flora Runnels White
(no dates)
&
"Son"
Robert M. White
1875-1950

Talbert Runnels White
Mar 12, 1898
Jul   1968
(Woodfin FH)

John F. Baldwin
Jun 16, 1865
Mar 21, 1931
&
Mary J. Baldwin
Nov 24, 1855
May 25, 1929

Wesley N. Blackburn
1882-1954
&
Bettie W. Blackburn
1890-19

Lula Stovall Blackburn
Dec 19, 1881
Feb 6, 1907

William M. Crews
Aug 17, 1879
Dec 4, 1930
&
Effie C. Crews
Nov 26, 1879
Jul 10, 1906

Elmer F. Crews
May 4, 1900

J. C. Crews
Died Jun 7, 1922
aged: abt 70 yrs.
&
Martha Jane Crews
Aug 9, 1855
Feb 19, 1941

"Brother"
Grover C. Crews
Feb 19, 1885
Mar 15, 1915
&
"Sister"
Emily Mary Crews
Jun 23, 1891
Aug 18, 1911

William Estel Crews
Tennessee
WT1 U.S.Navy W.W.II
Jun 23, 1903
Jul 17, 1973

Lois Christine Crews
Jan 28, 1926

J. M. Runnels
1857-1924

Tennie P. Runnels
1866-1942

D. W. Shriver, Jr.
Mar 25, 1881
Apr 18, 1919

William T. Dye
1870-1955
&
Mollie H. Dye
1875-

Grant Norris
1891-1941
&
Nannie Norris
1888-1957

Mary H. Norris
1940-1944

Walter D. Sharp
May 30, 1918

&
Lytle B. Sharp
May 15, 1906

William Arthur Stepp
1883-1964

Tennie C. Stepp
1884-1968

Willella Stepp Hatcher
1914-1940

Kirty Crews Broyles
Jul 7, 1887
Aug 31, 1962

W. W. Crosslin
Mar 13, 1900
Mar 6, 1920

J. W. Crosslin
May 28, 1893
Dec 28, 1917

John T. Crosslin
Jul 16, 1885
Jul 3, 1957

Lillard T. Crosslin
Oct 27, 1901
Jul 20, 1953

Emerson Edwards
1858-1936
&
Annie D. Edwards
1869-1959

Charles L. Edwards
1897-1936

Otto Rosenberg
Jul 15, 1885
Mar 6, 1947

Emma Rosenberg
Jul 19, 1892

Burrell T. Dye
Jul 11, 1896
May 20, 1951

James ----- Foster
1867-1948
(Thompson)

A. J. Roberts, Sr.
Dec 15, 1832
Jan 13, 1913

James E. Roberts
Oct 9, 1862
Jun 6, 1932

Thomas E. Russell
Nov 17, 1907
Jun 7, 1972
&
Jessie R. Russell
Nov 18, 1905

A. J. Roberts, Jr.
1870-1957

Lena A. Roberts
1877-1962

Lillian S. Roberts
1907-1924

Ruby E. Roberts
Jan 16, 1904

Thomas P. Crosslin
Jun 16, 1862
Nov 18, 1931

Bettie S. Crosslin
Feb 20, 1860
Apr 17, 1944

Mary E. Crosslin
May 30, 1897
Jun 7, 1927

Prentice Edwards
Mar 14, 1887
Sep 6, 1971
&
Vera Velma Edwards
Aug 1, 1892
Jan 23, 1957

Joe Ethridge Edwards
Dec 28, 1889
Nov 19, 1947

Albert Dwight Edwards
Jan 3, 1941
18 days

Pollard R. Runnels
Feb 11, 1824
Aug 7, 1907
& wife:
Martha Elizabeth Runnels
Jul 20, 1840
Aug 24, 1922

E. C. Bowling
Jul 26, 1869
May 29, 1957

Molita N. S. Bowling
Feb 20, 1870
Apr 7, 1965

Frank Douglas
1863-1943
&
Mary W. Douglas
1872-1942

Lucy C. Douglas
Sep 9, 1910
Dec 31, 1913

Tempy West
1870-1950

C. A. Hummel
A native of Saxony, Ger.
1838-1911
& wife:
M. C. Whitworth
1842-1898
&
Fred C. Hummel
1869-1947
&
Patra F. Hummel
1883-1965
&
Walter A. Hummel
1906-1909

George Franklin Gregory
1877-1948

Elizabeth Hummel Gregory
1875-1954

J. W. "Watt" Harrison
Jul 2, 1879
Apr 4, 1961

Nannie Mae Harrison
Jul 29, 1884
Jan 2, 1957

J. W. Harrison, Jr.
1919-1919
&
Janie M. Harrison
1921-1926

Martin L. Bush
Jun 23, 1879
Jan 9, 1962
&
Mae P. Bush
Sep 23, 1883
Jun 15, 1973
married Feb 16, 1902

J. E. Tarpley
Jun 22, 1853
Aug 21, 1927
& wife:
Elizabeth Yeargan Tarpley
Aug 19, 1862
Jan 26, 1950

"Father"
J. A. Gannaway
1824-1911
&
"Mother"
M. R. Gannaway
1830-1920

Lee Fox
1883-1961
&
Lucy Fox
1886-1969

Cornelia Fox
Jul 8, 1916

L. C. Fields, Sr.
1850-1907

Sarah Fields
1855-1904

Lemma Fields
1877-1907

Helen Fields
Jul 18, 1913

Mary Fields
1914-1915

L. Carter Fields
1882-1952

Charles Sanders
Oct 1, 1927
Jun 3, 1928

Mattie Jernigan Sanders
1885-1958

G. M. Jernigan
Oct 24, 1884
Feb 28, 1919

E. B. McCrory
1867-1931

Mary E. McCrory
1877-1951

Carl W. McCrory
Apr 8, 1900
Dec 15, 1972

Alva Eugene McCrory
Aug 12, 1895
Mar 29, 1897

Jane Coop
1852-1937

Mattie Estella, dau of
H. W. & Sallie Bush
Jun 18, 1905
Jul 3, 1914

Theodore Bush
Sep 3, 1909
Apr 3, 1910

Mark Bush
Dec 4, 1903
Jul 18, 1918

Charles Henry North
(no dates)
& wife:
Mary Cassie Gannaway North
Oct 1, 1864
Jul 17, 1918

George T. Burnett
Nov 24, 1891
Dec 2, 1950
&
Essie Ann Burnett
Feb 27, 1893
Apr 5, 1958

William Ransom
Oct 29, 1846
Dec 12, 1935
&
Mary Huff Ransom
Sep 13, 1851
May 25, 1941

Cornelius H. Bomar
Dec 15, 1872
Sep 18, 1961
&
Sarah R. Bomar
Dec 9, 1873
Nov 17, 1964

Ras Jones
1892-1974
&
Margaret Jones
1898-1938

Sam D. Jones
1919-1938

Willie Warren, Infant dau of
W. C. & E. D. Erwin
Jan 7, 1887
Jul 24, 1887
age: 6m & 18d.

Francis May, dau of
Robert & Ella M. Erwin
Nov 9, 1902
Feb 20, 1907

Marvin Erwin
1913-1937

G. B. Erwin
1857-1921

A. S. Erwin
Jul 31, 1869
Apr 8, 1926
& wife:
Callie Erwin
Aug 29, 1883
Nov 10, 1922

Joe Y. Parker
1860-1934
&
Martha E. Parker
1856-1941

Mattie Belle, dau of
J. Y. & M. E. Parker
May 12, 1895
Aug 14, 1910

Benjamin Allen Clary
1854-1929
&
Nannie Gannaway Clary
1862-1940

William C. Vannatta
1884-1944
&
Ophelia H. Vannatta
1884-1972

Guy Vannatta
Mar 9, 1916
May 2, 1973

Reuben L. Wallace
Mar 15, 1899
Dec 3, 1966

Craig Vannatta
Oct 24, 1946
Dec 24, 1946

Robert Lee McCarty
1873-1958

Judy Alma McCarty
1883-1931

Evelyn Gregory Claxton
1916-1947

R. Grier Peoples
1869-1939

Alla C. Peoples
1869-1954

William Crawford Erwin
1850-1897
& wife:
Emma Erwin Paty
1859-1943

Margaret S. Erwin
Aug 18, 1825
Jun 21, 1897
age: 71y, 10m, 3d.

Robert L. Erwin
1869-1912

Mary L. Erwin
Jul 31, 1858
Jan 2, 1926

Stephen Dunbar Thach
Mar 31, 1866
Oct 1, 1900

Alma Terrill Thach, wife
of Stephen D. Thach
1870-1958

Elam Jackson
1886-1949
&
Lena Jackson
1886-1971

Idella Hazlett
Mar 4, 1873
Apr 21, 1956

Kiziah Fleming Kinnard
1829-1913

Frank G. Robinson
Feb 2, 1886
Dec 2, 1947

Doak Richard
Jan 1, 1863
Jul 9, 1932
&
Mattie P. Richard
Dec 15, 1867
Jan 20, 1938

James C. Redden
Dec 1, 1879
Jul 6, 1953

Alice T. Redden
Nov 20, 1876·
Feb 8, 1926

Mary V. Redden
Oct 18, 1928
Nov 27, 1928

Roy L. Redden
Jan 31, 1904
Feb 14, 1926

Mildred Ann Burnett
Nov 2, 1924
Jan 25, 1928

Gerald Webb Follin
1891-1962
&
Grace Cleveland Follin
1890-1955

M. T. Stubblefield
Jun 23, 1844
Feb 16, 1915

Mattie M. Lynch
19-2-1955
(TM)

Bettie Linch*
1887-1973
(Gowen-Smith)
(Born Sep 13, 1887
Died Nov 8, 1973)*

J. Henry Bomar
Feb 9, 1897
Nov 4, 1961
&
Lizzie G. Bomar
Apr 25, 1902
Jun 24, 1961

No Marker:*
Sarah Davis Linch Runnells
Born Mar 7, 1863
Died Nov 21, 1934

No marker:*
Walter S. Runnells
1863-1935

No marker:*
Jesse Linch
1886-Jan 25, 1936

No marker:*
Patra Linch
(no dates)

Joe Henry Adcoc
1854-1904
&
Mary Adcoc
1847-1929

Tom Lynn Bingham
1888-1973
(Gowen-Smith)

Sadie C. Bingham
1889-1970
(Hoover)

Stanley E. Kwapinski
1887-1972

Irene Douglas Kwapinski
1898-1940

B. Silas Beachboard
Jul 17, 1888
Jul 15, 1970
&
Lucile Thomas Beachboard
Nov 5, 1892
Aug 23, 1970

William Dennison Lee
Mar 6, 1885

&
Aggie Graham Lee
Jun 4, 1881
Mar 24, 1970

Joe Estill Lee
Feb 2, 1885
Dec 20, 1972

Sallie Fields Lee
Jul 26, 1885
Dec 29, 1972

J. E. Lee, Jr.
Apr 11, 1919
Nov 15, 1945

Ephriam M. Wood
1866-1938

Mary Pruett Wood
1868-1944

L. M. Lynch
1895-1974
(Howell)

Mary Woodward Lynch
Sep 17, 1898
Dec 24, 1929

Robert W. Lynch
1920-1971
(Hoover)

No marker:*
Patra Linch
(no dates)

No marker:*
Lela Linch
1884-(no date)

Claude Haithcock
1889-1948
&
Carrie Haithcock
1902-19

Finis E. Parker
1874-1948
&
Sallie H. Parker
1879-1925

Robert S. Pruitt
1901-19
&
Ruby C. Pruitt
1901-1949

William Travis Hazlett
Feb 6, 1876
Oct 31, 1927
&
Hattie Parker Hazlett
Jun 20, 1878
Jul 26, 1945

William Clyde Hazlett
Oct 31, 1906
Apr 21, 1970

Rachel E. Wallis
1850-1931

Jasper M. Wallis
Mar 26, 1880
Nov 28, 1952

Sadie M. Wallis
Jan 8, 1876
Jan 18, 1950

Daisy Dean Wallis
Nov 14, 1872
Nov 5, 1962

Della Freeman Wallis
Oct 22, 1888
Mar 4, 1959

Ada Birdy Wallis
Sep 25, 1884
Jan 6, 1953

James Sim Lynch
Mar 31, 1851
Jul 3, 1929

Josie McKee Lynch
Sep 2, 1857
Nov 12, 1947

William Thomas Wilson
Jul 22, 1865
Sep 2, 1930

Bina Wallace Wilson
Apr 23, 1865
Jan 30, 1950

John E. Wilson
1887-1971

W. Jackson Lynch
Mar 25, 1899-Jun 5, 1957

James Hatchett
Jul 1851
Feb 28, 1934
&
Flora Hatchett
Jun 15, 1854
Jan 3, 1937

Albert L. Hatchett
Nov 22, 1889
May 4, 1963
&
Leera E. Hatchett
Feb 27, 1894
(TM----1975)
(Gowen-Smith)

N. C. Hatchett
Sep 18, 1831
Aug 18, 1919
"Rest Soldier, Rest
Thy Warfare Oer."

John Rufus Batte
Apr 18, 1850
Mar 23, 1926

Ella Knott Batte
Oct 16, 1856
Feb 11, 1937

Jerry Joyce
Oct 4, 1946

Ray Joyce
Aug 11, 1958
Aug 13, 1958

Lela Linch
1884-1963
(Hoover)

Drennon Lynch
Apr 2, 1900
Jul 15, 1966
&
Nell C. Lynch

Robert W. Muse
1905-1971
&
Eliza A. Muse
1906-

James C. Spann
1869-1926
&
Mary E. Spann
1871-1960

Ira Linch
1893-1964

Julia Linch
1901-1974

Sammie Carylon Bomar
Born & Died
Oct 5, 1942

Mary Kelly Lynch
Jan 19, 1874
Aug 21, 1958

Robert Iota Lynch
Nov 18, 1869
Apr 28, 1934

Thurman Webb Lynch
May 5, 1934

Robert Webb Lynch
Feb 25, 1893

Addie Bell Staland Lynch
Aug 15, 1900
Sep 24, 1964

R. F. Wallis
Mar 17, 1832
Feb 24, 1911
&
S. C. Wallis
Jan 6, 1838
Mar 11, 1905

Latimer W. Beachboard
1907-1932

Archie Ray Prince
Apr 17, 1903
Dec 26, 1956
&
Susie Belle Prince
Sep 6, 1904

Marion Ray Prince
Mar 21, 1927
May 18, 1927

J. G. Miller
Jun 22, 1875
Jun 6, 1939

Nannie Bingham Miller
Jan 7, 1878
May 14, 1960

Leone Miller
Aug 31, 1898
Nov 15, 1964

Arch Latimer
Jun 21, 1874
Feb 4, 1930

Mary Latimer Johnson
Jan 19, 1877
May 4, 1959

Carl Johnson
Jul 11, 1903
Dec 27, 1962
&
Lucille Johnson
Dec 19, 1905

S. R. Rucker
1898-1940

Charles Rice Wood
Apr 26, 1893
Jun 26, 1939

Charles J. Fulks
1867-1948

Evelyn K. Fulks
1875-1955

J. H. Armstrong
May 8, 1853
Aug 28, 1923

Kate Thweatt Armstrong
Dec 8, 1868
Aug 28, 1923

J. F. Armstrong
Jan 31, 1884
Jul 22, 1956

Lula P. Armstrong
Mar 12, 1882
May 6, 1967

Thomas W. Helton
1887-1968

Thomas W. Helton, Jr.
1921-1939

James Wesley Crosslin
Sep 9, 1878
Sep 30, 1971
&
Era Johnson Crosslin
Jul 9, 1897

Charles M. Hatchett
Mar 3, 1898
May 12, 1973
&
Alene M. Hatchett
May 9, 1901

Sophia, wife of
Jno. P. Mankin
Mar 5, 1869
Apr 6, 1895

Samuel G., son of
J. D. & N. C. Bingham
Sep 5, 1873
May 14, 1877
age: 3y, 8m, 9d.

John D., son of
J. D. & N. C. Bingham
Mar 31, 1871
May 15, 1877
age: 6y, 1m, 15d.

Guss M. Coop
1883-1958
&
Lula Coop
1882-1935

Bibb D. Bomar
Apr 27, 1875
Apr 19, 1944
&
Ethel L. Bomar
Sep 13, 1885
Oct 14, 1955

J. D. Orr, Jr., Infant son
of J.D. & Jessie L. Bomar
1941

James E. Nance, Sr.
1864-1956

Emma Todd Nance
1874-1961

James Emmett Nance, Jr.
Tennessee
Maj. 63 Ordnance GP W.W.II
Nov 3, 1900
Oct 15, 1954

Sam Bell Vincent
1899-1973
(Gowen-Smith)

Patricia Ann Fox
1951-1960
(Hoover)

Dee Fox, Sr.
Feb 6, 1883
Feb 21, 1968

Emma Fox
Aug 13, 1886
Dec 23, 1963

Sammie B. Fox
May 25, 1891
Apr 30, 1966

Roy B. Bingham
Dec 28, 1883
Feb 28, 1940

Queenie Lynch Bingham
1883-1967

Margaret E. Bingham
Born in McLinburg Co., N.C.,
Oct 22, 1814, moved to
this County March 1816
Died Jan 15, 1883
age: 68y, 2m, 23d.

John D. Bingham
May 28, 1821
Oct 2, 1901
&
Nancy C. Bingham
Jun 30, 1835
Aug 10, 1901

Matilda B., dau of
J. D. & N. C. Bingham
Apt 7, 1860
Aug 7, 1864
age: 4y & 4m

Harvey L. Haggard
1857-1934
&
Etta I. Haggard
1861-(no date)

George Bacon Moon
Jun 16, 1832
Nov 7, 1901
& wife:
Apr 15, 1827
Jun 17, 1913

J. H. H. Thweatt
1840-1908
&
Martha J. Thweatt
1848-1920

Robert C. Butner
Mar 9, 1893
Dec 13, 1954

Mary Henderson Butner
Jan 27, 1907
Nov 2, 1955

Lawrence Butner
1915-1939

William Arch Arnold
Dec 29, 1880
Feb 27, 1952
&
Kate L. Arnold
Jun 3, 1881
Feb 23, 1948

Albert W. Arnold
Jan 13, 1915
Jan 1, 1932

J. B. Lewis
1861-1934

Isabella, dau of
J. D. & N. C. Bingham &
wife of J. B. Lewis
Aug 16, 1866
Jul 29, 1899

Mary Belle, dau of
J. B. & Isabella Lewis
Jul 9, 1896
Jun 16, 1916

Nola, dau of
J. L. & M. A. Goodrum &
wife of J. B. Lewis
Jun 13, 1877
Dec 17, 1905

Joseph E. L., son of
J. D. & N. C. Bingham
Apr 10, 1876
May 16, 1876
age: 1m & 6d.

Mary Jane, dau of
J. D. & N. C. Bingham
Jun 11, 1862
Jun 30, 1864
age: 2y & 19d.

W. W. Williams
1880-1931

No marker:*
Daisy Hoover Williams
1833-1974

* Family Record

William C. Ellis
Dec 1, 1891
Oct 18, 1957

Racheil B. Ellis
Apr 3, 1897
Aug 3, 1968

Edith R. Ellis
Nov 9, 1933
Nov 7, 1960

Nancy E. Ellis
Oct 13, 1924
Apr 10, 1937

Lillie M. Timmons
Nov 16, 1877
May 15, 1962

E. H. McCulloch
1847-1931

William Clarence McCulloch
1884-1960

Mary Elizabeth McCulloch
1882-1949

F. S. Harris
Jan 29, 1854
Apr 15, 1939
&
Cassie Spence Harris
Jul 4, 1861
Jul 15, 1903

Sue Kay Harris
1861-1944

Randolph Claxton
Oct 30, 1902
Nov 23, 1921

W. F. Sutton
1840-1890

W. B. Sutton
1869-1933

Elizabeth F. Sutton
1872-1963

Rev. A. F. Rankin
Jul 22, 1827
Nov 13, 1901
&
Mary H. Rankin
May 6, 1828
Oct 22, 1906

David S. Miller
Died Jun 10, 1911
(no age given)

William A. Anderson
1871-1945
"Father"

Fannie B. Anderson
1877-1934
"Mother"

Zachry Taylor Beachboard
Dec 22, 1847
Nov 21, 1899
&
Eliza Lynch Beachboard
May 31, 1849
Jan 1, 1932

Maude (Beachboard)
Mar 2, 1887
Aug 8, 1897

Nell Beachboard Bingham
May 3, 1881
Mar 9, 1924

Adolph P. Zazzi
1881-1955

Louis E. Beachboard
May 21, 1887
Feb 27, 1940

Mamie Beachboard Bass
Mar 23, 1875
Sep 26, 1913

Elmer E. Eaton
Sep 26, 1881
Oct 31, 1955

Octa Lee Eaton
Sep 25, 1880
Dec 29, 1962

Mervin E. Eaton
Sep 15, 1911
Jan 10, 1957

Sewell L. Troxler
Jan 10, 1918
Jul 10, 1930
&
Nelle L. Troxler
May 6, 1895
Apr 3, 1972
&
George Troxler
Oct 12, 1895

Robert L. Arnold
1894-
&
Laura E. Clark Arnold
1892-1971

J. A. Jordan
1855-1924
&
Jesse M. Jordan
1868-1955

Charles S. Miller
1870-1890

Rally M. Butner
1905-1931

Mrs. Sallie B. Bingham
1895-1959
(Thompson)

G. C. Bingham
1864-1928

Olive Gilmore, wife of
G. C. Bingham
1870-1936

William Winfield Bingham
Mar 16, 1858
Sep 16, 1944

Margaret W. Bingham
Sep 29, 1876
Dec 7, 1962

Ida W. Bingham
Dec 25, 1871
Jan 22, 1903

Katharine B. Paty
Jun 28, 1898
Mar 29, 1920

W. T. Paty
1858-1910

Lina K. Paty
1869-1947

Gordon Johnson
1922-
&
Frances Johnson
1921-

Infant Son of
Gordon & Connie Johnson
Oct 15, 1972

William Berry Sharp
1877-1923
&
Jennie Phelps Sharp
1877-1947

Johnie B. Sharp
Oct 6, 1905
Sep 16, 1918

John W. Paty
1856-1932

Emma R. Paty
1855-1899

John W. Paty
1887-1964
&
Lavinia B. Paty
1891-1963

Joe C. Miller
1839-1916

Adah S. Miller
1845-1916

William V. Barrett
Tennessee
Pvt 1 Cl 156 field Arty
81 Div 1892
Dec 13, 1936

John Wright Douglas
1890-1973

Emmett Douglas
1858-1936

Cora W. Douglas
1867-1951

Margaret Douglas
1887-1932

Myrtle Douglas
1885-1968

Nicholas C. Ellis
Born & Died
Sep 12, 1932

William Winfield Bingham, Jr.
Jan 22, 1913
Jul 16, 1965

James A. Hatchett
Oct 29, 1892
Apr 5, 1932
&
Della D. Hatchett
Apr 12, 1892
Apr 14, 1957

William B. Steiner
1916-
&
Ethel J. Steiner
1917-1943

"Ned" E. B. Dolby
1858-1938
&
Ella R. Dolby
1866-1949

Moses Woodfin
Mar 8, 1829
Jan 30, 1908
&
Rachel Anna Clark Woodfin
Aug 9, 1835
Dec 4, 1920

Alice Woodfin
1869-1942

Mollie Woodfin
1858-1945

J. M. Woodfin
"Payne"
1874-1973

Mary M. Webb
1875-1908

Mabel M. Fletcher
1872-1920

Rufus A. Hoover
1843-1901
&
Mary Kay Hoover
1865-1937

Nona Kay, child of
R. A. & M. K. Hoover
Jun 19, 1891
Dec 24, 1894

Sarah C. Kay
Feb 1, 1831
Apr 23, 1909

Joe F. Hoover
1858-1932

Emma W. Hoover
1861-1949

Walter R. Hoover
Feb 6, 1893
Apr 25, 1922
30 Div 117 Reg Co.
M.A.E.F.

Frances R. Hoover Gregory
Jul 4, 1899
May 30, 1973

Emma Josephine Gregory
Born Jul 18, 1829
(no death date)

Walter Y. Partee
Oct 4, 1893
Apr 26, 1963
&
Ella H. Partee
Oct 10, 1884

William Carroll Partee
1890-1934

Oscar Partee, Jr.
1902-1926

Mattie H. Partee
1866-1927

W. D. Partee
1861-1933

Randy, son of
Mr & Mrs P. R. Crosslin
1948-1949

Jimmie, son of
Mr & Mrs C. C. Crosslin
1942-1944

Daniel D. Hoover
Mar 5, 1833
Aug 28, 1905
&
Mary E. Hoover
Oct 26, 1834
Dec 21, 1914

John Morton Whiteside
Jan 14, 1888
Apr 17, 1961

Grace H. Whiteside
Feb 26, 1884
Mar 15, 1972

S. R. Whiteside
1847-1929

Kate Tune, wife of
S. R. Whiteside
1852-1921

Mabel Kate Whiteside
Feb 3, 1879
Mar 1, 1960

Lyda Louise Whiteside
1886-1901

Esther Vesey Whiteside
1890-1950

Samuel Porter Whiteside
Mar 25, 1883
Jan 5, 1970

Louise Weisiger Whiteside
Oct 7, 1881
Sep 12, 1972

Rodolph G. Partee
Nov 20, 1894
Jan 11, 1952

Ida Lee H. Partee
Jul 4, 1899
Jul 9, 1969

R. M. Crosslin
Jul 7, 1856
Dec 25, 1921
&
Eliza Ann Crosslin
Apr 24, 1853
May 8, 1922

Orin Crosslin
1924-1927

Silas Robert Crosslin
1888-1968
&
Parthenia Eaton Crosslin
1887-19

J. Freeman Brandon
Feb 7, 1895
Jan 28, 1967
&
Mattie Sue Brandon
May 24, 1905

J. T. Haile
Sep 24, 1868
Jul 3, 1939
&
Ella Beachboard Haile
Feb 20, 1881
Jan 13, 1908

Susan J. Jordan
1845-1936

Annie Jones Woodfin
1908-1936

S. N. Woodfin
1866-1924

Tennie J. Woodfin
1872-1960

John P. Jarman
Jan 5, 1858
Feb 21, 1917
&
Annie Jarman
May 18, 1866
Jun 6, 1918

Dwight Jarman
Jun 4, 1898

&
Sophia L. Jarman
Jan 12, 1893
Jul 24, 1969

Rollie A. Crosslin
Aug 16, 1881

&
Lucy Gay Crosslin
Jan 20, 1895
Feb 28, 1956

William Odie Butner
Oct 16, 1884
Feb 13, 1958
&
Zora B. Lee Butner
Jan 15, 1883
Feb 16, 1965

George W. Jarman
1862-1938
&
Lou C. Jarman
1864-1938

William John Hoover
Jun 11, 1856
Mar 1, 1906
&
Sallie Peacock Hoover
Mar 16, 1861
Jul 27, 1932
&
Rebecca Banks Hoover
Apr 26, 1891
Nov 19, 1894

T. R. Freeman, Jr.
Sep 1, 1874
Jun 25, 1933
&
Zenobia Freeman
May 19, 1879
Dec 2, 1951

Sue F. Bingham
Apr 13, 1853
Dec 31, 1925

Lester Freeman
Jul 10, 1905

Mary Nettie Freeman
Aug 9, 1892
Dec 1, 1956

John Bess
Feb 25, 1888
Dec 5, 1925

Arthur H. La Mouria
Sep 5, 1901

&
Adeline R. La Mouria
Aug 23, 1895

Gartha A. Richards
1864-1957
&
Thomas S. Richards
1861-1929

Allie T. Whitaker
Jun 21, 1890
May 14, 1963

Eva E. Whitaker
Jun 30, 1895
Aug 15, 1962

P. E. Whitaker
Jun 2, 1866
Jun 23, 1938

Josephine F. Whitaker
Oct 13, 1866
Oct 12, 1956

Frank Claxton
1868-1934

Fannie H. Lisenby
1878-1968

Helen Hoover Douglas
Jul 3, 1899
Jan 23, 1973

Pauline, dau of
Dr. W. C. & C. T. Hoover
Aug 27, 1887
Aug 7, 1891
&
W. C. Hoover
1856-1908
&
Kate P. Hoover
1858-1933

William D. Hoover
Tennessee
Pfc 4 Co 153 Depot
Brig W. W. I
Jan 5, 1891
Oct 4, 1970

Adria Black
Mar 10, 1865
Jul 25, 1937

D. E. Hoover
1859-1933

Lottie Hoover
1862-1921

Kathleen Hoover
1888-1965

Edwin Hoover
1894-1965

Valleria Hoover
1890-1963

Sophia B. Foltz
1888-1953

Tappie Moore Wright
Jul 26, 1879
Nov 22, 1958

Ernest Bowlin Wright
Jun 18, 1881
Nov 21, 1956

Aubrey W. Wright
1902-1975
(Howell)

Henry Pearl Sain
May 27, 1913
Dec 8, 1968

Caleb E. Clifford
Feb 18, 1906
Apr 28, 1959

Doris Clifford
Apr 11, 1940
Nov 12, 1949

R. Marvin Osteen
Jan 1, 1884
Feb 17, 1949

Mary F. Osteen
Mar 15, 1899

William R. Coop
Jan 19, 1849
Nov 28, 1931

Susan Coop
Jun 23, 1856
Aug 21, 1931

James J. Coop
Oct 6, 1876
Jun 16, 1916

Jennie F. Coop
May 30, 1894
Mar 10, 1947

Z. R. Pickens
Jun 11, 1859
Feb 25, 1936

Nancy Lou Pickens
Jan 4, 1862
Sep 25, 1944

Robert E. Epps, Sr.
May 23, 1855
Aug 16, 1929

Lou Miller Epps
Dec 22, 1865
Sep 17, 1939

Robert E. Epps, Jr.
1896-1950

Kathleen Epps Rhodes
1891-1974
(Gowen-Smith)

A. E. Buttner
1865-1927

Martha Buttner
1865-1938

Myrtle S. Buttner
1891-1945

Alice Buttner
1898-1962

Jim Wilson Bomar
Nov 9, 1880
Dec 31, 1969
&
Tennie C. Bomar
Apr 14, 1885
Jun 13, 1953

Jesse H. Powell
1897-1975
(Gowen-Smith)

Elam Wright
1867-1963

Ella Maye Wright
1888-1949

David W. Wright
1853-1933

Mattie B. Wright
1854-1928

"Children of William R. &
      Susan Coop"
Ella Coop   John H.
Hattie Nelson   James J.
Lula Hoover   Guss M.
Annie Arnold   William F.
Kate Knox   Robert W.
Jennie Coop   Tom L.
Susie McDonald   Volney T.

John H. Coop
Feb 12, 1875
Jul 1, 1941

Sophia A. Coop
Dec 21, 1881

Z. R. Pickens, Jr.
Sep 9, 1890
Oct 26, 1943

William Gray Vance
1883-1960
&
Annie Lou Epps Vance
1889-1972

J. A. Bush
1873-1926

Tythia A. Bush
Jan 4, 1876
Jan 1, 1960

Thomas L. Bush
Aug 4, 1897
Apr 18, 1969

Leighton J. Bush
Apr 30, 1925
Aug 1, 1960

Chas. R. Faulkner, Sr.
May 8, 1861
Oct 4, 1943

Mary S. Faulkner
Sep 24, 1876
(no date)

Wilburn B. Carroll
Dec 21, 1858
Oct 1, 1940

Gordon M. Carroll, Jr.
Jun 10, 1923
May 29, 1941

Gordon M. Carroll
Tennessee
Lt. 6 Regt F.A. Repl Depot
W. W. I
Oct 13, 1899
Sep 14, 1966

T. L. Faulkner
1852-1940

Addie J. Faulkner
1857-1921

Ella Jacobs
1865-1943

Robert L. Bingham
1869-1925

Rosa Lee Miller Bingham
1871-1936

Irene Bingham
1902-1920

James Daniel Batte
1881-1908
&
Ida Landis Batte
1883-(no date)

Homa W. Pickens
Jun 27, 1839
Dec 10, 1955

W. R. Stovall
Sep 22, 1877
Feb 24, 1951

Beulah P. Stovall
Sep 13, 1889
Oct 4, 1972

Etta McConnell, wife of
W. R. Stovall
Oct 8, 1884
Jul 7, 1924

Jessie T. Stovall
1872-1924

D. H. Stovall
May 4, 1843
Dec 16, 1916
& wife:
Lettie C. Terry Stovall
Nov 15, 1849
Jun 11, 1901

William E. Draper, Jr.
(William Estill)
Tennessee
Capt. U.S.Army   W.W.II
Jul 30, 1918
Apr 13, 1970

Mary C. Smalling
1851-1940

Stella B. Smalling
1855-1936

Clarence A. Smalling
1890-1971
&
Alice L. Smalling
1898-

Ben R. Smalling
Mar 22, 1926
Mar 1, 1951

William F. Buchanan
1879-1938

John Morton Whiteside, Jr.
1912-1941

Iva Mai Alexander
1912-1970

William H. Landis
Jan 16, 1841
May 15, 1915
&
Janet H. Landis
Sep 25, 1851
May 3, 1931

Maggie Lula, dau of
W. H. & J. Landis
Jan 10, 1877
Sep 11, 1892

Virginia Haile Starnes
Aug 15, 1829
Sep 14, 1901

Lizzie E., wife of
G. W. Douglas
Mar 26, 1857
married Dec 13, 1887
Died Jan 17, 1890

Exine Wyche, wife of
J. M. Nuckolls
Oct 17, 1841
Jan 6, 1896

Exine, dau of
J. M. & Exine Wyche Nuckolls
1865-1936
&
Louise Nuckolls, wife of
T. N. Blake
Feb 9, 1863
Apr 25, 1894

Nell S. Hartman
1896-1921

William H. Payne
1866-1945
&
Lavadah H. Payne
1865-1945

Oscar Walton Beachboard
Nov 8, 1873
Jan 18, 1954

Dera Lynch Beachboard
Sep 24, 1878
Jan 29, 1965

Addie V. Keysaer
1881-1965

Nellie E. Keysaer
1878-1940

J. C. Keysaer
1838-1924

Nancy R. Keysaer
1848-1943

Abner B. Keysaer
1876-1951

Annie B. Keysaer
1875-1951

Lytle Warren Woodfin
Sep 3, 1886
Aug 30, 1960

Elizabeth Y. Woodfin
1857-1918

Ephie Kirk Woodfin
Feb 25, 1886
May 22, 1952

Abner Waite Yell
1853-1930
&
Bessie Rice Yell
1865-1956

Ann Lowe Yell Clary
May 31, 1897-Sep 8, 1929

Elizabeth F. Morgan
1907-1970

Marian Freeman
Jan 24, 1910
Jul 29, 1910

Dr. John Knox Freeman
Jul 10, 1872
Oct 23, 1954

Ethel Holder Freeman
Sep 9, 1878
Mar 11, 1949

Horace J. Epps
1891-1926

Eula E. Shofner
1865-1948

Thomas N. Epps
Dec 29, 1850
Sep 28, 1916

Charles I. Mullins
Sep 9, 1895
Jan 11, 1959
&
Maude P. Mullins
Jan 1, 1896

Charles I. Mullins, Jr.
1927-1972

Sallie Beachboard Gallagher
Oct 26, 1858
Jun 3, 1947

Robert Morris Paty
1862-1946

Zula Muse Paty
1866-1940

Annie May Paty, wife of
E. H. Travis
1892-1919

Patty, Infant of
E. H. & A. M. Travis
1919

Leone Paty Mann
1888-1971

Wayne A. Paty
1900-1970

Infant Son of
R. R. & A. M. Paty
1923

Sidney G. King
Feb 28, 1873
Nov 10, 1926
&
Alice King
Apr 30, 1876
Apr 5, 1955

"Father"
(J. H.) Holder
1847-1899

"Mother" Holder
1843-1913

Leonard Lee Holder
Jun 28, 1880
Jan 3, 1881
&
Robert Holder
Jun 2, 1890
Jun 26, 1890

Robert L. Taylor
1895-1968
&
Saidee Shoffner Taylor
1897-1962
married Aug 1, 1921

John Peyton Crigler
May 21, 1886
Dec 31, 1940

Caroline Grimmett Crigler
Dearest of Mothers
(no dates)

Arthur P. Kay
1878-1949

Elizabeth Kay
1914-1966

John F. Coffman
1914-1948

Annie Mae Coffman
1884-1929

W. C. Coffman, Jr.
1912-1929

William C. Coffman, Sr.
1885-1968

J. L. Coffman
1918-1944

Clyde Muse
1881-1950

Jennie M. Muse
1885-1965

Infant of
Robert & Eliza Muse
Oct 14, 1928

Evelyn, dau of
Clyde & Jennie Muse
1909-1915

William Perry Muse
Tennessee
SK1 U.S.Navy W.W.II
Jan 30, 1922
Feb 7, 1970

Mary E. Osborne
1843-1920

Madison H. Webb
Feb 5, 1836
Sep 13, 1891

Jane Ellen Webb
1847-1938

John L. Sutton
1865-1938

Maggie W. Sutton
1868-1952

J. Mat Sutton
1895-1918
13th Regt U.S.Marine

Eugene B. Shoffner
1870-1953

Evie A. Shoffner
1868-1956

Elmer C. Johnson
May 25, 1895
Nov 10, 1918

Grover C. Joyce
1889-1974
(Howell)

Brenda Lucille Burks
Jan 5, 1973
Jan 5, 1973

Lucille Burks
1921-1949

Spencer A. Turrentine
1868-1965
&
Agatha T. Turrentine
1872-1954

Thomas H. Still
1869-1930
&
Emma Payne Still
1868-1952

John L. Payne
1871-1938
&
Jennie P. Payne
1877-1939
&
Nannie E. Payne
1881-1956

William Simeon Ashley
1862-1946

Tennie C. Carlisle, wife
of J. S. Ashley
Jul 19, 1868
Dec 5, 1920

Mattie Carlisle Ashley
1866-1948

James H. Edwards
Jun 14, 1856
Dec 28, 1916

"Father" Yell
1829-1907

"Mother" Yell
1830-1889

James Monroe Braden
1851-1922
"Brother"

Emma Braden Freeman
1851-1912
"Mother"

William Rucker Freeman
Jan 5, 1848
Dec 31, 1902
&
Adella Braden Freeman
Sep 20, 1849
Jun 6, 1931

Roy Freeman
1880-1956

Alma V. Freeman
1879-1971
(Hoover)

Will Stephenson
1878-1967

Jannie Gragg, wife of
W. S. Stephenson
1897-19

Irene Shipley, wife of
W. S. Stephenson
1894-1954

Josephine Stephenson
1850-1923

Comer Williams
1891-1925

Minnie Williams
1893-1943

L. B. Williams
1854-1944
& wife:
Letsie T. Brittain Williams
1857-1926

Clifford H. Ashley
Dec 23, 1875
Jan 25, 1960
&
Mattie W. Ashley
Sep 20, 1894

Lena E. Jacobs
1878-1947

Thomas Eugene Norvell
1869-1947

Mary Burr Norvell Smith
Dec 25, 1848
Oct 2, 1940

T. R. Freeman
Jun 1, 1830
Jul 8, 1916
age: 86y, 1m, 7d.

Rebecca S., wife of
T. R. Freeman
Apr 11, 1844
Feb 23, 1899
age: 54y, 10m, 12d.

Dr. T. F. Frizzell
1855-1887

Sadie Clay Frizzell
Dec 10, 1881
Sep 26, 1973

Sallie F. Smalling
1858-1946

Robert A. Wright
Apr 20, 1848
Oct 18, 1918
&
Jesse Thomas Wright
Jan 13, 1884
Jul 28, 1884
&
Johnnie L. Wright
May 25, 1862
May 5, 1910

Novella McAdoo Wright
Aug 5, 1861
Oct 1, 1921

Robr't A. Shipley
1897-1969

James W. Stephenson
1871-1944

Maggie Loyd
1868-1942

Mollie S. Loyd
1875-1934

"Father"
Frank Euless
Nov 5, 1850
Jan 10, 1923

"Mother"
Mattie F. Euless
Sep 1, 1856
Jan 3, 1923

Herbert F. Euless
Jun 10, 1883
Jan 14, 1926

W. R., Jr., son of
W. R. & Clara Mingle
Feb 10, 1921
Sep 17, 1921

James C. Mingle
Feb 13, 1852
Apr 2, 1922
& wife:
Emma Gaither Mingle
Oct 17, 1858-Sep 29, 1913

Andrew W. Smith
1885-1936

Willadel F. Smith
1887-1959

Elizabeth F. Carney
1854-1937

Robert Carney
May 14, 1854
Jan 4, 1895

Susie, dau of
B. T. & Lizzie Carney
Died Apr 30, 1890
age: 11m & 20d.

Kate Carney
1881-1970

George D. Stephenson
Tennessee
Pvt Co C 307 Inf W.W.I
Jan 7, 1890
Apr 18, 1966

Lula L. Stephenson
Nov 24, 1896
Mar 20, 1957

Tom Lynn Stephenson
May 21, 1899
Mar 1, 1974

Iola D. Stephenson
May 13, 1866
Feb 4, 1956

David C. Williams
Aug 22, 1881
Nov 21, 1971
&
Daisy Anthony Williams
Jun 26, 1882
Mar 5, 1964

Jasper Ernest Smith
1885-1971

Lockie Powell Smith
1893-1952

Olin W. Smith
1880-1941

Myrtle W. Smith
1883-1973

Martha Ellen Smith
1944-1951

John S. Norvell
1875-1945

Lula M. Norvell
1883-1963

Don Norvell
1900-1949

S. P. Jones
Oct 18, 1860
May 28, 1913

Thomas G. Moseley
1824-1908

Drucilla Moseley
1830-1878

Mathew W. Moseley
1859-1911

Annie M. Couch
1865-1954

Hattie B. Moseley
1870-1932

Tommie Drue Muxen
1861-1937

Andrew Muxen
1859-1954

Sara M. Phillips
1888-1956

Jesse C. Henderson
1878-1935

Stella Overby Green
1847-1919

Stella Green, wife of
Fred Pearson
1883-1915

Nisbett Plot, with 2
unmarked graves.

Dan B. Vance, Sr.
1845-1921

Betty B. Vance
1850-1941

Dixon C. Vance
1877-1940

Zora Vance
1869-1954

Rev. D. B. Vance
Feb 20, 1845
Jun 20, 1921

Lt. Amos H. Taylor
1910-1942

W. M. Cortner
1873-1945

Annie McQuiddy Cortner
1884-1971

W. M. Cortner, Jr.
1915-1965

W. B. McQuiddy
1853-1933

Chappell Wade McQuiddy
1857-1934

Iowa Rogers Jones
1864-1917

Charles Leslie Jones
1891-1944

William John Davis
1864-1955

Birdie Rathbone Davis
1873-1943

Rucker Harris
Aug 9, 1855
May 8, 1921

Lilburn L. Miller
Oct 1, 1870
Dec 8, 1938

Bettie Miller Bingham
1880-1968

Rosa Fields Bingham
1878-1950

Granville H. Bingham
Mar 13, 1853
Apr 28, 1919

Delilah, wife of
G. H. Bingham
Jan 1, 1854
Dec 21, 1917

Mary Adla Bingham
1885-1965

Roberta Bingham
1898-1973

T. S. Stephenson
Mar 23, 1842
Nov 13, 1913

S. E. Stephenson
Jul 26, 1847
May 9, 1913

_.(J) A. Stephenson
1867-1946

Lurton Busch Hinkle
1892-1957

B. Porter Hinkle
1889-1918
"Killed in Action at
Boise De Harville, France,
Nov 11, 1918"

Martha Cheatham Hinkle
1858-1932

T. Iverson Hinkle
1879-1951

J. W. Anthony
1880-1951

Mary Anthony
1880-1957

William Parker
Oct 30, 1861
Nov 25, 1944

James Miller Wilson
1857-1933

Emma D. Wilson
1860-1935

James Miller Wilson, Jr.
1890-1914

Robert George Coop
Apr 9, 1907
May 6, 1907

Infant Son of
Mr & Mrs R. M. Coop
Sep 1, 1900

John W. Coop
Died Feb 26, 1905
age: 83 yrs.

George W. Coop
1846-1923

Laura H. Coop
1858-1925

Horatio E. Coop
Aug 19, 1881
Sep 24, 1910

Corrie M. Coop
Apr 29, 1883
Aug 12, 1897

Lillian K. Coop Whitsett
Jun 5, 1885
May 16, 1948

Jesse T. Parker
1870-1927
&
Alvie S. Parker
1871-1935

Infant Son of
Mr & Mrs J. A. Whittemore
Mar 17, 1919
Dec 2, 1920

Thomas Marshall Hinkle
1858-1932

Lucie Mai Hinkle
1891-1948

Herschel S. Hinkle
1883-1939

Erin Ashley Hinkle
1888-1967

J. F. Anthony
1849-1927

Amanda S. Anthony
1858-1951

Peter G. Anthony
1877-1956

Emma P. Anthony
1879-1956

John T. Clary
1878-1974

Eva Clary
1874-1967

Dr. William Franklin Clary
1830-1910
&
Tennie Little Clary
1842-1928

Alfred D. Fugitt
Nov 8, 1813
Feb 13, 1897
&
Jane M. Fugitt
Sep 3, 1814
Jan 5, 1889
married Jan 10, 1837

A. T. Fugitt
1859-(no date)

Ida H. Fugitt
1869-(no date)

Pearl Fugitt
1866-1887

Infant Son of
A. T. & Ida H. Fugitt
(no dates)

Mary Ward Fugitt
1894-1896

Miles Hathcock, Jr.
1894-19
&
Jewel Hathcock
1897-1940

Elmer Hathcock
1892-1918

Willie Hathcock
Mar 21, 1899

Miles N. Hathcock
1851-1930
&
Jossie T. Hathcock
1884-1927

B. G. Bingham
Feb 22, 1882
Aug 2, 1945

Ora Edwards Bingham
Aug 16, 1882
Sep 4, 1947

Palmer Bingham
1890-1943

Lillian Vaughn Bingham
1891-1948

Emma Bingham
1891-1938

Evelyn Bingham
1914-1929

William A. Webb
1867-1919

Mary Clary, wife of
W. A. Webb
1871-1919

Ethelwyn, dau of
William A. & Mary C. Webb
1909-1910

J. C. Freeman, son of
J. H. & H. Freeman
Aug 11, 1863
Jan 23, 1881

Hattie, dau of
J. H. & Harriett Freeman
Apr 7, 1870
Nov 6, 1887
age: 17y, 6m, 9d.

Jos. H. Freeman
Apr 19, 1822
Nov 4, 1895
age: 73y, 6m, 15d.
& wife:
Harriet Freeman
Apr 12, 1825
Jul 2, 1873
age: 48y, 2m, 21d.

Jennie Coop Freeman
1841-1920

Mary E. Freeman
1886-1968
(Hoover)

Mary E. Frothingham
Mar 6, 1845
Aug 1, 1927

Merrill Frothingham
Jun 12, 1881
Mar 22, 1920
& wife:
Jennie England Frothingham
Jan 20, 1880

Ulysses C. Frothingham
1902-1930

Calvin H. Winnette
Jul 7, 1867
Aug 6, 1925

Horace Winnette
Jan 8, 1894
Oct 11, 1926

William Granville Bingham
Jul 4, 1876
Jul 16, 1940

Pearl Johns Bingham
Apr 11, 1880
Jun 17, 1967

Pearl E. Bingham
May 11, 1914
Jan 27, 1926

William F. Clifford
1874-1934
&
Annie E. Clifford
1876-1948

Buford A. Clifford
Sep 11, 1901
Dec 6, 1966

Robert B. Clifford
Nov 1, 1897
Nov 5, 1918
U.S.A. Co E
6th Inft 5 Div.

Robert Brank Scruggs
Jun 5, 1882
Mar 29, 1916

Frederick Moore Scruggs
Oct 6, 1880
Aug 13, 1904
&
Mary Scruggs Owen
Feb 7, 1869
Jul 6, 1900
&
Laura B. Scruggs
Jun 14, 1873
Feb 8, 1875
&
W. F. Scruggs
Jun 4, 1841
Jan 22, 1882

Mother Scruggs
(no dates)

William Robert Webb, Jr.
Aug 4, 1874
Oct 31, 1960

Louise Manning Webb
Jan 25, 1872
Nov 4, 1958

McDugald McLean
Jan 20, 1886
Sep 8, 1922

Serena German Porter Hulme
Mar 16, 1813
Sep 30, 1892
"Erected by G. L. Beale."

Thomas K. Munsey
1860-1916

Cora Lee Munsey
1874-1934

J. E. Elkins
1872-1949

Mittie Watson Elkins
1873-1929

Charlie Elkins
Oct 8, 1902
Jul 17, 1922

Sadie Elkins
Dec 4, 1896-May 16, 1920

Erby Smith Brown
1856-1935

Mollie P. Brown
1856-1927

Lonnie A. Brown
1882-1957

Katharine Brown
1885-1920

Finis E. Brown
1902-1969

Lon A. Brown, Jr.
California
CRM U.S.Navy W.W.II
Jul 17, 1912
Jan 19, 1942

Townzin F. Smalling
1845-1930

Aline Smalling
Feb 16, 1884
Jan 11, 1970

Price P. Manley
Sep 25, 1899
Sep 23, 1969
&
Ruth F. Manley
Jan 22, 1904
Apr 11, 1972

Baby Girl of
R. T. & V. H. Webb
1920

Alla Webb
Oct 2, 1875
Mar 15, 1944

William Robert Webb
Nov 11, 1842
Dec 19, 1926

Emma Clary Webb
Apr 17, 1846
Apr 3, 1937

Mary Moffatt, wife of
Rev. J. T. Curry
Sep 13, 1863
Apr 1, 1902

James B. Hunter
Apr 27, 1838
Feb 3, 1905
&
Mary Cooper Hunter
Aug 20, 1847
Jun 23, 1934

Ida Lee Hunter
Jul 22, 1868
May 15, 1954

Spencer M. Elkins
1899-1970
&
Bera H. Elkins
1897-1971

Edmond Jones Mash
Tennessee
Cpl Army Air Force W.W.II
Dec 28, 1905
Dec 30, 1952

John J. Mashe
Feb 23, 1877
Nov 24, 1961

Emma Dean Mashe
1885-1938

Herbert H. Mashe
Mar 30, 1904
Sep 23, 1925

Linda Fay (no last name)
(no dates-in Mashe-Dozier
                    plot)

L. T. D.
(footmarker -no dates)

T. W. D.
(footmarker-no dates)

Moores Peacock
May 14, 1878
Dec 13, 1952

Harriet Peacock
Jan 31, 1882
Oct 13, 1964

Cassie Fugitt Peacock
1850-1899

Samuel M. Linch
Mar 21, 1901
(no date)
    & wife:
Ella Brabson Linch
May 13, 1923
(no date)

Infant Son of
S. M. & E. B. Linch
Nov 12, 1886

Caleb R. Faulk
1877-1940
&
Sallie A. Faulk
1879-1958

Fred Hoover Faulk
Nov 10, 1906
Apr 30, 1908

William R. Bomar
1843-1934
&
Betty F. Bomar
1852-1927

William H. Bomar
1877-1956
&
Xennie Pickens Bomar
1884-19(no date)

Martin Payne
1874-1937

W. G. Davis
1837-1904

Mary E. Davis
1842-1921

Francis Pruitt Davis
Jul 8, 1867
Mar 1, 1934

C. E. Davis
1861-1914

T. E. Mullins
1863-1933
&
Lula Mullins
1874-1905

Beuna D. Mullins
1901-1905

M. A. Clifford
Oct 8, 1839
Nov 5, 1921
& wife:
M. J. Clifford
Sep 15, 1827
May 19, 1906

Marie Kate Thaxton
1876-1919

Henry Fox
Jun 21, 1860
Jul 10, 1930
&
Harriet Fox
Jun 28, 1850
May 14, 1915

John Fox
Aug 15, 1894
Sep 4, 1920

Harriette, dau of
Dee & S. B. Fox
1913-1926

Cora Jane Parsons, wife of
T. E. Mullins
Apr 25, 1877
Apr 19, 1915

Horace Reagor
1908-1961

Anna Mullins
1883-1969

Ruby Mullins
Infant
1924

John M. Mullins
1922-1923

Andrew B. Payne
1888-1963
&
Mattie M. Payne
1878-1968

George W. Parker
Cook U.S.Army
Jan 29, 1893
Oct 2, 1974
&
Mary L. Parker
1915-

Addie M. Lowe
1874-1928

"Father"
T. H. Parker
Mar 25, 1864
Mar 3, 1920

"Mother"
Tennie L. Parker
May 6, 1870
Sep 13, 1928

Stonewall M. Parker
Nov 2, 1891
Jan 13, 1960

Fugitt Plot,
3 graves, unmarked.

Frank Lee Richard
1874-1951
(Thompson)

E. N. Richards
1879-1918

Ibbie, wife of
E. N. Richards
1886-19

"Father"
Dr. Caleb C. Murphree
Aug 2, 1860
Jan 15, 1900
"Graduated with higest
honors from Medical Dept.
University of Tennessee,
April 12, 1888."
& wife:
Emma S. Murphree
Mar 10, 1856
Jan 22, 1900
&
Doak, only son of
C.C. & E.S. Murphree
Feb 10, 1886
Jan 23, 1900

Elizabeth Murphree
"Bess"
1890-1973

F. M. Pruett
Apr 28, 1828
Apr 22, 1900

Mary Catherine Pruett
Jun 23, 1836
Nov 27, 1912

Emma Williams
May 15, 1875
Aug 6, 1933

"Father"
Barton Fulks
Mar 10, 1890
Nov 7, 1965

"Mother"
Annie Espy Fulks
May 31, 1899
Aug 17, 1937

F. Walter Parker
Feb 18, 1893
Sep 10, 1963
&
Pearl S. Parker
Jan 10, 1891
Apr 27, 1968

Nora, dau of
J. T. & S. S. Parker
Sep 13, 1900
Apr 15, 1918

John T. Parker
Jun 23, 1857
Oct 22, 1936
&
Sarah I. Parker
Dec 13, 1860
Aug 8, 1929

Joseph D. Murphree
1869-1949

Virginia E. Murphree
1829-1915

William D. Murphree
Nov 20, 1819
Jul 21, 1904

W. C. Alexander
1832-1904

Fannie Murphree Alexander
1863-1939

W. C. Alexander, Jr.
1883-1955

Mary E. Patterson Spence
1843-1925

Belle Kenny
1852-1926

Johnnie F., son of
F. M. & M. C. Pruett
Aug 2, 1864
Aug 4, 1864

Willie E., son of
F. M. & M. C. Pruett
Sep 14, 1856
Aug 10, 1871

Herbert W. Davis
1879-1908

Lytle Davis
1880-1885

Georgie Mozelle Espy
1903-1970

George U. Espy
Mar 6, 1865
Aug 8, 1938
&
Callie B. Espy
Nov 20, 1876
Sep 25, 1954

Nina Espy Dunn
1917-1967

Drue Tolbert Robinson
1877-1963

Alberts Gill Robinson
1891-19

Albert Benoist Gill, Jr.
1902-1926

James Lafayette Goodrum
1844-1914

Malida Cooper Goodrum
1848-1921

Emma Goodrum
1884-1924

George C. Troxler, Jr.
Tennessee
S Sgt U.S. Air Force
Vietnam, A.M.
Oct 20, 1943
Jun 20, 1973

Robert M. "Mitch" Powell
Apr 30, 1895
(TM) 1974
&
Elizabeth O. Powell
Dec 7, 1896
Dec 21, 1966

Charles G. Lance
1864-1932
&
Clara J. Lance
1867-1961

Mary Lizzie, dau of
Mr & Mrs G. L. Anderson
Jun 23, 1900
Apr 5, 1905

Rev. W. W. Graves
Mar 1, 1836
Nov 6, 1906
& wife:
Annie Kenney Graves
Oct 27, 1844
Jan 9, 1918

Lutie Graves
1870-1917

J. N. Graves
1872-1912

Douglas A. Graves
1877-1947

Joseph Thomas Lynn
Dec 4, 1863
Aug 15, 1926

Flora Lynch Lynn
May 5, 1882
May 4, 1965

Sophia Peacock Cooper
1850-1917

Albert Benoist Gill
1868-1946

Ella Cooper Gill
1868-1946

William Charlie Cooper
Oct 1, 1844
Sep 13, 1905
"Member Forest's Escort
1861-65."

G. Clifford Troxler
Nov 27, 1908
Jan 24, 1961

Sarah Whiteside Troxler
Dec 16, 1907

Margaret Helen, dau of
J. E. & Margaret R.
                  Whiteside
Apr 21, 1926

Ida Goodrum Whiteside
1878-1939

Ida Whiteside Drake
1906-1935

Emmett E. Whiteside
1872-1944

John Thomas Moseley
1860-1938

Frances Pruett, wife of
J. T. Moseley
1860-1924

John Howland White
Oct 6, 1849
Jan 21, 1907

Francis Pruett, son of
J. H. & Mattie B. White
Feb 10, 1881
Jan 31, 1885

Mrs. Mary M. White
Dec 11, 1820
Nov 1, 1903

Baby Burrell, son of
B. G. & Jennie C. White
May 20, 1911
Aug 18, 1914

Jennie C., wife of
B. G. White
Aug 26, 1879
Jun 16, 1917

James J. Whiteside
Dec 15, 1844
Dec 24, 1900
& wife:
Nannie L. Stokes Whiteside
Jul 17, 1854
Apr 11, 1935

Mary Cooper Whiteside
1901-1902

Thomas Roe Curtis
1851-1916

Anna Kethroe Curtis
1852-1948

Helen Curtis
1887-1942

Catherine Thom Taylor
Dec 30, 1894
Oct 6, 1973

Sam J. Bingham
1886-1954
&
Bennie May J. Bingham
1888-1952

Henry W. Adcock
Mar 6, 1893
Apr 20, 1965
&
Effie M. Adcock
Nov 27, 1891
(no date)

Rebecca Evelyn Reed
1958-1959

B. Cleve Cawthron
Mar 9, 1888
Jun 24, 1967
&
Maggie E. Cawthron
Feb 21, 1884
Oct 18, 1968

Kenneth S. Phillips
Jul 18, 1926

&
Muriel M. Phillips
Feb 11, 1927
Oct 9, 1969

Mrs. Lightie R. Douglas
Died Jun 16, 1971
age: 82 yrs.
(Woodfin)

Martha Louise Parker
Mar 2, 1914
Dec 26, 1974

Barbara S. Parker
1943-1967
(Howell)

Melvin Ray Parker
May 7, 1959

John W. Davis
1854-1886

Lucy N. Davis
1858-1886

Jessie R. Plummer
1838-1910

Francis, wife of
Jessie R. Plummer
1850-1908

William H. Elkins
May 18, 1912

&
Sarah M. Pruett Elkins
Nov 2, 1917
Jul 11, 1972

Robert L. Elkins
1894-1941

Edw. H. Elkins
1870-1943

Johnnie E. Elkins
1876-1940

Winford E. Woodfin
1903-1972
&
Lula C. Woodfin
1913-

Walton Chunn Woodfin
1906-1954
&
Laura K. Coop Woodfin
1910-

John T. Stephenson
1855-1939

Martha A. Stephenson
1858-1902

Alpha E. Williams
1875-1941

Mary S. Williams
1878-1972

John W. Brandon
Aug 20, 1891

&
Eunice H. Brandon
Oct 10, 1890

C. Cecil Crosslin
1909-1961
&
Mary L. Crosslin
1915-19

William C. Smith
Jul 31, 1887
Oct 4, 1959

------- Prince
---- - 1958
(McFarland-Thompson)

Asbury C. Couey
1856-1928

Dr. T. H. Woods
1867-1940

Jennie L. Murphree, wife of
T. H. Woods
1865-1914

John W. Peacock
Mar 18, 1844
Feb 10, 1913

Ora Peacock
Oct 20, 1863
Oct 30, 1947

Z. T. Crouch, Jr.
1883-1956

Joseph Crouch
1886-1960
&
Jeannette Shoffner Crouch
1894-19

John H. Crouch
1873-1936

Maud S. Crouch
1879-1965

S. Alton Crosslin
May 12, 1910
Nov 27, 1966
&
Mary W. Crosslin
Apr 28, 1911

Clara Belle Puryear
1881-1951

Sam W. Lowe
1849-1937

Maude K. Frizzell
May 11, 1871
Aug 13, 1901

Adah Frizzell McCarver
Nov 7, 1883
Oct 20, 1920

James H. Hood
Mar 13, 1886
Oct 14, 1962
&
Bernice L. Hood
Oct 12, 1899

James Sewell Linch
Sep 7, 1932
Jun 19, 1970

Henry Clayton Jarman
Tennessee
Cpl 1 Co 20 Engineers W.W.I
May 13, 1894
May 17, 1963

J. H. Cunningham
Sep 3, 1838
Jun 6, 1897
&
Louisa J. Cunningham
Jan 23, 1840
Feb 18, 1909

T. W. Cunningham
1863-1919

John Cunningham
Died-1939

Sallie Cunningham
Died 1950

Z. T. Crouch
1847-1926

Malissa T. Crouch
1846-1938

Addie M. Crouch
1876-1965

Sadie R. Crouch
1881-1968

W. A. Crouch
1870-1950

Mabel B. Crouch
1890-1954

Archer Chaffin Frizzell
Mar 27, 1852
Mar 16, 1937

Jesse Edwin Frizzell
Oct 25, 1857
Jan 6, 1952

Kate Blair Frizzell, wife
of Jesse Frizzell
Jan 6, 1857
Jun 24, 1929

Lucile Frizzell Jacobs,
wife of Herbert Jacobs
Oct 2, 1882
Jan 30, 1970

Ruby Provence Jacobs, wife
of Blair Jacobs
Jun 1, 1899
Oct 5, 1962

Carl Rogers Stovall
Tennessee
Pfc Co C. 31 Inf 196 Lt
Inf Bde, Vietnam, P.H.
Sep 24, 1947
May 23, 1967

J. M. "John" Hill
May 31, 1903
(no date)
&
Florence W. Hill
May 22, 1903

George C. Smith
Tennessee
Cpl Hq Co 117 Inf W.W.I
Oct 27, 1894
Jun 27, 1961

Alla W. Haskins
1897-1975
(Howell)

Mary Cecile Messick
Dec 16, 1936
Dec 12, 1973

Thomas Drennon Pruitt, Sr.
Apr 13, 1906

&
Annie E. Prince Pruitt
Dec 7, 1907
Jul 16, 1971

Danny Dale Kelton
May 17, 1953
Mar 8, 1975

Clarence D. Edwards
Nov 19, 1869
Jul 23, 1960

H. F. Brown
Sep 18, 1860
Sep 10, 1927
& wife:
Rebecca Brown
Nov 29, 1863
Mar 17, 1924

Robert M. Prater
Tennessee
Pfc 315 Bomb Wing A A F
W. W. II
Nov 16, 1918
Apr 5, 1964

Joe Henry Mashe
Sep 10, 1899
Dec 17, 1968
&
Rebecca D. Mashe
Sep 25, 1901

Andrew J. Dearing, Jr.
Jul 12, 1911
Dec 10, 1969

Acey J. Prater
Mar 13, 1882

&
Sallie G. Prater
Jun 10, 1881
May 8, 1973

Georgia Ruth Delk
1915-1973
(Gowen-Smith)

Kate Coop Knox
1888-1975
(Gowen-Smith)

Robert W. Coop
Jan 14, 1892
May 20, 1954
&
Eva M. Coop
Feb 22, 1890
Mar 4, 1969

Richard D. Calvert
Nov 27, 1935
Feb 24, 1974
&
Sue C. Calvert
Aug 28, 1938

James W. Earls
1898-1969
(Powell)

George Melvon Mitchell
Jan 15, 1882
Jun 17, 1951
&
Lucy Jane Simpson Mitchell
Mar 12, 1879
Feb 18, 1961

Rebecca A. Taylor
Feb 16, 1851
Apr 11, 1924

William Frank Brymer
Jan 22, 1925

&
Della M. Brymer
Nov 11, 1925

Maggie Brymer
1887-1963

Don Douglas Mason
Apr 13, 1894
Sep 5, 1963

Jerry Lee Ensley
1963-1963
(Gowen-Smith)

Willie R. Delbridge
Oct 25, 1897
Jan 12, 1974
&
Zettie H. Delbridge
Dec 11, 1908
----
married Jul 31, 1927

William H. Fox
Aug 29, 1911
Sep 2, 1972
&
Olga Carter Fox
Oct 5, 1911

Margret E. Smothermon
Jan 17, 1922
Feb 23, 1924

Oman H. Harrell
Jul 19, 1903

&
Lucille U. Harrell
Jan 6, 1906

June Harrell
Tennessee
Cox U.S.Navy W.W.II
May 29, 1926
Jun 26, 1969

Marie P. Harrell
Dec 29, 1927
Jun 28, 1967

Harold Erle Paty
Tennessee
QM1 U.S.N.R.F.   W.W.I
Apr 14, 1894
Feb 3, 1961

Joseph Warren Thompson
1872-1952
&
Fanny Smith Thompson
1876-19(no date)

A. Burton Norris
Feb 24, 1921
Jun 3, 1962

Catherine C. Norris
Feb 27, 1922
Sep 19, 1973

William B. Wilson
May 8, 1895
Jul 1, 1968
&
Carrie H. Wilson
Jan 15, 1895

Coma L. Richards
Jun 3, 1891
(no date)
&
Pearl C. Richards
Sep 13, 1895
Jun 20, 1970

Lucille Richards
Jan 28, 1915

William Everett Young
Apr 12, 1908

&
Alma Cribbs Young
Mar 9, 1903

Bennee Lee Sasnett
Apr 10, 1935

&
Mary Joy Young Sasnett
Aug 4, 1936
Jul 27, 1970

David F. Bush, Sr.
Jan 28, 1900
Apr 20, 1959

David F. Bush, Jr.
Sgt U.S.Marine Corps
Dec 17, 1928
Oct 21, 1974

Orman C. Neal
Aug 20, 1898
Jun 12, 1968
&
Ella Mai T. Neal
Dec 14, 1901
Jan 10, 1974

Waldon E. Blackburn
Apr 5, 1894
Mar 8, 1962
&
Elsie Mae Blackburn
Dec 29, 1895
Jan 15, 1970

Lee Nix Clifford
Jun 8, 1908
Sep 3, 1967

Mary J. Clifford
Jan 10, 1909

Billy L. Clifford
Nov 2, 1939
Aug 17, 1961

Ike G. Lowery
Dec 30, 1904
Mar 1, 1970

Frankie Lynn Brown
Apr 5, 1962
Dec 7, 1962
(Picture)

Cathy J. Clifford
May 5, 1961
Mar 12, 1964

Patsy P. Clifford
Nov 30, 1942
Mar 12, 1964

Infant Son of
Joe & Belva Vance
Dec 7, 1968

Margaret Vance Martin
1915-1966

Ferrow H. Himes
Jan 9, 1906
Aug 24, 1971

Ella Church
1905-1944

Archie R. Winnett
1918-1975 (Gowen-Smith)

Kacy R. Farless
1910-1975 (Gowen-Smith)

Arthur Clarence Stacy
1892-1974
(Gowen-Smith)

Rosie A. Stacy
May 30, 1896
Dec 13, 1961

Dorris H. Stacy
May 2, 1935
Feb 22, 1962

John A. Butner
1875-1917

Charles L. Stacy
Feb 22, 1920
Apr 21, 1921

Morris Stacy
May 2, 1935
May 5, 1935

Billie Stacy
Aug 10, 1938
Aug 24, 1938

Kathy D. Todd
Sep 13, 1953
Feb 5, 1969

Evelyn Teresa Todd
Sep 16, 1955
Aug 7, 1956

Will Dye
1954-1954
(Thompson)

Benjamin Bingham
1882-1970
(Hoover)

T. Emery
1861-1931

6 OLD SALEM CEMETERY   Map # 8
Located at Bell Buckle, Tennessee

(Continued)

No marker:*****
Sarah Campbell Majors, dau
of Robert & Sarah Majors
(no dates)

No marker:*****
Evelyn Phillis Smith
Born Feb 21, 1923
Died Sep 18, 1933

***** by Mrs. Walter Parrish.

No marker:*****
Martin David Payne(no dates)
Clara Jane Mason Payne (no dates)
Mary A. Payne (no dates)
Sallie A. Payne (no dates)
Leahr B. Payne (no dates)

No marker:*****
Claudia Bomar Payne (no dates)
Ruth Payne (no dates)
Mary Ellen Payne (no dates)

8 UNKNOWN CEMETERY   Map # 8
Located near where the Railroad Track crosses Fairfield Pike.

Defo----
C. C. (never finished)

3 or 4 unmarked graves.

9 MUSE CEMETERY   Map # 8
Located about 2 miles West of Fairfield, Tenn.

George P. Muse
Jan 29, 1844
Mar 8, 1922

Mary J. Wright Muse
Dec 14, 1845
Aug 22, 1898

Oscar Muse
Sep 22, 1867
Aug 12, 1890

Infant Baby Muse of
O. W. & Lizzie M. Muse
Aug 13, 1903

Orville W. Muse
Nov 5, 1869
Nov 10, 1928

Lizzie M. Shriver, wife of
Orville W. Muse
Sep 11, 1872
Aug 14, 1903

Grace Muse Reaves
Aug 5, 1882
Jun 2, 1959

Shriver Muse
Aug 1889
Mar 1900

Katie May Muse
Jan 1897
May 1897

10 BATES-FINCH-MUSE CEMETERY   Map # 8
Located about 1½ miles Southwest of Fairfield, Tenn.

T. H. Clay
Apr 22, 1832
Nov 19, 1881
age: 49y, 5m, 30d.

Lizzie R., dau of
T. H. & M. R. Clay
Sep 8, 1879
Jun 17, 1881

Nannie, dau of
B. C. & Lucy Slaughter
Died Feb 26, 1876
age: 6m & 15d.

E. F. Scruggs
Died Dec 9, 1875
age: 46y, 8m, 23d.

Ludolphus C. Muse
Jun 5, 1839
Oct 18, 1856

Henry Norvill Muse
Jan 26, 1854
Nov 17, 1860

James O. Muse
Dec 27, 1851
May 26, 1870

Margaret H., wife of
E. F. Scruggs
Died Jun 10, 1873
age: 40y, 7m, 15d.

Mary Fugit, wife of
Towsend Fugit & former wife
of Matt Scruggs, was born
15th Dec 1776, married Matt
Scruggs 9th Dec 1793, and to
T. Fugit in 1839, joined the
Baptist Church in 1812. She
was an acceptable member until
Sep 2, 1852

Elizabeth Woods
Jun 1, 1854
Dec 12, 1867

Lula Allice, dau of
T. H. & E. L. Woods
Died Nov 24, 1872
age: 3y, 6m, 27d.

W. B. Moore
Born in Greensburg, Ky.
Jul 22, 1839
Sep 15, 1878

Gabriel Glen Osborne
1803-1879
   & wife:
Nancy Jones Osborne
1802-1860

Sarah J., wife of
Thomas Booher, born in
Washington Co., Va.,
Sep 19, 1848
Sep 22, 1879
age: 27y & 3d.

131

Arvill Muse
Nov 13, 1806
Oct 23, 1855

Malinda M. Muse
Apr 26, 1809
Jan 31, 1857

Martha E. Muse
Aug 1, 1842
Dec 31, 1856

Many unmarked graves.

William H. Finch
Apr 2, 1823
Nov 26, 1876

Several fieldstones, no inscriptions.

Mary E. Finch, dau of
M. S. & Julia A. Finch
Oct 13, 1843
Oct 23, 1843

11 NEW HOPE CHURCH CEMETERY   Map # 8
Located at the New Hope Church, Fairfield, Tenn.

Wetheston Cooper Orme
Born Birmingham, Ala.
Feb 17, 1902
Died Fairfield, Tenn.
Aug 22, 1956

Elizabeth Sara Cooper
Born in Fairfield, Tenn
Feb 4, 1878
Died in Manchester, Tenn.
Jan 11, 1966

Dr. Robert L. Singleton
Born in Halifax Co., Va.
Oct 2, 1813
Jan 20, 1858

Sarah Elizabeth Scott, wife
of Dr. Robert L. Singleton
Dec 28, 1818
Aug 4, 1900

"My Husband"
Benj. F. Davis
Jul 5, 1846
Aug 15, 1881

Kittie, wife of
B. F. Davis
Died Jan 22, 1875
age: 25y, 9m, --d.

John S. Davis
Nov 15, 1818
Apr 17, 1867

Nannie S., dau of
J. S. & F. L. Davis
Apr 8, 1851
Apr 9, 1872

Henry Davis
Born --- --, 1844
Died Aug 23, 1872

Charlie C. Scruggs
1886-

Claude M. Scruggs
1894-1922

Mary Agnes Scruggs
1845-1936

Jack E. Scruggs
1851-1933

Maggie R. Scruggs
1860-1943

Virginia F. Hawkins
1876-1944

Wetheston Greer Orme
Born Grassy Cove
Jun 27, 1854
Died Fairfield, Tenn.
Jan 2, 1939

Constance Cooper Orme
Born Rileys Creek
Nov 29, 1868
Died Fairfield, Tenn.
Jan 17, 1955

John Singleton
Apr 13, 1847
Apr 27, 1915
"Joint discoverer of Yellow
Aster Gold Mine, Randsburg,
Calif."

Martha D. Singleton
May 12, 1836
Nov 4, 1898

S. P. Davis
Apr 7, 1857
Jun 29, 1909
"A loving Husband, a Father
dear, lies buried here."

Emily Paralee, wife of
S. P. Davis
Aug 11, 1861
May 19, 1895

Little Pattie Walker, dau of
S. P. & E. P. Davis
Jun 22, 1894
Feb 19, 1895

Infant dau of
S. P. & E. P. Davis
Born & Died
Sep 9, 1891

Mrs. Sarah A. Waite
15 June 1790
14 Jan 1823

John E. Scruggs
Mar 5, 1802
Jul 15, 1889

"Mother"
Mary J., wife of
J. E. Scruggs
Feb 24, 1810
Apr 20, 1897

A. M. Tillman
(no dates)
(Name on wall around grave.)

James Orme
Born Mar 10, 1793
Died (no date)
&
Catharine T. Orme
Born Mar 5, 1783
Died (no date)

Sally Singleton
1845-1927

Kate Singleton
Jan 29, 1840
Oct 23, 1890

John Sehorn Singleton
Lt. 3rd Inf U.S.A.
1882-1918

Robert L. Singleton
1842-1919

M. A. Butner
Jan 21, 1869
Apr 5, 1919

William J. Osborne
Oct 20, 1823
Dec 6, 1898
& wife:
Elizabeth V. Osborne
Feb 17, 1823
Dec 22, 1887

Melissa F., wife of
H. P. Osborne
Dec 21, 1849
Jan 14, 1884

Mary Campbell, dau of
H. P. & Ida C. Osborne
Nov 4, 1890
Oct 3, 1891

J. Meadows
Died Oct 11, 1819
aged: 59
(fieldstone)

Eliza F., dau of
Philip & Mary J. Dedman
Dec 3, 1833
Mar 9, 1896

John B. F. M. Shaw, son of
C. & Mary Shaw
Died Sep 9, 1820
age: 1m & 27d.

N. L.   E. L.
(no dates-rock slabs)

A. A. Cooper
1832-1915
& wife:
Mary E. Cooper
1838-1923

Robert S. Cooper
1863-1922

Alex Alvin Cooper, Jr.
Jan 2, 1875
Apr 21, 1888
age: 13y, 3m, 19d.

Fanny Singleton, wife of
F. Jeter Martin
Dec 4, 1853
Jun 16, 1893

Rosamond, dau of
Fanny S. & F. Jeter Martin
Apr 9, 1878
Apr 19, 1878

Clement, Infant of
C. B. & E. C. Osborne
Nov 6, 1885
Oct 6, 1886
age: 11m.

Nannie E., dau of
C. B. & E. C. Osborne
May 6, 1881
Feb 3, 1887

G. Glen Osborne, III
1852-1923
&
Lola Rutledge Osborne
1863-1900

Frank B. Morgan
Sep 22, 1883
Jul 18, 1956

Myrtle Morgan
Mar 4, 1868
Apr 10, 1952

W. H. Morgan
1841-1883
&
Edna J. Morgan
1839-1913

Rebecca A., wife of
W. J. Shofner
Mar 16, 1839
Jun 24, 1903

Jemima Wood
Oct 19, 1771
Sep 3, 1831

Sacred to the Memory of
Christopher Shaw who was
born in Guinette Co., S.C.
on the 25th October 1765,
Removed to Bed. Co., Tn.1808
and departed this life 22nd
Feb 1832. "At an early age
Capt S. engaged in the
struggle of the Revolution
on the side of Liberty and
continued through life to
be an upright honest citizen,
faithful in the discharge of
his duties, setting an example to all around of in-
dustrius perseverances &
frugality. He was for many
years a member of the Baptist
Church at New Hope and fin-
ally died in the triumph of
faith in his blessed Redeemer."

J. F. Scruggs
Nov 13, 1853
Jul 1, 1879

I. M. Clark
Nov 9, 1852
May 6, 1897
&
Ann E. Clark
Jan 22, 1855
Apr 9, 1936

Rufus A., son of
J. M. & A. E. Clark
Sep 1, 1888
Jul 19, 1889
(J. on marker)

Lizzie, dau of
I. M. & A. E. Clark
Dec 15, 1882
Nov 27, 1910

Juliet M. Cakrothers
Born 1810
Died Jan 6, 1856

Joe S. Foster
1864-1940

Hattie K. Foster
Mar 5, 1869
Dec 30, 1955

Bailey Foster
1893-1935

Claude Bailey, son of
Bailey & Sadie Foster
Nov 15, 1923
Jun 16, 1928

Joe Hiles
1868-1929

Walter Hiles
1877-1940

Mary Hiles
1871-1958

Lena Hiles
1878-1967

Mary, wife of
Christopher Shaw
Born 1779
Died 1861
age: 82 yrs.

David W. J. B. Shaw, son of
C. & Mary Shaw
Died Jan 3, 1826
aged: 16y, 5m, 18d.
"This Memorial of respect &
love is erected by his Father,
C. Shaw."

William C. Shaw, son of
George W. & Sophia Shaw
Jul 6, 1833
Aug 21, 1852

W. R. Walker(J.R.)
Aug 5, 1833
Jun 27, 1904
& wife:
Lucinda Powers Walker
Oct 7, 1838
Apr 12, 1877

Lida Walker
1862-1920

Maurice L., son of
Mr & Mrs Dewey Johnson
Mar 8, 1930
Aug 10, 1934

John C. Lemmons
Mar 27, 1882
Jan 18, 1932

Martin Jones
1882-1929

Lucretia Jones
1860-1937

W. J. Jones
1858-1920

Raymond Keithley Crosslin
Mar 13, 1917
Feb 13, 1921

Thelma Inez Crosslin
Feb 5, 1919
Feb 9, 1919

Nettie Jane Harris
May 12, 1869
Mar 3, 1910

Nellie Hall Haggard
Oct 29, 1903
Feb 14, 1904

Annie Lee Haggard
Dec 17, 1907
Nov 1, 1910

O. W. Haggard
Mar 29, 1880
Feb 16, 1911

Infant of
A. F. & Mattie B. Euless
Born & Died Aug 2, 1890

Infant dau of
H. R. & Huldah Green
Died Apr 26, 1831

Elizabeth, wife of
William Pepper
Died 11 day Nov. 1843
she fell a sleep.
Born 29 June 1805

William G. Dolby
Co D
23 Regt Tenn Inf
C.S.A.
Aug 9, 1835
Nov 27, 1893

---------------(name gone)
Died --- 13, 1884
age: -- -- 20d.

Lula M., dau of
J. R. & L. Walker
May 20, 1875
Mar 18, 1875

Nannie E., dau of
J. R. & Lucinda Walker
Oct 3, 1860
May 24, 1877

T. P. Walker
Jul 6, 1858
Dec 21, 1890

John C. Foster
1880-1943

Eliza Foster
1863-1945

Mrs. Sallie Foster
1892-1974
(Gowen-Smith)

James L. Taylor
Oct 27, 1885
Aug 22, 1950
&
Maggie Ann Taylor
Jun 20, 1887
Feb 22, 1969

Infant Sons of
J. L. & Maggie Taylor
Born & Died
Oct 8, 1919

James N. Foster
Mar 15, 1856
Apr 12, 1925
&
Maggie G. Foster
Aug 9, 1860
Jan 11, 1917

Son of
Mr & Mrs J. S. Foster
May 10, 1907
Jul 25, 1907

Daisy Hiles
1880-1948

Macajah Thomas Cooper
Born in Rowan Co., N.C.,
Dec 28, 1806
Feb 16, 1873
&
Sara Vincent Cooper
Mar 31, 1809
May 22, 1864

Susan Love Cooper
1849-1867

S. B., dau of
J. R. & Lucinda Walker
Jan 28, 1869
Mar 11, 1889

Joseph Baker Walker
May 14, 1865
Jan 1, 1934
&
Janie Stephens Walker
Sep 24, 1871
Sep 12, 1951

James W. Isom
1847-1923
& wife:
Mary E. Walker Isom
1857-1922

G. W., son of
J. W. & M. E. Isom
Apr 10, 1891
Feb 8, 1891

M. L. Isom
Jun 14, 1895
Feb 11, 1897

Alice Marion Isom
age: 23 yrs & 20 days
Died Jan 30, 1910

William Walker Isom, Jr.
Nov 2, 1933
Oct 29, 1934

Mattie Lyde, dau of
J. W. & M. E. Isom
Jun 14, 1895
Feb 11, 1897
(same as M.L. Walker, above)

Eddie Foster
Feb 4, 1889
Jul , 1908

Gertrude Foster
1897-1903

Lawson Foster, Jr.
1930-1931

Porter Foster
1895-1896

Ida J. Foster
1891-1915

James W. Foster
1924-1926

Wilburn Hiles
Jul 30, 1826
May 30, 1889
&
Minerva Hiles
Sep 18, 1843
Feb 27, 1924

Claude T. Brooks
Jun 17, 1870
Nov 28, 1928

Mattie Brooks, wife of
P. G. Byers
Feb 24, 1878
Dec 11, 1913

T. J. Lee
Sep 25, 1840
Aug 31, 1910
&
Mrs. T. J. Lee
Sep 25, 1843
Jan 20, 1922

Robert E. Lee
Jun 15, 1866
May 27, 1909
&
Mary E. Lee
Jul 15, 1878
Apr 3, 1907

R. Aubrey Lee
Aug 12, 1869
Feb 18, 1959
&
Mary W. Lee
Jan 19, 1874
Dec 27, 1968

Bartlett Bird
Feb 13, 1818
Apr 2, 1881
age: 62y, 1m, 20d.

Sallie Thomas, oldest dau
of Asa & Caroline Thomas
Mar 5, 1852
Jun 14, 1900

Winn Thomas, 5th son of
Asa & Caroline Thomas
Oct 8, 1846
Oct 4, 1875

John Thomas, 2nd son of
Asa & Caroline Thomas
Nov 8, 1839
Aug 11, 1884

David Thomas, 6th son of
Asa & Caroline Thomas
Mar 12, 1849
married Bettie Bramble
Mar 15, 1874
Died May 17, 1874

James A. Hord, son of
Edmond Hord
Dec 14, 1826
Aug 31, 1849

James M. Brooks
1838-1921
&
Rebecca A. Brooks
1844-1886

J. T., son of
J. M. & R. A. Brooks
Jun 26, 1873
Dec 21, 1891

M. Scruggs
Born ---------
Died --- --, 1884
(illegible)

Jonnie Stone, son of
H. P. & Josie Scruggs
Nov 25, 1889
Sep 16, 1891

Eddie Lee, dau of
H. P. & Josie Scruggs
Feb 18, 1881
Jun 30, 1890

H. P. Scruggs
May 7, 1852
Jun 2, 1898
age: 40y, 1m, 1d.

Josie Stone, wife of
H. P. Scruggs
Mar 1, 1854
Mar 27, 1895
age: 41y, 26d.

Sara Electra Lee, wife of
J. A. Chilton
Apr 8, 1872
Apr 10, 1912

Martha Thomas, wife of
Bartlett Bird
Feb 28, 1821
Oct 19, 1870

Asa Thomas
Nov 2, 1811
Dec 17, 1888

Sarah Caroline Clark, wife
of Asa Thomas
Feb 18, 1818
married Jan 31, 1838
Died Nov 15, 1898

David Thomas,
A Native of Virginia
Died Jan 29, 1856
Age: 79 yrs.

Martha, wife of
David Thomas
Died Jan 19, 1837
age: 57 yrs.

"Brother"
S. S. Whitworth
Feb 22, 1819
Oct 31, 1894
&
"Sister"
Martha C. Wilkinson
Dec 30, 1826-Sep 8, 1897

Mitchell D. Brittain
Dec 29, 1822
Sep 26, 1883

Nancy B., wife of
M. D. Britton
Dec 18, 1830
May 30, 1917

Betsey Cannon
Mar 1800
Aug 27, 1875

L. F. Dillard
Mar 23, 1826
Jan 13, 1888

Paralee Dillard, dau of
L. F. & P. Dillard
Jan 4, 1863
Feb 23, 1887

Jim Record
1863-1933
&
Willie B. Record
1877-1953

Henley W. Record
Nov 26, 1894
May 9, 1936

Clara Reckord
1896-1939

Jimmie Allene Record
Jan 29, 1915
Jan 1, 1933

Thomas W. Mason
Sep 18, 1807
Aug 7, 1853
&
Huldah, wife of
T. W. Mason
Dec 31, 1809
Oct 7, 1857

L. P. Fields, Sr.   and
Jan 24, 1820
Feb 22, 1889
&
Mary Fields   and
Feb 9, 1824
Jan 13, 1876
&
Thomas B. Fields   and
Jan 24, 1846
Dec 24, 1848
&
L. P. Fields, Jr.   and
Oct 25, 1849
Mar 26, 1894
&
E. L. Fields
Sep 20, 1872
Sep 16, 1889

Ola Sparkman, wife of
W. L. Baker
Apr 9, 1871
Jun 17, 1900

J. M. Lane
Feb 16, 1795
Jun 17, 1869

Rachel P. C., wife of
John M. Lane
Mar 19, 1811
Jun 2, 1880

Joseph Walker
May 29, 1827
Oct 7, 1898

Elizabeth M., wife of
Joseph Walker
Oct 30, 1832
Oct 25, 1881

W. B. Walker
Mar 21, 1838
Mar 3, 1926
&
Martha Lane Walker
Jul 22, 1835
Oct 31, 1922

Herbert R., son of
J. B. & Janie Walker
Nov 2, 1890
Jul 10, 1892

Mary Louise, Infant dau of
Audry & Elizabeth C. Walker
Jan 6, 1936
Feb 6, 1937

John Tillman, son of
L. & M. C. Tillman
Aug 13, 1843
Oct 21, 1852

Irvin P. Green
Oct 19, 1849
Jan 7, 1929

Mary S. Fields
Nov 21, 1858
Oct 1, 1875
&
Maggie L. Fields
Apr 11, 1862
Nov 1, 1862
&
Infant Dau :
Oct 24, 1853
Jan 19, 1854
&
Mrs. R. A. Fields
Aug 14, 1850
Jun 20, 1880

Earnest G. G. Gober
Sep 28, 1878
Nov 21, 1886

Lizzia Gober
Jul 10, 1875
Sep 15, 1877

In Memory of
Edmond Hord, was born the
22nd of July, 1763
Deceased the 6th of Sept.
1838.

In memory of Mary Hord,
Consort of Edmond Hord
was born the 7th of March
1784, deceased the 14th of
July 1850.

Samuel Clement Cannon
Jul 8, 1858
Jul 4, 1894
&
John Scott Cannon
Jul 8, 1858
May 22, 1894
&
Cora Yell Cannon
Aug 23, 1865
Nov 26, 1955
"Children of Clement, Jr. &
Mary Yell Cannon, Grand-
children of Archibald Yell,
2nd Governor of Arkansas &
Mary Scott Yell."

Mary S. Yell
Died Jan 5, 1823
age: 18y & 2d.

H. L. Walker
1877-1939

Mattie Walker
1875-1971

S. D. Gallagher
Jul 17, 1838
May 26, 1894

A. M., wife of
S. D. Gallagher
Aug 21, 1836
Jan 6, 1900

James Armstrong Word, son
of J. C. & C. T. Word
Oct 11, 1844
Sep 14, 1845

-----. T. Montgomery (H.T.)
Born 1808
Died (no date-after 1850
census)

Marker now gone:**
Lucretia H. Montgomery
Born June 15, 1803
Died (after 1850, census)
(copied in 1961 by Mary Bass)

S. C., dau of
A. J. & S. C. Jones
Jan 29, 1894
Oct 18, 1896

J. R. Jones
Nov 28, 1873
Oct 29, 1902

Alexander Hord, son of
Edmond Hord,
Born 11 of Nov 1806
Died 26 Aug 1825

Thomas H. Hord, son of
Edmond Hord,
Born 26 Sept 1818
Died 10 April 1833

Archibald Yell, our 2nd
born, Died May 31, 1852
age: 19m & 10d.
Clement & Mary S. Cannon
&
Sarah Blythe, our 1st born
Died Mar 6, 1849
age: 2y, 1m, 13d.
Clement & Mary S. Cannon

Archie Yele (Yell)
Died Mar 23, 1862
age: 6y, 1m & 2 weeks
C. & M.S.Cannon

Catharine J. Scott
Died Sep 11, 1822
age: 7y, 5m, 5d.

Mary Carroll
Died Feb 26, 1816
age: 52y & 11m.

John W. Ragsdale
1800-Sep 5, 1846
age: 46 yrs.

Sarah A. Ragsdale, dau of
J. G. & Mary Walker
Jan 10, 1821
Jul 21, 1849
age: 28y, 6m, 17d.

Winnie V. Butner
1889-1919

Sarah Francis, wife of
T. E. Butner
Nov 2, 1868
Oct 16, 1913

Vincent Smith
Oct 27, 1778
Jun 17, 1857
age: 78y, 7m, 20d.

Sophia W. Shaw
Born Nov 18, 1839
Died of Scarlet fever
Feb 13, 1840
age: 1y, 2m, 25d.

W. A. Parks
Dec 2, 1862
Mar 2, 1915

Arthur Lee, son of
W. A. & C. A. Parks
Mar 12, 1897
Nov 21, 1910

W. Alex McMichael
1875-1932
&
Pearl McMichael
1881-1936

Clyde Vernon McMichael
Sep 24, 1883
May 26, 1943

Carmack, son of
W. A. & P. McMichael
Jun 4, 1908
Jun 30, 1921

Joshua P. Scott
Died Feb 24, 1849
age: 35y, 7m, 17d.

Mary, wife of
Joshua P. Scott
Died May 8, 1887
age: 74y, 3m, 5d.

Infant Son of
W. B. & M. Walker
Oct 4, 1865
Oct 22, 1865

Infant Son of
W. B. & M. Walker
Oct 2, 1864
Oct 19, 1864

Infant Son of
J. & E. Walker
Sep 15, 1870
Sep 21, 1870

Emily P. Walker, dau of
J. G. & Mary Walker
Jan 27, 1840
Aug 5, 1860
age: 20y, 6m, 9d.

No marker:*
Joseph Walker
(no dates-SOR)

John G. Walker
Jan 6, 1797
Aug 7, 1855
age: 58y, 7m, 1d.

Mary, wife of
J. G. Walker
Mar 30, 1801
Sep 23, 1879

L. Armstrong
Born Aug 18, ----
in Rutherford Co., Tenn.
Died of Cholera
Jul 1, 1855

Infant of
W. A. & C. A. Parker
(no dates)

Mildred Foster
Feb 22, 1807
Jan 2, 1885
age: 77y, 10m, 10d.

Uriah A. Duncan
May 27, 1856
Feb 15, 1929

Mabel Duncan
Sep 11, 1881
Apr 23, 1962

John Scott
Died Jun 5, 1865
age: 88y, 9m, 19d.

Sarah, wife of
John Scott
Died Feb 9, 1842
age: 62y, 5m, 9d.

Robert C. Scott
Died Aug 10, 1853
age: 8y & 4d.

Minnie Lee Shelton
Aug 15, 1876
Oct 4, 1933

Fannie V. Shelton
Dec 20, 1871
May 24, 1947

Lucinda Walker, dau of
J. G. & Mary Walker
Nov 11, 1836
May 30, 1837

W. R. Walker, son of
J. G. & Mary Walker
Nov 27, 1825
Jun 8, 1826
age: 6m & 11d.

Two Twin Infants
Son & Daughter of
J. G. & Mary Walker
Born & Died
Jun 27, 1835

John B. Walker, son of
J. G. & Mary Walker
Jul 5, 1831
Jun 27, 1835
age: 3y, 11m, 22d.

Bertie Mai, wife of
Dave Payne
Jan 6, 1896
Nov 9, 1922

Gertie J., wife of
Emmitt Elliott
Jul 24, 1894
Oct 8, 1918

F. E., dau of
A. J. & S. C. Jones
Feb 26, 1872
Nov 13, 1875

Elmer Lafayette, son of
J. W. & M. A. Reynolds
Sep 23, 1898
Mar 19, 1908

Riley Jones
Apr 11, 1830
May 15, 1901
&

Bettie, wife of
Riley Jones
Nov 13, 1835
Jan 12, 1885

Parthena Montgomery
Died Nov 22, 1848
age: 14y, 5m, 7d.

J. T. Barton
May 25, 1839
Jul 24, 1899
"A Confederate Soldier,
a loving Father, a true
Husband, a faithful
Christian."

W. J. Gibson
Nov 5, 1856
Jun 22, 1937

F. C., son of
W. J. & M. F. Gibson
Jun 15, 1890
Nov 12, 1893

Ensel Brookshier
Dec 30, 1846
Mar 21, 1912

Amandy E. Earls,
Born Apr 26, 1850
married to Ansel Brookshier
Dec 9, 1874
Died Jan 25, 1899

Martha Brookshier
Feb 28, 1843
Apr 8, 1918

B. N. Beachboard
Oct 24, 1815
Dec 28, 1891

Eliza A. Beachboard
Jan 9, 1820
Nov 25, 1877

W. A. Ashby
Born in Spencer Co., Ky.
Jul 8, 1840
Died Feb 18, 1863
"Capt. Johnston's Co.
Bufords Brigade
C.S.A."

W. D. Ashby
Born 1743
Died 1818
(W.P.A.Records, copied this
marker, which is now gone)

Sallie McFerrin, dau of
Mr & Mrs W. H. Evans
Nov 16, 1842
Oct 11, 1886
age: 43y, 10m, 25d.

T. G. W. Wright   and
Jun 23, 1817
Jul 12, 1854
&
Mary A. Farrell
Mar 7, 1822
May 20, 1839
&
Clamenza T. Hoover
Feb 14, 1831
Aug 12, 1909

Carl Winnette
Oct 25, 1899
Nov 13, 1967

Clyde Wade Winnette
1927-1936

H. L. Smith
Apr 3, 1827
Dec 11, 1902

Dilliah, wife of
H. L. Smith
Feb 3, 1827
Jan 19, 1912

James Driver
Oct 17, 1871
Jan 5, 1956

Della R. Driver
Aug 2, 1878
Dec 25, 1950

Alex Dye
1886-1940

Sidney W. Todd
Feb 10, 1881
(no date)
&
Julia A. Todd
Feb 7, 1881
Mar 13, 1955

Infants of
Mr & Mrs R. M. Gordon
Infant
Born & Died
May 9, 1901
&
Infant
Born & Died
May 24, 1902

William Smith
Feb 11, 1819
Mar 28, 1876
age: 57y, 1m, 17d.

T. J. Todd
1852-(no date)
& wife:
Mary Ann Todd
1857-(no date)
& Son:
T. N. Todd
1894-1925
(Picture of all three)

Richard Farrell
Nov 30, 1798
Aug 8, 1838
& wife:
Mary Ferrell
Oct 6, 1797
Dec 1, 1875

Christine Bell Jordan
Jul 6, 1904
Nov 3, 1909

William H. Ogles
May 13, 1892
Nov 27, 1916

J. M. Brookshier
Sep 15, 1855
(no date)
& wife:
Eliza Brookshier
Jan 6, 1874
Aug 8, 1901

E. D. Bishop
June 22, 1906

&
M. J. Bishop
Oct 13, 1905

Alex Elliott
Jul 23, 1881
Apr 19, 1937

Delar Elliott
Jan 19, 1884
Aug 13, 1913

Macy Elliott
1841-Nov 18, 1918

Matthew, son of
M. P. & Mattie Stricklin
Dec 5, 1905
Mar 10, 1912

Estil Teal
1934-1935
&
J. L. Teal
1921-1929

James Napper
Nov 12, 1889
Nov 12, 1914

Martha A. Napper
May 18, 1838
Aug 2, 1912

Infant of
Jno. G. & S. E. Arnold
Born & Died
Apr 19, 1887

J. W. Jernigan
May 31, 1854
Oct 29, 1908
& wife:
Sarah T. Alford Jernigan
Apr 14, 1856
Nov 16, 1910

Eunice, dau of
E. G. & M. C. Fletcher
Jun 27, 1894
Aug 27, 1895

M. H. Harris
1872-1923
& wife:
Mai Gordon Harris
1882-(TM-Lilly G. Harris
1884-1973)
& their Son:
Edwin Harris
1905-1929

J. E., son of
E. G. & M. C. Fletcher
Oct 12, 1881
Jan 7, 1882

A. B. Taylor
Oct 29, 1842
May 13, 1893
& wife:
Elizabeth Katherine Moore
Apr 19, 1851
Oct 10, 1934

J. R. Elliott
Nov 9, 1874
May 10, 1914
&
S. A. Elliott
Feb 13, 1888
Aug 18, 1913

Edd Elliott
Nov 4, 1873
May 11, 1924

Jefferson C. Jernigan
Nov 13, 1844
Feb 25, 1909

Sophronia H. Jernigan
Jun 13, 1856
Aug 19, 1916

S. A. C.
(footstone-headmarker is
face down, on ground.)

Lula Pearl Todd
Feb 19, 1892
Dec 12, 1917
&
Emma Nola Todd
Apr 5, 1890
Mar 26, 1922
"Daughters of M.A. &
T. J. Todd."

Lester Fugitt Todd
Jun 4, 1897
Aug 1, 1909
&
Sarah Elizabeth Todd
May 5, 1879
Mar 29, 1914

Sarah E., wife of
John G. Arnold
(broken away)

E. H. Gallegly
Sep 27, 1833
Jul 12, 1917

Mary R., wife of
E. H. Gallegly
Oct 10, 1843
Aug 21, 1905

No marker:**
Thomas B. Holland
Born Mar 17, 1846
Died May 27, 1903
(broken-copied in 1963 by
        Mary Bass)

No marker:
Major James L. Armstrong
aged: 46 yrs. Volunteer in
the Mexican War, died near
Fairfield and buried at
Church Cemetery.
from-Shelbyville Commercial
        Jan 12, 1872

W. H. Summers
Jan 5, 1819
Jan 11, 1888

Hillary D. Moseley
May 1, 1862
Sep 5, 1912

No marker:**
James Jakes, who was borned
the 10th of February 1788,
departed this life the 5th
of Sept. 1847.
aged: 58y, 8m, 5d.
(copied in 1964 by Mary Bass)

No marker:
Dr. James L. Armstrong,
Died 1868
Buried in Church Cemetery
Born abt 1782
from-Shelbyville Commercial
        Jan 12, 1872

Mary Louise Tenley
Jun 29, 1886
Oct 13, 1922

Mary Lula, dau of
J. A. & M. C. McDonald
Sep 8, 1881
Oct 9, 1899

No marker:*
Elijah Green, Father of
Elizabeth Keller who was the
wife of John M. Keller, A
Soldier of the Revolution
from North Carolina, came to
Tennessee in 1802 and at his
death in 1842, was buried at
the New Hope Primitive Baptist
Church at Fairfield, Tenn., in
Bedford County.Born 1752.
    * by-Klyne Jack Keller

J. A. McDonald
May 25, 1842
Oct 19, 1918
    & wife:
Mary C. McDonald
Mar 20, 1849
May 16, 1909

William J. McDonald
Jun 24, 1876
Jun 30, 1920

No marker:**
Mary Keeling, wife of
Thomas Keeling, dec'd.
Born in Maryland 1776
married Vincent Smith
Dec 25, 1850
Died Jun 13, 1853
age: abt 77 yrs.

* by Klyne Jack Keller
** by Miss Mary Bass

12 McMAHAN CEMETERY   Map # 8
Located about 1½ miles Northwest of Fairfield, Tenn.

W. J. Davis
Oct 11, 1824
Apr 3, 1877

Bettie, dau of
S. & S. J. McMahan
Dec 20, 1847
Dec 21, 1876

Lettia Watson, dau of
T. W. & L. M. Jordan
Dec 14, 1864
Jul 17, 1865

Samuel McMahan
Sep 7, 1813
Apr 22, 1858

Abram McMahan
Apr 13, 1809
Apr 22, 1880
age: 71y & 9d.

Thomas Watson, son of
T. W. & L. M. Jordan
Mar 14, 1858
Jul 15, 1858

R. M. Stephens
Sep 6, 1799
        1857
age: 58y, 2m, --d.

Sophia Rebeca, dau of
T. W. & L. M. Jordan
Apr 18, 1856
Dec 15, 1856

Thomas B. Mosley
Apr 22, 1788
Jul 7, 1866

Infant Son of
T. W. & L. M. Jordan
Mar 25, 1863
Jun 8, 1863

Mary, dau of
T. W. & L. M. Jordan
Feb 5, 1860
Mar 29, 1860

5 large slabs inside
Rock Wall with the Jordan's
& Mosley's. no insc. Ed.

13 UNKNOWN CEMETERY   Map # 8
Located 2 miles North of Fairfield, Tenn.

        No markers.

14 MARTIN CEMETERY   Map # 8
Located about 2½ miles North of Fairfield, Tenn.

Sacred to the Memory of
Col. Barclay Martin, a native
of Virginia. Born June 13,
1756. He emigrated to South
Carolina during her colonial
dependency, and at an early
period, was identified with
its cause of the Revolution
and served his Country with
the zeal and fidelity of a
Patriotic Soldier and a Merit-
orious Officer to its close.
He was a kind, sincere friend
and devoted Husband. A Deacon
of the Baptist Church. His
life was an example of Piety
and unselfishness. Died on
the 16th of Nov. 1815, in the
full hope of the blest, in-
heritance of the Just. His
memory will ever be sacred.

Sacred to the Memory of
Capt. Matt Martin, born 26
of December, 1763. At an early
age of 16 years, He became a
Soldier in the defense of his
Country during her struggle
under Gen. Greene, in the
Battle of Gilford and under
Clark and Sumpter in many
other Battles. He continued
to discharge the duties of
a Patriotic Soldier until the
close of the War. He was a
humane Master, a kind neigh-
bor and unwavering friend.
Tender and affectionate
Father and devoted Husband.
Died 16th of October 1846 in
the esteem of all who knew him.
Kind to his children, a friend
made evidence in his last days.

the Consoling reflectiona that
their loss was his infinite
gain.
"Revolutionary Soldier
    1763-1846
Placed by Belle Meade Chapter
        DAR"
(DAR Marker now gone)

Mrs. Sally Martin, wife of
Capt. Matt Martin, Born Nov.
16, 1765. Member of the
Baptist for near a half Century. Died Jan 2, 1842.

L. B.
(fieldstone-Lucy Bradford)

Mary H. Tillman, dau of
John & Rachel P. Tillman
Died Apr 6, 1826
    age: 13y, 8m, 26d.

William D. Martin, son of
Henry P. & A. J. Martin
Born 17th ---, ---- (1805)
Died Sept 17, 1822
age: 17y & 10m.(illegible)

Sarah Harris Mullins, dau of
Jas. Harris
Born July --, 1811 (day gone)
Died Feb 11, 1867

Henry C. Martin
Nov 25, 1806
Sep 4, 1835

Eliza Henry Clay Martin,
dau of Henry C. & Sarah H.
Martin.
Mar 28, 1836
Feb 9, 1841

Sally C. Bradford, dau of
Theodrick F. & Lucy G.
Bradford
Died Oct 26, 1830
age: 17y, 7m, 21d.

Frances Harrison Sutton, dau
of Theodrick F. & Lucy G.
Bradford
Born Sep 30, 1811
Died May 22, 1834
age: 23y, 9m, 11d.

Mary H. Tillman, dau of
John & Rachel P. Tillman
Died Apr 6, 1826
age: 13y, 8m, 26d.

Several graves, with fieldstones.

Mrs. Sarah C. M., Consort
of Henry Cannon & dau of
John & Rachel P. Tillman
Died Jan 19, 1836
age: 21y, 1m, 4d.

15 SHAW CEMETERY   Map # 8
Located near the Fairfield & Bell Buckle Roads. On Old Stage Coach Road.

C. G. W. B. Shaw
Born Oct 29, 1811
Died Oct 6, 1852
(1850 Census, born in Tenn.)

No marker:
Martha, wife of
C. G. W. B. Shaw,
Born abt 1811 in Pa.
Died after 1850 (1850 Census)

16 ROUTON CEMETERY   Map # 8
Located about 1½ miles Northeast of Fairfield, Tenn.

A. B. Routon
Dec 10, 1793
Sep 26, 1811
age: 17y, 9m, 16d.

Several unmarked graves.

No Marker:
William Rowlette,* A Soldier
of the American Revolution.
Born-
Died-1811
Index to application for
pension--William Rowlette
Served in Virginia, R8607.

* Some question on this
  burial as he was in
  Shelby County, TN in
  1840.

17 UNKNOWN CEMETERY   Map # 8
Located about 2 miles East of Fairfield, Tenn.

Dovey R. No----------
dau of W. & M. A. Nort-----
          (Norton)
Feb 8, 1828
Sep 16, 1841
age: 13y, 1m, 8d.

Only grave, in yard beside Road.

18 SHELTON CEMETERY   Map # 8
Located about 2 miles East of Fairfield, Tenn.

Tom O'Neal
Dec 29, 1846
Jan 3, 1917

B. J., dau of J. & F. C.
Shelton
Jan 1, 1882
Feb 15, 1883

Jessee Shelton
Born abt 1800
Died Jul 13, 1865
    & wife:
Nancy Shelton
Born 1805
Died Oct 17, 1876

H. Gibson
Nov 26, 1831
Jan 17, 1891

Harriett C., wife of
H. Gibson
Aug 29, 1837
Feb 22, 1875

Ida Alice, dau of
George & S. J. Shelton
Oct 18, 1881
Oct 8, 1891

Elmer Lee, son of
J. W. & Nannie Bell
Aug 5, 1894
Oct 1, 1899

George A. Shelton
Dec 23, 1832
Apr 2, 1900

Rachel C., wife of
G. A. Shelton
Nov 7, 1859
Jan 31, 1924

Martha Ada, dau of
George & S. J. Shelton
Apr 28, 1865
Aug 11, 1891

Several graves with fieldstones,
no inscriptions.

Claud, son of
G. A. & R. C. Shelton
Jul 29, 1894
Aug 17, 1894

Susan Jane, wife of
George A. Shelton
Oct 19, 1842
Sep 18, 1892

William J., son of
G. A. & S. J. Shelton
Mar 26, 1874
Mar 21, 1878

Several unmarked graves.

19 SHILOH CEMETERY   Map # 8
Located at the Tower at Shiloh, Tenn.

(gone) Thompson
1869-1957
age: 88y, 10m, 8d
(Cothran-Thompson)

Pauline Seagroves
1904-1942

John W. Anderson
1881-1947
&
Effie M. Anderson
1884-1969

Willie B. Ledbetter
June 1936
Sept 1938

Eula Bell McCart
1882-1954
(Thompson)

Ernest Hayes Foster
Missouri
Pvt 64 Depot Brig
Mar 31, 1936

Doris Jeanette Seagroves
Died Feb 22, 1938
age: 1m & 3d. (TM)

Wiley T. Jolly
Jul 15, 1878
May 19, 1922

Saline J. Mangrum
Dec 25, 1871
Mar 9, 1902

About 10 unmarked graves.

20 CAWTHRON CEMETERY   Map # 8
Located East of Shiloh, near Coffee County Line.

Fannie P., wife of
W. W. Cawthron
Dec 17, 1849
Dec 7, 1878

"Mother"
Nannie, wife of
W. R. Ledbetter
1865-1903

Jim Ledbetter
Oct 24, 1890
Mar 25, 1918

NOTE: This Cemetery was a
large Cemetery at one time,
but all markers are now gone.

21 KEELING CEMETERY   Map # 8
Located East of Shiloh, near Coffee County Line.

Thomas A. Keeling   and
Oct 1, 1847
Sep 24, 1910

Lizzie Keeling
Sep 7, 1867
Mar 19, 1920

22 VANCE CEMETERY   Map # 8
Located near Lake Bedford.

Samuel Vance
Apr 18, 1783
Mar 13, 1849
(another grave beside above
grave, could be his wife:
Christiana Vance, Born 1789,
Died after 1850, census)

Robert B. Vance
Aug 18, 1825
Sep 24, 1852

Departed this life
Dec 12, 1855
Priscilla Caroline, wife of
Willis Blanton & dau of
Sam'l & Christiana Vance
aged: 41y, 5m, 17d.

Departed this life by
drowning in the Barren Fork
of Duck River near Normandy
Nov 1, 1859
Elizabeth Caroline, dau of
Willis & Caroline Blanton
aged: 6y, 8m, 10d.

23 HORD CEMETERY (Col)   Map # 8
Located near Hord Chapel, Union Ridge.

James Frierson
Died --- --, 1965
(TM-Nashville)

James Hord
Died Jun 26, 1951
age:---(gone)
(Scales)

Joe Hord, Jr.
Tennessee
Tec 5 1327 Engr Ten SVC
Regt   W.W.II
Apr 25, 1908
Aug 4, 1967

Thanks to Mr. Comer Hord.

Joe A. Hord
Feb 26, 1862
Feb 7, 1966
&
Bobbie Hord
Born 1878
Died Aug 15, 1951

Andrew J. Hord
Dec 23, 1951
(Scales)

Loretta K. Hord
Feb 22, 1955
Jul 27, 1955
(Welton)

24 KELLER CEMETERY   Map # 8
Located near Kellertown, East of Wartrace, Tenn.

Estel Ferrell
1883-1962
(Howell-Thompson)

Evie E. Ferrell
1888-1928

H. P. Jones
Sep 12, 1846
Aug 15, 1900

S. J. Jones
Apr 21, 1867
May 21, 1899

Lela Mai, wife of
W. R. King
Jul 26, 1890
Aug 28, 1921

Mattie Jewell King
Oct 5, 1914
Jul 14, 1915

J. L. Throneberry
Mar 24, 1845
Feb 15, 1919
&
Bettie Throneberry
Aug 11, 1861
Jul 1, 1938

Elizabeth Throneberry
Mar 3, 1918
Dec 16, 1919

Hazel Throneberry
Mar 18, 1917
Oct 16, 1918

E. M., dau of
I. B. & D. E. Foster
Nov 18, 1898
Jul 21, 1899

Luther, son of
N. B. & S. A. Hawkins
Aug 16, 1899
Jun 22, 1918

Lola, wife of
J. A. Keller
May 26, 1889
Jan 29, 1922

Rena Odell, dau of
W. F. & Carrie Keller
Jun 26, 1918
Dec 1, 1918

Mary Elizabeth Keller
Jan 31, 1864
Aug 31, 1915

F. A. Bramblett
Jul 13, 1850
Sep 7, 1911

Emma S. Morgan, wife of
F. A. Bramblett
Oct 18, 1853
Jul 11, 1916

John Alvin Stephens
Jun 7, 1857
Feb 5, 1932
&
Sallie Rippy Stephens
Mar 14, 1861
Apr 27, 1924

Grace Alenne, dau of
Grace Lawrence & Alvin
Stephens
May 8, 1921
May 11, 1921

Rachel May, dau of
John & Sallie Stephens
Nov 18, 1887
Apr 5, 1889

William D. Bramblett
Nov 9, 1875
Oct 2, 1934

Betty Y.
she died -------
(fieldstone)

Sally Bramblett
Died 30 Oct 1845
age: 33 yrs.

Willie M., son of
R. H. & Melvina Stephens
Dec 17, 1869
killed by overhead bridge
on N. & C. R. R.
Apr 25, 1890
age: 22y, 4m, 8d.

Melvina, dau of
Jas. & Mary Green & wife of
R. H. Stephens
Jul 25, 1841
Dec 25, 1909
age: 68y & 5m.

R. H. Stephens
Nov 24, 1843
Jan 25, 1912

Laban Jones
dec'd 1886
(fieldstone)

Elizabeth Smith
(no dates-fieldstone)

Daniel Cortner
Apr 22, 1813
Feb 9, 1843

Elvira A. Cortner
Dec 25, 1818
Jul   1840

Infant son of
Daniel & Elvira Cortner
Born & Died
Mar 1840

Jacob Keller
Oct 20, 1797
Mar   1869

Fannie B., dau of
R. H. & Elvira Stephens
Jun 24, 1872
Sep 3, 1875
age: 3y, 2m, 9d.

Betsy Turner
Dec'd 1821
aged: 6
(fieldstone)

W. K.
1813
(fieldstone)

Daniel Stephens
Feb 9, 1809
Sep 29, 1894

James M. Stephens
Mar 29, 1834
May 6, 1917
&
S. Emeline Stephens
Jan 28, 1835
Jun 8, 1915

Emeline Stephens
Mar 26, 1864
Jun   1866

Nancy J. Stephens
Nov 16, 1854
Aug 3, 1865

Infant Dau of
J. M. & S. E. Stephens
Born & Died
Nov 16, 1854

Ja. K.*
dec Apr 26th 1846
age: 86 yrs.
(fieldstone)

* Keller Records:
Jacob Keller
Died Apr 26th 1846
aged: 86 yrs.
&
Vira Lovicy Keller
Born abt 1760
Died abt 1850

No marker:*
James A. "Jim" Keller
died 1913
age: 73 yrs.
&
Mary Jane Gallager Keller
(no dates)
married Apr 2, 1859

* Keller Family Records.

Polly Kelley*
(no dates)
(Fieldstone)

* Keller Records:
  Polly Kelley, died 1815
              age: 27 yrs.

R. K.*
Dec Nov 1815
age: 52
(fieldstone)

* Keller Records:
Rev. Reuben Kelley (SOR)
Died Nov 11, 1815
age: 52 yrs.

James F. Stephens
Mar 19, 1866
Oct 31, 1874

Sarah C. Stephens
Sep 23, 1853
Oct   1854

No marker:**
Hosea Garrett
Died Dec the 17th 1827
aged: 45 yrs.
(fieldstone)

** copied by Mary Bass,
   Nov 27, 1960

N. A. V. Daniel
dec Oct 1846
age: 18 yrs.
(fieldstone)

W. M. Rippy
Aug 28, 1827
May 29, 1873

Eliza A. Keller, wife of
W. M. Rippy
Apr 22, 1840
Apr 5, 1910

Infant dau of
W. D. & S. C.
(no other information)

Many unmarked graves.

Many fieldstones, no insc.

** Miss Mary Bass.

B.A.G.
Dec'd Nov -- 1844
(fieldstone)

Mary Jones
aged: 30
Dec'd Nov 1815
(fieldstone)

Roda Marie Jones
Dec'd Feb 1813
(fieldstone)

James Edgar Bramblett
Apr 19, 1869
Aug 19, 1870

Elanora Caroline Bramblett
Dec 24, 1872
Apr 29, 1875

James Bramblett
Oct 30, 1826
Oct 12, 1899

Rachel C., wife of
James Bramblett
Sep 11, 1826
Aug 6, 1886

G. D. Bramblett
Jan 2, 1856
Apr 22, 1919

J. B. M. Keller
died 27 July 1850
aged: 27y, 5m, 15d.

F. H. Keller
Nov 18, 1794
Sep 22, 1856

Sarah Keller
Oct 19, 1800
Jun 6, 1863

Thomas A. Stephens
May 25, 1844
Oct 14, 1877

Robert Alexander, son of
Thomas A. & M. J. Stephens
Jan 26, 1873
Jul 22, 1875

25 COUCH CEMETERY   Map # 8
Located at Kellertown, East of Wartrace, Tenn.

Sarah J., wife of
John A. Couch
Mar 1, 1836
May 15, 1863

Kittie P., dau of
J. A. & S. J. Couch
(no dates)

E. B. (fieldstone)

John W. Couch, son of
Jas. & Abigail Couch
age: 4mo. & 13d.

Joel Thronebery
1841-1923
&
Alice Thornebery
1857-1923

David Thorneberry
Jan 1, 1815
Oct 13, 1870
age: 55y, 9m, 12d.

Elizabeth, wife of
David Thorneberry
Jun 6, 1818
Oct 16, 1887
age: 69y, 4m, 10d.

Rev. John Bramblett
Feb 6, 1791
Nov 20, 1861

Jane Bramblett
Jan 3, 1792
Dec 28, 1861

Isaac N. Couch
Aug 17, 1835
Jan 21, 1859

John M. Green
Nov 15, 1826
Apr 10, 1852

Mrs. Rhoda F. Green
Mar 5, 1832
Aug 23, 1852

N. Couch
Died Oct 3, 1840
(no age given)

W. G. Keller
Aug 4, 1837
Aug 28, 1887
age: 50y & 8d.

N. C., wife of
W. G. Keller
Jul 29, 1838
Dec 13, 1887

Reuben D. Stephens
May 22, 1863
Sep 19, 1878
age: 15y, 3m, 27d.

Gracie B. Stephens
Jul 5, 1875
Aug 27, 1878
age: 3y, 1m, 16d.

James Patton
Died Aug 9, 1827
age: 63 yrs
"Left 12 children"

Sarah Patton
Died Aug 13, 1825
age: 60 yrs.
"Leaving her Husband &
12 children"

Sarah N. Couch
Aug 17, 1835
Jun 21, 1839

Rhoda J. Couch
Nov 30, 1825
Jun 25, 1840

Nancy Stephens, wife of
David Stephens
Mar 30, 1815
Nov 15, 1840

No marker:**
Mary C."Kittie" Keller
Born Jan 14, 1866
Died (no date)

Many unmarked graves.

Isaac Couch
Dec 24, 1799
Sep 30, 1841

Rhoda Couch
Mar 1786
Oct 1845

William L. Couch
Aug 4, 1842
Aug 21, 1858

R. D. Hayes
died Mar 1839
(Rock Slab)

M. E. Hayes
died 1828
(Rock Slab)

John P. Stephens
Born Aug 13, 1830
killed by lightening
Aug 19, 1904
age: 74y, & 6d.

Rhoda C. Stephens
Jun 30, 1829
Aug 29, 1888
age: 59y 1m, 29d.

Mary Stephens Couch
May 1, 1861
Mar 16, 1935

Elizabeth C., wife of
E. W. Jennings & dau of
Thomas & Rhoda Couch
Died Jul 18, 1846
aged: 24y & 9m.

Sarah E. Cunningham, wife of
John W. C. Cunningham
Born Sep 1823
married Aug 17, 1837
Died Aug 20, 1840

J. W. C. Cunningham
Mar 27, 1812
Oct 10, 1855
age: 43y, 6m, 8d.
"Leaving Wife, 2 sons &
2 daus."

Mary L., dau of
_. B. & S. R. Woods
Aug 23, ----
Jun 28, 1854

** by Klyne Jack Keller.

many graves with fieldstones, no inscriptions.

J. L. Couch
May 30, 1821
Jun 6, 1863

Eliza Ann Couch
Apr 4, 1824
Jan 23, 1859
"Leaving a Husband &
7 children."

Joseph Couch
Oct 9, 1787
Mar 9, 1861

Catharine Couch
Jul 10, 1796
Mar 10, 1886
married Nov 4, 1813

James Patton Anderson
Mar 1, 1827
Oct 9, 1855

Jacob Moffit Anderson
Nov 11, 1835
Sep 29, 1855

Rhoda Cunningham
Born Mar 1733
Died Jan 1831

Pumphrey Meadows
Born May   1806
Died Aug 17,1834

James M. Meadows
Mar 1832
Jun 1835

Turner N. Meadows
Mar 1832
Jun 2, 1835

Pumphrey Meadows, Jr.
Apr 3, 1835
Aug 2, 1854

Sarah L. Meadows
Jun 28, 1814
Oct 17, 1840

Thomas M. Couch
Aug 13, 1818
Dec 26, 1821

No marker:**
Daniel Keller
Born Jun 17, 1870
Died Nov 30, 1874

Thomas Edgar Davis
Apr 10, 1870
Oct 18, 1898
&
Lizzie Keller Davis
Sep 9, 1877
Jul 17, 1902

Infant of
Thomas Edgar & Lizzie Davis
Born & Died
Sep 9, 1895

Nancy E. Keller
May 11, 1823
Jul 31, 1850

Robert C. Maupin
Dec 14, 1834
May 5, 1905

Emily A., wife of
R. C. Maupin & dau of
Joseph & Catharine Couch
Jan 1, 1839
Jun 2, 1862
&
Samuel C., son of
R. C. & E. A. Maupin
Sep 20, 1860
Nov 1, 1861

Jacob Anderson
Apr 22, 1799
Aug 31, 1839

Abigail Anderson,
Born in Buncombe Co., N.C.,
Dec 11, 1800
Died in Bedford Co., Tenn.
Mar 31, 1875

James Couch
Apr 29, 1789
Jun 8, 1837

N.(Newton) Couch
Dec 1784
Oct 3, 1848

W. D. B.
died 1838

S. F. B.
died (illegible)

N. B.
died 1836

No marker:**
Sam Keller
Born Aug 2, 1875
Died Dec 4, 1879

26 UNKNOWN CEMETERY   Map # 8
Located South of Kellertown, East of Wartrace, Tenn.

Several fieldstones, no inscriptions.

27 CLEVELAND CEMETERY   Map # 8
Located about 1 mile East of Wartrace, Tenn.
(continued on next page)

J. Cleveland   and
1877
&
S. E. Cleveland
1840
&
M. Cleveland
1847
&
M. H. Cleveland
1862

J. Cleveland, Jr.
1862
&
M. Cleveland, Jr.
1847

Mary Alice Cleveland
Jul 24, 1873
Jan 14, 1874

William P. Pepper
Sep 30, 1846
Aug 29, 1847

William Pepper
Dec 15, 1801
Mar 13, 1862

Jane Rebecca Pepper
May 28, 1826
Jul 18, 1852

Walter H., son of
J. G. & Mary R. Sims
Jul 12, 1881
Apr 17, 1882
age: 9m & 5d.

Elizabeth H., dau of
J. G. & Mary R. Sims
Mar 27, 1883
Sep 30, 1884

28 BETHSALEM CEMETERY   Map # 8
Located about 1 mile from Wartrace, at Knob Creek Road.

Robert Murphy
Jun 20, 1840
Mar 2, 1894
&
Julia Murphy
Nov 13, 1833
Sep 7, 1852
&
Alonzo Murphy
Dec 17, 1835
Jan 20, 1889

T. J. Myers, Jr.
son of Thomas & Agnes
Davidson Myers
Aug 24, 1883
Mar 6, 1886

Henry, son of
William & Janie Stone Pepper
Jul 28, 1849
Feb 9, 1936
&
Mary, dau of
William & Elizabeth Bush
Osborne
Aug 5, 1854
Oct 31, 1929
married Nov 22, 1876
&
Henry Pepper, Jr.
Apr 29, 1881
Oct 28, 1932

Jane Stone Pepper
Feb 7, 1893
Mar 24, 1893

"Mother"
Lula Selvidge, wife of
George N. Hall
May 29, 1860
Sep 15, 1882
&
"Son"
Charles W. Hall
Sep 11, 1882
Oct 27, 1904

James Ruby, son of
W. H. & Ella Morris
Jan 22, 1915
Oct 29, 1922

W. H. W.
(footstone)

Jane R., wife of
Archibald Murphy, dec'd
Jan 29, 1812
Mar 30, 1873

Patrick A. Murphy
Jul 30, 1855
Apr 9, 1900

Ellen C. Murphy
1851-1940

Mary C. Myers
Dec 6, 1844
Apr 8, 1872

Hettie N. Myers
Jul 2, 1852
Jan 4, 1853

Katharine Rowland, dau of
Mary Osborne & Henry Pepper
Oct 29, 1894
Jan 28, 1911

William Bush Pepper
Sep 28, 1877
Jul 25, 1883

Herbert Osborne Pepper
Sep 12, 1890
Feb 8, 1959

Lewis W. Hall
Oct 22, 1802
Jun 4, 1886

Lucy E. Hall
Sep 14, 1812
Nov 24, 1878

Annie C., dau of
J. E. & E. J. Hall
Apr 10, 1866
Oct 5, 1874

Margaret Jane, Consort of
Calvin E. Jenkins
Aug 2, 1837
Sep 12, 1857
age: 20y, 1m, 10d.

Eliza Davidson, wife of
Dr. Jas. O. Norton
Apr 7, 1833
Aug 20, 1884

Adelaide Robertson Murphy
Mar 26, 1884
Feb 25, 1913

Annie Robertson, wife of
C. B. Murphy
Aug 14, 1861
Sep 8, 1895

Jonas Myers
Nov 12, 1795
Apr 18, 1870
&
Prudence Hall Myers
Jan 14, 1813
May 18, 1878

Lizzie Myers
Dec 16, 1829
Aug 9, 1855

Jerry Cleveland Pepper
Apr 28, 1879
Jul 26, 1893

Elizabeth Pepper
Mar 17, 1884
Sep 22, 1885

Osborne Pepper
Apr 24, 1886
Dec 24, 1889

John Q. Davidson
Jun 26, 1808
Oct 12, 1879

Susan S. Davidson
Jul 10, 1811
Jul 27, 1884

James Munro
Born at Novar, Ross Shire,
Scotland
Sep 9, 1848
died at Tallahassee, Fla.
Aug 28, 1894

Kate Munro
A Native of Ross Shire,
Scotland
Died at Macon, Ga.
Dec 16, 1892
(no age given)

Elizabeth H. Stevens
Mar 25, 1831
Mar 31, 1862
age: 31y & 6d.

William Kirby, son of
Joseph W. & Elizabeth H.
Stevens
Jun 2, 1854
Aug 21, 1854

John Bell Myers
Sep 30, 1849
Sep 4, 1856

Emma E. Myers
Jan 18, 1854
Oct 2, 1861

George L., son of
J. E. & J. L. Chilcoat
Died Jun 29, 1886
aged: 6m & 7d.

Robert B. Campbell
Jan 4, 1861
Jun 3, 1880

James Cauble Anderson
Apr 21, 1868
Dec 23, 1873

Perry Davidson Arnold
Dec 7, 1874
Sep 24, 1878

Susan P. Harris
Born --- 15, 1858
Died (broken away)

Robert Munro
Born in Ross Shire, Scotland
Jan 12, 1823
died near Fairfield
Jul 29, 1898
&
Mary, wife of Robert Munro
Born in Ross Shire, Scotland
December 1817
died near Fairfield
May 4, 1887
"Erected by her son."

Willie W. Whitson
Jul 17, 1865
Oct 17, 1866
&
John G. Whitson
Feb 1, 1868
Jul 30, 1868

Robert Emmet Whitson
Apr 28, 1858
Dec 2, 1889

Mary Hall Whitson
Sep 7, 1835
Jul 1, 1888

Panthea and the little
Infant Charles Murat, that
sleeps in her arms, wife of
C. C. Carter, and youngest
daughter of Daucey & Martha
Adams,
Born in Halifax Co., N.C.
Dec 28, 1828
married Dec 22, 1854
Died Mar 23, 1856
aged: 27y, 2m, 24d.

[The Bethsalem Presbyterian Church
started here under the leadership
of the Rev. George Newton]

Many unmarked graves.

29 ERWIN CEMETERY   Map # 8
Located about 1 mile Southeast of Wartrace, Tenn.

Nancy Payne, Consort of
Walter Payne
Died Jan 25, 1832
age: 21y, 7m, 8d.

[Andrew Erwin, from Buncombe Co.,
NC, to GA, to TN]

Abraham Hoffman
Died Jan 20, 1829
in the 37 year of his age.
"Formerly of Shandoah Co.,Va."

Mary Jane Porter, wife of
James Porter of Louisiana &
youngest daughter of Andrew
& Jane Erwin of Tennessee,
who departed this life July
7, 1856, in the 26 year of
her age.

Sacred to the Memory of
Col. Andrew Erwin, who
died April 19, 1834, in the
61st year of his age.

NOTE: On side of Tomb of
Mary Jane Porter:

Mary Eliza Porter
Jul 27, 1835
Jul 23, 1836

Mrs. Jane Erwin, Consort of
Col. Andrew Erwin
Born in Ireland
May 27, 1770
Died in Bedford Co., Tenn.
Oct 8, 1859

There are 2 or 3 graves
inside the wall of the
Erwin's plot, no markers.
Fieldstones, no insc.

30 WAITE-FRIENDSHIP CHURCH CEMETERY Map # 8
Located about 1 mile North of Wartrace, Tenn.

Sacred to the Memory of
enesteemable Worth
William G. Wood
A Minister of the Gospel
& Pastor of the Baptist
Church at Rowesville who
departed this life
Feb 8, 1845, in the 48th
year of his age.

No marker:*
Zadoc Wood, A Soldier of
the American Revolution.
Born Mar 7, 1766 in
Frederick Co., Va.
Died after 1840 (Census)

Mary Jane Stokes
(no dates)
"Erected by Vannie Warren"

William Waite
Nov 4, 1786
Aug 6, 1845

Mary H. Waite
Oct 21, 1799
Dec 30, 1835

10 Hewn Rock, stacked
Vaults. no insc.

Jane C. Galbreath
Died Jul 16, 1833
age: 7m & 28d.

Roxanna, wife of
R. L. Lovel
Sep 11, 1856
Oct 28, 1882

Many unmarked graves.

31 HOLLYWOOD CEMETERY   Map # 8
Located at Wartrace, Tennessee. This is the City Cemetery.

South-West Section:

Robert T. Walker
1869-1951
&
Maude F. Walker
1877-(no date)

Jesse Clay Walker
Sep 30, 1901
Apr 5, 1962

Clarence E. Fletcher
1888-1950
&
Lillie D. Fletcher
1895-1963

William D. Dye
1865-1939
&
Sarah E. Dye
1876-1942

William D. Dye, Jr.
Apr 2, 1913
Nov 18, 1936

William Guy Frye
1888-1957
&
A. W. F.(footmarker)

Jas. Terrell Tanner
Jun 9, 1897
Sep 13, 1958
&
Mary C. Tanner
Feb 19, 1904

John A. Overall, Sr.
Nov 30, 1892
May 8, 1941

George H. Davis
Jul 29, 1922
Jan 1, 1961

J. Scott Davis
1880-1950
&
Ollie White Davis
1884-1946

"Husband"
Albert Wesley Webster
1847-1904
&
Mattie Davis Webster
1869-1951
"Interred in Three Fork
Cemetery"

Jesse R. Overall
1868-1945
&
Nora C. Overall
1867-1938

"Father"
J. Clyde Landis
1875-1934
&
"Mother"
Myrtle Landis
1874-1951
& "Daughter"
Evelyn Landis
1900-1925

Joe K. Morris
Mar 3, 1889
Feb 21, 1973
&
Pearl D. Morris
Jan 22, 1890

James H. Beasley
1883-1943
&
Dedie F. Beasley
1890-19

J. Clarence Beasley
1901-1973
&
Clara F. Beasley
1913-

Charles Homer Dye
Nov 17, 1917
Nov 29, 1946

Carl Woods Claxton
Nov 7, 1913

&
Margaret Davis Claxton
Sep 26, 1911
Aug 30, 1967
married Jul 29, 1934

Infant dau of
W. A. & Maxine Odle
Apr 28, 1963

William Minos Leatherman
Tennessee
SF2 U.S.N.R.   W.W.II
Sep 30, 1910
Nov 24, 1966

Joe Ramsey Leatherman
Tennessee
A1C 79 AIR SVC Sq A.F.
Feb 9, 1940
Nov 27, 1967

Willie Arnold Leatherman
Nov 12, 1887
Feb 17, 1963

William Jefferson Morrow
1878-1948
&
Effie Shelton Morrow
1881-1959

Ervin P. Thomas
1865-1942
&
Sallie A. Thomas
1866-1956

Henry C. Kubley
Sep 4, 1851
Aug 8, 1934

Alice Holt Kubley
1870-1961

Mary Lee Kubley, wife of
K. L. Harrison
Oct 9, 1893
Jan 17, 1929

David Murphy Alderman
1877-1954

Sadie Stephens Alderman
1891-1963

D. M. Alderman, Jr.
May 12, 1920
Oct 15, 1944

Samuel M. Chitwood
1884-1955

Eula Blanche Chitwood
1924-1926

Eula Wright Chitwood
1884-1926

Mary Catherine Chitwood
1913-1931

John Percy Bramblett
Jul 6, 1882
Nov 19, 1955
&
Willie A. Bramblett
Nov 28, 1885
Nov 15, 1967

William Percy Bramblett
Sep 25, 1912
Feb 22, 1961
&
Mary F. Bramblett
Nov 25, 1912

Addie B. Slater
Dec 15, 1884
Mar 19, 1973

Edd Bert Slater
Nov 4, 1889
May 17, 1956

William E. Beck
1903-1963

James L. Bramblett
Mar 6, 1878
Sep 9, 1952
&
Alberta G. Bramblett
Sep 9, 1881
Aug 19, 1971

Roscoe Rippy Stephens
Mar 28, 1885
Mar 8, 1944

Irma Crowell Stephens
Feb 15, 1890
Nov 16, 1926

J. F. Bowen
1863-1939

Bettie Bowen
1865-1930

Lena B. Hoebel
1892-1953

J. H. Alderman
Sep 15, 1833
Jul 2, 1910

Mary Alderman
Feb 27, 1847
Feb 22, 1924

Mary Bailey Alderman
Jan 10, 1884
Jul 14, 1963

Jennie A. McCall
1869-1954

Nellie Alderman
1872-1931

Olivia Alderman
1880-1948

Abbie Lee Holt
1876-1934

Sue Ellen Holt
1877-1961

Elizabeth Holt
1885-1967

R. Bennett Troxler
Sep 1, 1892
Nov 20, 1961
&
Ethel Lee Troxler
Dec 29, 1895

Jack Kubley
1894-1942

John Alvin Stephens
1895-1949
&
Grace L. Stephens
1900-

John Everette Roberts
Died Jan 31, 1944
&
Annie Davis Roberts
Apr 29, 1878
Jul 20, 1961

Johnny Carolyn Armstrong
Dec 17, 1932
Apr 3, 1938

Mary Strother Stephens
Apr 11, 1894
Oct 23, 1953

Paul Bramblett Stephens
Jun 19, 1890
Dec 17, 1956

Jeanne Jones Stephens
Jun 9, 1888
Apr 14, 1962

Horace V. Stephens
1882-1973
&
Nell W. Stephens
1890-

"Mother"
Margaret Jenkins, wife of
H. V. Stephens
1883-1930

E. L. Keeling
May 1, 1846
Aug 29, 1925
& wife:
Laura G. Oden Keeling
Feb 18, 1866
(no date)

Rev. L. B. Jarman
1845-1920

Fannie McLean Jarman
1849-1935

Walter Smotherman
1875-1949
&
Tennie Smotherman
1881-19(no date)

Charlie D. Faulk
Aug 3, 1894
(no date)
&
Mary A. Faulk
Jan 30, 1904
Sep 19, 1963

Sam Baker Crockett
Apr 1, 1907
Mar 8, 1955
&
Margaret Jane Crockett
Jan 3, 1919

Mary Ann, Infant dau of
Lem & Mary Parks
Aug 18, 1934

J. H. W. Crowell
Mar 14, 1861
Jun 23, 1941
&
Laurah Crowell
May 22, 1862
Sep 12, 1939

Samuel Frank Crowell
Mar 10, 1906
Jan 21, 1974

Orville P. Davis
(no dates)

Olive E. Davis
(no dates)

Verner Lee Davis
(no dates)

Thomas S. Davis
1847-1927
&
Jane Bobo Davis
1846-1928

T. Lynn Davis
1897-1947
&
Kate J. Davis
1902-1967

Almattie Jarman
1871-1947

Elizabeth Vance Jarman
1875-1935

William Bilbro Jarman
1877-1955

Walter Jarman
1888-1920

Adella Millett Bomar
1852-1913

"Brother"
John G. Walker
1908-
&
"Sister"
Betty M. Walker
1890-1971

John G. Walker
Mar 21, 1863
Jan 26, 1918
&
Nelie S. Walker
1867-1943

Grover Cleveland Shelton
Apr 12, 1889
Jul 31, 1959

William Forrest Shelton
Apr 7, 1887
Jul 18, 1947

Ethel Shelton Wilson
May 15, 1900
Mar 17, 1971

W. H. Shelton
Dec 27, 1855
Jul 13, 1937
& wife:
Francis E. Shelton
Oct 11, 1853
Mar 14, 1925

Stephen Shelton
1876-1947
&
Rebecca Shelton
1881-1954

Robert L. Lovell
1852-1937
&
Rachel T. Lovell
1857-1940

H. Grady Lovell
Aug 25, 1891
Nov 11, 1914

Shirley H. Lovell
Tennessee
Y3 U.S.Navy   W.W.I
Nov 9, 1889
Oct 6, 1956

Robert W. Lovell
Tennessee
Pvt 39 Co 163 Depot Brig.
W. W. I
May 10, 1888
Oct 14, 1959

Birdie F. Lovell
Mar 5, 1897

William L. Robertson
1882-1962

Jonnie H. Robertson
1883-1949

Virginia Seabright Wells
Apr 28, 1885
Mar 21, 1966

Herbert John Wells
Jan 12, 1885
Sep 5, 1952

Agatha Pepper Wells
Nov 18, 1888
Nov 20, 1915

William R. Martin
Dec 27, 1871
Feb 18, 1951
&
Elizabeth K. Martin
Oct 13, 1881
Jan 12, 1968

Leonard O. Shelton
Aug 17, 1896
Sep 26, 1966
&
Louise B. Shelton
Aug 8, 1915
----
married Apr 11, 1942

Henry Shelton
1892-1931
&
Dollie (Driver) Shelton
1904-1928

William Carl Shelton
Dec 23, 1901
May 24, 1954

W. W. Phillips
Feb 20, 1852
Jul 20, 1933
&
Mary E. Phillips
Sep 23, 1857
Apr 5, 1926

William C., son of
William M. & Mary E. Phillips
Nov 11, 1876
Apr 29, 1907

Eugenie Lovell
Tennessee
Pfc 310 Infantry   W.W.I
Sep 2, 1895
Jul 7, 1957

Jimmie Lee Chilton Lovell
Dec 7, 1900
Dec 7, 1958

Ruby S. Healan
Sep 5, 1903

William Leslie Robertson
1910-1911

Roger Holt Robertson
1912-1915

Bryant Elvis Rushing
Nov 3, 1862
Feb 13, 1916

Willie Short Rushing
Nov 14, 1862
Jun 4, 1953

John D. Phillips
Aug 11, 1896

&
Georgia D. Phillips
Sep 27, 1900
Jul 4, 1972

Gloria Virginia Phillips
Oct 28, 1922
Sep 15, 1923

Infant Dau of
K. M. & Betty Phillips
Sep 19, 1964

Charlie Green Bishop
1872-1958
&
Susan Jane Bishop
1878-1958

William J. Pannell
Aug 15, 1849
Jun 2, 1935

Sarah E. Pannell
Sep 6, 1853
Oct 3, 1920

Clarence Pannell
1885-1923

Catherine S. Pannell
1915-1968

Barbara Ann Pannell
Jan 23, 1949

Rena B. Phillips
Sep 5, 1880
Sep 18, 1912

Annie E. Phillips
Apr 17, 1889
Jan 17, 1919

Will P. King
1857-1942
&
Mary C. King
1865-1957

James R., son of
W. P. & M. C. King
Oct 26, 1889
Apr 21, 1914

Artie D. King, Sr.
1882-1963
&
Elnora P. King
1881-1969

Charlie Short Wilson
Jan 22, 1886

&
Juanita Scott Wilson
Jun 19, 1881
Mar 21, 1959

Infant Son of
M. R. & J. T. Carothers
Oct 26, 1915

Infant Son of
M. R. & J. T. Carothers
Mar 21, 1912

John Thomas Carothers
Sep 24, 1888
Dec 26, 1965
&
Ruth Espy Carothers
Sep 1, 1889
Jan 25, 1971

Silas Parker
1858-1925
&
Belle Parker
1864-1943

Jesse Parker
1894-1954

John C. Pannell
1877-1951

Charles R. Pannell
Apr 21, 1881
Nov 7, 1921

Mamie Shoffner Pannell
Jan 16, 1883
Oct 21, 1972

Robert H. Miller
1901-1946

Lyddia C. Bomar
Apr 21, 1892
Jul 15, 1918

George N. Blanton
1880-1953
&
Susie L. Blanton
1893-19

Clyde H. Shoffner
1877-1951

Mary D., wife of
Clyde H. Shoffner
1878-1912

Siquard A. Sundstrom
1883-1920
&
Lucy V. Sundstrom
1885-1972

G. D. Searcy
Mar 23, 1847
Jul 27, 1910

143

Frenchie D. Fowler
Dec 25, 1890
Oct 20, 1939
&
Bose L. Fowler
Jun 10, 1876
Feb 19, 1935

Thomas Clyde Crenshaw
1881-1957

Sarah Grider Crenshaw
1892-19

Sarah Arnold Crenshaw
1879-1920

Frances Arnold Carson
Oct 23, 1878
Aug 19, 1927

Edward Blackman Grider
1898-1966

Willia Barnes Grider
1895-19

Elizabeth W. Sutton
1878-1930

H. K. Stokes
1839-1930
& wife:
Frances Stokes
1843-1935

Edd C. Stokes
1870-1954
&
Julia C. Stokes
1872-1928

"Sisters"
Josie Clark
Sep 23, 1892
Dec 23, 1962
&
Sallie Clark
Sep 12, 1890
Jul 13, 1969

Carl R. Clark
Nov 21, 1880
(no date)
&
Pearl W. Clark
Aug 5, 1889
Aug 17, 1968

M. G. Plumlee
1860-1899

Jerry Michael Lovell
Tennessee
Sp4 Co D 187 Inf 101 ABN Div
Vietnam BSM PH
Oct 20, 1946
May 18, 1969

Owen Brown Wisdom   and
Mar 3, 1882
Dec 13, 1916

J. Newton Smith
Sep 11, 1874
Jan 24, 1940

Emma May Smith
May 8, 1893
Sep 28, 1936

Jasper Stokes, son of
Mr & Mrs J. N. Smith
Oct 12, 1902
Oct 1, 1909

Lettie, wife of
J. N. Smith, Jr.
May 12, 1879
Mar 20, 1911

John G. Arnold
Died Mar 19, 1900

Sarah E. Arnold
Died Apr 21, 1887

William A. Arnold
Jan 9, 1892

James Curry Yell
Dec 31, 1842
Jun 11, 1909
&
Ada Waite Yell
Mar 7, 1859
Oct 22, 1934

Warren S. Yell
1882-1950

Sadie Waite
Aug 16, 1889
Nov 22, 1904

W. S. Waite, Sr.
1862-1930

Warren S. Waite
1887-1955

Alda C. Waite
1880-1926

John Samuel Guy
Aug 20, 1823
Jul 23, 1904

Amelia Ann Guy
Sep 17, 1831
Feb 6, 1908

Mark Guy
1850-1939

William Arthur Hoyle, Jr.
Jul 23, 1914
Nov 12, 1971
&
Virginia Christian Hoyle
Jul 3, 1920

Virginia Brown Wisdom
Mar 28, 1912
Feb 28, 1913

L. T. Throneberry
1842-1920

Atlanta A. Thorneberry
1840-1921

John H. Grider
Dec 27, 1841
(no date)
C.S.A.
(Southern Cross,1861-1865)
&
Sarah J. Grider
Feb 12, 1844
Feb 24, 1927

Andrew Jackson Grider
1868-1931

Rebecca Arnold Grider
1868-1943

Sgt. John H. Grider
Co I 17 Tenn Inf. C.S.A.
1839-1923

Jimmie Ruth Yell Robertson
Aug 10, 1895
Jul 12, 1970

Shelley Jean Robertson
Apr 3, 1951
Jun 27, 1953

Willis K. Pruitt
Sep 10, 1858
Dec 2, 1904

Sallie E. Smith, wife of
W. K. Pruitt
Jun 2, 1871
May 10, 1917

Delia May Christian
Mar 8, 1885
Feb 2, 1905

W. M. Sehorne
1842-1926

"Mother"
Lena Sehorne
1861-1940

"Husband"
Charley Edward Seahorn
Mar 19, 1869
Sep 28, 1911

William Hoyle
Oct 3, 1857
Feb 28, 1917
&
Sarah Jane Hoyle
May 4, 1854
May 2, 1920

William Arthur Hoyle
Jun 19, 1888
Feb 6, 1964
&
Docia Phillips Hoyle
Oct 27, 1888
Aug 28, 1959

Georgia, wife of
F. W. Dardis
Oct 22, 1866
Dec 5, 1902
"Dau of L. T. &
A. A. Throneberry"

Alberta, dau of
W. E. & Mollie Russell
Sep 6, 1902
Aug 3, 1911
age: 8y, 10m, 27d.

Walter E. Russell
1874-1942

Mollie T. Russell
Jan 3, 1876
Jan 31, 1953

G. E. Waite
(no dates)
&
Mackie Phillips, wife of
G. E. Waite
1864-1910

Warren Waite
Jun 9, 1827
Feb 4, 1896
&
Ruth S. Waite
1838-1922

James W. Waite
1869-1933
&
Minnie T. Waite
1867-1954

Marion Allen Kimbro
1920-1929

Allen S. Kimbro
1889-1975
(Tullahoma FH)

Willie Kimbro
1893-1975
(Tullahoma FH)

Isaac Heylan Erwin
1864-1931

Adele Nuckolls, wife of
Heylan Erwin
1872-1949

John Milton Erwin
1899-1967

Albert A. Hoyle
Apr 5, 1881
Feb 6, 1900

Maggie Hoyle
Oct 8, 1882
Jan 16, 1914

Aileene Hoyle
Nov 15, 1910
Sep 12, 1915

W. B. Chilton
Apr 22, 1860
Mar 18, 1930

Martha Jane Rippie, wife
of W. B. Chilton
May 8, 1863
Jun 4, 1919

J. N., son of
W. B. & M. J. Chilton
Nov. 27, 1900
Apr 18, 1902

Eliza Ruth Chilton
1903-1903

Ada Lee Rippey
1896-1921

John Carothers
Jan 25, 1831
Feb 15, 1909
&
Lettie Carothers
Feb 25, 1842
May 31, 1902

John M. Carothers
Aug 20, 1865
Oct 29, 1908

Corrie S. Carothers
Jul 4, 1869
Nov 13, 1945

John H. Morgan
1870-1953
&
Anna Blanton Morgan
1874-1949

S. P. King, M.D.
Feb 12, 1837
Jun 25, 1894

Emma Josephine, dau of
Dr. S. P. & R. R. King
Sep 2, 1876
Jul 26, 1889

David A. Dement
Tennessee
Sgt U.S.Air Force, Vietnam
Nov 10, 1946
Mar 12, 1972

Infant dau of
J. T. & Elizabeth N.
          Livingstone
Mar 4, 1942

James Stephens Justice
Tennessee
1st Lt. Co B 371 Inf W.W.I
Feb 6, 1886
Mar 4, 1970
&
Lucy Macrae Justice
1900-

Mary F. Nuckolls, 2nd wife
of L. T. Webb
1870-1961

James G. Moore
May 15, 1860
Dec 17, 1957

Elizabeth S. Moore
May 10, 1866
Mar 12, 1938

Infant of
J. G. & Elizabeth Moore
Feb 23, 1898

J. Glenn Moore, Jr.
Jul 6, 1903
Nov 2, 1967

Don S. Carothers
Apr 30, 1896
Jan 13, 1949
&
Ruth O. Carothers

Mary C., wife of
T. L. Kimbro
1875-1914

R. L. Blanton
1876-1921

William B. Morgan
Tennessee
Pvt Btry F 19 Field Arty
W. W. I
Jan 22, 1898
Dec 6, 1964

B. W. Blanton
Nov 22, 1835
Oct 8, 1901
&
Elizabeth J. Blanton
Jan 7, 1834
Sep 22, 1892
&
Annie E. Blanton
1848-1925

Mary H. Blanton
1840-1907

Arthur I. Neel
Mar 12, 1880
Feb 15, 1946

Vera Moore Neel
Dec 3, 1890
Jan 19, 1971

Laura Edna, dau of
M. P. & Dolly Davis
Mar 4, 1892
Jul 16, 1896

Frank Fletcher
Feb 28, 1885
Jan 15, 1954
&
Marie R. Fletcher
Dec 23, 1883
Sep 4, 1968

Ida J. Waite Keathley
1873-1927

John Casto Keathley
Apr 13, 1874
Oct 3, 1908

Harry Allen, son of
J. C. & Ida J. Keathley
Born & Died
Sep 8, 1900

Aunt Sally Phillips
1868-1949

Locke Clayton
1858-1910

Ellen C. Stephens
1866-1961

Vida Elizabeth, dau of
Lock & Ellen Clayton
Dec 26, 1905
Sep 3, 1907

Calvin Green Mitchell
1812-1887

Mary Olivia Mitchell
1827-1890

Sara Elizabeth Mitchell
1856-1910

Lee Mitchell
1868-1896

Robert P. Webster
1858-1945
&
Sallie S. Webster
1858-1947

Sallie Rowena Webster
Apr 26, 1895
Mar 2, 1899

Hattie Cleveland Webster
Oct 24, 1888
Jan 15, 1891

Infant Son of
Adelaide & Vannoy Webster
Sep 27, 1922

Jesse Goggie Webster
Dec 23, 1917
Jul 26, 1919

R. W. Couch
Mar 22, 1840
Sep 8, 1910

Mary A., wife of
R. W. Couch
Feb 12, 1863
Feb 4, 1898

William Henry Davis
1886-1962

Henry A. Justice
Apr 23, 1827
Apr 25, 1901

Grandma Justice
1838-1922

John H. Justice
May 29, 1862
Sep 29, 1942

Vina E., wife of
J. H. Justice
Aug 14, 1866
Dec 19, 1917

J. G. "Dock" Justice
1899-1951

Robert Vance Davidson
1858-1931

Annie Mitchell Davidson
1858-1928

Mary Sue Davidson
1886-1904

Margrett Cordeliar Vaughn
1835-1913

Vannoy Cleveland Webster, Jr.
Apr 30, 1925
Oct 28, 1956

Vannoy C. Webster
Jul 9, 1884
Jan 15, 1963
&
Adelaide G. Webster
May 4, 1883
Jul 10, 1964

Charles H. Hodge
Tennessee
Pvt Infantry W. W. II
Oct 12, 1929
Oct 5, 1969

Charley H. Griffy
Oct 30, 1860
(no date)
&
Mary Wiser Griffy
Aug 10, 1874
(no date)

Othal C. Griffy
Aug 29, 1892

&
Pearl C. Griffy
Jan 6, 1894
Jun 11, 1973

Frank Hall Fletcher
Apr 29, 1909
Jul 19, 1924

Ralph Fletcher
Feb 15, 1916
Jun 3, 1969

R. N. Phillips
1861-1927

Dora S. Phillips
1871-1923

James Berry Phillips
Apr 22, 1900
Feb 2, 1901
&
Ralph Phillips
Aug 10, 1896
Sep 1, 1896
"Sons of R. N. &
Dora Phillips"

R. S. Phillips
1904-1928

Mrs. Mary Webster
Mar 2, 1848
Dec 17, 1900
age: 52y, 9m, 15d.

Annie May York
Jan 22, 1879
May 15, 1904

James Arnold
1843-1915
& wife:
Nannie Frances Arnold
1848-1913
&
Thomas Francis Arnold
Jun 7, 1871
May 30, 1895
&
Hugh Turney Arnold
1874-1912

C. J. Shriver
1850-1927

Belle Shriver
1856-1926

Alley T. Culley
1873-1929

D. J. Shriver
Feb 28, 1854
Sep 2, 1894

Mabel, dau of
John R. & Alma E. Shriver
Mar 17, 1907
Jun 27, 1907

Mama Justice
1841-1926
& Son:
W. E. Justice
1875-1900

Wright Sims
1887-1966
&
Dewees Sims
1885-1947

Lucius B. Sims
1893-19   and

Dr. S. K. Whitson
1823-1900

Marshall H. Whitson
1869-1928

Isaac Brittain, son of
C. M. & Lula B. Gleaves
Jan 30, 1908
Nov 7, 1909

Jennie Clark Gleaves
Feb 19, 1887
Apr 3, 1974
&
Clyde M. Gleaves
Dec 22, 1879
Apr 21, 1962
&
Lula Clark Gleaves
Aug 22, 1879
Jul 8, 1921

Infant Son of
J. F. & S. A. Anthony
Feb 10, 1899

Thomas Francis, Infant son of
Hugh & Matchie Arnold
Died Aug 24, 1899
age: 2 months.

I. Herbert White
1893-1970
&
Jeanette B. White
1901-

Pat Barnett
Born in S. C.,
Feb 14, 1825
Died in Tenn.
Dec 15, 1898
&
Jane Barnett
Born in Tenn.
Aug 25, 1828
Died in Tenn.
Jul 22, 1900

Ethel Sunshine, dau of
C. J. & J. B. Shriver
Oct 1, 1884
Sep 15, 1891
age: 7 yrs.

Thomas Edward Harris
Aug 8, 1892
Sep 11, 1952
&
Ethel Arnold Harris
Oct 9, 1895
Mar 15, 1958

Newton C. Harris
Dec 22, 1814
Apr 4, 1891

Elizabeth C. Harris
Apr 7, 1818
Nov 1, 1892

Fannie M. Sims
---- - ----

John W. Shriver
Sep 31, 1858
Oct 4, 1897

Sarah B. Hensley
(no dates)

Maj. William Woods
(no dates)

Barnet F. Cleveland
Aug 11, 1846
May 17, 1929

Elizabeth Pepper Cleveland
Feb 14, 1851
Jan 1, 1938

Jesse F. Cleveland
1881-1952
&
Margaret Cleveland
1891-1942

William Pepper Cleveland
Nov 3, 1877
Oct 18, 1907

Isaac Hensley White
1851-1916

Bettie E. White
Nov 30, 1852
Mar 17, 1900

Margie Belle White
1881-1957

Alpha S. Barnett
(no dates)

Huston W. Barnett
(no dates)

Minnie S. Barnett
(no dates)

Kate J. Barnett
(no dates)

S. N. Stephenson
Jan 18, 1837
Feb 11, 1917

Elizabeth M., wife of
S. N. Stephenson
Nov 7, 1837
Apr 6, 1889

Thomas Overton Harris
Jun 30, 1860
May 24, 1947
&
Kate Miller Harris
Oct 17, 1866
Sep 1, 1945

John E. Justice
1858-1948
& wife:
Rachel Stephens Justice
1858-1945

Annie Moore, wife of
G. Elmer Slater
Aug 4, 1884
Sep 18, 1956

Lena Moore Hart, wife of
James W. Hart
1874-1952

Fannie Moore Osburn
1876-1912

Eliza Miller, wife of
J. K. Moore
Feb 10, 1852
Apr 10, 1904

J. K. Moore
Apr 1, 1845
Sep 1, 1941
"A Confederate Soldier"

Martha W. Cleveland
Tennessee
Nurse Army Nurse Corps
W. W. I
Jan 18, 1875·
Mar 3, 1957

Eliza Cleveland Tate
Aug 8, 1884
Sep 20, 1963
"Interred in Richmond, Va."

F. W. Smartt
Died 1925
(no age given)

Mabel Arnold Smartt
1877-1946

James C. Shriver
Feb 17, 1826
Oct 19, 1905
&
Catherine Shriver
Aug 6, 1830
Nov 2, 1916

Rachel J. Stephenson
May 1, 1850
May 16, 1912

L. B. Stephenson
Oct 7, 1879
May 14, 1919
"In U.S.Army, 19 yrs."

Susanah Alice Stephenson
1869-1929

Lillie Stephenson
Aug 14, 1874
Feb 14, 1885

Bessie Harris, wife of
C. W. Stooke
1891-1920

Mabel Justice Blackman
Sep 26, 1884
Jun 26, 1966

Mary Margaret S. Hailey
Jun 26, 1895
May 6, 1974

Jennie Phillips Hailey
Feb 4, 1866
Jul 30, 1941

Millard Fillmore Hailey
Jun 24, 1857
Jan 13, 1905

Samuel R. Hailey
Born Nov 15, 1815
in Halifax C., Va.
Died Dec 20, 1885

John G. Sims
1854-1939
&
Mary W. Sims
1856-1944

Sadie, dau of
O. P. & A. L. Arnold
1888-1894

Infant Son of
O. P. & A. L. Arnold
Oct 14, 1888

Rachel Tarver Vallotton,
wife of O. P. Arnold
1819-1896

Elmer C. Culley
1894-1895

Tennie L. Culley
1860-1905

Paul L. Culley
1897-1918

W. L. Culley
1844-1937
"A Confederate Soldier"

Infant dau of
Jesse & Lizzie H. Cleveland
(no dates)

Thomas Stone Cleveland
Apr 25, 1840
Sep 11, 1907

Annie E. Wright, wife of
T. S. Cleveland
1848-1902

Lizzie Harper, wife of
Jesse Cleveland
Mar 28, 1870
Dec 24, 1894

North-West Section:

Lawrence W. Arnold
Feb 29, 1892
Sep 20, 1951

Clayton Walker Arnold
Apr 27, 1893
Mar 30, 1964

Thomas Hardin Jones
Jan 30, 1837
Sep 24, 1909
&
Elizabeth F. Jones
Oct 26, 1840
Sep 12, 1916

Roger F. Crosslin
1947-1950
(Howell)

Deborah Ann Crosslin
1955-1959
(McFarland-Thompson)

E. W. Smith
Nov 3, 1884
Feb 19, 1911

Kittie Russell Smith
1858-1942
(Daves-Culberson)

"Mother"
Eliza C. Osborne
Nov 31, 1855
Aug 22, 1907
& "Son":
William W. Osborne
Oct 16, 1889
May 30, 1907

Clement Bush Osborne
May 3, 1856
Jun 2, 1912

Fannie T. Smotherman
Jan 15, 1861
Nov 21, 1951

Geneva M. Smotherman
Jun 23, 1903

John Gilbert Martin
Sep 7, 1889
Dec 25, 1951

Kitty Taylor Martin
Apr 8, 1893

Dr. Thomas W. Ryall
1874-1934
"Dentist"

Oliver F. Finney
Feb 19, 1872
Jun 30, 1955
&
Zella M. Finney
May 3, 1877
Sep 16, 1933

Paul Carroll
1901-1975
(Gowen-Smith)

Elizabeth Carroll
1912-1942

Alice Carroll
1869-1940

G. Glen Osborne
Apr 24, 1893
Mar 6, 1974
&
Bess H. Osborne
Jan 13, 1895
(no date)

Samuel M(McMinn) Hill
May 22, 1871
(TM-   1965, Gowen-Smith)
&
Ida D. Hill
Mar 12, 1870
May 30, 1965

Tommie H. Hill
Sep 20, 1902

&
Beatrice F. Hill
Aug 1, 1903
Jan 24, 1962

Buford Taylor
Sep 17, 1904

&
Pearl U. Taylor
Dec 2, 1906
Sep 16, 1971
married Dec 22, 1922

William R. Baker
Jan 11, 1906
May 24, 1964
&
Jewell H. Baker

----
married Jun 7, 1925

William H. Beckman
Aug 24, 1855
Jun 20, 1938
&
Sarah Elizabeth Beckman
Sep 2, 1869
Sep 4, 1952

R. Charles Beckman
1871-1936
&
M. Lillie Beckman
1876-1949

Walter R. Jamison
Apr 11, 1857
Mar 29, 1933

Virginia A. Jamison
Jan 24, 1866
Apr 23, 1940

Charles H. Stephens
1865-1934
(Note: another adult grave
beside this grave, unmarked)

Carrie E. Jamison
May 30, 1869
Nov 29, 1927

Roy W. Stephens
1892-1927

A. L. Stephens
1882-1919

William N. Bryant
Mar 17, 1881
Jan 12, 1956
&
Effie T. Bryant
Apr 30, 1895
(TM-   1972)

J. L. Satterfield
Jun 26, 1909
Dec 22, 1956

David Randall Ferrell
Apr 9, 1959
Sep 15, 1973
(color picture)

Daniel Clyde Thomas
Aug 11, 1897

&
Mary Effie Thomas
Dec 30, 1899
Mar 23, 1972

Salvatore Peter
Christopher Sicignan
M.M.3 U.S.N.R.
Oct 12, 1926
May 16, 1974

Joseph A. Kelly
Jan 20, 1893
Jun 1, 1964

Sammie B. Kelly
Sep 12, 1893
Oct 12, 1956

Leon Shriver
Mar 17, 1902
Dec 13, 1973
&
Christine S. Shriver
May 11, 1905
----
married Oct 6, 1929

Emma Jean Shriver
Oct 31, 1931

Infant Son of
W. D. & Emma A. Smotherman
May 23, 1908

Orr Dee Jordan Henry
Dec 12, 1903
Aug 15, 1973

James Hugh Maupin
May 24, 1894
Nov 22, 1957
&
Suma Jordan Maupin
Dec 6, 1906

Elmer S., son of
Mr & Mrs E. S. Robertson, Jr.
1919

W. S. Russell
May 23, 1867
Sep 24, 1910
& wife:
Mary B. Thompson Russell
Nov 9, 1867
Nov 2, 1908
& Dau:
Hattie Virginia Russell
Feb 4, 1903
Feb 20, 1903

Aubrey Lee Russell
Nov 25, 1892
May 20, 1940

J. W. Holt
Feb 22, 1855
Apr 7, 1938

Blanche Halback, wife of
J. W. Holt
1860-1923

Cecil Rupert Holt
Nov 22, 1882
Sep 20, 1905

Herbert F. Holt
Mar 29, 1884
Apr 17, 1931

Fanny Pauline Finch
1855-1895

Emma Susan Davis
1859-1915

Thomas Burt Davis, Jr.
1885-1887

Thomas Burt Davis
1849-1903

Alice Elizabeth Finch, wife
of Thos. Burt Davis
1854-1891

Capt. G. A. Cortner
Nov 24, 1838   and
Apr 18, 1911
&
Mary C. Cortner   and
Jul 20, 1844
Aug 30, 1893
&
Claude Cortner
Dec 3, 1872
Nov 15, 1902

Joseph Herman Couch
Oct 23, 1902
Jul 13, 1974

Ruben C. Couch
Mar 20, 1879
Sep 11, 1959
& Wife:
Eudocia K. Couch
Aug 1, 1878
Dec 8, 1958
& on reverse side:
W. T. Keller
Apr 3, 1848
Sep 17, 1920
&
Mary L. Keller
May 3, 1854
Dec 26, 1929

Robert David Maupin
1860-1900

Grace Landess Maupin
1865-1901

Robert N. Cleveland
1855-1940
&
Martha E. Cleveland
1859-1945

Harmon H. Landess
Jul 22, 1818
Jan 18, 1892

J. H. Stephens
May 27, 1859
Dec 24, 1904

A. G."Bud" Landess
1856-1936

Carrie E. Landess
1869-1900

Maggie R., wife of
William B. Bates
Feb 15, 1856
Dec 22, 1881

John Lane Walker, M.D.
1871-1949

Leola Arnold Walker
1872-1959
DAR Marker

Leola Arnold Walker
1905-1970

Infant dau of
A. J. & M. F. Cortner
(no dates)

Fannie E. Cortner   and
May 28, 1869
Dec 13, 1892
&   and
Minnie Cortner
Nov 7, 1874
Aug 15, 1894

Robert E. Couch
1918-1920

Mary R. Couch
1914-1915

R. C. Couch, III
1907 age: 6m.

Herbert E. Keller
1886-1944
&
Lillis S. Keller
1886-(no date)

Nancy E., dau of
W. T. & M. L. Keller
Apr 1, 1876
Dec 6, 1906

Eugene N. Cannon
Dec 31, 1892
Apr 25, 1959
&
Kathleen S. Cannon
Mar 21, 1904

Vinnie R. Cannon
Sep 20, 1877
Jul 13, 1949

John E. Hall
May 11, 1831
May 12, 1891

George N. Hall
Feb 22, 1840
Jul 29, 1909

B. Gordon Blackman
Sep 15, 1872
Oct 11, 1959

Margaret J. Blackman
Nov 5, 1870
Jan 29, 1954

Wynn Thomas
1879-1906

Mattie Thomas
1884-1897

Mary Thomas
1881-1882

Willie Thomas
1882-1891

Kate Thomas
1871-1891

Daniel F. Cortner
1871-1938
&
Cora Lee Cortner
Jul 19, 1874
Jan 13, 1947
&
Dorothy C. Williams
Jun 6, 1910
Jan 17, 1957

James D. Cortner
Sep 26, 1872
May 24, 1956

Della M. Cortner
1877-1926

Katie M. Cortner
1901-1903

Barnet D. Jakes
Mar 22, 1898
Feb 28, 1899

Lizzie C. Jakes
Apr 7, 1869
Jul 17, 1932

"Father"
William H. Cannon
Mar 29, 1847
Dec 24, 1907

"Mother"
Ida A. Cannon
Jan 22, 1851
Dec 30, 1928

Newton M. Cannon
Apr 20, 1879
Apr 20, 1928

Charlie L. Cannon
Feb 9, 1883
Dec 7, 1933

William H. Ellington
Dec 21, 1854
Dec 13, 1927

Mollie Ellington
Dec 11, 1865
Aug 21, 1957

William Thomas
1844-1926
&
Sarah Couch Thomas
1846-1932

Carrie Thomas
1889-1908

Ella Thomas
1873-1920

Elizabeth Thomas
1875-1957

Laura Thomas
1891-1960

Baby Son of
D. F. & C. L. Cortner
Jun 13, 1894

Robert Jennings Davis
1922-1944

Julia H. Davis
1890-1891

Benjamin Franklin Davis
1878-1943

Mary J. Boyle Davis
1886-1972

Fannie L. Davis
1882-1922

John Sims Davis
1855-1930

Julia M. Davis
1856-1932

Mary A. Davis
1884-1968

Hugh Albert Davidson
Jan 8, 1839
Oct 1, 1910

Ella M. Davidson
1856-1924

Thomas James Myers
1841-1914

Agnes Davidson Myers
1844-1930

Albert J. Uselton
1865-1946
&
Isora Uselton
1871-1955

Charles Hudges
1846-1919

Clarsie J. Hudges
1848-1924

Lou Belle Hudges
Oct 7, 1872
Aug 16, 1960

Robert Hampton Hudges
1871-1959

Hattie Smith Hudges
1876-1967

Samuel Emmett Burks
May 8, 1896
Jun 8, 1945
&
Vassie Marr Burks
Jun 27, 1899
May 12, 1960

James F. West
1879-1926
&
Josie S. West
1878-1952

William L. Bell
Tennessee
Cpl 2509 Base Unit AAF
W. W. II
Apr 20, 1906
Apr 29, 1969

Albert Miller Dement
Jun 1, 1868
Mar 16, 1940

Mina Preston Dement
Jun 7, 1871
Dec 2, 1944

Ruby McSpadden Dement
Oct 11, 1893
Sep 1, 1949

Robert Clarence O'Steen
Mar 11, 1881
Oct 17, 1925
&
Beulah Williams O'Steen
Nov 22, 1887
Sep 29, 1965

William Lee O'Steen
Tennessee
GM1 U.S.Navy W.W.II,
Korea PH
May 23, 1922
Dec 5, 1956

John Thomas Parker
1897-1918
(Old Marker: John Thomas
Parker, Died in France,
Pvt 331 Inf 83 Div.
Dec 29, 1918)
&
Dosia Kathryn Parker
1892-1919

Virgie Lena Cope
Mar 14, 1880
Aug 6, 1928

B. T. McCollum
1864-1920
& wife:
Mary Elizabeth Hudges McCollum
1876-1964

Thomas E. Butner
1872-1946
&
Ida Belle Butner
1877-19(TM 1971)

Willie Elmore White
Born & Died
Nov 3, 1958

Jearline B. White
Feb 22, 1925
Sep 10, 1969

Clarence E. West
Aug 30, 1908
Sep 16, 1963
&
Myrtle K. West
Jul 24, 1909

George D, Ferguson   and
Jul 25, 1898
(no date)

Freddie D. Dennis
1964-1964(Howell-Thompson)

C. R. Brevard
1863-1953

Annie M. Brevard
1874-1968

Thomas B. Spiers
1880-1952
&
Lillian R. Spiers
1881-1960

Roy V. Spiers
1892-1934

Albert Sidney Shriver
Jul 31, 1887
Feb 20, 1966

Thomas Abraham Shriver
Sep 22, 1843
Aug 22, 1929

Elizabeth Holt Shriver
Oct 7, 1850
Jan 16, 1929

Frank G. Parker
1866-1944

Annie S. Parker
1867-1946

William B. Parker
1906-1937

Houston F. Fox
Aug 13, 1886
Nov 19, 1972
&
Dora Lee Fox
Feb 7, 1880
Oct 19, 1951

Leroy S. Brown
1840-1921
&
Mary A. Brown
1850-1934

Joe C. Glenn
Mar 19, 1870
Aug 24, 1950
&
Hattie F. Glenn
Sep 5, 1875
Mar 21, 1959

Walter Caruthers
1878-1943
&
Mary Caruthers
1887-19

Virginia Caruthers
1915-1923

Mae O. Ferguson
Mar 6, 1899
Dec 31, 1963

E. A. Moseley
Apr 5, 1836
Jun 22, 1910

Mary F. Moseley
Dec 16, 1839
Jul 8, 1922

Mattie R. Moseley
Mar 26, 1870
Feb 1, 1911

Lottie Belle, wife of
J. J. Phillips
Jul 1, 1879
Feb 7, 1911

W. W. Hord
1844-1919

Sallie M. Hord
1847-1923

Rosella Hord
1874-1942

Elizabeth Hord
1868-1964

E. Cooper Stephens
Mar 29, 1869
Feb 4, 1959
&
Mary K. Stephens
Sep 8, 1882
Jul 16, 1973

Thomas J. Stokes
Jul 1, 1871
Jul 30, 1961
&
Viola E. Stokes
Feb 12, 1884
Nov 3, 1948

John A. Elkins
1889-1965
(Gowen-Smith)

Georgia Elkins
1886-1972
(Gowen-Smith)

Stanley W. Elkins
Tennessee
S Sgt 89 Depot Repl
Sq AAF W.W.II
Jan 30, 1920
Jun 2, 1968

Clarence Johnson
Nov 25, 1893   Seaman 2cl
Jun 21, 1941   U.S.Navy
&
Mary M. Johnson
Feb 24, 1897
Mar 28, 1971
married Oct 29, 1920

Henry Dean Ferguson
1873-1957

Rachel Ann Ferguson
1870-1948

Joe Freeman
1905-1952

Maude Freeman Ciantar
1903-1928

John L. Freeman
Sep 28, 1870
Aug 30, 1962
&
Nancy L. Freeman
Oct 30, 1880
Feb 12, 1951

Will Chitwood
1889-19(no date)
&
Kattie B. Chitwood
1873-1960

Raymond O. Barnes
Apr 14, 1898
Apr 9, 1965
&
Mary E. Barnes
Oct 14, 1897

Katie E., wife of
C. L. Davidson
Aug 25, 1872
Aug 10, 1894

Jesse C. Chockley
Born in Richmond, Va.
Jan 20, 1810
Died Mar 12, 1890

Mary, wife of
Jesse Chockley
(no dates)

Mattie Lou Alley, wife
of W. A. Hardy
Died Jan 2, 1927
(no age given)

Albert R. Alley
Mar 22, 1822
Jun 2, 1902
&
Martha A. Alley
Dec 2, 1827
Jun 10, 1903
&
Walter C. Alley
Oct 19, 1857
Feb 21, 1876

William Patton Clark
Tennessee
Pvt U.S.Army W.W.I
Mar 23, 1889
Jul 29, 1966

Marion Stone
1844-1914
&
M. Elizabeth Stone
1843-1925

Robert S. Clark
1849-1924
&
Mattie B. Clark
1856-1923

Sanford Porter Norton
May 24, 1885
Jan 22, 1916

John H. Morgan
Feb 14, 1857
Apr 14, 1932
&
Rosa M. Morgan
Mar 6, 1872
Apr 5, 1955

Everett F. Morgan
Aug 5, 1884
Jul 20, 1914

Lillard T. Morgan
Sep 18, 1894
May 22, 1915

James Robert Isom
Feb 4, 1889
Jan 9, 1968
&
Mollie Green Isom
Jan 31, 1891

Alex Mackey
Jan 28, 1871
Dec 10, 1907

Robert S. Clark
(no dates)

Sarah B. Clark
(no dates)

Gordentia Waite Clark
1855-1940
&
Lydie Little Clark
1859-1940

Robert Little Clark
1882-1948

Lucie C. Clark
1884-1924

G. Waite Clark, Jr.
1886-1916

Carlton C. Sims
Sep 30, 1890
Aug 16, 1960
&
Sarah Clark Sims

James S., son of
Marion & M. E. Stone
Oct 27, 1874
Jan 25, 1891

Jane Blanton
1852-1899

Paul Baker
1897-1927

W. B. Walker
1867-1923

Fruzie C. Walker
1878-1949

C. French Walker
1893-1949

Mary Stokes
&
Paul Stokes
Jan 23, 1945

Clemmie A. Jones, wife of
W. A. Parks
May 18, 1876
May 22, 1961

W. R. Jones, Husband of
Katy S. Jones
Jan 28, 1869
Feb 9, 1908

A. J. Jones
1847-1934
& wife:
Susan C. Jones
1851-1927

Willie Mai Jones
1908-1939

Joe L. Jones
Tennessee
Sgt 83 CML Bn W.W.II
Dec 19, 1921
May 24, 1944

Ernest B. Jones
Apr 1, 1884
Jan 22, 1924
&
Sarah C. Jones
Feb 18, 1891
Feb 6, 1964

Robert S. Clark
Jun 14, 1827
Sep 22, 1892
&
Sarah P. Clark
Apr 29, 1829
Mar 13, 1900
&
Julia Clark
Jan 30, 1860
Sep 19, 1890

Infant Son of
H. A. & Lizzie Clark
Died Aug 12, 1892
(no age given)

R. H. Hale
Sep 28, 1866
Sep 15, 1871

W. G. Carothers
Jan 31, 1873
Apr 4, 1922

Minnie Carothers
Jan 2, 1874
Mar 6, 1943

William Floyd Carothers
1902-1944

James Thurman Jones
Jun 25, 1924
Oct 31, 1931

Cecil E. Hackathorn
May 14, 1905
Sep 23, 1967
&
Louise M. Hackathorn
Dec 20, 1904
Jan 2, 1970

Alexander J., Husband of
Josie Drumright
Jun 6, 1827
May 12, 1892

Josie Drumright
1857-1925

A. M. Harrison
1863-1893

Etta Harrison
1875-(no date)

A. G. Harrison
Died Jul 10, 1893
(no age given)

Louise Clark
Mar 7, 1887
Nov 20, 1904

Joseph C. Clark
Tennessee
Pvt 5 Regt U.S.M.C. 2 Div
W. W. I
Nov 15, 1888
Jun 23, 1950

Lizzie Cunningham, wife of
H. A. Clark
Mar 23, 1862
Apr 4, 1909

Henry Anthony Clark
Mar 28, 1857
Sep 20, 1952

James H. Cortner
Sep 30, 1887
Jan 30, 1969
&
Julia C. Cortner
Sep 21, 1891
Feb 3, 1960

J. Harvey Bomar
Apr 27, 1869
Sep 12, 1903

Nannie Stone Bomar
Dec 24, 1869
Apr 28, 1954

Thomas R. Wade
1871-1953

Emma Jordan Wade
1871-1920

A. J. Cortner
Dec 28, 1876
Oct 28, 1967
&
Margaret Florence Cortner
Oct 10, 1879
Nov 30, 1920

Clarence Cortner
1884-1954
&
Oveida S. Cortner
1892-19

Emmett E. Cortner
Sep 4, 1902
Nov 20, 1929

Daniel Cortner
Oct 26, 1843
Nov 18, 1930
&
Bettie E. Cortner
Sep 8, 1844
Apr 4, 1923

Edd M. Black
Oct 10, 1881
Nov 17, 1962
&
Betty E. Black
Aug 13, 1887
Jan 8, 1960

Frances Marion Black
Sep 12, 1888
Nov 8, 1956

John Christofer Black
Jan 29, 1874
Mar 16, 1943

Erin O. Black
Aug 23, 1891
Jun 11, 1969

James N. Black
1876-1961
& wife:
Alice C. Hill Black
1882-1929

Viola Mullins Pruitt
1877-1949

Fannie B., wife of
H. R. Kinnard & dau of
S. C. & F. M. Phelps
Sep 8, 1872
Jan 1, 1902

John W. Tilford
Sep 8, 1829
Jul 14, 1917
& wife:
Eliza Maupin Tilford
Mar 12, 1846
Jun 23, 1934

William H. Tilford
Nov 6, 1853
May 22, 1895
&
Mary R. Tilford
Nov 25, 1859
Sep 15, 1896

Isham Morrow
1874-1923
&
Tina E. Morrow
1880-1970

Lawrence D. Daniel
1889-1950
&
Flaudie M. Daniel
1889-19

Lawson Baucom
1882-1955
&
Leland Baucom
1887-1933

Tildia Richardson Baucom
Jul 29, 1894
Aug 6, 1963

William B. Holt
Aug 9, 1872
Jan 9, 1936
&
Lula B. Holt
Apr 4, 1872
Oct 8, 1958

Joseph Newton Holt
Dec 21, 1857
Sep 3, 1942

Horatio S. Stokes
Tennessee
Pfc 17 Co 157 Depot Brig
W. W. I
Dec 13, 1892
Nov 15, 1959

Ann S. Barbee
1893-1972
(Howell)

Marshall Stokes
1908-1924

John J. Stokes
1865-1946

Frances B. Stokes
1870-1953

Mary A. Kinnard
Jan 24, 1859
Dec 3, 1902

Albert S. Justice
1866-1952

Mary Justice
1875-1971

Myrtle Grubbs McGee
1888-1915

J. T. Grubbs
1849-1921

Jane Grubbs
1845-1926

Everett L. Grubbs
1870-1956
&
Rebecca S. Grubbs
1868-1937

J. P. West
1864-1950
&
Jane West
1875-1924

James W. West
1887-1949

James Phillips West
1914-1929

Lettadene West
May 19, 1919
Nov 23, 1955

Robert Nealy Uselton
1881-1962
&
Mary Ethel Uselton
1883-

Erma Uselton
1909-1938

James L. Sutton
1865-1954
&
Etta W. Sutton
1873-1960

Miss Jayne Ruth Sutton
Died May 10, 1975
age: 60 yrs.
(Memphis FH)

Andrew E. Mullins
Sep 25, 1875
Mar 16, 1941
& wife:
Jennie Kinnard Mullins
Feb 2, 1880
Mar 18, 1918

James Mullins
Feb 7, 1841
Oct 3, 1915

Tom Mullins
1885-1947

James Mullins
Jan 6, 1872
Dec 22, 1945

Nannie May Isom
May 26, 1877
Feb 7, 1956

John Rufus Farrar
1861-1946
&
Louella Yell Farrar
1874-1959

Emery "Sunshine", son of
J. R. & Ella Farrar
Aug 14, 1903
Oct 26, 1920

Everett A. Farrar
Tennessee
Pvt U.S.Army   W.W.I
Jan 28, 1895
Sep 2, 1968

Jackie, son of
Mr & Mrs I. M. Farrar
Sep 26, 1929
Feb 5, 1930

Annie L. West
1907-
&
Arch H. West
1896-19
&
Emma S. West
1894-1967

Murray Gilbert
1935-1935

John Edward Green
Feb 2, 1881
May 13, 1964

"Sister"
Alice H. Green
Dec 27, 1889
Nov 1, 1931

John T. Bomar, Sr.
1860-1935

Kate T. Bomar
1856-1927

Ernest E. Winigar
Sep 13, 1883
Feb 13, 1956
&
Carrie F. Winigar
Nov 9, 1888
Jan 24, 1961

Porter Winigar, Jr.
Sep 30, 1919
Dec 4, 1920

John L. Winigar
Sep 30, 1858
Jun 30, 1929
&
Rachel E. Winigar
Jun 13, 1859
May 12, 1927

H. C. Kinnard
Apr 25, 1824
Aug 15, 1887

Mary F. Kinnard
Jan 14, 1828
Apr 11, 1894

Francis Y. Phillips
1871-1875

E. B. Phillips
Jul 26, 1829
Jul 19, 1896

E. M., wife of
E. B. Phillips
Dec 16, 1841
Jan 11, 1875

Lettitia, wife of
E. B. Phillips
Aug 25, 1843
May 2, 1913

"Brother"
L. D. Campbell
1869-1964
&
"Sister"
Annie Campbell
1872-1961

Lucy O. Campbell
Oct 19, 1866
May 1, 1891

William A. Campbell
Sep 19, 1857
Jul 1, 1930

Elvira M. Campbell
Sep 18, 1833
Mar 10, 1910

Andrew E. Myers
Mar 15, 1841
May 22, 1923

Cora C. Butner
1888-1974
(Howell)

Walter B. Butner
1885-1968
(Howell)

Rego L. A. Butner
1888-1953
(Gowen)

John H. Haggard
Mar 28, 1875
May 2, 1942
&
Fannie Mai Haggard
Jun 23, 1882
Jan 27, 1948

Nannie P. Sain
1878-1961

Larry L. Thrower
1942-1942

Loddia, son of
John D. & S. A. Culley
Born & Died
Jul 11, 1892

Little Willie F., son of
J. D. & S. A. Culley
Born & Died
Mar 1, 1875

Embree C. Arnold
Jul 1, 1890
Dec 21, 1973

Jamie Arnold
Nov 19, 1892

Bettie D. Arnold
1887-1965

Clarence Hall
Apr 14, 1889
Feb 28, 1958

Lillian Houston Hall
Jan 25, 1899
Oct 19, 1973

Dr. R. E. Davidson
Aug 3, 1836
Apr 22, 1911

Susan D. Davidson
May 30, 1845
Apr 1, 1893

Albert A., son of
William M. & Martha M.
Davidson
Aug 14, 1867
May 8, 1893

Charles B. Edmondson
Oct 12, 1922
Mar 4, 1969
Tennessee
Sgt 2140 Base Unit AAF W.W.II

W. A. Butner
Mar 2, 1861
Oct 1, 1926

Jewel Umberger
Dec 23, 1902
Feb 16, 1936

Nellie H. Snooks
1893-1955

John E. Williams
1916-1929

H. Alton Uselton
Sep 4, 1893
Sep 23, 1967
&
Mattie H. Uselton
Jan 16, 1884
Dec 29, 1972

Elizabeth   & Edna J. Arnold
Died 1920   Died 1932

Joseph Medley
1852-1925
&
Nannie Medley
1858-1933

Joseph O. Arnold
Nov 31, 1848
May 11, 1939

Bettie Davidson, wife of
J. O. Arnold
Sep 13, 1851
Jun 25, 1917

Alberta A. Hooser
Jul 20, 1880
Jan 11, 1948

B. I. Hall
Feb 5, 1848
Jun 12, 1934

Alice V. Hall
Apr 22, 1859
Aug 6, 1932

Ben I. Hall, Jr.
Jan 10, 1895
Feb 26, 1944

Harry P. Hall
May 9, 1882
Jun 10, 1957

Ralph H., son of
B. I. & Alice V. Hall
1885-1888

Anderson Parks Gammill
Nov 11, 1899
Dec 30, 1974
&
Gertrude Grubbs Gammill
Jun 7, 1899

Garland M. Rutledge
Mar 21, 1874
May 20, 1956
&
Martha S. Rutledge
Nov 28, 1877
Jun 4, 1959

Cornelius Rutledge
1905-1926

G. Cleve Jernigan
Dec 1, 1888
Apr 20, 1956
& wife:
Edna P. Jernigan
1894-1955

Manie Jernigan
1885-1927

James W. Bess
Jan 17, 1913
Nov 7, 1972
&
Emma Lou Bess
Nov 10, 1908

Thos. E. Moore
Aug 2, 1871
Mar 16, 1891
age: 19 yrs.

A. T. Moore
1875-1895

Mrs. T. E. Moore
1848-1915

H. T. Moore
1851-1925

Joseph H. Walker, Sr.
Jul 9, 1874
Feb 23, 1959

Nora A. Walker
Jul 8, 1883
Oct 2, 1954

Elizabeth Josephine, dau of
John L. & Leola A. Walker
Feb 26, 1901
Oct 27, 1901

Ethel Grubbs Arnold
Apr 25, 1897
Feb 21, 1919

Vincie Searcy Arnold
May 27, 1909
Oct 1, 1935

Glen Philip Arnold
1915-1968

Richard E. Edmondson
1870-1948
&
Lizzie G. Edmondson
1873-1922

James Coleman
Dec 8, 1855
Feb 22, 1931

Betty Coleman
Dec 19, 1975
Nov 28, 1925

James E. Coleman
Jul 4, 1892
Jul 22, 1932

Henry J. Miller
Jul 1, 1850
Jul 20, 1930
&
Fannie B. Miller
Oct 21, 1863
Oct 16, 1936

Joe B. Miller
Jan 16, 1892
Mar 7, 1974
&
Frances Elizabeth "Lizzie"
Miller
Apr 20, 1892

Ida Bell Johnson
Apr 26, 1873-Jan 2, 1944

Henry C. Arnold
Aug 8, 1897

&
Nona M. Arnold
Jun 7, 1902

John H. Flippo
May 3, 1866
May 12, 1942
&
Laura M. Flippo
Nov 11, 1875
Mar 15, 1968

Paul Gore
Tennessee
Cpl Co F 113 Engineers
W. W. I
Jul 29, 1894
Nov 20, 1961

James E. Grubbs
May 14, 1866
Jun 23, 1945

Mary Alice Dye Grubbs
1884-1938

Elen J., wife of
J. E. Grubbs
Dec 14, 1865
Nov 24, 1906

Abram Myers
1856-1935

J. D. Myers
1862-1919

Samuel Myers
1876-1938

H. A. Myers
1871-1910

William T. Myers
Jul 5, 1828
Jun 1, 1893

Mary J. Myers
1834-1920

Elizabeth Myers
1859-1940

J. F. Briggs
Jan 9, 1843
Aug 17, 1893
age: 50y, 7m, 8d.

Theodosia Coffy Halliburton
1858-1941

John Stevenson
1877-1944
&
Kittie Stevenson
1882-1949

Etheridge H. Still
1888-1971
&
Annie P. Still
1890-1970

Jane Still
1861-1948

William J. Still
1862-1912

James P. Taylor
1868-1931
"Doctor"

Edith S. Taylor
1870-1937

Charles Coble
1880-1951
&
Neely Coble
1872-1960

Maggie Coble
1870-1933

Lettie Mae Eason
1880-1923

Lewis C. Eason
1852-1922
& wife:
Mary Ann Allen Eason
1855-1925

Anthony Edward Eason
1875-1941

Ella M., dau of
James & Lizzie Scruggs
Jan 25, 1889
Aug 19, 1891

Orman H. Gilmore
Tennessee
Pfc Co D 11 Inftry 5 Div
W. W. I
Jul 18, 1895
Oct 18, 1958
&
Lillian Lee Gilmore
1895-1954

W. M. Halliburton
Dec 17, 1850
Jul 2, 1911

Sud C. Stokes
1850-1938

W. Mumford Stokes
Aug 30, 1875
May 14, 1926

Izzie A. Stokes
Jul 16, 1884
Nov 16, 1958

William Harry Jarman
Nov 14, 1861
Nov 6, 1911

Malona Teems
1834-1918

Roy Jarman
1894-1916

Nannie Jarman
1871-1910

J. M. Jarman
1871-1944

John E. Medley
1900-1935

Rosa Mae Medley
1903-1964

William Morton Griffith
Jul 8, 1882
Mar 4, 1954

Mary Moore Fields Griffith
Jul 25, 1886
Aug 4, 1971

Ella M. Fields
Sep 24, 1852
Aug 25, 1932

Ernest Gould Roberts
Feb 22, 1882
May 9, 1964
&
Emma Virginia Roberts
Nov 27, 1882
Jan 14, 1963

J. Cleveland Sims
1885-19
&
Myrtle G. Sims
1890-1969

W. Frank, son of
W. M. & Dosia Halliburton
Jan 14, 1889
Dec 26, 1889

Mrs. Hattie Jordan
1880-1951
(Thompson)

H. L. Dye
1861-1928

Mrs. Jane Dye
1870-1945

Lena Stanfield Ramsey
1867-1933

Stephen Marion Gill
1873-1931

H. Jasper Allen
1850-1915

Harriet E. Allen
1854-1919

Jessie E. Allen
1891-1926

Janie Allen
Apr 13, 1887
Sep 14, 1907

Martha C. Cassidy
1889-1975
(Howell)

William Penn Hart
1887-1918

B. F. Moore
May 18, 1824
Jan 23, 1895

Mary J. Moore
Dec 10, 1825
Mar 8, 1913

Robert G. Moore
Jul 9, 1855
Aug 22, 1908

Charlie M. Moore
Apr 17, 1861
Apr 22, 1893

Robert O. Jordan
Oct 25, 1873
Dec 26, 1898
& wife:
Mattie Jordan
May 26, 1876
Dec 31, 1899

South-east Section of Hollywood Cemetery:

Florence L. Brantley
Mar 6, 1878
Oct 5, 1914

Walter S. Alley
Died 1882 age: 23 days

Ruth Couch Brantley
May 28, 1855
Jan 25, 1906

Orlando R. Alley
1886-1887

Joseph P. Brantley
Jan 12, 1849
Jul 9, 1915

Albert S. Alley
1890-1891

J. Thurman Brantley
Jul 6, 1884
Sep 6, 1905

Alice G. Brantley
Sep 29, 1880-May 13, 1885

Mrs. Ida Elam
(no dates)

Orlando C. Alley
1850-1918

Selena R. Alley
1848-1920

Dr. John R. Fletcher
1832-1890
&
Alice L. Fletcher
1843-1908

Mary Olivia Fletcher
Aug 1, 1874
Oct 4, 1875

In Memorium
Dr. James S. Sandidce
(no dates)

"Mother"
Frenchie A. West
1892-1947

W. H. Puryear
1877-1937

Thos. Edd Bomar
1873-1939
&
Addie R. Bomar
1874-1967

Ethel Espy Holden
and
Infant Daughter
Sep 11, 1884
Apr 22, 1964

Susan A., wife of
E. R. Carroll
Jun 26, 1857
Aug 11, 1897

William W. Cawthron
Nov 7, 1849
May 13, 1932
& wife:
Maria Cawthron
Apr 5, 1855
Mar 14, 1908

Jennie Cawthron, wife of
W. W. Cawthron
1864-1941

Annie F., dau of
W. W. & Fannie P. Cawthron
Oct 23, 1873
Aug 10, 1897

Joshua W. Smith
Aug 12, 1846
Apr 6, 1912

Lawrence, son of J. R. &
A. J. Smith
Jun 15, 1887
Jul 17, 1887

John R. Couch, son of
Dr. R. W. & L. W. Couch
Feb 27, 1864
Sep 13, 1885

Kittie, wife of
J. A. Pearson
Feb 28, 1866
Dec 2, 1894

Sammie Lee, dau of
H. K., Jr. & A. L. Stokes
Died Sep 17, 1897
age: 3y, 7m, 24d.

Mrs. E. J. Zellner, mother
of Mrs. J. W. Templeton
Nov 10, 1817
Oct 30, 1901

Audry S. Walker
Mar 26, 1902
Sep 16, 1972
&
Elizabeth C. Walker
Jun 23, 1903
----
married Dec 9, 1922

Walter D. Newman
1876-1947
&
Abbye M. Newman
1882-1966

Arch H. Carothers
1861-1949

Rachel V., wife of
A. H. Carothers
Jun 16, 1867
Jul 18, 1922

John W. Caruthers
Jun 5, 1895
Jan 31, 1922
&
Lennie Mai Caruthers
May 25, 1895
Feb 18, 1959

Rachel Virginia, dau of
J. W. & Lennie Mai Caruthers
Born & Died
Aug 10, 1922

Brantley Stephens
1883-1937
&
Lena C. Stephens
1889-1932

George Gore
May 2, 1899
Jun 6, 1929

Mary E., wife of
R. W. McClure
Jul 26, 1823
Sep 13, 1887
age: 64y, 1m, 17d.

Dr. Robert W. Couch
Mar 13, 1834
Jul 7, 1899
&
Lucy W. Couch
Oct 8, 1837
Nov 16, 1905

Robert Lewis Couch
Mar 1862
Nov 1927

Ella L. Couch
1874-1925

William J. Couch
1868-1950

John A. Chilton
1862-1945

Ollie Chilton, wife of
John B. Bramblett
1849-1921

William J. Allen
1868-1961
&
Lillie L. Allen
1871-1935

Darling Edith Allen
1906-1918

Baby French Allen
1897-1899

James W. McQuiddy
1843-1926
& wife:
Nannie G. McQuiddy
1847-1927

H. C. Stokes
1844-1927
&
Fannie Stokes
1852-1932

M. C. Stokes
1848-1928

Sallie Stokes
1857-1935

Martha Smith
1832-1928

Infant Son of
G. R. & Sadie Cortner
Jan 14, 1932

Ernestine Norvell
1921-1923

Charlie W. Smith
Apr 15, 1891
May 7, 1914

Joe B. Smith
Oct 26, 1843
Feb 27, 1894
age: 50 yrs.

"Daddy"
J. E. Russell
1873-1933

"Mother"
Mabel M. Russell
1879-1951

John Russell, Jr.
1904-1961

W. F. Russell
Nov 10, 1834
Jan 21, 1912

"Granny"
Martha J. Russell
1838-1923

Robert Townes, son of
Emmet & Bertha Russell
May 13, 1896
Mar 30, 1899

W. E. Russell
Dec 19, 1862
Aug 19, 1886

Lawrence L. Lee, Sr.
1882-1945
&
Nora Bob Lee
1883-1951

Charles C. Richard
Sep 18, 1886
        1974 (TM)
&
Frances A. McQuiddy Richard
Aug 29, 1890
Nov 18, 1952

H. A. Shepard
Oct 31, 1860
Feb 16, 1930

Lucy Shepard
Apr 11, 1869
Jan 19, 1956

Malinda A. Forman
May 8, 1842
Jun 1, 1907

Forman Norvell
1895-1970
&
Tommie A. Norvell
1907-

Arguyle Reedy Norvell
Feb 20, 1847
Apr 26, 1915

Grover Cleveland Norvell
Jun 8, 1892
Mar 30, 1910

Lucy Norvell Morgan
1899-1944

James Lester Morgan
1900-1975

Robert H. Armstrong
1871-1953
&
Nannie E. Armstrong
1872-1952

Thomas M. Armstrong
Feb 20, 1900
Nov 1, 1970
&
Mildred C. Armstrong
Oct 20, 1904

Samuel G. Blackman
1844-1880
&
Amanda B. Smith Blackman
1849-1936

James M. Blackman
1848-1896

Addie Blackman
1847-1928

Annie Mai Blackman
Dec 29, 1877
Sep 17, 1906

Hugh, Infant Son of
C. Milton & Anna E. Dean
Oct 21, 1901

A. M. McKnight
1861-1945

Grace Blackman McKnight
Sep 19, 1878
Jun 9, 1960

Ernest Lytton Blackman
1876-1934

Welburn W. Wileman
1888-1960
&
Sarah Jessie Wileman
1887-1958

John W. Wileman
1913-1974
(Gilmore)

Oscar N. Ashley
1876-1944
&
Addie S. Ashley
1878-1964

Joe Chadwick Ashley
May 8, 1902
Feb 6, 1972
&
Lucile K. Ashley
Mar 20, 1904
----
married Dec 12, 1923

"Mother"
Malissa Manning
Died Jun 3, 1897
age: 69 yrs.

Elsie French, dau of
T. S. & S. E. Ferrell
Sep 22, 1869

Nannie Hord Bramblett
1856-1937

Arthur M. Dye
Tennessee
Pvt U.S.Army   W.W.I
Sep 17, 1895
Apr 21, 1974

Dr. Philip H. Manier
Jan 18, 1822
May 20, 1886

William Thomas Cunningham
1879-1952

Josephine Justice Cunningham
1888-1959

James Arnold Cunningham
1843-1929

Margaret McKeand Cunningham
1856-1929

Casper Milton Dean
Nov 1, 1862
Sep 10, 1940

Anna Blackman Dean
Jul 30, 1868
Aug 10, 1951

William Gallagher
Oct 12, 1871
Apr 29, 1930

Annie W. Gallagher
Jun 29, 1836
Aug 29, 1912

James T. Stephenson, Sr.
1877-1947
&
James T. Stephenson, Jr.
1919-1943
Lt. U.S.Navy
"Lost at Sea"
&
Vanderlyn P. Stephenson
1892-19

Albert Thomas Brimm
Dec 8, 1874
(no date)
&
Willie Lillian Brimm
Apr 18, 1871
Mar 15, 1928

Fannie B. Barker
1846-1890

William David Nichols
1880-1925
&
Cora Elizabeth Nichols
1877-1938

F. W. Cunningham
1850-1917

Della Cunningham
1867-1945

W. H. Cunningham
1888-1913

C. E. Cunningham
1890-1924

O. P. Cunningham
May 5, 1845
Nov 18, 1882

Lucinda W. Cunningham
Jul 9, 1820
Mar 29, 1902

Belle, wife of
N. J. Roberts
Oct 9, 1867
May 29, 1897

William A. Arnold
1853-1919

Iva Roberts Arnold
1863-1937

Charles T. Hulan
1885-(on footstone,Sep 27,1961)
&
Iva E. Christian Hulan
1885-1946

Oscar F. Winigar
Nov 7, 1881
Oct 1, 1960
&
Sallie W. Winigar
Feb 27, 1873
Jan 1, 1954

Thomas W. Harmon
Jan 5, 1877
Sep 12, 1959
&
Elizabeth D. Harmon
Jul 9, 1882
Oct 8, 1965

Thomas W. Harmon, Jr.
Nov 28, 1922
Jul 7, 1923

J. N. Bramblett
Oct 2, 1861
married Nov 28, 1885
Died Jul 2, 1898

Little Beulahland Bramblett
Jul 12, 1897
Sep 16, 1898

Jonnie A. Bramblett
Mar 18, 1889
Jan 24, 1892

Thomas Barnes
Sep 22, 1842
Nov 13, 1887

William Henry Crowell
Mar 1, 1874
Feb 12, 1961

Infant of
A. D. & S. M. Brown
Died Nov 13, 1888

Charlie Brown
May 26, 1890
May 3, 1964

Walter D. Brown
Jan 22, 1894
Jan 23, 1921

Sarah M. Brown
Jul 28, 1854
Aug 13, 1919

Douglas Brown
Aug 3, 1860
May 5, 1935

William Allen Christian
Died Feb 6, 1873
age: 20y, 6m, 5d.

J. A. Christian
1848-1928
& wife:
Fanny Christian
1854-1922

Barney V. Christian
1875-1937
&
Sibbie M. Christian
1875-1950

Thomas Lee Isom
Tennessee
AE1 U.S.Navy
Aug 21, 1936
Jan 24, 1964

Catherine M. Chitwood
1918-1950

Marshall O. Lawrence
1868-1946

E. Clifton Throneberry
Feb 20, 1908
Aug 13, 1970
&
Ollie M. Throneberry
Mar 2, 1914
----
married Apr 8, 1935

Joe L. Taylor
1860-1947
&
Sarah L. Taylor
1869-1945

Lilly Helan Ashworth
1865-1898

W. A. Hardy
Mar 18, 1854
Jul 3, 1933

"Wife"
Kate Healan Hardy
Died Jul 16, 1887
age: 26 yrs.
& Daughter:
Kate Healan, dau of
W. A. & Kate Hardy
Died Sep 23, 1887
age: 8 months

"Brother"
Ralph H. Healan
Mar 16, 1867
Dec 22, 1911

Sarah Jennings Healan Leet
Oct 27, 1833
Dec 20, 1909

Maj. A. S. Healan
May 14, 1818
Apr 19, 1876

Clarence H. Gallagher
Mar 11, 1903

&
Mary Horace Gallagher
Oct 12, 1917
Apr 3, 1973
married Sep 7, 1940

Herbert A. Gallagher
1906-1925

John M. Gallagher, Sr.
1866-1941

Mammie D. Gallagher
1872-1911

William R. Erwin
Sep 6, 1892
Apr 5, 1914

Robert L. Justice
1862-1932

Jasper N. Smith
Nov 8, 1828
Feb 12, 1912
&
Sarah E. Smith
Dce 2, 1836
Jul 8, 1888

A. S. Brown
1861-1943
&
Augusta Brown
1862-1934

Helen K., wife of
T. H. Harris
Jun 3, 1859
Feb 22, 1893

John E. King
Aug 7, 1842
Oct 27, 1906
"A Rebel Soldier"
&
Sarah Jane King
Oct 2, 1851
Sep 8, 1938

Walter Wood, son of
W. H. & Jennie C. Jarman
Aug 20, 1878
Oct 15, 1896

Alfred Ogle
Nov 13, 1832
Oct 28, 1891

Mary V., wife of
Albert Ogle
Nov 20, 1838
Dec 22, 1918

Coleman Warner
1912-1913

Culley C. Warner
1912-1912

"Papa"
Porter C. Warner
1873-1944

"Mama"
Jennie Culley Warner
Sep 8, 1857
Jan 31, 1938

Jennie C. Warner
1893-1920

Elbert B. Lovell
Tennessee
Pfc 10 Chemical Service Co
W. W. II
Jan 30, 1917
Aug 17, 1945

Mandie J. Lovell
1886-1970

Henry Frizzell
Jun 6, 1905

&
Anna Mae Frizzell
May 1, 1909
Jun 3, 1967

J. J. Mallard
Oct 6, 1868
(no date)
&
Lula Mallard
Dec 24, 1871
Jun 28, 1922

Robert J. Searcy
1886-1912

Daniel C. Searcy
1882-1909

Emmett F. Searcy
1889-1921

Dan C. Searcy
Died Jun 23, 1891
age: 36y, 1m, 29d.

Thomas A. Gattis
Jul 9, 1825
Jan 25, 1898
& wife:
Julia B. Gattis
Aug 12, 1827
Jul 5, 1910
&
Ormie Cecil McCullough
Jul 31, 1883
Jan 22, 1906

Olive D. Hazelton
Aug 19, 1906
Sep 4, 1906

John Y. Blacknall
May 26, 1831
Mar 2, 1880

Thomas J., son of
J. Y. & C. E. Blacknall
Oct 7, 1861
Oct 25, 1888
age: 27y & 18d.

Louannie Mallard
1875-1944

Ethel, dau of
J. J. & Lula Mallard
Jan 31, 1899-Sep 7, 1899

32 HENRY-JARMAN CEMETERY   Map # 8
Located about 1½ miles North of Wartrace, on Railroad.

[Once the old Moseby Harris place] Hiram Henry
(no dates)

Harriett Jarman
Sep 22, 1814
Oct 10, 1877
"Member of Primitive
Baptist Church."

Copied by John Anderson
Joyce.

33 ARNOLD CEMETERY   Map # 8
Located about 1½ miles South of Bell Buckle, Tenn.

Jas. Arnold
Mar 10, 1783
Oct 9, 1841
age: 58y, 6m, 30d.

M. M. Arnold
Nov 19, 1794
Aug 28, 1855

L. M. Arnold
Dec 14, 1824
Aug 30, 1855

Jas. F., son of
O. P. & Rachel T. Arnold
Apr 4, 1855
Nov 3, 1858

34 CHAMBERS CEMETERY   Map # 8
Located about 1½ miles Northwest of Wartrace, Tenn.

Robert Chambers
Nov 25, 1781
Died (no date)
(after 1850 census)

Judeth, wife of
Robert Chambers
Born Apr 19, 1788
Died (no date)(after 1850)
"A Wife & Mother"

Robert G. Chambers
Apr 25, 1816
Mar 9, 1889
age: 73 yrs.

P. F. Chambers
Mar 16, 1829-Jul 19, 1892

H. C. Chambers
Nov 23, 1831-Apr 17, 1896

35 PRUITT CEMETERY   Map # 8
Located about 2 miles Northwest of Wartrace, Tenn.

J. A. Pruitt
1860-1945

Nannie, wife of
J. A. Pruitt
Mar 13, 1857
Apr 7, 1897

Forrest Pruitt, Sr.
Feb 8, 1888
Dec 12, 1959

Lizzie M. Pruitt
Born & Died
Aug 10, 1927

A. Pruit
Sep 2, 1819
Dec 3, 1893
&
Elizabeth Pruit
Oct 28, 1820
(no date)

Haskel Pruitt
Jan 1, 1925
May 20, 1931

Mitchell Pruitt
Mar 22, 1926
Aug 4, 1926

36 WALLIS CEMETERY   Map # 8
Located about 1 mile Southwest of Bell Buckle, Tenn.

Rev. Allen Wallis
Jan 14, 1792
Sep 1, 1868

Sarah Wallis, Consort of
Rev. Allen Wallis
Apr 16, 1797
Jan 27, 1879
"She was a Member of the
Church Militant, 61 yrs."

Miria Thompson, Consort of
J. P. Thompson & dau of
Allen & Sarah Wallis
Born Apr 2, 1817
Died Sep 14, 1850
age: 33y, 5m, 12d.

5 graves with fieldstones,
no inscriptions.

37 HOLT CEMETERY   Map # 8
Located about 1 mile Northwest of Wartrace, Tenn.

Mary M., wife of
Henry Kubley
1808-1893

Berry Douglas Holt
Mar 4, 1824
Aug 25, 1912

Mary, wife of
Berry D. Holt
1841-1919

Charles B. Holt
Feb 2, 1848
Nov 18, 1876

James Berry Holt
Jul 13, 1861
Jan 1, 1914

T. T. Moore
May 20, 1827
Sep 30, 1883

Mrs. T. T. Moore
1833-1915

T. W. Tarpley
Feb 16, 1836
Mar 26, 1885

W. C. Holt
Apr 1, 1820
Jun 20, 1891
&
Elizabeth Holt
Feb 14, 1824
Nov 23, 1894

C. C. Holt
Jul 29, 1846
Jan 18, 1884

Elizabeth Holt
Jul 22, 1803
Jun 15, 1887
age: 83y, 10m, 13d.

Henry Holt
Died Mar 1, 1864
age: 72y, 1m, 19d.

Eliza Ann Holt
Nov 18, 1825
Aug 10, 1841
age: 15y, 8m, 22d.

Henry W. Holt
Died Aug 19, 1842
age: 2 weeks

Eliza Ann Holt
Died Mar 17, 1857
age: 4y & 11m.

John Thomas Holt
Died Sep 28, 1856
age: 8y & 6m.

Lillian A., dau of
T. A. & Elizabeth Shriver
Mar 20, 1873
Oct 2, 1893

James H. W. Holt
Died Mar 29, 1857
age: 7 months.

[John & Frances Holt, parents of
Henry Holt. John died 1823]

38 COFFEE CEMETERY   Map # 8
Located near Wartrace, Tennessee

Barthena, wife of
W. P. Raney
Oct 13, 1827
Jun 11, 1888

Nannie, dau of
W. P. & Barthena Raney
Jan 14, 1862
Aug 10, 1882

P. C. Coffee
1885-1962
(Howell-Thompson)

Rice Coffee
Born April 1766 in
Amherst Co., Va.
Died Jul 29, 1853

G. R. Coffee
Age: 69 yrs.
Died Feb 10, 1916

R. E. Coffee
Jun 15, 1833
Sep 10, 1910

Miss Sallie B. Coffee
1882-1972
(Howell)

Sallie R. Coffee
Apr 3, 1807
Mar 31, 1892

Several unmarked graves.

William E. Coffee
Feb 26, 1838
Mar 25, 1887

Mary A. Coffee
Nov 11, 1840
Mar 1, 1901

Andrew J. Grider
Co I
17 Tenn Inf
C.S.A.

Mary C. Kendall, dau of
R. & S. Coffee
Oct 12, 1797
Oct 22, 1878

Martha D. Coffee
May 18, 1845
Oct 16, 1891

Jane P., wife of
John W. Tilford
Apr 20, 1835
Aug 26, 1872

Robert W., son of
William & M. Tinsley
died Apr 10, 1865
age: 9y, 6m, 5d.

1 large marker, face down,
couldn't be moved.

39 LEE-STOKES CEMETERY   Map # 8
Located about ½ mile South of Wartrace, Tenn.

N. S. Lee
Aug 20, 1848
Nov 15, 1907

Martha C. Lee
Oct 18, 1846
Feb 8, 1921

Roy K. Stokes
May 2, 1891
Oct 12, 1913

L. Mollie Stokes
Jul 31, 1884
May 14, 1911

Kitchen Stokes
Died Oct 3, 1863
(no age given)
(70 yrs in 1850, born in
Va.)

Sara F. Stokes
Mar 24, 1860
Dec 5, 1862
age: 2y, 8m, 12d.

R. P. Lee
Mar 10, 1828
Jun 22, 1907

Louisa J. Lee
Oct 9, 1827
Nov 26, 1895

Terry L. Stokes
Jun 18, 1880
Dec 27, 1912

Nannie C. Stokes
Mar 11, 1889
Mar 6, 1912

Nancy Stokes
Died Jul 4, 1868
(no age given)
(68 yrs in 1850, born in
N. C.0

Sallie Stokes Lee
Jun 12, 1877
Jul 12, 1964

Several unmarked graves.

T. M. C. Lee
Jul 16, 1851
Feb 2, 1899

William B. Lee
Nov 2, 1855
Feb 22, 1926

Mary Susan Stokes
Jan 2, 1857
Feb 5, 1912

Roy P. King
May 18, 1855
Nov 1, 1887

Mary A. King
Mar 29, 1829
Dec 8, 1907

Jane Young, wife of
Rev. Acton Young
Jul 19, 1809
Mar 28, 1841
age: 32y, & 10d.

John M.(Munford) Stokes
Sep 15, 1814
Aug 5, 1878

Rebecca G.(Gant), wife of
J. M. Stokes
Feb 3, 1812
Aug 21, 1875

Mrs. Nannie Stokes
Aug 10, 1848
Jun 25, 1910

Thomas K. Stokes
Jun 25, 1864
Aug 11, 1868
age: 4y, 1m, 17d.

Lucy, wife of
W. T. Brawley
Sep 20, 1877
Jan 10, 1909

Lou Alice Stokes
Jul 31, 1884
May 14, 1911

40 ARNOLD-KING CEMETERY   Map # 8
Located about 2 miles South of Wartrace, Tennessee
near Mt. Olivet Church.

Laura Belle Searcy
1858-1924

No Marker:*
Robert Searcy
Died Feb 1890
* Newspaper

Robert Eugene Thompson
1877-1940

Ada Reba Thompson
1885-1969

P. A. Snelling
Tennessee
Pvt Co H 5 Tenn Regt Cav
   Civil War
1831-1909

Polly Tuck Snelling, wife
of P. A. Snelling
1849-1915

P. A. Dean
1840-1913

Nannie Dean
1865-1925

W. B. Dean
Sep 26, 1891
Aug 20, 1918

James K. Snelling
Tennessee
Pvt Co F 5 Regt Tenn Cav
   Civil War
1839-1862

Rev. D. P. Searcy
May 7, 1828
Oct 9, 1883

Mary L. Robinson, wife of
Rev. D. P. Searcy
May 2, 1832
May 9, 1899

R. J. Milloway
Feb 27, 1853
Jul 19, 1907

W. W. Grissom
Sep 12, 1828
Jan 5, 1901

John W. Milloway
1859-1930

James A. Milloway
1865-1927

A.(Adaline) E. Snelling,
wife of J. H. Milloway
Born --- --, 1829
Died Oct 25, ----
(21 yrs in 1850 census)

Mary Dean
1901-1901

Lottie Roach
1896-1919

Mrs. Jane Mullins, Consort
of Matthew Mullins
Born Nov 2, ____(1784)
Died _____

Vinson E. Searcy
Oct 18, 1861
May 19, 1863

Alice E. Searcy
Nov 3, 1859
Jul 1, 1860

James C. Searcy
Apr 3, 1826
Jan 26, 1888

Mary A. Searcy
Mar 4, 1828
Oct 6, 1901

Katie May Searcy
Feb 7, 1885
Jul 10, 1885

Lawrence Snelling
1925-1930

Sammie J. Snelling
Aug 30, 1920
Dec 22, 1921

Col. James Mullins
3rd Son of Mathew &
Comfort Mullins
Born in Bedford County, Tenn.
Aug 3, 1807
Died Jun 26, 1873

John King
Born Feb 11, 1770
Died Aug 18, 1811
age: 41y, 6m, 7d.
"Member of Baptist Church"

Hattie E. Slater
1864-1955

J. S. Conwell
Mar 1, 1854
May 2, 1930

Roxie Searcy, wife of
J. S. Conwell
Mar 7, 1863
Mar 10, 1910

Sarrah Ada McBee, dau of
Rob & Lula McBee
May 13, 1915
Jul 8, 1922

Zelmer Jones Snelling,
2nd wife of Will B. Snelling
1873-1909

James T. Snelling
1888-1958
(McFarlin-Thompson)

Mary N. Snelling
1890-1931
(McFarlin-Thompson)

Matthew Mullins
Born in Albermarle Co.,Va.
Dec 26, 1779, Died
Jun 23, 1853
age: 74y, 5m, 27d.
"Embraced Religion, Mt.
Reserve Camp Ground in 1817,
joined the Methodist E.
Church."

Lemuel Snelling
Tennessee
Drummer 1 Regt West
Tenn. Militia
War of 1812
1786-1860

Sallie King Snelling,
wife of Lemuel Snelling
1801-1874

J. T. Snelling
Nov 8, 1854
May 1, 1908

R. J. Snelling
Aug 1, 1826
Jun 28, 1908
&
Ellen L. Snelling
Mar 18, 1826
Jun 29, 1904

Adilade Searcy
Feb 10, 1825
married to Vinson Searcy
Feb 10, 1843
professed Religion 1845
joined the C.P.Church,
Died May 5, 1885
(Next to Vinson Searcy)

Eldridge Lee Morton
Tennessee
SEA U.S.Navy   W.W.I
Feb 9, 1894
Feb 25, 1963

A. L. Grubbs, son of
J. T. & M. J. Grubbs
Jul 16, 1872
Jan 5, 1895

Luisa H. wife of
P. A. Dean
Dec 15, 1816
Apr 5, 1890

Wife of
James H. Arnold
1806-1873

John M. Arnold
Tennessee
MM2 U.S.Navy   W.W.I
Aug 10, 1892
Feb 13, 1919

Luther Gregory
Aug 25, 1890

&
Lula Mai Gregory
Dec 29, 1887
(no date)

Doris Ray Gregory
Jul 23, 1940
Oct 21, 1940

Clarence M. Gregory
Feb 28, 1921
Oct 14, 1923

"Snelling"
1755-1841
Hugh Snelling came to Bedford
County, Tenn, in 1820 from
Granville Co., N. C., Lemuel,
his son, left N.C. on horse-
back with 5 slaves in 1811.
Hugh was wealthy & was the
owner of over a thousand acres
in this Vacinity when he died.
His heirs were: Lemuel, John,
Susanna Searcy, Frances
McConnell, Louisa Harriet
Arnold, & Elizabeth Snelling."

J. A. Tuck
Co F
5th Tenn Cav

John Dean
Tennessee
Pvt 29 U.S.Vol. Inf
Jul 9, 1939

Louisa J. Reed
Jul 19, 1819
Jun 15, 1896

James Robert Morton
Jun 24, 1864
Dec 27, 1959
&
Belle Koonce Morton
Oct 14, 1869
Apr 23, 1952

W. H. Morton
Nov 14, 1839
Jul 17, 1902
joined M.E. Church in 1867
& wife:
L. H. Arnold Morton
Apr 1, 1843
Jan 28, 1899
joined M.E. Church 1858

G. M., son of
W. H. & L. H. Morton
Aug 25, 1865
Dec 20, 1866

Hayden P. Arnold
1838-1910

Mary A. Snelling Arnold
1st wife of Hayden Arnold
1833-1880

James May
Jul 25, 1942

&
Bertie Marie May
Sep 14, 1945
Mar 5, 1971

R. S. McConnell
Jul 21, 1817
Dec 11, 1891
"Joined M.E. Church, South."

John W. Norvill
Born Oct 8, 1829
Died Sep 12, 1840
age: 10y, 11m, 3d.

David C. Norvill, son of
John W. & America Norvill
Apr 21, 1833
Oct 6, 1840
age: 7y, 5m, 15d.

Alexander B., son of
John W. & America Norvill
Mar 31, 1835
Aug 3, 1847

Frances Swan
Aug 8, 1860
Oct 12, 1934

Thomas Rittenberry
Dec 9, 1884
May 1, 1904

Infant Son of
J. D. & Mary E. Rittenberry
Sep 12, 1901
Sep 24, 1901

James Daniel Rittenberry
1861-1912

Alford Arnold
Jun 6, 1912

&
Annie L. Arnold
Sep 22, 1914
Aug 23, 1973
married Feb 18, 1934

John Holt Morton
Tennessee
Pfc U.S.Army   W.W.I
Mar 14, 1892
Aug 6, 1956

W. W. Koonce
Co F
Tenn Cav

Lilly Mai Cruse
1894-1944

Dorothy May Tenpenny
1949-1949
(Thompson)

H. B., son of
M. & Lula S. Mullins
Jan 4, 1879
Feb 27, 1879
age: 23 days

Molly Tenpenny
1886-1967
(Gowen-Smith)

Ernest R. McConnell
1881-1948

Mrs. Nancy McConnell
1884-1966
(Gowen-Smith)

Nancy King
Born Dec 11, 1772
Died Aug 21, 1841
Died a Regular Member
of the C. P. Church.
age: 69y, 6m, 13d.
(Her grave is beside that
of John King)

William Searcy
1790-1840
&
Susanna Searcy
1790-1865

Vinson Searcy
Born Jan 25, 1824
Professed Religion & joined
the M.E. Church at Bethel
1841, Died Mar 30, 1855
(next to Adilade Searcy)

Anderson D. Bush
May 8, 1885
Jan 15, 1949

Emmet Eustace, son of
Alford & Annie Arnold
1 Day Old
1940

Dennis Lee, son of
Alford & Annie Arnold
1 Day Old
1946

Little Willie, son of
J. R. & L. B. Morton
Apr 29, 1888
Jul 15, 1889

Jack B. Morton
Jul 2, 1925
Nov 5, 1934
"Son of Ralph B. & Hazel
Morton."

Lillie Arnold
1st wife of T. J. Arnold
1865-1901

T. J. Arnold
Sep 16, 1857
Nov 2, 1936

Sallie Eunice Arnold
Apr 10, 1879
Mar 14, 1945

Aderine Lelia Arnold Bush
Mar 14, 1887
Mar 4, 1957

Charlie Arnold
Dec 21, 1890
Apr 2, 1963

Grady L. Arnold
Dec 7, 1898
Aug 27, 1968

Fanny, wife of
R. S. McConnell
Jun 18, 1818
joined M.E. Church, South
in 1835, Died Sep 25, 1888

Hugh L. McConnell
Apr 9, 1839
Jan 12, 1863

John F. Boswell
1892-1959
(Gowen-Smith)

Lillian Mae Boswell
1897-1967
(Gowen-Smith)

James C. McConnell
May 31, 1847
Jun 20, 1868

Walter Woosley
1891-1940

Roxie Arnold Bennett
Aug 26, 1902
Jun 3, 1968

Jimmie Doyle Foster
May 19, 1948

Ruth Daniels
Nov 8, 1913
Jul 30, 1968

Earl B. McConnell
1916-1973
(Gowen-Smith)

Ruben (R.B.) Arnold
Oct 4, 1898
Sep 4, 1938

Rev. Berlin T. Arnold
1898-1922

Nellie Flora Arnold
Sep 8, 1900
Nov 6, 1934

Donald Simpson
May 23, 1942

Houston Foster
Mar 13, 1904
Mar 31, 1931

many unmarked graves.

Robert A. Arnold
1859-1934
&
Nannie C. Arnold
1868-1929

Kathleen Arnold
Jun 20, 1898
Sep 20, 1932

James R. Arnold
Dec 12, 1892
Apr 19, 1968

Mary Foster Simpson
Aug 29, 1903
Jan 8, 1968

41 CANNON CEMETERY   Map # 8
Located on Tilford Farm, on Fay Creek, near Butler Creek.

"Servant"
Sendy Hooser
1814-1910

William Hooser
Born April 30, 1779, pro-
fessed Religion & joined
Methodist Church in 1821 &
departed this life March 10th
1847 A.D.
age: 67y, 10m, 10d.

Rebecca Hooser
Born April 5th 1783
Died Nov 1st 1845
age: 62y, 6m, 26d.

Susan Rebecca Hooser, dau
of C. L. & M. A. Cannon
Born Mar 30, 1844
Died Monday July 12th 1852
at 15 min 4 o'clock A.M.
aged: 8y, 3m, 12d.

Robert T. Cannon
Born Jan 8, 1814
Died Dec 12, 1888

Letitia M., wife of
Robert T. Cannon
May 1, 1827
Aug 6, 1852
"Daughter of William &
Rebecca Hooser, left 3 child-
ren: M. R. Cannon
       L. C. Cannon
       J. M. Cannon"

Charles Lock, son of
C. L. & Mary Cannon
Died Saturday Oct 24th 1857.
aged: 1y, 8m, 17d.

Charlie Bowdon, son of
C. L. & M. A. Cannon
Nov 23, 1864
Jul 13, 1888
aged: 23y, 1m, 20d.

John M. Cannon, son of
Letitia M. & R. S. Cannon
Mar 25, 1852
Jul 21, 1854
age: 2y, 3m, 26d.

Thomas C. Cannon, son of
C. L. & M. A. Cannon
Died Monday July 22nd, 8
o'clock, 50 minutes P.M. 1869
age: 18y, 5m, 5d.

John Henry, son of
C. L. & Mary Cannon
Died Tuesday Oct 11th 1862.
aged: 11y, 8m, 19d.

Charles L. Cannon
Born Feb 14, 1813
Died Aug 24, 1897
(Note: Maria S. Cannon could
be on this marker, it is face
down and buried too deep.)

Juliet, Infant dau of
W. S. & M. L. Ryall
Born & Died
Jan 11, 1877

Maria Laura Ryall, wife of
William S. Ryall
Sep 3, 1843
Jan 13, 1877
age: 34y, 4m, 10d.

Infant Ryall

Mary Scudder, dau of
W. S. & M. L. Ryall
Jan 1, 1870
Jun 30, 1870
age: 6m.

1 grave with fieldstone,
no inscription.

42 WEST CEMETERY   Map # 8
Located about 1 mile West of Wartrace, Tenn.
NO MARKERS IN THIS CEMETERY.

No marker:*
William Cecil West
born 1846
died 1909
age: abt 62 yrs.

No marker:*
Jane Lovell West
(no dates)

*by Mr James Stevenson

No marker:*
Infant Boy, Stephenson
(no dates)

No marker:*
Infant of
John West
(no dates)

43 PHILLIPS CEMETERY   Map # 8
Located about 1½ miles West of Wartrace, Tennessee

Dr. John K. Phillips
Capt. of Co. 2nd Arka. Regt.
         C.S.A.
Born Feb 22, 1831
Killed in the Charge of his
Regt. at the Battle of
Franklin, Tenn.
Nov 30, 1864

"War is honorable in those
who do their native rights
maintain."

This was the only grave.

44 AULT CEMETERY   Map # 8
Located about 1½ miles West of Wartrace, Tennessee

[Old Mt. Hebron Church stood
near this cemetery]

This Cemetery was large.

Here lies the body of
John Ault, who departed the
8th day of August 1829. He
expired in the triumphs of
faith. aged: 42y, 3m, 6d.

Susan E. Ault
Mar 22, 1827
Aug 31, 1848

(Colored)
Viola Rankin
Nov 6, 1893
Sep 6, 1904

1 NOWLIN CEMETERY   Map # 9
Located about ½ mile Southwest of Wheel, Tenn.

Peyton P. Nowlin
Sep 21, 1826
Mar 11, 1848
age: 22y, 5m, 10d.

Jabus Nowlin
Aug 17, 1789
Sep 1, 1848
age: 59y & 13d.

Washington B. Nowlin
Jun 22, 1813
Apr 2, 1816
age: 3y, 9m, 20d.

Lucy L. Nowlin
Apr 12, 1836
Aug 12, 1838
age: 2y & 4m.

Edward B. Nowlin
Dec 7, 1823
Jul 19, 1846
age: 23y, 7m, 10d.

Mary L. Nowlin, wife of
Jabus Nowlin
Aug 16, 1796
Sep 23, 1859
age: 63y, 1m, 7d.

Mattie, dau of
J. S. & M. W. Nowlin
Died May 9, 1874
age: 5 yrs.

Light T. Nowlin
Dec 24, 1832
Oct 7, 1854
age: 22y, 9m, 17d.

Robleyd, son of
B. W. & R. E. Nowlin
Jan 3, 1848
Dec 26, 1848

Mary Jane, dau of
B. W. & R. E. Nowlin
--- 7, 1859 (broken away)
Jan 7, 1860

Edward P., son of
B. W. & R. E. Nowlin
Dec 6, 1845
Dec 18, 1848

Allen L., son of
B. W. & R. E. Nowlin
Oct 28, 1849
Dec 2, 1855

2 WHEEL CEMETERY   Map # 9
Located at Wheel, Tennessee

Clarence Claiborne
Jun 19, 1904
Sep 8, 1960

Sallie A. Darnell
Feb 4, 1855
Dec 8, 1913

Cordelia Pressley
May 1, 1883
Aug 18, 1969

Gertie Mai Claiborne
Nov 19, 1893
May 3, 1914
"Dau of J. W. &
Margrett Claiborne"

Parilee Darnell
Nov 1, 1898
Feb 8, 1918

Clayton James McBride and
"Buck"
Feb 8, 1912
Apr 9, 1971
Tennessee
Pfc U.S.Army   W.W.II

Gladys Mae Herrin McBride
Sep 27, 1923

&
Haskel Lee Herrin
Jun 13, 1921
Apr 21, 1969
Michigan
S1 U.S.Coast Guard Res
W.W.II

J. W. Claiborne
Sep 27, 1837
Oct 22, 1914
&
Margret A. Claiborne
Dec 15, 1860
(no date)

Ollie Lee Darnell
May 2, 1893
Jun 27, 1964
&
Della P. Darnell
Nov 14, 1894
Mar 16, 1970

Riley L. Herrin
Nov 1, 1895
Mar 19, 1963
&
Avo P. Herrin
May 11, 1903
Nov 29, 1967

"Father"
Benton G. Peoples
Feb 18, 1893
May 23, 1963
&
"Mother"
Minnie R. Peoples
Feb 10, 1888
Jan 8, 1973

Mae Pyland Claiborne
Oct 19, 1907
Feb 14, 1927

Norman Pugh
1923-1949
(picture)

James L. Glasscock
1868-1919
&
Mary Lou Glasscock
1867-1950

Claud H. Claiborne
Aug 4, 1907
Jul 15, 1939

Frank Thomas Cook
Jan 23, 1948

"Brother"
L. D. Peoples
Feb 10, 1921
Oct 17, 1963
&

Joel Stallings
Nov 26, 1817
Apr 26, 1886

S. B. Word
1853-1924
&
Annie Word
1861-1934

John C. Anderson
1867-1956
&
Viola W. Anderson
1880-1964

"Sister"
Faynell Peoples
Dec 12, 1922
Sep 18, 1973

W. J. Stallings
Jan 21, 1854
May 30, 1911

Allie May, dau of
Annie & S. B. Word
May 11, 1883
Jan 11, 1921

Kathleen Bell Jakes
Jan 19, 1908
Feb 3, 1962

Telitha Stallings
Jun 27, 1892
Dec 11, 1897

James Ronald Bell
Feb 24, 1943
Jun 20, 1943

Audell Peoples
1938-1950

Lemuel N. Stallings
Apr 4, 1886
Oct 29, 1886

Olin Preston Bell
1968-1968
(Gowen-Smith)

Joseph C. Bell
Apr 11, 1873
Mar 21, 1953

David Ervin Cook
Born & Died Dec 1, 1955

Roger L. White
1946-1947

Colon W. Neeley
May 6, 1907
(Gowen-Smith-1974)
&
Mamie B. Neeley
Jan 1, 1906
May 26, 1959

Leo V. Anderson
1921-1975
(Gowen-Smith)

Doris M. Anderson
Oct 13, 1949
Oct 30, 1950

William Kenneth Cook
Apr 13, 1958

C. R. Pickle
Aug 3, 1887
Oct 26, 1961
&
Rosie C. Pickle
Oct 1, 1889
Jan 12, 1961
(picture)

George Washington, son of
T. J. & M. E. Blackwell
May 16, 1886
Apr 20, 1887

Addie, dau of
T. J. & M. E. Blackwell
Mar 28, 1887
Apr 7, 1888

Elly, dau of
T. J. & M. E. Blackwell
Jul 29, 1888
Aug 30, 1888

Mary E., wife of
T. J. Blackwell
Jul 29, 1865
Jun 29, 1896

Thomas J. Blackwell
1862-1941
&
Sallie Lou Blackwell
1876-1961

James H. Darnell
Jan 4, 1886
Feb 2, 1961
&
Pearlie L. Darnell
Jun 6, 1888
Dec 18, 1915

Harvey H. Darnell
Sep 27, 1910
Nov 28, 1952
&
Cleara F. Darnell
Dec 16, 1913

James R. Irwin
1874-1951
&
Dora H. Irwin
1874-1937

Phillip C. Harvey
Jul 15, 1913

&
A. T. Bell Harvey
Feb 7, 1916
----
married Apr 27, 1935

Charnel M. Glasscock
1874-(no date)
&
Elizabeth T. Glasscock
1886-1947

Roy T. Glasscock
Jul 15, 1908
Aug 14, 1970
&
Mary E. Glasscock
Aug 10, 1910

Marvin N. Whitehead
1893-1893

Henry F. Whitehead
1852-1923
&
Arminta Whitehead
1854-1909

John Henry Blackwell
Jul 2, 1883
Jan 10, 1965

Lillie M., wife of
J. H. Blackwell
Feb 8, 1883
Dec 23, 1920

Nannie B. Gold Blackwell
1886-1931

William "Tom" Darnell
Aug 4, 1888

&
Jeannie E. Darnell
Jan 3, 1892
(Gowen-Smith-1974)

William J. H. Darnell
Jun 19, 1855
Jan 1, 1930
&
Emily Darnell
Feb 6, 1862
Feb 27, 1942

Infant son of
Mr & Mrs Lesie Darnell
Born & Died
Jun 4, 1937

Imogene D. Neal
Sep 18, 1912
Oct 30, 1952

Joel Newsom Pickle
Apr 15, 1879
Aug 19, 1884
age: 5, 4m, 4d.

Robert C. Pugh
Apr 22, 1885
Apr 27, 1972
&
Beatrice H. Pugh
Aug 12, 1889
Apr 14, 1967

Earnest C. Harber
Jan 2, 1882
Mar 20, 1910

Willie Frances Harber
Aug 1, 1844
Apr 27, 1913

Thomas Harber
Feb 13, 1851
Nov 3, 1933

W. Cleveland Harber
Jul 9, 1888
Sep 23, 1958
&
Lou Ella C. Harber
Nov 10, 1892

Infant Son of
W. C. & Ella Harber
1915

Chesley T. Adams
Dec 12, 1889
Mar 2, 1965
&
Ruth B.(Alma Ruth) Adams
Jul 7, 1900
Nov 24, 1967

W. James Young
Jan 21, 1909

&
Lela Young
Apr 10, 1914
----
married Nov 18, 1933

Willard Young
Oct 20, 1934
Jun 7, 1938
(picture)

Emma Young
1877-1940

Maggie C. Condra
1868-1950

William E. Pickle
Jan 21, 1867
Mar 12, 1927
&
Margaret H. Pickle
Mar 31, 1866
May 6, 1952

Ethel, dau of
W. E. & M. H. Pickle
Nov 2, 1896
Jan 30, 1897

Harvey Canady, Sr.
Mar 20, 1903
Aug 29, 1969
&
Minnie P. Canady
Aug 18, 1911
----
married Apr 8, 1928

John A. Campbell
1868-1942
&
Lela H. Campbell
1880-1965

Sherlock Arnold
1912-1950
&
Hazel C. Arnold
1910-1967

Sam Dudley Campbell
Jan 9, 1919

&
Evelyn Cook Campbell
Oct 11, 1926
Dec 9, 1961

Clarence Curtis
Apr 27, 1898
Jun 24, 1968
&
Josie B. Curtis
Dec 6, 1898

Frank Cook
Jun 6, 1887
Feb 12, 1962
&
Florence Cook
Feb 28, 1892
(Gowen-Smith-1974)

"Our Father"
Squire Thomas Pickle
Died Nov 7, 1921
(no age given)

Charles Pickle
(no dates)

Thomas J. Pickle
1883-1947
&
Hattie N. Pickle
1885-1947

George W. Pickle
1870-1936
&
Janie C. Pickle
1871-1945

Henry Clay Pickle
Feb 12, 1842
Aug 29, 1920
&
Margaret Elon Pickle
Oct 6, 1842
May 20, 1924
(picture)

William Clifford Darnell
Jun 18, 1908

&
James H.(Herman) Darnell
Jul 27, 1934
Apr 29, 1936
&
Mazelle C. Darnell
Aug 19, 1910
        1974 (TM)

Fred T. Darnell
Mar 5, 1907

&
Rosie E. Darnell
Feb 26, 1909
----
married Nov 2, 1924

Thomas J. Darnell
May 11, 1837
Mar 11, 1910
&
Nancy E. Darnell
Aug 19, 1839
Sep 30, 1928

William Thomas Barnell
Feb 26, 1863
Jun 10, 1884
&
Joel Newsom Darnell
Mar 20, 1865
Nov 19, 1884
"Sons of T. J. &
N. E. Darnell"

Malcom "Billy" Neill
Aug 12, 1910
Mar 14, 1970
&
Dorothy D. Neill
Sep 18, 1915

E. Huffman Stephenson
Apr 4, 1916

&
Louise H. Stephenson
Apr 27, 1918

Donald Ray Stephenson
Nov 11, 1947
killed in Vietnam
May 5, 1968
Tennessee
Sp 4 Co A 50 Inf 173 ABN
BDE   Vietnam

John Dryden
1866-1936
&
Kate Dryden
1865-1948

Albert Anderson   and
Dec 14, 1855
Jan 18, 1900

James E. Neill
Feb 25, 1905
Nov 7, 1971
&
Gladys Neill
Oct 11, 1905

B. T. Darnell
Jul 4, 1877
Nov 22, 1943

Lela J. Darnell
Jun 8, 1879
Nov 25, 1966

Lora A. Darnell
1893-1894

Sadie M. Darnell
1910
age: 17 days

Infant of
W. H. & M. E. Robertson
1906
age: 4 days

Medie D. Robertson
1895
age: 12 days

Johnnie B. Robertson
1891
age: 1 month

Homer L. Darby
1898-1951
&
Pearl R. Darby
1902-

George W. Stephenson
Oct 27, 1886
Jul 12, 1963
&
Genettie D. Stephenson
Jul 13, 1894

W. R. Dryden
1886-1937

Hannah Elizabeth, dau of
R. N. & Willie Dryden
Dec 22, 1873
Dec 25, 1906

Robert N. Dryden
Dec 14, 1834
Sep 7, 1898

Willie, wife of
R. N. Dryden & dau of
William & T. Stallings
Feb 26, 1842
Jul 19, 1900
age: 58y, 4m, 23d.

Mary Anderson
Apr 13, 1853
Apr 26, 1936

Larry George Darnell
Sep 1, 1947
Dec 12, 1947

Maggie Elizabeth Darnell
Oct 8, 1905
Nov 8, 1905

Twin Daughters of
Fred & Rosie Darnell
Jul 14, 1925

David A. Darnell
1871-1948
&
Mary J. Darnell
1871-1957

Herman Lee Darnell
1899-1921
F.B. 19th Artillery
(picture)

Edith Bell Carlton
Jul 11, 1902
Apr 18, 1936

Charles Hurbert Bell
Jul 6, 1904
Sep 23, 1933

Minnie Frances Bell
Dec 20, 1900
Jul 20, 1920

Laura D. Bell
Sep 23, 1873
Mar 11, 1963

William Frank Harris
Aug 28, 1885
Jun 9, 1971
&
Maggie Robertson Harris
Nov 9, 1889

Aaron Harris
May 28, 1915
Aug 30, 1916
&
Louise Harris
Sep 26, 1917
Jul 15, 1919

William Stallings
Jan 11, 1815
Oct 5, 1886
&
Talitha Stallings
Apr 10, 1818
Oct 16, 1893

"Father"
Chamberlaine T. Clay
Jun 9, 1827
Mar 3, 1900

"Mother"
Catherine Pickle
Mar 31, 1813
Oct 17, 1896
age: 83y, 6m, 16d.

Louise E. Pickle Ratcliff
Nov 27, 1911
Oct 8, 1939

Baby T. P. Ratcliff, Jr.
Nov 23, 1930
Nov 25, 1930

Clara May Pickle
Jun 14, 1908
Jul 14, 1908

Minnie E. Pickle
Nov 3, 1879
Sep 19, 1965

"Mother"
Margaret E.Darnell
      Pickle Taylor
May 12, 1861
Oct 8, 1938

Joshua Musgrave
1784-Aug 25, 1857
&
Prudence Musgrave
Jan 25, 1788
Apr 15, 1867

Rufus J. Shelton
1889-1938
&
Clarissa Shelton
1899-1964

W. H. Robertson
Jul 22, 1868
May 18, 1967
&
M. E.(Mary Etta) Robertson
Apr 18, 1869
Oct 27, 1951

Rev. Jesse W. Roberts
1874-1959
&
Harriet A. Roberts
1879-1949

Carrie L. Bills,
Feb 15, 1884
married to G. W. Stallings
Feb 15, 1917
Died Oct 17, 1918

Rev. G. W. Cook
Nov 14, 1833
Jul 26, 1902

Mary E. Pickle, wife of
G. W. Cook
Jan 27, 1835
Oct 23, 1919

John C. Pickle
Feb 15, 1888
Aug 10, 1965
&
Hattie L. Pickle
Jun 6, 1900

"Father"
T. N. Pickle
May 6, 1840
Nov 13, 1918
&
"Mother"
P. E. Pickle
Sep 17, 1849
Sep 18, 1912

Jennie Pickle
Aug 23, 1835
Apr 8, 1918

"Mother"
Delia Ann Kail
Feb 15, 1876
Apr 5, 1952

Charlie C. Neill
Jul 16, 1906

&
Ruby Gertrude Neill
Nov 13, 1909

Edna Frances Neill
1931-1949

Earl Neill
1934-1934
&
Charles Neill
1928-1928
&
Hazel Neill
1930-1930

Allie B. Hopper, Sr.
Tennessee
Pvt 324 Field Hosp. W.W.I
Jul 23, 1894
Sep 2, 1956

Maudie Elinor Hopper
Feb 10, 1892
Jan 22, 1893

Hazel Estell Roberts
Oct 8, 1927
age: 1 day

Virgil A. Darnell
1925-
&
Virginia M. Darnell
1926-1947

Charles Darnell
Feb 6, 1947
Feb 24, 1947

George W. Darnell
Mar 11, 1884
Dec 26, 1943
&
Nancy Ann Darnell
Sep 23, 1884
Nov 10, 1959

Lillie May Darnell
Apr 6, 1900
Jan 29, 1936

Charlene O'Donniley
1936

Clara Brewer O'Donniley
1907-1936

Horace, Jr., son of
Horace & Clara O'Donniley
1934-1935

Martha Ella O'Donniley
1875-1945

James H. Taylor
Dec 19, 1918
Sep 1, 1961
Tennessee
S1 U.S.N.R.   W.W.II
&
Violet L. Taylor
Oct 23, 1919

Samuel T. Neill
1853-1934
&
Jennie T. Neill
1872-1957

Earnie Wendell Neill
Jun 3, 1908
Feb 1, 1968
&
Clara Estelle Neill
Oct 18, 1912
Nov 22, 1955

S. D. Durham
Oct 11, 1844
Apr 17, 1925
&
Emily M. Durham
Oct 31, 1837
Dec 21, 1914

Edward S. Burgess
Feb 13, 1919
Jan 13, 1964
&
Ruth H. Burgess
Aug 3, 1912
----
married May 2, 1948

Robert Ewell Darnell
1879-1957
(Cotheran-Thompson)

Martha A. Darnell
1879-1903

Willie T. Cox
Jan 1, 1894
Oct 17, 1918

G. J. Cox
Apr 29, 1895
Dec 23, 1926
(picture)

Hubert Yoes
Born & Died
Jul 4, 1915

Elizabeth Glasscock
Jan 24, 1829
Feb 8, 1901
age: 72y & 15d.

Cleve (R. Cleveland) Perryman
1887-1947
&
Mary (Neill) Perryman
1887-1974

Adult grave, TM marker,
in Neill plot, information
now gone. Ed.

Andrew L.(Rue) Neill
Jan 23, 1877
Aug 15, 1968

James Ewell Neill
Dec 1, 1908
Feb 13, 1956

Thomas Baxter
Feb 17, 1833
Jan 29, 1911
&
Emily Baxter
May 16, 1835
Jan 4, 1922

Corp. Jessie N. Arnold
with A.E.F.
Jul 1, 1893
Oct 20, 1918

Robert W. Glasscock
1872-1927
&
Ella M. Glasscock
1876-1954

Jacob T. Cook
1849-1931
&
Mary L. Cook
1852-1940

August H. Balinger
1914-1942

Theodore D. Balinger
Sep 7, 1885
Jun 25, 1967
&
Susie E. Balinger
Mar 23, 1891

Robert Lewis, son of
L. J. & W. D. Cox
Jun 21, 1908
May 9, 1909

L. J. Cox
Jun 12, 1864
Sep 4, 1935

Winnie D. Cox, wife of
L. J. Cox
Jun 15, 1871
Sep 17, 1928
(picture)

J. L. Perryman
Jan 1, 1877
Jan 1, 1957
&
Margaret Ann Perryman
Jun 22, 1877
Sep 17, 1953

Hershel H. Perryman
Jul 21, 1907
Oct 7, 1966
&
Christine S. Perryman
Jul 9, 1919

Robert H. Perryman
Jun 15, 1888
Mar 30, 1969
&
Ellen W. Perryman
Jun 27, 1890
----
married Oct 7, 1923

L. J. Swinney
1856-1936 ·
&
Mattie Swinney
1863-1931

Howard Carlton
Jan 13, 1877
Jan 10, 1906
&
Ellie F. Swinney Carlton
Mar 9, 1887
Jul 23, 1905

Mrs. Sally --------
1864-1946
(Thompson)

Walter .T. Hodge
1872-1957
&
Nora Alice Hodge
1881-1957

Anna Harris Webb
Jun 15, 1876
Mar 13, 1953

Charlie Presley
1905-1973 (TM)
&
Lassie B. Presley
1906-1958

Horace L. Neill
1898-19
&
Vera Mai Neill
1906-1956

J. Clarence Yoes
Jun 13, 1891
Jun 2, 1964
&
Jennie Mai Yoes
Jul 3, 1892
Feb 7, 1953

Robert C. Yoes
Mar 9, 1937
Jul 11, 1938

John S. Yoes
Oct 9, 1849
Mar 5, 1927

Nora E., wife of
J. S. Yoes
Mar 25, 1870
Sep 14, 1897

Emma L., wife of
J. S. Yoes
(no dates)

John A. Yoes
Nov 23, 1912
Jan 26, 1970
&
Clara I. Yoes
Oct 2, 1912

Vernon L. Yoes
Mar 27, 1914
Jul 27, 1953
&
Helen L. Yoes
Jan 31, 1918

Annie Lois Neeley
1926-1949

J. W. Glasscock
May 25, 1878
Sep 8, 1948

Ella Glasscock
1876-1921

Lillie Mae Glasscock
Jan 15, 1888
Jun 13, 1974

Thomas Glasscock
1900-1920

Margaret Glasscock
1902-1932

Larry Wayne Neill
Tennessee
Pfc H.H.C. 3 B.D.E.
L.R.R.P., Vietnam
B.S.M. Ph
Apr 2, 1948
Feb 2, 1969

Melanie Kaye Collins
1968-1968
(Gowen-Smith)

John M. Harris
Jan 7, 1882
Dec 12, 1969
&
Carrie Mai Harris
Sep 29, 1903

J. Clarence Moore
Aug 10, 1889
Sep 7, 1959
&
Eula V. Moore
Oct 25, 1894
Apr 15, 1972

Glenn Moore
1918-1920

J. F. Neill
1873-1956
&
Maggie Neill
1872-1938

W. T. Neill
Aug 4, 1900

&
Alma Neill
Feb 7, 1917
Apr 14, 1972

Infant Dau of
C. B. & E. L. Darnell
Born & Died
Sep 16, 1901

Charlie R. Darnell
Oct 2, 1872
Mar 12, 1921
&
Emma L. Darnell
Sep 22, 1877
Feb 18, 1953

George Glasscock
May 12, 1847
Mar 1, 1929
&
Amanda E. Glasscock
Aug 17, 1847
Apr 16, 1900

J. H. Glasscock
Feb 27, 1871
Jul 7, 1914

Florence Yoes Glasscock
1865-1935
&
Inda Mae Glasscock
1903-1970

"Brother"
John C. Clay
Dec 11, 1879
May 29, 1937
&
"Sister"
F. E. "Tinie" Clay
Jan 30, 1873
Dec 22, 1958

Martha M. Clay
1843-1922

Thomas Liggett Clay
1910-1963
(London)

Bessie D. Gant
Mar 7, 1886
Jun 10, 1919

James Darnell
1828-1909
&
Nancy M. Darnell
1834-1920

Swanson C. Darnell
Mar 9, 1868
Nov 25, 1898
&
Martha B. Darnell
1864-1955

S. L., son of
Jas. & N. M. Darnell
Jul 23, 1878
Oct 20, 1898

Infant Son Darnell
Born Nov 19, 1896
&
Infant Dau Darnell
Born Jan 5, 1898
Children of
C. R. & E. E. Darnell

Marcus E. Darnell
Jul 12, 1900

&
Mary Lee Darnell
Mar 8, 1906
Aug 20, 1968

Sam F. Liggett
1883-1939
&
Eula M. Liggett
1881-1950

Ruth I. Liggett
1915   age: 9months & 4 days

Earl D. Claiborne
Sep 20, 1915
Apr 27, 1918

Leonard Vernon Claiborne
Dec 6, 1906
Jan 8, 1909

Frank Hill
Nov 7, 1893
Mar 23, 1965
&
Minnie Avo Hill
Sep 22, 1884
Aug 12, 1961

Edd L. Cook

&
Annie Clay Cook
1877-1964 (TM)

Johnny Darnell
1956-1970 (Lawrence)

Robert E. McKnight
Sep 1, 1884
Dec 4, 1948
&
Allice Y. McKnight
Aug 28, 1880
(no date)

Ransom Arnold
Mar 27, 1901
Aug 18, 1961
&
Bessie Arnold
Nov 1, 1905

(picture)

Haskel Collins
Oct 14, 1910
Aug 27, 1960
(picture)
&
Inez Collins
Jul 10, 1925

Creasy Liggett
1879-1898
&
Isabell Liggett
1854-1919
&
William S. Liggett
1854-1917

John M. Liggett
Oct 31, 1891
May 21, 1954
&
Lottie M. Liggett
Feb 11, 1902

Clarence Thomas Liggett
Nov 5, 1909
May 18, 1951

James T. Rittenberry
Sep 20, 1875
Mar 16, 1961
&
Ella Ervin Rittenberry
Aug 22, 1886
Jul 2, 1959

Charlie C. Rogers
Oct 19, 1896
Oct 20, 1967
&
Ethel N. Rogers
Feb 15, 1900

Sidney M. Head
1901-
&
Mary O. Head
1900-

Edwin Morris Clay
1873-1923
&
Mattie Belle Clay
1880-1932

Mary J. Presley
May 7, 1912

Fred B. Clay
Dec 9, 1912
Aug 31, 1913
&
Elgan T. Clay
Nov 25, 1908
Nov 27, 1910

J. N. Blackwell
Oct 5, 1828
May 6, 1910
&
Martha Jane Blackwell
Apr 17, 1833
Apr 27, 1909
age: 76y & 10d.

J. N. Blackwell
Oct 5, 1828
May 6, 1910
&
Martha Jane Blackwell
Apr 17, 1833
Apr 27, 1909
age: 76y & 10d.

Infant Sons of
S. J. & Carrie Blackwell
Infant: Sep 20, 1889
Infant: Aug 4, 1901

James Glenn White
Jan 6, 1950
Jun 20, 1970

Douglas Gardner
May 6, 1899
Jan 7, 1970
&
Ozzie H. Gardner
Feb 23, 1907
Mar 25, 1971

C. A. Shaw
1852-1949
&
Addie Shaw
1854-1928

Marshall L. Luna
Apr 4, 1892

&
Bertie Lee Luna
Aug 5, 1893
Aug 18, 1972
married Dec 9, 1910

Timothy A. Dunn
Jul 3, 1903
Mar 20, 1972
&
Demmie T. Dunn
Oct 3, 1906

Earl Shaw
1885-1956
&
Elsie Shaw
1902-

Robert L. Herron
Jan 26, 1936
Apr 28, 1968
&
Norma J. Herron
Nov 11, 1940

John Ross Herron
Jun 16, 1932
Apr 28, 1968
&
Elsie N. Herron
Jun 31, 1936

Several unmarked graves.

Several fieldstones, no inscriptions.

3 UNKNOWN CEMETERY   Map # 9
Located about 1½ miles West of Whitaker, South of Wheel.

Fieldstones, no inscriptions.

4 WOOD-MAYES CEMETERY   Map # 9
Located about 1½ miles South of Whitaker, South of Wheel.

J. P. Wood
Sep 20, 1838
Mar 28, 1916

M. C. Wood
Dec 6, 1841
May 23, 1910

J. A. Mayes
Apr 25, 1854
Dec 10, 1898

M. L. Mayes
Nov 2, 1866
(no date)

Copied by Jerry Wayne Cook.

5 ADAMS CEMETERY   Map # 9
Located 2 miles Northwest of Richmond, Tenn.

James L. Adams
Feb 12, 1828
Oct 4, 1909

Catharine Adams
Jun 17, 1827
Apr 10, 1872

Matilda C. Adams, 2nd wife
of J. L. Adams
Jan 5, 1841
Jul 27, 1880

Margaret E. Adams
Feb 14, 1850
Oct 18, 1867

Margaret, dau of
J. L. & Cathren Adams
Feb 14, 1850
Oct 18, 1867
age: 17y, 8m, 4d.

Nancy M., dau of
J. L. & M. C. Adams
Aug 19, 1873
Aug 6, 1880

Infant son of
Z. & M. E. Davis
Sep 23, 1876
Nov 11, 1876
age: 1m & 12d.

Lemuel Rice Hill
Jan 20, 1857
Apr 17, 1917
&
Fannie Adams Hill
Apr 11, 1862
Jul 9, 1945

Earnest Hill
Jul 8, 1893
Apr 21, 1921

Gertrude Hill
Jul 6, 1892
Sep 13, 1944

Charles P. Yancey
May 17, 1857
Jan 5, 1860

Elizabeth A., wife of
Gabrel Eddins
Mar 28, 1810
Jun 6, 1893

Frank Eddins
Feb 2, 1854
Nov 2, 1878
age: 24y & 8m.

Martha E. Yancey
Oct 24, 1840
Oct 25, 1850

Rachel A. Yancey
Sep 18, 1858
do do do
(Died same day)

168

1 GAUNT CEMETERY   Map # 10
Located about 1 mile East of Wheel, Tenn.

Lewis Gaunt   and
Dec 28, 1803
Feb 20, 1860

Mary S., wife of
Lewis Gaunt
May 2, 1816
Jan 29, 1873

Edmon Cooper Gaunt   and
Sep 9, 1853
Feb 9, 1924

Infant dau of
Ernest & Alla Cooper
1916

Martha Jane Gaunt
Jul 6, 1850
Aug 15, 1925

About 12 unmarked graves.

2 O'NEAL CEMETERY   Map # 10
Located about 2 miles West of Bedford, on Sinking Creek.

J. M. O'Neal   and
Sep 16, 1816
Jul 28, 1898

Elizabeth O'Neal
Mar 11, 1835
Jul 28, 1923

Copied by Jerry Wayne Cook.

3 PISGAH CEMETERY   Map # 10
Located near Lebanon Church, in 18th District.

Sacred to the Memory of
Henry Pickle, who departed
this life Sept 27, 1854
aged: 74 yrs.
&
Rachel, wife of
Henry Pickle
Died May 1859
aged: 80 yrs.

William Grant
Jan 5, 1794
May 16, 1875

No marker·*
Theophilus Williams
Born ca 1817
Died ca 1885
[Daniel & Benjamin Earnhart
said to be buried here]

No marker:*
James B. Jones
Born May 2, 1809
Died (no date)

Thomas J., Infant son of
G. T. & Rebecca Neeley
Died Jun 30, 1842
aged: 1y, 1m, 25d.

Hannah Neeley
Dec 6, 1789
Jul 8, 1845
aged: 55y, 6m, 2d.

James M. Neeley
Apr 4, 1817
Dec 24, 1880

No marker:*
Lear Williams, 1st wife of
Theophilus Williams
Born ca 1821
Died before 1863

No marker:*
Mary "Polly" Allen Jones
Born Nov 28, 1812
Died (no date)

David L. Clifft
Sep 20, 1818
(no date)*Jul 12, 1885

Dianah Clifft
Sep 19, 1819
Mar 20, 1900

Aged: 11mo, 20da.
George H. Baxter
Died Sep 30, 1843

No marker:**
Icy H., consort of
J. M. Neeley & dau of
Aaron & Elizabeth Bledsoe
Born Feb 19, 1820
Died Aug 25, 1878
aged: 58y, 6m, 6d.
(copied in 1960)

Many unmarked graves.

* by Jerry Wayne Cook
** by Mrs. Joe Neeley

Henry J. Earnhart
Apr 8, 1869
Dec 8, 1923
&
Emma M. Earnhart
May 22, 1869
Mar 27, 1921

Aged: 4mo, 20da.
Almira Jane Baxter
Died Dec 7, 1846

No marker:*
William H. Neeley
Born abt 1837, son of
James & Icy H. Neeley
(no death date)

No marker:*
Tom Berlin
(no dates)

4 STEPHENSON CEMETERY   Map # 10
Located about 3/4 mile Southeast of Lebanon Church, in 18th District.

Edward Stephenson
Born Sep 9, 1774
Died May 25, 1868
aged: 93y, 8m, 16d.

Rebecca, Consort of
E. Stephenson
Born Feb 8th 1784
Died Sep 9th 1845
aged: 61y, 7m, 1d.

James R. Pickle
Mar 7, 1854
Dec 22, 1856

Many unmarked graves.

E. I. Stephenson
Dec 20, 1839
Sep 6, 1916

Catherine M., wife of
Joshua Crowel
Jun 2, 1823
Apr 3, 1849
aged: 26y, 10m, 1d.

William H. Pickle
May 16, 1856
Sep 6, 1856

George W. Stephenson
Nov 23, 1810
Feb 12, 1880
aged: 69y, 2m, 19d.

Milley Stephenson
Apr 25, 1813
Sep 28, 1855

Lucinda B. Pickle
Apr 9, 1824
Jan 5, 1875

William N. Stephenson
Dec 11, 1834
Sep 5, 1855

R. J. Stephenson
Oct 9, 1844
Mar 11, 1937

M. E. Stephenson
May 15, 1844
Aug 28, 1912

Emma Stephenson Paschal
1875-1918

Bod Stephenson
Jun 7, 1870
Oct 18, 1902

5 WILSON CEMETERY   Map # 10
Located about 1 mile North of Coleman Cemetery.

James N., Infant of
M. M. & Mary N. Wilson
Born & Died
Jan 10, 1850   3 or 4 unmarked graves.

6 BROWN CEMETERY (Col)   Map # 10
Located on Sims Road, at Thompson Grove School & Church.

-------------(name gone)
Born 19--   (gone)
Died 1965   (TM)

James Harvy Peacock
1890-1941

Lovie Greer, wife of
Stalling Greer
Nov 18, 1879
Feb 1, 1919

Many graves with fieldstones,
    no inscriptions.

Idella Anderson
1887-1969

Mr. Andy G. Smith
Died Sept 1955

Tom Brown
Mar 15, 1850
Jan 2, 1939

Letsie Brown
Jan 1, 1854
Nov 26, 1945

7 UNKNOWN CEMETERY (Col)   Map # 10
Located at Corner of Comstock & Sims Road.

This Cemetery was located in a space along the road between
the Coleman Cemetery and Sims Road. This Cemetery was plowed
under several years ago.   by Jerry Wayne Cook.

8 COLEMAN CEMETERY   Map # 10
Located near Sims Road and on Comstock Road.

W. M. Damron
Feb 25, 1871
Feb 16, 1911

William Henry, son of
S. N. & E. M. Stephenson
Feb 17, 1861
Jul 4, 1864

Eli W., son of
S. N. & E. M. Stephenson
Feb 26, 1866
Mar 4, 1866

W. M. Pylant
Sep 1, 1857
Jun 12, 1907

Will P. Pylant
Mar 16, 1886
Mar 16, 1905

Fannie Phelps Pylant
Died Sep 30, 1890
age: 29 yrs.

Samuel F. Pittman
Feb 14, 1932
Mar 15, 1934

Nancy M., wife of   and
H. W. Bruster &
C. R. Head
Jan 29, 1840
Dec 12, 1900
        &
N. M., wife of
F. F. Cooper
Mar 17, 1880
Jun 12, 1908

John S. Delk
May 23, 1870
Nov 24, 1935
        &
Inez Landers Delk
Feb 12, 1879
Mar 30, 1918

N. S. E. Delk, wife of
W. M. Pylant
Feb 4, 1873
Jun 17, 1903

J. L. Anderson
Dec 28, 1845
Aug 28, 1921

M. F. Anderson
Aug 19, 1842
Jan 4, 1924

Lue & Lou Craig
1948-1948

Janie Annie Mai Craig
1947-1947

H. L. Williams
Dec 8, 1891-Apr 23, 1914

H. L. Williams
Jan 20, 1884
Jan 10, 1900

Nannie Ruth Williams
1916-1916

Ozella Williams Parker
Nov 18, 1897
Aug 25, 1917

M. M. Wilson
Mar 14, 1822
Feb 19, 1893
"Mexican Soldier"
        &
Mary A., wife of
M. M. Wilson
Feb 26, 1823
Feb 24, 1892

Z. T. Williams
Mar 20, 1850
Oct 25, 1890

Thomas Lee Williams
May 13, 1848
Sep 5, 1920

Mahala S. Williams
Dec 13, 1811
Aug 3, 1893

L. T. Williams
Feb 22, 1816
Oct 7, 1901

Effie A. Barnett
Feb 21, 1882
Dec 30, 1889

Maggie C. Barnett
Mar 29, 1874
Dec 7, 1875

W. J. Barnett
Aug 17, 1844
Jul 26, 1918

Nancy E. Barnett
Oct 4, 1847
Dec 14, 1899

Mary Altha, dau of
J. L. & R. J. Wilson
Sep 29, 1878
Oct 4, 1881

Eli H. W. Hanaway
Jun 15, 1842
Jan 2, 1863

L. H. (footstone)

Alice Farmer Curtis
1872-1911

Sallie M. Curtis
1885-1956

Altie E. Curtis
1921-1921

Thomas L. Curtis
1904-1923

Sarah L. Curtis
1916-1921

Zula B. Curtis
Nov 25, 1894
Sep 26, 1895

Oliver G. Curtis
1923-1923

Joe G. Curtis
1867-1948

James Luther Poplin
Jul 17, 1905

        &
Auda Muriel Poplin
Sep 28, 1913-Oct 18, 1969
married Dec 24, 1932

Kittie W. Williams
Nov 2, 1861
May 2, 1935

T. Marvin Williams
1882-1960
&
Auda Lee, wife of
Marvin Williams
1885-1971

James H. Williams
Oct 24, 1873
Nov 7, 1901

Johnie, son of
D. M. & M. S. Temple
Jan 23, 1882
Jan 4, 1883

Iva D. & Ima Lee, Infant
Daus of Mr & Mrs J. B.
Elliott
1918

Dorothy J. Thompson
1945-1945

Cappie T. McNatt
1895-1972
(Gowen-Smith)

Bettie, wife of
T. G. Clanton
Mar 11, 1884
Jan 11, 1919

Thos. G. Clanton
Jul 22, 1883
Jun 8, 1951

Everett Patterson
1892-1961
&
Vesta A. Patterson
1894-

Hattie R., dau of
J. T. & M. B. Damron
Apr 28, 1879
May 11, 1879

Plesant K., son of
J. T. & M. B. Damron
Jan 8, 1878
Mar 28, 1878

Robert Russell
1893-1962
&
Mary Elizabeth Russell
1907-1959

Claude Walters
Dec 13, 1896

&
Margaret Walters
Aug 4, 1899

Otis Clanton
1907-1971
&
Ruby L. Johnson Clanton
1912-

Martin Luther Clanton
1886-1973
&
Mattie C. Clanton
1883-1962

Several unmarked graves.

John Damron
Sep 26, 1882
Nov 10, 1959
&
Irene Damron
Jan 13, 1907

Lizzie Damron
Aug 8, 1880
Nov 15, 1908

Tom Damron
May 27, 1855
May 2, 1909
&
Bettie Damron
Mar 1, 1858
Jun 19, 1910

Sarah Jane Hoover
Nov 26, 1886
Feb 3, 1937

Stoney R. Hoover
1885-1958

Effie Pitts
Oct 7, 1884

&
Della D. Pitts
Feb 11, 1885
Jun 20, 1967

C. D. Walters
Feb 6, 1894
Jun 26, 1969
&
Eula M. Walters
Jun 3, 1904

Orville A. Hunnicutt
Jun 20, 1915

&
Bessie H. Hunnicutt
Nov 24, 1913
Mar 7, 1965

Madlon Fay, Infant Dau of
Mr & Mrs O. A. Hunnicutt
May 3, 1943

Alvin T. Hunnicutt
1885-1943
&
Minnie L. Hunnicutt
1887-1951

J. T. Hunnicutt
Jul 19, 1911
Nov 6, 1932

James W. Anderson
1850-1947

Laura Jane, wife of
J. W. Anderson
Dec 29, 1851
Nov 6, 1890

Hollis L. Prince
1898-1967
(Howell-Thompson)

Finis Clanton
Oct 22, 1914
Feb 25, 1936

James Walter Clanton
1916-1919

9 STEPHENS CEMETERY   Map # 10
Located about 2 miles West of Sim's Bridge.

John Stephens
Died May 12, 1831
aged: abt 55 yrs

Martha A. Culley, wife of
John Stephens, Sr.
Born Feb 21, 1796
Died Aug 29, 1879
aged: 83y, 6m, 8d.

Several unmarked graves.
Several fieldstones, no
inscriptions.

10 NEW BETHEL CEMETERY   Map # 10
Located at Bedford, Tenn.

Era Gertrude Jennings
1894-1924

Margaret Ellen Falcon
May 19, 1861
Aug 16, 1951

Julia G. Finney
1896-1936

George Walters
1865-1923
&
Zade Walters
1866-(no date)

Joseph P. Gambill
Feb 13, 1855
Sep   1901

Henry D. Gambill
Feb 23, 1898
Mar 24, 1899

Maggie M. West
Died Jul 23, 1911
age: 58 yrs.

Sherman Walters
1889-1965
(Gowen-Smith)

Malissa F., wife of
T. J. Berlin
Apr 14, 1829
Aug 14, 1907

W. M. Berlin
Dec 30, 1866
Mar 1, 1902

Infant of
W. M. & M. M. Berlin
Died Dec 12, 1900

Robert A. Neill
1878-1918

Clarence Delffs
Tennessee
S1 U.S.N.R.   W.W.II
Aug 2, 1918
Dec 24, 1965

Alice Perryman Adams
Sep 27, 1867
Oct 18, 1913

William Perryman
Co E

"Mother" (between 2 Neills)
1868-(Thompson Service)

S. M. Delk
Nov 12, 1853
Aug 24, 1940
&
J. J. Delk
May 6, 1838
Feb 7, 1911

Mrs. Hattie Delk
1870-1961
(Gowen-Smith)

Fannie F. Neill
Aug 24, 1879
Jan 29, 1961

A. A. Hunicutt
Jan 18, 1842
Nov 21, 1916
& wife:
Sarah E. Hunicutt
May 25, 1844
Feb 18, 1914

C. S. Chapman
1911-1951
(Gowen)

Mrs. Hettie Chapman
1874-1950
(Thompson)

J. Herman Dryden
1897-19
&
Bessie B. Dryden
1895-1956

Thomas W. Muse
Feb 26, 1826
Mar 26, 1886
(marker now gone)

Jane, wife of
T. W. Muse
Aug 1, 1823
Dec 29, 1883

William Chester, son of
A. W. & S. E. Morris
Born Oct 3, 1886
age: 8m & 18d.

James E. Cooper
Co C. 4 Tenn Mtd Inf
Oct 20, 1848
Oct 30, 1936
age: 88 yrs.

Jane D., wife of
J. E. Cooper
Mar 20, 1849
Jun 2, 1899

Mattie S. Cooper
Mar 8, 1864
Apr 11, 1931

Infant dau of
J. E. & M. B. Cooper
(no dates)

Mattie Kimmons
1887-1933

Georgia Cleek
1902-1932

Rosa Ethel Cleek
Dec 12, 1887
Oct 14, 1917

Robert L. Jones
Tennessee
Pvt 105 Trench Mortar Btry
30 Div
Aug 6, 1922

A. A. Turner
1870-1924

Harris Henslee
Dec 22, 1819
Jan 3, 1902
&
Bettie Henslee
May 15, 1817
Jun 29, 1899
&
Ann Denniston Henslee
1819-1897

Joe F. Dryden
1876-1903
&
Inez Dryden
1879-1960

Eugene Campbell
1896-1947
&
Alonzo N. Campbell
1897-19

"Father"
I. A. Givens
Jan 26, 1826
Jun 2, 1893
age: 66y, 4m, 7d.
&
"Mother"
H. C. Givens
Jul 21, 1826
Dec 15, 1884
age: 58y, 4m, 24d.

Nannie M. Liggett
Mar 4, 1857
Oct 16, 1884
(The information is almost
gone on this marker)

Ola Trice
Oct 3, 1881
Jan 2, 1904

Effie Trice
Oct 21, 1885
Jun 1, 1917

Martha Ann Couch
Jun 19, 1832
Jan 13, 1914

S. T. Word
Apr 21, 1835
Jan 12, 1904

Minter Lee Cleek
Aug 20, 1876
Jun 10, 1914

Mary E. Cleek
Jun 12, 1858
Jul 10, 1937

Infant Son of
Minter & Alvin Cleek
1914-1914

3 graves just South of
W. T. Daughtry, no markers:
Joseph Turner
(No dates)

Jane Turner
(No dates)

Dave Turner, son of
Joseph & Jane Turner
(no dates)

Jack Blackwell
(gone)-1892
(Gowen)

Susan Van Blackwell
1889-1910
(Gowen)

J. Lavoy Campbell
1902-1948
&
Mary B. Campbell
1902-19

Shirley S. Turner
Tennessee
Wagoner Sup Co 167 Inf W.W.I
Ph
Aug 27, 1894
Oct 15, 1956

Hiram G. Culbertson
"Father"
(no dates)
&
Annie Culbertson
"Daughter"
(no dates)

N. C. Gambill
May 28, 1846
Apr 20, 1900

Lucy A., wife of
N. C. Gambill
Dec 29, 1851
Feb 26, 1896
age: 44y, 1m, 27d.

Nanny L. Ladd, wife of
N. C. Gambill
Mar 11, 1840
Jun 6, 1893
age: 53y, 2m, 26d.

Michael Robinson
Oct 12, 1834   and
May 27, 1910

Jos. B. Cleek
Co F
4 N.Y. Prov. Cav.
1842-1910

J. L. Helton
Oct 2, 1856
Oct 23, 1918
&
Hattie Helton
Jun 7, 1872

Infant dau of
J. L. & H. H. Helton
Born & Died
Dec 29, 1909

E. W. Cooper
Sep 16, 1875
Jul 17, 1905

Virgie Lentz Cooper
Oct 30, 1895
Nov 8, 1927

Samuel A. Berlin
1864-Aug 22, 1938
&
Donnie S. Berlin
1867-(no date)

William C. Campbell
1872-1948
&
Mattie E. Campbell
1873-1966

Joe M. Turner
1870-1936
&
Caroline L. Turner
1867-1952

Thomas J. Barnett
1846-1918
&
Sarah M. Barnett
1848-1892

J. H. Campbell
Mar 6, 1842
Mar 18, 1889
&
Mrs. L. A. Campbell
Nov 9, 1849
Apr 29, 1940

Sallie J. Russell
Oct 9, 1866
Jun 30, 1891

Marlin Prince, Sr.
Sep 11, 1879
Aug 26, 1959
&
Alta Curtis Prince
May 25, 1881
Apr 24, 1939

Mary J. Robinson
Oct 23, 1837
Jan 8, 1924

Boyd Hooten
1904-1940
&
Ruby Hooten
1903-

William "Bud" Kimmons
Died Jun 21, 1974
age: 91 yrs.
(TM)-Wm. M. Kimmons
1883-1974
(Gowen-Smith) 2 markers.

"Our Idol"
Robert Cuthbert, son of
W. H. & M. J. Miller
Aug 14, 1895
Mar 2, 1898
age: 2y, 7m, 7d.

Margaret A., wife of
J. C. Corrunker
Aug 20, 1869
Mar 31, 1904

Willie B. Hill
Aug 18, 1885
Feb 22, 1962
&
Vera C. Hill
Apr 11, 1887
----
married Dec 24, 1904

Patie May, dau of
N. C. & Mattie Thomson
Died Mar 20, 1901
age: 14y, 8m, 2d.

Mary Alice Craig
Sep 11, 1892
Oct 28, 1918

L. M. H.
(no dates)

C. R.
(no dates)

Ethel J. Blackwell
Jul 10, 1904
Jun 6, 1950

Henry C. Craig
Jul 12, 1838
Sep 16, 1916
&
Martha J. Craig
Sep 26, 1859
Aug 22, 1936

Carrie Stallings, wife of
Harold H. Hansen
Aug 27, 1895
Nov 18, 1938

Edmon Wayne Pylant
1919-1944
(Thompson)
Tennessee
Pfc 12 Inf 4 Div W.W.II
Jul 12, 1919
Jun 15, 1944

Thomas E. Lents
1886-1941
&
Gertrude Lents
1898-19

J. M. McCall
Dec 15, 1848
Apr 13, 1911

W. P. McCall
age: 75 yrs.
(no dates)

Fannie McCall
age: 76 yrs.
(no dates)

Martha Ellen Word
Aug 10, 1877
Apr 12, 1897

C. C. Word
Jul 26, 1832
Apr 1, 1909
&
M. S. Word
Nov 6, 1831
Feb 18, 1909

Mary E., wife of
S. A. Johnsey
Apr 17, 1863
Aug 1, 1905

Willie & Katie Howard
(no dates)

Della Howard
(no dates)

John M. Howard
(no dates)

Nannie Stofle
May 8, 1871
Jun 8, 1953

Jas. Puckett
Co C
5 Tenn Cav.

Dan Shriver Gant
Aug 9, 1882
Jan 3, 1899

Ethel Lee Gant
Jul 26, 1886
Jun 11, 1901
age: 14y, 10m, 15d.

Ernest C. Gant
Jun 23, 1892
Jan 9, 1896

Mollie E. Gant
Oct 17, 1870
Oct 5, 1953

J. Morgan Pylant
1895-
&
Betty S. Pylant
1898-1973

John Blackwell
Mar 10, 1854
Jan 27, 1928

Hoyle Howard
Jul 7, 1890
Sep 28, 1926

William Howard
Died Apr 21, 1896
age: abt 78 yrs.

Samuel Johnsey
(no dates-Thompson FH)

James Houston Johnsey
Tennessee
Pfc U.S.Marine Co W.W.II
Aug 25, 1927
Aug 4, 1957
&
Carmen Chao Johnsey
May 18, 1928

John T. Johnsey
1888-1952
&
Jessie C. Johnsey
1887-19(no date)

Ashby, son of
J. J. & Mamie Word
Apr 10, 1908
Aug 13, 1910

J. J. Word
Jul 23, 1865
Sep 13, 1922
age: 57y, 1m, 21d.
&
Mamie Wade Word
Oct 20, 1870
Aug 20, 1945

P. C. Blist, son of
J. J. & Mamie Word
Mar 5, 1899
Jun 9, 1900

C. S. Chapman
Oct 20, 1840
Jan 11, 1924

Algie O. Chapman
Apr 13, 1895
Apr 24, 1896
&
Etta May Chapman
Jun 8, 1877
Jun 15, 1896

James N. Stallings
1848-1928
&
Belle N. Stallings
1869-1942

John F. Henslee
Tennessee
Pfc U.S.Army W.W.I
Sep 13, 1891
Feb 7, 1969

Mary Elrod, wife of
A. M. Campbell
Mar 11, 1840
Jun 6, 1893
age: 53y, 2m, 26d.

Eddie L. Campbell
Apr 5, 1874
Mar 21, 1919

Chas. E. Campbell
1885-1935
&
Eula Campbell
1888-19

"Father"
J. E. Campbell
Feb 7, 1835
Mar 13, 1890
&
"Mother"
E. E. Campbell
May 22, 1841
Mar 16, 1920

James Stallings
Nov 6, 1818
Jun 16, 1890
&
Elizabeth C. Stallings
Jun 26, 1829
Jan 11, 1897

Joe T. Stallings
May 14, 1859
Dec 13, 1892

C. T. Stallings
Jun 4, 1864
May 1, 1912

Martha Eleanor Stallings
1845-1928

Annie Blackwell Madison
Oct 22, 1902
Apr 27, 1920

Thomas L. Blackwell
1869-1940

Sallie Blackwell
1872-1951

Stanley Stallings
Feb 21, 1862
Mar 17, 1935
&
Tish A. Stallings
Jan 2, 1863
Mar 16, 1935

Bonnie L. Stallings
May 23, 1892
Sep 12, 1893

Jennie Loucille Stallings
Jan 20, 1908

Mary Ann Cook
Aug 8, 1897
Apr 19, 1972

Ezekiel Stallings
1881-1950
&
Beulah Stallings
1884-1968

Letha Bell Stallings
Sep 5, 1896
Jan 3, 1897

E. C. Stallings
Aug 14, 1870
Dec 16, 1938

Allice Stallings
Died Apr 22, 1914
age: 37 yrs.

William Dee Griffin
1876-1922
&
Susan Anne Griffin
1886-1949
&
Earl Griffin
1905-1944

R. L. Griffin
1911-1957

Sarah L. Griffin
Sep 5, 1908
Sep 8, 1972

Caroline Waters
Died Apr 9, 1918
age: 59 yrs.

Ernest C. Stallings
1891-1955
&
Ophelia E. Stallings
1891-1973

J. E. Stallings
Son of Ernest & Ophelia
Stallings
1915-1920

Thomas L. Henslee
Nov 14, 1849
Apr 17, 1942
&
Katie L. Henslee
Oct 4, 1868
Apr 23, 1956

H. W. Head
Jul 31, 1846
Mar 5, 1912
&
Buenia V. Head
Dec 19, 1850
May 4, 1901

Neely Gibson
1872-1941
&
Lizzie Gibson
1875-1948

B. Gambill
Apr 17, 1822
Sep 6, 1909
& wife:
Sarah C. Gambill
Died May 10, 1890
(no age given)

Annie B. Gambill
Oct 19, 1864
Feb 6, 1952

Charles Franklin
1935
age: 9 months

James L. Gant
Sep 1, 1874
Nov 23, 1927
&
Georgia L. Gant
Feb 16, 1882
Oct 10, 1972

Hugh Gant
Aug 12, 1904
Nov 10, 1922

Edgar Gant
1901-1941

William G. Pierson
Aug 27, 1866
Nov 21, 1955
&
Rosy E. Pierson
Apr 9, 1880
(no date)

Artie Lee Pierson
Sep 8, 1899
Mar 23, 1917

C. M. Kincaid
Dec 24, 1830
Jan 19, 1897

Elizabeth, wife of
C. M. Kincaid
Jan 24, 1835
Aug 12, 1905

R. M. Pylant
1881-1960
&
Donnie Pylant
1881-1958

Arrie P. Anderson
Aug 14, 1887
1974(TM)

Baby Bell
1899

W. T. Daughtrey
Aug 8, 1849
Mar 18, 1939

Ailsey P. Daughtrey
Sep 29, 1848
Mar 6, 1912

Mr. L. T. Gaunt
Mar 15, 1852
Jun 9, 1907
&
Mrs. M. E. Gaunt
Feb 11, 1854
Mar 29, 1938

J. H. Griffin
Co A
4th Tenn Mtd Inf

Anna Griffin
Sep 5, 1876
May 27, 1900

Mattie May Griffin
Jun 5, 1884
Jul 17, 1903

Mary E. Griffin
Jul 3, 1846
May 27, 1912

Baby Griffin
(no dates-McFarlin-Thompson)

Lee Russ
(no dates)

William Prince
1852-1927
&
Lettie Prince
1862-1931

Fred Prince
Jun 20, 1886
Aug 25, 1918

Walter Prince
1882-1943

Buford Henslee
1897

Ruth Henslee
1901

Lucy Henslee
1900

Lee F. Stallings
1883-1959
&
Gracie A. Stallings
1894-19

Tom S. Stallings
Tennessee
Corpl 83 Field Art
Sep 15, 1926

William T. Stallings
1879-1960
&
Sydney C. Stallings
1884-1944

John F. Arnold
1884-1933
&
Una T. Arnold
1887-1960

Infant of
Mr & Mrs W. E. Brown
(no dates)

Infant of
Mr & Mrs W. E. Brown
(no dates)

S. E. Cox
Oct 25, 1839
Oct 11, 1900

J. T. Griffin
Feb 16, 1872
Nov 13, 1960

Mary Lillian Griffin
Jun 30, 1915
Mar 4, 1918

Mrs. J. T. Griffin
(no dates-McFarlin-Thompson)

Jeff Prince
Sep 19, 1884

&
Essie Floyd Prince
Feb 25, 1890
Mar 28, 1967

William Thomas Prince
1909-1955
(Cothran-Thompson)

Myrtle Prince Lindsey
1889-1970
(Gowen-Smith)

Harris Henslee
Tennessee
Corp 317 Field Arty 81 Div
Jul 7, 1886
Jun 28, 1939

Mrs. Aulsey Thorne
1865-1948
(Beasley)

John Helton
Mar 17, 1847
May 14, 1915
&
Hettie Helton
Aug 15, 1847
Apr 13, 1925

John E. Stallings
Mar 27, 1851
Jul 18, 1928
&
Erie K. Stallings
Mar 14, 1864
Jun 15, 1933

Lillie T. Turner
1917-1920
&
Ivie R. Turner, Sr.
1884-1959
&
Emma L. Turner
1896-1964

William L. Davis
Apr 15, 1870
Jun 20, 1943
&
Mollie E. Davis
Sep 10, 1862
Oct 5, 1916

Oliver Lay
Dec 16, 1874
Mar 26, 1912

Victoria B. Lay
Jul 5, 1855
Feb 14, 1931

Paul R. Smith
Mar 10, 1894
Dec 25, 1929
(picture)

J. E., son of
R. F. & E. N. Smith
Jun 5, 1911
Jul 25, 1911

John Green
(no dates)

J. M. Pendley
Jun 20, 1840
Nov 12, 1912

Mary J. Head, wife of
J. M. Pendley
Oct 14, 1831
Aug 28, 1902

Ruby C. Harris
1911-1925

Eugene Harris
Mar 22, 1879
Mar 25, 1951
&
Demia Harris
Sep 12, 1883
Aug 18, 1973

Eva E. O'Neal
Apr 19, 1915

Nellie A. O'Neal
Apr 8, 1909

John O'Neal
Apr 22, 1874
Nov 12, 1923

Mary E. O'Neal
Mar 29, 1881
Dec 5, 1970

Medora O'Neal
Oct 29, 1911
May 30, 1972

Susan Brame Givens
1832-(no date)

T. A. Frances Brame Muse
1818-1902

James E. Poff
1848-1937
&
Mary Poff
1846-19(no date)

James Poff
Tennessee
Pvt 26 M.G. Bn 9 Div
Oct 24, 1918

Stella Helton
Feb 13, 1905
Sep 11, 1910

Infant Son of
C. C. & L. A. Winford
Born & Died
Jan 7, 1901

Curthburth C. Stallings
1864-1952
&
Ida May Stallings
1871-1947

C. T. Hastings
Oct 8, 1868
Apr 22, 1917
& wife:
Lizzie Pendley Hastings
Feb 17, 1870
Jan 7, 1919

Melville O. Hastings
1908-1945

Nowlin Boyd William
1867-1933
&
Sarah Elizabeth William
1834-1936

Edna E. Walters
1896-1942

J. W. Arnold
May 8, 1933
Dec 24, 1937

Claude H. Arnold
1903-
&
Lillie B. Arnold
1914-1956

Leonard Arnold
1902-1933
&
Maggie Arnold
1905-1955

Irene Russell
Mar 21, 1914
Dec 19, 1967

Sam T. Russell
1848-1933

Robert Lee Tucker
Aug 22, 1875
Dec 20, 1953

R. S. Arnold
1909-1942
&
Lucille Arnold
1917-

O. Clayton Curtis
1913-1923

John B. Baker
Apr 27, 1872
Oct 8, 1935
&
Nannie Baker
Aug 2, 1884
Jan 10, 1938

German Baker
Co H
5th Tenn Cav

Eathan A. Lawell
Jul 10, 1836
May 23, 1902
&
Mary T. Lawell
Apr 2, 1850
Dec 18, 1919

J. F. Berlin
Feb 25, 1852
Jan 12, 1927
& wife:
Mattie J. Berlin

(color picture of both)

W. F. Brown
1866-1941
& wife:
Eva Brown
1869-1943

George E. Gambill, Jr.
1945-1945
(Thompson)

Ernie Lee Blanton
Tennessee
Pfc XXI Corps Comp SVC Co
W.W.II
Oct 17, 1908
Dec 18, 1970

Hettie Blanton
1883-1972
&
Eunice Blanton
1879-1943

Otto Delffs
1872-1945

Mattie Delffs
Sep 29, 1893
Sep 3, 1933

Arnold Delffs
Hosp. Ster'd
5 Tenn Cav.

Martha Delffs
1846-Oct 12, 1912

James Leaper Lowe
1850-1923
(Thompson)

Mattie A. Lowe
1853-1929
(Thompson)

Lester Morris Pylant
1924-1926

S. P. Pylant
1849-1940

Aulcy Thorn
Feb 1, 1842
May 27, 1907

W. L. Smith
1860-1949
&
Mattie Smith
1862-1937

C. G. Berlin
Nov 16, 1860
Jan 30, 1921

Maggie Z. Gambille, wife of
C. T. Berlin
Apr 8, 1880
Mar 16, 1917
age: 36y, 11m, 23d.

James T. Henslee
Feb 16, 1888
May 12, 1963
& wife:
Vera F. Hastings Henslee
Jul 3, 1892
Oct 11, 1914
& wife:
Sallie V. Henslee
Apr 29, 1880
Feb 21, 1922

W. Forest Uselton
1895-1945
&
Gertrude Uselton
1899-19

"Mother" Sarah Ervin
(no dates)

No marker:
John Ervin
Died abt 1939
(information given at a
decoration)

Tom Ervin
1877-1953

Mary Etta Ervin
Jun 5, 1880
Jan 2, 1971

Volley Ray Ervin
May 12, 1916
May 27, 1945

Nellie Delffs, wife of
J. T. Ervin
Sep 2, 1883-Feb 2, 1904

Clarence Gant
1889-1940
&
Robbie Gant
1898-1970

Edwin C. Gant
Tennessee
Tec 4 U.S.Army   W.W.II
Feb 10, 1927
Aug 11, 1970

Wilson Curtis
Jul 24, 1824
Nov 16, 1914
&
Elizabeth Curtis
Jan 26, 1845
Sep 17, 1921

Willie Curtis
May 1, 1872
May 29, 1911

Rufus L. Shaw
1875-1946
&
Vera Shaw
1895-(no date)

R. Eugene Smith
Aug 5, 1888

&
Bettie H. Smith
Oct 28, 1893
Aug 1, 1966

William Smith
1856-1931

John Henry Wingo
Jul 22, 1871
Apr 21, 1941

Kietha Ann Burns
1948-1949

V. S. Davis
1852-1918

H. L. Freeman
May 13, 1841
Jan 16, 1908
&
Harriet Freeman
Jul 17, 1847
May 31, 1916

Gilbert B. Henderson
Mar 8, 1900

&
Carrie L. Henderson
Feb 4, 1906
Mar 11, 1971

John W. Cooper
1871-1936
&
Ellie N. Cooper
1872-1954

Paul F. Dryden
Jan 8, 1910
Sep 23, 1965
&
Lucille G. Dryden
Aug 21, 1915

Sarah L. Curtis
Nov 15, 1904
Jul 29, 1906

Mrs. Essie Curtis
1894-1946
(London FH)

Lessie Blackwell Dryden
May 27, 1881
Aug 12, 1932

George W. O'Neal
1870-1950
&
Ida May O'Neal
1887-1935

George A. O'Neal
Nov 8, 1894

&
Bessie T. O'Neal
Nov 23, 1896
Dec 30, 1971

Frank A. Helton
Nov 2, 1905
Feb 23, 1970
&
Edith G. Helton
Jul 4, 1910

John H. Helton
Apr 6, 1877
Mar 24, 1944
&
Edna F. Helton
Oct 26, 1872
May 12, 1938

Infant of
C. C. Stallings
(no dates)

Infant of
C. C. Stallings
(no dates)

Infant of
C. C. Stallings
(no dates)

Infant of
C. C. Stallings
(no dates)

Ernest Cooper
1893-19
&
Alla F. Cooper
1897-19

O. N. & Hattie Arnold
(no dates)

James P. Snoddy
Jun 24, 1909
Jan 14, 1974
&
Louise E. Snoddy
Jul 19, 1908
Aug 24, 1972
married Jun 21, 1937

Clarence M., son of
Mr & Mrs Joe Delk
Sep 3, 1915
May 26, 1916

Arthur Lee Delk
Feb 4, 1926
Oct 5, 1926

Joe P. Delk
Aug 26, 1883
Sep 21, 1967
&
Kitty P. Delk
Mar 25, 1892
Mar 28, 1968

_____Rogers
(no dates)

Lucille Rogers
(no dates)

Mattie Love Rogers
(no dates)

Doyle Rogers
(no dates)

A. B. Rogers
1877-1943

Susie Dean Rogers
(no dates)

Harvey H. Throneberry
Sep 11, 1899
Nov 10, 1957
&
Nannie F. Throneberry
Mar 14, 1901

Thomas Daughtrey
1885-1924
&
Bonnie Daughtrey
1890-19

Lillian E. Adams
1920-1955

"Brother"
John C. Craig
Dec 28, 1897
Jul 9, 1962
&
"Sister"
Annie M. Lawrence
Dec 31, 1889

Susie F. Moore
1864-1951

Donald Ramsey
(no dates)

Charley C. Snoddy
1874-1950
&
Ann Eliza Snoddy
1880-1973

J. F. Adcock
1864-1936

Mary E. Adcock
1864-1951

W. M. Jennings
May 30, 1857
Mar 12, 1924

Willie Ann Jennings
Oct 27, 1871
Dec 23, 1935

J. C. Price
Jan 2, 1862
(no date)
&
Mrs. Harriet Elizabeth Price
May 10, 1861
Apr 9, 19(never finished)

William H. Jones
Nov 22, 1844
Mar 23, 1933
&
Mary A. Jones
Feb 1, 1862
Jun 13, 1939

John Green
(no dates)

Elnora C. Campbell
1874-1956
&
T. Ozro Campbell
1875-19(no date)

I. Hoyt Campbell
Apr 9, 1896
Nov 2, 1908

R. W. Barnett
1854-1933
(Gowen-Smith)

Mary Barnett
1855-1924
(Gowen-Smith)

Jarmon M. Barnett
1905-1954
&
Mary E. Barnett
1906-

John T. Favors
1867-1956
&
Adella Favors
1869-1940

B---- & Betty E. Arnold
(no dates) 1946-1946

Patricia Gibson
1944
&
Donnie Ray Gibson
1941

Bennie F. Ray
Oct 24, 1883
Oct 12, 1963
&
Maud L. Ray
Nov. 2, 1887
Jul 29, 1969
married Nov 17, 1907

Walden J. Cooper
1883-19
&
Annie T. Cooper
1889-1959

Mitchell Cooper
1913-1940
&
Louise Cooper
1913-19

Thomas B. Turner   and
1872-1948
[See Addendum]

Donald Durbin
Jun 28, 1945
Jul 25, 1946

John Robert Mooneyham
May 1, 1879
Feb 15, 1957
&
Jossie Emma Mooneyham
Aug 11, 1880
Feb 22, 1945

Ida Landers Turner
1876-19(no date)

Ella Mae Adcock
Mar 16, 1900
May 30, 1971
"Church of God of Prophecy"

"Mack"
Mrs. Frances Welch,
Richmond Rd.

Emma P. Damron
1879-1949
&
J. Myrtle Damron
1875-1947

11 DAVIS-REDD CEMETERY   Map # 10
Located on Comstock Road, about 1 mile East of Bedford.

John Redd*
Dec 30, 1850
Sep 8, 1881
*-Husband of Martha Tennessee
Davis Redd.

No marker:*
Wife of Young Davis
(no dates)

No markers:*
4 children of
W. R. & Mary Smith
(no dates)

No marker:*
Goodrum Davis²
Born Sep 22, 1812
Died Apr 29, 1889

No marker:*
Goodrum Davis, Jr.
Died ca 1890
aged: 12 yrs.

Cemetery almost gone

* Marsh Family Records.

No marker:*
Henrietta Pryor Davis,
Born Jan 8, 1815
Married to Goodrum Davis
Sep 14, 1834
Died Feb 18, 1866

No marker:*
Young Daughter of
Goodrum Davis
(no dates)

No marker:*
Pattie Davis Ellis
Sister to Goodrum Davis
(no dates)

No marker:*   [Jesse]
Members of the William's
Family buried here before
Davis Family.

²Son of Abel & Mary Davis
of Rutherford Co., TN

12 MARSH CEMETERY   Map # 10
Located near Bedford, Tenn.

Michael Marsh
Jul 26, 1800
Aug 31, 1859
&
Elizabeth Marsh
Nov 5, 1800
Sep 22, 1875

George L. Marsh
Sep 24, 1832
Jun 28, 1852

Caladonia Marsh
Feb 13, 1841
Jun 16, 1852

T. J. Robinson
Mar 9, 1824
Aug 16, 1891
&
Elizabeth Robinson
Aug 15, 1839
Apr 6, 1871

Several fieldstones, no
     inscriptions.

[See Addendum]
For Marsh & Jordan family.

13 MADISON CEMETERY   Map # 10
Located on Comstock Road, about 1 mile East of Bedford.

W. Don, son of
Levi & Nancy J. Madison
Sep 7. 1852
married Fannie A. Jennings
Aug 6, 1882
Died Apr 15, 1887
leaving 2 little daughters
Vera Don & Nanie Lee
     & reverse side
"Our Son, My Husband
     Our Papa."

Nancy J.,Wife of
L. Madison, Born
Aug 11, 1829
Died June 22, 1893
aged: 63y, 11m, 11d.

* by Mr Tom Stallings, He
said that Levi Madison's
wife was the daughter of
the Colliers.

Infant of C. M. &
E. Kincaid
Born & Died
Feb 12, 1878

No marker*
Wife of Sam Wade
(no dates) This grave is
just outside the Iron Fence. Ed.

No marker:*
William Collier
(no dates)
     & wife:
Polly B. Garrett Collier
(no dates)
NOTE: These Collier's are
buried in Collier Cemetery,
See page 178.
1 adult grave marked with
fieldstone, no insc.

14 DOUGAN CEMETERY   Map # 10
Located near the Comstock Road and Lewisburg Highway.

Silvania S. Dougan
(fieldstone-dates gone)

---------------(name gone)
Died 1853
(fieldstone)

Other Dougan's graves destroyed when the Highway was built.

15 BRAME CEMETERY   Map # 10
Located about 2 miles East of Bedford, Tenn.

Melchisedec Brame
Who was born in Caroline Co.,   [Other graves here are probably, the widow,
Va. 21st of April 1773,   William Brame & Jemima Light, brother &
removed to Tenn. in 1817,   sister of Melchisedic Brame. Only one marker]
Died on the 16th April 1845
age: 71y, 11m, 25d.

16 COLLIER CEMETERY   Map # 10
Located off Harrison Road, about 2½ miles East of Bedford, Tenn.

No marker:*   No marker:8   No marker:*   No marker:*
William Collier   Polly Garrett Collier   Jane Collier   George Collier
Born 1800 in Va.   Born 1805 in Tenn   Born 1821   Born 1825
Died after 1886   Died (no date)   Died (no date)   Died (no date)

                     No marker:*
                     Richard Collier   * by Mr Tom Stallings.
                     (no dates)

17 KNIGHT CEMETERY   Map # 10
Located on Knight Campground Road, off Lewisburg Highway.

[Rev.William Knight was   William Knight   and wife: Elizabeth Knight
a pioneer Methodist   Died Nov 14, 1839   Died Nov 1st 1839
Minister]   aged: 77 yrs.   aged: 71 yrs.

18 MUSE CEMETERY   Map # 10
Located about 3 miles West of Shelbyville, on Lewisburg Highway.

Rev. John T. Muse   Aaron Muse   and   Jessie Muse   H. L. Williams
Apr 19, 1791   Co M 5th Tenn U.S.Cav. Vol., Mar 11, 1798   Co E 10th Tenn Inf.
Sep 4, 1850   Apr 6, 1844   Feb 4, 1862
                     Killed at Shelbyville, Tenn. age: 63y, 10m, 24d.   Sallie R., wife of
J. R. Curtis   Dec 12, 1864   &   ------- Smith
Oct 27, 1857   aged: 20y, 8m, 5d.   Jessie A. J., son of   Jan 20, 1846
Jan 7, 1869   Aaron & Lottie Muse   Jun 28, 1874
                                                Feb 20, 1864   age: 28y, 5m, 8d.
                     Fieldstones, no inscriptions. Jul 20, 1865
Many unmarked graves.   age: 1y & 5m.

19 THOMPSON CEMETERY   Map # 10
Located at Thompson Shop.

Joseph Thompson   Robert Oliver Shines Thompson Charles Lafayette, son of Alexander Winn, 5th son of
Dec 7, 1809   son of Jos. & Ann E. Thompson Jos. & Ann E. Thompson   Newcome & Lavenia Thompson
Mar 3, 1877   Jun 20, 1849   Born Feb 8, 1847   Apr 14, 1862
                     Dec 27, 1857   Died May 19, 1853   Mar 10, 1863
Ann E. Thompson   age: 8y, 6m, 5d.   age: 6y, 3m, 11d.   age: 10m & 26d.
Sep 13, 1812
Mar 15, 1876   Newcome Thompson, 2nd.   Alice Cary Butler, 3rd dau of James N., son of
                     Nov 12, 1812   Newcome & Lavenia Thompson Newcome & Lavenia Thompson
Lavania M. Thompson Jan 13, 1882   Apr 25, 1855   Jul 22, 1857
Oct 10, 1818   Aug 17, 1873   Dec 28, 1857
Sep 4, 1894   1 Box Type Vault   age: 18y, 3m, 3d.   age: 5m & 6d.
                     (illegible)   [Samuel Thompson brd.here]

                     10 graves in all.

20 OWENS CEMETERY   Map # 10
Located at Thompson Shop.

Berry C. Owens
Died Dec 13, 1861
(no age given)   This is the only grave.

21 SIMS CEMETERY   Map # 10
Located about 3/4 mile West of Sim's Bridge, on Sim's Road.

Jane N. Sims
Mar 18, 1813
Apr 15, 1852

Sarah L., Consort of
William A. Allen
Oct 2, 1832
Jun 18, 1854

About 20-25 graves with
fieldstones, no insc.

22 WHITESELL-WILHOITE CEMETERY   Map # 10
Located ½ mile West of Sim's Bridge, on Sim's Road.

John Whitesell
Nov 30, 1777
Apr 5, 1842

John Whitesell
Aug 2, 1814
Sep 22, 1840

Eveline Whitesell
Died Jun 25, 1832
age: 27 yrs.

M. V. T. Thomas
      &
   Child
Died Mar 2, 1834

This Cemetery is in very bad condition. Ed.

Jacob Wilhoite (Patriot)
Dec 22, 1751
Sep 30, 1821

Milly Wilhoite
Apr 7, 1762
Sep 30, 1822

Huldah B. Wilhoite
Jan 12, 1812
Mar 21, 1844
age: 32y, 2m, 9d.

Louisa J. Wilhoite
Died Oct 29, 1832
age: (broken away)

Infant Son of
John & Huldah B. Wilhoite
(no dates)

William Wilhoite
Mar 1, 1804
Jun 12, 1839
"left wife & 2 sons"

Infant Son of
William & Adaline Wilhoite
Dec 8, 1829
Dec 10, 1829

Emily J. Gambill
Born Jan 29, 1832
age: 7 yrs.

[Jacob Wilhoite native of Orange Co.,
NC, built first mill here ca 1812]

F. S. Gambill
Born --- 1, 1780
Died Nov 27, 1830

Maria Gambill
Died Mar 27, 1832
age: 27 yrs.

Thomas W., son of
Flower & Katharine Swift
Oct 22, 1811
Feb 21, 1840
age: 28y, 4m, 2d.

Kezira K., dau of
J. W. & H. F. Swift
Apr 5, 1813
Nov 1, 1813
age: 6m & 27d.

23 TALLEY CEMETERY (Col)   Map # 10
Located about 1 mile West of Shelbyville, on Fishingford Road.

No markers with inscriptions.

24 ROBINSON CEMETERY   Map # 10
Located about 2 miles West of Shelbyville on Fishingford Road.

Henry S. Thompson
Jul 11, 1880
Dec 19, 1928
      &
Algie Thompson
Mar 30, 1879
Jan 16, 1948

Ruth Thompson, Infant dau
of H. S. & Algie Thompson
Mar 9, 1905
Mar 31, 1905

Margaret Caledonia Purvis
Aug 13, 1895
Feb 27, 1897

James E., son of
T. D. & E. J. Robinson
Sep 13, 1874
Nov 20, 1875

R. J. Robinson
Mar 16, 1836
Mar 31, 1907
      &
Nancy C. Robinson
Mar 11, 1846
Aug 9, 1931

Ethel, dau of Ransom &
Mary E. Stephens
Feb 16, 1893-Feb 21, 1894

John Isaac Winsett
1864-1941

John Ernest Winsett
1901-1929

Ervin Winston Anderson
Aug 10, 1894
Nov 12, 1898

Jennie, dau of
Alex & Margaret Holt Sanders
1874-1881

Thomas D. Robinson
Sep 7, 1843
May 17, 1907
    & wife:
Elizabeth Robinson
Dec 25, 1853
Jul 25, 1936

Littie, Infant dau of
R. J. & N. C. Robinson
May 17, 1880
Jun 30, 1880

Infant Son of
Mildred F. & Joe H. Stephens
1895

John Robinson
Jan 29, 1770
Aug 24, 1839

Rachel Robinson
Dec 2, 1775
Mar 2, 1843

John Robinson
Dec 5, 1805
Jul 4, 1875

Eliza Robinson
1807-Aug 5, 1883

Emily Jane, wife of
Thomas D. Robinson
Mar 14, 1850
Oct 4, 1874
age: 24y, 6m, 20d.

Ruffus E., son of
R. J. & N. C. Robinson
Jun 29, 1884
Feb 25, 1885

J. M. L. Stephens*
(John Marcus Lafayette)
1831-1922

Jane Robinson, 1st wife of
Alex Sanders
Born 1812
married Dec 22, 1829
Died Aug 20, 1848

Eliza J. White, 2nd wife of
Alex Sanders
Oct 24, 1814
married Oct 11, 1849
Died Dec 28, 1862

Joseph Robinson
Nov 22, 1809
Mar 10, 1848
age: 39 yrs.

R. J. Robinson
Jan 1, 1813
Jun 29, 1835

Catherine Parson
Aug 10, 1838
Jul 25, 1920

Barnett, Infant son of
Ransom & Mary E. Stephens
Dec 6, 1891

Margaret F. Robinson, wife
of Jno. M. L. Stephens
Oct 12, 1840-Jan 1, 1891
age: 50y, 2m, 19d.

Thomas Thompson Aug 2, 1824 Aug 21, 1884	Caledonia H. Thompson Aug 10, 1839 Jan 5, 1922	Mary C. Thompson Jul 15, 1864 Sep 21, 1898	Willie J. Winsett, Sr. 1904-1973 (Gowen-Smith)

25 GREER CEMETERY   Map # 10
Located on Pleasant Grove & Greer Road, on Sugar Creek.
(Once known as Sugar Creek Cemetery)
NOTE: This Cemetery is the Oldest Marked Cemetery in Bedford County.

W. C. Delk
1838-1910
&
Mary E. Delk
1841-1901

H. T. Robinson
1826-1899
&
Letsey A. Robinson
1838-1914

C. Harris Hide
Died Dec 30, 1861
(no age given)

Joseph Morton
Dec 12, 1801
Dec 18, 1865
age: 64y & 6 d.
&
Annie Morton
Sep 16, 1802
Apr 1, 1869
age: 66y &6m & 18d.

William H. Robinson
Nov 5, 1856
Apr 18, 1883
age: 26y, 5m, 13d.

Jennie V. Gaither
Jun 26, 1877
Aug 24, 1909

Annie Gaither
Apr 22, 1870
Oct 5, 1902

Thomas L. Gaither, son of
Lee & Era Gaither
Sep 7, 1906
Sep 7, 1906

James McKissick Greer
Jul 14, 1819
Oct 14, 1837

George W. Greer*
Died Mar 1888
age: abt 75 yrs.
Son of Thomas Greer

* Newspaper
[Chancery court records state that William Stewart
brd.here in 1834,wife Peggy probably here also]

John Chapman
Mar 19, 1822
Oct 15, 1900
&
Anne Chapman
Dec 24, 1819
Mar 1, 1894

Caroline D. Hasting
Died Feb 4, 1861
(no age given)

John W. Greer, son of
R. J. Greer
Dec 17, 1818
Aug 17, 1876
&
Nancy M. Greer, dau of
Wm. Woodward & wife of
John W. Greer
Apr 30, 1819
Mar 12, 1883
"An affectionate wife, Step
Mother, Christian Woman."

Sammie C. Freeman, son of
D. F. & B. A. Freeman
Mar 31, 1879
Jul 2, 1880

Thomas Greer
Nov 28, 1770
Oct 16, 1848
"Oldest Man, 77 yrs."
&
Catherine R. Greer
Nov 8, 1781
Dec 16, 1865
"Oldest Woman, 84yrs & 28 da."

Benjamine F. Greer
Jun 25, 1817
Apr 14, 1880
age: 62y, 9m, 19d.

R. Wade
Died Sep 13, 1861

E. G.
(fieldstone, no insc.)

Thomas A., son of
G. W. & A. J. Greer
Mar 22, 1848
Aug 15, 1849

Louis V. Greer, son of
G. W. & A.J. Greer
May 21, 1851
Sep 21, 1852

George W. Greer
Dec 6, 1852
Dec 26, 1854

Joseph H. Greer, son of
G. W. & A. J. Greer
Dec 11, 1849
Jan 6, 1851

D. D. Delk
Died Feb 15, 1862
(no age given)

Thomas Hastings
Dec 15, 1822
Jan 30, 1871

A. J. Greer
Aug 2, 1824
Aug 2, 1884
&
Effie A. Greer
Dec 3, 1842
Jun 24, 1867
"An affectionate daughter,
Sister, Wife & Mother"erected
by her Husband, A. J. Greer.

Mrs. Rachel Greer,
wife of Dr. L. V. Greer
Died Aug 1, 1848
age: 21 yrs.

Eglantine C. Greer
Nov 22, 1809
Apr 21, 1816

Many unmarked graves.

[Old Sugar creek Bpt.church
located near this grave yard]

T. A. Greer
(Child, footstone)

W. S. Lacy
Co A.
4th Tenn Mtd Inf

B. H. Greer, son of
J. W. Greer
Feb 10, 1845
Sep 6, 1846

D. D. (footstone)

Willie B. Robinson
Aug 16, 1869
Jul 24, 1891
&
Jennie A. Robinson
Jan 31, 1872
Oct 22, 1891

H. P. Greer
(Harrison P.)
Dec 30, 1853
Feb 6, 1878
age: 24y, 1m, 7d.

A. J. Greer, son of
A. J. & Effie A. Greer
Mar 3, 1865
Dec 1, 1875

Adeline M. Greer, wife of
John A. Greer
Died Aug 26, 1843
(no age given)
&
Infant Daughter Mary, dau
of J. A. & A. M. Greer
abt 27 yrs (no dates)

Elizabeth Greer
Dec 6, 1803
Sep 6, 1805
&
Mary B. Greer
Jan 31, 1801
Apr 29, 1816

Many fieldstones, no
inscriptions.

26 WORD CEMETERY   Map # 10
Located about 1 mile North of Pleasant Grove, Tenn.

Sarah L., wife of
J. J. Adams
Aug 17, 1846
Aug 3, 1887

William B. Nance
Oct 22, 1829
Mar 26, 1874

M. J. McLure
Died Apr 17, 1834
(no age given)

A. R. McLure
Died Sep 25, 1835
(no age given-child)

Andrew Morrison   and
Apr 14, 1782
Feb 23, 1833
&
Thomas A. Morrison
Born 1816
Died 1824
Son of Andrew Morrison

Andrew Morrison *
Died Mar.6, 1833
age, 24 [no marker]

* National Banner

Wesley Sutton
Sep 8, 1799
May 1, 1882

Jane, wife of
Wesley Sutton
Dec 11, 1810
Nov 15, 1895

Lemuel Sutton
Apr 23, 1835
Nov 20, 1895

Alex N. Robinson, Infant Son
Born 1834
Died 1834

Harriet M. Morrison   and
Born 1808
Died 1825
Dau of Andrew Morrison

William Word
Jan 27, 1804
Nov 28, 1873

"Our Father"
Edmond Word, Born in Halifax
Co., Va. Oct 1801, Died Jan 9,
1892. age: 90y, 3m, 6d.

Amanda A. Word, wife of
J. H. Word
Nov 11, 1842
Oct 16, 1882

Jas. T., son of
J. H. & A. J. Word
Dec 29, 1866
Nov 22, 1870
age: 3y, 10m, 23d.

H. Ogilvie
Died 1830
(no age given)

Emily A. Morrison   and
Born 1818
Died 1836
Dau of Andrew Morrison

S. W. Edmondson, wife of
William Word
Born Mar 14, 1809
married Feb 26, 1826
Died Jan 12, 1900

Jesse Brown
May 11, 1828
May 22, 1843

Mary J. Phillips
May 7, 1838
Oct 15, 1873

Annie E. Wallace, wife of
William Phillips
Dec 1, 1847-Aug 4, 1882

Mary C., wife of T. C. Wood
& dau of M. W. & Louisa
Lucas
Feb 11, 1841-Jan 31, 1891

James H. Morrison
Born 1814
Died 1823
Son of Andrew Morrison

Infant Son of
Thomas C. & M. C. Word
Born & Died
Oct 9, 1876

Asenath Word dau. of Sampson
& Martha Smith, born N.C. Feb.
24, 1808, mrd. Edmond Word
1826, d.May 5, 1877.

27 ADAMS CEMETERY   Map # 10
Located about 1 mile West of Pleasant Grove, Tenn.

Nancy E. Adams
Feb 27, 1832
Mar 15, 1849

No marker:*
Edwin Wesley Adams
Born abt 1815
Died abt 1894

Mary Jane Adams
Dec 8, 1833
Mar 28, 1849

No marker:*
Winnie Mariah McTeer Adams
wife of Edwin Wesley Adams
Born abt 1824
Died after 1880

Talitha C. Adams
May 28, 1836
Jul 28, 1860

Several unmarked graves.

* by Mrs Carlyle Langley, Sr.

"Patriot"
Stephen P. Gatlin
Vol in Co I 123
Illinois
Reg. Killed in Battle of
Farmington, Tenn.
Oct 7, 1863
age: 45y & 6m.

28 DYER CEMETERY-BIG SPRING CEMETERY   Map # 10
Located near Pleasant Grove, Tenn.

Jesse H. Evans
Apr 8, 1862
May 10, 1897
age: 35y, 1m, 2d.

Effie J. Evans
Dec 21, 1868
Oct 6, 1893
age: 24y, 9m, 15d.

Alexander Greer Evans
Aug 20, 1864
May 31, 1891
age: 26y, 9m, 11d.

Bettie Evans Wright
Apr 22, 1857
Jan 1, 1895
age: 37y, 8m, 9d.

Viola Tinney
(large stone face down)

Kittie Evans Raby
Jan 2, 1860
May 21, 1930

Jesse Evans
Sep 14, 1821
Jun 14, 1890
age: 68y & 9m.
&
Sallie H. Evans
Nov 14, 1840
Oct 22, 1895
age: 54y, 11m, 8d.

"Erected by Members of
Cottage Grove Cumberland
Presbyterian Church, In
Memory of Our Beloved Pastor."
Rev. David Foster Jackson
Sep 3, 1830
Jun 15, 1866

John W. Wiggins
Dec 26, 1812
Jul 26, 1890
age: 77y & 7m.
& wife:
Mary S. Wiggins
Dec 25, 1811
Sep 15, 1885
age: 67y, 3m, 10d.

William O. Forbes
Jun 12, 1823
Oct 16, 1851
age: 31y, 4m, 4d.

N. C. Scales
Dec 7, 1825
Apr 14, 1875
age: 49y, 1m, 23d.

Harbert Wiggins
Jan 26, 1824
Apr 17, 1903

Matilda Wiggins, wife of
Harbert Wiggins & dau of
Randolph & Nancy Newsom
Feb 15, 1834
Apr 25, 1899

Elizabeth A., Consort of
Harbert W.Wiggins & dau of
Jeremiah & Edy Forbes
Aug 9, 1834
Sep 21, 1854
age: 20y, 1m, 12d.

Elizabeth L., dau of
Harbert & Matilda Wiggins
Jan 19, 1858
Jul 3, 1859

Harrel Wiggins
Born in Granville Co., N.C.
Apr 25, 1788
Died May 19, 1851
age: 63y & 24d.

Sarah Wiggins, wife of
Harrel Wiggins
Born in Granville Co., N.C.
Apr 3, 1789
Died Jan 11, 1870
age: 80 yrs, 9mo, 11da.

Eliza J. Word, dau of
J. W. & P. S. Wiggins
Born Apr 10, 1846
married to T. G. Word
Jan 11, 1870
Died Oct 1, 1873

Infant son of
John W. & Mary S. Wiggins
Died Oct 1838
age: 3 days

Hundley Wiggins
Deceased Sept 26, 1839
aged: 20 yrs.

Lizzie Bond, wife of
R. L. Damron
Jan 11, 1866
Jul 18, 1895

Minnie Coats Damron
1870-1909

John Henry Damron
age: 42 days
(no dates)

Minnie E. Damron
age: 14 months
(no dates)

Mary, dau of
R. L. & L. B. Damron
Born Jul 17, 1895
age: 1 month

Elizabeth Neely
Apr 11, 1803
Apr 12, 1857

William W. Neely
Oct 30, 1831
Feb 1, 1855

Jane Nix
Died Jun 7, 1841
age: 20 yrs.

B. B.
(Adult-no dates)

Henry Brim
Dec 1868
Mar 9, 1926

Ida Brim
Jan 1878
1938

Nancy C. Russell
Apr 24, 1837
Sep 27, 1860

James G. Russell
Sep 16, 1833
Feb 21, 1864
age: 31 yrs.

John William Harrel, son of
John W. & Mary S. Wiggins
Jun 14, 1851
Jul 14, 1855
age: 4y & 1m

Sarah A., dau of
J. W. & M. S. Wiggins
Feb 23, 1857
Sep 23, 1857
age: 7 months

Thomas J. Gabert
He was born Feb 26, 1814
& Died Mar 11, 1849
age: 34y & 15d.

1 child grave near the
Galbert (illegible)

Mary Catharine, Consort of
A. W. Bonds
Mar 7, 1834
Aug 5, 1869
age: 35y, 5m, 28d.

Infant dau of
A. W. & M. C. Bonds
Jul 29, 1869
Jul 30, 1869

Samuel Neely
Died Sep 3, 1894
age: 88y, 9m, 8d.

Mary A. Neely
Aug 17, 1821
Oct 12, 1906

Matthew C. Neely
Apr 22, 1830
Feb 15, 1858

Elizabeth Jane Neely
1842-1927

Nancy B. Neely
May 12, 1811
Jul 1, 1833
age: 22y, 1m, 18d.

Lewis Allen
Died Jan 9, 1814
age: 46 yrs.

William Bird
(no dates)

Samuel Bird
Apr 12, 1830
Mar 11, 1877

Mary H. Bird
Oct 31, 1834
Jun 15, 1890

Noah Scales
Apr 6, 1801
in Rockingham Co., N.C.
Died Jun 1st 1852

Elizabeth A. Scales
Jan 10, 1811
Feb 19, 1852

Joab Scales
May 18, 1828
Jan 24, 1851
age: 22y, 9m, 6d.

Infant dau of
Noah & Elizabeth Scales
Born Nov 1831

Violette J. Scales
Nov 4, 1816
Sep 6, 1847

Noah C. Scales
Feb 18, 1850
Nov 26, 1854
age: 4y, 9m, 8d.

Eull D. Scales
Oct 4, 1851
Jun 2, 1874

Little Winston, son of
J. H. C. & Minerva Scales
Dec 10, 1872
Oct 25, 1882

2 graves unmarked

Sallie A. Scales, dau of
J. H. C. & Minerva Scales
Jul 22, 1882
Apr 23, 1884

Caldonia A. Scales, Consort
of J. H. Scales
Oct 12, 1831
Jan 4, 1851

John B. Neely
Nov 24, 1842
Jan 21, 1855

Fines E. Neely
Apr 24, 1845
Sep 16, 1851

Mary Louisa Evans
Born Jan 27, 1859
age: 20 months & 25 days

Wynn D. Williams
(no dates)

Mary B. Williams
(no dates)

4 Rock type vaults, Infants,
beside the Williams graves.

NOTE: There are about 100
graves with fieldstones, no
inscriptions, in the most
eastern section of Cemetery.
Ed.

S. H. Neeley
Jul 28, 1842
Mar 24, 1904
&
Mary E. Neeley Wallace
Mar 7, 1845
Dec 25, 1920
&
R. D. Neeley
Nov 11, 1837
Mar 31, 1914
&
Mary E. Neeley
Feb 17, 1849
Feb 23, 1913
&
Lula E., dau of
R. D. & Mary E. Neeley
Sep 8, 1880
Sep 23, 1900
&
William Sammie, son of
R. D. & M. E. Neeley
Jun 1, 1889
Aug 13, 1889

Cintha Hasting, wife of
Joseph H. Hasting
Oct 17, 1814
Nov 27, 1849

Samuel A. Hasting, son of
Joseph & Cintha Hasting
Dec 25, 1848
Sep 10, 1849

Mary R. Thompson
May 12, 1811
Jul --, 1833
age: 22 yrs.

James C. Snell
Dec 8, 1816
Apr 7, 1887
age: 70y, 3m, 29d.
& Wife:
Sarah H. Snell
Oct 11, 1825
Jul 22, 1899

Mary C. Smith
Jan 2, 1846
Aug 8, 1852

Thomas Brown
May 30, 1783
Oct 12, 1833
& wife:
Mary Brown
Jan 21, 1801
Jul 21, 1853

Martha Williams
1849
(Rock Log type vault)

Larry Williams
Nov 8, 1855
Mar 19, 1856
(Rock Log type vault)

Andrew J. M. Williams
Mar 16, 1843
Aug 10, 1854
(Rock Log type vault)

David Allen
Apr 24, 1854
Mar 20, 1893
age: 38y, 10m, 27d

Samuel G. Dyer
Mar 30, 1810
Nov 2, 1879
age: 69y, 7m, 2d.

Esther G. Dyer
Feb 10, 1803
Aug 27, 1882

Ernest Garland, son of
J. H. & B. A. Dyer
Apr 22, 1873
Jun 4, 1880

Many unmarked graves.

Elijah Williams, son of
J. T. & S. Cunningham
Jun 12, 1876
Mar 26, 1895

Clarence Verner, son of
J. T. & S. Cunningham
Oct 2, 1893
Jul 14, 1897

Roenah Dyer
Feb 10, 1803
Aug 27, 1882

Harry Dyer, son of
J. H. & B. A. Dyer
Apr 6, 1873
Apr 26, 1873

Many fieldstones, no inscriptions.

A. M. R.
(fieldstone)

R. J. R.
(fieldstone)

W. H. Dyer
May 4, 1817
Oct 1, 1880

Harriet Dyer
Jan 2, 1819
Aug 4, 1856

Eugenia A. Dyer, dau of
W. H. & H. Dyer
Oct 7, 1853
Jan 9, 1873

James Dyer
May 8, 1779
Mar 4, 1817
age: 37y, 9m, 26d.
&
Martha Dyer
Nov 11, 1780
Nov 5, 1852
age: 71y, 11m, 24d.

Daniel D. Dyer, son of
W. H. & H. Dyer
Mar 29, 1849
Feb 17, 1880
age: 30y, 10m, 18d.

Infant Son of
J. W. & E. Woodward
Born & Died Aug 15, 1877

29 GABBERT CEMETERY   Map # 10
Located on Sandusky Road, near Pleasant Grove.

William Gabbert
Nov 10, 1794
Jan 26, 1852
age: 58y, 2m, 16d.

Matilda, wife of
William Gabbert
Aug 9, 1809
Aug 5, 1849
age: 40y, 11m, 27d.

William Taylor, son of
James & Elizabeth Carlilse
(Carlisle)
Dec 10, 1851
Jan 25, 1852

3 or 4 other unmarked
graves.

30 BARRETT-CARLISLE CEMETERY   Map # 10
Located on Robinson Road, East of Pleasant Grove.

John Barrett
1796-Nov 16, 1840
age: 46 yrs.

Barrett Child
Died Jul 5, 1841

Frances Barrett
Jan 18, 1796
Oct 9, 1846
age: 50y, 8m, 21d.

Carlisle Double marker
(deep in ground)(James & Elizabeth)
one date: Died Aug 17, 1885
one date: Died Oct 2, 1881
marker by: F. J. Scholz
Evansville, Ind.

William Carliles
Jun 8, 1785
Feb 27, 1867
aged: 81y, 8m, 19d.

7 graves in Cemetery.

Mary Carliles
Nov 27, 1790
May 16, 1869
aged: 78y, 5m, 19d.

31 EVANS CEMETERY   Map # 10
Located about 1½ miles Northeast of Moores Chapel, on Sandusky Road.

Nathan Evans
Died Feb 28, 1862
age: 74 yrs.

Elizabeth P. Evans
Nov 19, 1808
Apr 10, 1880

1 large marker down, footstone
has: R.M.E. & N.C.E.
(no dates)

2 Old Sand Stones (illegible)

Virgie Lou, dau of
J. H. & R. M. Evans
May 8, 1878
Apr 10, 1879

Archie Greer, son of
J. H. & R. M. Evans
Nov 9, 1875
Jan 3, 1885

32 MOORE CHAPEL CEMETERY   Map # 10
Located on Blue Stocking Hollow Road.

Walter H. Evans
1875-1951
(Thompson)

---------, wife of
W. H. Evans
(stone damaged, stone has
been removed when updated, in
1975)

William N. Bradshaw
1849-1929
&
Julia W. Bradshaw
1856-1949

Willie Logan
Dec 18, 1892
Dec 25, 1892

Robert S. Taylor
May 3, 1849
Jan 28, 1916
&
Permelia H., wife of
R. S. Taylor
Jan 8, 1862
Feb 18, 1909

Clay L. Kellogg
1893-1950

Baby Mary Mullins
1921-1923

Annie Mullins
1921-1921

J. H. Logan
Apr 30, 1855
May 26, 1914
&
Elizabeth Logan
Dec 12, 1867
Jul 4, 1941

Evelyn E. Logan
Sep 14, 1911
Jun 22, 1912

Lizzie Ruth Logan
Dec 20, 1895
Oct 31, 1907

Nellie D. Logan
Apr 4, 1900
(in ground, deep)

Annie B. Logan
Oct 11, 1897
Nov 21, 1900

L. A. Farrar
1838-1912

Tennie V. Farrar
1843-1912

I. G. Davidson
1846-1874

Susan J. Davidson
1817-1891

Bessie Davidson
1911-1911

Carlton Davidson
1912-1914

W. E., son of
C. T. & N. L. Snell
Jan 15, 1890
Oct 29, 1895

Nannie Lee Snell, wife of
C. T. Snell
Jun 16, 1871
Dec 30, 1902

"Father"
George E. Adams
Jan 7, 1857
Sep 17, 1942
&
"Mother"
Nannie Davis Adams
Sep 27, 1862
Aug 19, 1931

Alton Adams
1898-1899

Rosa Adams
Apr 2, 1860
Aug 19, 1917

J. J. Adams
Jun 29, 1846
Feb 8, 1923

Fred A. Mullins
Oct 22, 1890

&
Mary L. Mullins
May 10, 1890
Mar 25, 1955

Matte A. Robinson, wife of
J. H. Logan
May 27, 1863
Apr 27, 1904

W. W. Evans
Feb 7, 1828
Dec 27, 1896
&
Malissa A., wife of
W. W. Evans
Oct 4, 1836
Aug 20, 1893

Walter L. Evans
Dec 24, 1858
Sep 6, 1883
aged: 24y, 8m, 12d.

Nathan A. Evans
Mar 7, 1857
Apr 29, 1859
aged: 2y, 1m, 22d.

William D. Davidson
Nov 16, 1873
Nov 24, 1950
&
Annie R. Davidson
Jan 12, 1874
Jul 18, 1931

N. L. Dryden
1839-1916
&
Sarah J. Dryden
1844-1916

Daniel D., son of
N. L. & S. J. Dryden
Oct 2, 1879
Mar 30, 1884

Lewis N. Dryden
1885-1914

Hannah E., wife of
James C. Dryden
Jan --, 1826
May 6, 1849

Allie Berry Gaither
1872-1951
(Gowen)

Carrie Adams, wife of
Sam Pickle
Aug 19, 1888
Jan 1, 1923

George Robert, son of
Carrie & Keith Vaughn
1942

"Father"
W. W. Winford
Oct 12, 1836
Jul 28, 1910
&
"Mother"
Mary Frances Anderson Winford
Jun 26, 1837
Feb 28, 1910

C. C. Winford
Apr 3, 1868
Jul 24, 1922
&
Mrs. E. A. Winford
Mar 20, 1871
Mar 29, 1914

Virginia Lee Winford
Apr 30, 1913
Oct 1, 1914

Bess Winford
1898-1944

Charles C. Winford, II
Tennessee
S2 U.S.N.R., W.W. II
Aug 25, 1909
Nov 7, 1960

Lewis Bryant Hale, Infant son
of J. D. & Thelma Hale
1932

Maggie A., wife of
J. M. Bradshaw
Mar 7, 1847
Jul 8, 1870

Airy I. White
Sep 22, 1854
Apr 27, 1863

J. L. White
Dec 11, 1865
Feb 22, 1887

Mary White, wife of
T. A. White
Mar 15, 1825
Jul 12, 1853(second marker)

Thomas Dryden
Nov 8, 1796
Sep 15, 1868

Mary H., wife of
Thomas Dryden
Sep 21, 1806
Jul 6, 1878

Isabelle M., dau of
T. & M. H. Dryden
Nov 6, 1844
Aug 4, 1848

Eleanor Dryden
Jul 23, 1849
Jul 6, 1940

Coleman B. "Joe" Williams
Jan 19, 1875
Jun 23, 1913
&
Minnie Pearson Williams
Oct 11, 1874
Dec 30, 1965

Henry C. Elleott
Apr 1, 1843
Jan 28, 1846

Edmun C. White, son of
Joseph & Ruth White
Oct 15, 1853
Sep 19, 185-

Sarah J. White
Mar 25, 1838
Sep 23, 1862
age: 24y, 5m, 28d.

Beulah F. Barrett
Nov 18, 1871
Jul 8, 1908
"She hath done what she
could."

Andrew Kelso White
Jul 12, 1904
Apr 3, 1910

Louise Pitts
1858-1928

Airy, wife of
T. A. White
Mar 15, 1825
Jul 12, 1853
&
T. A. White
May 15, 1819
Jul 22, 1899
& .
Margaret, wife of
T. A. White
Dec 19, 1830
Jul 8, 1916

Thomas A. White, Jr.
Jan 31, 1887
Jul 24, 1889
age: 2y & 6m

S. S. White
Sep 17, 1824
Dec 15, 1863

Jane B. White
Nov 29, 1828
Jul 19, 1858

Mrs. Ruth White
Dec 6, 1818
Jun 6, 1890
aged: 71y & 6m.

Ethel D. Gambill
1881-1931

Infant dau of
George & Eliz. Gambill
1938

James A. Gambill
Tennessee
Pvt Co K 5 Regt Inf
Spanish American War
Apr 8, 1879
Jan 27, 1951

John W. Bledsoe
Feb 14, 1880
Oct 21, 1928
&
Sallie Ann Bledsoe
Feb 14, 1892
Nov 5, 1922

J. C. Bledsoe
Born -----
Died May 7, 1874
&
E. J. Delk, wife of
J. C. Bledsoe
Nov 13, 1836
Aug 29, 1870

Jacob Bledsoe, Jr.* (SOR)
Mar 28, 1762
Died -------(illegible)
(copied in 1968, now gone,
        in 1976) Ed.

*Death date of Jacob Bledsoe
listed as 1848-
     by Tom Muse.

Aaron Bledsoe
Feb 6, 1787
Jul 27, 1867

Elizabeth, wife of
Aaron Bledsoe
Nov 15, 1791
Mar 29, 1865

Willie Laurence Cummings
Feb 23, 1884
Jan 26, 1893
&
Vera Cummings
Dec 3, 1891
Nov 2, 1892
&
Lemuel H., son of
H. A. & M. E. Cummings
Oct 3, 1889
Oct 3, 1890

"Father"
George Newton Davidson
Jan 11, 1836
Jul 5, 1917
&
"Mother"
Nannie Jane Davidson
Jul 6, 1850
Jul 16, 1915

K. T. Bledsoe
Aug 19, 1870
Sep 14, 1870

M. A., wife of J. A. Bledsoe
Apr 10, 1867
Apr 21, 1890

J. H. Moore
Mar 21, 1828
May 22, 1893
&
Frances Moore
Died Oct 20, 1893
age: 60 yrs.

Sarah, wife of
Anthony Bledsoe
Jan 22, 1782
Aug 20, 1861
age: 79y, 6m, 28d.
"F.J.Scholz,Evansville, Ind."

T. L. Bledsoe
Jan 2, 1878
Feb 7, 1878

H. Bledsoe
Jul 1, 1869
Sep 17, 1883

Beulah Mae Adcock
Jan 19, 1916
Oct 1, 1922

Lee Brown
1872-1931
(McFarlin-Thompson)

Della Brown
1873-1958
(McFarlin-Thompson)

Many unmarked graves

Joseph D. Adams
Mar 14, 1838
Mar 23, 1900
&
Mary Elizabeth White
Born Sep 18, 1843
married to J.D.Adams
Jan 26, 1864
Died Nov 6, 1902

Thomas F. Dryden
1883-1937
&
Emma May Dryden
1885-1971

Thomas A. Bradshaw
Sep 18, 1840
Mar 18, 1915

Martha D. Bradshaw
Jun 11, 1840
Oct 22, 1872

Cassie Bradshaw
Nov 17, 1871
Oct 17, 1959

Hillsman Bledsoe
Jun 14, 1818
Nov 23, 1895
&
M. H.(Martha H) Bledsoe
Oct 30, 1820
(no date)(Nov 1907)

Susan F., dau of
H. & M. H. Bledsoe
Oct 14, 1856
May 12, 1872

Lucindy E., wife of
W. R. Bledsoe
Oct 31, 1859
Jul 9, 1883

Josie Patton
Born Feb 11, 18--
Died Dec 10, 188-
(fieldstone)

[NOTE from Charles Hummel: Unmarked
graves inside rockwall are: Nathaniel
White & wife Polly, children Nancy,
Margaret, and Jane White, Lewellyn
and little daughter Lena, also
Sherman White, sister of Nathaniel]

John Whitfield Dryden
1870-1934

Benjamin Adams
Jan 26, 1808
Dec 24, 1881
age: 73y, 10m, 28d.

Martha S., wife of
Benjamin Adams
Oct 27, 1811
Aug 6, 1889
"Bless the Lord O my Soul,
Which were the last words
she Spake."

Margaret Dryden Willis
Dec 27, 1906
Mar 30, 1971

Zack S. Morton
1861-1907
&
Martha A. Morton
1866-1950

Finis E. Farrar
1868-1948

Belle B. Farrar
1867-1930

Doyle C. Farrar
1897-1916

James W., son of
H. & M. H. Bledsoe
May 14, 1846
Oct 2, 1868

John W., son of
H. & M. H. Bledsoe
Aug 22, 1843
Nov 15, 1853
age: 10y, 2m, 24d.

33 BRADSHAW CEMETERY   Map # 10
Located about ½ mile South of Moore Chapel, off Blue Stocking Hollow Road.

[This was site of the old Blue-
stocking or New Providence Presbyterian Church. Old Church Records
show a beginning date of 1811]

Bell Bradshaw
Sep 22, 1851
Jan 18, 1861

R. E. Bradshaw
Jul 17, 1806
Nov 24, 1850

5 other graves, with
fieldstones, no insc.

34 SHEARIN CEMETERY   Map # 10
Located 2 miles Southwest of Pleasant Grove.

Edmund C. Shearin
Apr 4, 1851
Jan 26, 1883

35 GANT CEMETERY   Map # 10
Located about 1 mile South of Blue Stocking Hollow Road,
Off Petersburg Highway.

James Gant, Sr.
Born Dec 31, 1783
Murdered July 27, 185-(gone)
&
Elizabeth Gant
Born Oct 20, 1787
Died Jun 4, 1869

A. J. Gant
Mar 27, 1830
Feb 10, 1863

Several unmarked graves.

John Gant
Jul 17, 1786
Aug 25, 1836
&
Sarah Gant
Dec 28, 1796
Jul 20, 1857

Thomas Shearin
Jan 17, 1848
Sep 19, 1852

John A. Gant
Oct 4, 1809
Feb 11, 1860

Malinda Caroline, wife of
James Carlisle, & dau of
James & Elizabeth Gant
Mar 25, 1824
Sep 20, 1849 (Box Type Vault)

James M. Shearin
Jan 18, 1864
Nov 5, 1869
age: 5y, 9m, 18d.

Mathew Shearin
Dec 22, 1810
Jan 23, 1886

Mary L. Shearin
Apr 13, 1869
Jul 5, 1873
age: 4y, 2m, 22d.

Elizabeth, wife of
M. Shearin & dau of
J. & E. Gant
Nov 27, 1818
Jan 30, 1873

36 INGLE CEMETERY   Map # 10
Located about 1 mile East of Richmond, Tenn.

B. B. Ingle, dau of
E. L. & S. J. Ingle
Apr 5, 1871
Sep 13, 1872

[Ingle often spelled England]

5 graves with fieldstones, no inscriptions.

37 RICHMOND CEMETERY   Map # 10
Located at Richmond, Tennessee

Mrs. W. L. Davis
1885-1939
(R.H.Beasley)

W. L. Davis
Aug 1, 1842
Jun 13, 1918
&
S. M. Davis
Sep 13, 1851
(no date)

Fannie L. Davis
1889-1936

James Roland Davis
1867-1929
&
Virginia Ingle Davis
1867-1917

Mary J., wife of
H. H. Holt
Aug 12, 1839
Dec 22, 1863
age: 24y, 4m, 10d.

Infant of
John R. & Mary A. Smith
Born & Died
Jun 5, 1857

Infant of
John R. & Mary A. Smith
Born Mar 3, 1852

Infant dau of
William R. & Narcissa A.Smith
Nov 1, 1853
Apr 14, 1855 age: 13 months
after 7 O'clock P.M.

W. J. Freeman
Dec 23, 1839
Nov 16, 1922

Elizabeth Freeman
Died Oct 20, 1911
(no age given)

Hattie Freeman
1880-1936

Larena, dau of
W. J. & E. J. Freeman
Aug 7, 1883
Feb 9, 1907

W. R., son of
J. G. & M. H. Smith
Jun 11, 1869
May 1, 1873

J. R. Smith
Jul 27, 1824
Aug 30, 1866
age: 42y, 1m, 3d.

Gustavous Ann, dau of
John R. & Mary A. Smith
Mar 23, 1854
Mar 3, 1864

Infant of
John R. & Mary A. Smith
Born Jul 31, 1851

Narcissa Adaline, wife of
William R. Smith
Sep 12, 1822
Sep 1, 1857

Robert L. Hutchinson
Sep 20, 1912
Oct 13, 1922

Moses Darnell
Oct 19, 1868
Sep 27, 1928

Robert M., son of
M. & D. Darnell
Sep 20, 1895
Aug 10, 1901

Sarah E., wife of
G. R. Raney
Dec 20, 1842
Jan 27, 1871

Sarah, wife of
J. S. Brown
Sep 16, 1808
Feb 4, 1872
age: 63y, 1m, 18d.

Nancy Jane, dau of
John B. & Sarah Brown
Mar 18, 1837
Jul 30, 1864
age: 27y, 4m, 12d.

John R., son of
John S. & Sarah Brown
Aug 24, 1844
Jul 13, 1846
age: 2y, 9m, 11d.

F. R. Freeman
Nov 3, 1844
Apr 4, 1867
age: 22y, 5m, 1d.

James E. Hutchinson
1872-1913
&
Loretta K. Hutchinson
1877-1913

Lizzie King
1860-1934

Corp'l W. C. Reavis
Co A
4th Tenn Mt'd Inf
Jul 18, 1840
Nov 9, 1898

Nancy Reavis, wife of
Wm. C. Reavis
Nov 24, 1839
Dec 24, 1877

Johnson Reavis
Jul 21, 1810
Feb 20, 1877
age: 66y, 5m, 29d.

Jillana, wife of
Johnson Reavis
Sep 2, 1817
May 2, 1878

Rezin Smith
Mar 5, 1781
Jan 5, 1851

Sarah, wife of
Rezin Smith
Nov 8, 1800
Feb 8, 1873
age: 72y, 3m, 2d.

Joseph Dunham
Aug 28, 1812
Sep 21, 1832
age: 20 yrs.

Milla Dunham
Oct 27, 1811
Jun 21, 1840
age: 29 yrs.

Mary Dunham
Died 1840
age: 66 yrs.

Galaca, wife of
W. W. Gant
Nov 23, 1833
Oct 12, 1871

Edna E., dau of
W. W. & Galaca Gant
May 14, 1867
Sep 7, 1894

John Gant
Feb 9, 1829
Aug 9, 1853

John P. Gant
Jun 20, 1858
Sep 15, 1868

Mary Gant
Feb 19, 1869
Jun 10, 1869

Vance J. Wallace
Jul 8, 1865
Jan 20, 1923

Mattie M. Wallace
Sep 2, 1866
Nov 15, 1907

Lean E., dau of
John S. & Sarah Brown
Jul 31, 1834
Aug 26, 1844
age: 10y, 9m, 5d.

J. C. Gilbert
Mar 8, 1839
Jan 18, 1863

Rezin B. Roberts
Mar 18, 1837
Jan 9, 1870

Sarah Roberts
1832-1904

Peter Roberts
Nov 29, 1800
Dec 4, 1859

Lethe, wife of
Peter Roberts
Jan 21, 1808
Dec 20, 1873

Rachel, dau of
Peter & Lethe Roberts
Oct 23, 1844
Jan 26, 1863

Lethe, dau of
Peter & Lethe Roberts
Dec 1, 1853
Aug 7, 1853

I. S. Davidson
Apr 25, 1816
May 7, 1889
age: 73y, & 12d.
&
Martha R. Davidson
Jun 4, 1829
Apr 9, 1890
age: 60y, 10m, 5d.

P. Z. Roberts
Dec 15, 1864
Jan 1, 1887
age: 22y & 16d.

Ruth, dau of
Zaccheaus & Sarah Roberts
Apr 19, 1859
Apr 27, 1859

Joannah, dau of
Zaccheaus & Sarah Roberts
Feb 17, 1855
Oct 8, 1863

Infant dau of
Zaccheaus & Sarah Roberts
Oct 29, 1857
Nov 5, 1857

Mary R., dau of
Peter & Lethe Roberts
Jan 3, 1833
Mar 23, 1853

Isom, son of
Peter & Lethe Roberts
Sep 23, 1841
Aug 11, 1842

W. H. Redd
1848-1907
&
Josephine Redd
1847-(no date)

Martha Shaddia
1818-1905

Infant dau of
J. P. & S. A. Carlisle
Mar 14, 1884
Mar 18, 1884

[Old John Robert's Place]

John Morton
Nov 16, 1806
May 23, 1879
age: 72y, 6m, 7d.

Susanna, wife of
John Morton
Jun 23, 1807
Sep 30, 1891

R. A. Morton
Nov 2, 1849
Apr 28, 1926
&
F. A. B. Morton
May 1, 1850
Apr 6, 1920

Jessie Morton
Nov 5, 1873
Aug 10, 1874
&
Infant Son of
R. A. & F. A. B. Morton
Born & Died
Mar 21, 1886

William Morton
May 27, 1829
Jul 26, 1911

Sarah Morton
Apr 21, 1834
May 5, 1901

John C. Morton
May 13, 1851
Feb 19, 1855

W. C., son of
Z. S. & M. A. Morton
Mar 10, 1884
Jul 13, 1884

SECTION ACROSS THE ROAD, OF RICHMOND CEMETERY:

Robert L. Moore
Jul 23, 1884
Nov 25, 1952

Eula Nelms Moore
Aug 9, 1890
Feb 1, 1973

Lois A. Moore
Feb 17, 1911

Edward C. Moore
Apr 29, 1841
Jul 16, 1925
&
Mary H. Moore
Nov 16, 1849
Mar 3, 1926

J. W. Steele
Jul 25, 1934
Aug 28, 1935

Willie D. Crawford
1883-1931

John W. Nelms
1861-1941
&
Mary F. Nelms
1864-1950

Lillian Nelms Smith
1888-1933

John E. Moore
1875-1953
(Howell-Thompson)

Mrs. Bonnie Moore
1903-1950
(TM)

James C. Curtis
1882-1944

Ammie Curtis Cowers
1873-1952
(Thompson)

R. Curtiss Dysart   and
1887-1969

James Franklin Davis
Dec 11, 1871
Jun 2, 1928
&
Mary Ellen Davis
Mar 23, 1873
(no date)

Louis N. Evans
Feb 14, 1881
Jan 22, 1938
&
Lillian C. Evans
Feb 20, 1889
Jul 8, 1961

Noah Darnell
Oct 19, 1861
Feb 2, 1937
&
Lizzie Darnell
Jun 16, 1862
Sep 12, 1921

Gertrude Redd Dysart
1880-1931

Rebeccah D. Wallace
Jun 27, 1829
Sep 22, 1907

Mamie T. Wallace
Oct 3, 1877
Jan 10, 1912

Claude Brince Wallace
1870-1943

Elizabeth Kimmons
Dec 29, 1909
Dec 18, 1911

T. J. Dysart
Nov 15, 1830
Mar 16, 1910

Geo. Eva Dysart, wife of
H. L. Douglass
May 5, 1866
Jul 15, 1901

James A. Dysart
1866-1942

Blanch Kimmons
Nov 4, 1862
May 3, 1919

Sophia Phillips, wife of
Thomas Johnson
Jan 4, 1810
Aug 31, 1898

J. G. Richerson
Mar 31, 1828
Sep 6, 1909
age: 81y, 5m, 5d.

W. T. Richerson
Jun 1, 1826
Oct 21, 1906

Martha J. Richerson
Dec 11, 1871
Oct 30, 1894

Mary E. Richerson
Oct 8, 1869
Sep 12, 1894

Sarah Ann, wife of
John T. Stephenson
Apr 12, 1851
Apr 18, 1898

Jesse W. Stephenson
Jul 22, 1872
Sep 28, 1890
age: 18y, 2m, 6d.

F. A. E., wife of
T. J. Dysart
Mar 22, 1844
Sep 29, 1889

Minnie, wife of
W. H. Riggs
May 7, 1858
Jan 4, 1888

Mary T., dau of
T. J. & F. A. E. Dysart
age: 7m & 16d.
(no dates)

P. J. T.
(footmarker)

M. A. P.
(Headstone for
Mary A. Phillips, gone)

John Phillips
Born 1811
Died(illegible)

John P. Gambill
Nov 23, 1836
Dec 20, 1870

Izory Jones, dau of
W. & S. P. Gambill
Aug 4, 1860
Mar 8, 1863

Joseph R., son of
A. & M. Mosley
Feb 5, 1845
Jan 29, 1864

Jesse Phillips
Nov 28, 1811
Jun 21, 1889
age: 77y, 6m, 23d.

R. M., wife of
Jesse Phillips
Aug 2, 1840
Jul 19, 1904

Ida Phillips
Sep 25, 1872
Aug 9, 1893

Ellen D., wife of
William T. Richerson
Jun 7, 1824
May 2, 1884

E. L. Ingle
1847-1892
&
S. J. Ingle
1849-1916

Maud Z. Davis
1869-1937

John B. Smith
Aug 5, 1880
Jun 4, 1910

Hunter Smith
Feb 6, 1857
Sep 2, 1937
&
Elizabeth Smith
Oct 26, 1861
Feb 24, 1935

Arthur E. Smith
May 25, 1878
Oct 9, 1929

Jesse Phillips
Born Feb --, 1840
Died Dec --, 1864
age: 24y, 9m, 17d.

Miles Phillips
Born Oct 30, 1806
Died Sep 1, 1863
age: 56y, 10m, 1d.

John Phillips
Born --- --, 1774
Died (after 1850,census)

Elizabeth, wife of
John Phillips
Died Jul 31, 1853
aged: 66y, 10m, & 3 weeks

Nancy, wife of
Jesse Phillips
Jan 8, 1815
Mar 11, 1843
aged: 28y, 2m, 9d.

Minnie Lela, dau of
L. R. & S. N. Johnson
Jul 6, 1876
Sep 25, 1878

B. M. Curtiss
Jul 7, 1849
Jun 17, 1913
&
Sarah E. Curtiss
Jul 7, 1849
Jun 3, 1886

Mary F. E., wife of
J. R. Dyer
Apr 13, 1864
Jul 3, 1891

Willie Loving, son of
T. J. & M. L. Huddleston
Mar 21, 1873
Dec 20, 1878

Georgie Ann, dau of
T. J. & M.L. Huddleston
Oct 5, 1877
Mar 24, 1900
age: 22y, 5m, 20d.

James Leonard Williams
1913-1970 (TM)

Nina Williams Delffs
1918-1945

James R. Williams
1881-1946
&
Sarah E. Williams
1892-1963

Teresa Curtiss
Oct 22, 1824
Apr 15, 1908

J. H. Curtiss(James H.)
Born Nov 12, 1810
Died Aug 13, 1866
age: 56y, 9m, 1d.

Newton Gambill
--- --, 1812
--- --, 1861
(bad shape)

Manerva, wife of
Newton Gambill
Aug 27, 1815
Jan 22, 1867

Armantha Matilda Gambill
Jun 6, 1857
Feb 14, 1863
age: 5y, 9m, 8d.

Susan J. Ray
Jan 16, 1854
Oct 20, 1857

Mary Ray
Aug 16, 1834
Nov 1834

Newton C. Darnell
May 3, 1862
Feb 7, 1863
age: 8m & 7d.

Thomas Davis
1825-1895

Elizabeth Davis
1834-1887

Jackson Wallace
Nov 4, 1819
Jun 29, 1881

Elizabeth Wallace
Sep 7, 1820
Aug 20, 1892

Beauna Vista, dau of
Jackson & Elizabeth Wallace
Sep 22, 1851
Aug 8, 1878
age: 26y, 10m, 16d.

German Woodward
1846-1927
& wife:
Julia Freeman Woodward
1849-1898
& Dau:
Julia Wm. Woodward
1881-1882

Mary J., wife of
Dock Farrar
Jul 28, 1859
Mar 7, 1951

Leland Farrar
1892-1911

To the Memory of
Lucy Mosley, who Died
July 19, 1858
aged: 30 yrs.

Lucy A. Mosley, dau of
A. & M. Mosley
Nov 22, 1856
Oct 12, 1863

Infant dau of
A. & M. Mosley
Apr 22, 1858
Nov 26, 1858

Infant of
E. D. & F. E. Moore
Born & Died
Jan 15, 1870

Jane Ray
(illegible)

Sarah Ray
(illegible)

Alexander Ray
Jul 13, 1803
Jul 30, 1857

Joseph R. Ray
Sep 11, 1830
Sep 5, 1852

Julia, dau of
J. H. & M. A. Moore
(no dates)

A. Freeman (Alsa)
Jan 5, 1815
Sep 9, 1863
age: 48y, 8m, 4d.

Mary E. Freeman
Dec 5, 1828
Nov 3, 1867
age: 38y, 10m, 28d.

George C. Newsom
Mar 20, 1859
Sep 12, 1873
age: 14y, 5m, 22d.

No marker:**
Thomas Leonard Davis, son
of Thomas Davis
Born Dec 12, 1867
Died Apr 19, 1890

No marker:**
Robert Miles Davis
Born Mar 3, 1866
Died Feb 22, 1939

Green B. Newsom
Mar 12, 1818
May 22, 1866

Martha F. Newsom
Mar 10, 1845
Nov 24, 1866

W. R. S., son of
G. B. & E. J. Newsom
Feb 6, 1852
May 22, 1870
age: 18y, 3m, 18d.

No marker:*
Sadie Louise Davis
Born Oct 21, 1906/7
Died Oct 10, 1910

No marker:*
Marvin Curtis
Born Sep 1911
Died   1942
"First Casuality of Bedford
County, Tenn. Died at Camp
 Stewart, Ga. Army."

Nancy A. Newson, wife of
George N. Davidson
Oct 24, 1847
Apr 25, 1877

Bettie, dau of
J. H. & M. A. Moore
May 20, 1864
Dec 1, 1876

No marker:*
Dorothy Ellen Anderson
Born & Died July 1930

No marker:*
William Thomas Smith
(no dates)

No marker:*
Izora Jane Capps Smith, wife
of William Thomas Smith
(no dates)

Many unmarked graves.

* by People at Decoration Day.

Genevia, dau of
J. W. & B. V. Brown
Oct 8, 1865
Sep 11, 1874
age: 8y, 11m, 3d.

No marker:*
Carl King, son of
Mr & Mrs Hiram King
(no dates)

No marker:*
Mary Frances King, dau of
Mr & Mrs Hiram King
(no dates)

No marker:**
George Wesley Davis
Jul 11, 1872
Dec 11, 1897(has marker)

Many fieldstones, no insc.

**by Miss Maggie Davis

Colored Section of Richmond Cemetery

Johnson Gentry
Mar 7, 1835
Nov 16, 1892

Several unmarked graves.

Henry Woodard
March 1833
Sept 1890

Many fieldstones, no insc.

Stephen Medaris
1803-May 7, 1895

Cathren, wife of
Stephen Medaris
Died Nov 7, 1885
aged: 71 yrs.

S. S. Medaris
Jun 10, 1862
Apr 30, 1898

38 TALIAFERRO CEMETERY   Map # 10
Located north of Richmond, TN off Adams Road.

Benjamin Taliaferro, native of Georgia, and wife Adra buried
here. Benjamin in 1824. John Williams, SR. (SOR) died here.

39 BARRETT CEMETERY   Map # 10
Located about 1½ miles West of Pleasant Grove, Tenn., on Adams Road.

John E. Barrett
Jul 7, 1825
Jan 18, 1904

No marker:**
Louis Whitsell
Born 1805
Died (after 1850)

** by Ralph Whitesell

Elizabeth, wife of
J. E. Barrett
Dec 16, 1834
Mar 28, 1905
age: 60y, 3m, 12d.

Margaret J. Barrett
Oct 1, 1853
Oct 19, 1854

Sallie E. Barrett
Sep 3, 1859
May 26, 1898

No marker:*
In Memory of
Milla Whitsell
Born 20 Nov 1782
Died 22 Mar 1865

*Copied by Mary Bass in 1962

40 RUSSELL CEMETERY   Map # 10
Located about 2 miles South of Bedford, Tenn., off Bethleham Road.

William Woodward
Dec 13, 1833
Sep 30, 1866
age: 32y, 9m, 17d.

William M. Woodward
Departed this life
Jun 11, 1877
aged: 18y, 7m, 5d.

Jannie Head, wife of
M. A. Thompson
Apr 5, 1856
Mar 2, 1915

Rebecca S. Ursey
Aug 19, 1853
May 26, 1873

Charley Stapp
Jan 14, 1873
Nov 22, 1875

Mary D. Stapp
Died Jun 14, 1876
age: 40y, 7m, 8d.

Wiley J. Ursey
May 1, 1826
Apr 15, 1900

Adaline Ursey
Nov 30, 1825
Feb 22, 1880

Wiley Nuton Haynie
Mar 20, 1895
Feb 1, 1900

E. C. Barnett*
Jul 10, 1822
Aug 8, 1900
*(Emily Whitesell, wife of
W. F. Barnett)
&
W. F. Barnett
Mar 30, 1819
Jan 3, 1863

Herbert Shaw, son of
G. A. & S. A. Shaw
Aug 17, 1883
Sep 3, 1894
&
Infant Son of
G. A. & S. A. Shaw
Born & Died
Nov 9, 1883

Bessie, dau of
G. A. & S. A. Shaw
Aug 8, 1890
Aug 16, 1896

Infant Son of
J. W. & Zella Shaw
May 16, 1900

Susan Montgomery
Feb 1806
Sep 24, 1888
"After suffering 5 weeks"

D. N. Logan
Born Mar 8, 1828
Died Oct 12, 1831

In Memory of
Benjamin Gambill
Was born Sep 4, 1781
Dec'd Apr 30, 1846
aged: 64y, 7m, 16d.

Nancy Gambill
Dec'd Nov 20, 1830
aged: 44 yrs.

"Father"
John B. Nance
Dec 23, 1831
Apr 10, 1908

"Mother"
Kate Snell, wife of
John B. Nance
Nov 25, 1850
Jul 20, 1934

Thomas J. Nance
Mar 25, 1834
Sep 8, 1853

Nancy E. Nance
Apr 28, 1843
Aug 27, 1872

NOTE: This Cemetery is in very
bad condition, open to cattle,
most stones are down & broken.-Ed.

Rhoda S., wife of
B. F. Adams
Mar 15, 1854
Mar 11, 1892

Large Monument:
Sacred to the Memory of
Martha F. Russell, dau of
William M. & Martha Russell
Born March 24, 1835, lived an
exemplary member of the
Christian Church and departed
this life Sept. 21, 1855
aged: 20y, 5m, 27d.

George W. Blackwell
Aug 16, 1866
Aug 24, 1882

Mary Ellen Blackwell
Oct 7, 1874
Sep 22, 1882

Sally Etta Blackwell
Dec 4, 1868
Oct 10, 1882

William Wood
Feb 6, 1804
Nov 26, 1874
age: 70y, 9m, 20d.

Elenor Wood
Jan 31, 1806
Sep 24, 1890
age: 84y, 7m, 23d.

James T. Wood
Dec 21, 1828
Dec 24, 1852
age: 24y & 3d.

Jessie Wood
Died Jul 23, 1899
age: 17 days

Infant Son of
J. E. & Emma Moore
Jul 14, 1913

Infant dau of
W. C. & Mary Thomas
Apr 6, 1904
Oct 16, 1909

J. Y. Nance
Jul 8, 1886
Jul 21, 1886

Angeline Nance
Apr 1, 1819
Sep 2, 1847

Nancy A. Nance
Dec 19, 1836
Aug 31, 1853

Estella, dau of
A. & C. A. Reynolds
Sep 19, 1876
Jun 1, 1906

James R. Head
1848-1925
&
Mary J. Head
1863-1945

Nannie Belle Head
1895-1899

Stella May Head
1893-1896

John Trice
May 28, 1791
Aug 12, 1848

Elizabeth Trice
Sep 8, 1797
Aug 27, 1890

Joseph Trice
Jan 13, 1817
Sep 14, 1895

Sarah Trice
Jun 1, 1819
Apr 7, 1895

Nancy T. Trice
Dec 12, 1820
Feb 26, 1900

Samuel D. Wood
Sep 21, 1845
Sep 9, 1891
&
Martha D. Wood
Nov 26, 1842
May 28, 1935

Nancy F. Wood
Mar 10, 1841
Jun 10, 1842
age: 15 months

Sarah Annie Laura, dau of
W. B. & Amanda Gambill
Oct 30, 1869
Sep 6, 1883
age: 13y, 10m, 6d.

W. H., son of
W. B. & Amanda Gambill
Aug 14, 1871
Jul 13, 1896

John Nance
Mar 4, 1798
Feb 7, 1873

Ann Nance
Dec 24, 1796
Dec 28, 1836

P. L. Damron
Aug 24, 1830
Oct 9, 1903
age: 73y, 1m, 15d.

Sallie R. Coleman
Nov 13, 1824
Sep 15, 1904

M. A. Russell* wife of
J. H. Gambill
Jan 6, 1850
Apr 25, 1897
age: 46y, 3m, 19d.
*(Margaret Ann, wife of
James Hill Gambill)

Children of
J. A. & E. T. Gambill
Mattie Ruth Gambill
Aug 27, 1910
Feb 5, 1911
&
Infant Son Gambill
Jun 12, 1907

"Our Mother"
Mary C. Trice, wife of
F. F. Fonville
Sep 2, 1829
Sep 27, 1901

M. A. Trice, wife of
W. S. Hix
Mar 8, 1838
Aug 24, 1899

Anna E. Trice, wife of
William Phillips
Feb 2, 1836
Aug 25, 1861

Elizabeth Elen Ellis
Apr 30, 1840
Dec 1841

George W., son of
W. B. & Amanda Gambill
Mar 2, 1886
Dec 10, 1890
age: 4y, 9m, 8d.

Mattie Rowena, dau of
W. B. & Amanda Gambill
Mar 14, 1878
Jun 15, 1878

Thomas V., son of
W. B. & Amanda Gambill
Oct 2, 1879
Sep 17, 1880

Ida Vesta, dau of
W. B. & Amanda Gambill
Jul 19, 1895
Nov 8, 1897

Minnie E., dau of
T. J. & Lucy Gambill
Nov 17, 1877
Oct 16, 1879

Elmer Damron
Feb 7, 1868
Aug 13, 1868

Martha Ann Damron
Dec 7, 1827
Feb 9, 1868
age: 40y, 2m, 2d.

No markers:*
William M. Russell, Sr.
Born abt 1780
Died 3 Jan 1842
(William Madison Russell)

Many unmarked graves.

No marker:*
Martha Calloway Russell
Born- abt 1785
Died 10 Oct 1841

Many fieldstones, no insc.

No marker:*
Mary Whitesell Russell
(no dates)

* by Ralph Whitesell

No marker*
Joel Calloway Russell
Born 11 Feb 1823
Died 1 Mar 1863
married to
Margaret E. Trice
27 Aug 1844
Born 4 Apr 1823
Died 2 Mar 1910

41 CUNNINGHAM CEMETERY   Map # 10
Located about 2 miles East of Bethleham Church.

--------Cortner
Sep 14, 1815
Aug 24, 1889

Josephas A. Cunningham and
Mar 6, 1822
Oct 25, 1880
&
Elizabeth M. G. Cunningham
Dec 1, 1826
Jun 28, 1897

Frederick Brown*
Born Nov 24, 1818
Died (no date)
&
Margaret M. Brown*
Born Sep 15, 1817
Died Oct 27, 1888
&
"Our Children"   and
Margaret M. Brown
Apr 14, 1841
Jun 30, 1842
&
Nancy M. Brown
Jan 19, 1857
Dec 5, 1878
&
Jennette Brown
Nov 2, 1848
Aug 13, 1852

Margarett Hall
Nov 21, 1847
May 24, 1872

Margaret E.A.Cunningham
Aug 12, 1843
Feb 2, 1847
Dau of J.A. & E.M. Cunningham

Mathew Kinney
(no dates)

James Kinney
(no dates)

John Kinney
(no dates)

Margaret J. Brown
Jan 14, 1852
Mar 6, 1878
&
William D. Brown
Mar 31, 1855
Sep 29, 1873
&
John F. Brown
Mar 31, 1855
Dec 7, 1879

W. D. B.
(fieldstone)

C. W. B.
(fieldstone)

J. F. B.
(fieldstone)

A. J.--gyann Smith
Died 1828 age: 83 yrs.
(fieldstone)

Thadeus A. Blackwell, son of
R. B. & Mary J. Blackwell
Jun 4, 1861
Jun 9, 1862

Elizabeth, dau of
R. B. & M. J. Blackwell
Born & Died
Apr 30, 1857

Many fieldstones, no inscriptions.

Many unmarked graves.

* by Miss Mary Bass.

M. C. (fieldstone)

H. C. (fieldstone)

W. H. C. (fieldstone)

J. B. C. (fieldstone)

J. F. C. (fieldstone)

J. C. (fieldstone)

J. K. C. (fieldstone)

Josephine, dau of
R. B. & M. J. Blackwell
Jul 30, 1855
Feb 15, 1856

[This was the old Humphrey
Cunningham place]

42 PORTER-CORTNER CEMETERY   Map # 10
Located about 2 miles North of Richmond, on Old Merideth Gentry Farm.

T. S. Mayes
Dec 11, 1814
Jan 28, 1897
& wife:
Hannah M. Mayes
1827-(no date, after 1850)

Tommie A., dau of
T. S. & H. M. Mayes
Jan 8, 1872
Jul 6, 1873

Sallie C., dau of
T. S. & H. M. Mayes
Sep 27, 1866
Sep 8, 1867

Rozaner P., dau of
T. S. & H. M. Mayes
Feb 18, 1856
Feb 2, 1862

M. A. C. & L. L. C.
(footmarker)

Hattie, wife of
J. D. Stephens
Jul 21, 1863
Dec 31, 1905

William A. Wood
Died Nov 23, 1867
age: 1m & 2d.

John Cortner
Died Aug 1, 1892
(no age given, 1850:born abt
                1820)
&
Mary D. Cortner
Died Nov 12, 1842
age: 20 yrs.

Thomas N. Porter
Born Dec 21, 1822
Died (no date, after 1850)

E. E. C.
(footmarker)

Lewis L. Cortner
Died Sep 15, 1860
age: 74 yrs.
&
Mary A. Cortner
Died Mar 22, 1856
age: 60 yrs.

Eliza Cortner
Died Mar 17, 1865
age: 30 yrs.

Kitty Porter
Born Jul 4, 1795
Died (no date, before 1850)

John T. Porter, son of
Nathaniel & Sarah Ann Porter
Born Sep 7, 1841
Died Oct 1, 1842

Sarah Ann Porter
Born 1822 Died (no date,after
                    1850)

J. K. P. Moore
Aug 11, 1835
Jul 5, 1863

Alsy Jane Moor_
Feb 1, 1831
Oct 22, 1843

Nathaniel Porter
Born Feb 19, 1760
Died (no date) (1813)

Nancy Porter
Born Mar 29, 1761
Died (no date, before 1850)

Nancy Porter
Born Jan 1, 1797
Died (no date, before 1850)

(See addendum)

W. A., son of
S. D. & -. -. Wood
Oct 21, 1867
Nov 23, 1867

M. D. C. & J. C.
    (Footmarkers)

Peter Cortner
Mar 18, 1818
Aug 6, 1890
    &
Susanah Cortner
Mar 13, 1828
May 12, 1903

Many field stones no insc.

B. F. Johnson
Apr 24, 1844
Sep 4, 1889

* Bedford County 1850 Census.

Many unmarked graves.

No marker:*
Newcomb Thompson
Born 1825
Died after 1850

S. C.(Susan), Consort of
N. _. Thompson (Newcombe)
Apr 11, 1825
Jun 13, ---- (after 1850)

43 UNKNOWN CEMETERY   Map # 10
Located about ½ mile Northeast of Bethleham Church, on Sinking Creek.

Only fieldstones, no inscriptions.

44 HARRISON CEMETERY   Map # 10
Located about ½ mile Southeast of Bethleham Church, near Sinking Creek.

James Harvey Harrison   and
Nov 1, 1819
Jan 24, 1897

Hanah Medlin
Dec'd 1819

Margaret Thomas Harrison
Nov 20, 1826
Sep 3, 1853

Joseph M. S. Diunham
Dec 1820
age: 46 yrs.

Sarah A., wife of
J. H. Harrison
Aig 1, 1834
Mar 8, 1879

3 or 4 other graves.

Olive, Infant dau of
F. O. & Gladys Harrison
age: 4 days
(no dates)

T. F. H. (fieldstone)
[Harrison, d. Sep 22, 1933, age 80]

F. A. H. (Fieldstone)

45 HARPER CEMETERY   Map # 10
Located just North of Bethleham Church, near Sinking Creek.

Matilda Harper
Aug 7, 1813
Oct 25, 1892
age: 79y, 2m, 18d.

20 or more graves, with
fieldstones, no inscriptions.

46 HELTON CEMETERY   Map # 10
Located about 2 miles Northwest of Richmond, Tenn.

Elizabeth Gabbert, Infant
dau of Nelson & Rebecca
Gabbert
Apr 24, 1851
Jul 4, 1852

"Father"
Louis Cortner
Jun 7, 1860
Jul 7, 1916

"Brother"
Thomas Cortner
Sep 20, 1867
Nov 15, 1919

Daniel D. Helton
Nov 14, 1819
Mar 24, 1862
    &
Malinda E. Helton
Oct 28, 1829
Oct 29, 1899

Several unmarked graves.
(about 20-25 graves)

James H. Helton
Aug 9, 1852
Jun 9, 1853

George B. Helton
Nov 2, 1856
Apr 8, 1857

Several fieldstones, no
inscriptions.

James Cortner
May 20, 1865
Oct 25, 1954

47 DAVIS CEMETERY   Map # 10
Located about 2 miles South of Bethleham Church.

Isaac Newton Jones
Jul 11, 1822
Aug 21, 1898

Mary Ann, wife of
I. N. Jones
Nov 9, 1827
Aug 7, 1909

Mary Newton Jones
Oct 21, 1861
Jun 25, 1863

Eliza Ann Jones
Aug 28, 1865
Aug 13, 1868

M. L. Ophelia Jones
Dec 20, 1856
Apr 26, 1882

Martha F. Brown
Jan 27, 1852
Jul 8, 1853

Lucy Brown
Sep 7, 1820
Jul 15, 1857

Margaret M. Brown
Died May 20, 1901
aged: 83y, 4m, 19d.

2 Infants graves, with
fieldstones, no insc.

Nancy Ray
Jul 26, 1815
Nov 26, 1833

Daniel B. Davis
Mar 10, 1813
Sep 24, 1841

Frances Davis
Dec 26, 1822
Aug 22, 1834

Zachariah Davis
Dec 16, 1786
Mar --, ----(after 1850,
(broken away)   census)

Rebecca Davis
Oct 4, 1791
Mar 5, 1855

1 adult grave, with
fieldstone, no insc.

Minerva H. Davis
Mar 6, 1858
Nov 3, 1860

abt 15-20 graves with
fieldstones, no
inscriptions.

48 ARMSTRONG CEMETERY   Map # 10
Located about 2 miles West of Richmond, Tenn.

Walter Grey Freeman
Jul 6, 1871
Apr 14, 1901

Stacy Grey Freeman
Sep 14, 1895
Aug 15, 1896

1816
Margret Hatley, dau of
Robert & M. Ann Hatley
Died Feb 25, 1816
age: 3y, 3m, 13d.

1816
Mary Ann Hatley
Mar 15, 1791
Oct 29, 1816
age: 20y, 7m, 18d.

William Armstrong
Oct 23, 1822
May 2, 1895

Martha E. Armstrong
Oct 17, 1844
Jan 31, 1915

J. H. Armstrong
Died Jul 20, 1860
age: 6 yrs.

1816
Caty Donaldson, dau of
W. & Margret Hall
Died Dec 1, 1815
age: 31y, 9m, 29d.

Many unmarked graves.

C. M. Reese
Born Aug 18, 1835
Died (no date)

M. A. E. Reese
Sep 6, 1846
Mar 17, 1885

1816
Parish & Gincy Garner's
Child
Died 11 days Old 1816

Griffen Randle*
Born Mar 9, 1779
Died Jul 21, 1856
*-Wife: Elizabeth Randle
in 1850 census, was 70yrs.

Moses Darnell
May 7, 1806
Feb 15, 1877

Gincy, wife of
Moses Darnell
Dec 2, 1805
Sep 12, 1889

1816
Gincy Garner, wife of
Parish Garner
Died Feb 21, 1816
aged: 30y & 11 days.

1824
Matilda Armstrong
Died Jul 4, aged: 4 days.

49 BROWN CEMETERY   Map # 10
Located about 1 mile Northwest of Richmond, Tenn.

T. Y. "Tom" Brown
    Co. F.
1st Ala Cav   This Cemetery has been plowed.

50 UNKNOWN CEMETERY   Map # 10
Located on same Farm as the above Cemetery.

6 fieldstones standing, no inscriptions. (See Addendum for Reavis)

1 WILLOW MOUNT CEMETERY   Map # 11
Located in the City of Shelbyville, Tennessee.
NOTE: This Cemetery was copied in Sections, please see Section Map opposite p. 194.

SECTION "A"

Clarence H. Snell
Tennessee
Pvt 701 Tank Destroyer Bn
W. W. II
Nov 11, 1920
Jul 24, 1944

T. M. Snell
Oct 12, 1845
May 26, 1920

Alice Carlisle Snell
1854-1936

A. Moody Snell
1890-1956

"Mother"
Anna E., wife of
Moody Snell
Jan 19, 1895
Nov 22, 1930

John Phillip Hart
Apr 10, 1924

&
Margaret Craig Hart
Dec 19, 1923
Feb 10, 1956

J. Sumner Hart
Aug 16, 1889
Sep 17, 1939

Susan Lynn Brown
Feb 17, 1973
Apr 15, 1973

E. C. Thompson
1852-1937
&
Tennie Thompson
1879-1940

William McClure Hart
Sep 28, 1858
Jun 29, 1927
    & wife:
Anna E. Barnes Hart
Oct 1, 1858
Aug 1, 1931

James Robert Moore
Dec 31, 1878
Mar 6, 1952

Elizabeth C. Moore
Jan 15, 1878
Mar 12, 1964

"Mother"
Malinda E. Smith
1851-1940
    & Daughter:
Susie B. Woods
1875-1939

James Beauregard Boone
1862-1921

Marie Clark, Infant dau of
J. B. & L. N. Boone
Dec 13, 1918

James William Baskette
Oct 2, 1844
Jan 12, 1890
    & wife:
Bettie Cannon Baskette
Sep 1, 1848
Jun 3, 1905
    & Son:
Edwin Ewing Baskette
Sep 19, 1871
May 5, 1882

John Baskette
1879-1941

Rufus B. Koonce
1879-1937
&
Ora Bell Koonce
1879-1952

John C. Cooper
1852-1925
&
Bettie Cooper
1868-1940

Sunshine Cooper
Jul 2, 1900
Jul 22, 1922

Florence C. Wortham
1892-1937

Robert A. Wortham
Jul 29, 1887
Sep 24, 1965
&
Jessie D. Wortham
Jul 2, 1894
Jul 20, 1973

Lilly S. Bates
Oct 17, 1892
May 10, 1971

Ethel Frost C. Bates
Jan 18, 1892
Dec 9, 1923
"She did what she could."

William Ollie Arnold
1904-1922

William B. Arnold
1875-1942

Webbie Butts Arnold
1877-1944

George Raymond Arnold
Jan 1, 1902
Apr 4, 1969
&
Maude Jarman Arnold
Mar 29, 1904

Infant Son of
Raymond & Maude Arnold
1925

"Mother"
Ella B. Stephenson Foster
1870-1940

Billy Foster
1905-1924

James W. Arney
1872-1950
&
Della T. Arney
1886-19

Annie G. Arney
1905-1942

Birdie Moore Woods, wife of
F. B. Woods
1881-1947

T. E. Hoffman
1865-1941

John U. Naron
1854-1942
&
Jane C. Naron
1860-1947

Nadge D. Naron
Mar 28, 1878
Jan 7, 1972

Annie B. Naron
Nov 20, 1879
Oct 11, 1971

Lillie Naron
Jul 24, 1882
Jan 3, 1961

Elijah Williams
1860-1921
&
Betty Williams
1872-1953

Joseph H. Alexander
1832-1940
&
Dora H. Alexander
1881-1965

J. D. Alexander
1916-1921

Betty Jane Holton
1931-1936

Ben K. Arnold
Nov 26, 1852
May 18, 1935
&
Bettie E. Arnold
Apr 23, 1855
Jan 16, 1935

James Spence M. Elrod
1882-1923

William Hobart Harber
Nov 14, 1899
Mar 7, 1948
&
Evelyn Anderson Harber
Apr 7, 1903
Sep 14, 1941

"Father"
James L. Yoes
1862-1934

"Mother"
Sallie A. Yoes
1870-1924

Billy Marshall
1861-1929

Nannie Marshall
1870-1945

Herbert P. Dean
1901-1948
&
Virgie M. Dean
1906-19

William Wiley Troupe, Jr.
May 10, 1908
Oct 31, 1941

Raleigh Naron
Aug 9, 1884
Dec 24, 1928

John W. Naron, Jr.
Nov 26, 1890
Jul 17, 1922
Old marker:
Tennessee Seaman
2Cl U.S.N.R.F.

Gregory W. Medley
1961-1963
(Gowen-Smith)

Dartha Ratcliffe
1963-1963
(Gowen-Smith)

Raby Bryant Shearin
Tennessee
Pvt Co E 129 Inf W. W. I
Jan 14, 1892
Oct 14, 1964

Grayson H. Shearin
1859-1925
& wife:
Madora Shoffner Shearin
1862-1949

"Father"
Walter Edmond Shearin
1882-1941

"Mother"
Nora Shofner, wife of
W. E. Shearin
1880-1927

Maymie C. "Catherine" Anthony
Dec 20, 1896
Jan 15, 1937
&
Carl H. Anthony
Oct 14, 1898
Oct 6, 1971
&
Mary Belle Anthony
Mar 3, 1909

William H. Thompson
1872-1937
&
Eula T. Thompson
1881-1974

George Reaves
1898-1956
&
Edd C. Reaves
1862-1942

"Father"
Harve M. McAdams
1865-1923
&
"Mother"
Sam McAdams
1873-1924

Arthur McAdams, Sr.
1903-1966
(Gowen-Smith)

------- McAdams
(TM almost destroyed)

Christine Hanson Tolar
1892-1957
(Cothron-Thompson)

Thomas V. Tolar
Apr 19, 1911

&
Glenon W. Tolar
Feb 5, 1913
Sep 29, 1972

John Lisles Vogel
Nov 1, 1894
Apr 3, 1966
&
Lizzie Simmons Vogel
Sep 21, 1892
Oct 15, 1964

Louise Elizabeth Estes
Apr 20, 1918
Sep 28, 1920

John A. Thompson
1886-1943
&
Valona M. Thompson
1888-1971

John A. Thompson
Aug 5, 1909
Oct 22, 1970
(color picture)

Lawson "Dick" Gregory
Oct 11, 1904
Jan 22, 1969
&
Ruby E. Gregory
Mar 25, 1908

Carl Calahan
1895-1974
(Gowen-Smith)

Mary T. Calahan
Sep 16, 1896
Nov 6, 1968

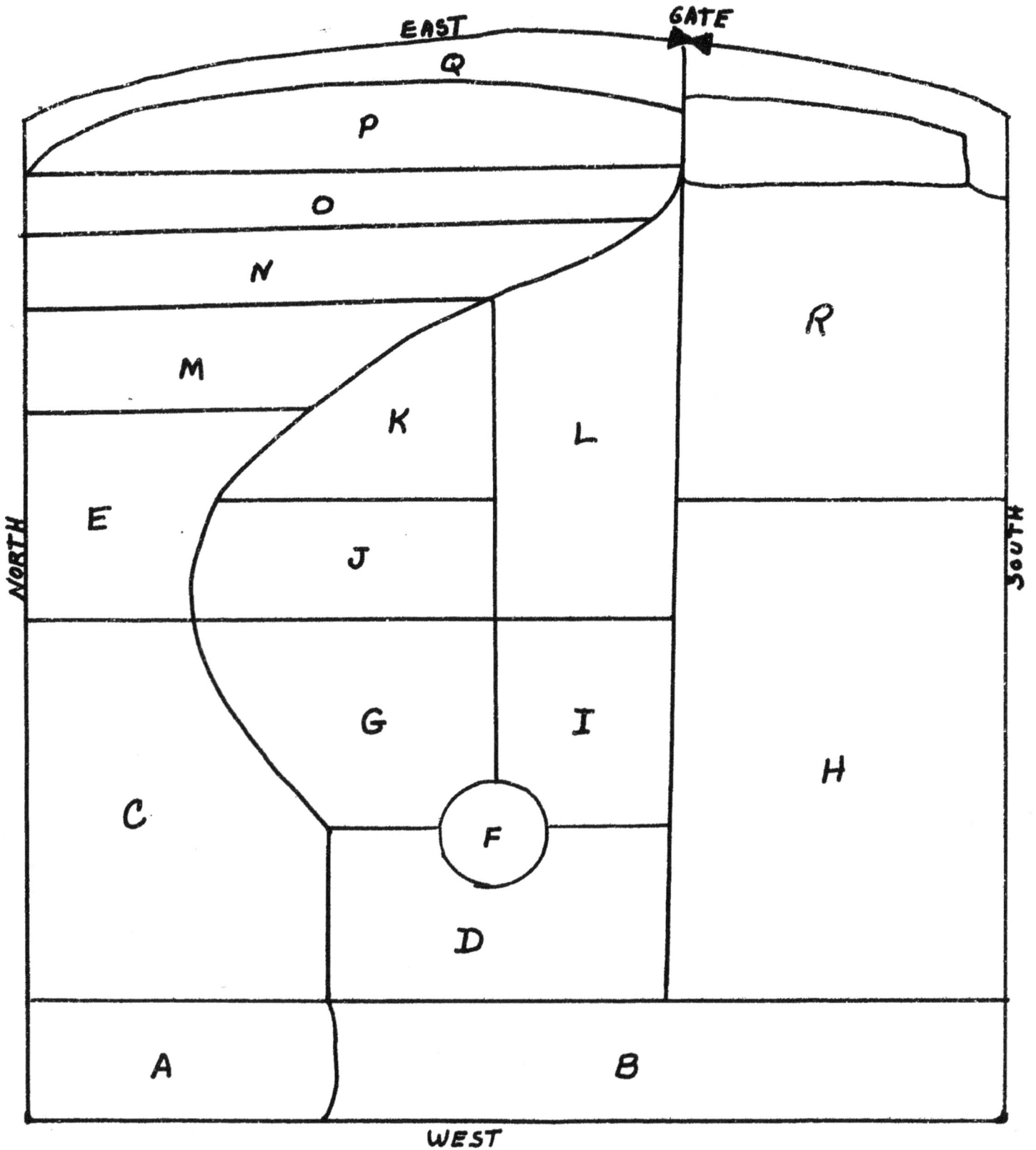

MAP OF WILLOW MOUNT

Jenny Ruth Calahan
1921-1927

Dorothy Lee Calahan'
1923

Douglas Calahan
1928-1944

Walter Kevin, infant son
of Fred & Jean Calahan
Jun 21, 1958

Infant Calahan, Jr., son of
James & Anne Calahan
May 23, 1970

Nathaniel Bradford
1845-1929
&
Jeanette Bradford
1846-1934

Peter La Paglia
1909-1942

Hershal B. Neely
Aug 20, 1907
Jun 26, 1950
&
Lavesta B. Neely
Nov 30, 1907
Nov 16, 1942

Laura Irene Moore
1939-1939

Mary E. Moore
Aug 17, 1883
May 24, 1968

"Father"
Robert Gallagher
1855-1922

"Mother"
Nannie H. Gallagher
1859-1921

Joe C. Harrison
1851-1922
&
Luticia Harrison
1853-1945

Elbert G. Harrison
Dec 18, 1902
Dec 7, 1967

A. Clarence Harrison
Sep 19, 1881
Dec 10, 1971
&
Minnie P. Harrison
Apr 14, 1879
Feb 6, 1970

John W. Moore
Jul 21, 1850
Apr 13, 1927

Elizabeth J. Moore
Sep 30, 1848
Jan 6, 1927

Drucilla Moore
Mar 24, 1896
Nov 8, 1957

William Jacob Moore
1887-1957

Luna, wife of
Jake Moore
1884-1922

Jim G. Reed
Sep 11, 1859
Aug 12, 1936
&
Martha Ann Reed
Jul 26, 1881
Oct 12, 1870

Roy Brown
Apr 12, 1896
Feb 27, 1970
&
Mary B. Brown
Apr 28, 1898
Oct 25, 1969

Hugh Parker
1880-1964
&
Etta Parker
1886-1932

M. W. A.
Raymond O. Parker
1904-1923

Robert Lee Gaither
Aug 18, 1868
Oct 18, 1959
&
Era Harrison Gaither
Jul 21, 1874
Jul 14, 1957

James Thomas Gaither
Feb 23, 1874
Jan 29, 1966
&
Lois Snell Gaither
Nov 2, 1882
Aug 11, 1962

F. O. Thompson
1889-1925

Newton O. Thompson
1858-1944
& wife:
Jodie D. Thompson
1864-1934

John Mayfield Thompson
1884-1922

Joe Winford Thompson
Dec 8, 1886
Apr 9, 1964
&
Nannie R. Thompson
Jun 18, 1889
Jan 27, 1975

Solon L. Landers
1848-1939
&
Holland L. Landers
1864-1926

Everette W. Snell
1883-1945

Ruby D. Snell
1889-1967

Thomas W. Snell
Apr 5, 1858
May 4, 1933
&
Ida Snoddy Snell
Apr 3, 1861
Mar 8, 1939

(end of Section "A")

SECTION "B"   (Colored Section)

William H. Mott

&
Eunice C. Mott
1896-1930

W. Burlin Holland
1886-1892

Dr. William Key
"Trainer of Jim Key"
1833-1909

Lucinda Davis, M.D.
wife of William Key
Born Feb 24, 1859
Died Aug 21, 1896
"What ever happens to me
My Dear, it is well with
my soul."

Sallie Cannon
Died Jan 17, 1889
age: about 20 yrs.

Robert L. Suggs, D.D.S.
Apr 2, 1888
Feb 15, 1969
Tennessee
Pfc U.S.Army W.W.I
&
Jamie E. Suggs
Dec 20, 1902

Maggie Davis Key
1865-1935

William Davis
Jul 1, 1857
Feb 6, 1886
age: 28y, 7m, 6d.

Fannie Bell, dau of
George & Harriet Davis
Mar 28, 1875
Jun 2, 1894

Sims Family

Arthur L. Davis, Sr.
Tennessee
MOMM2 U.S.N.R.
W. W. II
Oct 21, 1914
Oct 16, 1963

Essie C. Davis
1890-1952

Sam A. Davis
1880-1952

George Davis
1828-1905
&
Harriet E. Davis
1841-1912

Thomas R. Davis
1861-1916

Charley Davis
Jun 30, 1863
Feb 16, 1957

John D. Thompson, Husband
of Emma L. Thompson
Died Oct 1, 1900
age: about 50 yrs.

Annie May, dau of
J. D. & E. L. Thompson
Died May 9, 1890
age: 1y, 8m, 9d.

"Mother"
Martha J. Talley
Passed: 1903

Clark Talley
Died Mar 18, 1883
age: 55 yrs.
"Life's Labor Done."

Henry G. Davis
1868-1926

Irving J. Davis
1870-1939

195

Mary B. Harris
Nov 14, 1900
Jan 5, 1966

W. M. Nowlin
Aug 22, 1858
Oct 10, 1907
age: 49 yrs.

Cleveland Cowan
Apr 10, 1891
Jan 4, 1918

H. H. Bellanfant
Jan 22, 1866
Jun 24, 1891

M. E. Gill
Aug 27, 1877
Mar 8, 1918

Louis Hutton
1866-1895

Emma Hutton
1838-1905

C. Washington Talley
1827-1903
&   and
Lucinda Talley
1830-1913
&
Martha J. Talley
1852-1879

Martha E. Brown
Mar 6, 1858
Nov 9, 1949

Frances Mary, wife of
Lewis Wooley
Nov 16, 1844
Dec 18, 1881

Sgt. David Wilson
Co C
66 U.S.C.I.

Levi Myers
Co H
19th U.S.C.T.

J. A. Holder
Sep 3, 1876
Dec 17, 1910
&
J. D. Holder
Sep 17, 1872
Sep 3, 1902
&
Harriet Holder
Died Jul 22, 1889
age: 62 yrs.

Luther P. Talley, A.B.
1861-1888

Sylvester V. Talley
Jun 29, 1855
Sep 11, 1936

In Memory of
Tom Porter & Family
(no dates)

Mattie Wooley, wife of
H. Wiggins
May 18, 1870
Nov 24, 1893

Isaac N. McAdams
Sep   1838
Feb 14, 1909
&
Delilah McAdams
Jan 1, 1833
Jun 10, 1922

Brazier W. Robert
1902-19

"Mother"
Henrietta Motley
Died Sep 29, 1888
age: 88 yrs.

Prof. Religh Purdy
1870-1969
&
Annie Purdy
1876-

Alice Sims
Died Nov 22, 1956
(no age given)

Annie, wife of
Harvy Neil
Married Mar 1887
Died Nov 11, 1897
age: 38 yrs.

John Newton, Infant son of
John C. & Lizzie H. McAdams
Jul 8, 1886
Aug 2, 1887

J. C. McAdams
Oct 1860
Dec 1940
"Graduated from Fisk University, B. A. 1883, M. A. 1886 Proffessor in Mississippi State Schools 8 years, Principal in Shelbyville Public Schools 36 years, admitted to practice Law in all the Courts of the State."

(end of Section "B")

SECTION "C"

Joseph H. Moore
Oct 22, 1885
Aug 20, 1961
&
Esther B. Moore
May 25, 1888
Sep 24, 1966

William M. Noblitt
Nov 19, 1906

&
Margaret B. Noblitt
Nov 4, 1907

James D. Stephens
1875-1913
&
Minnie Ola Stephens
1882-1937

James D., Jr., son of
J. D. & Ola Stephens
Mar 3, 1914
Sep 19, 1915

William Fred Hughson
Aug 23, 1894
Dec 27, 1972
&
Mary Thompson Hughson

J. Edd Burris
1881-1957

Nancy Burris
1834-1946

Robert Cecil Burris
May 2, 1909
Oct 10, 1914

Richard Burris
1906-1946

Robert C. Burris
1926

James J. Gammill
Mar 26, 1834
Dec 6, 1913
&
Jennie Gammill
Jun 19, 1844
Jul 14, 1926

James R. Hix
1855-1945
&
Ola Smiley Hix
1863-1953

W. G. Smiley (William, C.S.A.)
Apr 1, 1833
Jan 5, 1915

W. T. Burris
1860-1914

Rebecca Burris
1857-1929

Edwin Burris
1911-1943

Betty Jane, dau of
Edwin & Marie Burris
1934-1935
(picture)

Elie Davenport
(fieldstone)
Elnora Davenport
1881-1945

William L. Kimbro
1858-1919 (TM)

Tennie J. Kimbro
1855-1944
(Gowen-Smith)

Marvin L. Kimbro
Oct 19, 1879
May 31, 1912

John W. Bomar
Jun 1, 1883
May 26, 1913

Oscar C. Kimmons
Aug 5, 1887
May 15, 1956

R. E. Kimmons
1861-1918

Curtis Kimmons
1908-1927

A. D. Curtis, II
Jan 28, 1927
Jan 2, 1929

Jean Curtis
Oct 15, 1924
May 23, 1927

Billy Bass
Aug 27, 1917
Jul 24, 1926

Alice Kimmons Bass
1891-1968

Ottie Glyn Collier
Jan 14, 1901
Jun 26, 1972
&
Virginia Vaughan Collier
May 30, 1905
Aug 15, 1961

Marks Hughson
1890-1952

Jimmie C. Hughson
1897-1913

Effie Vincent
1867-1946

Samuel Milton Lewis
Aug 29, 1936
Jan. 7, 1937

Bessie Lee Dye
May 5, 1907
Jun 30, 1973

"Mother"
Ada Poplin
Jun 21, 1872
Mar 28, 1965

"Artist"
Lizzie Evans
1865-1941

James G. Evans
Feb 27, 1861
Sep 9, 1936
&
Mary Bird Evans
Jan 14, 1868
Aug 16, 1949

J. B. Moulder
1858-1931

Sophronia P. Moulder
1863-1953

Euless M. Molder
1881-1967

Minnie W. Molder
1883-1965

Daisy W. Molder
1885-1971

Rufus G. Arnold
1865-1925
&
Mary E. Arnold
1865-1941

Willie C., son of
R. G. & Mary E. Arnold
Sep 16, 1892
Nov 22, 1909

Dorothy L. Arnold
dau of Louise Arnold Rugg
1926

Margaret Reeves, wife of
Acton Snell
Jan 12, 1844
Dec 5, 1929

Lelah Stewart
Nov 7, 1875
May 11, 1971

Ernie D. Collier
Apr 17, 1898

&
Pauline H. Collier
Sep 28, 1905

Reuben T. Collier
Dec 18, 1894
Dec 15, 1970

Barry L. Collier
1865-1923
& wife:
Ellen G. Collier
1869-1950

Russell S. Bryant
Aug 27, 1911

&
Sue Hudson Bryant
Feb 17, 1912
Nov 20, 1971

Pink Wheeler
1853-1941

Cynthia Wheeler
1857-1943

L. M. Creek
Jan 25, 1875
Nov 24, 1931
&
Sofronie Isora Creek
Oct 3, 1870
Nov 6, 1917

Gladys V. Snell
Nov 27, 1914
Oct 28, 1914

Sudie M. Snell
Nov 12, 1883
Mar 19, 1968

Rufus Arnold
1892-1937

Gracie Arnold
1892-1925

L. K. Arnold
Sep 20, 1875
Jun 6, 1911
"Soldier in Philippines,
Co F. 21 Infantry".

Joseph Lawson Hutton, Sr.
Alabama
Pvt U.S.Army W.W.I
Jun 9, 1899
Jan 7, 1974

Joseph Lawson Hutton, Jr.
Tennessee
Pfc 397, Inf 100 Div W.W.II
Dec 24, 1924
Dec 16, 1944

Walter P. Thompson
Sep 2, 1902
Jan 19, 1969
&
Eva C. Thompson
Nov 14, 1902

John W. Moore
Feb 20, 1883
Jul 19, 1951
&
Inda B. Moore
May 5, 1893
May 4, 1973

Joe B. Moore
Aug 2, 1860
Aug 26, 1921

Joe Hutton Moore
California
Pvt Inf W.W.I
Aug 31, 1912
Nov 12, 1968

Alice W. Martin
1877-1943

1 marker in ground, deep.

Alice M. Taylor
Oct 19, 1880
Dec 26, 1917
"Mother"

A. W. Sorrells
1887-1916

-------- Sorrells
(all other info gone)

Hoyt H. Sorrells
1891-1958

Ollie Turrentine Williams
Oct 9, 1870
Mar 21, 1968

Emmett M. Williams
May 29, 1867
Jan 29, 1934

Earl McGee Hurt
Jan 17, 1905
Jun 12, 1975
"son of Fannie McGee &
J. W. Hurt,Sr."
&
Mary Word Hurt
Mar 1, 1908

"dau of Clara Arnold &
Henry Lucas Word"

Henry L. Word
1878-1955
&
Clara A. Word
1885-1941

B. Franklin Parsons   and
Aug 12, 1889
Feb 15, 1965

Clarice, dau of
P. C. & Myrtle Claxton
1915-1922

William Finis Bryant
Sep 8, 1874
Jul 7, 1932

Mary Elizabeth Bryant Barnes
Apr 14, 1886
Jun 10, 1957

William R. Gardner
1867-1951
&
Sallie T. Gardner
1874-1946

Infant Bowling
1971-1971
(Gowen-Smith)

Drue Moore
Sep 13, 1860
Feb 18, 1941
&
L. F. Moore
Aug 22, 1853
Aug 27, 1919

George W. Snell
Oct 27, 1922
Nov 6, 1922

Willie B. Smith
Sep 1, 1891
May 11, 1940

Z. Taylor Cannon
1849-1926

Mary S. Cannon
1865-1937

George W. Montgomery
Dec 27, 1841
Jan 17, 1914

E. V. Montgomery (C.S.A.)
Mar 18, 1848
Apr 2, 1924

Thomas Edward, son of
Floyd & Bertha Miles
Oct 26, 1907
Oct 26, 1910

"Mother"
Bertha L. Miles
Mar 14, 1888
Jan 9, 1918

Eugene Haynes
Jul 14, 1885
Jul 22, 1942

Rebecca S. Haynes
Mar 8, 1877
Jun 21, 1965

Lillie Mae S. Parsons
Mar 1, 1892

Thomas G. Stewart
Oct 22, 1843
Aug 22, 1907
&
E. C. Stewart
Apr 4, 1844
Nov 8, 1910

Infant daus of
J. E. & Katherine Burton
1936

Joseph E. Haynes
1867-1935
&
Laura B. Haynes
1870-1930

Joseph Lee, son of
J. L. & Rubye Haynes
May 16, 1921
May 23, 1921

Ollie B. Haynes Burton
Apr 6, 1902
Aug 18, 1928

Pvt Levoy B. Haynes
1894-1918
"While in Service
with the A.E.F."

Robert Morgan
1920

Howard B. Green
Aug 3, 1890
Jun 11, 1960
&
Bennie Jo R. Green
Sep 16, 1902

Melba May Green
1910-1913

Lewis D. Green
Feb 20, 1852
Jun 25, 1934
&
Lucy W. Green
Jan 3, 1855
Jul 19, 1941

Melody Brents, Infant dau of
Leo & Juanita Reed
Sep 1, 1968

Robert Elam Bumpus
Jan 17, 1920
Sep 7, 1920

Leonard S. Bumpus
Aug 31, 1896
Jan 10, 1970
&
Euna Brents Bumpus
Oct 7, 1896

Thomas Elgan Winn
Mar 9, 1896
Mar 18, 1959
&
Jennie R. Winn
Dec 4, 1890

Elizabeth Robinson
Feb 22, 1881
Nov 26, 1965

"Father"
Fate Jackson
May 13, 1867
Jun 11, 1912

"Father"
Eugene Troupe
Oct 13, 1864
Sep 24, 1946

"Mother"
Mrs. Willie Troupe
Jun 19, 1863
Aug 6, 1926

Dessie Hazlett Morgan
May 19, 1900
Aug 20, 1920

Ben F. Hazlett   and
1871-1930

W. T. Thompson
1842-1914
&
H. B. Thompson
1844-(no date)

William Purdy Thompson
1882-1944

Jesse N. Taylor
Jul 27, 1906

&
Ruth W. Taylor
May 23, 1911

Robert L. Gaither
Jan 28, 1841
Oct 25, 1931
& wife:
Martha Jane Gaither
Jan 7, 1845
Mar 20, 1920

Robert G. Mudge
1908-1964
&
Willie H. Mudge
1902-1965

Dona Hazlett
1873-1947

(end of Section "C")   (continued on page 203)

SECTION "D"

Pvt Guilford T. Johnson
Q.M.C. Corp 302 Co 4
Born Dec 7, 1897
Died in France
Oct 11, 1918

Claude Johnson
Tennessee
Pvt 324 Inf Regt W.W.I
Dec 3, 1895
Mar 26, 1954

James A. Sanders
Mar 25, 1842
Mar 28, 1928
&
Sarah E. Harper Sanders
Nov 28, 1847
Mar 9, 1931

"Father"
Eunice A. Puckett
Nov 25, 1890

&
"Mother"
Jennie M. Puckett
Nov 16, 1898

Harold M. Searcy   and
Sep 19, 1912
Jun 24, 1967

Thomas Johnson
Jan 12, 1864
Dec 6, 1934
&
Nettie Johnson
Jul 28, 1868
Feb 4, 1931

B. T. Thompson(new marker)
1867-1923
Blanch Thompson(old marker)
Oct 19, 1876
Apr 28, 1923

"Father"
Byrom Haynes
Apr 11, 1900
Aug 18, 1933(picture)

"Mother"
Ethel L. Haynes
Feb 6, 1907
Dec 26, 1928 (picture)

"Daughter"
Inda Bell Haynes
Jan 18, 1932
May 14, 1936

Louise P. Searcy
Dec 8, 1913

John Dudley Tarpley
1864-1937

Tennie J. Tarpley
1863-1941

Eleanor Jean Parker
Jun 5, 1925
Nov 29, 1925

John B. Stong
1854-1920

Julia G. Stong
1865-1947

William F. Stong
1878-1972
(Howell)

W. W. Gant
Mar 14, 1832
Apr 3, 1926
&
Mrs. W. W. Gant
Mar 11, 1840
Oct 31, 1925

Maude Bell Perry
1891-1974
(Gowen-Smith)

"Mother"
Nancy E. Barnes
Nov 15, 1837
Nov 29, 1922

A. T. Barnes
1858-1948

E. T. Barnes
1860-(no date)

Bloom F. Deason
1874-1964
&
Centha A. Deason
1873-1946

James E. Deason
Nov 29, 1898
Jan 16, 1920

Hazel, dau of
Clarence & Kathleen
Deason
Apr 29, 1928
Jul 23, 1939

Richmond D. Naron
Apr 2, 1867
Mar 27, 1947
&
Celia P. Naron
Aug 16, 1870
Aug 30, 1952

"Husband & Father"
A. V. Cunningham
Sep 9, 1885
Feb 26, 1920

Martha A. Cunningham
Mar 12, 1886
Feb 11, 1959
"She did what she could"

Ben Kingree
1873-1943
&
Mary Kingree
1883-1967

Ben Kingree, Jr.
Jan 28, 1910
Nov 26, 1959

Martha T. Kingree
Oct 29, 1913
Nov 5, 1956

G. Haywood Alford, Jr.
Dec 16, 1909

&
Elizabeth B. Alford
Apr 24, 1902
Apr 19, 1917

Frank Evans
Mar 11, 1859
Sep 2, 1860
&
Mabel Evans
Dec 16, 1857
Aug 26, 1860
"Children of
Dr. R. F. & J. G. Evans"

"Father"
John W. R. Bird
Oct 31, 1853
(no date)
&
"Mother"
Ella D. Bird
Apr 12, 1873
Sep 11, 1942

Milton R. Bird
1876-1958
&
Ethel M. Bird
1877-1939

Infant Sons of
W. R. & Ella D. Bird
John Bird
May 18, 1899
Jun 21, 1899
&
Golie Bird
Born & Died
May 18, 1899

Stella Eakin, dau of
Evander & Emma F. Shapard
May 25, 1891
Jan 14, 1895

W. R. Dennis
Mar 17, 1884
Apr 24, 1920
"Sailor Memorial"
&
Mrs. W. R. Dennis
Mar 18, 1892

John H. Woosley
Jan 3, 1838
Feb 21, 1872
"His last words was 'Farewell
Vain World'"

Elijah Cortner Huffman
Jul 17, 1874
Mar 2, 1958

Bettie Mullins Huffman
Nov 8, 1879
Jun 27, 1973

James Edgar Huffman
Nov 4, 1905
Jun 29, 1906

Dr. Robert Frank Evans
1821-1893

Mary Frances Evans
Jan 1, 1874
Jul 2, 1956

Julia G., wife of
Dr. R. F. Evans
Oct 31, 1828
Oct 12, 1859
"Wife & Mother"

Alex Sanders
Died Mar 11, 1899
age: abt 96 yrs.
&
M. A., wife of Alex Sanders
Jul 9, 1824
Sep 14, 1895

Jennie Ann Ednie Laura
Emma Saunders
Feb 19, 1865
Aug 12, 1867

Evander Shapard, Sr.
Nov 2, 1843
Aug 15, 1921

Emma L. Shapard
Jan 26, 1852
Feb 12, 1942

Emma Shapard Trawick
1879-1905

"Our Little Fannie"
Fannie Lipscomb, dau of
Evander & Emma F. Shapard
Aug 25, 1881
Jun 18, 1883
age: 1y, 9m, 23d.

Jennie P. Blakemore
1868-1948

John T. Fuqua
Jul 14, 1835
May 17, 1882
age: 47 yrs.

Elizabeth Ann, wife of
John Fuqua
Died Nov 17, 1874
age: 32y, 1m, 8d.
"Her last words were "Heaven
Sweet Heaven", She made Home
Happy"

Cora C. Fuqua
Aug 6, 1867
Feb 12, 1895
Age: 18 yrs.

Lillie E. Fuqua
Mar 20, 1871
Jan 9, 1885
age: 14 yrs.

John Hanley Fuqua
1865-1947

"Mother"
Eliza A. Fuqua
Sep 4, 1816
Jul 15, 1883

Mary E. Fuqua
Mar 3, 1837
Nov 27, 1873

John M. Shapard, son of
R. P. & P. Shapard
Jun 25, 1851
Jan 9, 1858
&
Ava, dau of
Rev. W. & E. H. Shapard
Dec 22, 1858
Apr 7, 1862

Robert Paine Shapard
Born in Caswell Co., N.C.
Jan 9, 1805 & died
Sep 18, 1871
&
Parthenia Shapard
Born in Person Co., N.C.
Jan 12, 1809 & died
Apr 27, 1872

Charlotte Frierson, wife of
Robert P. Shapard
May 3, 1872
Nov 21, 1898

Annie R, dau of U.E. &
S. J. Peacock
Jan 24, 1864
Jul 21, 1864

Mary D., dau of U. E. &
Sallie Peacock
Died Mar 31, 1873
age: 14y, 2m, 19d.

Agnes R. Peacock
Sep 17, 1873
Dec 11, 1961

J. T. Arnold
Apr 17, 1857
Feb 22, 1918
& wife:
Lula Arnold
Dec 7, 1858
Jul 7, 1934

Pleasant Thaddus Arnold
Oct 26, 1878
Nov 12, 1878
&
Nellie Elizabeth Arnold
Dec 2, 1894
Feb 12, 1895

Thomas Eldridge Arnold
Mar 8, 1883
Sep 14, 1959

John Cullom Floyd
Jul 14, 1891
Jul 20, 1965
&
Margaret Huffman Floyd
Sep 16, 1903

John Campbell Coldwell
Jan 23, 1792
Jul 12, 1867
married Jul 13, 1819
&
Jane Northcott Coldwell
Oct 25, 1799
Aug 30, 1867
"by their loving daughter,
Mary"

Mary Coldwell Evans
1835-1907

Jacob C. Fite
Jul 28, 1829
Jan 24, 1863
"Capt. C.S.A."
marker by:Shirley-Shane,
Nashville.

Jane Fite Moore
1859-1921
"Daughter of Captain Fite,
C.S.A. & Wife of Dr. Moore,
U.S.N."

Uncas E. Peacock
Sep 7, 1833
Nov 1, 1922

Sarah J. Peacock
Feb 6, 1838
Mar 11, 1928

William J. Peacock
1884-1934

Sarah L. Peacock, wife of
Lewis A. Tillman & dau of
Uncas E. & Sarah J. Peacock
Oct 9, 1870
Apr 10, 1893

Jas. J. Elliott
Mar 29, 1860
Aug 4, 1896
"Husband"

"Father"
Joshua Kimmons
Sep 21, 1820
Aug 29, 1889
&
"Mother"
Isabel McClintock Kimmons
Feb 18, 1828
Jan 12, 1910

Beryl Maurine Bass
Aug 1, 1914
Sep 3, 1915

Thomas G. Kimmons
Dec 27, 1879
Feb 4, 1924

Ethel Kimery Rogers
Aug 6, 1890
Apr 13, 1973

Kate Kimery
Aug 4, 1893
Nov 12, 1972

Robert Samuel Robinson
1872-1946

Julia Jennings Robinson
1878-1939

Mary Emma Robinson
1900-1958

R. H. "Bob" Brown
1870-1943

Bessie M. Brown
1874-1919

Georgie W. Brown
1879-1945

Hattie T. Brown
1867-1933

R. Henry Brown, Jr.
1896-1970

Mary S. Brown
1899-1950

"Our Mother"
Harriet P. Wisener
married to William H. Wisener
Nov 17, 1839
Died Nov 16, 1868
&
Ruth Whitney, mother of
Mrs. Wisener. "Both of
whose remains quietly sleep
beneath this Monument."

William H. Wisener, Sr. and
Apr 22, 1812
Dec 24, 1882

Walter S. Lipscomb
was born in Fredericksburg,
Va., Mar 14, 1833 & died in
Shelbyville, Tenn. Nov 29,
1872

Harriet E., wife of
W. S. Lipscomb & dau of
Dr. Thomas & Mrs R.Lipscomb
Born in Shelbyville, Tenn
Aug 26, 1835 & died
Jun 29, 1873

A. O. Murdock
1854-1915

Alice, wife of
A. O. Murdock
Mar 3, 1857
Jan 12, 1914

J. Wilson Sanders
1867-1918
&
Nancy Edens Sanders
1877-1961

James, Infant son of
B. A. & Mina Reichenbach
1943

W. P. Reed
Sep 3, 1868
(no date)
& wife:
Mattie Lula Reed
Oct 25, 1874
May 5, 1918

J. Thomas Fisher
1891-1942
&
Agnes R. Fisher
1900-

Oliver Perry Arnold
1817-1884

Col. James Arnold
(no dates)

Nancy Caldonia Haynes
Nov 17, 1863
Mar 26, 1946

Troy Martin
Jul 15, 1940
Oct 26, 1940

M. Elizabeth McAnally
1919-1920

Joe D. McAnally
1899-1948
&
Argie S. McAnally
1898-1972

Mrs. M. V. Wisener
Died Mar 12, 1886
age: 49 yrs.

Dr. George W. Fogleman
May 5, 1804
Oct 28, 1853

Thomas G., son of
G. W. & M. V. Fogleman
Mar 1, 1847
Sep 26, 1849
age: 2y, 6m, 26d.

Benjamin -., son of
G. W. & Mary V. Fogleman
Jul 19, 1853
Jan 20, 1855

William Asbury Sanders
Oct 4, 1865
Dec 31, 1947

Myrtle Jernigan Sanders
Oct 24, 1886
Oct 26, 1948

Elsie Jernigan, wife of
W. A. Sanders
Nov 17, 1870
Nov 11, 1914

Charles W. Renegar
Oct 16, 1874
Oct 27, 1963
&
Willie C. Renegar
Jun 24, 1886
Feb 26, 1975

Geneveive R. Renegar
1923-1961

Donald M., Infant son of
C. & W. Renegar
Oct 18, 1913
Apr 6, 1916

Elijah M. Riddle
Sep 9, 1880
Mar 22, 1968
&
Katie V. Riddle
May 20, 1888
Jun 29, 1936

Daniel N. Martin
Sep 18, 1903
Apr 9, 1975
&
Bessie H. Martin
Jul 11, 1903

&
Edith Martin
Jul 26, 1930

George W. Swing
1908-1963

Margaret Lou Swing
1875-1948

M. Beatrice McAnally
1929-1951

George W.Fogleman,Jr, son of
G. W. & M. V. Fogleman
May 16, 1848
Sep 23, 1849
age: 1y, 4m, 7d.

Samuel Fogleman, Jr., son
of G. W. & Mary V. Fogleman
Oct 28, 1845
Sep 24, 1846
age: 10m & 26d.
(Oldest Marker in Cemetery)

Another Fogleman marker,
inscription broken away.

"Mother"
Etta Mai May
Mar 19, 1883
Feb 3, 1969

Reba, dau of
J. E. & Ettie M. May
Sep 26, 1903
Jan 4, 1918

Kenneth Wade May
Mar 5, 1922
Aug 11, 1944

Cecil G. Taylor
Aug 31, 1899

&
Jayne H. Taylor
Oct 18, 1904

Lelan Hargis
Sep 1, 1897
Dec 9, 1918

Ella Hargis
Sep 8, 1858
Jul 29, 1928

Arch Coldwell
1856-1937
&
Tennie Green Coldwell
1860-1934

Harry Coldwell
1892-1919

A. Eugene Umble
Sep 12, 1891
Oct 5, 1962
&
Virginia E. Umble
Nov 18, 1899
Jul 19, 1953

J. B. Umble
Jun 25, 1918
May 10, 1941
&
Thomas H. Hill
Mar 30, 1915
May 10, 1941

William H. son of
William H. & Harriet P.
Wisener
Sep 13, 1840
Mar 1, 1880
&
Infant son of
William H. & Isabella
Wisener
Born & Died
Aug 17, 1874

Frank O'Neal
1872-1941

Pearl O'Neal
1885-1929

Frank O'Neal, Jr.
Sep 5, 1916

Lucy F. Fitts, wife of
Joseph W. Nowlin
Mar 17, 1864
May 20, 1892
"Her Babe sleeps with her"

James Alexander Tate
Feb 26, 1860
Jan 25, 1951

Laetitia Cornforth Tate
Dec 31, 1868
Feb 23, 1934

James Alexander Tate, Jr.
Aug 17, 1894
Mar 21, 1919

Infant son of
James Guy & Gertrude Huff
(no dates)

Nucomb T. Brittain
Apr 13, 1845
Nov 5, 1916
&
Jason T. Brittain
Apr 3, 1853
Aug 2, 1926

Mary Ann Brittain
Dec 28, 1821
Apr 13, 1900
age: 78y, 3m, 16d.

"Mother"
Mary A. Russell
Feb 23, 1852
Mar 2, 1929

"Our Father"
Elbert G. Warren
Jan 20, 1814
Oct 13, 1880
age: 66y, 8m, 24d.

Charles A. Warren
Sep 16, 1845
Sep 17, 1909
&
Letitia Warren
Aug 10, 1846
Jan 18, 1923

Horace S. Hammond
Oct 3, 1872
Apr 11, 1922

"Mother"
Mary Wisener Hammond
Died Jun 27, 1880
(no age given)

Elizabeth Sutton
1833-1921

John W. Sutton, M.D.
1863-1942

Gwynn Rosson Sutton
1870-1958

Dr. J. S. Nowlin, M.D.
(no dates)

Mattie W., wife of
Dr. J. S. Nowlin
Jan 31, 1839
Feb 2, 1888

Gordon McLaurin Stewart
Aug 15, 18, 1957
son of James T. & Louise M.
Stewart, Grandson of Mr & Mrs
G. G. McLaurin, Dillon, S.C.

Bain Stewart
Nov 16, 1886
Jun 1, 1948

Rose Tate Stewart
Mar 2, 1890
Mar 24, 1867

"Mother"
Emma R. Morton
1865-1946
&
"Daughter"
Ethel Morton
1894-1950

James W., son of
J. T. & M. A. Brittain
Apr 16, 1846
Jun 10, 1873

Martha J., dau of
J. T. & M. A. Brittain
Sep 29, 1855
Apr 14, 1888

(Name gone)
1875-1950
(Gowen-Smith)

James Fred Nance
Nov 10, 1890
Jun 19, 1968

Edith Goggins Nance
Dec 18, 1890
Mar 28, 1941

Alfred Ranson Nance
1860-1946
&
Mollie G. Thompson Nance
Died 1924

"Mother"
Mary Powell Thompson
1874-1951

Lucy J., wife of
S. T. Powell
May 22, 1849
Jun 11, 1911

William W. Powell
Aug 19, 1854
Mar 27, 1890

Mollie Congo
1876-1952

W. M. Thompson
Mar 29, 1837
Dec 16, 1910
&
Cynthia Thompson
Apr 10, 1838
(no date)
&
Idella Thompson
Sep 29, 1863
Nov 17, 1887
&
B. J. Thompson
Oct 28, 1863
(no date)
&
Minnie S. Thompson
Apr 14, 1868
(no date)

Barbara Lee, dau of
Henry & Elizabeth Walls
Jun 17, 1949
Feb 26, 1962

Brown W. Minatra
1912-
&
Mary "Jiggs" Minatra
1919-1946

Sallie Green
1853-1923

W. Emerson Wilson
1878-1948
&
Vera W. Wilson
1882-1972

Willis Cannon
Feb 4, 1792
Feb 4, 1876
age: 84 yrs.

Nancy J., wife of
Jason T. Cannon
Feb 28, 1846
Sep 23, 1883
age: 37y, 6m, 25d.

Mattie George, dau of
A. R. & M. G. Nance
Apr 1, 1839
Oct 3, 1889

Robert A. Powell
Oct 3, 1906
Nov 22, 1912

Lillie Powell, wife of
Jno. F. Thompson
(no dates)

"My Husband, Our Pa"
W. J. Powel
Born in Richmond, Va.
Jul 14, 1820
Died Jul 24, 1874

Mildred Shapard Alexander
1876-1919

Jacob Fisher Thompson
Jun 12, 1833
Jun 8, 1880

Newcomb Thompson
Dec 27, 1792
Sep 8, 1869

Mrs. Amy Thompson
May 22, 1805
Mar 20, 1886

Jo. A. Thompson
1841-1921
"Confederate Soldier"

James Thomas Harper
1853-1935
&
Ida McMurray Harper
1854-1933

William Harper Oakes
Dec 30, 1920
Jan 7, 1922

Will A. Landers
Tennessee
Sup. Sgt 324 Inf 81 Div
Aug 17, 1892
Jun 5, 1943

"Father"
William Sullivan
Jul 5, 1844
May 1, 1883

"Mother"
Alice Thompson Sullivan
Nov 10, 1849
Dec 5, 1905

Dixie Connon(Cannon)
Mar 15, 1899
Jun 16, 1899

Johnie, youngest child of
J. W. & Mary J. Thompson
Feb 19, 1861
Jul 7, 1873

Elizar J., wife of
M. G. Thompson
Sep 5, 1851
Oct 22, 1882

Infant of
A. R. & M. G. Nance
Died Sep 15, 1837

George W. Thompson
Feb 1, 1823
Mar 10, 1908
age: 85y, 1m, 10d.

Martha M., wife of
G. W. Thompson
Mar 7, 1826
Aug 13, 1874
age: 48y, 5m, 6d.

Edwin Thompson Nance
Dec 25, 1892
Jul 21, 1971
&
Ruth Evans Nance
Jan 17, 1896
Dec 28, 1965

Henry L. Hanson
1866-1941

Ada L. Hanson
1871-1964

Clarence Edwin Hanson
May 25, 1890
Apr 27, 1904

John M. Hudson
Aug 15, 1888
Jan 9, 1964
&
Turley S. Hudson
Nov 18, 1889

Mary Hudson Wilson
1891-1918

Horace E. Landers
Mar 21, 1870
Jun 9, 1943
&
Annie B. Landers
Mar 29, 1874
Sep 2, 1949

"Father"
Elgin C. Landers
Jan 6, 1841
Apr 27, 1922

"Mother"
Mary E. Landers
Oct 3, 1846
Sep 7, 1896

William Jason, son of
J. H. & Amy W. Gill
nee Brittain
Jan 11, 1892
Oct 8, 1918

J. H. Gill
May 26, 1862
Apr 3, 1928
& wife
Amy W. Gill
1858-1945

Martha Washington Thompson
Dec 29, 1848
May 24, 1852
&
Joseph Newcom Thompson
Mar 10, 1851
May 13, 1860
"Children of G. W. &
Martha M. Thompson"

Mattie Mariah, youngest
dau of G. W. & Martha M.
Thompson
Dec 9, 1858
Oct 10, 1883

George Hobbs Cowan
1873-1957

John B. McDougal
1859-1932
"He was true to his
obligations"

Alec L. McDougal
1863-1917
&
Florette H. McDougal
1859-1933

George Hobbs "Sug" McDougal
1898-1951

Jas. S. Gillis
Apr 12, 1839
Jan 1, 1915

Eliza B. Gillis
Jan 29, 1842
Feb 26, 1913

George D. Gillis
Jun 9, 1867
Jun 1, 1891

Jno. D. Gillis, Jr.
Feb 29, 1876
Jun 27, 1893

"Father"
Silas A. Bivins
Apr 30, 1824
Oct 13, 1863
& wife:
"Mother"
Lucy W. Gannaway Bivins
Mar 20, 1826
Feb 7, 1885

Levoy B. McFarlin
1896-1968

Pauline D. McFarlin
1910-1944

Addie B. McFarlin
1909-

Eula C. McFarlin
1898-1927

John Kelly Breast
Aug 21, 1903
Dec 7, 1977

Joshua Edgar Huffman
Jun 12, 1879
Feb 21, 1955

Sarah Young Huffman
Aug 16, 1885
Jul 31, 1960

Ruth Trimble Huffman
Jun 3, 1889
Dec 2, 1922

Francis, dau of
J. & C. M. Wortham
May 6, 1843
Oct 19, 1844

Nellie, Infant dau of
R. C. & M. F. Wortham
Nov 9, 1882
Jan 10, 1883
age: 2 months

Shellie, son of
R. C. & M. F. Wortham
1885-1910

F. S. Landers
1842-1927

Sallie J. Landers
1852-1914

Albert Sidney Landers
Sep 10, 1877
Nov 18, 1896

Ella Laura, dau of
F. S. & S. J. Landers
Feb 29, 1884
Jul 28, 1888

James Harry, son of
F. A. & M. A. -------y
was born --- 5, 1864
died May 25, ----
(very bad condition)

Lona Lewis, Sister of
Tom Cox
(no dates)

Fannie Cox (b. 1863)
(no dates)
&
Maggie Cox (b. 1866)
(no dates)

Thomas Cox
1827-1910
&
Sarah Cox
1835-1901

Sallie Cox
1868-1870

Robert Lee Joyce
1869-1957

Mrs. R. L. Joyce
1870-1938

Major John Wortham
Born in Graves Co., Ky.
Aug 31, 1840 & died
Dec 7, 1868
"Rest Soldier"

Kitty McNairy Wells, dau of
J. & C. M. Wortham
Born in Shelbyville, Tenn.
Apr 2, 1838
Died in Atlanta, Ga.
Nov 23, 1866

Captain James Wortham
1813-1873
&
Catherine Cannon Wortham
1816-1885

Robert Cannon Wortham
1858-1939
&
Mary Fruzie Wortham
1860-1934

John W. Fletcher
Dec 28, 1825
Sep 8, 1863

James Laurence Whittier
Jun 14, 1896

"Father"
Henry L. Graves
Feb 17, 1832
Dec 2, 1882
& wife:
"Mother"
Georgie Bradley Graves
Died Dec 7, 1915
(no age given)

Sidney Landers
Nov 7, 1912
Jan 8, 1953

Sarah E. Landers
1906-1908

Finis Marks Landers
Dec 4, 1874
Dec 14, 1953
&
Nora Green Landers
Jul 29, 1882
Apr 21, 1915

Samuel E. Green
Feb 8, 1854
Nov 29, 1948

Margaret R. Green
Jul 7, 1858
Aug 10, 1931

Effie Green Stapp
Dec 25, 1883
Mar 2, 1920

Fay Elizabeth Perryman
1923-1924

Rose Wallace
1899-1924

Joseph L. Haynes
Pvt U.S. Army
Apr 13, 1892
Sep 21, 1972
&
Rybye J. Haynes
1897-

Mamie Wallace, wife of
J. B. Spradlin
1901-1928

Isabelle Nash Bobo
Sep 15, 1908
Jul 26, 1950

Robert Lee Jones
Oct 1, 1889
Feb 4, 1973
&
Bessie Lee Jones
Jan 17, 1897

Donald Crowell
Apr 7, 1931
Aug 7, 1932

Charlie B. Whitmon
Dec 7, 1897
Jun 26, 1954
&
Jennie Mae Whitmon
Apr 20, 1901

William Henry Shepperson
Jan 18, 1845
Mar 31, 1918
&
Eliza Katherine Shapperson
Jul 16, 1844
Apr 10, 1918

William Franklin Patterson
Apr 19, 1919
Apr 8, 1924

Frank Patterson
Sep 10, 1866
Sep 10, 1928
&
Annie Patterson
Nov 10, 1862
(no date)

Willie Patterson
1891-1962
(Thompson)

Henrietta Molley
Died Sep 20, 1888
aged: 88 yrs.
"Rest Mother"

Wayne Crowell
May 1, 1920
Apr 24, 1936

Brownie Crowell
Dec 17, 1921
Oct 30, 1933

Lucy, wife of
William Key
Feb 1832
Aug 17, 1885
"She was but words are wanting
to say what think, what a wife
should be, she was that."

Bud Morton
1865-1932

"Father"
C. C. "Pete" Foster
Jul 1, 1869
Feb 2, 1938

"Mother"
Allie Foster
Feb 21, 1874
Sep 29, 1932

Elmore Foster
Jan 26, 1914
Nov 20, 1934

Jonnie F. Osteen
Mar 12, 1906
Sep 29, 1934

Infant son of
Jonnie-Frank Osteen
(no dates)

Eddie, son of
J. D. & G. T. Kimmons
Dec 5, 1875
Jan 15, 1877

Arabella Davidson, was born
in the year of 1800, Died
Sep 17, 1882
"Erected by her affectionate
children-William & Lucy Key"

D. B. Shepperson
Born 1816
Died Jan 7, 1861
aged: 45 yrs.

M. E. Shepperson
Mar 10, 1843
Dec 16, 1888

220	219
80	77
81	218

James, son of
John & Mary Haberlin
Jan 26, 1864
Oct 9, 1875

Emmett Haberlin
1868-1938
&
Josephine Haberlin
1879-1955

J. D. Kimmons
Dec 1, 1854
Jan 9, 1929

Gracie T. Kimmons
Jul 30, 1854
Feb 6, 1881

Tint Kimmons
1886-1974
(Gowen-Smith)

Nancy, wife of
Henry McLain, Born 1833 &
Died Oct 30, 1885
"Erected in token of love
and affection by her brother:
William Key"

William Kirk Shepperson
Sep 6, 1892
Dec 16, 1892
age: 3m & 10d.

(end of Section "D")

SECTION "C" (continued)

"Father"
Rev. B. J. Gaston
1841-1910
&
"Mother"
Elizabeth Gaston
1844-1905

Marvin R. Gaston
1876-1892

Robert Y. Gaston
1879-1889

Willie J., son of
J. F. & S. J. Turrentine
Feb 7, 1898
Aug 18, 1902
&
Fred R., son of
J. F. & S. J. Turrentine
Apr 4, 1888
Jul 18, 1901

Ellie Trolinger
1875-1942

P. H. Reaves
1828-1896

Caroline, wife of
P. H. Reaves
1827-1904

John F. Turrentine
1864-1958
&
Jennie Turrentine
1866-1946

"Father"
W. J. Turrentine
Mar 1, 1837
Mar 8, 1898
&
"Mother"
Mary Turrentine
Sep 14, 1840
Sep 25, 1915

Mary A., wife of
T. L. Elam
Jul 2, 1851-Jul 11, 1903

Callie, wife of
D. H. Anderson
1849-1937

Minnie M., dau of
D. H. & Callie Anderson
1880-1884

Thomas J. Brown
1868-1945
&
Susie R. Brown
1874-1910

"Our Mother"
Sallie Haynes, wife of
Dr. W. J. Miller
Died Feb 18, 1890
(no age given)

Little Myrl, Infant dau of
W. J. & Sallie Miller
Apr 7, 1888
Jul 25, 1888

Alice Sullivan
May 20, 1872
Aug 4, 1922

Belle Stout
Feb 5, 1862
Jan 14, 1916

Rev. B. M. Stout
Mar 12, 1836
Dec 5, 1893
&
Eliza J. Stout
Nov 7, 1843
Mar 3, 1929

Bronson E. Stout
Jul 30, 1886
Oct 15, 1904

Thomas C. Martin
1880-1940

Emma Elam Martin
1884-1974

Moody Ventress
1856-1931

Dana Ventress
1858-1932

Letitia, wife of
John K. Ventress
Apr 22, 1824
Feb 25, 1900

James A. Thompson
Feb 26, 1836
Dec 11, 1911

Martha Ventress, wife of
James A. Thompson
May 22, 1848
Mar 19, 1893

Aunt Josie McAuliff
left us Jan 23, 1908
(no age given)

Eugene S. Beatty
1867-1947

Mary J. Beatty
1870-1929

Aubrey Robert Moon
Feb 10, 1900
Mar 23, 1930
&
Louise Brown Moon
Apr 17, 1903

Pleasant Bacon Moon, Sr.
Jun 24, 1874
Feb 22, 1951
&
Leno Carpenter
Mar 30, 1874
Dec 5, 1959

Infant son of
Mr & Mrs P. B. Moon
1903

Albert Clifford Green
1893-
&
Gladys Moon Green
1898-1925

Daniel B. Stewart
Feb 6, 1851
Mar 8, 1903
& wife:
Nancy McCrary Stewart
Feb 29, 1864
Mar 11, 1946
& son:
Daniel Grayson Stewart
Oct 26, 1893
Nov 20, 1958

Joseph D. Brown
May 25, 1903
Sep 7, 1965
&
Mary D. Brown
May 2, 1905- 1976 June

John A. Moore
1866-1935
&
Mattie J. Moore
1869-1958

Mary D. Moore, wife of
Glenes Cates
1900-1930

Newcomb Cary Thompson
1870-1919
&
Lizzie Dixon Thompson
1872-1950

Nathan Evans, son of
Thomas & Lizzie Thompson
Aug 23, 1868
Dec 23, 1870

Thomas Thompson
Born Jul 1, 1841
married to Lizzie Evans
Jan 19, 1865
Died Aug 19, 1870

L. J. Osburn
Feb 18, 1853
Jun 9, 1935
&
Mattie Elmore Osburn
Sep 13, 1852
May 3, 1903

Nettie Osburn Hix
1878-1919

Florence P. Burrow
Sep 24, 1876
Mar 24, 1938

Margaret Mai Burrow
Nov 16, 1902
May 10, 1904
"Daughter of Warder &
Florence Burrow"

Bettie Nelson
Dec 3, 1870
Jun 9, 1905

Clifford E. Gates
Jul 5, 1883
Apr 4, 1904

Robert C. Wright
1849-1905
&
Georgia Ruth Wright
1844-1880

Wiley Elliott Bell
May 4, 1881
Apr 11, 1972
&
Lula Bell
Mar 4, 1894

Wendelle T. Williams
1915-1975
(Howell)

Ewin Burrow
1871-1900
&
Will Burrow
1865-1917

J. Riley Burrow
Nov 12, 1830
Mar 5, 1905
&
Harriet E. Burrow
Feb 5, 1840
Dec 26, 1915

Ella Burrow
1878-1918

Charlie Floyd Reagor
Mar 30, 1880
May 29, 1934
&
Rhoda Reaves Reagor
Oct 3, 1882

Mildren Reagor, dau of
Mr & Mrs H. H. Jones
Jun 16, 1900
Aug 23, 1904

Robert Lee Sanders
Jun 4, 1878
Feb 6, 1954
&
Elma Osburn Sanders
Sep 14, 1881
May 10, 1966

Eugene M. Hairston
1875-1950
&
Eula May Hairston
1880-(no date)

Mary E. Hairston
Jul 20, 1844
Dec 19, 1899

E. J. Hairston
Mar 29, 1870
Jan 6, 1912

Bertie Hairston
Nov 19, 1870
Sep 23, 1948

James H. Castleman
Feb 19, 1866
Oct 4, 1923

Henrietta R., wife of
J. H. Castleman
Born Jun 10, 1872
age: 41y, 2m, 4d.

Starling T. Marbury
1905-1971
&
Elizabeth A. Marbury
1908-19

Lafayette Reagor
Jul 24, 1856
Sep 19, 1915
&
Fannie Burrow Reagor
Feb 25, 1862
Dec 20, 1950

"My Husband"
Henry Walker Rumbley
Nov 7, 1865
Apr 16, 1903

Lavinia Rumbley Rice
May 7, 1867
Jan 1, 1926

"Father"
Joe A. Reagor
May 10, 1838
Aug 12, 1907
& wife:
"Mother"
Sallie Gardner Reagor
Nov 22, 1839
Jun 7, 1903

"Father"
W. T. Snell
May 28, 1828
Dec 30, 1902
&
"Mother"
F. E. Snell
Jun 30, 1832
Jan 29, 1917

Annie Belle McCullough
May 29, 1905
Mar 15, 1906

Fred A. Reaves
1873-1918

Bettie Reaves Dennis
1878-1947

J. Reaves
Mar 26, 1848
Jan 19, 1905

Rebecca Reaves
Jan 30, 1850
Nov 4, 1909

G. W. Edwards
1926-1971
(Gowen-Smith)

Edward Dudley Tarpley
1833-1894
&
Alice Bivins Tarpley
1849-1930

Thomas A. Tarpley
Oct 3, 1877
Oct 30, 1901

Napoleon B. Tarpley
Oct 4, 1869
Jan 12, 1895

Lealon D. Stephens
Sep 5, 1895
Jan 3, 1965
&
Alice W. Stephens
Oct 17, 1898
Nov 25, 1968

Edna R. Davis
Jul 31, 1871
May 17, 1911

William C. Lane
Mar 5, 1874
Dec 6, 1933

William Holeman Lane
Feb 26, 1909
Jun 25, 1912

Carrie Scudder
(no dates)

George D. Scudder
(no dates)

Jennie D. Scudder
(no dates)

Daniel B. Stewart
Mar 1815
Nov 19, 1890
age: 75 yrs.

Harriett, wife of
Daniel B. Stewart
May 1833
Nov 11, 1887, age: 54 yrs.

Mary, wife of
D. B. Stewart
Died Sep 18, 1870
age: 50y, 5m, 3d.
"She was a member of the
Cumberland Presbyterian
Church for 30 yrs."

Abraham Frankle
1847-1928
&
Elizabeth Y. Frankle
1858-1945

Jimmie Bryant, dau of
W. P. & A. M. Yancy
Jun 6, 1880
Jun 13, 1884

Charles Pearson
1880-1947

Ethel R. Pearson
1882-1952

Alma Raby, wife of
Jas. B. Parsons
1895-1921

"Our Mother"
Mrs. Susan Burt
Mar 13, 1797
Nov 30, 1876

R. B. Wilhoite
Apr --, 1836
Aug 10, 1883
&
Tennie G. Wilhoite
Sep 18, 1840
Nov 2, 1909

Sara T. Wilhoite
Feb 24, 1915
May 30, 1927

Col. James L. Scudder
Born in Shelbyville, Tenn
Mar 23, 1823 & Died
Dec 5, 1882
"Father"
& wife:
"Mother"
Caroline Davidson Scudder
Born in Shelbyville, Tenn
Sep 9, 1833 & Died
Jul 20, 1919

Richard Phillips
1794-1872
&
Elizabeth Pool Phillips
1794-1869
& (reverse side)
David Richard Phillips
1858-1863
&
William Word
1803-1883
&
Mary Cunningham Word
1801-1876
&
Cuthbert Burney Word
1824-1866
&
Eliza Ann Phillips
1851-1855
&
William Milton Word
1848-1882

R. N. Wallace
Apr 8, 1805
Nov 8, 1883

Eliza Jane Hollins, wife of
Dr. R. N. Wallace
Oct 30, 1813
Aug 26, 1899

Mabel C. Robson
1861-1946

James Russell Brown
Jul 28, 1879
May 5, 1883

Nash H., son of
William & Susan Burt,
Father of Hardy M. &
Nash H. Burt
Jun 27, 1832
Jul 31, 1903

Thomas W. Dyer
1877-1923

John G. Cannon
1874-1933
& wife:
Jessie Cannon
1877-1958

A. Edward Chunn
Sep 29, 1877
Sep 3, 1957
&
Jennie S. Chunn
Mar 15, 1886
Oct 10, 1970

Tennie Chunn
Feb 24, 1854
Jan 23, 1939

James S. McClelland
Oct 4, 1854
Jul 31, 1886

Jennie E. McClelland
Sep 28, 1856
Jun 6, 1938

Jimmie, son of
J. S. & Jennie McClelland
Jul 16, 1886
Aug 24, 1886

William Bryant Woosley
1904-1972

Harry Lee Woosley
1870-1935

Mattie Bryant Woosley
1870-1952

W. M. Bryant
1836-1917

Martha J. Bryant
1851-1921

M. A. Bryant
1875-1928

Jesse L. Bryant
Aug 31, 1872
Sep 12, 1872
&
James M. Bryant
Nov 6, 1873
Jan 26, 1874
"Sons of W. M. &
M. J. Bryant"

Martha R. Bryant, dau of
J. P. & Mollie B. Fyff
Nov 27, 1890
Jan 30, 1895

Richard Burt, son of
William & Susan Burt
Nov 4, 1836
Dec 16, 1888

Edwin H. McGowan
Sep 26, 1842
Jun 8, 1903

Stevens Hubbard Walker
1850-1900
&
Huldah Wilhoite Walker
1861-1895

Nannie Greer Butler
Jan 31, 1848
Jun 12, 1924

Thomas Newcome Greer, Jr.
Dec 15, 1909
Dec 28, 1954

Thomas Newcome Greer
Jun 13, 1875
Jul 10, 1932

Minnie Taylor Greer
May 28, 1875
Aug 12, 1932

Infant son of
T. N. & Carol Greer
1935

Arrie Vance, Infant dau of
M. T. & T. N. Greer
Jan 29, 1898
Jan 10, 1899

David Swain Blakemore
1862-1905
&
Hattie Bryant Blakemore
Mar 25, 1867
Nov 15, 1907

Horace J. Rowzee
Nov 19, 1869
Dec 1, 1890
age: 21y & 12d.

James Yancy
1816-1874
&
Martha Wilhoite Yancy
1823-1910

Sallie E., wife of
W. V. Raby
Oct 27, 1875
Sep 21, 1903

Hettie A., wife of
John R. Raby
Jul 9, 1829
Oct 4, 1901

Mary, dau of
Vance & Sallie Raby
Feb 17, 1899
Jul 11, 1900

Cassie, dau of
William & Susan Burt
Mar 6, 1829
Jan 15, 1905

Luna Burt, wife of
Edwin H. McGowan
1840-1910

James Harrison Dyer
Apr 8, 1841
Oct 3, 1901
&
Belle A. Dyer
Nov 25, 1841
Dec 26, 1906

Roy O. Dyer
1880-1921

James H. Dyer, M.D.
1875-1955

Thomas Wesley Buchanan
Jan 14, 1817
Nov 4, 1884
&
Sarah A. Buchanan
Mar 29, 1820
Mar 6, 1903

Samuel, youngest son of
T. W. & Sarah A. Buchanan
Oct 7, 1857
May 6, 1876
age: 18y, 7m, less 1 day.

Thomas L. Buchanan
1871-1874

Lawson L. Buchanan
1844-1875

Richard A. Bartlett
Jan 10, 1859
Mar 17, 1899

Ella Bartlett
1861-1933

"Mother"
Mary H. Hendon
Died Jul 28, 1894
(no age given)

John C. Hendon
1846-1924

Kate Hendon
1844-1921

John B. Jackson
1873-1920
&
Glenn M. Jackson
1882-1962

John M. Jackson
1902-
&
Mary H. Jackson
1907-

Wilson W. Brown
Sep 19, 1859
May 26, 1909
&
Susan E. Brown
Mar 30, 1856
May 28, 1921

Fred Deery Brown
Mar 28, 1893-Nov 20, 1948

John L., son of
William & Susan Burt
Oct 21, 1830
Feb 2, 1906

Mary J.C., dau of
T. S. & M. C. Burt
May 17, 1848
Jan 16, 1889

Joel J. Blackwell
Feb 19, 1826
Aug 2, 1873

Joe, son of
Jas. S. & Mary Miller
Sep 27, 1860
Died in Augusta, Ga.
(dates broken away)

Lewis Vance Fogleman
Jun 10, 1850
May 21, 1880

Geraldine Fogleman, dau of
L. V. & Lettie Fogleman
Mar 3, 1878
Dec 27, 1880

Josephine Fogleman Rawlings
1878-1914

George W. Fogleman
1875-1940

Mary S. Fogleman
1876-1922

"Father"
Tom Pettus
1853-1916

"Mother"
Lucy Pettus
1855-1893

"Sister"
Virginia Pettus
1888-1908

E. S. Pettus
Aug 1, 1829
Jan 13, 1908

Elizabeth E. Pettus, wife of
J. K. Randolph
Jun 22, 1862
Mar 12, 1931

Marshall L. Morton
1841-1895

Lee G. Morton
1851-1884

Martha Ellen Brown
Nov 5, 1895
Nov 2, 1966

Drucilla, dau of
F. D. & M. E. Brown
Died Mar 31, 1921

William E. Sims
1835-1902

Lucy B. Sims
1837-1913

W. Ola Sims
1877-1907

Luna M. Sims
1871-1915

Richard P. Stephenson
Feb 7, 1808
Mar 27, 1882
& wife:
Martha J. Stephenson
May 27, 1824
Oct 11, 1882

The Tribute of the South to
S. A. Cunningham
founder & Editor of the
"Confederate Veteran" Jan 1893
to Dec 1913. He gathered the
History of his people written
in tears but radiant with
Glory.
A Member of Co. B., 41 Tenn.
Inf. Army of Tennessee, Part-
icipated in & captured at the
Battle of Fort Donalson when
exchanged, he returned to the
Army & engaged in the One
Hundred Days Battle, from
Dalton to Atlanta, Ga., march-
ed with the Army to Tenn., &
was in the Battles of Franklin
& Nashville.
Summer Archibald Cunningham
A Gallent Confederate Soldier
Born 1843 & Died 1913
"In 1893, he established the
"Confederate Veteran" and
owned & Edited it until his
death." " On Fame's eternal
Camping ground his silent tent
is spread, and Glory Guards,
in solemn Round, the Bivouac
of the Dead."

W. F. Buchanan
1848-1919

Ellen C. Buchanan
1850-1898

Joe H. Evans
1843-1908

John Massey
Nov 11, 1866
Jun 21, 1933

Ann Elizabeth Parsons
May 11, 1871
Mar 5, 1909

Joe E. Snoddy
1862-1937
&
Willie A. Snoddy
1871-1937

Virgil J. McRee
Died Jun 23, 1875
age: 37y, 3m, 4d.

Catherine Ann, wife of
V. J. McRee, & dau of
William & M. B. Galbraith
Sep 16, 1838
Dec 2, 1878
"She hath done what she
could."

A. E., wife of
V. J. McRee
Feb 16, 1835
Aug 18, 1873

Thomas McRee
Mar 18, 1869
Sep 1869
&
Sarah R. McRee
Jul 6, 1870
Jun 1872

J. H. McRee
Apr 20, 1863
Dec 30, 1885

Little Mary Cunningham
Mar 15, 1873
Oct 28, 1875
& (reverse side)
Patented July 3, 1877
A. M. Buchanan, Moberly, Mo.

Mary Buchanan, wife of
B. W. Sutton
Jan 8, 1872
Apr 13, 1896

"Mother"
Mary A. Cunningham
1820-1889
"She did what she could."

Samuel Buchanan
1876-1900

Marcus Buchanan
1877-1900

T. W. Buchanan
1885-1925

Lois D. Buchanan
Jul 10, 1882
Jun 29, 1964

James E. Buchanan
1883-1916

Elizabeth Irene Bittick
Mar 19, 1894
Dec 11, 1971

Phillip Jason Altman
Apr 19, 1950
Mar 1, 1973

B. L. McFerrin
Feb 20, 1812
Jul 24, 1881

"Brother"
Howard Lee Gibson
1939-1940
&
"Brother"
Deery Gibson Tucker
1937-1944

Richard Samuel Stapp
Oct 22, 1878
Feb 19, 1956

Helen Temple Stapp
Sep 25, 1851
May 1, 1932

Charlie M. Reid
Jun 6, 1875
Nov 21, 1958
&
Bettie R. Reid
Aug 26, 1877
May 10, 1963

Nannie Kate Tillman, dau of
W. G. & M. A. Miller, wife
of G. N. Tillman, mother of
Aileen Tillman
Born Nov 14, 1853
married Oct 14, 1875
Died Jun 14, 1880
age: 26y & 7m.

Lewis Tillman
Aug 18, 1816
May 3, 1886
& wife:
Mary C. Tillman
Mar 1, 1823
Dec 7, 1902
marker: Dooley & Ayers,
        Fishkill Landing,
        N.Y.

"Our Mother"
Mary McFerrin Reagan
Born Apr 10, 1846
Married Nov 28, 1864
Died Oct 8, 1876

H. W. Smith
Apr 21, 1848
Apr 6, 1903

J. B. Temple
Jul 1, 1860
married to Ella Williams
Mar 19, 1893
Died Dec 19, 1893
age: 33y, & 6m.

Rebecker G., wife of
T. R. Smith & dau of
W. H. & M. H. Anderson
Aug 26, 1853
May 26, 1880

Mary C. Tillman, dau of
L. & M. C. Tillman
Aug 29, 1853
Feb 18, 1858

John Marshall Tillman, 7th
son of Lewis & Mary C.
Tillman
May 27, 1861
Feb 17, 1877
age: 15y, 8m, 21d.

Blount Garriett Green
Oct 4, 1815
Jul 1, 1906
&
Selina Floyd Stewart Green
Mar 25, 1820
Sep 24, 1906

Warner G. Storey
Nov 24, 1889

&
Lynn S. Storey
Jun 14, 1911
Feb 20, 1963
&
Nina H. Storey
Oct 7, 1898
Jan 6, 1934

John Tillman
Born in Edgefield Dist., S.C.
Feb 5, 1786
Died Oct 3, 1854 at his house
near Fairfield, Bedford County,
Tenn.
&
Rachel P. Tillman
Born in Edgefield District,
S.C., May 16, 1789 & Died
Nov 10, 1881 at the house of
her son Lewis Tillman, near
Shelbyville, Tenn.
"John Tillman & Rachel P.
Martin were married Jan 17,
1810 at the Residence of her
Father, Capt. Matt Martin,
Bedford County, Tenn. They
became members of the New
Hope Baptist Church at Fair-
field in its infancy were
members of the same at their
deaths & Died in full assur-
ance of there long cherished
Faith in Christ." Erected in
1883 by their only surviving
sons: Lewis & Barclay M.
Tillman.

James Story
Nov 29, 1801
Oct 27, 1889
age: 87y, 10m, 23d.
    & wife:
Diadma A. Story
Died Wednesday 3 o'clock
A.M. March 25, 1862
aged: 54y, 1m, 14d.

Thomas C. Allison
Feb 5, 1828
Apr 9, 1908
&
Evaline Allison
Aug 6, 1827
Jan 26, 1895

W. W. Ivie
Nov 27, 1850
Nov 17, 1919

"Sister"
Bettie Miller Ivie
Dec 29, 1856
Feb 13, 1880

T. B. Ivie, Jr.
1880-1928

(end of Section "C")

SECTION " E "

Mattie R. Hinson
1848-1873

Elizabeth R. Hinson
1843-1884

Benjamin, son of
Samuel & Elizabeth Little
Jul 10, 1808
May 19, 1861

Chauncey, son of Samuel &
Elizabeth Little
Jul 18, 1814
May 19, 1861

Benjamin L. Russell
1811-1887
&
Ermin Gill Russell
1816-1876

Fannie C. Little, wife of
John R. Wallace
1853-1914

Fannie Stevenson, Infant dau
of William C. & Jennie C.
Little
Dec 20, 1874
Nov 14, 1878

William Clary Little
Born in Bedford County, Tenn.
Jan 14, 1839 & Died in
Shelbyville, Tenn. Oct 27,1880

Thomas H. Coldwell*
Died Mar 10, 1891
(no age given)
* Born Aug 29, 1822, by
  Mrs. Amie McGrew.

Carrie Hopkins Coldwell*
Died Dec 10, 1884
(no age given)
* In 1880 Census, 35 yrs old,
  by Mrs. Amie McGrew.

Virginia C., wife of
William C. Little & dau of
Thomas & Rebecca Lipscomb
Dec 21, 1840
May 9, 1893

Mary H., wife of
Thomas H. Coldwell
Died Oct 4, 1874
age: 53y & 4m.

Ernest Coldwell
1859-1937

Josephine Warren Coldwell
1873-1957

William Street Ransom
Feb 2, 1880
Aug 2, 1929

Caroline Caldwell Ransom
Sep 1, 1876
Jun 10, 1953

Hugh Lawson White, son of
William & Lucy C. Little
Jun 21, 1840
Aug 13, 1873
&
Montgomery, son of
Samuel & Elizabeth Little
Jul 18, 1825
Mar 8, 1863

Bennie Little
May 9, 1851
Jun 19, 1867

"Father"
William, son of
Samuel & Elizabeth Little
Jan 29, 1806
Sep 1, 1875
& wife:
"Mother"
Lucy Caroline, dau of
William & Nancy Clary
Feb 4, 1818
Jan 23, 1878

Sallie, dau of
Thomas C. & Agnes (Sir name
not on Stone)
Born Oct 1, 1869
Died Mar 25, 1870
(in Little plot)

In Memoriam
Sarah Little, wife of
Richard A. Wilkes
Born in Bedford County, Tenn.
Jan 16, 1850 & Died in
Culleoka, Tenn.
Apr 9, 1883

R. S. Miller
Jul 23, 1835
Sep 3, 1896
& wife:
Roxanna Miller
Nov 13, 1855
Feb 23, 1935
marker by: Hummel & Son of
        Huntsville, Ala.

H. E. B. (in Miller Plot)

William H. North
1871-1935

Emma V. North
1872-1962

George Denny Dysart
Apr 28, 1839
Jul 17, 1900
"A Brave Soldier of the
Confederate Army & a beloved
Citizen of Bedford County."
&
Robert A. Dysart
Dec 31, 1840
Oct 5, 1914
"A Brave Soldier of the
Confederate Army & a beloved
Citizen of Bedford County."

Bruce K. Brantley
Oct 19, 1874
May 9, 1928

Maggie M. Brantley
1881-1960

Clarence E. Brantley
Tennessee
Pvt 1cl 115 Field Arty 30 Div
Feb 16, 1938

Albert E. Fuqua
Apr 7, 1874
May 31, 1874
&
Edner M. Fuqua
Dec 9, 1875
Dec 27, 1875

Sarah E., wife of
G. W. Fuqua
Sep 11, 1844
Dec 20, 1875

Harry L. Fuqua
1891-1902

Ella Fuqua
1863-1926

George Fuqua
1842-1924

Alice Fuqua
(no dates)

Edwin R. Bearden
(no dates)

Walter Scott Bearden
Jan 10, 1843
Dec 15, 1919
&
Margaret Whiteside Bearden
Nov 21, 1840
Jul 22, 1919
&
Mary H. Bearden
Mar 7, 1878
Jan 15, 1948

"Our Darling Little Margie"
Margie R. Bearden
Died Dec 29, 1881
age: 5y & 4m.

Ada C. Whiteside, wife of
James Wylie Mather
Died Apr 13, 1887
(no age given)
&
Margaret Robinson, dau of
James W. & Ada C. Mather
Sep 4, 1880
May 13, 1899

J. M. Jordan
1840-1923
Tenn Inf. 1861-1865

Patrick R. McKenna
Born near Dublin, Ireland
Feb 24, 1819
Died Nov 19, 1870
    also his Son:
Richard McKenna
Died Mar 15, 1865
age: 7 days

Elmer Neeley
Nov 20, 1900
Jun 25, 1927
&
Madgie Neeley
Jun 5, 1898
Jun 25, 1927

Hugh Jones
Dec 24, 1810
Nov 19, 1892

Jesse Ely
1837-1897
    & wife:
Mary Whiteside Ely
1837-1893
    & Their Son:
William Edward Ely
1878-1881

Mary Mitchell Ely
1867-1943

Henry C. Whiteside
Dec 3, 1842
Feb 23, 1905

Ruth Whiteside
Jul 3, 1876
Jun 28, 1967

Annie Robinson, Infant dau
of H. C. & A. L. Whiteside
Jan 23, 1871
Jul 1, 1873

Ruth Whiteside, wife of
Jesse Ely
Died Apr 8, 1873
age: 30 yrs.
&
Ruth
Apr 5, 1873
Nov 21, 1873

T. C. W., Junior (Whiteside)
(no dates)

James R. Whiteside
Jun 25, 1849
Nov 28, 1892

David Jenkin Whiteside
May 22, 1851
Mar 9, 1930

Robert S. Rollings
Oct 16, 1842
Mar 9, 1919
&
Joann Rollings
Sep 1, 1853
Mar 9, 1936

Pearl Phelps
1890-1972

Lucy M. Phelps
1892-1954

W. T. Heard
Oct 16, 1850
Feb 10, 1912
&
Sallie R. Heard
Jan 19, 1854
(no date)

T. Leigh Thompson
Jul 26, 1862
(no date)
&
Nellie Ely Thompson
Nov 5, 1870
Aug 8, 1927
&
Infant Daughter
Jul 7, 1905

Charles R. Shapard
Sep 27, 1883
Jul 17, 1934

Ada Whiteside Shapard
Aug 28, 1881
Aug 2, 1954

Birdie Whiteside
Mar 28, 1868
Sep 11, 1954

Agnes Louise Whiteside
entered into Rest
Aug 7, 1930
(no age given)

Agnes Lipscomb Whiteside
Aug 14, 1843
Jan 12, 1932

"Father"
Thomas Cooper Whiteside
Jun 29, 1809
Jan 10, 1885
&
"Mother"
Margaret A. Whiteside
Jul 5, 1821
May 30, 1894

Capt. Thomas R. Mitchell
Jan 19, 1834
Wounded Dec 6, died Dec 9,
1864.

Annie S., dau of Thomas C.
& Margaret A. Whiteside
Jul 19, 1862
Jul 5, 1863
&
Annie, dau of
Thomas R. & Mary E. Mitchell
Feb 25, 1862
Apr 5, 1863

J. P. Huffman
Apr 21, 1835
Dec 16, 1906

N. E. Huffman
May 12, 1850
Feb 22, 1929

In Memory Our Confederate Dead, in Plot of about 500* numbered
Memorial Markers.

* No list of names to the
500 exists today.

L. A. Horton
of
Pleasant Ridge,
Green Co., Ala.
(no dates)

Capt. W. H. Keiter, C.S.A.
A Native of Virginia, was killed
by the bursting of the gun Lady
Polk at Columbus, Ky.,
Nov 11, 1861

Dr. Wayne T. Robinson
1885-1973
&
Olive Lane Robinson
1893-1932

C. N. Allen
1816-1898
&
Lucy C. Allen
1820-1895

W. V. Allen
Feb 7, 1857
Aug 24, 1900
age: 43y, 6m, 17d.

John W. Allen
1860-1892

"Father"
Robert Payne Frierson
Aug 24, 1843
Jun 26, 1893
&
"Mother"
Mollie Little Frierson
1844-1935
&
Robert Payne Frierson, Jr.
Apr 29, 1875, lost in
Alaskan Waters June 1898
&
Robert Payne Frierson, IV
1899-1950
&
Lizzie Mai Ransom, wife of
J. B. Frierson
1874-1943
&
John Burton Frierson
1870-1952

Fayne Holt Parsons
1896-1961
&
Leola Farrar Parsons
1902-1952

Jack, Infant son of
Fayne & Leola Parsons
Nov 20, 1933

Humphrey T. Farris
Apr 5, 1864
Feb 10, 1930
&
Mildred R. Farris
Jun 30, 1868
Dec 29, 1958

Lucie Maud, dau of
J. R. & M. F. Scott
Apr 20, 1885
Jul 16, 1886
age: 1y, 2m, 26d.

"Father" T. B. Ivie
Jun 30, 1825
Sep 5, 1907
age: 82y, 2m, 10d.

"Mother" Matilda J. Ivie
1827-1912
age: 84y, 6m, 15d.

Mollie Ivie Coleman
1855-1930

Charles S. Ivie
1857-1933

Laura Ramsey, wife of
C. S. Ivie
Died Oct 6, 1905
(no age given)

Harry B. Graves
Mar 30, 1860
Mar 14, 1935

Lizzie Ivie, wife of
H. B. Graves
Died Dec 28, 1893
(no age given)

Allie Mullins Taylor
1896-1972

Kathleen Limbo Taylor
Dec 27, 1896
Dec 14, 1962

D. Luke Jacobs
Feb 24, 1885
Apr 17, 1960
&
Leila F. Jacobs
Jul 19, 1891

Mildred Ann Jacobs
Aug 1, 1915

Mattie F. Scott
1854-1888

Charles A. Warren
May 21, 1820
Oct 29, 1883
&
Amie Warren Ransom
Died May 14, 1898
(no age given)

George Warren
Died Mar 2, 1897
(no age given)

Winston Gill Evans
1867-1914

Carrie F. Evans Sandusky
1872-1963

Winston Gill Evans, Jr.
Mar 11, 1903
Jan 13, 1973

Benjamin Franklin Robinson
Aug 19, 1865
Nov 9, 1942
&
Martha Elizabeth Robinson
May 11, 1872
Jan 16, 1953

Thomas Earl Robinson
Jul 27, 1895
Mar 28, 1896

C. Clark Robinson
Nov 17, 1903
Jul 23, 1969

William H. Limbo
May 9, 1873
Aug 18, 1933
&
Inda Holt Limbo
Sep 28, 1874
Dec 27, 1964

(end of Section " E ")

John Wilson Weatherly
Apr 29, 1859
Mar 10, 1932
&
Sarah Baird Weatherly
Apr 22, 1871
Dec 21, 1964

William E. Weatherly, Jr.
Jan 1, 1926
Apr 15, 1974

E. A. Coldwell*
(no dates)
(Emmet Abiram Coldwell*
Born May 18, 1841
Died after 1882-mrd. Nov 8,
1870)
Nettie Brame,*wife of
E. A. Coldwell
(no dates)
(Annett Brame* Born abt 1845,
in 1850 census, 5 yrs old)

* by Mrs. Amie McGrew.

Mary Annette Coldwell
(no dates)

W. B. Coldwell**
(no dates)
(Will Brame Coldwell**
Died in late 1920's)

** by Mrs. William Hope, Sr.

Mollie Brame
(no dates)

James S. Brame
(no dates)

Robert A. Taylor
1872-1948
&
Lydia T. Taylor
1873-1904

Clifton Taylor
Tennessee
Corp 117 Inf. 30 Div
Jun 27, 1937

James A. Kimery
Dec 19, 1927
Feb 19, 1928

William F. Kimery, Jr.
Oct 12, 1924
Aug 30, 1962
&
Ruth C. Kimery
Apr 22, 1928

Caleb M. Thompson
Dec 17, 1882
Oct 29, 1959

Beniva M. Thompson
Jun 6, 1890
Jul 21, 1973

Grace Thompson
1888-1973

Frank Kimery
Military marker:
William F. Kimery
Tennessee
Sgt Quartermaster Corps
W. W. I
Jul 12, 1888
Sep 7, 1959
&
Bertie Kimery
Jul 3, 1893
Jul 16, 1973
married Jul 11, 1919

Effie Mae Landers
May 11, 1888
Mar 13, 1932

William B. Landers
Nov 21, 1882
Dec 3, 1965

Ella A. Landers
Mar 12, 1890
Nov 25, 1964

Jesse P. Walling
1862-1933

Della Walling, wife of
J. P. Walling
1865-1927

Howard Alfred Farrar, M.D.
Mar 29, 1899

Virginia Snell Farrar
Oct 21, 1909

Clarence Snell
1879-1940

Estelle Moore Snell
1881-1938

George H. Hulan
Nov 22, 1869
Dec 31, 1950

Bessie H. Hulan
Aug 17, 1877
Jan 6, 1970

James Howard Hulan
Feb 22, 1895
Dec 12, 1965

Arthur Bell Tarpley
Aug 18, 1860
Dec 16, 1936

Lula Deery Tarpley
Jun 29, 1860
Feb 8, 1932

(end of Section " F ")

SECTION " G "

John Martin Sehorn
Mar 6, 1815
Aug 11, 1885
& wife:
Mary Biddle Coldwell Sehorn
Nov 20, 1832
Mar 14, 1903
& Son:
Nathaniel Coldwell Sehorn
Dec 14, 1865
Oct 14, 1888

Edward Bowlin Maupin
1886-1942
&
Mary Kennedy Maupin
1887-

John Streater, son of
H. C. & C. S. Shapard
Mar 4, 1875
Aug 25, 1876

Henry C. Shapard, Jr.
son of Henry C. & Cassie S.
Shapard
Mar 24, 1878
Jun 22, 1884

H. C. Shapard
Feb 12, 1843
Sep 29, 1913

Cassie Shapard
Jun 20, 1851
May 13, 1916

Rufus L. Martin
Oct 21, 1869
Jul 6, 1870

Sallie Sehorn, wife of
Robert L. Singleton
1856-1942

Sophia W. Davidson
Jun 25, 1804
Jul 12, 1870

Nora Bass Noland
1864-1946

Robert C. White
May 17, 1837
Sep 28, 1870
age: 33y, 4m, 11d.

"My Husband"
G. W. Buchanan
Feb 27, 1820
Aug 2, 1868

Little Hugh, only child of
G. W. , V. S. Buchanan
aged: 12 months.
(no dates)

Lewis Shapard
1879-1953
&
Bessie N. Shapard
1889-19

Crete Jean Shapard
1889-1972

Frank B. Shapard
1888-1943

Frank Butler Shapard, Jr.
Aug 4, 1913
Aug 7, 1915

John Campbell Coldwell
Apr 20, 1820
Feb 12, 1880
& wife:
Sarah Annie Martin Coldwell
Apr 26, 1834
Oct 26, 1863

Henry Abiram Coldwell
Mar 19, 1863
Mar 29, 1902

Robert Coldwell Bradshaw
May 20, 1880
Jan 5, 1906

Robert Samuel Bradshaw
Oct 8, 1845
Jan 8, 1905
&
Sara Coldwell Bradshaw
Dec 19, 1845
Mar 4, 1925

William H. Martin
Dec 10, 1828
May 3, 1901

Mary B., wife of
W. H. Martin & dau of
L. B. & M. B. Knott
Dec 14, 1834
Sep 18, 1884
age: 49y, 9m, 4d.

James B. Martin
Jun 22, 1853
Jul 19, 1853

George W. Jones
1852-1916
&
Nannie Coldwell Jones
1853-1922

William E. Chunn
1875-1952
&
Mattie V. Chunn
1871-1955

A. L. Chunn
1847-1921

Eliza Chunn
1846-1929

W. H. Driver
Died Feb 28, 1874
aged: 68y & 16days
& wife:
Tibatha G. Driver
Died Jul 4, 1859
aged: 46y, & 27 days

Charles Clifton Smith
Sep 14, 1879
Jun 29, 1956

Carrie Ryall Smith
Aug 6, 1885
Mar 27, 1975

"Our Mother"
Sarah Smith
Jul 27, 1809
Oct 2, 1870

"Papa"
Benjamin F. Smith
Aug 27, 1831
Feb 9, 1898
&
"Mama"
Georgia Smith
Jul 28, 1851
Dec 21, 1929
&
Albyn Smith Clark
Jan. 10, 1870
May 30, 1957

Mayme Smith Ervin
Aug 3, 1874
Sep 22, 1967

Miss Sue C. Clark
Jan 1, 1825
Oct 25, 1895
age: 70y, 9m, 24d.

George Albert Woods,
Husband of Fannie Sandusky
Woods
Apr 11, 1867
Mar 19, 1927

Fannie Sandusky, wife of
George Albert Woods
Dec 15, 1871
Oct 5, 1927

James Albert Woods, Husband
of Cornelia W. Woods
Sep 3, 1897
Jun 21, 1964

Cornelia W. Woods, dau of
Albert & Cornelia Woods
Jan 21, 1927
Oct 19, 1927

Mary Ellen Green
1874-1971
(Gowen-Smith)

J. Frank Green
1886-1926

Jessie Green
1916
age: 4 days

Thomas J. McLean
Jul 31, 1891
May 19, 1934

Thomas Lipscomb
Born in Louisa Co., Va.
Jul 22, 1808
Intered into life eternal
Dec 22, 1891
in Shelbyville, Tenn.

Rebecca, wife of
Dr. Thomas Lipscomb
Born in Ireland Oct 1814
Died in Shelbyville, Tenn
Dec 6, 1880

Anne Ruth, wife of
J. I. Campbell
Mar 15, 1870
Aug 7, 1901

Sam M. Cannon
Jul 12, 1902
Nov 19, 1955

S. T. Cannon
1871-1936

Mary C. Cannon
1880-1962

Dr. Roy C. Brittin
1877-1938

Lillie Brittin
Aug 27, 1852
May 7, 1938

James Allen Woods
1861-1929

Lettie B. Woods
1854-1932

Clemmie Woods
Aug 1866
May 1904

George Bedford Woods
Dec 22, 1831
Aug 12, 1880

Margaret M. Woods
Dec 15, 1826
Oct 18, 1905

Horace C. Parsons
Jun 19, 1883
Dec 4, 1969
&
Jessie G. Parsons
Sep 16, 1884
Mar 7, 1970

James B. Green
1856-1931
&
Tennie M. Green
1856-1941

A. B. Mitchell
Apr 12, 1910

&
Gladys Holt Mitchell
Dec 31,----

Willie E., son of
Dr. T. & R. Lipscomb
Apr 14, 1846
Nov 26, 1864
"From a Mortal wound received
in a charge made by Forrest's
Escort of which he was a
beloved Member."

John W. Ruth
Feb 27, 1839
May 14, 1906
&
Fannie E. Ruth
May 27, 1843
Apr 27, 1910

Albert Hayden Ruth
Sep 24, 1866
Dec 25, 1936

Gertrude Hammond Ruth
Oct 17, 1876
Mar 15, 1957

Miss Jennie Hutton
1838-1920

John P. Hutton
May 27, 1823
Dec 24, 1892
&
Francis M. Hutton
Dec 12, 1828
Nov 5, 1907

Albert C., son of
J. P. & Frances M. Hutton
Nov 19, 1862
Jun 11, 1865

R. N. Hutton
1852-1916

Nannie W. Hutton
1866-1936

Mary A., dau of
William & Eliza Gallagher
Jun 17, 1844
Oct 26, 1873

William B., son of
William & Eliza Gallagher
Jul 29, 1847
Nov 22, 1877
age: 30y, 3m, 24d.

A. J. Trolinger
1867-1935

Lizzie M. Trolinger
Feb 17, 1879
Feb 9, 1963

G. W. Trolinger
1884-1929

S. H. Trolinger
1878-1918

H. M. Trolinger
1841-1924

Margaret Ann, wife of
H. M. Trolinger
1848-1905

John Wesley, son of H. M. &
M. A. Trolinger
Sep 18, 1870
Jun 29, 1897
age: 26y, 9m, 11d.

Weakley Ruth
Nov 18, 1876
Oct 9, 1954

Lyde Frierson Ruth
May 28, 1879
Jun 30, 1953

Samuel Moody Ruth
Born in Shelbyville, Tenn.
Mar 3, 1848
Died Jan 27, 1881

Sophia Winford Ruth
1852-1882

Grace Ruth
1875-1909

Levi G. Anderson, D.D.S.
Feb 25, 1857
Jan 5, 1886

Katherine Greer, wife of
Granville Cecil Woods
Jun 19, 1901
Sep 16, 1973

John Henry Neely
Died Dec 30, 1908
(no age given)

Susan Neely
Jan 28, 1848
Jun 30, 1899

William Gallagher
Born 1812
Died Apr 4, 1886
age: 74 yrs.
& wife:
Elizabeth Gallagher
Born 1815
Died Apr 16, 1899
age: 84 yrs.

Mary E. Gallagher
1875-1936

Will J. Muse
Dec 5, 1844
May 15, 1913

Nannie R. Muse
Jun 24, 1852
Jul 20, 1924

Willie Hontas, dau of
Will J. & Nannie R. Muse
Died Nov 29, 1884
age: 4 yrs.

Fannie Stevenson, youngest
dau of Thomas & Rebecca
Lipscomb
Nov 21, 1858
Jun 22, 1894

Thomas Lipscomb, son of
John & Mary A. Davidson
Aug 7, 1851
Jul 31, 1853

Mary Ann, wife of
John Davidson & Eldest dau
of Dr. Thomas & R. Lipscomb
Born Mar 30, 1833
Died Oct 14, 1852
marker by: W.L.Shelton,
          Nashville, Tenn.

Thomas Chalmers Lipscomb
Mar 10, 1855
Dec 12, 1912

Laura Butler, wife of
Thomas C. Lipscomb
Nov 27, 1871
Aug 21, 1905
      &
Thomas C. Lipscomb, Jr.
Dec 30, 1903
Jun 21, 1905

Ella Gordon Morton
Oct 6, 1857
Sep 7, 1889

Mary C. Crowell
1836-1921

William J. Gordon
May 8, 1846
Nov 26, 1908
      &
Mary D. Gordon
Mar 23, 1859
Nov 10, 1900

Florrence S., dau of
W. J. & M. D. Gordon
Apr 1, 1894
Jul 12, 1894

Samuel Clifford, son of
W. J. & M. D. Gordon
Sep 19, 1890
May 24, 1904

Hugh Lawson Dayton
1859-1927

Lida McConnell Dayton
1865-1905

Eva Shapard Dayton
1883-1952

Owen Sharky
Died July 1879
age: 55 yrs.
Gardner to
J. D. Wilhoite

C. B. Freeman
Oct 8, 1879
Mar 28, 1914

James H. Evans
1844-1912

Mary B. Evans
1842-1918

Hiram H. Evans
Apr 25, 1876
Jan 29, 1907

Rastic L. Shearin
Dec 30, 1883
Feb 23, 1918

Rose Shearin
Mar 22, 1877
Apr 7, 1904

Horace Shearin
Mar 12, 1871
Feb 13, 1937

Mary V., wife of
Horace Shearin
Sep 29, 1886
Jan 25, 1905

Georgetta S. Sprowl
Jul 22, 1865
Sep 24, 1945

Luvicie M., wife of
J. M. Shearin
Sep 2, 1845
Oct 10, 1892

"Mother" "Father" "Our Darling"
(in Shearin plot, no dates or
          names.)

Scott Sanders
1855-1939
      &
Emma Sanders
1860-1932

John D. Hanson
Feb 3, 1844
Apr 9, 1929

Albyne H. Watson
Dec 14, 1904
Sep 2, 1969

George Ashley
Oct 7, 1882
Jun 29, 1953

J. P. Gregory
Aug 5, 1809
Jan 6, 1884

Annie Abigal, wife of
B. T. Gregory & dau of
N. J. & J. E. Calhoon
Aug 15, 1860
Oct 10, 1886

Joseph Julian, son of
B. T. & Annie Gregory
Jul 9, & Died Nov 18, 1884

George L. Evans
1874-1946

Kate Haynes Evans
1879-1974

Martha Lovell, wife of
D. W. Jarrell
Jan 15, 1812
Oct 1, 1891
age: 79y, 8m, 16d.

Emmet Word
Jun 29, 1869
Oct 28, 1904

Mrs. Annie Lee Word
Feb 13, 1871
May 4, 1900

Helen Demuth
Jul 23, 1897
Feb 10, 1900

W. A. Black
Dec 13, 1827
Feb 15, 1898
      & wife:
Jane P. Black
Died Dec 22, 1905
(no age given)

James Lawrence McCall
Mar 13, 1893
Jan 6, 1972
      &
Emma Gordon McCall
Jan 26, 1893
Feb 17, 1932

Edwin Shapard
Aug 16, 1890
Sep 8, 1947

"Father"
Dr. A. P. Ryall
1840-1909

"Mother"
Lozena Burrow Ryall
1859-1945

S. K. Brantley
1872-1941

Louise J. Brantley
1880-1963

Louise Brantley
1903-1906

Harold Brantley
1919-1943

Myrtle Brantley Pressgrove
1900-1973

A. J. Jarrell
Mar 15, 1845
Mar 11, 1901
age: 55y, 11m, 26d.

Helen G., wife of
A. J. Jarrell
Dec 5, 1849
Sep 5, 1881
age: 31y, & 9m.
"6 little ones I leave behind to mourn a Mothers loss."

Jennie Jarrell
(no dates)

R. W. Jarrell
Died 1917
(no age given)

Josephine Ramsey
Aug 14, 1840
Apr 8, 1892

Fannie Ramsey
May 10, 1843
May 11, 1907

Ellen B. Ferrell
Died in Shelbyville, Tenn.
Jun 7, 1882

"Father"
Joseph Ramsey
Aug 1, 1804
Jan 15, 1892
age: 87y, 5m, 14d.
      &
"Mother"
Hanah Ramsey
Dec 27, 1800
Jun 17, 1880
age: 79y, 5m, 20d.

John Andrew Gordon
Oct 3, 1898
Dec 31, 1969
      &
Ruth Stewart Gordon
Jul 8, 1904

W. J. Gordon, Jr.
1897-1933

"Father"
Samuel B. Gordon
Feb 14, 1813
May 20, 1890
      &
"Mother"
Amelia Gordon
Jun 18, 1818
Dec 23, 1898

Samuel B. Gordon
Mar 19, 1855
Sep 9, 1926

W. S. Gordon
Dec 16, 1848
Apr 6, 1909

Crawford A. Talley
Born in Halifax Co., Va.
Jan 9, 1828
May 24, 1887

Kate Burrow Jarrell
Aug 20, 1881
Jun 14, 1905

Horace L. Jarrell
1883-1911

Alice Pauline, wife of
H. R. Jarrell
Jul 16, 1869
Aug 19, 1897

Thomas Andrew, son of
A. B. & Pearl Jones
1904-1909

Bernice, wife of
W. E. Hight
Aug 2, 1877
Sep 24, 1902

Charles P. Adams
1877-1954
&
May Shearin Adams
1879-1972

E. J., wife of
A. B. Knott
Died May 9, 1871
age: 46y, 1m, 17d.

E. F., dau of
A. B. & E. J. Knott
Apr 2, 1854
Jun 8, 1855

C. Eugean, son of
A. B. & E. J. Knott
Sep 4, 1850
Oct 9, 1851

Arthur Alexander McCorkle
Aug 16, 1860
Oct 2, 1932
&
Ida Stephens McCorkle
Jun 27, 1872
Oct 23, 1931

Sallie McCorkle Wood
Nov 7, 1890
Oct 18, 1942

Ida Wood
Aug 25, 1916

Robert W. Davis
Jun 1, 1855
May 22, 1933
&
Beulah M. Thompson Davis
May 22, 1877
Dec 30, 1965
married Aug 9, 1900

Henry H. Jones
1875-1942
&
Argie R. Jones
1878-1947

William Richard Bearden
Feb 13, 1917
Mar 18, 1932

James Marshall Crutcher
1865-1943
&
Lillian Raby Crutcher
1887-1968

Mary Maud Mathews
1918-1920

Georgie Payne, dau of
J. R. & Mattie Burdett
Feb 24, 1888
Apr 25, 1889

Lalia Marvia, dau of
J. R. & Mattie Burdett
Jun 1, 1880
Mar 7, 1882

J. R. Burdett
1848-1912

Mattie Ann Burdett
1859-1929

Ledbetter

Thomas Smith Sharp
1835-1893
&
Palestine McKnight Sharp
1836-1925

Mary R., wife of
J. M. Hobbs
Jun 11, 1832
Jun 30, 1873

John B. Fuller
Died in Nashville, Tenn.
Apr 16, 1897
(no age given)

Elizabeth C. Fuller
Died in Nashville, Tenn.
Nov 17, 1895
(no age given)

Elizabeth C. Fuller
Died May 27, 1889
(no age given)

Swain Gunter, son of
E. W. & E. C. Fuller
Nov 28, 1884
Jul 18, 1885

Emma Gunter, wife of
E. W. Fuller
May 18, 1862
Feb 8, 1885

James Lewis Hix
1833-1906

Huldah A., wife of
J. L. Hix
Nov 28, 1836
Aug 16, 1883
age: 46y, 8m, 19d.

Frances Pollock
Jul 9, 1908
Apr 30, 1909

William H. Parsons
1902-1965
&
Helen H. Parsons
1907-1971
married Dec 10, 1927

John T. Stephens
Mar 25, 1833
May 8, 1911

Annie Cowan Stephens
Mar 13, 1836
Enterred Dec 28, 1908
&
Sallie E., wife of
John T. Stephens
Mar 1, 1835
Feb 8, 1880

Samuel S. Morton
Aug 11, 1816
Jan 10, 1888

Pauline C. Morton
Jan 11, 1824
Nov 11, 1907

George W. Morton
Died Sep 1, 1881
age: 23 yrs.

Andrew B. Trolinger
Apr 15, 1865
Feb 20, 1872
&
Charles Augusta Trolinger
May 8, 1878
Aug 27, 1880
&
Willie Edwin Trolinger
Sep 29, 1887
Aug 4, 1900

John Fox Wheatley
Sep 19, 1896
Jan 5, 1969

Jane Allen Marks Wheatley
Aug 24, 1901
Oct 27, 1968

J. Alvis Crowell
1913-1944
&
Mary S. Crowell
1918-

Infant dau of
J. H. & A. B. Neil
1901

James H. Neil
1860-1925
&
Annie B. Neil
1861-1930
"Parents of J. W., H. L.,
& E. C. Neil"

James L. Russ
Jun 30, 1843
Feb 12, 1883

Mrs. Ella Russ, wife of
James L. Russ
Dec 19, 1851
Jun 29, 1880

"Mother"
Elizabeth Scales Boone
Dec 28, 1854
Mar 14, 1905

Gusta
(all on stone)

A. B., son of
T. F. & M.J. Trolinger
Apr 15, 1868
Feb 20, 1872

Joe Trolinger
1840-1881

Martha Trolinger
1840-1881

(end of Section " G ")

SECTION " H "
(Colored Section)

Lear Moton
Died Sep 21, 1908
(no age given)

Esquire Tally
Apr 30, 1823
Oct 31, 1898

Robert Henry, son of
Squire Tally, was born
Aug 12, 1859 & Died
Nov 14, 1868

Washington Buchanan, son of
Squire Tally, was born
May 1, 1856 & Died
Apr 14, 1865

W. H. Tally, step-son of
Squire Tally
Jun 8, 1867
Mar 26, 1875

Horace Morton
1906-1945

James H. --------
Born Jan ---, ----
Died(Illegible)

Thomas Sutton
    Co K 1st Tenn Inf
Mexican War

Ann Davidson
Died Sept 1870
age: 49 yrs.

Sallie J. Sutton
Jul 19, 1842
Dec 25, 1908

-------------(name gone)
Who died Shelbyville, Tenn.
Oct 22, 1876
age: 50y, 8m, 9d.

Perry Knott & Family
(no other information)

(end of Colored Section)

Mrs. M. E. Davis, wife of
A. E. Davis
Jan 23, 1845
Sep 23, 1869
age: 24y, & 8m.
"Sister of J. R. Ivie"

Rufus T. Farrar
Oct 30, 1866
May 22, 1944
    &
Lillian B. Farrar
Nov 17, 1869
Jan 3, 1941

William F. Farrar
1864-1936
    &
Mary E. Farrar
1875-1969

Eula B. Lloyd
1908-1929

Gertrude Wagster
1885-1937

David Ruth
Apr 1, 1790
Mar 11, 1862

George C. Snell
Jun 5, 1860
Jul 15, 1927
    &
Mary H. Snell
Jan 15, 1871
Aug 4, 1937

Joe H. Snell
Dec 13, 1911
Nov 26, 1967

"Mother"
Bertha Jones
1898-1926

"Our Infant Son"
James W. Jones
1926-1926

Josephine Anderson Fitzgerald
1882-1966
(Note: A new unmarked grave
  beside the above grave)

Thomas N. Gregory, Jr.
Born & Died
Nov 17, 1918

Sam M. Evans
1851-1919

Ailcy J. Evans
1853-1919

John C. Farrar
Nov 14, 1871
Oct 11, 1945
    &
Addie Farrar
Feb 6, 1872
Mar 15, 1945

John I. Farrar
1834-1920
    &
Ellen J. Farrar
1845-1922

Melvin Parker
Feb 2, 1864
Jun 30, 1930
    &
Ella M. Parker
Dec 23, 1871
Dec 28, 1952

"Father"
R. P. Clemons
1845-1927

"Father"
William O. Green
1838-1903
    &
"Mother"
Katherine Green
1850-1944

"Father"
John Thompson Snell
Mar 17, 1889
Mar 10, 1937
    &
"Mother"
Lena May Snell
Aug 30, 1899

Robert Emmitt Snell
Mar 3, 1921
Oct 9, 1969

J. M. Brantley
    Co H. 1 Ala Cav
Dec 29, 1844
Apr 26, 1902

John H. Massie
Sep 21, 1885
Sep 11, 1937

S. T. Campoell
Feb 29, 1872
Sep 14, 1873

J. Campbell
Died Feb 13, 1866
age: 2 yrs.

Lewis Franklin Gilliland
Nov 4, 1861
Oct 28, 1946
    &
Henrietta Farrar Gilliland
Dec 7, 1869
Aug 8, 1944

Mattie B. Bryant, wife of
O. F. Gilliland
Oct 23, 1895
Aug 9, 1926

Forrest C. Bryant
1900-1975
    &
Glyndon B. Bryant
1905-19

Henry R. McKamey
Dec 10, 1878
Mar 7, 1929
    &
Vercie McKamey Harden
Feb 2, 1900

    &
Buford G. Harden
May 27, 1897

Gladys Rilla McKamey
Apr 21, 1925
Apr 13, 1927

Thelma Irene McKamey
Mar 24, 1921
May 9, 1927

Sarah Z. Kelly
Jan 24, 1858
Mar 22, 1926

George A. Anderson
1887-1955

W. F. Anderson
Dec 25, 1854
Apr 23, 1901
"Husband & Father"

Elizabeth W. Anderson
1851-1937

Frank W. Anderson
Feb 22, 1882-Jun 18, 1927

James H.(Harrison) Campbell
Jan 28, 1840
Jun 30, 1873
    &
Martha F. Campbell
Jan 31, 1840
Jul 1, 1873

J. Frank Turner
Aug 20, 1845
Oct 31, 1928
    &
Sarah Parsons Turner
Feb 20, 1854
Feb 4, 1931

Morgan L. Stewart
Nov 28, 1878
Aug 25, 1940
    &
Martha E. Stewart
May 18, 1886
Aug 10, 1973

B. F. Tiller
    Co M 5th Tenn Cav
Jul 7, 1847
Jul 25, 1879

Marie E. Tiller
Mar 4, 1845
Jan 28, 1940

William M. Tiller
Feb 20, 1876
Jan 19, 1901

"Father"
George W. Young
1892-1926

"Mother"
Amelia Lynch Haynes
Jun 22, 1896
Feb 7, 1965

"Father"
Joe Estill Williams
Apr 11, 1894
Apr 24, 1934

Thomas N. Gregory
Jan 7, 1892
May 22, 1969
    &
Addie M. Gregory
Aug 15, 1895

Ophelia Anderson Covington
Feb 22, 1887
Dec 23, 1963

R. Claude Thompson
Jun 2, 1896

&
Kate M. Thompson
Mar 23, 1898
May 16, 1969

Hester Brymer
Mar 30, 1929
Jul 3, 1929

Sammie Pratt Faulk
May 13, 1913
Jun 8, 1936
"Given by Sister in law,
Aline Ballard."

"Mother"
Leona Wiser
Nov 25, 1897
Mar 10, 1930

Robert L. Clay, Jr.
1938-1940

Billy Anderson
1939

Mary B., wife of
James Clark, Mother of
Howard
Feb 10, 1907
Apr 24, 1930

"Brother"
Beady Meadows
1862-1935

Eva Savage Stacy
1916-1957

Sam Bell Parsons
1898-1935
&
Mary Joan Parsons
1898-1929

Volney S. Parsons
1852-1926

Bettie W. Parsons
1857-1933

James B. Parsons
Tennessee
2d Lt. Co K 324 Inf. W.W.I
Jun 9, 1895
Jun 6, 1961

Inda Lavina Vincent
Jul 17, 1898
Sep 30, 1972

Joseph W. Bailey
Tennessee
Pvt Co H 167 Inf 42 Div
W. W. I
Jun 17, 1894
Mar 6, 1963

Summer M. Bailey
Aug 8, 1900
Jan 10, 1968

J. T. Massie
Oct 21, 1849
Dec 28, 1925
&
Tennie C. Massie
Jul 26, 1877
May 10, 1940

Gread Lee Gulley
1940-1940
(Gowen)

Daughter: Dot.
Born Dec 1, 1937
Died --- 19, 1939

Hazel R. Wilson
1921-1938

B. A.

Charles Cecil Adams
1942-1943
(Gowen-Smith)

Drennon Jordan
1903-1947
(Thompson)

Opel F. Ortner, dau of
J. C. & B. E. Ortner
Jan 6, 1922
Feb 25, 1929

Rosetta McAdams
1918-1936

Lige Savage
Jan 9, 1884
Feb 24, 1930

Josephine Savage
1881-1970
(Gowen-Smith)

"Father"
Archie Savage
1906-1937

James W. Savage
1928-1929

"Daughter"
Susie L., dau of
J. M. & J. L. Savage
1910-1926
(picture)

John F. Puckett
1892-1966

Nellie Mai Williams Puckett
Sep 21, 1893
May 10, 1917

John Burton Puckett
Dec 11, 1917
Dec 19, 1969

William M. Brown
1842-1926
&
Eliza L. Brown
1862-1935

Sarra "Sallie" L. Vernon
Aug 10, 1885
Feb 23, 1973

"Father"
J. M. Vernon
1852-1926

"Mother"
Tennie Vernon
1855-1928

"Daughter"
Mrs. E. W. Goodwin
1888-1932

Jack Vernon
Tennessee
S Sgt U.S.Air Force, W.W.I&II
Korea
Aug 19, 1892
Mar 19, 1970

Mattie S. Kirkpatrick
1878-1930

J. S. M. (all on stone)

Sursie Rayburn
Died Jan 10, 1914
age: 24 yrs.

W. F. Freeman
Born Nov 20, 1900,08(on stone)
Died (deep in ground)
(fieldstone)

Martha E. Freeman
Apr 25, 1931
Jun 9, 1932

Ernest E. Eakin
Jun 22, 1885
Jun 17, 1964

Mary P. Eakin
Sep 8, 1888
Oct 8, 1956

Volney P. Eakin
Tennessee
2d Lt. Arty, W.W.II
Apr 3, 1909
Jul 25, 1952

James Jakes
1857-(no date)
&
Annie Jakes
1858-1919

Annie Garner
1856-1919

Evan Hiles
1869-1930

E. C. "Pone" Campbell
1861-1950
&
Mattie S. Campbell
1868-1940

Hiram Rittenberry
1873-1940 &
Beulah V. Rittenberry
1880-1943

Clarence Helton
Jun 8, 1914
Aug 18, 1931

Billy Joe Helton
1941-1941
(Thompson)

James C. Freeman
1880-1940
(Thompson)

Cecil Mae Dyer
1938-1939

Suddie Dyer
1900-1940

Ransom O. Dyer
1896-1974
(Gowen-Smith)

William Ramsey
1868-1933

Dulcenia Harris
1916-1935

Norma Jewell Long
Oct 16, 1927
Apr 11, 1934

James M. Smotherman
1888-1928
&
Bonnie B. Smotherman
1890-1956

Harold B. Smotherman
1921-1950

Mark L. Raby
Mar 29, 1851
Oct 21, 1946
&
Jennie Nease Raby
Aug 21, 1856
Feb 6, 1929

J. Buford Manley
1910-1963
&
Wilma S. Manley
1918-

J. B. Williams
Apr 2, 1872
Sep 10, 1935
&
Cynthia E. Williams
Nov 13, 1866
Nov 13, 1943

Merle A. Nelson
1895-1925
&
Florence Nelson
1894-(no date)

Lark Lindsey Stanton
1893-1970

Gladys Bennett Stanton
1902-

Edd McAdams
1889-1958
&
Addie McAdams
1885-

Allen Cook
1911-1960
&
Prietta Cook
1918-1945

Margaret Ann Seibers
Mar 17, 1956
Oct 8, 1956

Thomas Pruitt Lane
Feb 25, 1921
Mar 4, 1921
&
Addie Lee Lane
1899-1921
"Wife & Son of
Robert A. Lane"

Robert A. Lane
1892-1970

Jane Ruth Lane
Jan 10, 1927
Jun 17, 1928

Maime L. Lane
1904-1946
&
Infant Dau: Laura Lane
1946

Robert S. Wright
Mar 8, 1875
Apr 12, 1955
&
Mamie B. Wright
Sep 9, 1879
May 11, 1964

Robert, son of
R. S. & Mamie B. Wright
1918-1919

William Thomas Wright
Aug 16, 1926
Feb 3, 1927

Frank Gammill
1897-1968
&
Alene Gammill
1897-1948

James M. Gammill
1872-1937
&
Fannie L. Gammill
1877-1966

Mary S. Jones
1890-1928

Maurice Mitchell Nelson
1900-1925

Julia Brown Loyd
Mar 27, 1879
(no date)
(picture)

Horace B. Freeman
Tennessee
Pfc Inf W.W.II
Sep 9, 1906
Apr 22, 1967

Lee Adona Freeman
1912-1943

Nancy S. Sutton
Feb 14, 1856
May 10, 1933

J. Thomas Lane
1862-1936

J. Lee Lane
1870-1938

Infant Son of
J. T. & J. L. Lane
Died May 4, 1905

Margaret Elizabeth Cates
"Lillie"
Nov 20, 1882
Oct 30, 1966

G. R. Reavis
1856-1927

Bettie Reavis
1855-1934

John Oliver
1865-1944
&
Minnie Oliver
1875-1950

James A. Kimbro
Sep 6, 1858
Feb 26, 1927
&
Lillie A. Kimbro
Feb 15, 1871
(no date)

Dewey Dean, son of
Dewey H. & Addie Kimbro
Aug 4, 1921
Sep 24, 1926

John T. Deason
1868-1932
&
Alice L. Deason
1869-1927

Samuel Thomas Deason
Sep 18, 1904
Jan 14, 1960
&
Minnie Etta Deason
Oct 3, 1902

Hubert Prosser
Jul 17, 1885
Dec 31, 1961
&
Mayola Prosser
Feb 24, 1889
Dec 7, 1943

Bill McAnally
Aug 27, 1895
Mar 3, 1954
&
Lorine N. McAnally
Nov 22, 1904

John B. Clanton
1872-1931
&
Nora B. Clanton
1878-1952

C. J. Clanton, Sr.
1874-1947

Esther Lane Mash
1897-1974
(Gowen-Smith)

Sgt Jas. Howard Lane
U.S.Army Air Corps
Jan 23, 1924
Lost his life in the line of
Duty in the South China Sea
Lat. 14° - 18' N.-Long. 114°-
35' E.
Mar 10, 1945

Jacob T. Lane
Oct 10, 1894
Mar 29, 1958
&
Sallie E. Lane
Oct 24, 1900
Dec 17, 1974

Ben M. Robinson
1896-1951
&
Annie P. Robinson
1900-

Charles W. Barber
1850-1939
&
Anna Barber
1836-1920

Rutledge Logan
1873-1940
&
Birdie Logan
1878-1962

Sergeant Clem Hope Wiggins
Born in Shelbyville, Tenn.
Sep 27, 1892

W. W. I, U.S.A., Marine Mess
Corps, W. W. II, U.S.A.,
Marine Guard Co.

J. P. Bell
Co H
5th Tenn Cav

T. C. A. Fowler
Jul 19, 1804
Sep 28, 1866
age: 62y, 2m, 9d.

Charlie R. Holder
Oct 6, 1915
Nov 12, 1942

Fred V. Woosley
Apr 5, 1905
Aug 22, 1955(picture)
&
Minnie C. Woosley
Jul 15, 1905
(no date)

L. B. Price
Nov 6, 1859
Nov 18, 1928
&
Sarah F. Price
Nov 8, 1859
Mar 29, 1945

Eliza Brown Epperson
1862-1935

Billie Gary Conder
1940-1940
(Thompson)

Elijah Damron
Nov 8, 1903
Feb 2, 1937

Lucy Henley Damron
Oct 30, 1908
Jul 22, 1971

Francies E. Damron
1914-1926
&
Mammie J. Damron
1911-1933

John Oscar Damron
Oct 28, 1878
Apr 15, 1958
&
Sarah C. Damron
Mar 23, 1876
Dec 15, 1957

Benjamin Lafayette Burdette,
M.D.
Born in Shelbyville, Tenn.
Sep 11, 1878, Died in
Shelbyville, Tenn. May 19,
1970. Sp. Am. War, Phili-
ppines, 1st Tenn. Vol.,
Infty. W.W.I, Siberia 27th
Infty.U.S.Army, Surgeon.
& wife:
Willa May Pomeroy, R.N.
Born in Nashville, Tenn.
Sep 1, 1899

John M. Perry
1887-1940

W. W. Brown
1842-192-(broken away)

Jeanette N. Hargis
1895-1931

Andrew Lee Gibson
Feb 4, 1873
Jan 17, 1951
&
Fannie Cora Gibson
Sep 14, 1883
Apr 5, 1965

Sterling Ray Gibson
1916-1944

Paul Shriver
1892-1950
&
Ida Jane Shriver
1893-1944

Frank W. Ogilvie
Jun 25, 1886
Jan 15, 1928

Sam W. Moore
1871-1962
&
Mandy J. Moore.
1881-(no date)

Eugene Moore
1906-1928

James O. Bartlett
1914-
&
Georgia O. Bartlett
1912-1945

Curtis Sims
1884-1964
&
Dixie L. Sims
1907-

Basil Sims
1894-1945
&
Genelle Sims
1913-

Milton Rucker
1906-1938

Dana Pruitt Rucker
1908-1955

Horace G. White
Tennessee
Sgt Co G 1 Regt Tenn Inf.
Sp. Am. War
Jan 19, 1872
Aug 26, 1958

Margaret Dryden White
1876-1948

Coleman Chambless
Apr 17, 1896
May 16, 1945
&
Gertrude Chambless
Sep 18, 1896

Robert A. Adcock, Jr.
1944-1945

Robert L. Thompson
1886-1973
(Gowen-Smith)

Thelma Thompson
Oct 12, 1927
Mar 28, 1928

W. L. Rucker
1875-1964

Robert D. Vandagriff
1892-1940

Mary B. Vandagriff
1898-1928

Andrew Herbert Smith
Jan 22, 1898

&
Ethel Mae Wade Smith
Jun 16, 1902

Ida Landers Turner
Oct 8, 1876
Aug 4, 1974

Milton W. Smith, Sr.
1923-1974
(Gowen-Smith)

W. G. Rucker
1851-1930

Malisia A. Rucker
1850-1927

E. H. Rucker
1882-1966

(end of Section " H ")

SECTION " I "

Richard Foreman
Dec 28, 1814
Jan 14, 1903

Mrs Sarah Forman
Mar 9, 1818
Jul 11, 1858

V. D. Foreman
(no dates-fieldstone)

Frances Emma, dau of
R. & S. A. Foreman
age: 5 yrs & 9 mo.
(no dates)

Jesse Hampton Goggins, Jr.
Tennessee
Mach. Mate 1 Cl U.S.Navy
Aug 2, 1939

Jesse Hampton Goggins
May 13, 1850
Dec 25, 1925

Elizabeth Smith Goggins
Sep 26, 1855
Oct 9, 1938

William Becton Goggins
Oct 21, 1884
Mar 27, 1888

Kathleen Goggins Butz
Aug 14, 1887
May 21, 1969

John M. Trolinger
May 1, 1827
Aug 22, 1(broken away)

Malinda C., wife of
J. M. Trolinger
Feb 3, 1826
Sep 26, 1863

Harvy James Neil, son of
J. M. & M. C. Trolinger
Dec 21, 1862
Nov 6, 1863

Martha Jane, dau of
J. M. & M. C. Trolinger
Apr 27, 1860
Apr 22, 1861

Pearl, Infant son of
S. M. & M. C. Thompson
aged: 5m & 15d. (no dates)
&
Nellie, only dau of
S. M. & M. C. Thompson
aged: 10m & 13d. (no dates)

S. M. Thompson
Sep 14, 1837
May 14, 1895

Maria E. Phillips
Oct 4, 1820
Mar 15, 1900

E. H. Silsbee , Born
Nov 11, 1826 at Dundee, N.Y.,
Died Dec 17, 1878 at Shelby-
ville, Tenn.

Fannie Hudson
Aug 24, 1881
Aug 7, 1902

Mamie Andrews
Jan 17, 1879
Apr 23, 1965

Charlie H. Jackson
Feb 7, 1882
Jan 6, 1956
&
Ida E. Jackson
Mar 6, 1896

George W. Jackson
Sep 28, 1845
Sep 28, 1913
age: 68 yrs.
& wife:
Mary Jane Jackson
Oct 27, 1844
Jun 13, 1917
age: 72 yrs.

George W. Jackson, Jr.
1873-1938

W. Frank Brown
1890-1955
&
M. Mattie Brown
1897-1947

James Alex Brown
Aug 29, 1925
Jul 13, 1956

W. Frank Brown, Jr.
Aug 3, 1916

Charles Wilburn Frost
Dec 21, 1913
Jun 4, 1917
&
Robert J. Frost
Aug 9, 1916

Harry Lee Thompson
May 2, 1866
Jun 6, 1892

Eoni Thompson
May 28, 1874
Jun 7, 1894

Fannie Thompson
1857-1939

Mary Louise Thompson
Infant (no dates)

Nannie White, dau of
Joseph H. & Mary A. Thompson
Oct 29, 1858
Apr 4, 1962
age: 3y, 5m, 15d.

Macon Cannon, wife of
Stanley Thompson
Nov 9, 1862
Nov 7, 1914

James A. Neil
May 27, 1827
Oct 21, 1903
(He was 1st Vice-President
of Bedford County Historical
Society)
&
Jane G.(Whitney) Neil
Mar 10, 1830
Oct 28, 1903
(They were married :
Mar 21, 1852)

Manerva Hall, dau of
James H. & Jane G. Neil
(no dates)

Rev'd S. Woodbury
Born in Winchendon, Mass.
Mar 20, 1798
Died in Shelbyville, Tenn.
Feb 11, 1873

Sarah King, wife of
Rev. Silas Woodbury
Born Dec 24, 1802 in
Suffield, Connecticut
Died Apr 15, 1886

Wiley J. Chockley
Born in Chesterfield Co., VA.
Oct 15, 1816
Died in Tullahoma, Tenn.
Nov 16, 1880

Pamelia, wife of
R. H. Tucker, fell asleep
Oct 4, 1867
aged: 44 yrs.
"Also her Infant Son
Harry, aged: 1m & 7d.

"Our Mother"
Maggie, wife of
John D. Hanson
Apr 16, 1844
Dec 29, 1887
(John D. Hanson is on page
212)

"Father"
Thomas Coleman Ryall
Apr 19, 1809
May 13, 1897

"Mother"
Elizabeth Scudder Ryall
Nov 30, 1819
Aug 14, 1857

Johnston Scudder Ryall
Oct 31, 1838
Dec 4, 1917

Josephine P. Bailey
1867-1933

"Father"
Joseph H. Thompson
1832-1909

"Mother"
1832-1917

Charles J. Thompson
1861-1933

"Father"
L. J. Marbury
1828-1866

"Mother"
A. C. Marbury
1834-1920

"Brother"
J. H. Marbury
1857-1910

"Brother"
Leonard J. Marbury
1860-1933

Shields W. Rambo
1889-1946
&
Katie Lee Rambo
1888-(no date)

Jim Alexander Rambo
Aug 10, 1928
Feb 9, 1930

Harry J., Infant son of
J. R. & Judith B.Huddleston
Born & Died
Jun 12, 1887

Judith B., wife of
J. R. Huddleston
Aug 17, 1859
Oct 9, 1890

Lillie C. Martin
Sep 14, 1866
May 9, 1936

Ollie E. Nelson
1869-1936

Nellie L. Nelson
1889-1932

Harry Clay Ryall
Dec 17, 1871
Sep 15, 1872

Nellie Moore Ryall
Aug 4, 1877
Feb 8, 1880

"Sister"
Elizabeth Rebecca Ryall
Mar 25, 1849
Jun 21, 1869

Hugh Davidson
1852-1923

Mollie H. Davidson
1854-1932

Rev. Wilson Turrentine
Born in N.C., 1804. Came to
Tenn. in 1808. Married Elvira
Harris 1829. Died 1898.

Wilma Foster
Oct 11, 1905
Jan 5, 1958

Jas. W. Gollithan
Apr 17, 1826
May 18, 1880

Isaac Newton Stanford
Co A 18 U.S. Inf
May 10, 1844
Oct 9, 1915
&
Mary Jane Stanford
May 20, 1843
Dec 11, 1928

Margaret Stanford
1920-1925

F. K. Stanford
Jun 2, 1885
Jan 30, 1907

Oscar Daniel Turnbow
Jan 12, 1920
Aug 12, 1970

Elizabeth Trolinger
Jan 21, 1839
Jun 24, 1864

Tennie S. Carpenter
Oct 21, 1855
Sep 28, 1942

B. F. Long
1871-1951
&
Julia A. Long
1868-19(no date)

Erastus Shields McRee
Apr 18, 1850
Dec 22, 1860
age: 10y, 8m, 4d.

Zuleka K. McRee
Feb 21, 1858
Apr 11, 1873

"Father"
Henry Clay Ryall
Feb 19, 1845
Nov 29, 1923

"Mother"
Frances Bomar Ryall
Nov 7, 1849
May 24, 1922

Joseph Cox
Born in County Longsford,
Ireland, Died Mar 31, 1907
(no age given)
&
Sarah Cox
Born in Shelbyville, Tenn.
Jul 19, 1864
Oct 16, 1890
&
Sarah, wife of
Joseph Cox, Born in Queens
Co., Ireland, Died Jan 23,
1888. aged: 55 yrs.
&
Catherine Cox, Born in
Shelbyville, Tenn.
Apr 19, 1862
Oct 1, 1887

Juley Annie, dau of
Joseph & Sarah Cox
Jun 17, 1859
Jan 31, 1864

Cadle Burrell
Co C
87 Ill. Inf.

Joseph Virgil Hastings
Nov 17, 1894
Sep 14, 1969

Ben Hastings
Dec 25, 1932
Apr 5, 1934

William E. Galbraith
Aug 12, 1834
May 9, 1875
& wife:
Virginia C. Evans Galbraith
Mar 30, 1834
Aug 27, 1861

David S. Evans
Born in Caroline Co., Va.
Nov 29, 1794
Died Aug 29, 1869
&
Judith B. Evans
Born in Caroline Co., Va.
Jan 5, 1797
Died Aug 27, 1870
married Feb 3, 1819

Anna B. Evans
Nov 27, 1829
Aug 2, 1873

Sarah E., wife of
Bartley Posey
Jul 22, 1828
Mar 13, 1865

Edwin W. Bearden
1875-1936

Juliet Ryall Bearden
1880-1955

"Father"
William J. Whitthorne
Born in Dublin, Ireland
Feb 22, 1798
Died Feb 19, 1872
&
"Mother"
Eliza J. Whitthorne
Born in Marshall Co., Tenn.
Feb 14, 1808
Died Oct 16, 1877
&
"Father"
Bromfield R. Whitthorne
Dec 17, 1850
May 20, 1924
&
"Mother"
Juliet R. Whitthorne
Aug 13, 1854
Jan 13, 1934
marker by:Calhoun Bros.

NOTE:On Whitthorne Lot in
a unmarked grave:
Frank Whitthorne, C.S.A.

Willie J., Infant dau of
S. H. Whitthorne
(no dates)

Felicia J. Whitthorne
Died Sep 8, 1886
(no age given)

Mattie Whitthorne Thomas
Died Nov 3, 1878
(no age given)

Dennis B. Phillips
1885-1947
&
Fannie D. Phillips
1887-1972

Joel Orval Fly
Jun 8, 1883
Oct 2, 1960

Carrie Funk Fly
Aug 24, 1884
Nov 7, 1973

"Mother"
Malinda S. Cannon
Nov 1, 1826
Jan 11, 1901
age: 74y, 2m, 10d.

"Father"
Jacob Walter Campbell
May 28, 1863
Jul 31, 1904
& wife:
"Mother"
Nellie Calhoun Campbell
Jul 20, 1867
Aug 6, 1904

Wilson W., son of
J. P. & Mary A. Calhoun
Born Sep 21, 18--
Died ----(gone)

James K. P. Whitthorne
Died Oct 13, 1847
(no age given)

Andrew J. Whitthorne
Died 1871
(no age given)

Edward F. C. Whitthorne
Died Sep 16, 1871
(no age given)

Juliet Whitthorne Grayson
Feb 15, 1881
Mar 12, 1963

W. W. Gunter
Feb 28, 1826
Jan 26, 1897
&
Mary E. Gunter
Jul 3, 1830
May 6, 1909

"Father"
Ed. Charles David Gunter
Dec 12, 1857
Aug 24, 1913
&
"Mother"
Belle Newton Gunter
Jan 5, 1863
Mar 4, 1914

James William Wallace
Aug 16, 1847
Nov 13, 1920
&
Mary White Wallace
Aug 22, 1855
Jul 3, 1919

Robert Cyrus, son of
J. W. & M. W. Wallace
Dec 13, 1871
Jan 2, 1872

Jones W. Wallace
Apr 7, 1818
May 20, 1857

Earl Frazer Warner
Nov 27, 1899
May 28, 1900

N. J. Calhoun
Jun 27, 1832
Dec 16, 1917

"Our Mother"
Joannah E., wife of
N. J. Calhoun
Feb 25, 1832
Oct 10, 1881
age: 49y, 7m, 15d.

Mary J., wife of
N. J. Calhoun
1850-1936

Florence Ozellor, dau of
N. J. & J. E. Calhoun
Sep 22, 1869
Oct 19, 1869

Searcy Wilson Judd
Oct 3, 1880
Aug 30, 1960

Elizabeth Whitthorne Judd,
wife of Searcy Wilson Judd
Apr 6, 1878
Jun 5, 1915

Julian, Infant son of
S. W. & E. W. Judd
Apr 26, 1915

Amos R. Witner
Apr 14, 1846
Sep 5, 1866
age: 20y, 4m, 22d.

William Harden Jones
1867-1925

Katie M. Jones
1869-1946

Robert Henry Jones
Jan 29, 1852
May 29, 1895

Harry Lee, son of
R. H. & Della Jones
Jun 25, 1881
Jun 10, 1885

Robert N. Jones
1818-1898
"Grand Pa"

Elizabeth Jones
1823-1919
"Grand Ma"

Pannie M. Carter, wife of
Rev. J. M. Carter
1856-1931

J. W. Shriver
May 30, 1878
Jul 10, 1878

Katie May Shriver
Jan 31, 1883
Aug 16, 1885

Claude Homer Lewis
Tennessee
Pvt 15 Co Recruit Depot, W.W.I
Mar 29, 1888
May 30, 1957
&
Lavinia Y. Lewis
1896-1943

Little Julin, son of
J. W. & Nettie Campbell
Apr 8, 1895
May 14, 1896

Mary, wife of
L. S. Brown
Apr 9, 1840
Dec 25, 1907

M. E. W.
(all on stone)

Sgt J. H. Galbraith
Co C
5th Tenn Cav.

Alice Gunter, wife of
J. H. Galbraith
Sep 18, 1852
Apr 27, 1885

Mrs. M. E. McMinn
Oct 16, 1834
Nov 22, 1870

William J. Walker
Mar 19, 1861
Oct 11, 1883

James A. Moore
Oct 20, 1835
May 31, 1872
age: 36y, 7m, 11d.

Mattie A. Moore
1844-1926

Arch Tully, son of
J. A. & M. A. Moore
Nov 16, 1868
Feb 16, 1869

Robert E. Clark
1929-1945

Roy E. Clark
1891-1939

J. P. Mankin
Co A
4 Tenn Mt'd Inf

John J. Mankin
1825-1898
&
Nancy E. Mankin
1827-1894

J. J. C. "Grit" Mankin
Died Nov 29, 1891
age: 29y, 9m, 15d.
"I have no fears, the
future is alright"

Richard S. Yancey
Dec 5, 1890
Jul 11, 1964

W. L. Yancy
1847-1910
& wife:
Sarah E. Yancy
1849-1920

Mike H. Yancey
1873-1953
&
Ella S. Yancey
1877-1962

E. W. Martin
Mar 26, 1890
Mar 6, 1914

Mishie, wife of
J. R. Martin
(no dates)

Little Joe, Infant son of
J. R. Martin
(no dates)

James Robert Martin
1850-1931
&
Mary Emma Martin
1861-1930

Margarete A., wife of
T. J. Walker
Jan 28, 1837
Jul 24, 1869

Ella F. Walker
Aug 21, 1852
Sep 6, 1870

Henry Etta Walker
1879-1907

Granville C. Neely
May 1, 1833
Nov 1, 1905
age: 72y & 6m.

Mary Jane Neely
Feb 31, 1835
May 18, 1909
age: 74y, 3m, 15d.

Mae Neely
Dec 20, 1871
Feb 11, 1873
age: 1y & 2m.

(end of Section " I ")

SECTION " J "

Samuel J. McDowall
Sep 6, 1856
May 8, 1936

Levonia C. McDowall
(no dates)

"Our Babe"
Infant Son of
S. J. & L. M. McDowall
Died Nov 22, 1878
aged: 2 days

John H. McDowall
Feb 21, 1861
Jul 17, 1889

William Hurt Riggs
Dec 12, 1855
Sep 23, 1898

Ruth Smith Riggs
Jun 19, 1867
May 25, 1952

Jesse P. Jacobs
1892-1934

Adam S. Riggs
Nov 14, 1882
Aug 1, 1940

Rev. A. S. Riggs
Jun 6, 1816
Oct 29, 1870
"He labored faithfully thirty
one years as Minister of the
Gospel in connection with the
Tenn. Annual Conference."

"Our Mother"
Sarah M., wife of
Rev. Adam S. Riggs
Apr 8, 1823
Mar 10, 1902

Mary Kelley, dau of
Jo D. & Sallie Riggs Steele
Feb 4, 1895
Oct 10, 1895

Johnnie Gill, Infant dau of
Jo D. & Sallie Riggs Steele
Apr 8, 1887
Jun 28, 1887

Mary H. Hendon
Sep 26, 1816
Jul 28, 1894

John C. Hendon
(no dates)

Kate Hendon
(no dates)

William Franklin McDowall
Feb 2, 1859
Jan 18, 1895

William McDowall
1st Lieut. U.S.Army
Dec 6, 1836
Apr 27, 1865

Mary E. McDowall
Jan 27, 1836
Aug 4, 1917

Adam S. Riggs, Jr., son of
Rev. A. S. & S. M. Riggs
May 7, 1860
Nov 24, 1885

Kelley, dau of
A. S. & S. M. Riggs
Jun 27, 1865
Mar 12, 1894

Sarah Steele Jacobs, wife of
Jesse P. Jacobs
Oct 11, 1892
May 18, 1961

Jo D. Steele
1855-1942
&
Sallie Steele
1862-1939

Joseph R., Infant son of
Jo D. & Sallie Riggs Steele
May 13, 1890
May 20, 1890

Josephine, Infant dau of
Jo D. & Sallie Riggs Steele
Nov 20, 1888
Jun 2, 1889

Walter Clifton Rhodes, D.D.S.
Feb 15, 1900

Elizabeth Stephens Rhodes
Sep 11, 1902
Feb 9, 1971

William Clifton Rhodes
May 9, 1928

Robert E. Rhodes
Tennessee
Sgt Infantry, Korea
May 9, 1928
Apr 19, 1970

Miss Mattie J. Briggs
Jul 5, 1835
Jun 7, 1888

Nancy, Infant dau of
E. H. & S. S. Stephenson
Dec 10, 1921
Dec 13, 1921

Susie Steel Stephenson
Sep 16, 1896
Jan 25, 1922

Jarrell Burrow
Sep 18, 1838
Apr 17, 1923
&
Nancy Burrow
Died Sep 17, 1899
aged: 62y, 6m, 2d.

John Thomas Alexander
Nov 21, 1873
Jul 15, 1965
&
Margaret Steele Alexander
Feb 4, 1895
Dec 18, 1968

"Happy"
Vera Endsley
Died Apr 30, 1914
age: 4y, 4m, 4d.

Wade Hampton Jennings
1858-1920

Thos. Moore
Co A
4th Tenn Mt'd Inf

Kittie, wife of
W. A. Landers
May 18, 1852
Apr 19, 1899

Earnest J. Williams
1879-1889

Wallace W. Lacy
1847-1925

John L. Lacy
May 7, 1868
Feb 2, 1900

"Our Loving Daughter"
Eva L. Lacy
Jun 8, 1875
Mar 1, 1899

Ernest C. Lacy
1886-1912

Robert S. Lacy
1884-1905

Minnie B. Lacy
1882-1901

William Ervin Hall
1880-1936
&
Kittie Clyde Hall
1885-1973

Hampton H. Evans
1853-1905
&
Margaret N. Evans
1854-1936

Nelle Evans
1885-1970

Mary Gault Sanders
Aug 29, 1932
May 16, 1973

Ben F. Shearin
Sep 2, 1879
Sep 10, 1916

Marion S. Shearin
Apr 16, 1902
Jul 16, 1958

"Father"
Amzira Reynolds
May 22, 1853
Dec 27, 1918
&
"Mother"
Clara Ann Reynolds
Feb 9, 1854
Apr 13, 1917

Thomas B. Reynolds
1894-1929

Josie Pierce Reynolds
1887-1970
on TM: Josie T. Pierce
1887-1970
(Howell)

Samuel H. Phillips
1875-1961
&
Idella T. Phillips
1871-1943

James Clarence, son of
S. H. & Della Phillips
Apr 16, 1903
Sep 13, 1925

Edna Gertrude, dau of
S. H. & Della Phillips
Sep 27, 1905
Apr 15, 1916

William E. Gant
Mar 24, 1860
Oct 5, 1940

Mary D. Gant
Aug 28, 1858
Mar 30, 1911

Edgar O. McLean
Feb 26, 1871
Jun 30, 1956

Stella G. McLean
Jan 9, 1885
Jul 23, 1973

William Edgar McLean
Jun 13, 1917
Mar 30, 1944

Infant dau of*
W. E. & Mattie Chunn
(no dates)
* Born & Died
Sep 18, 1897-by Wilma Chunn

Benjamin O. Vaughan, Jr.
1908-1963

C. E. Logan
1863-1937

J. R. Kingston
Jul 3, 1880
Dec 25, 1943

Vera Kingston
Jul 22, 1883
May 21, 1957

Louis H. Hickerson
Mar 20, 1891
Apr 15, 1970
&
Maude R. Hickerson
Jun 7, 1891
Sep 23, 1973

John L. Hickerson
Aug 14, 1921
Nov 21, 1921
&
Verdie D. Hickerson
Aug 15, 1930

Arthur Williams
Feb 17, 1910
Jun 29, 1964
&
Lilly Williams
Dec 13, 1903

Dixie Williams
1873-1950
&
Ella Williams
1878-1961

W. H. Word
1835-1923

Josie Word
1850-1928

W. H. Marbury
1865-1937
&
Tennie Marbury
1873-1928

William H. Marbury
Apr 1, 1903
Jan 28, 1971
&
Zannie E. Marbury
Oct 18, 1905

David A. Vaughan*
*David Ashley Vaughan
Mar 16, 1824
Nov 25, 1888
age: 61y, 8m, 9d.
&
America C. Vaughan*
*America Clementine Vaughan
Aug 19, 1840
Dec 26, 1918
* by Wilma Chunn

Kate A. Vaughan
1874-1945

Susie W. O'Neal
1874-1948

J. G. Landers
1868-1921

Janie M. Landers
1873-1955

Ester Madden, Infant dau of
J. G. & Janie M. Landers
May 29, 1904
Jun 8, 1904

James G. Landers
Tennessee
Pfc 332 MP Escort GD Co.
W. W. II
Jul 17, 1914
Jun 11, 1959

Terry D. Thompson
1875-1926

Mittie L. Thompson
1876-1914

Virginia L. Thompson
1905-1961

Fred W. Anderson
1876-1914

Edna O. Anderson
1879-1942

Infant son of
Fred & Edna Anderson
(no dates)

Josephine C. Anderson
1903-1948

S. D. Thompson
Jan 15, 1849
Jun 4, 1906
&
Kittie I. Thompson
Sep 3, 1849
May 26, 1916

Veola Thompson Randolph
1889-1950

William H. Thompson
Dec 31, 1886
Nov 20, 1955

Thomas Evans Kelton
1854-1911

Fannie Runnels Kelton
1865-1921

Benjamin Oscar Vaughan
1882-1949
&
Maude Flippen Vaughan
1885-1974

James Oliver Armstrong, Jr.
1895-1942

J. O. Armstrong
1865-1935

Bessie L. Black
1898-1938

Madelyn Black
1934-1937

Garland B. Willis
Dec 17, 1893
Aug 15, 1957
&
Leila Mai Willis
May 30, 1899

"Babe"
Albyne L. Willis
Mar 14, 1917

Cynthia G. Willis
Sep 16, 1868
Apr 14, 1953

J. W. Burrow
1854-1915

Julia A. Hooker
Jan 15, 1881
Dec 5, 1907

Kate Hooker
Apr 19, 1858
Feb 25, 1907

Dellie, wife of
Thomas Foreman
Feb 10, 1819
Mar 8, 1888
age: 69y & 23d.

Joe H. Robinson
1867-1950

Harve W. Robinson
1881-1952
&
Edyth H. Robinson
1887-19

"Wife & Mother"
Dollie Barrett
Mar 4, 1865
Sep 4, 1908
age: 43y & 6m

Oliver, son of
E. C. & Dollie Barrett
Aug 7, 1888
Jan 2, 1907

Earl H. Foster
1886-1957
&
Mabel A. Foster
1892-19

Helen Armstrong Foster
Mar 1917

Anna Chisholm Armstrong
1894-1922

Ama White Armstrong
1870-1946

Bob Sims Hart
Aug 24, 1887
Aug 23, 1967
&
Bettie Mai Hart
Jul 31, 1891
Jul 21, 1948

William A. Frost, Jr.
May 9, 1888
Mar 7, 1913

William A. Frost
1855-1935

Kate W. Frost
1861-1943

Charles R. Gunter
Jun 18, 1907
May 28, 1970

Ewald K. Gunter
Jul 15, 1900
Oct 3, 1952

Jo Reagor Gunter
Jul 25, 1908
Mar 14, 1972

Clyde Gunter
Mar 27, 1884
Jan 21, 1945

Kathryn Gunter Fox
Oct 27, 1897
Jul 15, 1963

Ulric Wilson Gunter
Aug 22, 1888
Apr 14, 1973
&
Lilly Green Gunter
Mar 27, 1891

Patricia Ann Lowe
Feb 7, 1951

Herbert L. McCall
Jan 14, 1890
Mar 7, 1973

Susan F. McCall
1880-1932

Corinne Frazier
Oct 21, 1886
Dec 31, 1967

John S. Frazier
Apr 29, 1847
Dec 17, 1910

"Mother"
Mildred S. Frazier
Dec 24, 1848
Mar 18, 1924

Cassie E. Frazier
1876-1946

Frank Yancy
1882-19
&
Ella R. Yancy
1881-1924

"Daughter"
Elizabeth Yancy
1916

T. Doyle Hawkins
Apr 2, 1888
Jul 5, 1951

Frank Yancy, Sr.
Jul 10, 1882
Oct 13, 1962

Faye J. Yancy
Apr 4, 1907

Frank Yancy, Jr.
Mar 7, 1927
Jun 25, 1947

W. T. Gunter
May 22, 1855
Nov 5, 1932

Mary Rees Gunter
Sep 15, 1866
Jun 14, 1912

Herbert C. Gunter
Jul 9, 1892
Jun 18, 1934

Adeline F. Gunter
Mar 8, 1894

Jasper N. McAdams
Aug 27, 1854
Sep 13, 1936

Virginia A. McAdams
Jan 10, 1873
Jul 19, 1909

Jasper Jordan McAdams, Jr.
Mar 15, 1922
Mar 30, 1922

William, Infant son of
Jordan & Grace McAdams
Nov 6, 1933

Mary Virginia, Infant dau of
Jordan & Grace McAdams
(no dates)

Jesse P. Frazier
1878-1947

Alice S. Frazier
1880-1959

Thomas C. Frazier
1902-1919

Infant dau of
Mr & Mrs J. P. Frazier
1915

J. R. Norvell
Feb 19, 1850
Jun 18, 1916
&
Fannie E. Logan Norvell
Dec 12, 1850
Sep 13, 1917

Sarah A. Jones, wife of
Rev. T. D. Jones
Dec 29, 1838
Jun 19, 1917

Horace Walter Carter
Sep 30, 1874
Jan 2, 1938
&
Hannah Ruth Carter
Aug 1, 1875
Dec 10, 1931

Charles Robert, son of
R. S. & V. A. Carter
Nov 28, 1870
Nov 20, 1885

Ida Ruth "Idy" Carter
1872-1951

Edna Smotherman Carter
1884-1956

Hugh Thomas Carter
1880-1922

Albert Allen
1881-1943
&
Nancy Allen
1882-1950

"Father"
Jason S. Cannon
Sep 10, 1851
Dec 22, 1911

"Mother"
Kate Cannon Clifford
Jan 30, 1879
Mar 4, 1971

Charles Newton Rice, Jr.
1899-1962
&
Olivene Reaves Rice

W. T. Solomon, Sr.
May 18, 1855
Jun 3, 1911

Sue B. Solomon
1858-1928

E. B. Solomon
1897-1956
(Oakes-Nichols)

W. T. Solomon, Jr.
1883-1941

James Pinckney McDonald,
Oct 29, 1859   D.D.S.
Aug 10, 1950

Lizzie D. Jones, wife of
Dr. J. P. McDonald
Oct 10, 1861
Nov 17, 1929

Marian B. Cowan, wife of
J. P. McDonald, Jr.
Nov 2, 1895
Aug 7, 1951

Col. James Pinckney McDonald,
Sep 19, 1894   Jr.
Feb 2, 1959

Elizabeth McDonald Clark
Oct 5, 1887
Jan 15, 1949

Courtney Janes Clark, Jr.
Oct 25, 1911
Oct 26, 1911

D. M. Temple
Oct 7, 1849
Mar 19, 1922
&
Margaret S. Temple
Nov 8, 1849
Dec 29, 1929

George M. Comstock
1869-1948
&
Annie L. Comstock
1874-19

Charles Coble, son of
G. M. & A. L. Comstock
May 18, 1898
Jun 30, 1912

Mary V. Cannon, wife of
William Jarrell
Jan 7, 1847
Feb 18, 1900

Charles N. Rice
Mar 22, 1856
Sep 21, 1932
&
Hattie F. Rice
Dec 23, 1857
Jan 6, 1939

Willie Rice, wife of
Horace Parsons & only dau
of C. N. & Hattie Rice
Dec 22, 1884
Mar 29, 1911

Francis Parsons
1909-1916

Vera M. Solomon
1883-1939

Thomas Tony Green
May 1, 1872
Jun 25, 1949
&
Mary Walker Green
Oct 17, 1874
Dec 2, 1971

Mildred Green
Oct 12, 1912
Jan 20, 1916

Charles H. Green
Nov 22, 1895
May 4, 1968

James W. Drake
May 24, 1881
Apr 2, 1964
&
Dona B. Drake
Oct 9, 1882
Aug 22, 1971

Clayton Drake
Apr 3, 1909
Nov 7, 1917

Ottie D. Gammill
1862-1936
&
Callie Wagster Gammill
1878-1946
married Dec 27, 1900

Ironie Gammill
1878-1952

Eula M. Gill
May 10, 1882
Dec 23, 1966

"Mother"
Sarah A., wife of
W. M. Gammill
Aug 16, 1852
Oct 27, 1930

Thomas W. Hix, Jr.
Jun 29, 1914
Mar 24, 1971
&
Charles R. Hix
Sep 23, 1916

William H. Anderson
Sep 27, 1882

&
Julia May Anderson
May 3, 1882
Aug 5, 1964

Mildred Evelyn Anderson
1921-1924

Roy A. Anderson
Mar 31, 1888
Apr 18, 1971
&
Jessie L. Anderson
Jul 22, 1894

"Father"
James Bailey Scudder
1865-1911
&
"Mother"
Margaret Henry Scudder
1869-1917

Allen D. McCall
Feb 13, 1859
Oct 14, 1945
&
Mollie V. McCall
Dec 6, 1858
Aug 29, 1917

James R. Hughes
Jun 22, 1881
Mar 1, 1969
&
Mary J. Hughes
Sep 30, 1881
Oct 9, 1940

Willie Tom Hughes
Apr 5, 1917
Sep 19, 1922

Robert C. "Bob" Overcast
Apr 27, 1879
May 8, 1971
&
Fannie R. Overcast
Dec 2, 1889
Oct 28, 1972

Martha Lois Jones, First
Born of Sarah A. Kimbrough
& Theophilus Davis Jones
Sep 25, 1858
Aug 5, 1943

Thomas M. Robinson
Jan 29, 1863
Jan 24, 1930

E. H. Kahl
Born in Eutin, Germany
Apr 6, 1849 & Died
Jul 21, 1911

Lester Sanders
Dec 14, 1905
Nov 2, 1966
&
Sara S. Sanders
Dec 28, 1910

W. W. Sanders
Jan 11, 1881
Jan 4, 1956
&
Dovie Sanders
Mar 13, 1881
Dec 31, 1936

Louella R. Sanders
1882-1945

John Lawrence Warren
Oct 9, 1910
Feb 17, 1970

Jesse G. Prosser
May 31, 1858
Jan 12, 1944
&
Sonia W. Prosser
Apr 7, 1864
May 18, 1944

Cassie, wife of
John Damron
Sep 8, 1892
Aug 16, 1923

Chanie G., wife of
P. C. Brown
Apr 22, 1859
Oct 1, 1922

Rena B. Arnold
Feb 20, 1890
Jan 27, 1926

Will Adam Reed
Sep 25, 1879
Dec 10, 1923

Jennie "Dainty" Reed
Mar 21, 1877
Sep 2, 1949

Monroe "Mike" Reed
Nov 5, 1871
Feb 16, 1936

Richard Dake Reed
Oct 22, 1920
Jun 19, 1924

Newell McNatt
1904-1939
&
Joy B. McNatt
1903-1970

J. Mitchell McNatt
Sep 3, 1906

&
Pearl B. McNatt
Jan 15, 1904
Oct 1, 1957

William Jerry, son of
W. N. & Joy McNatt
Mar 2, 1930

James Bobby, son of
J. M. & Pearl McNatt
Oct 9, 1930
Oct 10, 1930

Bayard E. Tarpley
Sep 24, 1881
Jul 29, 1966
&
Margaret H. Tarpley
Apr 7, 1882
Nov 24, 1971

Charles W. Tarpley
Dec 6, 1906
Feb 4, 1960

"Mother"
Mrs F. R. Bearden
1875-1922

H. H. Bearden
1893-1937

Finis R. Bearden
1861-1932
&
Marie E. Bearden
1882-1955

Mattie Wilson Mullins
May 1, 1889
Sep 4, 1970

Ewin George Thomas
1887-19
&
Ethel McNatt Thomas
1892-19

Susie F. Thomas
1894-1921

R. B. Stokes
1883-19
&
Lela Stokes
1891-1954

Henry L. Crowell
1901-1935

Ivonne Alford, wife of
A. T. Easley
1891-1929

Corinne Alford Stevenson
1886-1945

Willie B. Dugger
Sep 9, 1902

&
Jessie K. Dugger
Mar 13, 1905
Jul 5, 1970

Lonzo Reynolds
1878-1949
&
Ellie F. Reynolds
1879-1948

Claude Winford Brown
Jun 5, 1908
Jul 5, 1911
&
John Brown, Jr.
Oct 16, 1923
May 10, 1924

Effie Bagley
Aug 5, 1889
Jun 26, 1921

C. C. Moore
1849-1936

M. J. Moore
1855-1940

A. L. Moore
1877-1946

Delma Lorene Moore
Dec 7, 1923
Dec 1, 1932

Ruby D. Moore
Feb 22, 1920
Nov 16, 1923

J. E. Williams
Feb 5, 1856
Nov 2, 1913

Mollie K., wife of
J. E. Williams
Feb 22, 1852
Jul 5, 1932

Eustace Williams
Oct 7, 1886

Lillie W. Williams
Mar 2, 1887
Sep 19, 1967

John W. Johnson
1866-1930
&
Virginia Johnson
1875-1964

Mary E., dau of
J. W. & Virgie Johnson
Aug 3, 1908
Jun 29, 1910

J. K. Hope, Jr.
1879-1910
"Dear Husband, We part to
meet again"

Mary A. Grey
Jan 22, 1814
Jul 4, 1883
"A Stranger in a Strange
Land" A Token of Love from
her Children.

William T. Harrison
Jul 27, 1862
Oct 29, 1920

Vera Harrison
1890-1920

Mary Elizabeth Harrison
May 3, 1856
Dec 2, 1881

John Holt Raby
Jun 6, 1888
Jul 31, 1952

William B. Dixon
Mar 26, 1900
Jun 10, 1926

Robert E. Dixon
Jun 10, 1924
Jun 12, 1924

Robert W. Dixon
Apr 1, 1873
Nov 3, 1923

Mary E. Dixon
Sep 11, 1875
Nov 13, 1959

George H. Pickle
1840-1922

Dovie A. Pickle
1845-1924

J. Potter Harrison
1920-1924

Vernon Dorris
Jan 7, 1888
Jun 24, 1968
&
Alice C. Dorris
Feb 13, 1882
Aug 23, 1966

Helen Dorris Atwood
Sep 12, 1918
Feb 4, 1975

Fannie, dau of
John & Martha Harrison
Feb 14, 1860
married J. W. Proby
Oct 16, 1882
Died Aug 22, 1886

"Father"
John Harrison
May 30, 1835
Jan 20, 1889
&
"Mother"
Martha J. Harrison
Dec 8, 1836
Aug 26, 1910

Henry J. Davis
Sep 26, 1894
Jun 17, 1964
&
Daisy R. Davis
Apr 6, 1901
Jan 18, 1960

Horace C. Dixon
Jan 10, 1885
Apr 9, 1953

Bertha B. Dixon
Feb 13, 1885
Sep 16, 1973

J. L. Cooksey
1867-1960

Addie C. Cooksey
1867-1958

J. E. Puckett
1870-1924

Lucy Puckett
1878-1935

Joe M. Puckett
1881-1959
&
Margaret L. Puckett
1887-19

J. W. Trolinger
Co A
4 Tenn Mt'd Inf
Dec 17, 1826
Oct 16, 1905

Eula May Trolinger
Mar 15, 1899
Mar 19, 1920

Sam W. Trolinger
Aug 24, 1868
Oct 8, 1935
&
Janie Trolinger
Nov 25, 1868
Oct 9, 1959

Warner Thompson
Nov 14, 1877
Jul 8, 1911

T. J. Jackson
1860-1920

Tommie Knott Jackson
1863-1950

Roy Jackson
1894-1922

Thomas M. Womack
Mar 27, 1857
Jan 9, 1934

Martha H. Womack
Sep 2, 1856
Jan 4, 1944

Luther E. Womack
1881-1940
&
Nellie L. Womack
1881-1947

Ben F. Lentz
1857-1925
&
Bettye J. Lentz
1859-1927

Josephine L. Blue
Apr 11, 1910
Jul 18, 1910

W. F. McAdams
Aug 22, 1835
"Will sleep beside one
I loved"
Died Nov 2, 1916
& wife:
Mary C. W. McAdams
Jan 30, 1835
Aug 3, 1904

William Steel Sharp
May 24, 1853
Aug 5, 1882
"My Husband"

Minerva J. Steel, wife of
W. J. Sharp
Nov 13, 1831
Feb 6, 1900

(end of Section " J ")

SECTION " K "

Rev. Samuel S. Moody   and
May 1, 1810
May 7, 1863
"33 yrs a Member of Tenn.
Conference"
&
Mary E. Moody
Mar 19, 1855-Jul 24, 1876

Letitia T. Moody, wife of   &
Samuel S. Moody
Jan 30, 1817
married Oct 29, 1840 & Died
Jul 26, 1880
&   and
S. S. Moody
Feb 20, 1850-May 16, 1902

Georgie S. Moody   and
Jul 24, 1860-Apr 2, 1922
&
Winston G. Moody   and
Jan 2, 1882-Nov 8, 1972
&   and
C.J. Moody
Jul 2, 1845-Dec 28, 1922
(continued)

George W. Moody, M.D.
Nov 5, 1847-Mar 24, 1931
&
Rev. T. L. Moody
Nov 30, 1842-Sep 23, 1916
&
Louisa Moody
Oct 17, 1845-May 5, 1926

(on same Stone as Rev.
 Samuel S. Moody, page 224)
Sallie G. Moody
1859-1955

Samuel S. Moody, M.D.
1884-1943

Martha W. Moody
1890-1971

Thomas R. Sims
Jun 19, 1848
Jul 12, 1901

Eleanor Estelle Sims
Apr 6, 1846
Jun 8, 1895

J. S. Butler
Mar 13, 1832
Jan 2, 1900
&
Mary A. Butler
May 31, 1837
Dec 17, 1910
&
William S. Butler
Jun 29, 1880
Mar 21, 1882

Joe Simmons
Aug 9, 1893

&
Gracie W. Simmons
Jun 25, 1893
Apr 10, 1973

Charles E. Hale
Aug 28, 1909
Apr 14, 1966

"Father"
Spencer G. Gregory
Jul 10, 1874
Aug 29, 1929

"Mother"
Effie Gregory
Apr 27, 1881
May 13, 1954

Gene A. Burns
Aug 30, 1940
Dec 23, 1957

Cannon A. Burns
Jul 4, 1907
May 23, 1975

Mary Lou Burns
Mar 11, 1907
Apr 18, 1971

Cannon M. Burns
1932-1932

Martha F. Lentz
Jul 31, 1848
Dec 4, 1931

J. J. Armstrong
Nov 17, 1875
Feb 14, 1932
&
Margaret Ida Armstrong
Aug 30, 1880
May 31, 1914

E. Hayes Armstrong
Jul 9, 1902
Mar 26, 1967
&
Ruth Reed Armstrong
Mar 21, 1904

John T. Cannon, Sr.
Dec 7, 1835
Apr 26, 1900

Narcissa W. Cannon
Mar 12, 1838
Aug 6, 1890

John T. Cannon, Jr.
Jun 28, 1861
Jul 11, 1883

Mary T. Cannon
Died Feb 27, 1910
(no age given)

Mary Burns Haynes
1877-1948

"Father"
William R. Haynes
1844-1886

"Mother"
Mollie Haynes Haley
1854-1933

Ann Holt Haynes
Jul 18, 1927
Jun 29, 1928

William Edward Taylor
1912-1970
&
Willie M. Gregory Taylor

W. Carter Arnold
Sep 23, 1889
Oct 1, 1951
&
Estella L. Arnold
Sep 19, 1900

Masie Ruth Arnold
1926-1974
(Gowen-Smith)

William Fulton Arnold
1919-1929

Alla W. Parsons
Nov 25, 1892
Jun 24, 1944

Claude E. Thomas
Jul 25, 1896
Oct 13, 1965
&
Sallie P. Thomas
Jan 13, 1899
Aug 5, 1972

William L. Parker
1898-1975
(Howell)

Robert Henry Lee
1877-19(no date)
&
Louise Deery Lee
1882-1944

Walker Cannon Sanders
1874-1917

Edward G. Sanders
1872-1938

Elizabeth Sanders Driscoll
1901-1939

Sarah A. Burns
May 10, 1810
Jul 24, 1894

Saidee Haynes Neely
1884-1912

Jimmie Haynes
Oct 3, 1876
Aug 27, 1897

Nellie Haynes
Jul 8, 1881
Oct 2, 1882

William R. Haynes, Jr.
Jun 26, 1885
Dec 21, 1945

Elese I. Haynes
May 2, 1886
Nov 24, 1962

Virginia S. Haynes
Aug 10, 1909
Apr 1, 1957

"Mother"
Frances H. Parsons
1870-1928

William W. Lacy
1870-1932

Sue E., wife of
W. W. Lacy
1849-1932

Nora Lacy
1879-1930

John Vance Davidson
1883-1953
&
Lou Ella Lacy Davidson
1892-19

Mrs. Martha Lee Forde
Died Feb 10, 1975
(no age given)
(Griffin FH, Jackson, Tenn)

Annie Deery Dryden, wife
of Dr. D. M. Dryden
1858-1884
&
James Lewis Dryden
Infant Son
(no dates)

James E. Deery
Sep 22, 1852
Aug 9, 1918
&
Annie Deery
Jul 31, 1854
Apr 1, 1917

John Gilliland Coble
Oct 7, 1875
Feb 17, 1889
&
S. G. Coble
May 27, 1869
Feb 24, 1921
&
Neely B. Coble
Dec 6, 1837
Apr 22, 1900
&
Emma J. Coble
Sep 23, 1847
Apr 4, 1911

Thomas J. Coble, M.D.
1871-1940

Mabel Holt Coble
1882-1966

Thomas J. Coble, Jr.
1904-1927

George W. Coble
1878-1948

Henrietta S. Coble
1878-1958

William M. Shearin
1860-1927
&
Ida Lacy Shearin
1873-1945
&
Charlie Ivie Shearin
1894-1897

Edd. C. Stokes
1876-1929

Myrtle Stokes
1883-1918

William Pruitt Stokes
Oct 8, 1904
Feb 11, 1975

A. L. Adams
May 25, 1822
Mar 4, 1889
&
Famey A. Adams
Jul 5, 1823
Jun 26, 1894

Claude W. Raney
Jun 23, 1910
Apr 20, 1955

J. Morgan Raney
Dec 18, 1878
Dec 14, 1955
&
Maggie M. Raney
Jul 20, 1882
Oct 22, 1962

Liney Mangrum
Jan 16, 1816
Sep 4, 1887
"My Daughter, Lizzie Tune
lies at my left."

Elitha E., wife of
T. K. Tune
Dec 27, 1845
Apr 7, 1882
age: 36y, 3m, 10d.

Dr. John C. Jackson
1860-1927

Mary S. Lamb Jackson
1864-1943

Carrie Louise Jackson
1901-1966

Samuel J. McGrew
1854-1926
&
Dixie Darwin McGrew
1866-1942

Sidney Darwin McGrew
Mar 29, 1895
Jan 6, 1949

Elbert Brasseale
1832-1942

Sallie May Brasseale
1904-1939

Martha T. Wilhoite
Nov 8, 1908
Aug 16, 1926

William Lawrence Troxler,Jr
May 8, 1921

&
Frances Locke Troxler
Oct 26, 1919
May 19, 1968

Robert E. Elkins
1864-1936
&
Ora A. Elkins
1874-1957

William J. Moore, Jr.
Pfc U.S.Army
Mar 11, 1917
Dec 13, 1974

Richard O. Covington
1870-1926

(end of Section " K ")

SECTION " L "

Capt. Reuben C. Couch
Jan 13, 1830
Apr 12, 1918
&
Mary Josephine Couch
Died Feb 17, 1891
aged: 48 yrs.
&
Loula Dwiggins Couch
Died Jun 24, 1897
aged: 44 yrs.
&
Hettie Eugenia Couch
Died Oct 6, 1878
aged: 6 yrs.

Dr. E. W. Carney
Jul 19, 1870
Jun 15, 1910

Cora M. Carney
Nov 29, 1872
Apr 30, 1914

Mrs. M. C. Jenkins
1864-1921

James E. Martin
1891-1941
&
Evelyn K. Martin
1891-19

J. Ben Faulk
1883-1956
&
Florence Faulk
1888-1973

Noble C. Faulk
Tennessee
Pfc 1772 SVC Comd Unit W.W.II
Mar 4, 1918
Feb 4, 1964

Byron Bruce Brantley
Jan 19, 1876
May 8, 1959
&
Docia Hix Brantley
May 4, 1893

James Pearson
Co C
5th Tenn Cav.

"Father"
Elijah Wilson Carney
Died Mar 4, 1898
age: 71y, & 2d.
&
"Mother"
Amelia B. Carney
Died Jan 17, 1890
age: 50y, 10m, 11d.
&
"Son"
Elijah Wilson Carney
May 27, 1896
lost at sea
Jan 14, 1918

Joe, son of
J. & S. Singleton
Mar 18, 1863
Dec 30, 1880

Nellie E., Infant dau of
E. K. & Sue L. White
Jun 21, 1902
Aug 17, 1903

Martha Elizabeth, wife of
W. B. Spencer
Feb 8, 1840
Aug 16, 1874

Margaret W., dau of
W. B. & Elizabeth Spencer
Jul 31, 1859
Nov 31, 1871 age:12y & 4m.

Isaac Fuston
1888
&
Cordelia Fuston
1880
"Fuston Babies"

W. Cleo Fuston
Jun 8, 1881
Apr 14, 1933

Jeptha M. Fuston
Nov 2, 1841
Mar 8, 1927

Evaline B. Fuston
Jun 26, 1849
Dec 24, 1913

"Father"
George E. Calhoun
Jun 17, 1844
Mar 5, 1906
&
"Mother"
Cynthia A. Calhoun
Aug 16, 1843
Jan 14, 1923

Sarah, dau of
G. E. & C. A. Calhoun
(no dates)

George A. Calhoun
Aug 21, 1872
Jan 8, 1955

"Father"
R. D. Gordon
1854-1942
&
"Mother"
Callie Gordon
1856-1947

William H. Weaver
1885-1944

Ella W. Weaver
1873-1943

In Memory of our Dear Wife
& Mother
Addie Lee Weaver Tallman
Jul 12, 1883
Aug 27, 1934

Henry Weaver
Jan 10, 1846
Dec 20, 1921

Tempy A. Weaver
Born Sep 8, 1847
Died (deep in ground)

J. C. Weaver
Jul 19, 1874
Oct 14, 1876

David Guest
Oct 14, 1808
Sep 11, 1870

Elizabeth Guest
Died Jun 27, 1906
age: abt 89 yrs.

Tillman Guest
Sep 15, 1853
Sep 25, 1905
age: 52 yrs.

Kittie, dau of
D. & B. Guest
Apr 5, 1850
Jun 4, 1891

Frank Gordon Bramblett
1923-1947

Frank S. Bramblett
1891-1949
&
Kathleen G. Bramblett
1892-19

William M. Wilhoite
Jun 17, 1811
Jun 29, 1884
"A True Man. An Humble
Christian, a loving brother,
a devoted Husband has gone
from us to dwell above."
&
Mrs. I. C. Wilhoite
Jul 24, 1822
Feb 21, 1887
age: 64y, 6m, 27d.

Willie Doss, dau of
William C. & Anna Haley
Nov 6, 1880
Mar 27, 1883

Thomas P. Wilhoite   and
Oct 14, 1828
Jan 12, 1891
"True as a man, Husband,
Father, Brother, & Friend"

"Mother"
Carrie V. Wilmot
1839-1915
"She did what she could"

Lula Wilmot Walker
Aug 10, 1880
May 27, 1921

Dora E., wife of
P. C. Gillispie
Apr 18, 1874
Apr 20, 1918

Frank T. Walker
1917-1922

Walter N. Walker
1915-1922

John S. Walker
Aug 21, 1856
Sep 5, 1937
&
Margaret Walker
Jul 24, 1854
Feb 20, 1922

J. A. Campbell
1859-1926
& wife:
Effie A. Campbell
1865-1929

John Davidson Hutton
May 11, 1857
Sep 12, 1939

Annie Lane Hutton
Sep 21, 1869
Jun 16, 1912

James Artus Warder
Sep 24, 1843
Jul 15, 1891

Willie Eugenia, dau of
Jas. A. & Laura D. Warder
Died May 5, 1879
age: 11y, 6m, 13d.

S. M. Wilhoite
Mar 14, 1843
Sep 6, 1873
"He said, I will be waiting
and watching for you"

W. W. Wilhoite
Nov 3, 1808
Apr 6, 1893
"Dear Brother, you lived for
others"
&
J. R. Wilhoite
Mar 28, 1825
Oct 15, 1893

Virginia M. Wilhoite
Mar 27, 1841
Dec 11, 1934
&
Thomas P. Wilhoite, Jr.
Oct 30, 1878
Jan 21, 1882

M. L. Allison
1860-1939

Lizzie Wilmot Allison
1869-1938

William I. Campbell
1866-1947
&
Agnes M. Campbell
1870-1944

Leona Campbell
1900-1968

Ella Pollock
Apr 12, 1878
May 12, 1918

Sallie F. Stokes
Oct 25, 1852
Apr 15, 1919

"Mother"
Mattie E. Nance
Apr 15, 1833
Aug 11, 1912

Qualls W. Nance
Jul 13, 1868
Apr 27, 1924

Lizzie Hix Nance
Jul 27, 1873
May 26, 1917

Sallie McDonald Hutton
Jan 14, 1884
Dec 4, 1957

Joseph D. Wilhoite
Oct 10, 1820
Nov 13, 1891
&
Amanda Clark Wilhoite
Oct 6, 1833
May 12, 1894
&
Robert Clark, son of
Jos. D. & A. C. Wilhoite
Born Apr 30, 1868 & fell
asleep Feb 9, 1886 at
Bingham School, N.C.

Urn:
"Dear Robbie"

"Father"
Young Wilhoite
Died Feb 15, 1898
aged: 81y, 1m, 10d.
& wife:
"Mother"
Martha Keyser Shaw Wilhoite
Died Jul 22, 1893
aged: 87y, 5m, 21d.

Virginia Moore Kimbro
Apr 9, 1903
May 3, 1961

Virginia Wilhoite Lanham
Mar 26, 1882
Jul 25, 1964

Jordan Moody Moore
Feb 4, 1879
May 25, 1883
&
Annetta Russell Moore
Jul 25, 1888
Jul 25, 1888
Children of J. H. &
M. A. Moore

Jordan Holt Moore
Feb 20, 1844
Jun 12, 1916

Mariah Moore
Jun 20, 1847
Sep 23, 1920

Charlie T. Snell
1865-1941
&
Lula T. Snell
1886-19 (TM-Lula Moore Snell
            1886-1975,
            Gowen-Smith)

Esther L., dau of
Mr & Mrs Allen A. Smith
Sep 6, 1910
Mar 16, 1928 (Metal marker)

Arthur Smith
1893-1952
(Gowen-Smith)

Gilbert N. Johnson
Jul 11, 1891
Jun 2, 1918

Henry J. Thompson
Aug 30, 1871
Dec 6, 1944

Emma Clary Thompson
Dec 10, 1874
Jul 18, 1927

Clary Thompson
Aug 8, 1907
Jun 13, 1923

"Mother"
Sarah T. Thompson
1841-1920

Mary E., dau of
S. J. & Sallie F. Wilhoite
Dec 12, 1876
Sep 25, 1878
age: 1y, 9m, 13d.

William A., son of
Young Wilhoite
(no dates)

Lawson W. Kimbro
Oct 24, 1905
Jan 16, 1911

Nathan Peyton Evans
May 31, 1836
Mar 24, 1930

Mary Gill Evans
Jan 21, 1849
Jan 29, 1923

George Peyton Evans
Jul 10, 1869
Feb 21, 1950

Stella Bailey Evans
Jun 22, 1872
Jun 24, 1955

James O. Martin
1871-1956
&
Ella N. Martin
1887-1926

T. E. Martin
Aug 21, 1888
Aug 14, 1917

Dan Mack Howard
Jul 18, 1858
Sep 15, 1918
&
Jennie File Howard
Sep 27, 1860
Jan 7, 1923

Rufus Henderson Smith
1869-1952
(Gowen-Smith)

Vinie C. Smith
1870-1918

Virginia Garland Fisher
Sep 5, 1875
Mar 13, 1954

Thomas E. Fisher
1868-1939

Mattie C., wife of
T. E. Fisher
Nov 19, 1875
Jun 9, 1918

Horace Claude Johnson
Died May 9, 1931
(no date)

Addie M. Fisher
1873-1926

Charlie Churchwell
Mar 2, 1914
Jul 21, 1957
&
Maude Churchwell
Jan 8, 1906

"Father"
William R. Raney
May 24, 1867
Mar 9, 1921
&
"Mother"
Mollie J. Raney
Feb 1, 1869
May 9, 1937

Clyde Bailey Raney
Jan 13, 1898
Dec 13, 1919

Ethel May Raney
Jun 20, 1932
Nov 16, 1932

Roy Mitchell Bartlett
1900-1936
&
Iris Jackson Bartlett
1910-

Henry M. Bartlett
Apr 22, 1881
Jul 8, 1964

Callie Mai Bartlett
Sep 12, 1883
Apr 22, 1923

Lenard H. Boyce
Private in late War
Jun 26, 1894
Oct 13, 1918
(picture)

Joe H. Turner
1868-1940

Fannie J. Turner
Jan 22, 1871
Feb 26, 1920

W. F. Turner
Apr 9, 1856- Sep 20, 1921

Infant of
F. & Edna Woodward
(no dates)

A. P. Woodward
1868-1920

Eva Woodward
1875-1963

J. B. Woodward
May 27, 1893
May 5, 1927

Edith Woodward
Aug 13, 1907
Jul 4, 1908

C.S.A.
30

Tolbert W. Compton
Jul 27, 1884
Dec 21, 1960
&
Frances B. Compton
Nov 8, 1884
Aug 5, 1967

George G. Compton
1915-1918

Wayne F. Martin
1870-1943
&
Mary F. Martin
1872-1945

Nina Sue Martin
Nov 27, 1907
Jun 26, 1974

David H. Nowlin
1894-1969
(Howell-Thompson)

John S. Pettus
Nov 13, 1862
Nov 18, 1923
&
Daniel Pettus
Jul 11, 1851
Sep 6, 1931

Francis Henry, Infant son of
Roy & Iris Bartlett
1935-1935

William R. Middleton
1862-1921
&
Georgia B. Middleton
1878-1940

Hoyt Middleton
1919

Howard Middleton
1919

Mary Ann Turner
1927-1940

Charles H. Smith
1859-1933
&
Elizabeth S. Smith
1858-1936

R. P. Posey
1874-(no date)
& wife:
Della May Posey
1887-1934

"Father"
James Walter Bell
Jul 1, 1888
Oct 11, 1918

"Daughter"
Corrine Bell
Oct 18, 1910
Apr 20, 1929
NOTE: A new unmarked grave
in Bell plot. Ed.

John R., Infant son of
T. A. & Zilpha King
Nov 12, 1927

Thomas A. King
May 3, 1896

Zilpha Lane King
Oct 9, 1901
Oct 20, 1942

Ira D. Montgomery
Oct 19, 1887
May 12, 1943

Lena B. Montgomery
Mar 24, 1890
Nov 14, 1967.

Addie Montgomery
Jul 18, 1876
Aug 20, 1948

W. C. Scales
1875-1932

Wenona T. Scales
1880-1941

"Daddy"
James B. Capley
1871-1924

"Mother"
Minnie B. Capley
1889-1962

"Brother"
James W. Turner
1853-1936
&
"Sister"
Elizabeth A. Turner
1860-1943

Arter E. Zumbro
1889-1945

Elvis Chambless
Tennessee
Pvt ANTI ACFT Train Bn AAF
W. W. II
May 22, 1900
Aug 13, 1971

Joe Henry, son of
Mr & Mrs Joe Chambless
Oct 23, 1897
Jan 13, 1914

Golie, son of
Mr & Mrs Joe Chambless
May 30, 1902
Mar 18, 1918

"Father"
Joe H. Chambless
1875-1939
& "Mother"
Alice F. Chambless
1874-1935

William Thomas King
1860-1942
&
Ada Himes King
1872-1942

Arthur Coy Summerford, Jr.
1940-1942

John F. Thompson
1856-1918
&
Harriet Thompson
1846-1923
&
Lou Thompson
1865-1948

Arizona V., wife of
H. B. Freeman
Jun 18, 1868
Aug 15, 1922

Ben F. Perry
Dec 28, 1898
Jun 1, 1958

Minnie Long, wife of
J. P. Thompson
1842-1923

Joe H. Stephens
Aug 18, 1868
Dec 20, 1965
&
Mildred F. Stephens
Aug 18, 1868
May 24, 1932
NOTE: Above ground Vaults.

James D. Martin
Aug 12, 1899
May 10, 1964
&
Alieen C. Martin
Sep 9, 1899

Bedford H. Forrester
Feb 16, 1871
Feb 7, 1919
&
Addie S. Forrester
Nov 26, 1887
Jul 16, 1966

Ethel T. Blackburn
Mar 29, 1900
May 15. 1957

Henry L. Thomas
1863-1936
&
Maggie V. Thomas
1874-1944

George W. Martin
1835-1925
&
Tishie S. Martin
1877-1943

Basil C. Martin
Mar 16, 1905
Mar 5, 1956
&
Ruby K. Martin

Pettis N. Arnold
Jun 19, 1885
Jun 25, 1966

Hortense Arnold
1889-1949

Gallagher Arnold
Jan 11, 1906
Aug 11, 1968

Clarence Nelson
Nov 9, 1897
Jan 23, 1967
&
Ola C. Nelson
Sep 4, 1904

Jerry Nelson
May 11, 1940
Aug 31, 1962
(picture)

Jean Nelson
Sep 30, 1944

Clarence Nelson, Jr.
Tennessee
Pvt U.S.Army, Korea
Sep 6, 1926
May 6, 1970
(color picture)

Robert Edgar Alexander
Jun 15, 1875
Sep 15, 1954
&
Daisie Marks Alexander
Mar 13, 1889
Oct 31, 1952

"Father"
Jasper Ogilvie
1845-1926
&
"Mother"
Josephine Ogilvie
1847-1925

Mildred S. Purdom
Jan 30, 1920
Dec 27, 1925

William Harry Logue
1891-1924

Edd. Durham
1884-1945
&
Minnie Durham
1889-1974

Samuel Porter
1878-1944

"Mollie"
Mary Ann Wallis Hastings
1879-1971

Paul Wallis
1901-1966

G. Moody Arnold
Sep 16, 1883
Sep 11, 1969

Annie C. Arnold
Sep 14, 1885
Aug 15, 1953

George Moody Arnold, III
Dec 10, 1947
Dec 12, 1947

Timothy Joe Knox
1953-1960
(Gowen-Smith)

Louise Knox
1921-1965

Joel F. Parker
1874-1951
&
Della G. Parker
1878-1971

Robert L. Armstrong
1904-
&
Bessie Mae Armstrong
1907-

"Mother"
Maggie E., wife of
Turner Puckett
Jan 26, 1896
Jan 27, 1924

William Roy Alexander
1880-1963

Myrtle Marks Alexander
1887-1924

J. D. Zumbro
May 18, 1876
Nov 27, 1941
&
Nancy Zumbro
Oct 12, 1882
Oct 26, 1918

Louisa Bradley Gribble
1859-1924

Rosie A. Fitzgerald
1883-1958
(Gowen-Smith)

Sallie Ann Bradford, wife
of James L. Buckaloo
1883-1919

Herbert Coats
1879-1944
&
Julia Coats
1878-1969

Houston Reed
1880-1946
&
Birdie Reed
1886-1970

Paul Martin Gentry
Oct 28, 1934
Aug 7, 1964

Leland Jordan
1878-1941
&
Annie Jordan
1878-1939

Nancy Carol Trotter
Jul 23, 1942
Jun 6, 1944

John F. Elmore
Apr 9, 1832
Jun 23, 1955
&
Pearlie L. Elmore
Mar 25, 1884
Jun 12, 1957

Howard Elmore
Tennessee
Pvt 59 Armd Field Arty Bn
Jul 23, 1916
Sep 18, 1944

Harrison McLaughlin
1849-1929
&
Charity McLaughlin
1852-1931

James Garland Whitener
May 19, 1911
Jan 9, 1914

McCajar C. "K" Alexander
1844-1927
&
Mary Gault Alexander
1849-1920

Dr. Arthur Elmore Fuston
1876-1960

Maggie M. Gribble Fuston
1880-1936

William Fuston Braswell
Oct 2, 1923
Oct 18, 1923

Mary Lou Fuston Braswell
1906-1923

Aubrey James Fuston
1901-1937

Horace E. Rogers
Tennessee
Pvt 67 Infantry 9 Div
W. W. I
Nov 5, 1890
Jun 24, 1950
&
Mary Reid Rogers
Apr 14, 1903
Apr 29, 1969

Robert M. Rrince
Apr 20, 1914
Jun 3, 1963
&
Mary Lynn Prince

Ellis H. Lamb
1896-1945
&
Sammie B. Lamb
1901-

William Gordon Lamb
Tennessee
Sgt 1989 Comm Sq A.F.
Nov 3, 1947
Feb 11, 1968

Florence B. Lamb
Jun 26, 1923
Aug 23, 1967

Hugh Naron
Sgt U.S.Army, W.W.I
Nov 30, 1895
Mar 9, 1975
&
Nannie Gray Naron
Jul 17, 1900

Paul Hairston
1888-1966
&
Lena Hairston
1886-19

Oma Hairston
1890-19

Ada H. Hairston
Nov 19, 1871
Jun 4, 1923

Bessie Alexander Hix
1881-1969
(Gowen-Smith)

Elroy Mallard
Aug 31, 1877
Jun 12, 1906
age: 28y, 9m, 11d.

Arthur Clement, Infant son
of Arthur Landers
Jul 19, 1901
Sep 7, 1901

"My Wife"
Clemmie W. Landers
May 27, 1872
Aug 3, 1901

Winnie D. Woosley
May 30, 1890
Jun 19, 1920

Bessie Stewart Willis
May 19, 1878
Aug 12, 1899

Hattie C. Stewart
May 7, 1880
Jan 11, 1902

Sam G. Woosley
1880-1940

N. M. Woosley
1837-1888

T. A. Woosley
1842-1924

Belle Woosley
1853-1931

Richard Woosley
1867-1926

John W. Phillips
Oct 3, 1864
Oct 30, 1893

"Mother"
Bettie Cheshire Hight
Dec 31, 1854
Feb 3, 1901

"Mother"
Lucy J. Hight
Jan 26, 1846
Oct 4, 1894

Robert W. Edwards
1870-1912
&
Emma A. Edwards
1865-1940

Allice Evealine, Infant dau
of W. G. & L. J. Hight
Sep 6, 1878
Sep 17, 1879
age: 1y & 11d.

William G. Hight
1845-1928

Elizabeth R. Hight
1877-1965

Portia Hight McClure
1885-1902

Roberta, dau of
R. W. & E. A. Edwards
Jul 24, 1907
Sep 20, 1907

(end of Section " L ")

SECTION " M "

Charles Gregory Hummel

Olga Farrar Hummel

"Father"
Ernest Hummel
Feb 22, 1874
Mar 29, 1947

"Mother"
Alma G. Hummel
Sep 11, 1875
Jan 7, 1966

Phil J. Scudder, Sr.
1854-1931

Abbie Bright Wardlow, wife
of Phil J. Scudder, Sr.
1858-1936

Phil J. Scudder, Jr.
1890-1969

"Father"
Anthony Corbridge
Jul 6, 1841
Sep 8, 1895

"Mother"
Betty Corbridge
Feb 19, 1844
Jun 7, 1927

Charley Leroy Corbridge
Apr 18, 1882
Aug 28, 1882

Willie Eddelston Corbridge
Apr 22, 1878
Jan 4, 1933

H. P. "Ted" Moore
1912-1943

J. M. Fidler
1875
&
Loefler Fidler
1872-1876
&
Josephine Fidler
1875

Olaf Fogh
1857-1920

Olive Cowan Fogh
1876-1942

Robert Cown
Born in Co. Deery, Ireland
Sep 24, 1813 & Died
Aug 22, 1889

Leah Cowan
Died Nov 20, 1910
age: 77 yrs.
"Native of Ireland"

William B., son of
Robert & Easter Cown
Mar 20, 1840
Oct 13, 1889

Allice J., wife of
W. B. Cowan
Mar 19, 1854
Nov 30, 1875

Emma Jenkins
Sep 8, 1866
Jan 2, 1961

Pearl   Robbie
(no dates)   (no dates)
NOTE: Both of the above are
   in Corbridge Plot. Ed.

A. L. Stamps
1820-1904
& wife:
Mary Ann Motley Stamps
(no dates)
& Daughter:
Clemmie Stamps
1846-19(no date)

A. L., son of
A. L. & M. A. Stamps
Nov 17, 1861
May 20, 1863

Lucy Allen, dau of
A. L. & M. A. Stamps
Apr 29, 1852
Oct 20, 1854

M. E. L., dau of
A. L. & M. A. Stamps
Sep 26, 1853
Feb 23, 1855

Mary Kimmons Russell
Nov 11, 1875
Jun 10, 1957

Grace C. Kimmons
1904-1918

John A. Kimmons
Feb 18, 1903
Feb 20, 1903

Thomas Delacy Corbridge
Mar 12, 1876
May 15, 1931

Mary Frances Corbridge
May 4, 1919
Jan 7, 1921

W. H. Steele
Died Aug 25, 1867 age: 23 yrs.

Oliver Cowan
age: 83
Born in County Deery,
Ireland
(no dates)

Sallie Bryson, wife of
Oliver Cowan
age: 83
1841-1924

John Knox, son of
Oliver & Sallie B. Cowan
Dec 17, 1880
Nov 30, 1881

Ephraim, son of
W. B. & Allice Cowan
Mar 19, 1875
Aug 24, 1875

Alex Cowan
Mar 17, 1824
Dec 16, 1905
"Native of Ireland"

Lou Sheffield Cowan
Nov 17, 1838
Apr 21, 1931

John Cowan
2 days old
Born Nov 23, 1876

Robert L. Cowan
Nov 11, 1874
Jan 31, 1924

V. H. Steele
Feb 3, 1803
Mar 11, 1870
&
Mrs. S. L. Steele
May 15, 1815
Sep 15, 1877

Lucina J., dau of
V. H. & S. L. Steele
Died Aug 18, 1848
age: 2y, 7m, 10d.

Thomas DeLacey Wardlaw
Born in Warren Point,
Ireland Oct 31, 1826 &
Died Aug 29, 1879
& Wife:
Sarah Louisa Fisler Wardlaw
Born in Chester Co., Pa.
Apr 4, 1831
Died Mar 23, 1896

James C.
(no dates-in Wardlaw plot)

Samantha
(no dates-in Wardlaw plot)

James Preston Brown
Jul 30, 1838
Jan 7, 1896
age: 57y, 5m, 8d.

NOTE:In same plot as James
Preston Brown: no marker:
R. L. Brown
C.S.A.

Jamie, Infant son of
J. P. & Kate G. Brown
Dec 13, 1889
Jan 6, 1890

Annie L. Brown
Mar 23, 1883
Apr 7, 1915

J. H. Martin
Nov 26, 1853
Jan 4, 1916

R. J., wife of
J. H. Martin
Nov 5, 1856
Aug 31, 1885

Martha F., wife of
J. H. Martin
Aug 12, 1853
Jul 5, 18--(broken away)

"Mother"
Hatie Martin
1875-1950

C. F. Martin
Mar 2, 1873
Nov 21, 1896

Allie Martin
Jul 4, 1884
Oct 28, 1916

Sarah E. Woodward
Apr 25, 1847
Sep 12, 1868

Sandra Darlene, dau of
Ewing & Lanelle Woodward
1945-1959

Eugene Steele Blackwell
Oct 17, 1876
Feb 11, 1880
age: 3y & 3 weeks.

Albert R. Alley
1866-1926

Maude Wardlaw, wife of
Albert R. Alley
1868-1960

Carl Edwin Brandon
Jul 24, 1902

&
Sara Thompson Brandon
Sep 8, 1905
Jan 10, 1974

Charles C. Brandon
1869-1929

"Dean"
Virginia Brandon
1877-1960

William Brown
Born in Wake Co., N.C.
Jun 1, 1803 & Died
Feb 6, 1880
& wife:
Jane G. Brown
Feb 8, 1810
Feb 4, 1882

Minnie P., wife of
L. M. Brown
Oct 1, 1873
Oct 8, 1904

Newton T. Gregory
1873-1947

Mary E. Brantley, wife of
N. T. Gregory
1871-1895

Elizabeth Luttrell, wife of
N. T. Gregory
1879-1915

"Mother"
Sarah Belle, wife of
Wallace E. Walker
Dec 13, 1857
Jun 6, 1903

Sgt J. M. Jarrell
Co A
4th Tenn Mt'd Inf
Jul 8, 1831
Sep 6, 1884

Jno. W. Woodward
Jul 30, 1844
Oct 30, 1915

Emily D. Woodward
Apr 10, 1847
Jan 9, 1913

J. K. Hope
1839-1914

Cynthia E. Hope
1838-1913

Will M. Hope
1868-1913

Elizabeth M. Hope
1870-1932

O.(D)S. Thompson
1868-1897

Joseph Edwin Thompson
1870-1939

Sarah Hobson Thompson
1879-1955

Dr. Joseph H. Peebles
Entered into rest at 1 A.M.
Friday the 18th of January
1907. aged 42 yrs.

Clay Dyer Peebles
1894-1940

Mary, dau of
Clay & Mary Peebles
Oct 1922

E. E. Baker
Aug 19, 1875
Sep 14, 1918

Sarah M., wife of
E. E. Baker
Mar 26, 1883
Oct 26, 1902
& Son:
Paul Edward Baker
(no dates)

Christine Gregory Baker
                    Cothran
1887-1944

_. J. Armstrong
Jun 22, 1920
Dec 20, 1920

George William Todd
Jan 2, 1917
Jan 22, 1917

In Memory of
Capt. W. L. Brown, son of
Thomas & Mary Brown, Born
Feb 3, 1830 & Died
Mar 8, 1862
"At Camp Chase near Columbus,
Ohio. A Prisoner of War. His
remains is interred there."

Emily Diane, dau of
Ewing & Lanelle Woodward
1939-1940

Melanye Denise, dau of
Ewing & Lanelle Woodward
1958-1967

"Husband & Father"
William H. Mathews
Jul 29, 1844
Nov 10, 1891

"Mother"
Alice E. Mathews
Mar 17, 1845
Sep 6, 1896

Jo Stamps Houston
Jul 10, 1864
Jul 25, 1865
&
Byrd Houston
Aug 28, 1865
Jul 22, 1866
"Children of C. P. &
Jennie Houston"

Henry, son of
C. P. & Jennie Houston
Mar 28, 1870
Jun 29, 1870
age: 3m & 1d.

C. P. Houston
1842-1903
& wife:
Jennie Stamps Houston
1843-1830

Jennie Belle, wife of
W. D. Robinson
Aug 7, 1874
Dec 16, 1902

Infant of
W. D. & J. B. Robinson
Born & Died
Aug 10, 1902

Donald Dodd
Feb 22, 1889
May 30, 1964
&
Edwina Shearin Dodd
Jun 3, 1890
Jan 16, 1971

George W. Shearin
1854-1938

Ruth Snell Shearin
1857-1934

Allie J. Jarrell
1880-1935

"Father"
W. C. Raby
1849-1919

"Mother"
Maude S. Raby
1857-1944

Harvey D. Woodward
1875-1923

Emily E. Woodward
1875-1956

Harvey D. Woodward, Jr.
1909-1966

Martha T. Woodward
1909-1954

Mitchell H. Rice
Jul 28, 1851
Nov 30, 1923

Emma R. Walling
Jan 3, 1879
Jun 2, 1953

Finis E. Dunaway
Died Jul 28, 1882
age: 48 yrs.

"Father"
John H. Rice
May 23, 1828
Mar 17, 1912

"Mother"
Saidee, wife of
John H. Rice
Aug 12, 1830
Dec 9, 1912

James A. Rice
Sep 7, 1854
Feb 7, 1913

William G. Rice
Jan 4, 1853
May 24, 1927

Ada, wife of
W. G. Rice
Sep 21, 1850
Jun 12, 1900

Pauline B. Rice
1880-1972

Col. William Frierson
Mar 14, 1839
Jul 27, 1882

E. J. Frierson
(no dates)

L. S. Frierson
"Mother"
(no dates)

J. W. Frierson
(no dates)

Thomas S. Steele
Apr 15, 1839
Jan 30, 1881

Nannie F., wife of
Thomas S. Steele
Mar 9, 1838
Jul 5, 1918

"Father"
W. S. Jett
Dec 23, 1814
Feb 3, 1876

Eugene Blakemore
1852-1925

"Mother"
Ludie P. Newton, wife of
Eugene Blakemore
Jan 27, 1852
Sep 27, 1896

J. R. Blakemore
Jun 21, 1858
Dec 8, 1924

Nannie Barnes Blakemore
May 30, 1867
Dec 22, 1959

Dr. George E. Blakemore
Died Mar 7, 1875
age: 52 yrs. (broken)

Al B., youngest son of
Dr. Frank & Talitha C.
Blakemore
Died Nov 12, 1895
age: 25 yrs.

Alice Bates, wife of
Frank Buckner
Jun 21, 1878
Dec 10, 1943

Thomas F. Bates
Aug 21, 1822
May 23, 1897

James E. Bates
Mar 28, 1853
Sep 13, 1902

William B. Bates
Jan 15, 1851
Oct 14, 1917

Jennie M. Bates
Dec 8, 1864
Mar 15, 1939

William B. Bates, Jr.
Aug 23, 1880
Jun 6, 1927

Thomas Fletcher Bates, D.D.S.
Oct 27, 1876
Mar 7, 1964

Ethel Myers, wife of
Thomas F. Bates
Dec 22, 1881
Nov 6, 1972

Thomas Jett Steele
Nov 29, 1872
Apr 17, 1901
"Only Son of his Mother &
she a Widow"

"Mother"
J. C. Jett
Mar 10, 1815
Feb 11, 1876

"Mother"
Caroline Newton Shofner
Dec 3, 1821
Nov 7, 1902

Carolyn, dau of
Mr & Mrs E. D. Newton
Jun 29, 1906
Aug 10, 1907

"Father"
Ernest Driscol Newton
Nov 17, 1867
Jul 3, 1929

"Mother"
Ruth Neely Newton
Dec 30, 1869
Jul 7, 1939

Claude Nowlin Cunningham
Sep 30, 1891
Mar 21, 1954
&
Ida Camp Berry Cunningham
Died Jul 3, 1973
(no age given)

A. B. Cunningham
Feb 8, 1887
Jul 28, 1930

Dr. J. M. Cunningham
Jun 17, 1849
Jun 5, 1909
&
Lizzie L. Cunningham
Sep 17, 1852
Jan 11, 1929

H. L. Cunningham
Apr 8, 1885
Mar 2, 1945

James D. Hawes
1867-1929
&
Elizabeth F. Hawes
1869-1966

Frank Jacob Wallheiser
1889-1955

Margaret Cooper Wallheiser
1894-1964

Margaret Cooper Wallheiser
1918-1939

Ernest Bonner Cooper
1870-1951
&
Sara Vance Cooper
1873-1905
&
Lucy Bonner Cooper
1895-1939

Jane Caroline Jett
Oct 10, 1858
Oct 22, 1921

Mrs. Martha G. Dunaway
Apr 12, 1831
Mar 7, 1895

Claude D. Roberts
Jan 1, 1889
Nov 24, 1969
&
Pauline Wallis Roberts
Apr 26, 1892
Feb 13, 1964

J. Allen Wallis
1866-1946
&
Eunice E. Wallis
1870-1953

Nancy C. Coonce
Nov 30, 1859
Jan 4, 1885

Rev. John R. Shoffner
Nov 24, 1835
Died in Wilkes-Barre, Pa.
Jun 12, 1891
&
Hattie Shoffner
Dec 29, 1842
Dec 18, 1910

Anne Bates Boak
1919-1949
&
Anne Barringer Boak
1946-1949

M. N. Shriver
May 13, 1853
Feb 14, 1921
&
James Abram Shriver
May 14, 1859
Aug 18, 1918
&
Allie Grant Shriver
Oct 8, 1919
Nov 19, 1919

G. Thomas Alexander
1874-1947

Mollie Alexander
1869-1938

S. J. Shearin, wife of
D. W. Alexander
Sep 1840
Jun 1904
&
Una, dau of
D. W. & S. J. Alexander
Mar 13, 1871
Aug 2, 1889

D. W. Alexander
Nov 22, 1841
Feb 4, 1912

Mildred P. Jett
1849-1915

Sallie C. Jett
1861-1931

Mary, Infant dau of
D. F. & C. S. Jett
Sep 5, 1872
Mar 27, 1873
age: 6m & 22d.

Albert Frierson
1875-1932

Kate Fogleman Frierson
1875-1955

Albert Frierson
Jan 1900
Nov 1901

Richard S. Frierson
Aug 11, 1900
TM-1975 (Goven-Smith)
&
Genelle V. Frierson
Nov 29, 1913
May 13, 1959

Albert Frierson
Feb 6, 1841
Jan 2, 1836

Felicia Cowan, wife of
Albert Frierson
Sep 9, 1843
Oct 2, 1896

Little Albert Frierson
Nov 28, 1872
Jan 13, 1874

Christina S. Frierson
Died Jan 9, 1878
age: 2m.

Dr. W. G. Frierson
32°
Jul 27, 1875
Oct 21, 1916
"Shelbyville Benevolent Lodge
122 Tannehill Chapter
No. 40 Trinity Consistory
No. 2."

Frances C. Frierson Earthman
Nov 3, 1875
Aug 19, 1955

Frances Frierson
Died Jul 25, 1951
(no age given)

Robert Waite Clark
1862-1926
&
Anne Frierson Clark
1870-1942

John W. Frierson, Sr.
Sep 19, 1847
Aug 23, 1893
& wife:
Elizabeth Baskette Frierson
Jun 9, 1849
Mar 24, 1914

Irene Frierson
Sep 23, 1872
Feb 9, 1900

Henry Bryan Cowan
Jul 4, 1870
Nov 25, 1951

Mary Frierson Cowan
Aug 2, 1870
Aug 7, 1951

(end of Section " M ")

SECTION " N "

Mary E. Cooper
(no dates)
"She is not dead but sleepeth"

Dr. Charles T. Carney
May 11, 1876
Apr 25, 1941
&
Mary Thompson Carney
Mar 4, 1878
May 8, 1969

Emmett E., Infant Son of
Charles & Euline Carney
1941

Thomas M. Robinson
1870-1908
&
Nannie C. Robinson
1895-1909
&
Cassie P. Robinson
1876-1954

"Husband"
Rolin Martin
Feb 14, 1855
Aug 16, 1926

Lillie Martin Stephenson
Jun 2, 1873
Dec 22, 1962

"Our Son"
Bobby Overall
May 30, 1943
May 27, 1955

James E. Parsons
1870-1942
&
Martha E. Parsons
1875-1953

Eph L. Carney, Jr.
Apr 14, 1925
Mar 8, 1970
&
Jewel D. Carney
Oct 22, 1923

Eph L. Carney, Sr.
May 2, 1899

&
Mary C. Carney
Jun 26, 1899

James C. Halmontaller
Feb 14, 1905

&
Eva S. Halmontaller
Nov 9, 1903

James C. Halmontaller
Apr 19, 1924
Mar 9, 1941

P. A. Parsons
Apr 12, 1835
Nov 26, 1912
&
Catharine Parsons
Apr 12, 1837
Aug 29, 1908
&
B. E. Parsons
Mar 2, 1863
Mar 8, 1922

Mary P. Delk
Jul 15, 1857
Aug 26, 1913

Zach T. Carney
Aug 18, 1901
Mar 9, 1949
&
Elizabeth R. Carney
Sep 5, 1902
Aug 10, 1972

"Father"
Thomas N. McCord
Dec 3, 1836
Nov 24, 1889
&   and
"Mother"
Iva A. McCord
Jun 14, 1841
Mar 31, 1920
&
Ed. C. McCord
Mar 17, 1879
Jan 28, 1900

James Thomas Cunningham
Feb 23, 1846
Jun 12, 1918
&
Samantha Harrison Cunningham
Sep 28, 1851
Jul 21, 1927

Edgar Ewell Cunningham
Apr 2, 1868
Jun 16, 1923

Humphrey Davidson Cunningham
Oct 18, 1874
Nov 1, 1927

Ruth C. Cunningham
Aug 28, 1889

Zach Thompson
1844-1925

Lettie Cannon, wife of
Zach Thompson
Apr 9, 1850
Feb 22, 1943

Daisy L., dau of
Zach & Lettie Thompson
1890-1911

Price S. McCord
Apr 9, 1887
Apr 2, 1903
&
Iva L. McCord
Jan 25, 1881
Apr 14, 1903
&
Fannie K. McCord
Oct 26, 1884
Aug 22, 1904

Samuel G. Cunningham
May 28, 1888
Jan 23, 1950
&
Beulah A. Cunningham
Oct 29, 1892
Mar 1, 1963

Elizabeth Cunningham
Mar 2, 1924
Nov 20, 1963

Elizabeth Eakin Cunningham
Feb 8, 1905
Jul 26, 1910

Harvey Sephas Cunningham
Jan 13, 1871
Oct 3, 1917

G. A. Cleveland
Mar 1851
Jan 1919

Emma L. Cleveland
1852-1921

E. Albro Cleveland
1874-1923

Wiley J. Chockley
1881-1964
&
Inda Gunter Chockley
1884-1972

Arthur Lee, son of
P. A. & E. M. Chockley
Sep 9, 1876
Aug 10, 1881
(broken)

William Thomas, son of
W. J. & I. B. Chockley
Nov 18, 1908
Jan 15, 1909

W. H. Lane
1844-1923

Daisy Lane
1877-1928

R. T. Lane
Dec 4, 1847
Feb 12, 1886
age: 38y, 2m, 8d.

Violet R., wife of
R. T. Lane
Aug 19, 1847
Dec 19, 1880
age: 33y & 4m.

Warner G. Rutledge
1853-1926

Bettie K. Rutledge
1865-1925

Warner G. Rutledge, Jr.
1904-1949

John W. Rutledge
1822-1901

Mary Warner Rutledge
1832-1906

John W. Rutledge, Jr.
1851-1911

T. H. Smith
Mar 25, 1856
Jan 6, 1916
&
Nannie R. Smith
Jan 16, 1860
Apr 25, 1941

Lucille, dau of
T. H. & N. B. Smith
Died Nov 19, 1894
age: 5y, 11m, 21d.

Thomas B. Laird
Jun 6, 1830
Mar 21, 1867
&
Berta L., wife of
William Fox
Mar 18, 1857
Jul 12, 1880
&
Tommie Laird
Apr 9, 1859
Sep 13, 1878

Corp'l
M. J. Dryden
Co F
1st Ala Vid. Cav
M. J. Dryden
Mar 15, 1846
Jan 20, 1872
"He is gone but not forgotten"

Mary A. Dryden
Feb 13, 1840
Feb 3, 1921

Babe Dryden
Nov 25, 1860
May 7, 1909

J. C. Akin
Died Oct 22, 1900
age: 78y, 3m, 20d.

"My Dear Wife"
America Akin
Died Feb 6, 1892
age: 68y, 5m, 15d.

D. S. Curle
Jun 25, 1841
Jul 7, 1903

Emma R., wife of
D. S. Curle
May 20, 1853
Sep 19, 1892

Fannie J. Curle
Mar 20, 1863
Dec 1, 1944

Jas. Gordon Noblitt
Aug 31, 1888
Feb 22, 1966
&
Henrietta S. Noblitt
Feb 9, 1891

Henry Gordon Noblitt
Oct 12, 1914
Oct 24, 1914

Arthur Paul, son of
T. H. & N. B. Smith
Died Aug 25, 1901
age: 5y, 1m, 2d.

S. G. Butler, Jr.
Sep 12, 1896
Jul 13, 1897

John Franklin Boyd
Oct 18, 1852
Jun 29, 1936

Amie Dove Forman, wife of
John Franklin Boyd
Mar 30, 1856
Mar 12, 1953

Franklin Boyd
Jan 6, 1893
Sep 29, 1960

Kate Frierson Boyd
Jul 4, 1905
May 22, 1971

"Our Father"
Henry Yancy
Oct 16, 1816
Jan 4, 1894

M. E., wife of
Henry Yancy
Dec 28, 1828
Jan 28, 1891
age: 62y & 1m.

Tho's M. Coldwell
Dec 18, 1808
Mar 26, 1871

Mrs. Elizabeth W. Coldwell,
Consort of T. M. Coldwell
Who departed this life the
30th day of April 1849
aged: 30y, 6m, 7d.

Margaret Jane, wife of
T. M. Coldwell
May 4, 1819
May 26, 1893

Robert C. Russ
1824-1902
&
Euphamie M. Russ
1831-1900

Kate Greer Fay
1882-1962

Minos C. Fay
1882-1948

Nora Bell Fay
1906-1950

Adria J. Greer
Feb 12, 1825
Nov 26, 1885

Miranda T. Oakley
Oct 12, 1855
Aug 9, 1909

Sara Shapard Butler
May 31, 1874
Dec 27, 1936

W. A. Shapard
Jan 14, 1873
Jun 19, 1935

Yorke Poitevent Nicholson,
Mar 13, 1922   Jr.
Nov 27, 1929

Amie Boyd Nicholson
Sep 2, 1917
Feb 4, 1919

Martha C. Taylor, wife of
Bayard E. Tarpley
Jan 16, 1880
Mar 2, 1908

Jorden A. Jackson
Dec 1871
Jun 1917

James W. Taylor
Aug 20, 1856
Aug 12, 1927

Rebecca Jackson, wife of
James W. Taylor
Jun 4, 1859
Jul 25, 1925
"She lived for others"

Thomas C. Black
1845-1923
&
Addie C. Black
1860-1908

Emma Coldwell Black
1854-1920

Margaret Jane Coldwell
1861-1913

Eliza Guthrie
Nov 19, 1806
Apr 16, 1866

R. E. Fay
1846-1900

"Mother"
Rebecca M. Fay
1848-1940

Grover C. Fay
1884-1948

Clarence Fay
1875-1879

Robert E. Fay
1867-1928

P. O. Fay
Apr 26, 1869
Sep 17, 1923

David G. Shapard
Feb 28, 1846
Jan 21, 1919

Martha J. Shapard
Apr 20, 1853
Jul 29, 1941

Bertha B. Shapard
May 4, 1877
Jan 28, 1946

Henry C. Tilford
Aug 30, 1837
Apr 14, 1971

Lillian Moore Tilford
Mar 24, 1892
Jul 2, 1958

Sara Tilford Wetterstrom
Feb 4, 1893
Sep 24, 1972

Thomas J. Jones
1842-1916
   & wife:
Mary E. Jones
1845-1912

Dr. Sam R. Jones
1877-1927
   &
Myrtle R. Jones
1875-1954

Sidney Reagor Jones
May 2, 1901
Feb 4, 1902

George Bruce Fisher
Sep 15, 1883
Feb 25, 1958
   &
Cleo Pearson Fisher
Dec 23, 1873
Aug 2, 1958

J. C. Fisher
Jan 16, 1838
Jan 4, 1917
   &
Mattie B. Fisher
Dec 6, 1844
Jun 19, 1887

Stella, only dau of
J. C. & Mattie Fisher
Jun 12, 1875
Apr 3, 1882
age: 6y, 9m, 21d.

Harry Coble Calhoun
Tennessee
Fireman 3Cl U.S.Navy
Died Sep 30, 1941

Hattie, wife of
Harry C. Calhoun
(Dates in ground)

A. L. Calhoun
1866-1931

Hattie Calhoun Stephens
May 22, 1876
Feb 19, 1965

Gladys Stacy
Nov 26, 1896
Aug 29, 1959

W. D. Stewart
Jul 5, 1861
Apr 28, 1892

Mary Cannon, dau of
P. R. & Lettie Wilhoite
Apr 13, 1881
Dec 13, 1882

William Burton Demonbreum
1930-1931

Tabie Canon, dau of
Francis Marbrey
Died Jul 25, 1892
aged: 37 yrs.

Infant dau of
T. J. & Mary E. Jones
(no dates)
   &
Uriah G. Jones
Sep 13, 1865
Mar 9, 1867
   &
Thomas Jones
Nov 17, 1875
Oct 27, 1876
"Children of
T. J. & Mary E. Jones"

Erskine M. Alexander, Jr.
Jul 23, 1922
May 2, 1957

Charles Summer Lewis
Dec 19, 1957
Apr 16, 1958

Shirley Traylor
Aug 28, 1907
May 9, 1939

Shirley Glenn, Infant of
C. S. & B. M. Traylor
Jan 1931
Feb 1931

Thelma Ray
1898-1915
Died in Birmingham, Ala.
   &
Bunie Irene Reed, wife of
Albert A. Ray
Nov 25, 1878
Oct 27, 1903

Lula White, wife of
D. G. Ray
1862-1884

A. M. Prosser
and wife:
America Prosser
and Children:
Lou Mary & Sanford
(no dates)

Robert Harrison Jennings
1872-1937

Julia Sanders Jennings
1882-1975

H. J. Stewart
Jan 15, 1857
Dec 2, 1920

Thomas Somers Newman
Apr 12, 1888
Sep 22, 1959

Dorothy Bedell Newman
May 7, 1902
Nov 29, 1960

W. Otis Stricklin
May 16, 1886
Mar 3, 1912

Haley Harrison
and
Katherine Holt
(no dates)

W. F. Jackson
Feb 28, 1874
Aug 22, 1904

"Mammy"
Edith G. Jackson
1843-1927

"Father"
J. T. Allison
1862-1906
   &
"Mother"
Rosie J. Allison
1870-1913

W. J. Damron
1858-1900(see another marker
              below)
Mary F., wife of
W. J. Damron
1859-1938

G. B. Damron
  Co A
4th Tenn Mt'd Inf.

Mary B., wife of
G. B. Damron
1839-1930

W. J. Damron (2nd marker)
Died Feb 21, 1900
age: 42 yrs.

Bernice Damron
Aug 27, 1904
Nov 14, 1907

Allie F. Damron
Dec 4, 1883
Dec 15, 1937

Viola C. Damron
Feb 4, 1886

William Lee Stewart
Aug 12, 1897
Nov 7, 1966
   &
Katherine Fay Stewart
Sep 14, 1904
Feb 15, 1958

Effie Nelson
1874-1894

Christine Nelson
1906-1934

Kate M. Nelson
Died Mar 1, 1928
(no age given)
"Mother"

Tom Nelson
Feb 14, 1893
Apr 13, 1923

W. R. Marshall
1874-1930

Mary Gladys Marshall
1896-1897

James Ramsey, son of
Jno. B. & Susie E. Gunter
Nov 28, 1890
Jun 27, 1891

Littleton, son of
J. B. & S. E. Gunter
Jan 11, 1888
Oct 25, 1889

Annie G., wife of
J. S. Bell & dau of
C. C. & Mattie J. Grizzard
Dec 31, 1863
Nov 5, 1889

Georgie E., dau of
J. S. & Annie A. Bell
Oct 21, 1882
Feb 13, 1883

John S., son of
J. S. & Annie A. Bell
Feb 12, 1887
Aug 13, 1888

D. Lipscomb Sullivan
Jan 11, 1900
Jan 24, 1924

"Mother"
Dolly Sullivan
1855-1928

Daughters of
Mr & Mrs J. H. Sullivan
(no dates)

Mr & Mrs J. H. Sullivan
(no dates)

Horace Moore Sullivan
1883-1936

Samuel E. Stewart
1864-1924
   &
Lillie D. Stewart
1871-1949

"Father"
Eleazar J. Stewart
Dec 25, 1813
May 3, 1887
    & wife: "Mother"
Trecy Stewart
Nov 4, 1836
Aug 28, 1891

E. B. Patton
Feb 7, 1858
Jan 13, 1898

J. D. Martin
1830-1906

Alcy Martin
1833-1903

Tenny Martin
1855-1921

A. J. Martin
1861-1904

Joe P. Scales
1851-1952
    & wife:
Mollie C. Scales
1855-1924

Joel C. Evans
1867-1915

Thomas Batt Cannon
1815-1905
    &
Emily Janette Cannon
1819-1895

Virginia Cannon
1857-1915

Clement Wade
May 19, 1805
Sep 24, 1884
age: 79y, 4m, 5d.

Elizabeth Wade
1804-1884

"Our Mother"
Ida Thompson
Jul 14, 1864
Nov 5, 1902

J. W. "Bud" Sanders
1853-1944
    &
Mary C. Sanders
1859-1931

"Mother"
Bessie Jones
Oct 7, 1879
Sep 15, 1973

Anthony Tony Blessing
1943-1957
(picture)

G. P. Burdett
1857-1902

Guy F. Hill
May 31, 1909

    &
Betty Hill
Mar 14, 1910
May 5, 1970
married Jan 25, 1936

C. W. Cunningham
Aug 15, 1850
Jan 12, 1895
    &
Georgie Moody Cunningham
Aug 15, 1888
Jul 3, 1889

Susie May Cunningham
(no dates)

R. F. Hamilton
1830-1888
    &
Kate Hamilton
1837-1932

W. W. Scales
Apr 12, 1866
Mar 19, 1887

Reba Scales
Jan 8, 1888
Apr 8, 1890

Ruthy Scales
Dec 11, 1886
Jul 14, 1887

Marker:
Frankford
(all on tall marker, 3 graves)

Danial T. Warinner
Dec 12, 1852
Oct 26, 1930
    &
Sussie E. Warinner
Oct 22, 1858
Jan 27, 1942

Cecil Eugene Calahan
Mar 14, 1940
age: 5m & 6d.

Charlie Posey
1872-1939

Martha Posey
age: 39 yrs.
(no dates)

Josephine, wife of
Robert Posey
Died Sep 24, 1916
age: 31 yrs.

John J. Campbell
Aug 7, 1901
Sep 29, 1967
    &
Kathryn C. Campbell
Jan 28, 1906
Aug 19, 1968

Frank Ventress
1852-1921
    &
Lizzie Ventress
1860-1909

Willie Cooper Green
Jul 7, 1890
Nov 15, 1894
    &
Sadie Margaret Green
Jan 4, 1904
Jan 17, 1910
"Children of Joe C. &
M. F. Green"

Rev. T. B. Marks
1822-1902
    &
T. E. Marks
1834-1901

Samuel Bailey Marks
Jun 26, 1875
Apr 9, 1933

Martha Shapard Marks
Jun 29, 1879
Sep 24, 1924

Mother Mary A. Earnheart
age: 76 yrs.
(no dates)

Edwin Pickup
Born in England
May 15, 1847 & died
May 30, 1899
    & wife:
Alice Ann Pickup
Jun 20, 1846
Jun 5, 1900
    & wife:
Mary Jane Pickup
Died Aug 14, 1898
age: 39y & 11m.

James F. Calhoon
1826-1905
    &
Martha M. Calhoon
1827-1909

Mary H., dau of
J. F. & E. J. Calhoon
Oct 4, 1851
Apr 27, 1889

Mattie Calhoon
1864-1936

(end of Section " N ")

SECTION " O "

Joseph Moreau Blakemore
May 5, 1846
Jan 15, 1887

Gartha Barringer Blakemore
Born in Raleigh, N.C.
Sep 17, 1824
Died in Shelbyville, Tenn
Jan 21, 1873

Jehu Anderson Blakemore
Born in Fairfax Co., Va.
Jul 7, 1811 & Died in
Shelbyville, Tenn.
Feb 1, 1878

William White Blakemore
Aug 3, 1843
Apr 6, 1892

Daniel Laurens Barringer
Born in Mecklenburg Co., N.C.
Oct 1, 1788 & Died in
Shelbyville, Tenn
Oct 10, 1852

Nancy White Barringer
Born in Raleigh, N.C.
Jun 27, 1793 & Died in
Shelbyville, Tenn
Oct 18, 1860

Thomas Raleigh Myers
Jan 17, 1840
Aug 15, 1919

Anne Blakemore Myers
Oct 31, 1848
Oct 31, 1906

James B. Blakemore
Oct 27, 1902
Apr 1, 1969

Henry Blakemore Myers
May 17, 1873
Jul 12, 1873

Thomas Raleigh Myers, Jr.
Apr 1, 1888
Oct 21, 1888

Paul Barringer Myers
Mar 22, 1878
Sep 17, 1918

Hu Blakemore Myers
Colonel U.S.Army
Nov 13, 1875
Mar 30, 1936

Rebecca Lipscomb Myers
Sep 28, 1879
Nov 28, 1958

Jehu Anderson Blakemore, Jr.
Mar 27, 1858
Mar 12, 1906

Susan Blakemore Stephens
Jun 27, 1870
Aug 30, 1956

T. W. Oldfield
Sep 9, 1892
Apr 13, 1915

J. R. Oldfield
Apr 29, 1900
Oct 15, 1918

Thomas J. Oldfield
Mar 2, 1860
Sep 22, 1931

Mildred Oldfield
Mar 20, 1918
Dec 14, 1933

"Father"
Joseph Henry McGrew
Feb 13, 1826
May 30, 1889
   & "Mother"
Mary Belle McGrew
Oct 18, 1838
Jun 30, 1889
   &
James Henry McGrew
Jul 17, 1853
Dec 11, 1927
   &
May Baird McGrew
Sep 16, 1863
Jul 16, 1915
   &
James Henry McGrew
1839-1892

Edward Baird McGrew
1893-1943

Margaret L. McGrew
Mar 17, 1892
Sep 14, 1968

Samuel J. McGrew
1898-1975 (Howell)

William H. Trail
1863-1943

Retta Trail
Aug 12, 1877
Mar 16, 1953

J. O. Johnson
Jul 15, 1846
Apr 5, 1917

J. O. Johnson, Jr.
Feb 25, 1900
Dec 27, 1949

Walter Ray Bartlett
1942-1943

Ida May Bartlett
1921-1942

Lieut. J. M. Buckaloo
   Co B
3 Tenn Inf

William Kingston
Oct 9, 1824
Jan 10, 1902
   &
Malinda Kingston
Oct 28, 1823
Jul 7, 1911
   &
Sarah Kingston
Sep 24, 1853
Apr 11, 1908

Jno Sutton
   Co M
5th Tenn Cav.

Sarah R., wife of
John Sutton
Jun 14, 1849
May 25, 1908

"Father"
Jason L. Sutton
1867-1936
   &
"Mother"
Jennie L. Sutton
1879-1943
   & "Son":
William B. Sutton
1909-1930

John C. Shofner
Oct 10, 1854
Sep 15, 1925

Julia N. Shofner
1853-1933

Brenda Neil, dau of
Jno. C. & Julia N. Shofner
age: 7M & 12d.

Alsa W. Winford
1872-1963

Thomas R. Ray, M.D.
Jun 26, 1831
Feb 12, 1969

Emma E., wife of
J. C. Orrell
Nov 8, 1880
Dec 28, 1901
   &
Infant Son of
J. C. & E. E. Orrell
Born & Died
Dec 28, 1901

Frank Murray
Apr 30, 1872
Jul 24, 1891

W. J. Jackson
Jul 9, 1877
Feb 25, 1948
   & wife:
Annie Bomar Jackson
Jan 11, 1881
Aug 8, 1931

William A. Jackson
Oct 25, 1907
Jul 5, 1908

J. L. Jackson
Sep 13, 1909
Jun 18, 1912

"Mother"
Amanda F. Buckaloo
Jan 1, 1839
Feb 3, 1905

"Sister"
Amanda Buckaloo
Sep 22, 1869
Feb 3, 1905

W. M. Brantley
Sep 15, 1843
Apr 29, 1877
   &
Ella Brantley Reece
Dec 12, 1868
Jun 3, 1890

Mary Brantley Neely
Jul 5, 1851
May 1, 1933

Walton B. Buchanan
Mar 14, 1883
Nov 27, 1957

Annie Mae Buchanan
Feb 15, 1885
Jun 11, 1954

James Walton Buchanan
1914-1919

Polk Arnold
1844-1932
"Family Servant"

Jesse H. Cunningham
1858-1936
   &
Jennie N. Cunningham
1866-1931

Milton C. Hamer
Feb 23, 1835
Dec 5, 1890
"A good Husband, a loving
Father & a kind Friend"

Mary L. Goggins,
Born May 10, 1843
married Milton C. Hamer
Jul 24, 1873 & Died
Feb 5, 1905

William Goggins Hamer
Jul 25, 1874
Aug 10, 1874

Jessee Milton Hamer
Died Jun 22, 1880
age: 5months.

Sarah Elizabeth Hamer
Died Nov 9, 1876
age: 17 m.

Annie Florence Hamer
Died Oct 23, 1891
age: 9 yrs.

Rosa May Hamer
Died Jul 5, 1895
age: (broken)

Frank M. Jackson
Sec 21, 1873
Feb 27, 1950

Talitha T. Jackson
May 18, 1877
Sep 5, 1951

Julia E. Jackson
Jan 23, 1878
Dec 1, 1948

Clarence B. Ingle
May 22, 1890
Aug 12, 1970

Allie G. Ingle
Dec 23, 1893
Jun 30, 1946

Ruth G. Ingle
Feb 19, 1928
Dec 18, 1930

James P. Ingle
Aug 20, 1844
Apr 3, 1915

Virginia H. Ingle
Aug 6, 1854
May 21, 1927

Laura Cathleen Ingle
May 29, 1888
Nov 4, 1891

Ethel Gray Ingle
Apr 14, 1884
Nov 25, 1891

Lena Layton Ray
Dec 31, 1881
Apr 22, 1953

James W. Brantley
1867-1941

Helen G. Brantley
1871-1951

Daniel M. Brantley
1895-1930

Mary A. Overstreet
1844-1893

Oda --------(last name gone)
1888-(gone)
(Howell-Thompson)

Charles W. Marshall
Dec 12, 1869
was drowned in Duck River
Jul 9, 1883

Moses Marshall
Jan 28, 1811
Mar 2, 1901

Carrie E. Hill, wife of
Moses Marshall
Apr 26, 1825
Jun 11, 1909

James I. Marshall
Jan 1, 1864
Jan 6, 1941

Arch L. Marshall
Dec 22, 1859
Dec 24, 1941

Caroline Marshall Brock
Oct 19, 1867
Mar 31, 1961

Mary Lucy Stevenson
Oct 2, 1902
Jan 30, 1926

Mary Lillian Murdock
1880-1955

Annie Smalling Hoover
Jan 18, 1883
Jan 9, 1959

Annie Mae Hoover
Tennessee
Cpl Women's Army Corps
W. W. II
Jan 15, 1901
Oct 11, 1969

"Father"
J. S. McConnell
Apr 6, 1857
Nov 23, 1925

Lucy E. McConnell
Oct 8, 1865
Jan 30, 1956

William Clinton Rucker
Jan 25, 1901

Son of William Leon &
Katherine Sheppard Rucker
&
Mary Parker Rucker
Nov 24, 1902
Feb 4, 1971
Daughter of Charles G. &
Molly Reagor Parker

Tilden Prosser
1886-1974
(Gowen-Smith)

Argie Jackson
1915-1975
(Gowen-Smith)

James T. Prosser
Tennessee
Cpl Co F 349 Inf W.W.II PH
Aug 17, 1919
Apr 1, 1967
NOTE: another adult grave
beside the above grave,
TM marker ruined.

Dr. G. C. Sandusky, Sr.
Jan 25, 1834
Sep 8, 1904
"A Soldier of the Cross, A
Soldier of the Confederacy"

"Mother"
Ellen T., wife of
G. C. Sandusky, Sr.
Dec 12, 1834
May 10, 1911

Dr. John A. Sandusky
Jun 18, 1857
Sep 22, 1904
"Eldest Son of Dr. G. C. &
Ellen T. Sandusky"

Frederick Hoover, Jr.
1921
&
Marguerite Jane Hoover
1927-1930

Harvey Frederick Hoover
Sep 23, 1873
Apr 8, 1959

Cora I., wife of
H. F. Hoover
Dec 19, 1870
Feb 23, 1909
"She did what she could"

Thomas A. Rittenberry
Mar 29, 1835
Oct 8, 1903

Zilpha Rittenberry
1837-1909

Emma A. Landers
Jan 11, 1868
Jun 7, 1892

"Our Mother"
Elizabeth Scott
Oct 9, 1831
Apr 20, 1892
aged: 60y, 6m, 11d.

J. P. Cunningham
Aug 8, 1838
Feb 9, 1916

Ira D. Eley
Jul 29, 1883
Aug 1, 1946

Estella Darnell
Aug 12, 1889
Aug 16, 1910

John H. Miller
1873-1936
&
Pinkie D. Miller
1871-1960

Leonidas Thornton Reagor
1868-1941
&
Rose Dearing Reagor
1875-1941

Francis Marion Dearing
1839-1895
&
Mary Helen Dearing
1842-1907

Lillian Frances Dearing
1879-1950

Daisie Dearing
1884-1886

Richard Sandusky
1866-1935

Sarah Frierson, wife of
Richard Sandusky
Sep 19, 1867
Apr 30, 1912

John Thomas Rittenberry
1868-1951

Emma F. Rittenberry Phillips
Nov 18, 1870
Dec 15, 1897

William S. Rittenberry
1879-1956
&
Hattie Jane Rittenberry
1880-1951

Mary J., dau of
T. A. & Z. C. Rittenberry
May 24, 1863
Dec 23, 1882

Arthur L. Landers
1866-1959

Dayse R. Landers
1877-1955

Mattie Jordan
1876-1971

Edd Gregory
(no dates)

Kate Gregory
(no dates)

Rubie S. Gregory
1895-

Jimmie L. Ellis
Apr 3, 1880
Jul 27, 1893
age: 13y, 3m, 25d.

Ches. W. Lamb
Died Feb 17, 1893
age: 32 yrs.
"Shellered and safe from
sorrow"

Louis Arthur Neill, D.D.S.
1869-1957
&
Jessie Dearing Neill
1873-1944

Mrs. Elizabeth H. Thomas
Feb 17, 1815
Died in Shelbyville, Tenn.
Feb 19, 1886

Pleas M. Craigmiles
Jan 23, 1883
Nov 5, 1913
"Son of Walter & Annie S.
Craigmiles"

Dr. F. R. Sandusky, son of
G. C. & Ellen T. Sandusky
Sep 20, 1868
Aug 21, 1917

G. S. Sandusky, Jr.
30°
Jul 15, 1873
Mar 24, 1912

"Father"
Richard R. Adams
1848-1908

"Mother"
Tellah Wallace Adams
1859-1931

Koy Elgin Adams
Tennessee
Cpl 16 AERO Sq W.W.I
Apr 15, 1893
Aug 2, 1957

Bessie A. Adams
1888-1950

Samuel Thomas Brown
Jul 1, 1834
Jun 2, 1922

Alma Tune, wife of
Carl H. Holt
Jun 9, 1884
Mar 4, 1913

John H. Holt
May 3, 1855
Oct 2, 1908

Mollie Y. Holt
Jan 14, 1860
Jul 3, 1924

John Earl Holt
Oct 29, 1884
May 18, 1926

Barclay M. Tillman
Oct 31, 1825
Oct 2, 1901
&
Elizabeth F. Tillman
Dec 13, 1830
Jul 27, 1893

"My Husband"
Harry A. Tillman
Dec 2, 1860
Nov 6, 1892

Leona Sanders Stallings
Nov 9, 1896
Oct 2, 1919

Elijah A. Norvell
1844-1906
&
Bettie C. Norvell
1846-1897

F. M. Lane
(no dates, large marker)

Mrs. F. M. Lane
May 30, 1832
Jun 17, 1915

Robert H. Lane
Apr 12, 1874
Mar 19, 1913

Mary E., wife of
R. H. Lane
Sep 17, 1878
Aug 5, 1901
age: 22y, 10m, 17d.

Laura Lane
My darling girl
Died Jul 27, 1893
(no age given)

NOTE: James Cathey Lane:
as 2nd Husband of Frances
Mirande "Fannie" McCuistian,
her 1st husband was a Wynn.
James & Frances Lane are
buried in Willow Mount*

* by Mr John Lane.

Tennie McChristian
1854-1935

Walter G. Kirkpatrick
1904-1927

Lee Savage
Jul 29, 1887
Dec 24, 1915

Mattie S. Darnell
1887-1974

Vera Savage Vandagriff
1897-1916

Jordan A. Hale
1899-
&
Bernice M. Hale
1903-

W. W. Berry
Apr 21, 1837
Aug 30, 1916
"The best Heritage he left,
was a life well spent"
&
Adaline Hiles Berry,
wife of W. W. Berry
Oct 25, 1837
Dec 23, 1897

Kathleene Ingle Berry
Jul 4, 1906
Jul 24, 1906

William P. Trolinger
Aug 28 1868
Feb 11, 1915
"Remember friends, as you
pass by, as you are now,
once was I. As I am now
you soon shall be, prepare
for death and follow me"

Mary Ann Trolinger Gregory
Nov 22, 1875
Nov 23, 1961

Harris W. Trolinger
Jan 26, 1912
May 29, 1960

Blanch Trolinger, wife of
Aubrey L. Jordan
Nov 8, 1894
May 18, 1917

Howard T. Jordan
Feb 24, 1917
Aug 8, 1917

J. C. Lane
May 7, 1826
Jan 23, 1900

H. T. Coats
1877-1941

Elizabeth Kingree
Jun 10, 1899
Sep 22, 1900

Katie Lane Coats
Dec 4, 1868
Nov 26, 1948

Richard Lundy Lamb
Tennessee
Pvt Co E 310 Inf W.W.I
Dec 1, 1887
Apr 7, 1971
&
Lula L. Herron Lamb
Jul 10, 1906

Rachel Landers Philpott
1905-1931

Luther C. McLaughlin
Jan 14, 1876
Nov 18, 1955
&
Nora C. McLaughlin
May 13, 1876
Aug 19, 1961

Sadie G. Clanton
1882-1975
(Gowen-Smith)

J. N. Landers
Dec 2, 1881
Mar 23, 1910

"Father"
T. H. Berry
1861-1939

"Mother"
Ida Camp Berry
1866-1922

Will W. Berry
1868-1935
"Uncle Will"

Aileene Berry
Jun 22, 1896
Apr 18, 1916

Thompson Hiles Berry
Mar 10, 1904
Aug 29, 1904

William Felix Berry, Son of
T. H. & Ida Berry
Dec 2, 1891
Sep 8, 1892

George T. Parker
Nov 21, 1906
Aug 10, 1926
(picture)

William P. Parker
1873-1936

George W. Kingree
Jul 23, 1852
Apr 10, 1913
&
Nannie Lane Kingree
Dec 25, 1870
Sep 14, 1949

Anna Ruth McNatt
May 18, 1917
Jun 7, 1923

Billie Jane, dau of
Mr & Mrs H. E. Ward
Aug 17, 1942
Aug 18, 1942

W. C. "Bill" Haynes
1896-1948
&
Virginia Haynes
1898-19

Thomas Reed
1883-1945
&
Ellen Reed
1833-1948

W. A. Reed
1855-1931

Mary Elizabeth, wife of
W. A. Reed
Oct 9, 1856
May 30, 1910

Guy Reed
1905-1946

Alice Ruth Landers Reed
Jul 28, 1908
Mar 26, 1940

Almedia Stewart
Died Feb 18, 1910
(no age given)

W. W. Statum
Sep 19, 1847
Dec 29, 1918
&
Virginia Statum
Feb 7, 1873
Sep 22, 1901

Robert E., son of
Robert & Missouri Statum
Dec 20, 1891
Jul 3, 1893

"Father"
J. S. Chapman
Mar 14, 1874
May 14, 1928

Frances Marie, dau of
T. S. & F. K. Rowzee
1926-1927

Linda J. Drake
Feb 18, 1883
May 7, 1959

Edward L. Jordan
1872-1950
&
Willie F. Jordan
1879-19

Rev. John A. McNatt
Mar. 3, 1895

&
Lera J. Mcnatt
Dec. 29, 1898

James Erwin Lindsey
Sep 29, 1842
Jan 30, 1926

Martha Elizabeth Lindsey
Jan 8, 1839
Apr 30, 1920

Robert Hatton Holder
Tennessee
F2 U.S.N.R.F. W.W.I
Oct 6, 1896
Apr 29, 1958

Clarice Tune Holder
Jun 25, 1903
Jan 18, 1974

Claude J. Haynes
Jan 27, 1901

&
Sue Mai Haynes
Jun 17, 1909

Charles Andrew McLean
Apr 3, 1888
Jul 31, 1961
&
Elizabeth Hays McLean
Sep 20, 1888
Apr 23, 1972

Rev. C. S. Cromwell
1867-1923
& Wife:
Eliza J. Cromwell
1868-1957

F. Otis Pyrdam
1894-1952
&
Kate C. Pyrdam
1894-1962

Clevie Campbell
Nov 9, 1884
Nov 1, 1962

B. C. Campbell
Jan 17, 1883
Dec 6, 1961

Samuel L. Bryan
Feb 17, 1886

&
Christine S. Bryan
Jul 21, 1886
Feb 17, 1960

Dollie Delk Roden
Apr 23, 1874
Jul 28, 1963

Minnie Delk Capley
Feb 14, 1876
May 8, 1951

Benj. Mike Delk
Dec 24, 1844
Mar 19, 1919

Jessie R. Lindsey
May 22, 1867
Sep 29, 1918

Mary Brown Lindsey
May 6, 1888
Aug 6, 1918

Minnie Lindsey Eakes
Jul 16, 1898
Mar 14, 1921

Dewey Dozier Smith
Jan 10, 1905
Aug 17, 1961
&
Mary Thompson Smith
Feb 2, 1902
Jul 5, 1969

Alvis D. Evans
1875-1938
&
Chloe A. Evans
1875-1938

Lacie Evans
Jun 27, 1903
Oct 16, 1918

Joe F. Butts
1860-1952
&
Anna T. Butts
1870-1944

Ida T. Parsons
1870-1946

William P. Steele
Sep 27, 1873
Jul 5, 1941

Edith H. Steele
Apr 1, 1874
Nov 26, 1967

Argie T. Woodman
Aug 2, 1888
Oct 20, 1965

Marie T. Vollmar
Nov 29, 1914
Nov 2, 1966

"My Husband & Our Pa"
W. T. Tune
Dec 28, 1818
Mar 25, 1871

Christina E., wife of
William T. Tune
Jan 13, 1828
Jan 3, 1897

Kester Lewis Tune
Dec 6, 1829
Jun 2, 1905
&
Eliza Jane Tune
Oct 19, 1835
Aug 18, 1913

Callie Brown
1851-1928

William Samuel Tune
Mar 28, 1873
Apr 25, 1956

Hattie McLain Tune
Jul 27, 1879
Jan 30, 1974

Louise Lancaster
Dec 9, 1914
Nov 7, 1918

Sam J. Lancaster
Apr 5, 1885
Oct 28, 1918

Margrett Tune, wife of
J. A. McLain
1874-1926

Mary McLain
(no dates)

"Father"
P. C. Steele
Sep 8, 1848
Dec 2, 1919
&
"Mother"
Eliza T. Steele
Jan 17, 1851
Jul 11, 1933

John D. Steele
Feb 18, 1876
Nov 25, 1963

Katherine H. Steele
Apr 4, 1894
Jun 17, 1963

Guy Lewis Tune
Feb 8, 1891
Apr 8, 1928

Mattie Lee Tune
Jun 28, 1891
Apr 8, 1930

W. R. Tune
Oct 12, 1860
Aug 23, 1910

"Brother"
James C. Tune, Jr.
Sep 20, 1877
Feb 11, 1946

"Father"
James C. Tune, Sr.
Feb 24, 1847
Jul 30, 1908

"Mother"
Mary Powell Tune
Dec 18, 1856
Oct 2, 1923

"Uncle John"
John Morton Tune
Mar 20, 1858
Apr 24, 1917

Thomas L. Tune
Feb 22, 1899
Mar 9, 1970

Mary Dean Tune
Feb 14, 1900
Sep 5, 1962

M. D. L. Tune
Sep 24, 1831
Aug 29, 1907

John B. Tune
Apr 2, 1823
Jul 10, 1907

C. J. Tune
Jun 29, 1837
Sep 30, 1911

William P. Tune
Feb 6, 1864
Mar 20, 1931

Frances Tune Vannatta
Nov 6, 1860
Jun 1, 1919

Caleb L. Steele, II
Oct 4, 1880
May 17, 1934

Nannie F. Steele
Apr 1, 1879
Apr 15, 1953

(end of Section " O ")

Thomas Thompson
1866-1937
&
Corrie Thompson
1879-1955

George Eooton
1888-1937

Clifton Reed
Jun 15, 1903
Jul 3, 1966
&
Sallie W. Reed
Oct 16, 1906

(picture of both)

Martha Mae Reed
Oct 24, 1923

Burt J. Delk
Jul 5, 1889
Jul 9, 1939
&
Julia S. Delk
Dec 26, 1892
May 17, 1952

Horace Paul
1898-1940
&
Myrtle Paul
1898-1970

Arthur Lee Paul
Apr 1, 1924
Aug 4, 1939

Cicero D. Cowart
Mar 11, 1896
Nov 1, 1966

Ola Helton
1876-1939

Walter Locke
1877-1955
&
Dollie Locke
1882-1938

W. H. Locke, Jr.
Aug 13, 1909
Jun 22, 1959
&
Pansy W. Locke
Jul 5, 1912

John W. Wagster
1900-1961
&
Eva B. Wagster
1912-

Thomas H. Elam
Mar 14, 1913
Jun 24, 1939

Robert E. Compton
Jun 29, 1890
Sep 6, 1961
&
Lillian A. Compton
Jun 27, 1892
Dec 29, 1959

Othnel G. Chambless
1936-1936

Milton C. Renegar
1878-1947

Jennie L. Renegar
1883-1937

Roy L. Renegar
1903-1952

John Wesley Hammond
1875-1959
&
Nora Cannon Hammond
1879-1937

Geneva Hammond Hale
Feb 16, 1910
Jul 12, 1954

John W. Haggard
1874-1944
&
Alice L. Haggard
1881-1974

John Cecil Haggard
Aug 18, 1902
Dec 5, 1962

Lonzo W. Arnold
1895-1942

Mary Mitchell, wife of
R. L. Allen
1909-1967

Lottie Mitchell
1905-1942

John Ray Head
1889-1955
&
Pearl Swing Head
1898-

Minnie L. Head
1887-1937

Della Swing Lacy
1874-1949

"Son"
Winifred M. Lowe, son of
Emitt & Bessie Lowe
Jul 31, 1918
Jun 3, 1938

C. C. Sexton
1866-1937

Cad Crunk Bryant
1875-1936
&
Musa Hix Bryant
1889-19

Finis P. Hix
1857-1944
&
Virginia P. Hix
1868-1944

W. T. Mooningham
1858-19 (no date)
&
Dora M. Mooningham
1866-1939

R. K. Mooningham
1890-1938

Sadie L. Mooningham
1906-

Clyde Claxton
Apr 18, 1912
Dec 29, 1936

NOTE: A Plot with dates:
6-11-45, no Name.

Thomas M. Wheeler
Jul 29, 1883
Jan 10, 1958
&
Nezzie L. Wheeler
May 28, 1887
Feb 20, 1960

James T. Harrison
1864-1945
&
Elizabeth Moore Harrison
1881-1934

Thomas W. Beavers
Sep 5, 1883
Nov 22, 1934
&
Rena Potts Beavers
Mar 29, 1898
Mar 27, 1970

"Mother"
Margaret F. Beavers
Apr 9, 1858
Mar 5, 1943

Olin C. Lowe
Jul 9, 1888
Dec 25, 1969
&
Jessie C. Lowe
Sep 21, 1890
Feb 1, 1960

Julius N. Vincent
May 21, 1921
Jun 10, 1959

Roy F. Haithcote
Apr 26, 1896

&
Bertha L. Haithcote
Dec 1, 1907

William O. Lowe
1880-1934
&
Hattie Mae Lowe
1884-1940

"Father"
Howard Henley
1892-
&
"Mother"
Lucille Henley
1906-1938

"Mother"
Hazel L. Curle, wife of
Joe D. Brinkley
1896-1937

W. Luther Pope
1908-1937
&
Jimmie Lee Pope
1912-1939

Hayden M. Nelson
Mar 9, 1866
Aug 5, 1952
&
Jennie E. Nelson
Dec 9, 1868
Oct 8, 1948

Thomas George Nelson
Feb 16, 1934
Mar 28, 1934

Thomas L. Nelson
Jan 10, 1900

&
Inez L. Nelson
Jun 13, 1905
Apr 30, 1957

William R. Phillips
Mar 7, 1935
Feb 24, 1939
(picture)

James Green
Jan 23, 1896
TM-1975 (Gowen-Smith)
&
Dovie Green
Oct 1, 1893

Rosa Lee Peach
Feb 22, 1945

John E. Sexton
Aug 6, 1886
Sep 21, 1972
&
Nannie W. Sexton
Oct 17, 1895

Walter Dee Martin
May 2, 1890
Mar 16, 1954
&
Adaline E. Martin
Dec 14, 1892
Nov 10, 1961

A. D. Curtis
1873-1930

Nora Curtis
1878-1941

Martha Curtis
1911-1930

Frances Curtis Woodward
Dec 8, 1882
Mar 5, 1969

William D. Freeze
Jan 29, 1867
Jul 18, 1930
&
Laura F. Freeze
Oct 16, 1866
May 26, 1937
(picture of both)

Raht Freeze
Oct 23, 1903
Aug 10, 1951

Talmadge W. Freeze
Jul 14, 1896

&
Moselle L. Freeze
Sep 23, 1895
Apr 24, 1966

Betty Jean Harris
1931-1932

Elizabeth Harris
Jun 26, 1904
Mar 21, 1949

Newton J. Foster
1869-1946

Hattie F. Foster
1876-1942

"Daughter"
Juanita Kingston
Jan 28, 1926
Nov 7, 1932

Sewell Kingston
1897-1943

Arthur C. Jones
Jan 11, 1880
Sep 20, 1956
&
Mattie L. Jones
Jan 11, 1889
Jan 5, 1965

Calvin Jones
Jun 13, 1929
Jan 23, 1937

Jesse D. Evans
Jul 7, 1892
Jun 25, 1959

Gladys M. Evans
Mar 10, 1901
Nov 15, 1957

Mary Ann Evans
Nov 26, 1926
Jul 3, 1939

George O. Carroll
Oct 30, 1890

&
Julia Vera Carroll
Jul 15, 1901
Dec 17, 1956

Farris J. Nichols
1901-1933

John I. Parker, Sr.
Aug 12, 1887 Tennessee
May 10, 1971 Sgt Btry B,
&   318 Fd Arty W.W.I
Katie Mitchell Parker
Jan 6, 1898

Frances Parker
Mar 10, 1925
Jan 22, 1933

Orville Lee Raney
May 3, 1903

&
Nell Hitt Raney
Feb 2, 1905
Feb 3, 1974

William Everette Hitt
Jul 26, 1868
May 31, 1954
&
Brightie S. Hitt
Oct 18, 1877
Apr 6, 1964
married Aug 26, 1894

Joe H. Parker
Sep 26, 1888
Nov 22, 1944
&
Sue Mae Parker
Nov 9, 1893
Jul 23, 1959

Vernon Caldwell
1892-1966
&
Minnie Caldwell
1896-1924

Caldwell Infant
(no dates)

Daniel Lee Gunn
Jun 29, 1864
Nov 8, 1950

Annie Jane Gunn
Apr 10, 1875
Nov 11, 1931

William M. Glasscock
Apr 3, 1873
Jul 15, 1931
&
Annie L. Glasscock
Mar 23, 1879
Mar 10, 1974

Gertrude G. Hix
Sep 15, 1900
Jul 29, 1965

Den Helton
1872-19(no date)
&
Dona Helton
1880-1949

Neil McCrory
May 15, 1881
Jan 7, 1951
&
Mary McCrory
May 28, 1881
Dec 2, 1971

Charlie Jones
1885-1942

Johnnie R. Walker
Jan 31, 1907
Dec 23, 1970
&
Mattie L. Walker
Feb 26, 1909
Sep 2, 1958

Dorothy E. Walker
Nov 23, 1931
Jun 7, 1933

Sam W. Warner
1900-1972

Alberta F. Warner
1905-

R. A. Turpen
1868-1932

Allie R. Turpen
1871-1952

M. R. Turpen
1894-1941

Harry B. Henley
1904-1934

Nannie S. Henley
1865-1942

Boss Goodner
1874-1970
&
Maggie P. Goodner
1878-1950

Perry H. Scott
1880-1941

Bertie M. Scott
1893-

Infant Son of
Perry H. & Bertie M. Scott
Jul 28, 1930

Robert C. Agee
1875-1949
&
Rosa E. Agee
1877-1946

John H. Martin
Mar 6, 1902

&
Nell M. Martin
Jan 12, 1907

Roy Trolinger
Nov 22, 1903
Aug 4, 1970
&
Mary Lentz Trolinger
Jun 25, 1908
Dec 30, 1945

Peggy Trolinger
Jun 27, 1932
Sep 6, 1933

William Lawrence Troxler
Jan 23, 1892
Oct 23, 1931
&
Bonnie Hitt Troxler
Mar 25, 1896

Thomas A. Lyda
Feb 3, 1896
Jul 22, 1931

Ernest Marion Jackson
1927-1932

Lawson Clenney
Oct 29, 1899
Aug 3, 1938

Charles Howard, son of
Joe H. & Sue Mae Parker
1932
age: 2m & 20d.

J. Edgar Turner
1898-1967
&
Grace S. Turner
1898-1971

Louette Adams Slabbekorn
Feb 21, 1916
May 31, 1938

Marion C. Adams
Jan 5, 1885
Jan 11, 1970
&
Anna Lou Adams
Nov 25, 1890

A. Owen Woosley
Oct 19, 1875
Dec 26, 1954
&
Maude E. Woosley
Jul 4, 1873
Jun 9, 1969

Evelyn Woosley Nelson
Jan 20, 1908
Feb 15, 1931

Edgar D. Dye
1910-1943

Mary E. Dye
1910-1939

Barney O. Phillips
May 29, 1906
Jun 9, 1930

William Edd. Phillips
1861-1943
&
Sara Bell Phillips
1862-1936

James Wilburn Palmer
Jul 4, 1902

&
Pauline Harrison Palmer
Feb 17, 1906

James Alvin Palmer
Oct 15, 1936
May 11, 1970

W."William" Murry Fisher
Jun 14, 1902
Feb 14, 1976
&
Irene P. Fisher
Feb 18, 1903

Marvin Euless Philpott
Mar 6, 1900
May 9, 1970
&
Alvie Arnold Philpott
Jun 6, 1912

Albert Parker
Mar 22, 1888
Jul 21, 1963
&
Lula P. Parker
Mar 26, 1889
Feb 23, 1962

Florie W. Hoover
Jul 25, 1885
Mar 6, 1962

Raleigh Amos Holden
May 31, 1883
Feb 18, 1953
&
Fronnie Cannon Holden
Nov 12, 1890

James L. Cannon Holden
Aug 27, 1925
Nov 4, 1931

John Abner Brown
Mar 4, 1865
Aug 31, 1930

Nellie Isom Brown
Mar 6, 1882
Sep 7, 1950

John Clifton Brown
Aug 30, 1911
Dec 29, 1970

Fred Walker
Aug 18, 1894
Jun 11, 1961
&
Ethel P. Walker
Oct 22, 1898

W. E. Palmer
1876-1929

Mignon Palmer
1881-1929

Raymond R. Palmer
May 27, 1900
Oct 29, 1966
&
Ozelle E. Palmer
Apr 14, 1902

Fred Palmer Walker
May 28, 1921
Mar 7, 1969
&
Martha Hope Walker
Dec 3, 1922

David Philpott
1868-1942
&
Mary Philpott
1868-1929

John W. Watson
Jan 1, 1861
Jun 7, 1939
&
Rebecca F. Watson
Jun 13, 1872
Nov 3, 1932

Roy L. Watson
Feb 25, 1926
Jan 19, 1968

Miachel C. Watson
1952-1952

Walter G. Delffs
1877-1953
&
Maggie R. Delffs
1877-1965

Coy A. Delffs
1900-1973
(Gowen-Smith)

"Mother"
Georgie Delffs
1902-1930

Dixie Delffs Garber
Jun 1, 1916
Jul 19, 1945
(picture)

Cecil C. Simmons
1885-1949
&
Lottie J. Simmons
1895-1972

Margaret, dau of
Cecil & Lottie Simmons
Aug 18, 1917
Feb 3, 1932

James Marvin Simmons
1912-

Ruth Simmons
1918-1928

Ben F. Simmons
1875-1941

Lula Coats, wife of
Ben F. Simmons
1880-1945

Lera Whorley, wife of
Coy Simmons
1916-1942

Evelyn Joan, Infant dau of
Coy & Lera Simmons
1942

James Robert Phillips
1882-1953

Lillie Parker Phillips
1882-1961

Charles J. Chockley
Oct 3, 1878

&
Bessie Yates Chockley
Jun 20, 1889
Sep 9, 1930

Harold Y. Chockley
S/Sgt U.S.Army Inf.
Jun 6, 1922
lost in action
Dec 25, 1944

Earnest C. Swing
Mar 7, 1880
Mar 22, 1951
&
Dollie C. Swing
Jun 12, 1887
Oct 5, 1971

Edward Swing
Oct 26, 1907
Dec 22, 1930

Thomas B. Reese
Mar 29, 1903
Jul 31, 1954
&
Callie B. Reese
Aug 19, 1904

Lavern Compton
1928-1929

Mary M. Meacheam
1902-1929

Hiram L. Stephens
1879-1963
&
Sarah T. Stephens
1878-1958

Christy Lynn, Infant dau of
Donald & Betty Jo Cathy
Dec 9, 1972

Robert L. Damron
Jan 17, 1868
Oct 17, 1928
&
Fannie E. Damron
Oct 14, 1872
Jan 25, 1933

Major L. Burks
Died Nov 21, 1959
(no age given)
&
Katherine F. Burks

Ben R. Phillips
Jun 8, 1861
Jan 22, 1939
&
Mattie S. Phillips
Mar 7, 1863
Mar 20, 1949

F. G. "Dock" Phillips
Aug 13, 1857
Feb 20, 1931

Cordelia Phillips
May 1, 1861
May 1, 1942

Lizzie Phillips Aaron
Aug 31, 1881
Aug 1, 1953

Luther G. Phillips
Jan 31, 1891

Irene W. Phillips
Jun 1, 1895
Feb 14, 1974

William F. Phillips
Aug 7, 1883
Jun 25, 1969

D. Arthur Phillips
Jun 10, 1885
Mar 27, 1969

Bessie C. Phillips
Aug 1, 1889
Feb 7, 1951

Edward Troxler
Jun 9, 1880
Mar 7, 1944
&
Carrie Troxler
Dec 13, 1887
Sep 25, 1972

Edward B. Troxler
Nov 7, 1925
Jul 9, 1935

Lauran Raby
Jan 18, 1894
Dec 24, 1954
&
Lara Raby Dryden
Jan 8, 1896
Jan 16, 1973

Edwin Raby
1918-1940

William H. York
1861-1934
&
Alice B. York
1869-1944

Luna Mai Clanton
Dec 9, 1907
Apr 12, 1974
"From loved ones"

John P. Petty
1879-1944
&
Ruth M. Petty
1887-1954

Jas. W. "Jimmie" Armstrong
1930-1934

George Wesley Armstrong
Apr 16, 1885
Nov 29, 1957
&
Katie Gregory Armstrong
Feb 24, 1889
Sep 28, 1965

James R. Armstrong
1876-1938
&
Lena C. Armstrong
1880-1961

G. R. Armstrong
1854-1934

B. A. Lokey
1929-1931

William Lokey
Feb 19, 1912
Apr 5, 1934

Lydia P. Lokey
Oct 5, 1892
Sep 4, 1955

Neil C. Lokey, Sr.
Dec 10, 1891
Jan 27, 1958

Andrew J. Snoddy
Jun 7, 1901
Jul 1, 1963

Julius Snoddy
May 20, 1894
Jan 11, 1934
NOTE: New unmarked grave
     beside above grave)

James T. Snoddy
Feb 27, 1868
Jan 14, 1948

Blanch Womack Snoddy
Mar 12, 1872
May 5, 1932

James E. Loyd
1870-1948
&
Sallie N. Loyd
1877-1945

James Emit Loyd
May 21, 1903
May 3, 1974
&
Pearl Loyd
Mar 9, 1909

Malcolm Robinson
1883-1970
&
Mattie B. Robinson
1886-19

Evelyn Robinson
Nov 13, 1933

James Malcolm Robinson
Sep 8, 1928
Jan 23, 1929

Jeff D. Poplin
1861-1936

Alice B. Poplin
1868-1951

John Will Taylor
Oct 10, 1866
Nov 25, 1934

Lizzie Taylor
1871-1962

Samuel Davidson Wood
1873-1950

Martha Sue Wood
1873-1932

James Estill Penn
1878-1947

Tom Daniel
1866-1931

Mrs. T. A. Daniel
1887-195_(gone)
(Beasley)

Mike Shoffner Cannon
Oct 2, 1892

&
Myrtle Reaves Cannon
Aug 25, 1894

Wilburn Hoyt Cannon
Tennessee
Pfc Co A 114 Machine Gun Bn
W. W. I
Nov 16, 1893
Jul 4, 1953

Lillie Bell Loyd
Apr 26, 1901
Jan 3, 1932

Eugene Hix
Apr 19, 1866
Sep 23, 1961

Edwina Hix
1903-1933

James Polk Kee
1906-1968
(Gowen-Smith)
NOTE: a new unmarked grave
     beside the above grave.
     TM marker destroyed.

Tabitha Shriver Wilhoite
Jul 11, 1868
Sep 27, 1950

Oren Buford Wheeler
Jan 3, 1895
Sep 5, 1951
&
Gladys Wilhoite Wheeler
Jun 5, 1899
Jul 3, 1929

James H. Wheeler
1864-1950
&
Mary E. Wheeler
1873-1935

Robert Houston Smith
Mar 21, 1888

&
Blanche Poplin Smith
Feb 24, 1892
Mar 7, 1972
married May 6, 1917

Charlie C. Clark
Aug 31, 1878
Apr 15, 1958
&
Lizzie D. Clark
Oct 30, 1891
Feb 4, 1968

H. L. Jenkins
1853-1947
(Beasley)

Beulah Reaves
1871-19(no date)
&
Edna Reaves
1871-1937

Rev. Samuel L. Bell
Oct 3, 1877
Feb 14, 1965
&
Mattie Bell
Sep 10, 1882
Feb 8, 1957
&
Julius R. Bell
Jun 21, 1914
May 4, 1968
Tennessee
Pvt AT Co 383 Inf W.W.II

Jessie L. Kee
1895-1943

Charlie Kee
Jul 4, 1871
Oct 31, 1931
&
Lizzie Kee
Sep 21, 1871
Jun 21, 1955

Lockey Neese
1897-1934

244

George M. Phillips
1875-1947
&
Lizzie M. Phillips
1880-1953

George M. Phillips, Jr.
1914-1931

Maurice "Son" Limbo
Feb 10, 1902
TM-1975
(Gowen-Smith)
&
Bertie Lou Limbo
Feb 16, 1902
Oct 10, 1967

George Newton Gambill
Oct 8, 1908
Apr 21, 1970
&
Elizabeth Milton Gambill
May 30, 1914

Thomas D. Fann
May 26, 1884
Mar 17, 1958

Minnie Fann Temple
May 8, 1885
Jul 10, 1972

Cannon Reese
1908-1937

Joe Frank Williams
Aug 30, 1884
Feb 16, 1967

Agnes L. Williams
May 18, 1895
Jul 7, 1934

Eugenia C. Williams
Jun 1, 1905

James A. Stewart
Sep 14, 1846
Aug 26, 1933
&
Sarah M. Stewart
Jan 17, 1866
Aug 25, 1954

John L. Patton
Jun 26, 1887
Apr 4, 1955
&
Vassie V. Patton
Aug 28, 1887
TM-1975:V. Gammill
(Gowen-Smith)

Winnie Eva Patton
1911-1934
"Our Only Daughter"

C. C. Vannatta
1858-1939

Charlie C. Bell
1885-1946
&
Alice H. Bell
1888-1963

Eugene Bell
1863-1948
&
Mary Jane Bell
1864-1932

J. Hugh Hasty
1887-19(no date)
&
Pearl D. Hasty
1886-1960

Floyd G. Smith
Sep 8, 1903
Dec 27, 1939

"Father"
James A. McKay
Jul 27, 1876
Jan 25, 1940

"Mother"
Bertha J. McKay
Sep 4, 1886
Feb 9, 1968

William B. McKay
Jun 12, 1917
Jul 27, 1944
"Lieut in U.S. Air Corps"

Foster W. Smith
1922-
&
Virginia D. Smith
1922-1952

Byron L. Foster
Aug 4, 1891
May 28, 1956

Charlie R. Reed
Mar 2, 1872
Mar 16, 1941
& wife:
Amey Cannon Reed
Jul 22, 1872
May 8, 1937

Julius V. Yakmas
Nov 15, 1915
Feb 19, 1954

James E. Patton
Aug 2, 1913
Jan 26, 1967

James Owen Patton
Tennessee
S/Sgt U.S. Air Force
Vietnam, AFCOM
Dec 18, 1943
Jun 27, 1972

Vona Mai Cunningham
1925-1974
(Gowen-Smith)

D. P. Shapard
1881-1933

F. Boyd Justice
1911-1940

Thomas F. Beckwith
Tennessee
Cpl Btry A 316 Field Arty
W. W. I
Dec 16, 1888
Sep 10, 1959

Jesse M. Phillips
Dec 9, 1893
Feb 5, 1963
&
Margie P. Phillips
Oct 7, 1897

W. Thomas Cobble
Apr 17, 1870
Jun 14, 1950
&
Beatrice M. Cobble
Jan 18, 1879
Jul 28, 1938

James R. Raby
1881-1943
&
Fannie M. Raby
1887-1964

Henry C. Davis
1893-1966
&
Ruth S. Davis
1896-1934

Ella S. Davis
1898-19

George A. Lokey
Mar 15, 1896
Feb 14, 1932
&
Sara Lokey Ogles
Jul 21, 1898

&
Walter B. Ogles
Jun 10, 1894
Jun 5, 1970

John Clinton Moore
Mar 21, 1865
Dec 18, 1935
&
Lelia Brown Moore
Jun 20, 1875
Dec 31, 1936

Annie Frances, only child of
John C. & Lelia B. Moore
Jan 19, 1915
"Interred in Mt. Pisgah
Cemetery"

Julian Pinkston
Nov 15, 1933
Mar 11, 1934

Lester L. Pinkston
Feb 21, 1903
Dec 21, 1959

Thelma N. Norris
May 20, 1905
Jul 18, 1940

Charlie Robinson
1879-1945
&
Hattie Robinson
1882-1967

Evachel Williams
1880-1945
&
Nell D. Williams
1896-1969

Boss Jordan
May 7, 1892
Sep 30, 1956
&
Kathern Jordan
Mar 17, 1915
Aug 28, 1938

Thomas Jefferson Prosser
Mar 11, 1864
Mar 6, 1947
&
Dorah Newsom Prosser
Apr 22, 1871
Jan 19, 1939

Fred O. Gentry
1898-1961
&
Audra A. Gentry
1895-1946

Charles Orbin Gentry
1919-1963

Louis J. Lawell
Sep 2, 1883
Nov 9, 1966
&
Ettie S. Lawell
Jun 7, 1892
Jul 15, 1967

Eddie R. Lawell
Sep 18, 1895
Mar 29, 1974
&
Ida S. Lawell
Nov 19, 1894

Andrew J. Tillett
Dec 16, 1875
Apr 29, 1943
&
Jennye B. Tillett
Oct 5, 1882
Dec 23, 1962

David C. Daughtrey
1878-1952
&
Malissa P. Daughtrey
1883-1970

Joe Dean Byers
Mar 4, 1930
Jul 15, 1936

W. C. Pierce
1862-1938
&
Della Pierce
1865-1934

Shirley Ann Edwards
1935-1935

Sally Rachel Edwards
1971-1971
(Gowen-Smith)

Henry T. Posey
1876-1961
&
Fannie E. Posey
1886-1940

Thomas L. Melson
1888-1939

Lula Cashion Melson
1890-1949

Roland Lane Gibson
Dec 8, 1934
Jun 26, 1935

Thad Richard Smith
1874-1955
&
Pearl Wright Smith
1886-1953

Thomas Haskins   and
1882-19

Grady Davidson
Aug 6, 1900
Apr 2, 1971

Dryden Davidson
1902-1935

Robert Carl Howell
1935-1938

John M. Hutchison
1871-1940
&
Priscilla Hutchison
1872-1950
&
Lena M. Hutchison
1902-1948

Charles Etheridge
Oct 12, 1887
Apr 2, 1935

Ruby Etheridge Jones
Sep 23, 1910
Mar 16, 1970

Thomas Waters
1881-1941
(picture)
&
Mattie Lou Waters
1890-19

Lillie Mae Waters
Nov 25, 1910
Jul 31, 1961

William Lee Drake
1879-1939
&
Santafee Drake
1880-1954

Virgie Haskins   and
1886-TM-Virginia Ann, 1974
(Gowen-Smith)

Rhea Eaton Adams
1907-1935

E. L. Eaton
1868-1938
&
Beulah Eaton
1874-1965

Sumner A. Dillard
Mar 5, 1883
Mar 2, 1936

John W. Adams
1859-1938
&
America J. Adams
1867-1946

Doyle Swing
Jan 11, 1928
Feb 29, 1936

Leland R. Bledsoe
May 13, 1905
Aug 17, 1962
&
Sadie B. Bledsoe
Jun 29, 1910
May 11, 1964

James A. Bledsoe
1934-1936

William F. Smith
Tennessee
Tec 5 512 Ord Hv
Maint. Co.   W.W.II
Jan 16, 1913
Jul 11, 1949

Leona Reed Smith
Dec 1, 1915
Apr 28, 1939

Milford Haskins
1909-1939

Itys Reese Murray
1887-1939

"Daddy"
B. Douglas Gill
Nov 2, 1913
Jan 15, 1956

Leonard M. Gill
1888-1935
&
Ida C. Gill
1892-19

George Franklin Swing
1905-
&
Mattie E. Swing
1908-
&
"Father"
William Sim Waldrep
1879-1947
&
"Mother"
Margaret A. Waldrep
1882-1955
&
"Brother"
William Hubert Waldrep
1906-1969

William N. Wagster
Feb 15, 1878
Nov 6, 1956
&
Hattie N. Wagster
Nov 30, 1879
Jul 1, 1947

B. J. Wagster
May 31, 1912
Sep 19, 1938

Alta M. Wagster
Sep 29, 1909
Mar 7, 1970

Bonnie Marie Bartlett
Feb 13, 1966
Jun 2, 1966

(end of Section " P ")

SECTION " Q "

Joe V. Delffs
1897-
&
Mamie L. Delffs
1899-1974

Hazel Delffs Omdahl
1918-1951

Sgt. Joe V. Delffs
1920-1945

Will M. Sutton   and
Nov 9, 1880
Jul 23, 1967

Mrs. Hattie Cunningham
Oct 20, 1884
Nov 29, 1971

William A. Sutton
Nov 10, 1912

&
Loreen W. Sutton
Mar 19, 1912

Lizzie D. Sutton   and
Nov 10, 1883
Nov 11, 1962

Adam L. Davis
Apr 23, 1880
Jan 21, 1961
&
Pearl B. Davis
Dec 6, 1887
Oct 1, 1974

George Thomas Gray
1907-1963
(Gowen-Smith)

Eula Mae Sutton
Nov 16, 1910
Oct 27, 1911

Jas. Sol Womack
Jan 18, 1875
Aug 6, 1960

Media Womack
May 28, 1874
Mar 28, 1919

Woodard D. Womack
Nov 24, 1907
Jan 10, 1929

Scotty Shane Hay
Dec 6, 1970
Oct 30, 1971
(color picture)

Darlene Copeland Register
Jun 3, 1967
Jun 4, 1967
"Erected by her loving
Mother & Step-Father,
Julie & James Jones"

Charles David Nevill
1964-1964
(Howell-Thompson)

J. D. Watson, Sr.
1901-1943

Mathie Lee Claxton
Apr 24, 1905
Mar 12, 1974
&
Edith Trott Claxton
Nov 13, 1904

J. D. Claxton
1908-1935

C. Boyd Williams
Dec 27, 1886
Jan 1, 1962
&
Sarah C. Williams
Jun 5, 1900

Buren Williams
1938-1939

Charles Moore
Wagoner
1 Tenn Inf
Jun 15, 1870
Jan 27, 1943

Lillie Gwin Moore
Oct 4, 1882
Mar 12, 1957

Ernest Wilkes
1883-1944
&
Annie M. Wilkes
1893-19

Alton Wilhoit
1945-1945
(Thompson)

Jim Cunningham
1876-1942

Alice Cunningham
1877-1968
(Gowen-Smith)

Miles J. Lankford
1869-1948
&
Bettie Lankford
1874-(no date)

Charles Rich Adkins
Aug 10, 1942

Raybon Richardson, Jr.
1934-1943

Eddie Ray Hargrove
1963-1968
(Gowen-Smith)

Harold Lee, son of
Winfred H. & Ruby Cobb
Jan 3, 1968
Feb 10, 1968

Jean B. Feldhaus
1963-1963
(Gowen-Smith)

W. Houston Sudberry
May 24, 1904

&
Mary Jane Sudberry
May 1, 1907
----
married Dec 23, 1923

William H. Sudberry, Jr.
1933-1935

Lillie A. Reid Arnold
Apr 10, 1875
Apr 19, 1968

Albert Newton Reid
May 10, 1905
Jun 1, 1969

Walter Brawley
1878-1948
&
Hattie Brawley
1887-1964

Bettye Sue Grubbs
Sep 23, 1941
Sep 13, 1943

Gladys Marie Pittman
1943-1943 (TM)

Linda Rae Church
1947-1947
(Thompson)

R. Wiley Allen
1885-1962
(Gowen-Smith)

Nancy Allen
1890-1943

Rillie Roberts
1868-1951
&
Maggie Roberts
1879-1964

James N. Crowell
Dec 13, 1891

&
Carrie M. Crowell
Mar 16, 1887
Feb 25, 1956
(picture of both)

Hellen L. Holman
1944 age: 3 months

Shawn Bryan
1964-1967
(Gowen-Smith)

Infant Craemer
1966-1966
(Gowen-Smith)

Jeanie Ruth Nichols
Sep 16, 1963

Mattie H. Shearin
1911-1971
(Howell)

Cleburne Patterson
May 26, 1889
TM- 1970
(Gowen-Smith)

Elbert Patterson
Feb 15, 1887
Apr 19, 1967

Herschel Patterson
Nov 7, 1867
Feb 7, 1940
&
Willie Patterson
Mar 19, 1869
Jun 3, 1963

Ben P. Hoover
1879-1940
&
Lula L. Hoover
1881-1942

Slater D. Hoover
1881-1954

Felix Welton Hoover
Tennessee
Cpl SVC Btry 179 FA Bn W.W.II
Jun 17, 1916
Jun 18, 1962

Dorothy Marie Hoover
1927-1943

John N. Dunaway
1868-1951
&
Mary Matilda Dunaway
1864-1942

"Father"
Newton "Dick" Moore
Jan 26, 1901
Nov 8, 1941

Wencie Reid Johnson
1902-1943

Dale Wayne Church
1949-1949
(Thompson)

Janet Patricia, dau of
Lyle & Janet Widdowson
1942

Milton F. Sweeney
1873-1942

Richard Lee Smith
Jul 20, 1966
Jul 21, 1966

Charles Allen Joines
1964-1964
(Gowen-Smith)

Tony Glenn Hoover
1950-1950
(Thompson)

J. Virgil Hoover
1951-1969
(Howell-Thompson)

Gloria Gambill
1942

Jas. Joseph King
Feb 12, 1884
Jan 6, 1958
&
Ida Minnie King
Oct 23, 1889

Claude M. Woodward
1888-1956
&
Angie A. Woodward
1893-1939

Aline Faulk Woodward
1922-

Mildred E. Harris
1935- age: 8 months

Harmon Lokey
1887-1964
&
Myrtis Lokey
1892-1974

Cecil Lokey
1910-1936

James Morgan Dye
1914-1942

Rebecca Dye
1880-1970
(Gowen-Smith)

Timothy W. Dye
1958-1958
(Gowen-Smith)

Arthur Jackson Butler
1886-1943

William L. Townsend
1870-1944

William Fred Andrae
1942-1942
(Thompson)

Mary Elizabeth Herrin
1947-1947
(Thompson)

Luther Claxton
1880-1944
&
Mary Claxton
1886-1955

John B. Knox
1935-1945

Minnie Belle Starkweather
1923-1943

Mark O. Redd
1885-1957
&
Lettie M. Redd
1892-1953

Christlene Redd
1927-1943

A. Vance Nance
1879-1945
&
Ethel B. Nance
1883-1959

Kelly H. Woosley
1877-1964

Effie G. Woosley
1876-1945

James H. Hoover
1869-1947
&
Nellie F. Hoover
1891-1944

Deborah Shearin
1950-1956

"Father"
John Benton King
Jul 23, 1886

&
"Mother"
Nellie Florance King
Dec 4, 1892
Sep 21, 1944

Paul B. Clay
Sep 1, 1894
Oct 29, 1973
&
Dessie V. Clay
Apr 18, 1910
----
married Jun 6, 1931

Ernest O. Barrett
1906-
&
Jimmie R. Barrett
1915-

Margaret H., wife of
W. T. Tucker
1886-1952

Dorthy Jean Barrett
1935-1935

Charlie Oscar Marsh
Apr 3, 1877
Dec 27, 1943
&
Mattie Marsh
Nov 17, 1886
Nov 11, 1966

Carlos E. Helton
1945-1945

Coy M. Bonner
Nov 19, 1919

&
Margaret Bonner
Feb 2, 1919
Nov 24, 1973
TM-Frances Redd Bonner
   (Gowen-Smith)

Hoyt Redd
Tennessee
Pfc Btry D 210 AAA AW Bn
W. W. II
May 23, 1912
Jun 7, 1966

William Louis Dushane
1872-1957
&
Sarah May Dushane
1871-1953

Calvin Luther Nichols
Dec 31, 1873
Oct 3, 1919

Margaret Nichols Coop
Oct 6, 1884
Dec 11, 1944

Jim T. Sharp
Aug 2, 1880
Aug 15, 1931
&
Mary R. Sharp
Nov 27, 1877
Mar 21, 1965

Carl E. Reed
1903-1967
&
Irene C. Reed
1902-

Jasper P. Pittman
1873-19(no date)
&
Jane G. Pittman
1872-1944

Gus Pittman
1896-1959

Bettie Jane Pittman
1940-1944

Karen Lee Barrett
1956-1956

Mary M. Reed
1881-1939

David Edgar Clark
Aug 9, 1890
Jul 19, 1968
&
Edna Barry Clark
May 24, 1898
Aug 16, 1968

Nellon Charlton Clark
1920-1943

Carl Edward Blackwell
1943-1944

Elmer Fred Uselton
Tennessee
Tec 4 U.S.Army W.W.II
Apr 3, 1916
Oct 3, 1971

Mitchel E. Davidson
1881-1956
&
Estella A. Davidson
1883-1958

Marcus Lee Sipsy
1904-1944

W. H. "Buddie" Freeman
1882-1949
&
Ada W. Freeman
1883-1961

Mary Ann Cantrell
1942-1944
by-Johnny Cantrell

Arch W. Woosley
1876-1947
&
Edna R. Woosley
1879-19

Mary M. Covington
1889-

William M. Mack
1882-1949

Ruben M. Gordon
1872-1937
&
Lula T. Gordon
1885-1963

Sarah W. Gilley
Oct 13, 1878
Jun 9, 1944

David R. Bennett
1893-1937
&
Elsie D. Bennett
1909-19

Claude L. McBride
Jul 13, 1890
Jul 25, 1972
&
Myrtle M. McBride
May 16, 1896

Ollie P. Williamson
Jul 7, 1892
Dec 9, 1969

May Frances Williamson
1896-1949

William Faulk
1877-1944
&
Margaret Faulk
1879-1943

James Earl Faulk
1915-1971

Ernest E. Jackson
Aug 31, 1883
Sep 25, 1967
&
Maude G. Jackson
Sep 18, 1893
Jul 31, 1971

Thomas Grady Thompson
Jan 27, 1912
Mar 1, 1973
&
Ruth F. Thompson
Jul 19, 1918

Roy H. Thompson
Sep 17, 1887
Dec 20, 1956
&
Ida Mai Thompson
May 2, 1891

Floyd H. Gentry
1900-1944
&
Nona S. Gentry
1901-

Loucile Nelson
Jun 20, 1920
May 8, 1945

Wade I. Patton
Jun 20, 1914
Sep 8, 1961
&
Katherine G. Patton
Apr 24, 1918

James Alfred Patton
Infant Son
Aug 11, 1937

Isham Reaves
1860-1935
&
Nannie Reaves
1873-1949

Infant dau of
Luther & Maudie Goodman
Nov 30, 1944

Infants of R. C. &
Irene Parker (no dates)

Roy M. Moore
1923-1936

William Franklin Moore
Jun 13, 1921
Oct 22, 1956

Sam F. Moore
Sep 20, 1880
Feb 5, 1959
&
Maude W. Moore
Apr 12, 1883
May 5, 1959

William Thomas Troup
1904-1964
(gowen-Smith)

Lee Floyd Pyrdum
1883-1944
&
Daisy J. Pyrdum
1888-

"Father"
A. A. Fann
Apr 28, 1910
Nov 22, 1937

Annie C. Williamson
1863-1938

Susie Ann Warren
1875-1938

"Mother"
Clarice Fann Troup
Sep 14, 1908
Jun 26, 1949

(end of Section " Q ")

SECTION " R "

William B. Hasty
1893-1963
&
Bettie A. Hasty
1896-1944

Felix Ray, Infant son of
Oscar & Gertrude Hasty
1945

David G. Shapard, II
Oct 8, 1899
Jan 31, 1955

Loraine T. Shapard
Jul 16, 1904
Apr 6, 1968

Thomas B. Rowzee
1872-1925

Maude S. Rowzee
1874-1946

Roger P. Dale
1904-1965
&
Catherine J. Dale
1911-

John Brooks Kingston
1872-1942
&
Mary Brown Kingston
1887-19

W. Amos Brown
1889-1971
&
Blanche Lamb Brown
1895-

Minnie Neely Brown
1891-1929

William H. Brown
Sep 1, 1851
Feb 22, 1933
&
Fannie Curlin Brown
May 28, 1864
Oct 8, 1943

Odus Brown
Nov 15, 1883
Jun 21, 1925

Lula Wilks Collier
Jul 26, 1885

Elnora Graham
May 21, 1944
Dec 17, 1944

Lonnie O. Graham
Jul 5, 1889

&
Laura V. Graham
Jan 27, 1888

Howard D. Graham
May 12, 1911
Apr 3, 1972

John W. Landers
1871-1935
&
Callie Landers
1870-1928

Alice Landers
1862-1955

Samuel N. Landers
Jan 30, 1902
Nov 18, 1945

John W. Adams, Sr.
Tennessee
S2 U.S.Navy W.W.II
Aug 29, 1913
Oct 11, 1972

C. S. Adams
1886-1942

Edna Meadows
1867-1946

"Grandmother"
Francis Pollock
1856-1939

Herbert Pollock
Feb 10, 1876
Mar 10, 1937

Tess B. Hall
Nov 28, 1896

A. M. Partain
Oct 7, 1883
Feb 15, 1974
&
Day Partain
Sep 17, 1890
Dec 11, 1969

Henry Lee Stem
1904-1946
(Howell-Thompson)

Walter Pollard Jordan
Nov 16, 1901

&
Annie Ruth Jordan
Apr 14, 1902

Hugh Gaston Stowers
1883-1943

J. W. Arnold
1865-1940
&
Sallie M. Arnold
1869-19(no date)

Shannon, son of
E. B. & M. F. Nowlin
1933-1934

Sarah Ella, dau of
E. B. & M. F. Nowlin
1918-1937

Eddie Nowlin
Aug 22, 1896
Jul 23, 1967

Marshall G. Hill
Dec 31, 1917
Feb 15, 1974
&
Elizabeth H. Hill
Mar 23, 1920
Dec 14, 1973

John C. Lyell
1881-1959
&
Nellie F. Lyell
1890-

Morton Cobb
1919-1975
(Gowen-Smith)

Otis Tucker
1908-
&
Inez Tucker
1907-1943

Nancy F. Skinner
Mar 19, 1888
Sep 25, 1957

Albert Lenox Hurt
Tennessee
Pfc Co E 398 Inf BSM-PH
W. W. II
Mar 6, 1916
May 8, 1961

William Daniel Milton
1879-1954
&
Willie Dixon Milton
1887-1968

Charles A. Milton
1874-1932

Dewey L. Henry, Sr.
May 16, 1898

&
Jimmie F. Henry
Feb 27, 1899
Nov 16, 1962

Clarence D. Henry
Apr 18, 1872
Feb 28, 1952
&
Maude S. Henry
Jun 17, 1877
Nov 23, 1925

John C.,Jr., son of
J. C. & Nell Lyell
Nov 4, 1911
Oct 29, 1925

Henry H. Lyell
Jan 8, 1914
Mar 19, 1927

Newt Smelcer
1881-1925

L. M. Sipsy
1872-1940

Mary Ann Burrow
1897-1973
(Gowen-Smith)

Emma Clifton Reed
Jul 17, 1922
Aug 19, 1922

Shelburn M. Warner
Oct 10, 1913
Jan 13, 1948

Taylor C. Warinner
Feb 22, 1916
May 26, 1934

Eva Warinner
Aug 30, 1911
May 14, 1913

George, Jr., son of
George & Effie Warinner
1935-1935

Ed C. Warinner
Jan 28, 1882
Jun 28, 1950
&
Cora I. Warinner
Sep 27, 1888
Apr 22, 1975

Kirck H. Hogan
1879-1939
&
Addie M. Hogan
1877-1957

Warner L. Carpenter
Jan 15, 1876
(no date)
&
Jennie L. Carpenter
May 4, 1879
Dec 4, 1960

Annie May Carpenter
Feb 27, 1907
Nov 24, 1914

"Father"
William Riggs Newton
Jul 5, 1865
Jun 2, 1915

"Mother"
Mattie Huddleston, wife of
W. R. Newton
May 5, 1875
Jan 13, 1910
"Mother & Wife"

Vivian Burton Wilson
1931-1951

Margaret A. Hilliard
Died Nov 13, 1914
(no age given)

Leon B. Lacy
1879-1925
&
Emma Lacy
1882-1974

Baby Emma Lacy
Sep 15, 1918

Dora M. Lacy
Apr 20, 1877
Aug 29, 1912

"Father"
William R. Jones
1845-1904
&
"Mother"
Joanna Jones
1844-1930

William H. Jones, Jr.
Dec 8, 1872
Oct 5, 1903

Edward H. Ray
Feb 14, 1887
Dec 14, 1967
&
Vera Hicks Ray
Mar 3, 1885

S. T. Morton
Feb 4, 1855
Jun 28, 1922
&
Mollie E. Morton
Feb 11, 1859
Jul 24, 1934

Robert Ewing Rice
1889-1954
&
Myrtle Morton Rice
1893-1952

T. H. Lacy
Jan 28, 1857
Aug 7, 1939

"Mother"
Jennie Lacy
1857-1909

Florence Head, wife of
T. H. Lacy
1877-1929

Thomas J. Huddleston
Jan 20, 1838
Mar 12, 1914
&
Mary Newsome Huddleston
Sep 12, 1849
Apr 6, 1914

A. L. Anderson
Nov 14, 1875
Aug 9, 1913

James Raford Musgrave
Jan 20, 1877
Sep 9, 1938

Daisye Milton Musgrave
Jun 17, 1881

Infant Son of
J. R. & Daisye Musgrave
Oct 26, 1918

"Father"
Walter F. Harrison
1827-1912
&
"Mother"
Purlina Harrison
1835-1929

Joe W. Harrison
1878-1933

W. P. Harrison
Aug 10, 1855
Aug 10, 1900

Leonard Keith Potts
Oct 6, 1962

Fines M. Cates
1874-1956
&
Belle P. Cates
1881-1913

Frank M. Story
Mar 3, 1827
Jan 4, 1912
&
Mary Jane Story
Jul 20, 1855
(no date)

George E. Story
Jul 30, 1881
Mar 18, 1959

Olie Watson
1882-1944 (TM)

Barbara Faye Towery
1948-1948

Peggy Marie Towery
1937-1937

"Father"
J. T. Wheeler
Oct 14, 1864
Nov 1, 1925
&
"Mother"
Lee Wheeler
Nov 3, 1873
Feb 9, 1950

John Freeman Funk
1848-1934
&
Anna Margaretta Funk
1851-1935

W. S. Newsom
1855-1928

Kate Deery Newsom
1863-1930

Kathleen D. Newsom
1897-1897

John D. Caruthers
1866-1907

Beulah J. Caruthers
1870-1943

Lillian Kathleen Caruthers
1898-1900

Jesse F. Walker
1880-1961

Nugent Walker
1883-1953

Callie Walker
1877-1914

Thomas B. Morris
Oct 30, 1906
May 10, 1926

William H. Morris
Jun 27, 1901
Jun 15, 1956

Ruby Morris Floyd
Mar 7, 1907
May 2, 1971

Sallie L. Morris
Apr 9, 1867
Nov 7, 1925

R. L. Chockley
(no dates)

Willie Maud Herriford, wife
of J. H. Brantley
Aug 30, 1881
Sep 17, 1906

Mary Maud K. Brantley
Our Baby
Sep 10, 1906
Mar 18, 1907

J. H. Brantley
Oct 27, 1870
Feb 7, 1933

Turley A. Philpott, wife of
J. H. Brantley
Nov 13, 1888
Sep 7, 1921

Edwin Funk
1851-1912
&
Matilda J. Funk
1855-1928

Henrietta Funk, wife of
S. L. Sain
Mar 19, 1889
Jan 16, 1910

George Freeman Fly
Nov 20, 1909

&
Mary Esther Sanders Fly
Feb 2, 1910
Aug 7, 1975

W. J. Parks
Feb 27, 1866
Jun 10, 1935

J. A. K. Parks
Mar 31, 1867
Dec 6, 1934
"His Memory is Blessed"

Will I. Patton
1875-1936
&
Rosa M. Patton
1874-1948

"Father"
N. G. Terry
Sep 4, 1841
Oct 15, 1933
& wife:
"Mother"
Sallie J. Terry
Sep 2, 1843
Mar 25, 1906

Mamie E. Terry
Feb 14, 1874
Aug 24, 1913

Natt G. Terry, Jr.
Oct 5, 1881
Aug 17, 1918

S. P. Kirkpatrick
Jun 14, 1864
Dec 1, 1924

Mary Kirkpatrick
Mar 26, 1870
Jan 24, 1935

T. W. Warner
1838-1905

Emma P. Warner
1842-1928

"Mother"
Polly Shearin
Aug 1817
Apr 2, 1901

David N. Long
1849-1925
&
Sarah E. Long
1851-1923

Florence Long
Dec 15, 1891
Sep 15, 1894

William Fredric Fly
Mar 23, 1944
Mar 22, 1961

Joel O. "Snook" Fly, Jr.
Dec 15, 1915
May 19, 1970
&
Juanita Stong Fly
Feb 22, 1922

E. B. Parks
1843-1910

"Mother"
Sarah M. Parks
Mar 16, 1845
Jan 11, 1935

Ella M. Parks
Dec 20, 1874
Jun 23, 1912

S. H. Brixey
Oct 24, 1862
Feb 20, 1926

Ida I. Brixey
Jan 23, 1870
Feb 23, 1939

Francis D. Terry
Jun 9, 1869
Aug 8, 1931

Sallie F. Terry
Sep 23, 1876
Dec 14, 1941

Charles E. Hickerson
Nov 19, 1872
Jan 31, 1951
"Husband of Santafee
Hickerson"

John A. Hickerson
Nov 10, 1868
Aug 12, 1950

Thomas L. Thompson
1850-1912

"Mother"
Eunice Rutledge Thompson
Apr 27, 1855
Aug 11, 1899

Thomas L. Thompson, Jr.
1875-1935
&
Esther D. Thompson
1876-1952

Rutledge Thompson
Jul 1, 1889
Jul 16, 1959

Katharine Ruble, wife of
Aubrey J. Fuston
1894-1937

Raymond Ingle McGill
1901-1925

William Violett McGill
1905-1920

Robert P. McGill
1845-1922
&
Sarah Hix McGill
1852-1917

Lula C. McGill
Oct 1, 1875
May 13, 1965

William McGill
May 14, 1820
Jul 20, 1906
& wife: "Mother"
Mary H. McGill
Nov 1, 1820
Apr 19, 1893
age: 72y, 5m, 18d.

L. C., son of
William & M. H. McGill
Aug 19, 1853
Sep 28, 1874

A. W. Condra
Apr 30, 1876
Jun 9, 1905
age: 29y, 1m, 9d.

Frank Condra, Sr.
Feb 28, 1837
Mar 10, 1916
age: 79y & 11d.

Amanda Condra
Jun 12, 1839
Dec 2, 1919
age: 80y, 5m, 20d.

Frank Condra
1866-1931

Bright Condra
Feb 3, 1880
Jul 14, 1915
age: 35y, 5m, 10d.

Abby Coma Green
1879-1893
&
John Landis Green
1884-1899

Abbie L., son of
T. P. & H. N. Green
Jul 30, 1872
Oct 26, 1874

William A. Reed
1883-1952
&
Sallie J. Reed
1887-1950

P. L. Wade   Alabama Wade
1839-1904   1844-1892

J. A. McGill
1841-1926
&
Mary F. McGill
1847-1929

Allie Berry McGill
Oct 10, 1879
Nov 22, 1960
&
Virginia Branham McGill
Jul 23, 1893
Jul 16, 1978

William J. McGill
1873-1949

Mary Ingle McGill
1876-1949

Lois Evans Phares
1907-1909

T. B. McGill
1848-1919

Kittie E. McGill
1861-1941

Robert Thomas
Oct 9, 1869
Jan 19, 1915

Zadie McGill Thomas
Oct 30, 1871
Oct 11, 1937

Robert McGill Thomas
Aug 27, 1906
Jun 30, 1967

George W. Snoddy
1857-1938
& wife:
Anna J. Snoddy
1865-1924

Mary E., dau of
G. W. & Anna Snoddy
May 28, 1900
Oct 29, 1909

Joe Pressgrove
Dec 27, 1867
Mar 12, 1939
&
Mary A. Pressgrove
Mar 19, 1878
Mar 18, 1961

T. (Townsend) P. Green
1849-1934
&
Helen Narcissa, wife of
T. P. Green & dau of
A. L. & Nancy Landis
Jan 1, 1848
Oct 25, 1887
&
L. (Lanetta) M. Green
1860-1920

Ben G. Wade
1879-1952

Sallie, wife of
Ben G. Wade
1893-

"Father"
J. T. Cunningham
Jul 12, 1846
May 19, 1911
&
"Mother"
Elizabeth Cunningham
Jul 1, 1841
Jun 21, 1908

Ella Cunningham
May 13, 1874
Nov 15, 1916

"Brother"
S. T. Cunningham
Nov 15, 1872
Mar 24, 1938

Janie Cunningham
Jan 29, 1880
Jan 17, 1949

Ed L. Philpott
1873-1956
&
Ona C. Philpott
1882-1942

Edmund L. Philpott, Jr.
Dec 7, 1908
Oct 5, 1968

John G. Frost
Dec 3, 1893
Dec 12, 1962
&
Mary J. Frost
Aug 16, 1882
Dec 7, 1971

Tom W. Hix
Dec 7, 1884
Nov 22, 1937

Sue S. Hix
Feb 4, 1884
Nov 14, 1967

Carl J. Rainwater
1924-1930

J. Franklin Waite
Jan 30, 1892
Mar 2, 1955
&
Nell Lacy Waite
Sep 15, 1889
Feb 24, 1956

Charles Lee Mooningham
Nov 8, 1949
Nov 9, 1949

J. R. Kirkpatrick
Jul 17, 1873
Sep 17, 1903
&
Ada Kirkpatrick
Oct 27, 1873
Feb 24, 1949

Pearl, wife of
H. W. Pollock
Feb 12, 1884
Oct 16, 1935

Frances Iloi Holder
1918-1924

Avery Gragg
Oct 25, 1942

William Gragg
Aug 7, 1943

Martin J. Stanley
Nov 27, 1865
Jul 3, 1910

Sarah, wife of
John Hulan
Died Jan 24, 1941
age: 84 yrs.

Frank D. Raby
Tennessee
Pvt 383 Inf 96 Div
Jun 25, 1930

Anna W. Dixon
1860-1935

Lewis Rice
Oct 16, 1877
Jul 6, 1956

Hettie Dixon Rice
Jan 1, 1898
May 30, 1974

Walter W. Jordan
Sep 22, 1900
Apr 1, 1930
&
Susie W. Jordan
Jul 28, 1904
Jul 10, 1937

Fred Daniel Pyrdam
Nov 25, 1920
Jul 23, 1963

Robert H. Harrell
Feb 14, 1892
Mar 10, 1969
&
Ada Mai H. Harrell
Jan 4, 1900
Nov 20, 1970
married Jan 23, 1917

John Melson
1848-1929
&
Julia Melson
1853-1917

J. M. Moore
1838-1911
&
Nancy J. Moore
1838-1917

Aubrey Mitchell Moore
May 30, 1906
Mar 6, 1908

Wyatt H. Avery, M.D.
Feb 11, 1880
Sep 1, 1960
&
Clyde Park Avery
Jan 25, 1889
Oct 9, 1962

Wiley T. Hamilton
Tennessee
Pvt Div Sup Co Qm W.W.I
Feb 13, 1896
Sep 6, 1943

James L. Hamilton
Tennessee
Pfc 24 General Hospital
W. W. II
Mar 25, 1908
Sep 21, 1962

James F. Hamilton
1880-1951
&
Mary C. Hamilton
1886-

Ella Hamilton
Jun 1, 1875
Apr 16, 1915

J. C. "Dock" Lamb
1858-1945
&
Luna Lamb
1858-1951

William C. Wright
Aug 28, 1884
Nov 9, 1939
&
Sarah F. Wright
Apr 7, 1887
Jun 24, 1971

"Father"
Simon P. Martin
1870-1920

"Mother"
Mollie Martin
1872-1934

Simon S. Martin
1900-1917

Thomas Martin
(TM-Dates gone)

Charles E. Harrell
Aug 6, 1923
Mar 25, 1933

N. A. Potts
1873-1931

Nannie M. Potts
1870-1963

B. Cecil Potts
1903-1959

William L. Gammill
Oct 30, 1865
Jul 23, 1956
&
Bell R. Gammill
Oct 21, 1870
Feb 14, 1942
married Oct 1889

Annie Mai Gammill
1884-1915

Mary A. Harrison
Oct 10, 1856
Aug 3, 1951

Lizzie C. Harrison
Dec 21, 1876
Feb 1, 1933

William Harrison
Jul 10, 1883
Jun 29, 1950

Mamie D., wife of
J. W. Harrison
Jan 25, 1884
May 11, 1911
"Erected by the Sailors"

W. I. Winn
Sep 30, 1864
Aug 5, 1941

Sarah C. Winn
Oct 14, 1856
Oct 30, 1929

James M. Martin
1876-1930

Nellie G. Martin
1870-1954

John W. Bullion
Feb 9, 1860
Mar 14, 1933
&
Eliza J. Bullion
Mar 1, 1875
Jan 15, 1937

John D. Martin
Oct 9, 1866
Mar 23, 1938
&
Cyntha D. Martin
Mar 13, 1867
Dec 15, 1953

"Mother"
Jenn Ruben Scudder
Dec 24, 1890
Jun 7, 1923

Byrd Savage
Apr 18, 1892
Jan 28, 1961

Dovie Savage
Jun 12, 1894
May 27, 1934

Edwin Hix, son of
Ira & Alberta Stephens
Sep 30, 1915
Oct 11, 1915

William Clyde Tune
1900-1958
&
Alice Carter Tune

Clarence B. "Pete" Gambill
Aug 13, 1901

&
Lottie F. Gambill
Mar 20, 1907

Leroy Bonham Brown
1902-1967
&
Virginia Thomas Brown

Clarence Lee Thomas
Tennessee
S2 U.S.N.R.F. W.W.I
May 12, 1897
Nov 2, 1947

Thomas Marks Thomas
1866-1935
&
Stella Wallis Thomas
1872-1944

"Father"
Ernest C. Bradford
Aug 20, 1892
Oct 21, 1960

"Mother"
Nina Poarch Bradford
Oct 7, 1893
Mar 16, 1944

"Son & Brother"
William Nathaniel Bradford
Feb 24, 1920
Aug 27, 1936

Roy Roberts
Sep 6, 1890
Feb 4, 1930
&
Jennie Roberts
Jan 31, 1896

Lettie Trent Burke
Jul 26, 1874
Mar 7, 1960

Neal Bartlett
Nov 24, 1887
Sep 8, 1967
&
Susie Mai Bartlett
Mar 17, 1903
May 23, 1954

Charley Neal, son of
Mr & Mrs Neal Bartlett
Jul 8, 1934
Nov 12, 1934

Russell A. Cain
Dec 20, 1878
Mar 29, 1941

Leila E. Cain
Sep 17, 1887
May 8, 1973

Infant Daughter of
David & Jean Enochs
1936

Granville Thomas Carter
1876-1940

Virginia S. Carter Bird
1883-1968

Ben Newton Davidson
May 30, 1883
Sep 30, 1973

Bessie Tate Davidson
Dec 4, 1888
Mar 7, 1965

Frank C. Bobo
1887-1936

Eva Tate Bobo
1897-19

James F. Tate
1862-1936

Sallie M. Tate
1867-1950

Eual Crawford Tate
Jan 27, 1900
Apr 24, 1955

Joseph B. Crowell
Sep 23, 1903
Jan 11, 1974
&
Nola K. Crowell
Jan 20, 1912

John A. Overall, Jr.
Tennessee
Pfc Co K 60 Inf Div W.W.II
Jan 15, 1920
Jul 21, 1972
&
Mildred Reed Overall
Jul 30, 1923
Feb 27, 1971

James B. Hix
Mar 15, 1847
Jan 27, 1918
&
Sarah Caraline Hix
Feb 2, 1846
May 29, 1909

Lawson Hix
1882-1925

Hobert Thomas Scott
1847-1910
"The Cedar King"
"Erected by his Wife, Laura C.
Scott, his Baby girl Marguerite
& her Husband Mars Hill Bush"
& wife:
Laura C. Scott
1860-1937

Mars Hill Bush
Apr 19, 1885
Nov 14, 1962

Margaret Scott, wife of
M. H. Bush
Jan 9, 1885
Apr 24, 1933

Benjamin H. Kennamer Foster,
son of Mr & Mrs R. T. Scott
Sep 25, 1889
Jul 20, 1914

"Wife and Infant"
Nannie Lee Bush, wife of
M. H. Bush
Dec 1, 1885
Oct 2, 1904

Mitchell C. Reid
1864-1941

Effie H. Reid
1879-1967

John Z. Atnip
1900-1968
&
Virgie L. Atnip
1900-1954

Howard Atnip
1925-1941

John H. Atnip
Aug 29, 1859
Jul 2, 1943
&
Idella M. Atnip
Jul 6, 1868
Mar 15, 1951

Matthew Shearin
Feb 16, 1884
Apr 1, 1954

Lena Rivers Shearin
Nov 22, 1898
Oct 28, 1974

Sabrina Creighton Boggs
1858-1935

"Our Daughter"
Bell Hix Shearin
Mar 8, 1872
Jul 16, 1903

Mattie Boring
1885-1918

"Father"
Mathew S. Mullins
Mar 1843
Feb 21, 1910
&
"Mother"
Lula C. Mullins
Jul 21, 1851
Jun 27, 1913

Willie Mullins
1887-1908

Sarah Mullins
1882-1966

Lillie Mullins
1879-1918

Burtis Shofner
1889-1964
&
Ela K. Shofner
1891-1941

Nora M. Walker
1887-1975

Oliver C. Walker
1880-1963
&
Minnie V. Walker
1883-1942

W. Erskine Patton
Jan 26, 1877
Jun 25, 1953
&
Everett G. Patton
Jan 28, 1893
----
married Feb 1, 1919

Edd Richardson
1881-1950
&
May Richardson
1885-1935

Terry Lavon Richardson
Jul 5, 1908
Nov 15, 1967
&
Margaret Garrett Richardson
Feb 15, 1915

Infant Son of
H. A. & G. M. Scott
1937

John A. Harrison
1874-1962

Myrtle M. Harrison
1879-1923

George W. Shearin, Jr.
May 1, 1882
Oct 12, 1953

Judy Shearin
May 10, 1932
Jun 21, 1936

William N. Bearden
Feb 11, 1859
Jun 19, 1936
&
Mary E. Bearden
Jun 12, 1863
May 3, 1953

Roy Newman Bearden
Apr 23, 1897

&
Margaret E. Bearden
Jun 30, 1909
Oct 18, 1959

Eva Bearden
Feb 25, 1890
Feb 6, 1964

Julius Luna
Tennessee
Pvt 1 Development Bn W.W.I
May 28, 1889
Nov 15, 1951

William E. Brasseale
Tennessee
Pfc 625 A.F. ACFT Contl &
Ang Sq
Sep 15, 1932
Aug 17, 1950

Albert G. Hart
Feb 20, 1884
Sep 5, 1954
&
Fruella H. Hart
Dec 21, 1881
Jan 2, 1945

Morton Parsons
1912-1943

H. A."Shep" Parsons
1885-1939

Ella M. Parsons
1888-1956

Grady L. Parsons
1925-1944
"U.S.Marine Corps"

Hiram Burrow
1864-1941
&
Lula Burrow
1869-1940
&
Lula Pope Burrow
1911-19

"Father"
Christopher C. Hime
Mar 3, 1858
Mar 4, 1934
&
"Mother"
Annie Reed Hime
Feb 6, 1864
Jun 5, 1944

Hugh Ross Prosser
1895-1937
&
Nola Gill Prosser
1896-1958

Aldia Gammill Gill
1867-1953

W. Hoyt Raby
1884-1946
&
Mildred W. Raby
1893-1956

Willie T. Grooms
Oct 15, 1894
Jun 23, 1940
&
Sarah A. Grooms
Sep 26, 1896
Jun 15, 1966

Morgan Sandlin
1861-1945

Elizabeth L. Sandlin
1866-1939

Floyd Sandlin
1904-1963

Jas. Walker Hames
Oct 11, 1882
Dec 30, 1966
&
Annie Mae Hames
Oct 29, 1886
Dec 29, 1961

Miss Sallie Smith
1871-1943
(Thompson)
NOTE: above grave in
      Troup plot.

Charlie Troup
Apr 28, 1875
Feb 8, 1946
&
Lou Ellar Troup
Aug 25, 1868
TM-1972(Gowen-Smith)

Walter W. Troup
Jul 27, 1900
Aug 30, 1939

John W. "Buck" Foster
Mar 16, 1898

&
Valentine T. Foster
Feb 14, 1904-Oct 17, 1968

James A. Dillard
Jan 6, 1879
Jun 20, 1964
&
Lizzie M. Dillard
Dec 15, 1886
Dec 28, 1966

T. Minor Richardson
Died 1967
(no age given)
&
Lillian G. Richardson
Died 1967
(no age given)
"Parents of Fred &
Jimmy Richardson"
(Above ground Vault)

Lee Marshall
Jan 22, 1881
Feb 21, 1957
&
Florence B. Marshall
Feb 18, 1893
Feb 9, 1942

Jas. O. Anderson
1896-1941

Edwin Dixon
1882-1938
&
Mattie Dixon
1878-1971

Oscar Clenney
1897-1942

Fielding W. Lloyd
1901-1954

Edd B. Bearden
1861-1942
&
Kittie Bearden
1867-1939

Hubert A. Bearden
Nov 10, 1885
Sep 1, 1967
&
Vesta C. Bearden
Dec 7, 1889
Apr 12, 1971

J. W. Parker
Feb 12, 1896
May 9, 1940
&
Laura Parker
Jul 15, 1898
Nov 21, 1972

Winston Thomas Gant
May 9, 1920
Mar 8, 1941

Ethel Parsons Gant
Nov 10, 1881
Jun 15, 1964

"Mother"
Elizabeth Whitesell Thomas
1877-1936

Alric F. Mullins
1896-1959
&
Bessie Thomas Mullins
1898-19

Walter W. Higgins
1885-1942
&
Victoria W. Higgins
1887-1940

Neil C. Lokey, Jr.
Sep 2, 1916
Oct 15, 1957

Nancy Jane Lokey
Jun 14, 1940
Mar 18, 1941

Ernest Thompson
1881-1940
&
Jennie Thompson
1884-1956

J. Harrison Davidson
Nov 8, 1888
Nov 27, 1968
&
Clara W. Davidson
Apr 14, 1894

Cecil H. Gammill
Jul 6, 1890
Sep 26, 1972
&
Lillie M. Gammill

Vonceil D. Gammill
1904-19
&
Newell L. Gammill
1898-1958

William A. Thomas
Jan 23, 1874
May 7, 1939
&
Lena Faulk Thomas
Dec 25, 1875
(no date)

William F. Melson
1871-1940
&
Alice Melson
1879-1944

Rachael E., dau of
W. E. & Ethel Gant
Dec 3, 1916
Feb 18, 1917

Ella D. Thompson
1872-1941

Leonard L. Edwards
1895-1974
&
Bessie R. Edwards
1901-1940

Infant dau of
Leonard & Dorothy Bogg
Jun 18, 1941

Berry Shelby Gill
1875-1940

Gill
Born Aug 30, 1880
Died Nov 15, 1966
(on Rock)

Lily C. Bearden
1906-1942

Cleve Ray
1873-(no date)
&
Alla Ray
1878-19

Lula Blackburn
1881-19

Lonnie Teal
1897-1971
&
Alla Mae Teal
1900-

Earl Teal
1936-1943
(picture)

Jim B. Whitt
1888-1943
&
Beula Whitt
1896-1967

Grover C. Faulk
Mar 30, 1882
Aug 15, 1955
&
Iry M. Faulk
Aug 8, 1889
May 28, 1953

George M. Faulk
1911-1943

Hugh F. Searcy
Oct 3, 1911

&
Beatrice D. Searcy
Feb 7, 1912
Aug 10, 1962

Robert L. Jarrell
1870-1955
&
Della O. Jarrell
1875-1958

C. Frank Jarrell
Jun 13, 1900
May 18, 1916

Clifton C. Landers
Aug 21, 1905
Feb 25, 1972
&
Edith H. Landers
Aug 16, 1909

Cecil Browder Neely
Jul 1, 1925
Aug 5, 1943

-----------(Name gone)
1905-1962
(Howell-Thompson)

Lonnie, Infant son of
Nell & Phillip Pyrdum
1943

Walter Adkins
1912-1958

Mary F. Adkins
1922-1943

Infant Son of
Mr & Mrs Martin E. Elam
Oct 10, 1952

Harry S. Elam
Apr 12, 1891
Sep 26, 1942

Thomas Foster   and
1875-1956

Claud P. Barrett
1887-1940
&
Sallie K. Barrett
1894-19

Bell Thompson
Sep 30, 1894
Oct 19, 1973
&
Ruth J. Thompson
Jan 24, 1902
Apr 3, 1972

William Fred Searcy
1881-1941
&
Fannie B. Searcy
1891-1955

Fred A. Reed
1885-1960
&
Eula B. Reed
1887-1972

William T. Gregory
1868-1943
&
Edna F. Gregory
1872-1965

Lester C. Spence
1907-1948
(Gowen-Smith)

Lewis Richard Waters
1945-1945

William P. Waters
1891-1942
&
Sallie A. Waters
1893-1969

Robert Gleaves Adcock
Apr 23, 1911
Feb 2, 1943

Rev. B. W. Cole
1873-1950

Lillie M. Foster
1877-1963

* John T. Ledbetter, beloved
husband of Laura T.Ledbetter
Mar 12, 1861
Feb 9, 1915

W. Cicero Cooper
1857-1941
&
Alice Howland Cooper
1858-1940

John Ben Phillips
Apr 28, 1890
Jul 17, 1959
&
Margret Ozella Phillips
Aug 8, 1894

Allie A. Hasty
Feb 4, 1889
Jan 30, 1966
&
Gladys B. Hasty
Mar 30, 1890
Feb 5, 1972

Marvin G. Holt
Sep 27, 1888
Dec 17, 1945

George E. Gregory
Tennessee
Pvt U.S.Army W.W.I
Dec 14, 1893
Dec 27, 1973

Lula Belle Gregory
1899-1951

Thomas L. Waters
1943-1944

Paul Waters
Tennessee
Cpl U.S.Army Korea
Nov 8, 1917
Sep 2, 1971
"Son of William &
Sarah Waters"

Mary R. Gregory
1943

James Gregory
1941

* J. W. Hoskins, beloved
husband of Laura T.Hoskins
Oct 16, 1860
May 25, 1894

*copied in 1936 by:
Mrs Sara Jones

(end of Section " R ")

(See addendum for omissions)
page 331

Robert Marten Buttion
May 19, 1925
Jul 16, 1926

William R. Bailiff
1882-1928
(Thompson)

Mary Frances Bailiff
1928-1929
(Thompson)

Eldred W., son of
E. C. & N. Bell
Nov 22, 1924
Aug 13, 1925

Charles Bell
Dec 25, 1826
Aug 17, 1901
&
Mary J. Bell
May 3, 1838
Jan 15, 1905

James M. Welch
Nov 26, 1927
Mar 26, 1929

Hazel, dau of
Mr & Mrs L. G. Cunningham
(no dates)

Earl & Gerald Wilson
1956-1956
(Cothron-Thompson)

Leroy Trope
Born 1841
Died Dec 12, 1912
&
Eliza Trope
Born 1843
Died Jun 14, 1911

Mary J., dau of
C. & M. J. Bell
Jan 29, 1868
Jan 27, 1880

Cora Staggs
Jun 8, 1882
Jul 9, 1920

Melvin, son of
N. S. & C. M. Staggs
Sep 25, 1910
Sep 30, 1918

J. S. Sepsy
Feb 28, 1880
Apr 7, 1918

Mrs. Leona R. Campbell
1919-1943 (TM)

William T. Carroll
Sep 28, 1924
Dec 23, 1926

Thelma Irene Carroll
Jul 28, 1916
Jul 16, 1917

Allie Levoid Troup
May 17, 1881
Sep 12, 1898

Johannia, wife of
Babe Staggs
Sep 12, 1875
Jun 27, 1917

Rebecca Ann Banks
Died Jun 28, 1933
age: about 80 yrs of age

* by- Jerry Wayne Cook.

Tommie Lee Fisher
1893-1937 (TM)

Mrs. Willie Fisher
1896-1955
(Thompson)

Mary Ruth Fisher
1932-1956
(Cothron-Thompson)

Nathaniel Troup
Feb 18, 1828
Apr 7, 1889

Florance Troup
Nov 8, 1897
Apr 21, 1898

Annie Mitchell
Dec 18, 1908
Jan 20, 1915

No marker:*
John Cook
Born abt 1869
Died abt 1915

No marker:*
Zeelia Florence, wife of
John Cook
Born abt 18--
Died abt 1917

[Land deeds indicate that this
Cemetery was established by
the Samuel Patton family
relative of Ann Patton Balch,
wife of Amos Balch]

This Cemetery has been destroyed.
Copied by Wayne Lentz, several years ago.

This Cemetery was on, first, Patton then Doak then Wood
property, then for many years it was known as the P. Murry
Pickle Farm. This Cemetery is no longer there, it has been
destroyed and a large man-made Lake is there now.
John Theophillis Thompson, A Revolutionary Soldier was
buried in this Cemetery. He had a large Box-Vault type marker
on his grave.

John Theophillis Thompson
Born Dec 7, 1759
Died Apr 10, 1826
married to Mary Newcome

James W. Bradshaw
Died April 12, 1828
age 59-2-16

Amos Balch
Born Jul 20, 1758
married to Ann Patton
Died abt 1835
"A Revolutionary Soldier"

Mrs Jane Doak *
Died Apr 20, 1837
age: 55 yrs.

John W., son of
Samuel & Nancy Doak
Aug 10, 1830
Aug 28, 1848

Joseph, son of
Charles & Elizabeth McCarty
Apr 10, 1811
Aug 8, 1839
age: 28y, 3m, 28d.

*[Wife of David Doak]

William Gammill
Born Oct 10, 1801
Died of Flux
Oct 12, 1852

No marker:
Elly, wife of
William Gammill
Born 1803 in N.C.
Died (no date)

2 marked graves
(no inscriptions)

[Old Mt.Zion once stood here]

5 REED CEMETERY   Map # 11
This Cemetery is located about ½ mile Southeast of Shelbyville,
across Flat Creek, off Narrows Road.

William Thompson
Apr 25, 1834
Dec 28, 1855
age: 21y, 8m, 3d.

8 Long hewn Rock type Vaults.

W. M. Reed
Jan 12, 1828
Jan 15, 1905

Nancy J., wife of
W. M. Reed
Oct 11, 1836
May 2, 1899
age: 62y, 6m, 21d.

Malinda A., dau of
W. M. & N. J. Reed
Jan 21, 1861
Sep 8, 1861

Infant Daughter of
A. N. & L. A. Reid
(no dates)

Marion B. Reid
Jun 22, 1895
Apr 6, 1914

Cyntha, wife of
J. M. Stewart
Dec 7, 1817
Mar 22, 1894

Rhoda A. Haynes, wife of
C. R. Tribble
May 20, 1855
Mar 19, 1882

Infant Son of
W. M. & N. J. Reed
Born & Died
Oct 19, 1870

John A., son of
W. M. & N. J. Reed
Nov 1, 1856
Oct 8, 1880

A. N. Reid
Feb 28, 1861
Oct 15, 1916

Annie Gladdis, dau of
A. N. & L. A. Reid
Born Aug 15, 1893
age: 2m & 18d.

Virginia F., dau of
A. N. & L. A. Reid
Oct 9, 1916
Feb 24, 1917

Henry Coats
   Co C
41 Miss. Inf.
   C.S.A.

No marker:*
Betsy Lane, married to
Andrew Reed
(no dates)

"Father"
A. E. S. Hanes
1829-1876
   &
"Mother"
Cath. Hanes
1834-1900

Infant Son of
J. M. & E. A. Reed
Born & Died
Mar 7, 1861

J. W. Reed, M.D.
1873-1944

Tennie, wife of
J. D. Reed
Jun 20, 1879
May 3, 1918

William Henry Lee, son of
Mr & Mrs J. D. Reed
May 2, 1913
Aug 17, 1915

Elzira Reed
1837-1905

Malinda Coats
1841-1881

Infant Son of
Henry & Malinda Coats
(no dates)

No marker:**
Jahu Haynes
Born (no date)
Died 1900

James Reed
1841-1908
   &
Eliza A. Reed
1845-1939

Infant Dau of
J. M. & E. A. Reed
Born & Died
Jul 8, 1876

Talitha Emily, dau of
J. M. & E. A. Reed
Aug 14, 1869
Sep 28, 1869

Infant Son of
J. M. & E. A. Reed
Born & Died
Feb 7, 1868

"Mother"
Martha A. Reed
1862-1903

Tommie Lee, Infant son of
J. A. & M. A. Reed
Jul 15, 1901
Aug 25, 1902

Nancy C., wife of
J. H. Ivy
Aug 29, 1856
Feb 9, 1894

* by Mr. John Lane
** by Mrs. Buford Haynes

6 CANNON CEMETERY   Map # 11
This Cemetery is located inside the City Limits of Shelbyville,
off Lynchburg Highway.

Susan Locke Cannon, wife of
Clement Cannon
Born Jun 29, 1793
Died at residence of Mrs.
S. S. Moody, Mar 15, at
4:30 p.m. 1874 (Obit)
(Fieldstone, no inscription)

Doc. Abraham B. Morton
who departed this life
June 29th 1833, aged: 48 yrs,
8m & 11 days.
"He was a generous kind and
Charitable Friend to all of
his acquaintances, Died of
the Cholera.

Letcy Morton, Consort of
Doctor A. B. Morton, who was
born Nov 24, 1793 & departed
this life Feb 1st 185(3)8,
dau of Minos & Letticia
Cannon & Sister of Newton,
        (con't)

Clement Cannon *
Died Jun 19, 1860
in the 78 year of his age.

Infant son of
H. & A. F. Cannon
(no dates)

Infant dau of
H. & A. F. Cannon
(no dates)

        (Con't)
Clement, Minos, Robert &
Thompson Cannon & Famy
Cheatham.

Letticia Cannon
who died Apr 22, 1823
aged: 10m & 19d.
                    M.C.
*[Donated land for the town
  of SHELBYVILLE in 1810]

Mrs. Mary Locke, Consort of
Charles Locke, departed this
life Sep 6, 1852 in the 78th
year of her age. She was a
worthy Member of the M.E.
Church 62 yrs.....Illegible.

Sacred to the Memory of
------- Patience---, dau of
James & Maria Brittain
Died -----------, 1827
aged: 7m & 21d.

Sacred to the Memory of
John M. Cannon, Born Sep 3rd
1811 & died of cholera Jul 1st
1833. aged: 21y, 9m, 29d.
"He was a admirable Son &
affectionate Brother & will be
lamented by a large circle of
friends.   I.W.
                  R.T.C.
                  M.C.

Jason Thompson Brittain
Dec 1, 1821
Oct 6, 1858

James W. Brittain
Died 20(26) of Sept 1832
aged: 13m & 9 days

Catharine McNairy Brittain
dau of James & Maria
Brittain died --- --, 18--
aged: illegible

Robert, Infant Son of
Minos T. & Emma Cannon
Born Sep 14, 1860
Died May 30, 1861

Sacred to the Memory of
Minos Cannon, Esq.
who departed this life
April 7th 1823
aged: 37 yrs, 11m, & 24days.
"He was a kind husband &
Father & an affectionate
brother. He bid all his
friends & relatives that
were present Farewell &
closed his eyes in death.
    also
Sacred to the Memory of his
Daughter, Mariah T. Cannon
who died April 8, 1823
aged: 4 yrs & 11 days
"Both laid in one coffin"
                    M.C.
                    R.C.

Elizabeth Cannon
who departed this life on
Tuesday night 5th Dec 1826
aged: 2y, 4m, 7d.

America Livonia Cannon
died 27th Feb 1835
aged: 3 weeks & 1 day
Daughter of Robert &
Elizabeth Cannon

Sacred to the Memory of
Elizabeth Cannon, Consort of
Gen'l Robert Cannon & Mother
of Nancy S., Elizabeth M., &
Minos T. Cannon & the daughter
of the late Mr. Daniel & Mrs.
Nancy Scales of Wm'son County
who departed this life Friday
the 15th of June 1838
aged: 32 yrs 6m & 19 days.
"She was a kind affectionate
Compassionate Mother, Sister
& Friend. Her two little
daughters are here buried by
her left side"

Gen'l Robert Cannon
(Marker is illegible)

Mrs. Eliza Jane Cannon,
Consort of Gen'l Robert
Cannon & daughter of
R. H. & Sarah C. Major of
Te--. Who --------
18th day of Mar 18--
    (illegible)

3 graves with fieldstones,
    no inscriptions.

This Cemetery has a fence around it and is under lock & key.
it is being kept by the City.   Historical marker on
                Lynchburg Highway.

7 TROUP CEMETERY (Col)   Map # 11
This Cemetery is located about 1 mile South on Highway 82,
                Lynchburg highway.

Jim Ray   15-20 graves, all unmarked.
"Colored"
Tenn Pvt
1 Cl P.of W.
Escort Co A.S.C.
Mar 30, 1923

8 ZIVLEY CEMETERY   Map # 11
This Cemetery is located about ½ mile Southeast of Shelbyville,
                off Old Tullahoma Highway.

John H. Zivley
Who was born in Salem, N.C.
& departed this life
Dec 29, 1824
aged: 46 yrs, 5mos, & 19 days.

9 THOMPSON CEMETERY   Map # 11
This Cemetery is located on Fairoak Street, at Eastview
Baptist Church. Shelbyville.

Martha Thompson, Consort of   Nancy Newsom, Consort of   Sacred to the Memory of
Terry D. Thompson   Sterling Newsom   -----(never finished)
Born neare this place   who was born in N. Carolina
May 5, 1827, married Jan 20,   Aug 17, A.D. 1788   about 25-30 graves, unmarked
1846, died Mar 26, 18(broken) departed this life
"She died as she lived for   Feb 1st 1849   Several fieldstones, no insc
the last 16 years of her life,
a devoted Christian, Mother   ---(name broken away)---
of four Children whom are   Died Nov 31, 1844   8 Markers with only a
left with her bereaved   aged: 37 yrs.   Star.
Husband, to mourn her loss"

10 COWAN CEMETERY   Map # 11
This Cemetery is located behind the First Baptist Church, City.

Christina Strickler   Mrs. Sarah Cowan   M. McC. R.   Henry Cooper, Born in
Aug 15, 1835   Died May 2, 1864   (all on stone)   Maury Co., Tenn. Aug 22,
Jun 26, 1916   aged: 57 yrs.   1827, killed by bandits and
                                                   W. S. McC.   buried in Culiasaw, Mexico
John E. Strickler   William Guy Cowan   (all on stone)   Feb 3, 1884
Sep 3, 1827   Born in County Deery, Ireland   "U.S.Senator from Tenn.
Nov 14, 1851   Feb 11, 1811, died in Shelby-   1871-1878"
                           ville, Tenn. May 25, 1880

Ann Eliza Cooper, wife of
Henry Cooper
Born Aug 19, 1833
Died Feb 3, 1872

Charles D. Cooper
Jan 21, 1856
Nov 8, 1875
&
Sadie, wife of
W. B. Bryan, Jr.
Nov 24, 1858
Aug 16, 1884

John Cowan
Born in County Deery, Ireland
Aug 9, 1815
Died Aug 24, 1900

Alexander Eakin
Born in County Deery, Ireland
1800 & Died Sep 13, 1877
&
Margaret Deery Eakin
Born Jul 25, 1812
Died Aug 3, 1901

Samuel Cowan, son of
Alex & Mary Cowan, Born in
Londonderry, Ireland &
Died Mar 22, 1864
aged: 23y, 3m, 7d.

T. E. Cowan
Sep 24, 1846
Sep 12, 1873

Mary Cowan Lipscomb
Jul 4, 1834
Dec 11, 1906
&
Laura Cowan
Apr 7, 1843
Nov 1, 1934

George Newton Eakin
Nov 17, 1841
Mar 13, 1920
&
Frances Swift Eakin
Jun 4, 1846
Feb 3, 1925

This Memorial slab dedicated
by a disconsolate and bereaved Mother and the affectionate sympathies of his brothers & sisters underneath
which repose the earthly
remains of Spencer Eakin, an
intelligent & interprising
Merchant of Nashville, who
was born in Muff, County of
Deery, Ireland and emigrated
to Tenn. in 1819. He died
while on a visit to his
Mother in Shelbyville on the
27th day of June 1840, in
the 42nd year of his age.

Eliza McClelland
Died Dec 17, 1885
aged: 75 yrs.

Willie Spencer, only son of
J. I. & Eliza McClelland
Born in Huntsville, Ala.
Jul 4, 1847 & died in
St. Louis, Mo. Jan 31, 1866
&
James Irwin McClelland
Born in Franklin Co., Pa.
Sep 29, 1816 & died in
Huntsville, Ala. May 12, 1855

Mrs. Mary Cowan
Born in County Deery, Ireland
1791 & Died Feb 2, 1868
aged: 77 yrs.

Jane Cowan, Born in County
Deery, Ireland 1818 & Died
Sep 2, 1868
aged: 50 yrs.

John W. Cowan
Born in County Deery, Ireland
Jul 7, 1807 & Died
Jan 12, 1879

"My Wife"
Jane Eakin Cowan
Who fell asleep
Aug 22, 1868
(no age given)

Thomas Lindsey Eakin
Oct 17, 1838
Apr 9, 1857

John R. Eakin
Dec 27, 1872
Jul 30, 1890

Margaret Eakin Hood
1885-1918

Sarah Agnes, dau of
William G. & Sarah Cowan
Died Feb 11, 1842
aged: 13m & 2d.

Leah, dau of
John W. & Jane Cowan
Died May 8, 1842
aged: 3y, 4m, 20d.

John E. Eakin
died Jul 22, 1825
aged: 63 yrs.
"Came to America in 1822
from Ireland"

------(name gone)---
Died Jul 23, 182-
aged: 69 yrs.

Samuel A. Strickler
Died May 1, 1871
aged: 45 yrs.

Our Aleck (Eakin)

Annie, Infant dau of
C. & A. E. Moorman
(no dates)
&
Emma E., dau of
C. & A. E. Moorman
Dec 26, 1871
Sep 21, 1878

Nannie E. Eakin, wife of
Cyrus Moorman
Born May 30, 1839
married Apr 16, 1867
Died Jan 6, 1883

Cyrus Moorman
(no dates)

Margaret E. Moorman
1868-1953

William S. Eakin, Jr., son of
William S. & Lemira C. Eakin
Nov 22, 1853
Jul 2, 1854
aged: 7m & 10d.

Emmet A. Eakin
Died Dec 27, 1864
aged: 28 yrs.

Argyle Pearson Eakin
Aug 30, 1825
Jan 13, 1868

James Deery Eakin, Sr.
Nov 13, 1883
TM-1973
&
Cary Allmond Eakin
May 26, 1890
Mar 15, 1963

Mrs. Jane Eakin, Consort of
John Eakin, died Jan 11, 1846.
aged: 76 yrs. Born in Ireland,
County of Deery, immigrated to
this County with her Husband,
her youth in 1822, who together with a son, the beloved
of her heart, she now follows
to the grave.

Sarah Pearson,*
Died 25th July 1845
aged: 85y, 2m, 3d.
(very bad condition)

Sarah Jones Jacks Pearson*
was divorced from William
Pearson, SOR, in Union Co.,
S.C., in 1812.
* Records of William Floyd.

Mary Agnes Cooper
Jun 25, 1852
Jan 9, 1873

Benjamin Strickler Cooper
Feb 14, 1854
Feb 9, 1872

Spencer Eakin
1844-1907

Milbrey Erving Eakin
1846-1932

Spencer Eakin, Jr.
Jul 12, 1874
Feb 16, 1955

John Eakin, Born in the
County of Deery, Ireland
Nov 14, 1796, immigrated
to America 1816, Died
Sep 19, 1849.
&
Lucretia Pearson, wife of
John Eakin
Born Dec 15, 1802
Died Sep 13, 1895

Sarah Wardlaw
Died Nov 5, 1907
aged: 80 yrs.

Robert W. Cowan, Born in
Bally Gilly, Ireland
Died Aug 15, 1869
(no age)

Hannah L., wife of
Robert W. Cowan
Born in Bally Gilly, Ireland
Died Dec 23, 1870
(no age)

Mrs. Ann Nevins
Died Jan 2, 1856
aged: 63 yrs.
"A Native of Ireland"

"Sister"
Mary J.(Jane) Eakin
Died Jun 25, 1853
aged: 61 yrs.

Pamelia H. Roberts, dau of
Levi C. Roberts & Frances H.
Roberts.
Born Jun 22, 1815
Died May 12, 1826
aged: 10y, 10m, 20d.

Robert H. Roberts
Jun 7, 1823
Jul 12, 1824
&
Lindsey J. Eakin
Jan 15, 1824
Jul 17, 1824

This Cemetery is located behind the First Baptist Church,City.

"Father"
R. D. Deery
Feb 14, 1825
Jan 18, 1866
&
"Mother"
M. L. Deery
Nov 5, 1832
Mar 17, 1876

John R. Deery
Died Nov 11, 1841
aged: 26 yrs.

J. H. Deery
Died Mar 9, 1857
aged: 31 yrs.

John W. Hamlin
Jan 4, 1803
Aug 12, 1851

Theophilus R. Hamlin
Apr 18, 1834
Apr 19, 1854

Martha Elizabeth McKnight
Nov 25, 1842
Sep 2, 1851

M. L., dau of
P. H. & N. A. Odum
Mar 9, 1864
Aug 4, 1865

Elizabeth McCombs
Dec 1, 1776
Nov 17, 1861

Margaret L., wife of
D. G. Deason
Died Jan 31, 1858
aged: 32y, 1m, 6d.
"The Mother of 4 Children"

Mrs. Sophronia P., Consort
of Dr. G. W. Bacon & dau of
William & Jane G. Brown
Feb 17, 1832
Jun 30, 1853
aged: 21y, 4m, 13d.

H. Lawson Wood
Sep 10, 1836
Sep 28, 1855
aged: 19 yrs.

Maggie, dau of
W. B. M. & M. A. Brame
May 21, 1842
Oct 31, 1859

"My Wife-Our Mother"
Mary Ann Brame
Jul 20, 1817
Oct 16, 1867

William Edgar, son of
W. B. M. & M. A. Brame
Sep 20, 1856
Oct 5, 1857

Susan B. Peacock
Died Nov 13, 1842
aged: 42 yrs.

Adam Alexander, son of
Thomas A. Peacock
Died Mar 1, 1826
aged: 11 yrs.
(marker now gone)

John Sutton
Born --- --, 180-
Died --- 23, 1847
(hewn Rock type vault)

Narcissa J., Consort of
John B. Fuller
Sep 8, 1830
Oct 23, 1849
aged: 19y, 1m, 15d.

John Morgan
Born May 21, 1799
Died Jul 20, 1854
aged: 55y & 2m.

Mary Morgan
Born ---------(gone)
Died Apr 2, 1850

Elvaanah, dau of
John & Mary Morgan
Mar 9, 1836
Aug 13, 1851
aged: 15y, 5m, 4d.

Thomas Holland
Jul 16, 1797
Apr 23, 1875

Sarah, wife of
Thomas Holland
Dec 4, 1799
Jan 17, 1884

Alexander Holland
Jan 20, 1836
Dec 23, 1861

Sarah M., dau of
Thomas & Sarah Holland
Sep 6, 1842
Jun 7, 1856

Alice B. Brame
Born --- --, 1847
Died --------(after 1850)
(broken)

William Deery Brame
Nov 3, 1851
Dec 5, 1854
age: 3y, 1m, 2d.

E. R., Infant dau of
W. B. M. & M. A. Brame
Died Jul 29, 1841
(no age given)

James B. Lane, son of
Robert & America Lane
May 15, 1846
Nov 9, 1851
aged: 5y, 5m, 24d.

M. E. Lane
Died Sep 20, 1852
aged: 20y & 6m.

Patrick Fay
Born Mar 10, 1814 in County
Galway, Ireland. He emigrated
in 1837, married in 1845 &
Died Aug 25, 1865

No marker:*
Ella Fay
Died winter of 1908
(no age)

No marker:*
Julia Fay
Died abt 1910
(no age)

Martha E. McDaniel, wife of
W. P. McDaniel
Jan 1, 1824
Jun 2, 1853

Menetto Alice Russ
Oct 1, 1849
Jul 24, 1850
&
J. S. Russ
Jun 5, 1854
Sep 17, 1855
&
John Russ
Feb 6, 1858 ·
Feb 16, 1862
&
Edna Cora Russ
Mar 10, 1861
Aug 28, 1862
"Children of R. C. &
E. M. Russ"

T. S. Ragsdale
May 28, 1842
Jul 11, 1856

G. P. Baskette
Born in Fluvanna Co., Va.
May 3, 1810 & Died
Feb 24, 1873

Eliza J. Baskette
Jul 20, 1819
Sep 7, 1887

Frances A. Baskette
age: 6 mos. (no dates)

William Organ, Esq.
Born Aug 14, 1800
Died in Shelbyville
May 28, 1856
"Emigrated from Campbell Co.,
Va. to Texas."

James Deery, Born near
Muff, County of Londonderry,
Ireland, May 1777, emigrated
to Tenn. 1811, died Oct 31,
1857. Aged: 81 yrs.
(marker now gone)

Elizabeth Deery
Born Feb 23, 1783
Died Oct 2, 1873
aged: 90y, 7m, 9d.

John Ruth
Born Feb 27, 1839
Died May 4, 1906

Kenneth Anderson
Adj.
1 N.J. Mil
Rev. War

Nancy B. Marshall, wife of
Moses Marshall
Jul 24, 1809
Jun 18, 1855
aged: 45y, 10m, 24d.

Infant Marshall
(no dates)

"Our Mother"
Thursa Shapard
Nov 16, 1813
Feb 2, 1883

Lewis Shapard
(no dates)(marker now gone)

Robert L. Blackwell
aged: 22 yrs.
"Confederate Soldier,
Resting from Battle near
Murfresboro, Dec 31, 1862

Thomas Cheatham**
Dec 22, 1792
Oct 15, 1857
aged: 64y, 9m, 23d.
** His wife is buried in the
Garrett Cemetery, page 1.

James H. Graham, son of
James & Margaret Graham
Born in Rowan Co., N.C.
Feb 17, 1807 & Died
Nov 21, 1868

L. A. J., Consort of
J. H. Graham & dau of
George N. & Nancy Thompson
Died 27th May, 1851
aged: 35y, 2m, 7d.
&
M. L. A. J., Infant dau
Born May 20, 1851
Died Jan 5, 1855
aged: 3y, 7m, 6d.

M. F. Thompson
Nov 26, 1828
Oct 25, 1855

Letitia T., wife of
Dr. J. H. McGrew
Jul 17, 1834
Mar 1, 1857
"and her two Infant
Children lie buried here
together"

--------(name gone), Infant
son of M. F. & Martha
Thompson
Died 1852
(no age given)

E. J., Consort of
William A. Griffis & dau of
N. & A. Thompson
Jan 23, 1835
Jul 8, 1854

Mrs. Mary E., wife of
W. P. Coleman
Jun 8, 1846
Jun 2, 1932

Russell P. Whiteside
Nov 16, 1824
Apr 4, 1854
&
Mary Louise, Infant dau of
R. P. & M. A. Whiteside
Died Jun 27, 1854

William B., son of
John C. & Jane E. Anglin
Died Aug 15, 1847
aged: 11m & 8d.

Henry J. Anglin
Died May 11, 1852
aged: 24y, 10m, 8d.

Jane E., Consort of
John C. Anglin
Died Feb 13, 1847
aged: 21y, 2m, 12d.

Duglass R. Simms
& Wife(no name)
Born Sep 19, 1816
Died Jul 11, 1847

Mrs. Jane Moffat, Born in
Ireland May 12, 1775 &
Died Jun 30, 1845
age: 70y, 1m, 18d.

Robert Moffat, Born in
Philadelphia
Sep 8, 1813 & Died
Feb 1, 1853

Mary A. Moffat, Born in
Philadelphia Dec 21, 1807
Died Feb 23, 1855

L. A. Marshall
(no dates)

Samuel T. Cannon
Oct 20, 1823
Jul 8, 1855

Mrs. Letitia Cannon
Jun 19, 1799
Mar 7, 1863

Malida, dau of
Sidna Elliott & Eliza Cannon
Nov 24, 1839
Dec 24, 1853

Andrew Mathews
Oct 31, 1821
Apr 27, 1859
"A Native of Ireland"

Mary Ann, wife of
Robert Mathews
Died Apr 18, 1852
aged: 31y, 6m, 18d.

Mary Inez Mathews
aged: 5y & 2m.
Died Jun 17, 1864
"Following her Father &
Brother"

John Mathews
age: 2y & 21d.
Died Jul 19, 1859

Caroline Johnson, Consort of
James M. Johnson & dau of
James & Nicey Russ
Died Mar 4, 1846
aged: 19y, 6m, 23d.

William Hill Russ
Died Sep 11, 1840
aged: 19y, 6m, 16d.

James Russ, Sr.
Jun 29, 1790
Mar 16, 1854

Nicey Steeley Russ, Consort
of James Russ, Sr., Born in
Fayetteville, N.C., Oct 7,
1791 & Died in Shelbyville,
Tenn. Jul 8, 1872
aged: 81 yrs.

Emma S. Knott, dau of
L. B. & M. B. Knott
Born Jul 23, 1855
Died Aug 26, 1861
aged: 6 yrs.

Anna M. Knott, dau of
L. B. & M. B. Knott
Jul 7, 1844
Jun 1, 1864

Sarah E. Knott, dau of
L. B. & Mariah Knott
Died Nov 17, 1848
aged: 12y, 11m, 22d.

M. L. W.
(foot marker)

Isaac Dickerson, son of
Peter S. & Mary T. Law
aged: 11 months

Narcissa S. Davidson, youngest
dau of Robert P. Harrison &
Eliza Williams
May 3, 1829
May 8, 1867

Robert H. Davidson
Died Oct 6, 1905
(no age given)

Elizabeth H. Davidson
Mar 14, 1849
Feb 14, 1889

Maggie Mathews Armstrong
Jul 11, 1870
Oct 6, 1876

Margaret E., Consort of
Sgt. George F. Blakemore
May 18, 1830
Aug 20, 1849

John H., son of the
Rev. Daniel Stephens, D.D.
Born Jul 18, 1833, was
drowned while bathing in
Duck River May 22, 1851.

Zebulon Evans
Sep 3, 1809
Nov 29, 1874

Elizabeth, wife of
Zebulon Evans
Mar 19, 1819
Mar 22, 1900

W. B. Evans
Jun 9, 1844
Jul 14, 1846
aged: 2y, 1m, 5d.

"Brother"
Louis E. Evans
Apr 20, 1855
Oct 26, 1913

R. E., dau of
Z. & E. Evans
Oct 18, 1849
Mar 7, 1869

J. E., son of
Z. & E. Evans
Nov 19, 1847
Aug 25, 1849

L. B. Knott, Jr., son of
L. B. & M. B. Knott
Died Jul 1, 1861
Born Apr 17, 1848
aged: 15y, 2m, 15d.

Henry S. Knott, son of
L. B. & M. B. Knott
Jan 10, 1842
Mar 25, 1845
aged: 3y, 2m, 15d.

Ede H., Wife of
H. L. Davidson
Apr 25, 1821
Mar 15, 1858

Robert H., son of
H. L. & E. H. Davidson
Jul 7, 1839
Jun 20, 1863

Sallie Brame Davidson
Aug 12, 1838
Oct 6, 1904

Robert B. Davidson
Mar 17, 1817
Oct 3, 1900

Allen, Infant son of
Allen B. & Martha A. Coble
was born near Shelbyville
Jul 18, 1868
(no death date)

Darthuley M. Rayon, dau of
Th. R. & Malinda Rayon
Aug 29, 1848
Dec 18, 1849

Joseph S. Owens
Died Dec 23, 1861
(no age given)

Nancy E., Consort of
Joseph S. Owens
Jul 25, 1822
Aug 3, 1853

William T., son of
J. S. & N. E. Owens
Born Jun 17, 1849
age: 11 months.

L. B. Knott
Born Oct 24, 1810, Died at
his residence in Shelby-
ville, Tenn. Oct 2, 1871.
He was converted at abt age
18 yrs of age into the M.E.
Church, South.

M. B.(Mariah) Knott
Born Jul 11, 1814
Died Jul 4, 1897
(marker now gone)

Jesse L., son of
L. B. & M. B. Knott
Born Jan 11, 1852
Died Aug 6, 1853
aged 18 mos & 26d.
(part of marker now gone)

R. W. Knott, son of
L. B. & M. B. Knott
aged: 22y, & 2m
Born Feb 18, 1840, "He fell
at Shiloh in defence of his
Country in the action of
April 6, 1862. His body was
not recovered by his parents"

Eliza Ann Moffat, Born in
Philadelphia Nov 29, 1815
Died May 22, 1841
aged: 25y, 5m, 23d.

"Mother"
Martha A. McDougal
Oct 11, 1834
Jan 3, 1878
&
"Daughter"
Jannette McDougal
Sep 12, 1857
Nov 1, 1875

Willis Burks
Dec 19, 1799
Jan 12, 1861

J. L. Williams
Jan 7, 1853
Oct 21, 1855
aged: 2y, 9m, 14d.

Sallie Clay, dau of
B. M. & E. F. Tillman
Died Aug 11, 1856
aged: 2y, 11m, 22d.

Mary Elizabeth, dau of
B. M. & E. F. Tillman
Died Sep 15, 1876
age: 4y, 11m, 24d.

Sophia A., wife of
William O. Pepper
Died Mar 23, 1855
aged: 25y, 9m, 10d.
&
Inde, Infant dau of
W. O. & S. A. Pepper
aged: 1y, 3m, 2d.
(no dates)

William B. Sutton, Esq.[2]
Attorney at Law, who was
born 9th Mar 1801 in Prince
William Co., Va., & Died
29th Nov 1833.

Mrs. Marianne Sutton, wife of
William B. Sutton & dau of
Dr. J. L. Armstrong
Died 8th Oct 1825
age: 18 yrs & 8 mos.
"Leaving an Infant dau then
only 15 days old"

Marianne Sutton
Died 17th Mar 1830
aged: 4y & 6m.
"The Infant referred to on
the Tomb of Marianne Sutton"
"These Monuments erected by
Father & Husband, William B.
Sutton"

James A. Sutton
Died 11th May 1832
age: 1 month

P. B. Martin
Born Sep 26, 1824
aged: 13y, 8m, 23d.

Catharine, Consort of
John Jacobs
Born Mar 22, 1783
Died May 16, 1849
aged: 66y, 1m, 24d.

James Russ, Jr., who was
born in Fayetteville,Cumber-
land Co., N.C. Jun 13, 1818
& Died Aug 17, 1869

Margaret Elizabeth, Consort
of James Russ, Jr.
Died Aug 13, 1856
aged: 33 yrs.

Clara J. Russ
Apr 25, 1833
Sep 27, 1898

W. H. Russ
    Co C
5th Tenn Cav.

Emmett
(in Russ Plot, no dates)

Robert Tyler
(in Russ Plot, no dates)

Marianne, dau of
J. L. & M. P. Armstrong
Died 2nd Oct 1831
age: 1y, 7m, 8d.

James L., son of
J. L. & M. P. Armstrong
Died 29th Oct 1821
age: 10m & 15d.

Mrs. Sophia Armstrong *
Died Dec 12, 1815
aged: 32y, -m, -d.
    also
Henrietta Armstrong
who died 25th Aug 1816
aged: 5 yrs.
"These Testimonials of love
& respect were erected by
the Husband & Father,
Dr. J. L. Armstrong."

Birkett D. Jett
Nov 21, 1777
Jan 26, 1849
age: 71y, 2m, 5d.

Mrs. Mildred P. Jett
of Virginia, Born
Mar 7, 1788 & Died
Nov 10, 1820

John W. Williams
Born May 3, 1813
Died Mar 23, 1847
age: 34 yrs.

Anne M. W. Porter, wife of
Dr. J. M. Porter & dau of
R. N. & E. J. Wallace
Dec 5, 1843
Aug 20, 1870

Rev. O. E. Ragland
"A Regular Iteraerant of the
M. E. Church 15 yrs"
Died Nov 2, 1849
aged: 36y & 6m.

William Robinson Neil
May 5, 1856
May 18, 1858
age: 2y & 13d.
    &
James Robinson Neil
eldest Son
Sep 18, 1851
Sep 15, 1852
"Sons of John F. &
Sarah F. Neil"

John T. Neil
Nov 23, 1802
Nov 3, 1860

Mrs. Evaline M. Neil* widow
of late John T. Neil
Died July --, 1890
aged: 86 yrs.
*No marker-Newspaper Obit.,
            July 10, 1890

George W. Ruth
Born in Granville Co., N.C.
Oct 6, 1799 & Died
Aug 20, 1858
    &
Anne, Consort of
George W. Ruth, Born near
Baltimore, in the State of
Maryland, on the 1st day of
April 1804 & Died on the 1st
day of July 1863, in the 60th
year of her age.

Henry Rufus Wallace
Died 5th Nov 1841
age: 1y, 10m, 13d.
Son of R. N. & E. J. Wallace

Robert Warner Wallace
Died 8th Sep 1844
aged: 6y, 7m, 23d.

Elizabeth C. W., dau of
R. N. & E. J. Wallace
Died Nov 29, 1848
aged: 17y, 1m, 15d.

Spyker Hollins, son of
R. N. & E. J. Wallace
Jun 30, 1848
Feb 17, 1849
aged: 7m & 18d.

Mary Eliza, dau of
R. N. & Eliza Jane Wallace
Died Oct 15, 1854
aged: 1y, 10m, of fever.

Rush Wallace Porter
Sep 28, 1869
Jul 8, 1874

Mary Martin
Died Apr 9, 1837
aged: 31 yrs.

I. C. Brasfield
May 8, 1808
Aug 5, 1846

John H. Laird
Aug 15, 1802
Nov 2, 1845

No marker:(Newspaper obit)
Mrs. Nancy G. Laird
Died Oct 7, 1853
aged: 53 yrs.

Ervin J. Frierson
Feb 12, 1805
Dec 3, 1849

Ann P. Frierson
Apr 12, 1819
May 7, 1859

E. J. Frierson, Jun.,
Infant son of
E. J. & A. P. Frierson
Sep 17, 1845
Jun 15, 1848

Ervin J. Frierson
Nov 30, 1849
Jan 3, 1851

Elizabeth, Infant dau of
E. J. & Ann P. Frierson
Feb 28, 1837
Nov 21, 1839

Ann F., Infant dau of
E. J. & A. Frierson
Died 1839(no age given)

Robert P. Harrison
Oct 25, 1787
Aug 5, 1843
age: 55y, 2m, 11d.

Eliza W. Harrison
Oct 5, 1795
May 4, 1866
age: 75y, 7m, 2d.

Mary B., Consort of
W. Galbraeth
Feb 20, 1809
Sep 13, 1869

Sarah E. Galbreath
Died Jun 1, 1842
aged: 11y & 10m.

Lt. Col Rob't Galbraith
    5th Tenn Cav

John H. Galbreath
Died Jan 9, 1835
aged: 6y, 4m, 9d.

Dr. Joseph Kincaid
Born in Madison Co., Ky
May 5, 1794 & Died
Mar 31, 1844 (marker now
                        gone)
Mary E. S. Kincaid
May 9, 1839
May 24, 1855

*[Sophia (Smith) Armstrong, wife of Dr. J. L. Armstrong is first known
  burial in the area that was first Dr. Armstrong's private family graveyard in 1815]

[2]Atlanta J. Armstrong, 2nd wife of
W. B. Sutton, died July 1, 1833]

Pierce Gosling Wallace
Mar 5, 1834
Feb 27, 188-(gone)

Mary Eliza Wallace
Born Apr --, 1830
Died Dec --, ----
(illegible)

R. A. Evans
Born Sep 30, 1826
Died Jul 10, 1844
age: 17y, 7m, 10d.

Evva E., dau of
D. & E. J. Dillon
Jun 4, 1856
Jul 3, 1857
aged: 1y & 29d.

John B. Miller
A Native of County London-
deery, Ireland
Died 17th Nov 1840
age: 21 yrs.

Nathaniel Evans Coldwell,
Husband of Sophia Woodward
Peacock
Born May 29, 1794
Died of Cholera
Jun 28, 1833

G. Davidson, Jun.
Born 10 Apr 1829
Died 14 Jul 1846

S. C. Davidson

(Marker now gone)

Mrs. Caroline S. Davidson,
Consort of George Davidson
Born Dec 6, 1807
Died of Cholera in June 29,
1833. aged: 25y, 6m, 25d.

George Davidson
Mar 11, 1800
Nov 19, 1854

Elisha B. Spencer
Dec 25, 1838
Aug 14, 1851

C. B. Morton, son of
S. S. & P. C. Morton
Aug 16, 1843
Apr 2, 1850

William H. Koonce
Oct 16, 1835
Jun 22, 1859
aged: 23y, 8m, 6d.

F. D. Haggard
Jun 1, 1819
Mar 2, 1862

Ruth Marrs
Born --- --, ----
Died Jul 30, 1847
aged: 14y, 6m, 11d.

James C. Martin
Apr 28, 1804
Sep 2, 1874

Lucy H., Consort of
James C. Martin
Jun 17, 1811
Nov 3, 1862
aged: 51y, 4m, 16d.

E. H. Martin
Died Jul 25, 1841
aged: 1m & 26d.

Doctor Hall
Died Nov 13, 1826
aged: 29 yrs.
(sandstone)

M. Jane Hall
Died Sep 1, 1825
aged: 29 yrs.
(sandstone)

James D. McKisick, son of
Daniel & Margret B. McKisick
Died 24th June 1824
age: 1y, 5m, 7d.

Mrs. Harriet M. Brame,
Consort of W. B. M. Brame
Died Aug 30, 1835
aged: 15y, 7m, 21d.

James C. Terry, son of
J. R. & E. C. Terry
Died 1848

R. Moxley
Born 1818
Died ----(illegible)

C. F. Pratt, son of
E. M. & S. A. R. Pratt
Sep 8, 1868
Mar 10, 1871
aged: 2y, 8m, -d.

Isaac Thompson
Born 1813
Died 1866
age: 53 yrs.

Mrs. Sebrine Wilhoite, wife of
Young Wilhoite, Sen.
Born in N.C. in 1786 &
Died Sep 15, 1858
age: 72 yrs.

Eugene C., son of
J. D. & A. C. Wilhoite
Jan 13, 1857
Jul 25, 1858

Rufus Emmet, son of
J. D. & A. C. Wilhoite
Nov 27, 1858
Oct 25, 1863
aged: 4y, 10m, 28d.

Josephin, dau of
J. D. & A. C. Wilhoite
Nov 22, 1866
Jun 26, 1867

Ann Newton
Died Jul 5, 1831
aged: 34y, 1m, 19d.

Rev. George Newton
Died Dec 4th 1840, in the
75th year of his age. 50 years
preacher, and for the greater
part of the Presbyterian
Church in this Village....
(old marker)
New Marker:
Rev. George Newton
1765-1840
Pastor, First Presbyterian
Church, Shelbyville 1815-1840

Helen M. Newton
Wife of Rev. George Newton,
dec'd, who died April 2, 1859
at an advanced age.

Martha E. Seahorn, Consort of
J. M. Seahorn
Jan 3, 1818
Nov 24, 1850

Martha Ellen, Consort of
William A. Allen
Born 26 Oct 1821
Died 13 Feb 1846
age: 24y, 3m, 17d.

J. M. Wardlaw
Sep 2, 1830
Oct 4, 1860

Ned, faithful Servant
of John W. Cowan
Died Sep 1856

Elizabeth Brooks, wife of
H. B. Quimby
Born May 15, 1833
married Sep 6, 1851
Died May 1, 1896

Phillip Brooks
Dec 6, 1797
Sep 22, 1868

Mrs. Sarah, wife of
Phillip Brooks, born in
Washington Co., Va.
Jul 11, 1799 & Died
Aug 13, 1872
aged: 73y, 1m, 2d.

Martha Long
Born Nov 6, 1777 in the
State of N.C. & Died
Jan 11, 1841
aged: 63y, 2m, 6d.

Mary Elizabeth, Consort of
W. F. Long
Died 2 Jun 1839
aged: 37y, 4m, 3d.
"With her Infant Daughter
who lies here in her arms"

J. P. Calhoon
Nov 6, 1806
Jun 20, 1866

John W. Barber
Dec 4, 1836
Feb 20, 1863
&
Silvanus A. Barber
Jan 24, 1839
Nov 12, 185(6)2.

Francis J., dau of
T. J. & M. Barber
Feb 7, 1837
Sep 28, 1851

Samuel L., son of
T. J. & M. Barber
Oct 29, 1840
Jul 30, 1842

S. B.
(fieldstone)

T. B.
(fieldstone)

Joanna Barber
aged: abt 16 yrs.
Died Aug 25, 1838

Joannah L. Barber
May 16, 1807
Aug 11, 1874

William Strickler
Sep 20, 1831
Sep 12, 1832

Benjamin Strickler
Died May 11, 1836
aged: 47 yrs.

Lucy Brooks
Born 27 Nov 1767
Died 17 Aug 1844
aged: 76y, 8m, 20d.

Lynch Brooks, son of
Phillip & Sarah Brooks
Born Nov 29, 1825
Died Jul 2, 1848
aged: 24y, 6m, 10d.

James West, late of County
of Antrim, town of Mobill,
Ireland. Departed this life
Jany 19, 1816
aged: 24 yrs.
(marker now gone, copied in
1938, grave under a very
large tree)

Crece, wife of
Benjamin Cannon
Died May 22, 1824
aged: 30 yrs.

Franz Mankel, son of
L. & M. Mankel
Died Dec 10, 1859
aged --(gone)
(marker now gone)

Mary A., wife of J.P.Calhoon
Sep 3, 1806
Nov 14, 1874

George, was born
Feb 17, 1835 &
Died Apr 4, 1858
(Slave, only slave marker
that remains)

Jesse P. Gilman
Died Sep 23, 1857
aged: abt 45 yrs.

Mary E., dau of
D. & Ellen Cooper
May 27, 1867
May 12, 1873
age: 5y, 11m, 12d.

Mrs. Olive Duncan, Consort
of Lemuel H. Duncan
Died 14th Jul 1826
aged: 22y, 7m, 22d.

Susan T. Gibson, Consort of
H. Gibson & dau of T. P.
& Ann Holman
Died Aug --, ----(gone)
aged: 26y & 1m.

Infant dau of
-. J. & T. Gibson
(no dates)

No marker:*
Mary Jane Sharp
Died Sep 14, 1878
age: abt 76 yrs
"Aunt Polly"

* by Miss Bertha Henslee

Mary Jane Nisbett
Aug 27, 1818
Mar 5, 1857
aged: 38y, 6m, 8d.

Queen Victoria Nisbett
Mar 29, 1854
Aug 15, 1855

T. L. Henderson
Mar 21, 1829
Mar 14, 1855

Harriet Jane, wife of
J. A. Davis
Oct 14, 1847
Aug 5, 1864
age: 20y, 9m, 22d.
&
Caddy, Infant daughter
age: 2m & 5d.

------- Wolworth
Born -------
Died --- --, 186-
(illegible)

Dr. J. G. Barksdale
Sep 7, 1801
Feb 23, 1885

Eva Jane, wife of
J. F. Calhoon
Dec 20, 1826
Dec 19, 1856

Joseph B., son of
J. P. & M. A. Calhoon
Mar 16, 1841
Dec 3, 1857

Sarah E., wife of
W. L. Yancy & dau of
J. F. & E. J. Calhoon
Nov 9, 1845
Sep 27, 1865

Solomon Holland
age: 11 yrs.
(no dates)

Silvy Holland
age: 10 yrs.
(no dates)

Tolbert Holland
age: 26 yrs.
(no dates)

Polly Ann, wife of
Dr. J. G. Barksdale
1811-1896

(These two graves are on the North side of the Cowan Cemetery,
just within the Churchyard.)

Johanne S. B. McGhie
Abitt A.D. Plures VI
Cal Nov. MDCCCLVII (1858)
Non Apparet
Quia Tulit Eum Due
(stone under large tree)

George Barksdale, son of
D. B. & I. G. Hale
Died Jul 19, 1858
age: 5m & 27d.
(stone under large tree)

W. L. Welch
Oct 25, 1829
Apr 7, 1859

Frank B., son of
M. S. & M. A. Wallace
Dec 17, 1863
Jan 19, 1867

Jane Story
Died Dec 30, 1849
aged: 85 yrs.

Ann E. Story, wife of
T. M. Story
Sep 29, 1829
Mar 10, 1858

The Barksdale Tombs at the rear of the Educational Building
have attracted much interest because of their location. Mr.
O. C. Walker gives new light on this from an entry in some
Old City Minutes dated Nov 25, 1884. The entry reads:
"G. C. Sandusky & B. M. Tillman petitioned the Mayor and
Board of Alderman for permission to bury Dr. Barksdale and
Wife, when they die, in the Church Yard near the fence
separating it from the Cowan-Frierson Ground". After Dr.
Barksdale's death in February 23, 1885, Mrs. Barksdale
operated their large home as a boarding house known as
"Barksdale House". It was located where the Funeral Home
now stands(now 1975, a parking lot for the Baptist Church).
She followed her Husband in death in 1896. It is presumed
that they wished this place for their interment because of
their intence love for the Church in which both were so very
active. We are indebted to Mr. Walker for his interesting
information. He in turn credits Hon. John B. Templeton with
bringing the entry to his attention. We thank both of them
for this additional historical fact."

12 BLESSING-COATS CEMETERY   Map # 11
This Cemetery is located near Railroad Avenue, off New Tullahoma Hwy.

Sam'l Richards
    Co A
4th Tenn Mt'd Inf.

David Richards
Died Jul 30, 1871
age: 70 yrs.

Fannie T., dau of
J. M. & M. J. Brown
Apr 12, 1864
May 13, ----(broken)

Sam E. Green   and
1851-1936

J. M. Brown
Dec 13, 1827
Aug 4, 1906

Mary Jane, Consort of
J. M. Brown
Feb 22, 1834
Apr 16, 1876

Infant Son of
J. M. & M. J. Brown
(no dates)

Mary Frances Stewart Green
1859-1928

Tomie Thomas
Sep 27, 1807
May 23, 1863

Elizabeth Thomas
Dec 22, 1813
May 5, 1868

Lizzie Stewart, wife of
G. W. Grubbs
Oct 11, 1851
May 2, 1919

R. E. G.(Green)
(fieldstone, no insc.)

Mary A. Stewart
Jul 21, 1828
Jan 20, 1911

C. W. Stewart
Oct 17, 1849
Jan 12, 1871

Maggie A. Stewart
Jun 15, 1863
Mar 14, 1938

Henry G."Buddy" Blessing
Jul 7, 1890
Feb 11, 1947

W. W. C.(Wilson Coats)
(foot marker)

J. E. C. (Coats)
(foot marker)

Robert Earl Overcast
1951-1952
(Thompson)

Hugh L. Case
1948-1948 (now gone)

Elenor, Consort of
James P. Blessing & dau of
Isaac & Elizabeth Patterson
Sep 7, 1826
Sep 17, 1852

John Reed
Oct 2, 1803
Jul 29, 1860

Luvisa Reed
Feb 8, 1800
Aug 15, 1874
age: 74y, 6m, 7d.

Mrs. Minnie W. Johnson
1872-1944
(Thompson)

No marker:*
Mrs. Gilla Blessing, widow
of late H. C. Blessing, died
Friday April 14, 1899.
aged: abt 75 yrs.
*Shelbyville Gazette.

Sandra Kay Stewart
1944-1944
(Thompson)

Jim Nichols
1896-1942 (now gone)

Gail Stewart
1948-1948
(Thompson)

William Henry, son of
James P. & Elenor Blessing
Aug 27, 1848
Apr 21, 1849
age: 7m & 25d.

Narcisa L. McFarlin, dau of
J. & L. Reed
Oct 16, 1839
Jan 24, 1861

Mary S. Richards
Aug 18, 1856
Oct 13, 1857

Jessie Bryson Brown, Husband
of N. N. Brown & son of
J. M. Brown
Oct 19, 1861
Mar 21, 1886
age: 24y, 5m, 2d.(now gone)

Mrs. May Blessing Hay
1895-1951
(Thompson)

Sallie Blessing
Died Jul 29, 1938
age: 67y, 2m, 22d.

Shefter Kirk Blessing
1900-1950
(Thompson)

James B., son of
B. W. & C. A. Reed
Jan 21, 1858
Aug 29, 1861

Franklin B., son of
B. W. & C. A. Reed
Jan 23, 1859
Sep 3, 1861

Baly W. Reed
May 5, 1833
Aug 26, 1862

Harry C., son of
J. M. & Mary E. Brown
Sep 11, 1886
Sep 23, 1887

Unmarked graves:**
Wilson Coats and wife,
Celia --- Coats.
** by Mr. John Lane.

Nora Blessing
May 2, 1902
May 5, 1946

H. G. Blessing
Died Jun 20, 1903
age: 34y, 1m, 10d.

Albert Lester, son of
H. G. & E. Y. Blessing
Dec 6, 1909
Nov 30, 1918

Sabrina Hurst
May 11, 1813
Jan 24, 1884

Cassie A. Montgomery
Feb 13, 1827
Apr 2, 1898

Mary E. Brown, wife of
J. M. Brown & dau of
H. C. & Gilla Blessing
Sep 29, 1850
Apr 24, 1887

Mary Elizabeth, dau of
J. M. & M. E. Brown
Jan 5, 1882
Jul 1, 1882
age: 27 days

#13 HOLLAND CEMETERY   Map # 11
This Cemetery is located in the Industrial Park. City.

Jesse J. Deason
May 18, 1873
May 12, 1912

Franklin Deason
Co E
3 U.S.V.I.

Maggie Ruth Deason
Aug 16, 1908
Sep 13, 1910

James Holland
Mar 2, 1795
Jul 13, 1850

John W. McAdams
Aug 6, 1843
Sep 27, 1917

Martha McAdams
1851-1924

C. C. McAdams
Jan 17, 1879
Nov 2, 1896

Sarah F. McAdams
Apr 28, 1859
Jun 25, 1902

W. H. Lokey
Dec 28, 1876
Nov 18, 1903

Novella Lokey
Mar 10, 1901
Jun 18, 1902

Burton Lokey
Sep 27, 1903
Mar 6, 1904

John A. Patterson, Infant son
of E. M. & Lavina Patterson
Born Sep 15, 1861
Died May 30, 1863

James McAdams
May 31, 1809
Mar 13, 1885
age: 75y, 9m, 12d.

Martha M. McAdams
May 23, 1825
Mar 3, 1908

James N. McAddams
Feb 24, 1845
Jul 20, 1870

Annie B. Pratt
Feb 21, 1872
Mar 12, 1903

Melvin Pratt
1911-1934
"Drowned in Duck River"

Jessie Pratt
1907-1929
"Drowned in Duck River"

Michael Green
Born 1813
Died (gone) (marker now gone)

Elizabeth Green
Dec 16, 1828
Jun 12, 1871

J. -. Nelson
Aug 15, 1830
(fieldstone)

W. C.
(fieldstone)

Vergie, dau of
R. D. & N. Ellis
Jun 24, 1901
Dec 25, 1901

Walter Bearden Reed
1894-1942
(Thompson)

Nicey Davenport
1846-1921

Barbra Ann Brandon
1941-1941
(Thompson)

Letsy Butner
1841-Dec 14, 1911

E. N. M.
Died Nov 9, 18-7
(fieldstone)

C. A. Travis
Died Mar 18--
(fieldstone)

G. N. Marchl
Died May 25, 1846

No marker:**
Rev. James W. Lokey
Born 1847
Died at Shelbyville, Tenn.
Feb 10, 1925

** by Jerry Wayne Cook

[Thomas & Jane Nelson Holland
brd.here in unmarked graves]

No marker:*
Lizzie Adcock Woosley
Born 1878
Died Dec 21, 1928
      & Her Husband
C. Virgil Woosley
(no dates)

* Charlie Adcock

No marker:*
Effie Adcock McGee Landers
Born Mar 8, 1884
Died Dec 29, 1917
      &
John McGee
Born Oct 15, 1877
Died Jan 16, 1910
      & Baby:
Martha Landers
(no dates)

No marker:*
Charles Martin Adcock
Born abt 1830
Died Nov 5, 1914
      & 4th wife:
Polly Edde Adcock
Born 1857
Died Oct 6, 1926

14 UNKNOWN CEMETERY   Map # 11
This Cemetery is located in the Industrial Park, City.
(On Road between Horse Mt. Road and Eaton Yale Co.)

3 graves, no markers.

15 GRAY CEMETERY   Map # 11
This Cemetery is located at Gray's Crossing.

No markers.

16 YOUNG CEMETERY   Map # 11
This Cemetery is located near Butler Creek.

James Young
Born May 1779
Died April 11, 1844
35 minutes after 4 o'clock
P.M. aged: 65 yrs.

"Mother"
Eliza Catharine Young
Aug 30, 1825
Apr 1, 1904

Rebecca Eliza Young
Born Mar 30, 1848
Died Sep 20, 1848
at 11:00 o'clock P.M.
aged: 5m & 20d.

William Young
Died Jan 24, 1878
aged: 62y, 5m, 17d.

Anna, dau of
William & C. Young
Died Feb 9, 1865
age: 2y & 1m.

Little Medora, dau of
J. E. & M. E. Shoffner
Died Nov 16, 1873
aged: 5y, 1m, 6d.

James H. Young
Died Jul 4, 1892
aged: 26y, 10m, 4d.

Infant Son of
William & C. Young
Died Jan 11, 1856
age: 11 days

Eliza Swanson
Born in Tennessee
Sep 6, 1825
Died Aug 3, 1852
      also her Babe:
Born Aug 1, 1852

17 JENKINS CHAPEL CEMETERY   Map # 11
This Cemetery is located at Jenkins Chapel Lutheran Church.

Donald McBryde Street
May 17, 1886
Jul 23, 1949
      &
Annie Wells Street
Sep 23, 1889

John William Street
Jul 17, 1928
Oct 24, 1937

L. E. Wood
1870-1935

Walter B. Jenkins
1874-1918

Annie M. Jenkins
1879-1928

Gideon A. Brown
Apr --, 1856
May 3, 1911

Archibald G. Moore
Aug 3, 1838
Jun 11, 1915
      &
Mattie Tune Moore
Jan 27, 1849
Feb 23, 1928

A. G. Moore
Sep 1886
Jun 1904

Lewis Tune Moore
1889-1947

Omar Shoffner
Jun 22, 1830
Aug 18, 1915
      &
Eoline Shoffner
Mar 25, 1880
Nov 17, 1958

Hazel L. Shoffner Godwin
1904-1949

Blanche Miller Shoffner
1878-1950

Emmett Thompson
1874-1907

Hattie B. Miller
1872-1917

Wiley M. Miller
1834-1917
      &
Harriette J. Miller
1841-1933

Morris Miller
1870-1934

Thomas Boyers
Sep 29, 1817
Sep 10, 1868
age: 50y, 11m, 11d.

Mary Boyers
Feb 29, 1820
Mar 13, 1882 age:62y, & 14d.

Clarence L. Shoffner
1873-1943
      &
Bessie B. Shoffner
1878-1960

Charles Edward Shoffner
1918-1923

Dorothy Dare Shoffner
1913-1919

John H. Shoffner
Jul 15, 1906
Aug 29, 1973
      &
Lemay D. Shoffner
Jul 9, 1909

Oscar W. Searcy
Dec 25, 1880
Oct 18, 1930

[Located on part of the old
John Shofner farm]

Daniel Moody Searcy
Dec 12, 1878
Dec 19, 1915

Dennis Morton Searcy
Jan 6, 1888
Jul 4, 1911

Dennis Searcy
May 17, 1850
Dec 7, 1920
• &
Lee M. Searcy
Mar 29, 1860
Dec 24, 1901

Morton Brandon King
Sep 8, 1889
Dec 18, 1962
(footmarker: M.M.K.)

Hoyt Dale King
Mar 11, 1885
Mar 18, 1902

Charles Henry Armstrong
1869-1937

Joe Mullins
1867-1918
&
Mary Mullins
1875-1921

James M. Mullins
1916

John E. Shoffner
1847-1925
&
Mary E. Shoffner
1850-1926

R. E., son of
D. M. & E. R. Shofner
Jul 17, 1870
Oct 16, 1884

Annie M., dau of
D. M. & E. R. Shofner
Aug 17, 1860
Nov 7, 1861

Daniel M. Shoffner
1827-1889
& wife:
Rachel Brittain Shoffner
1836-1913

Sam D. Shoffner
Jan 1862
Oct 1915

Loton Shoffner
Born in the State of N.C.
Dec 26, 1813, moved to
Bedford Co., Tenn. 1815
Died Jul 30, 1898

Wileford Coleman   and
Feb 17, 1820
Apr 11, 1879

Joel Shoffner
Died Sep 16, 186-
age: 50y, 11m, 16d.
(broken)

Jacob Morton Shofner
Aug 2, 1841
Jul 8, 1916
&
Melissa Landis Shofner
Sep 4, 1844
Aug 28, 1912

Edna, Third dau of
J. M. & M. E. Shofner
Mar 26, 1867
Oct 17, 1868

Edward Bowlin Maupin
1860-1900
&
Emma Shofner Maupin
1864-1926

Edward Bowlin Maupin, Jr.
May 26, 1914
Apr 27, 1971

James M. Mullins
Nov 11, 1837
Jan 25, 1928
&
Lettie M. Mullins
May 6, 1841
Jan 21, 1911

H. T. Mullins
May 8, 1864
Dec 17, 1898

George S. Edmondson
Jul 25, 1888
Apr 21, 1890

Mitchael B. Shoffner
1856-1928

Henry Gaston Shoffner
1858-1928

John William Wirsching
1867-1913
&
Amelia Shofner Wirsching Holt
1875-1972

Sarah Elizabeth, wife of
L. Shoffner, Born in Kentucky
Jan 28, 1826 & died in Tenn.
Mar 28, 1846
aged: 20y & 2m.
&
Sarah Elizabeth, wife of
John W. Wells & only child
of L. & Sarah E. Shoffner
Born in Tenn. Mar 6, 1846 &
Died Sep 4, 1873
aged: 27y, 5m, 28d.

Jane Coleman Hester
Jul 3, 1834
Oct 30, 1911

Rev. R. J. King
Dec 24, 1810
Feb 13, 1887

Mary Ann King, wife of
R. J. King
Feb 2, 1819
Jan 20, 1885
age: 75y, 11m, 18d.

Maggie A., dau of
J. F. & F. T. King
Jan 21, 1859
Jul 18, 1877

Samuel Francis King
Died Jun 4, 1889
age: 20y & 20d.

Redden Dale King
Died Jul 4, 1895
age: 34y, 1m, 11d.
&
Alice Shofner King
1863-1932

Douglas, son of
Dale & Alice King
Died Oct 6, 1896
age: 4y, 6m, 9d.

John Mullins
Died Jul 6, 1883
age abt 76 yrs.
"Joined the Lutheran Church
1865 & was made an Elder & was
a Consistant Member until
death"

Fannie Mullins
Nov 8, 1878
Nov 9, 1878

W. L. Mullins
Oct 2, 1862
Nov 28, 1862

Ada Mullins
Oct 4, 1876
Nov 1, 1876

Othniel Wells
1868-1956
&
Irma F. Wells
1872-1933

John W. Wells
May 15, 1842
Jul 11, 1894

Margaret C. Wells
Sep 9, 1847
Apr 23, 1907

Edwin L. Bryan
Oct 23, 1825
Aug 24, 1854
&
Martha Dyer Bryan
Aug 5, 1829
Aug 8, 1899

William Prentice Cooper
Sep 27, 1870
Jul 3, 1961
Mayor of Shelbyville
1905-1907
Speaker House of Representa-
tives 1915-1917
Trustee University of Tenn.
1915-1958
&
Argentine Shofner Cooper
Apr 3, 1873
Apr 4, 1954
First Lady of Tennessee
1939-1945
U.S. Ambassadress of Peru
1946-1948

To the Glory of God
In loving Memory of
William Prentice Cooper, Jr.
Born 28 Sept 1895
Riverside, Bedford Co., Tenn.
married 22 April 1950
Died 18 May 1969
Governor of Tennessee
1939-1945
U.S. Ambassador to Peru
1946-1948
"Perserverenta Omnia Vincit"

Mildred, dau of
William P. & Argentine
Cooper
Sep 29, 1898
Oct 11, 1898

Benjamin Northcott, young
son of Dr. R. A. & Mary
Catharine Coldwell
1862-1868

Roy S. McTaggart
1888-1948
&
Jennie H. McTaggart
1887-
& Son:
Norris Wesley McTaggart
1926-1934

Sallie T. Groomes
May 12, 1865
Jun 26, 1913

John Shofner
Died Jan 6, 1857
aged: 69y, 10m, 17d.

Amelia Shofner, Consort of
John Shofner, Born in
North Carolina Mar 19, 1794
married Feb 18, 1810, moved
with her Husband to Tenn.
1815, & Died Aug 24, 1849.
"Was the Mother of Twelve
Children, eight of whom
with her Husband are left
to mourn her loss"

Little Isabella Shofner
aged: 5y, 4m, 20d.
(no dates)

Alex E. Coleman
Jan 6, 1853
Aug 31, 1880
age: 27y, 7m, 25d.

Anna Belle Shofner, wife of
Alex E. Coleman
Apr 26, 1852
Feb 11, 1943
age: 90y, 9m, 16d.

Little Emma
(no other information, in
Coleman plot)

Martha Coleman Lowe
Oct 27, 1872
Aug 13, 1958

Infant son of
T. B. & C. A. Carpenter
Apr 20, 1880
May 7, 1880

Neely S. McConnell
Sep 22, 1852
Sep 4, 1927
&
Martha J. McConnell
Mar 6, 1850
Apr 17, 1937

Fannie B. McConnell
Sep 26, 1875
Oct 31, 1948

Claude V. McConnell
Feb 14, 1887
Sep 1, 1905

Bennie A. McConnell
Sep 21, 1878
Oct 13, 1898

Claude H. Young
Aug 19, 1886
Aug 26, 1926

Grace Shofner Young
Feb 10, 1885
Sep 29, 1956

Grace Aline Young
Jul 6, 1915
Nov 11, 1936

Finis E. Shofner
Feb 10, 1850
Jan 16, 1918
&
Elizabeth E. Shofner
Feb 6, 1850
Jun 30, 1920

Freddie E. Moore
Dec 19, 1871
Apr 6, 1874

Lula J. Holt, wife of
John Penn & Joe Fulton
Aug 21, 1869
Jul 30, 1942

J. T. Arnold
1855-1926
&
Annie C. Arnold
1860-1929

Jimmie Ruth
age: 5 months

Infant Son
(no dates)
NOTE: The above 2 graves are
between the Arnold & Bobo's)

Mamie Mullins Bobo
1899-1920

Mary E. Glenn
1890-1956

Mike F. Shofner
Apr 8, 1861
Oct 10, 1862
&
Martha W. Shofner
Feb 22, 1851
Oct 6, 1854
"Children of Mike &
S. E. Shofner"

James J., son of
Michael & Sophronia F.
Shofner
Jan 14, 1853
Jun 11, 1853

Samuel Moody Holt
May 29, 1842
Apr 8, 1912
& wife:
Sophronia Ann Morton Holt
May 12, 1843
Sep 13, 1917

H. L. Shofner
1848-1915

Elizabeth Young Shofner
1857-1944

Hugh L. Shofner
1890

Elsie Shofner
1895

Young Shofner
1878

Victor Shofner
1888

George W. Holt
Hosp. Corps
Sp. Am. War
Jul 8, 1878
May 11, 1940

Lucy W. Sheridan
1865-1965

Albert F. Mullins
1874-1953
&
Irene S. Mullins
1875-1951

Harry Herschel Leiter
1891-1950
&
Laura Amrette W. Ailes Leiter
1907-
&
John Walter Ailes
1894-1947

Floy F. Webb
1885-1967
&
Lillian A. Webb
1889-1952

Mary Jane, wife of
John M. Phillips
Died Jul 30, 1873
aged: 30y, 5m, 8d.

Hugh W. Phillips
Sep 30, 1872
Apr 23, 1890
age: 17y, 5m, 7d.

Mikie S., son of
J. M. & M. J. Phillips
Sep 1, 1870
Sep 8, 1870

Horace J. Phillips
1860-1891

Frank E. Huffman
1900-1931

Jimmie M. Huffman
1870-1941

Ephraim S. Huffman
1867-1938

Infant of
J. F. & E. A. Moore
(no dates)

Mike S. Moore
Apr 24, 1866
Jun 18, 1890
age: 24y, 1m, 25d.

Andrew M. Moore
May 7, 1875
Nov 22, 1962

John F. Moore
May 14, 1841
Feb 24, 1905
&
Emma A. Shofner Moore
Oct 3, 1844
Nov 25, 1911

Jennie Moore Keeling
1873-1896

Harry Evans Thompson
1894-1938
&
Lorraine Webb Thompson
1896-19

Effie Webb Brown
1877-1919

Morgan Cofield Webb
1853-1942

Laura Shofner Webb
1856-1935

Michael Shofner
Died May 27, 1892
age: 73y, & 29d.

Sophronia E., wife of
Michael Shoffner
Born in Shelbyville, Tenn.
Sep 19, 1820 & Died
Nov 1, 1875

Benie Holt, Infant son of
S. M. & S. A. Holt
Jan 19, 1868
Feb 9, 1868

G. W. C. Morton
1818-1870
&
Julia B. Morton
1823-1891

Fannie A. Morton
Dec 29, 1864
Jan 30, 1884

William E. Dixon
1877-1945
&
Nancy C. Dixon
1878-1969

Daniel A. McConnell
Oct 25, 1849
Dec 11, 1912

Julia E. McConnell
May 19, 1852
Dec 21, 1916

Mary L. Shofner
1883

Verner Shofner
1877-1880

Ada E. Shofner
1873

W. H. Young
1853-1917
& wife:
R. E. Young
1857-1933
&
Baby Young
(no dates)

Frances M. Bomar
1852-1900

Mary N. Bomar
1857-1913

Elijah Bomar
1842-1929

Ann Taylor Bomar
1852-1921

James H. Bomar
Born in Halifax Co., Va.
Oct 13, 1814
Died Jun 21, 1898
age: 83y, 8m, 8d.
&
Eleanor Bomar
Jun 29, 1827
Feb 19, 1901

Piercy Yell Bomar, son of
Elijah & F. P. Bomar
Jul 20, 1867
Aug 3, 1896
age: 29y & 14d.

W. S. Bomar
May 30, 1857
Jul 14, 1915

Turley Euless Bomar
Sep 26, 1868
Nov 15, 1919

Charley A. Gill
1872-1932
& wife:
Elnora Young Gill
1877-1928

Ernest M. Hill
(no birth date)-1968

Carl L. Chappell
1913-1967

Ernestine M. Chappell

Henry K. Morgan
1873-1930

Tina W. Morgan
1879-1962

Baby Paul,
Died Mar 12, 1896
age: 2 months
Infant son of
Mr & Mrs E. B. Shoffner

May Agnes Crawford
1922-1927

Mary Elizabeth Crawford
Dec 24, 1906
Oct 11, 1907

Joseph S. Crawford, Jr.
Mar 1919
Mar 10, 1968

Nina Shoffner Crawford
Apr 18, 1885
Oct 20, 1962

18 MORGAN CEMETERY (CEDAR HILL)   Map # 11
This Cemetery is located on Arnold Lane.

Mrs. Rebecca Morgan, wife
of James Morgan, who was
born Dec 1, 1792 & died
Aug 3rd. 1852, & lived a
respectful Member of the
Baptist Church about 20
years, until her death.

E. M. Lacy (& wife, Catharine)
  Co F   (no marker)
5th Tenn Cav.

Rachel Morgan
(no dates)

L. B. Morgan
Oct 15, 1826
Feb 22, 1876
& wife:
Mary J. Morgan
Jun 13, 1834
Jun 2, 1912

This was a large Cemetery,
many graves marked only
with fieldstones, no insc.
Many unmarked graves.

[Cedar Hill Church once stood here]

19 REAVES CEMETERY   Map # 11
This Cemetery is located near Riverbend Country Club.

Almedia, wife of
J. H. Swing
Sep 8, 1854
Oct 24, 1885

Venoy C., son of
B. C. & Lettie McGill
Jan 1, 1887
Jul 19, 1887

William Reaves   and
Jun 4, 1814
Oct 12, 1887

Joel Coggins
(no dates-Marker now gone)

Elizabeth Reaves
Dec 24, 1819
Sep 9, 1888

many unmarked graves.

20 PISGAH CEMETERY   Map # 11
This Cemetery is located on Road between Flat Creek & Raus.

George Snell
1877-1940
&
Lena Snell
1883-1936

William R. Snell
Dec 3, 1836
Aug 27, 1859

Asahel C. Snell
Feb 3, 1824
Feb 16, 1852

Rev. Wiley B. Snell
Apr 30, 1798
Jan 18, 1881

Frances Snell
Nov 13, 1818
Jan 4, 1865

Johnnie Maye
1911-1936

L. C. Tribble
1859-1920

Fannie Tribble
1864-1892

Earnest Tribble
Jun 13, 1881
Jul 8, 1928

Jane Tribble
1836-1918

Elizabeth, wife of
W. B. Snell
Aug 12, 1796
Nov 7, 1851

R. D. Hitt
Aug 9, 1913
Aug 15, 1913

"Mother"
Winnie Bearden
1821-1903
& "Son"
James C. Bearden
1853-1908

Phillip Gilbert, son of
N. B. & Hattie Burrow
Aug 2, 1894
Mar 9, 1896
&
Jennie Vaden, dau of
N. B. & Hattie Burrow
Jun 17, 1891
Apr 16, 1896

Sarah A. Landis, wife of
Nimrod Burrow
Mar 19, 1822
Jun 26, 1894
age: 72y, 3m, 7d.

John E. Burrow
Jul 29, 1860
Aug 2, 1860
&
Infant Son
Feb 27, 1867
Mar 2, 1867
&
Samuel R. Burrow
Nov 11, 1873
Nov 19, 1875

Katharine Burrow
Mar 5, 1806
Oct 22, 1845

Nimrod Burrow
Sep 4, 1799
Oct 7, 1890
age: 91y, 1m, 3d.

J. C. Coleman
1823-1883

"Father"
W. S. Johnson
Mar 3, 1836
May 12, 1902
&
"Mother"
M. E. Johnson
Apr 6, 1841
Dec 27, 1905

Roy A., son of
W. L. & T. J. Kimbro
Jun 26, 1882
Aug 2, 1883

Alton G., son of
J. T. & H. F. Snell
Sep 26, 1900
Sep 11, 1901

Elga P., dau of
J. T. & H. F. Snell
Dec 22, 1891
Oct 17, 1904

Ola C., dau of
J. T. & H. F. Snell
Nov 20, 1881
Apr 11, 1903

B. F. Reed
Sep 28, 1842
Aug 31, 1920

Sarah Jane, wife of
B. F. Reed
Feb 2, 1843
Sep 27, 1914

M. B. Reed
Feb 4, 1874
Oct 14, 1946

Luvenia A. White
Jul 3, 1878
Oct 25, 1917

William Neil Brown
May 12, 1878
Aug 31, 1931
&
Ida Morgan Brown
Jul 6, 1879
Jun 11, 1944

Anna Frances, dau of
J. C. & Lelia Moore
Born & Died
Jan 19, 1915

A. G. Snell
Jul 22, 1820
Oct 16, 1855

Cassander M. Coldwell, wife
of Albert G. Snell
May 4, 1820
Feb 19, 1900

James T. Snell
Jul 12, 1854
Sep 12, 1919

Allie B., son of
J. T. & H. F. Snell
Sep 24, 1878
Jan 25, 1905

Orpha E., dau of
J. T. & H. F. Snell
Feb 9, 1879
Oct 20, 1904

Fred Kimbro
May 25, 1861
Jun 21, 1896

Infant of
A. J. & M. A. Gordon
Oct 7, 1887
Oct 28, 1887

Lillian Cobb
Sep 21, 1910
Oct 30, 1910
&
Christine Cobb
Oct 19, 1911
May 22, 1914
Daughters of Elisha &
Annie Lee Cobb.

G. T. Cobb
1846-1923
& wife:
C. E. Marr Cobb
1855-1929

James M. Cobb
Sep 7, 1878
Aug 6, 1923

John O. Bearden
1847-1898
&
Sarah A. Bearden
1850-1913

Maggie A., dau of
W. A. & E. A. Brown
Mar 28, 1869
Mar 23, 1870

Lydia C., dau of
W. A. & E. A. Brown
Dec 8, 1866
Mar 12, 1870

J. P. Brown
1826-Jun 4, 1894
&
Nancy E., wife of
J. P. Brown
Apr 20, 1826
Sep 22, 1868

J. R. Brown
1865-1934

Edwin E. Martin
Dec 12, 1833
Apr 4, 1908

Pascal Brown
1802-1887
&
Jim Brown
1839-1884
&
Kitty Pollard
(no dates)

R. M. Brown
Sep 14, 1841
Apr 26, 1907

Mary Jane Brown
Apr 28, 1851
Apr 29, 1916

J. T. Brown
1865-1897

Corp'l W. A. Brown
Co F 5 Tenn Cav.
Jun 23, 1834
Apr 15, 1905

Elizza A., wife of
W. A. Brown
Apr 4, 1841
May 18, 1914

Many unmarked graves.

Mary M., wife of
J. O. Blanton
Dec 2, 1848
Aug 4, 1902

Argyle H. Bearden
Oct 2, 1842
Jun 23, 1876

Walter E. Bearden
Oct 19, 1871
Sep 11, 1872

Margarette A. Kimbro
Oct 4, 1844
Dec 28, 1919

William P. Snell
Feb 22, 1856
Feb 24, 1909
&
Maggie A. Snell
Nov 24, 1858
(no date)

W. C. Snell
Nov 4, 1832
Jun 24, 1898

Cassie D., wife of
W. C. Snell
Jan 5, 1836
Aug 12, 1895

Nancy J. Snell
Apr 26, 1849
Dec 22, 1919

J. T. Snell, Sr.
Co F 5th Tenn Cav C.S.A.
Oct 4, 1846
Nov 20, 1918

Georgia A., dau of
J. T. & Nancy J. Snell
Jul 8, 1869
Nov 21, 1917

Infant Son of
Mr & Mrs W. N. Brown
Sep 18, 1904

Infant Daughter of
Mr & Mrs W. N. Brown
Jan 1, 1901

many fieldstones, no insc.

21 HASTING CAMP GROUND CEMETERY   Map # 11
This Cemetery is located on the New Hope Road.
New Hope Church Cemetery.

Giles Cates
Feb 1, 1838
Jul 20, 1866
&
Tennie Cates
Mar 10, 1856
Dec 31, 1968

W. C. Himes
Oct 4, 1839
Mar 24, 1915

Martha A. Himes
Oct 13, 1837
(no date)

Emmet L. Himes
Apr 27, 1871
Aug 7, 1875

Melvina E. Ray
Dec 12, 1842
Feb 2, 1863

Conl. John Hastings
Jan 26, 1801
Feb 5, 1863

Laurka Hastings, wife of
Conl. John Hastings
Apr 9, 1810
Mar 18, 1891

Susan Hastings, Consort of
John Hastings
May 13, 1804
May 17, 1839

John M., son of
John & Laurka Hastings
Feb 17, 1839
Aug 27, 1913

Joseph Hastings
Nov 10, 1782
Oct 13, 1868
&
Nancy Hastings
Aug 31, 1781
Sep 12, 1864
age: 83y & 11d.

Frances, dau of
Jos. & Nancy Hastings
Nov 26, 1803
Oct   1818

Talten W. Kimery
Aug 31, 1841
Jan 4, 1847
age: 5y, 4m, 3d.

Elizabeth Kimery
Aug 4, 1824
Aug 19, 1847
age: 23y & 15d.

Alcy Langley, dau of
Robert R. Pollock
May 6, 1826
Apr 21, 1886

Margret M. Hastings, Consort
of Robert Hastings
Sep 4, 1830
Oct 10, 1857
age: 27y, 1m, 6d.

John Kiser
Jun 15, 1826
Aug 23, 1863

H. R. Kiser
May 13, 1825
Nov 4, 1877

Jiles U., son of
William & C. Burrow
Oct 4, 18--(gone)
Jul   1875

Ider Lou, dau of
W. & F. C. Burrow
Jan 1, 1871
Feb 22, 1871

Isaac B. H. Hime
Infant Son of
Henry & --- F. Hime
(no dates)

Mrs. Dorothy Cobb
1932-1955
(Gowen)

Jos. Hastings
Nov 25, 1757
Jan 30, 1816
(Soldier of Revolution)

Susanah Hastings
1755-1842

Pherbe Hastings
Feb 23, 1816
Oct 26, ----(gone)

8 unmarked graves with the
long hewn rock over graves.

Mary, Consort of
J. Rogers
Aug 16, 1798
Jun 16, 1835
age: 36y & 10m.

John F., son of
S. & S. M. Rogers
Jun 29, 1855
Dec 7, 1857

William Hime
Mar 25, 1813
Mar 11, 1863

Sarah S. Hime
Jul 27, 1811
Jan 22, 1855

John Hime
Sep 13, 1826
Dec 23, 1899

Daniel K. S., son of
William & Sarah Hime
Feb 14, 1836
Jan 17, 1859

Robert McFarlin
Feb 18, 1776
Feb 28, 1850
age: 74 yrs.

Mary A. McFarlin
Dec 24, 1825
Sep 8, 1861

T. N. McFarlin
Jun 29, 1838
Jul 27, 1866
age: 28y & 28d.

W. J. L. McFarlin
Jan 6, 1864
Jul 18, 1866

Jacob Harbour Kiser
Dec 18, 1841
Nov 18, 1908
&
Maria Parkes Kiser
Aug 12, 1850
Oct 20, 1911

Buford, son of
G. S. & L. Womack
Oct 12, 1893
Jul 18, 1894

William H. Miles
Nov 30, 1806
Aug 16, 1854

James W. Miles
son of W. H. & C. H. Miles
Sep 16, 1827
Apr 1, 1845

Tho. B. Pitman
Born (gone)
Died (gone)

Nancy Pitman
Born (gone)
Died (gone)

William E. Woosley
Jun 8, 1812
Apr 13, 1856
age: 44y, 10m, 5d.

A. C. S. Woosley
May 9, 1855
Oct 1, 1861
age: 6 yrs.

William A. Hime
Apr 8, 1830
Dec 8, 1861

Sarah C. Hime
Jan 5, 1853
Oct 11, 1854

Amy Hime
Jan 3, 1835
Jan 18, 1835

John Dunaway
Died May 17, 1849
age: 50 yrs.

Mrs. Margaret Dunaway
Dec 15, 1802
Mar 17, 1832
age: 79y, 3m, 2d.

W. J. Kiser
Sep 3, 1876
Apr 24, 1916

Sallie Kiser
Jul 19, 1873
Dec 12, 1875

Elizabeth Kiser Webb
Jan 14, 1878
Aug 30, 1941

Jean Kiser
Sep 23, 1883
May 13, 1900

G. S. Womack
Jan 3, 1865
Dec 18, 1918

Lizzie Philpott, wife of
G. S. Womack
Aug 14, 1869
Jun 17, 1897

"Father"
T. S. Cates
1775-1843

"Mother"
M. Cates
1779-1818

M. M. Cates
1804-1921

M. H. Cates
1806-1843

Purlina Ellen, Consort of
Jos. Cates
Jul 22, 1833
Apr 26, 1864

M. Tap
1839-1846

S. P.
1801-1845

M. Runnels
(no dates)

F. D. Kimery
1784-1828
age: 44y & 4m.

Turly Kimery
Nov 26, 1786
Oct 11, 1857
age: 70y, 8m, 15d.

John Koonce
1782-May 15, 1846

Sarah, wife of
John Koonce
Jul 9, 1786
Feb 22, 1845

Alfred K. Koonce
Dec 25, 1834
Apr 4, 1855

Elizabeth J. Koonce
Jan 17, 1840
Oct 9, 1857
age: 17y, 8m, 23d.

Blackmon A. Koonce
Aug 1, 1837
Oct 15, 1857
age: 20y, 2m, 11d.

Jo. J. Kimery
Apr 4, 1840
Jul 8, 1869
age: 29y, 3m, 4d.

W. E. Kimery
Jan 6, 1846
Sep 23, 1868
age: 22y, 8m, 17d.

Infant Daughter of
G. S. & L. Womack
Jan 21, 1896
Jan 23, 1896

Thomas B. Philpott
Dec 7, 1847
Sep 5, 1917
&
M. R. A., wife of
Thomas B. Philpott
Dec 8, 1843
Aug 9, 1899

M. T. Cunningham
Apr 14, 1809
Oct 9, 1873

John Wallis
Jan 7, 1807
Sep 18, 1888
&
Mary Wallis
Jan 15, 1814
Feb 29, 1864

E. Lavoy, son of
J. P. & Fannie Wallis
Aug 13, 1833
Jan 8, 1838

Eustace W. Woosley
Aug 26, 1873
Aug 28, 1910

Mamie Dews, dau of
W. F. & E. M. Woosley
Jan 17, 1872
Dec 16, 1903
age: 31y, 10m, 29d.

William F. Woosley
Sep 17, 1835
Aug 18, 1903
age: 67y, 11m, 1d.
&
Elizabeth M. Woosley
Jul 8, 1846
Feb 4, 1925

Earnest M. Woosley
Jan 17, 1880
Sep 5, 1903
age: 23y, 7m, 18d.

Infant of
Earnest & Lizzie Woosley
Died Jun 8, 1903
(no age given)

Emma Woosley
1883-1955
&
Stella W. Shofner
1886-1955

William A. Haynes
Aug 7, 1834
Oct 24, 1884

Andrew J. Haynes
Mar 21, 1890
Sep 14, 1891

Ernest G. Haynes
Jul 3, 1894
Mar 15, 1896

Sarah N. A. Philpott, wife of
M. F. Hime
Dec 31, 1874
Jan 30, 1898

Ella May, dau of
M. F. & Nannie Hime
Mar 3, 1897
Jul 3, 1897

Joshua M. Hix
Nov 4, 1812
Nov 27, 1885
age: 73y & 23d.

Jane, Consort of
J. M. Hix, who died of fever
Sep 1, 1839
aged: 27y, 8m, 20d.

Mary E. Hix, who died of
fever, Sep 26, 1839
aged: 6m & 18d.

John E. Hix, who died of
Croup Aug 8, 1846
aged: 2y & 30d.

Isaac N. Hix, died of
Scarlet Fever
Jan 7, 1850
age: 9m & 11d.

Child's grave,
(marker destroyed)

Sarah C. Hix, wife of
J. M. Hix
Nov 30, 1821
Jan 30, 1913

William G. Hix
Nov 5, 1850
Feb 11, 1886
age: 35y, 3m, 6d.

Nannie J. Coats
Apr 6, 1841
Mar 12, 1879

William Russell
Dec 25, 1793
Feb 24, 1819

Nancy Russell
Aug 10, 1795
Sep 15, 182(7)

Elizabeth J., wife of
William H. McFarlin
Aug 9, 1832
May 9, 1868

B. G. C. McFarlin
Sep 24, 1858
Aug 30, 1861

Willie Philpott
Mar 1, 1900
Aug 3, 1900

Emmet A. Philpott
Aug 28, 1888
Jun 10, 1948

Ernest C. Philpott
Jan 26, 1832
Aug 14, 1898

Minnie M. Philpott
Dec 22, 1879
Aug 24, 1898

Genoah C. Brown
Feb 1, 1859
Dec 5, 1860

Caladonia C. Brown
Oct 5, 1835
Aug 20, 1864

J. W. Brown
Nov 31, 1832
Apr 19, 1863

Benjamin P. Stanfield
1835-1914

James T. Arnold
Jul 26, 1822
Oct 10, 1876

Julia, wife of
B. P. Arnold
Jan 1, 1833
Jan 2, 1904

John Hime
1811-1831

Minnie Lee Cawthron
1869-1959
(Gowen-Smith)

"Mother"
Eliza J. Cates
1832-1916
& "Son"
Samuel E. Cates
1872-1916

W. C. Cates
Aug 13, 1840
Nov 14, 1902
C.S.A. 1861-1865, Iron Cross.

Virginia B., dau of
Joseph & Susan Cates
Mar 25, 1869
Oct 18, 1872

Ricy Cathrin, Infant of
T. B. & Laura Philpott
Mar 30, 1904
Apr 10, 1904

Dollie May Philpott
Mar 18, 1890
Jun 4, 1900

William C. Philpott
1864-1931
&
Sarah C. Philpott
1858-1946
[Matthew Cunningham and Aaron Woosley
two Revolutionary Soldiers may be
buried here]

William S. Wallace
Aug 25, 1813
Mar 10, 1865

Mrs. Cynthia Wallace
Mar 11, 1814
Jul 29, 1884

M. A. B. Brown
Jul 3, 1855
Feb 3, 1874

M. L. G. Brown
Apr 2, 1857
May 26, 1872

Annie, wife of
Allen J. Thomas
Aug 6, 1863
Nov 8, 1902
"If she had a fault, her
husband never knew it"

Gordon Wallis
Sep 13, 1846
Oct 30, 1932
&
Caddie Wallis
Mar 7, 1854
Jan 18, 1931

Joseph Cates, Born in
Orange Co., North Carolina
Sep 28, 1812 & Died
Sep 30, 1889
&
Sophia, Consort of
Joseph Cates
Oct 3, 1820
Jan 28, 1858
age: 38y, 3m, 25d.

Joshua W. Woosley
Jul 11, 1807
Dec 21, 1870
&
Nancy Woosley
Mar 4, 1809
Jan 12, 1885
&
Lucinda M. Woosley
Jun 23, 1847
Aug 2, 1876
&
John C. Woosley
Apr 13, 1834
Nov 22, 1908
&
Ann E. Woosley
Jul 15, 1837
Aug 13, 1913

Infant dau of
Mr & Mrs J. P. Arnold
Feb 18, 1879
Mar 18, 1879

Fanny Frost Haynes
Mar 30, 1856
Sep 27, 1930

Andrew S. Haynes
Jun 22, 1856
Jan 10, 1919
&
Rachel M. Haynes
Apr 19, 1862
Apr 14, 1835

John L. Cannon
Jun 14, 1846
Aug 25, 1918
&
Kate Haley Cannon
1853-1913

R. A., son of
W. F. & Fannie Searcey
Aug 6, 1917
Nov 4, 1917

Erastus G. Woosley
Nov 7, 1849
Mar 1, 1918

Almeda K. Woosley
Jun 1, 1854
(no date)

J. M. Woosley
Sep 24, 1834
Mar 21, 1896

Robert E., son of
J. M. & Leatha B. Woosley
Mar 25, 1867
Jul 10, 1884

Albert B., son of
J. M. & Leatha B. Woosley
Nov 18, 1878
Mar 22, 1879

Henry Snoden, son of
J. C. & Laura V. Rogers
Feb 3, 1884
Oct 7, 1884

Stephen Rogers
Co F
5th Tenn Cav.

William Reaves
1854-1882

Donia Reaves
1856-1899

John Euless Rogers
Oct 17, 1886
Sep 11, 1912

Oscar D., son of
J. B. & Fannie Rogers
Sep 9, 1887
Dec 30, 1901

John S. Cates
Jan 12, 1808
Jun 1, 1830

Elizabeth Cates
Dec 25, 1809
Jan 14, 1901

Jane M., Consort of
Thomas H. Buckingham
Feb 20, 1825
Aug 22, 1852

Estel Thorneberry
1928-1929

S. H. Haggard
Apr 7, 1836
Apr 15, 1903

G. W. Reed
1837-1911

Jane Reed
1842-1925

L. N. Reed
Jun 17, 1864
Aug 15, 1876

C. R. Reed
Nov 27, 1871
Dec 12, 1891

S. S. Wallis
May 1, 1838
Mar 1917

A. E. Wallis
Sep 15, 1845
Jun 7, 1907

William A. Philpott
Tennessee
Sgt Co E 23 Reg Tenn Inf C.S.A.
Apr 3, 1836
Nov 16, 1926

Chas. T. McAdams
1955-1965

Roy Lee McAdams
1963-1963

Joe H. Hastings
Feb 1, 1836
Sep 28, 1925
C.S.A.-1861-1865

Mary Latitia Hastings
Aug 26, 1846
Jan 27, 1920

Humphrey Jerome Hastings
Dec 28, 1881
Sep 27, 1905

Tinie B. Hastings, dau of
J. H. & M. L. Hastings
May 3, 1874
Dec 10, 1875

Paulette Marie Frazier
1945-1945

Larry Dwight Lynch
1944-1944

James T. Brown
1878-1963

Mary Cates Brown
May 8, 1829
Apr 10, 1891

El-a Audena, dau of
Paschel & Mary E. Brown
Jan 10, 1872
Mar 2, 1875

R. A. Hasty
Jan 17, 1862
Jun 22, 1926
&
Margriet G. Haynes, wife of
R. A. Hasty
Sep 27, 1850
Feb 26, 1911

Weldon Cheshire
1876-1942

Mr. J. D. Reed
1909-1963

Annie Laura, wife of
J. D. Reed
Jul 20, 1883
Jun 20, 1905

W. P. Horsley
Apr 6, 1854
Jun 25, 1902

Sarrah Louise Horsley Rowell
Jul 31, 1916
Sep 1, 1938

Jimmie P. Horsley
1894-1922

Mutas Horsley
1891-19

S. F. Horsley King
May 27, 1858
Jan 8, 1936

Sallie E. Lindsey Reed
Died Oct 1, 1902
aged: 29 yrs.

Celia Ann Cheshire
Dec 5, 1854
Apr 20, 1903

William A. Philpott
1836-1926

Tacy A., wife of
William Philpott
1842-1876

Mary E., wife of
William Philpott
1851-1908

"Our Mother"
Nancy C. Puryear
Feb 22, 1856
Dec 16, 1891

Ibbie C. Himes
Mar 18, 1870
Aug 16, 1907

Martin Friddle
Dec 20, 1797
Oct 16, 1895
&
Dianna Friddle
Died Aug 20, 1880
age: 81 yrs.

Infant Son of
Alfred & Margaret Friddle
(no dates)

John R. Philpott
Apr 10, 1892
Apr 22, 1892

Willie Bryon, son of
M. P. & M. E. Reeves
Jun 1, 1891
May 3, 1899

Mamie Pearl Reavs, wife of
Lee Philpott
Aug 24, 1878
May 12, 1898

R. O. Philpott
1917-1967

T. E. Womack
Jun 9, 1873
Jun 4, 1899

Francis M. Johnson
Mar 17, 1829
Nov 4, 1914

John F. Johnson
Nov 22, 1841
Jul 21, 1914

Sarah D. Johnson
Feb 17, 1856
Jan 5, 1919

Jimmie Lee Philpott
1875-1957

Lela Mai, dau of
J. L. & Katie Philpott
Apr 12, 1907
Jul 1, 1907

George Allen Philpott
Feb 19, 1893
Oct 29, 1895

Ruby, dau of
F. Z. & Jennie King
Born & Died
Oct 28, 1887

N---- Woosley
May 9, 1846
Mar 7, 1835

Peter Lee Limbo
1847-1919

Charlie R. Hodge
1883-19

T. A. Himes
Jul 31, 1817
Sep 17, 1891

Mary Himes
Dec 14, 1822
Jul 17, 1890

Homer H. Reed
Oct 29, 1899
Feb 5, 1903

Maggie Perl Reed
Oct 8, 1902
Nov 22, 1902

Francis F. Arnold
Feb 7, 1829
Nov 25, 1899

Donnie, wife of
Francis Arnold
Sep 6, 1847
Mar 6, 1925

James Franklin Limbo
Apr 30, 1877
Nov 18, 1902

"Father"
G. W. Swing
Nov 8, 1839
Nov 13, 1916

"Mother"
Mary Warren Swing
Aug 10, 1839
Mar 22, 1917

John B. Swing
Jan 19, 1865
Jun 18, 1911

Robert H. A., son of
Rufus & Argie Swing
Apr 20, 1904
Nov 15, 1908

Several fieldstones, no insc.

Several unmarked graves.

W. C. Woosley
May 6, 1844
Jan 31, 1908

Mary J. Evans Woosley
Oct 14, 1850
Jun 25, 1892
"A loving wife, a Mother Dear
lies buried here"

Azzie Lee Woosley
Feb 28, 1879
Apr 29, 1902

Bettie Haynes Woosley
Oct 30, 1864
Jan 18, 1908

C. P. Woosley
1887-1963

Rox Anna Brown
1871-1936

1 unmarked grave.

George W. Hasty
Sep 24, 1850
Nov 10, 1918

Ella Josephine Hasty
Dec 17, 1857
Dec 4, 1923

"Father"
Edd Ewing Swing
Oct 31, 1877
Mar 21, 1907
&
"Mother"
Della Swing
Jun 29, 1874

James Carl Reed
Sep 4, 1932
Nov 13, 1933

John C. Haithcote
Tennessee Pfc U.S.Army
W. W. I
Aug 3, 1887
Apr 27, 1967

Thomas O. Reed
Dec 22, 1876
Mar 3, 1939

Ruth, wife of
T. O. Reed
Jul 8, 1884
Jan 29, 1908

Gene Reed
1876-1956

Nora Reed
1882-1940

Roy Glenn Reed
1930-1930

Lillian, dau of
G. N. & N. M. Reed
Jul 6, 1906
Oct 16, 1906

John H. Reed
1854-1924

Sophia I. Reed
1871-1944

Addie Himes, wife of
G. F. Himes
1862-1926 age: 64y & 3m.

Infant Son of
R. C. & M. L. Gordon
--------(dates gone)

John Bell McFarlin
1860-1919

Mattie C. McFarlin
1873-1954

William David McFarlin
Sep 6, 1913
Jun 15, 1915

Alice M. Haithcote
Sep 22, 1895
Apr 22, 1946

Robert Lee Young
1894-1957

Catheleen W. Young
Aug 16, 1897
Aug 1, 1923

Eula M. Woosley
Aug 25, 1894
Aug 4, 1896

Thomas B. Rogers
Apr 12, 1876
Apr 8, 1957

Berthie H. Rogers
Aug 26, 1888

Thomas Benton Rogers
Apr 25, 1920
Dec 31, 1937

John F. Dwyer
1856-1910

Caldonia C. Dwyer
Nov 2, 1850
Aug 3, 1896

Alfred Friddle
1837-1926

Margaret J. Friddle
1845-1915

Mary E. Mitchell
Jul 12, 1870
Feb 15, 1936

J. B. Rogers
1857-(no date)

Fannie L. Rogers
1863-1928

No marker:*
James Cheshire and 2nd wife:
Celia Blessing. (no dates)

* by Mr. John Lane.

About 100 yards back of the Main Cemetery, is the Slave Graveyard.

Maggie Berry, wife of
W. M. Berry
Dec 10, 1877
Sep 4, 1917

In Memory of George Washington
Basket, son of Mary, wife of
A. Basket. age: 1 month.

Several unmarked graves.

This Cemetery is located behind the Hinesville Church, Hinesville.

George Pratt
Mar 16, 1781
May 24, 1855

Jane, Consort of
George Pratt, Born in
Rockingham Co., N.C. & Died
Jan 15, 1851
aged: 65 yrs.

Phines O. Pratt
Sep 20, 1852
Aug 3, 1853

Several unmarked graves.

This Cemetery is located about 1½ miles Northwest of Flat Creek, Tenn.

Charlie Hix
1875-1947

W. S. Hix
May 14, 1825
May 9, 1913
& wife:
Martha Ann Hix
Jan 5, 1827
Apr 14, 1894

Sallie, wife of
W. S. Hix
Jan 1, 1848
Mar 25, 1907

Louisa F. Hix*
Mar 1, 1860
Sep 28, 1876
*Louisa Frances Hix

William W. Hix
1858-1926
& Wife:
Francis E. Hix*
1861-1934
*Francis E. Reagor Hix

Our Little Ernest L., son
of W. W. & F. E. Hix
Oct 10, 1882
Sep 28, 1885

Joseph S. Kimery*
*Joseph Steel Kimery
1859-1942
&
Laura J. Kimery*
* Laura J. Parks Kimery
1862-1935

William B. Kimery*
Tennessee
Pvt 117 Inf 30 Div
May 17, 1935
*Born Jun 16, 1888

Fanny Bird Kimery
Oct 31, 1902
Mar 30, 1904

Mitchel T., son of
J. E. & A. D. Frost
aged: 11m & 12d.(no dates)

William D. H., son of
J. E. & A. D. Frost
age: 1y & 4m. (no dates)

Frank Hix
Aug 7, 1851
Jul 5, 1916
&
Kate Hix
Aug 28, 1853
Jan 5, 1921

John E. Hix*
Died Aug 5, 1852
(no age given)
*Born Jul 7, 1848

Aseanith M. Hix*
Died Jan 23, 1861
(no age given)
*Born Oct 24, 1853

Martha N. Jane Nix (Hix?)
Died Jun 4, 1861
(no age given)

James E. Hix*
Died Jan 4, 1850
(no age given)
*Born Oct 30, 1849

Infant of
J. S. & L. J. Kimery
Born & Died
May 1, 1897

Joe Bryant, son of
J. S. & L. J. Kimery
Mar 25, 1897
Jun 24, 1899

Sidney Parkes, son of
J. S. & L. J. Kimery
Sep 27, 1890
Jun 5, 1892
aged: 1y, 8m, 8d.

Infant of
J. S. & L. J. Kimery
Sep 16, 1884
Sep 24, 1884

Bertie Lee, dau of
J. S. & L. J. Kimery
Apr 11, 1886
Nov 12, 1891
aged: 5y, 7m, 1d.

Malinda N., dau of
J. E. & A. D. Frost
aged: 2y, & 9m (no dates)

Eld. J. E. Frost
Apr 7, 1825
Mar 26, 1904
& wife:
Alcey D. Hix Frost**
Sep 29, 1826
Sep 6, 1899 **Dau of
Demarcus Hix

D. D. Hix
Jan 3, 1802
Sep 19, 1872
"In the 71st yr of his age"

Malinda Hix
Jan 8, 1804
Apr 30, 1874

Naomi E., dau of
D. D. & Maud Hix
Jun 9, 1878
Jul 17, 1878

Macy D. Gammill
1898-1932

Infant dau* of
Parks & Mary D. Gammill
1932
* Malinda Parks Gammill

Edwin Lee, son of
J. G. & H. F. Kimery
Sep 22, 1876
Jun 11, 1903
age: 26y, 8m, 19d.

Jackson Greer Kimery
1854-1939

Harriet Francis, wife of
J. G. Kimery
Oct 12, 1857
Dec 20, 1902

H. F., son of
J. G. & H. F. Kimery
Sep 22, 1876
Jan 11, 1908
age: 26y, 8m, 9d.

Frances C. Reagor, Consort of
William J. Reagor & dau of
D. D. & Malinda Hix
Dec 11, 1838
Oct 16, 1860

James E., son of
J. E. & A. D. Frost
aged: 3m & 22d. (no dates)

Dr. William J. Gordon
Feb 16, 1813
Aug 21, 1875
& Wife:
L. B. Gordon*
*Louise Black Gordon
Aug 2, 1829
Aug 25, 1911

Hettie Grace, Infant dau of
John F. & Dosid L. Shofner
Sep 9, 1880
Jan 9, 1881

Eula May, Infant dau of
John F. & Dosid L. Shofner
Jul 20, 1877
Sep 20, 1877
aged: 2months.

Albert N. Shofner
Jun 5, 1880
Mar 5, 1891
age: 10y & 9d.

Kate, wife of
G. F. Shofner
Mar 1, 1860
Sep 5, 1890
aged: 30y, 6m, 4d.

H. D., son of
H. H. & Lucinda Landess
Nov 27, 1851
Jul 16, 1852
age: 7m & 8d.

Lucinda S., wife of
H. H. Landers(Landess)
Oct 6, 1832
Jul 8, 1852
aged: 19y, 9m, 2d.

Ellen H., wife of
T. J. Stanfield & dau of
D. D. & Malinda Hix
Jul 13, 1836 & Died
Aug 30, 1855 of Typhoid
fever. age: 19y, 1m, 17d.

Infant Sons of
William J. & Louisa B. Gordon
(no dates)

Andrew J. Parks
Dec 11, 1855
Aug 17, 1901
age: 46 yrs.

Susan S., dau of
A. L. & Nancy M. Parkes
May 24, 1860
Dec 23, 1878
aged: 18y, 6m, 29d.

Dr. A. O. L. Parks   and   Nancy M. Parks
Jul 20, 1821   May 9, 1825
Jun 18, 1891   Jul 28, 1905

Several fieldstones, no
    inscriptions.

* by Roy Bearden Bible Records. ** by Newspaper.

Several unmarked graves.

24 CRANE CEMETERY   Map # 11
This Cemetery is located 1 mile Northwest of Flat Creek.

Nancy Crane
Born Jun 10, 1796
Died Aug 26, 1816

1 Adult grave beside N.C.'s
    no inscription.

Only 2 graves in Cemetery.

25 OLD FLAT CREEK CEMETERY   Map # 11
This Cemetery is in Flat Creek, off Hilltop Road.

Allie C., son of
William & Emma Farrar
Nov 3, 1892
Dec 7, 1895

Maggie M. Snell
Dec 15, 1850
Apr 19, 1912

Dora May, dau of
I. S. & Mary Parker
Jun 10, 1883
Oct 17, 1892

P. G. Williams
Sep 21, 1846
Apr 17, 1914

Marthy Jane, wife of
Thomas Word
May 13, 1827
Feb 13, 1913

R. F. Blankenship
Jun 2, 1854
Mar 24, 1905

Sallie Blankenship
Mar 5, 1860
(no date)

Asberry U. Blankenship
Oct 14, 1851
Jul   1852

Willie Blankenship
Jul 28, 1856
Apr 12, 1858

Nancy L. Blankenship
Sep 5, 1832
Aug 12, 1850

Dr. W. D. Frost
Died Sep 23, 1888
aged: 58 yrs.(broken)

Martha L., wife of
W. D. Frost
Died Sep 24, 1874
aged: 56y, 9m, 25d.

Horace Frost
Mar 5, 1864
Mar 29, 1884

Albert A. Ray
1861-1948

Dosia Parker, wife of
Albert A. Ray
Died Dec 22, 1890
aged: 25y, 8m, 28d.

"Mother"
Morning Bearden Glidewell
1827-1904
    & "Son"
Benjamin Franklin Glidewell
1857-1938

Rev. Joseph Hasty
Jan 22, 1817
Jul 2, 1881

Mary Hasty
Aug 2, 1820
Nov 4, 1886

Robert L. Gilliland
Oct 9, 1891
Sep 4, 1914

Willis Bearden
Jan 2, 1810
Jun 4, 1892
aged: 82 yrs.

Mahala, wife of
Willis Bearden
Died Aug 11, 1889
aged: 84 yrs.

Onez O., dau of
W. E. & Victoria Bearden
Apr 5, 1874
Jan 31, 1889

No marker:*
Revolutionary Soldier,
John Bearden
Born Mar 11, 1744 in
Spottsylvania Co., Va.
Died 1836 aged: 92 yrs.

M. J. B.(broken)
(no dates)

Mrs. Martha J. Cunningham
Jun 20, 1830
Nov 17, 1891

James P. Snoddy
Sep 14, 1814
Jan 29, 1876
    &
Julia A. Snoddy
Mar 7, 1830
Jul 3, 1913

Lena V. Bryant, Infant dau of
J. D. & M. A. Bryant
Sep 30, 1869
Feb 18, 1870

Elizabeth Bryant
Died Sep 10, 1868
age: abt 78 yrs.

Dennis Bryant
Born Sep 12, 1808
Died Jun 14, 1868

William M. Evins
Aug 11, 1787
Jun 26, 1852
    &
Elizabeth Evins
Oct 24, 1791
Sep 8, 1875

Manerva J. Evins
Apr 21, 182-(gone)
Jul 12, 1857

Elizabeth M. Evins
Dec 18, 1820
Jun 30, 1854

Mary E. Evins
Mar 14 1837
Aug 31, 1921

"Mother"
Sidney Gowen
May 16 1829
Jul 10, 1896
    & "Son"
George Gowen
Jan 3, 1859
Jan 21, 1931

Sophia, wife of
M. Hale
Jan 15, 1794
Jan 25, 1869
aged: 75y & 10d.

Thomas Dean
Oct 31, 1791
Jan 5, 1881
aged: 89y, 2m, 5d.

Cassander Dean
Born May 29, 1792
Married to Thomas Dean
Feb 18, 1817
Died Jan 5, 1884
aged: 91y, 7m, 6d.

Polly Grace Hurst
Sep 17, 1771
Jul 8, 1855
age: 83y, 9m, 10d.
"Member of the Baptist
Church for 70 yrs."

Note: The Revolutionary
Soldier, William Hurst, is
said to buried in this area.
Could the above be his wife?

Elizabeth Hurst
Aug 19, 1783
Married Jan 9, 1806
Died Dec 27, 1877
aged: 94y, 4m, 8d.

Addie Pauline, dau of
J. D. & S. B. Floyd
May 5, 1871
Mar 6, 1874

J. H. Farrar
Co C
Statesman

Elizabeth, wife of
John H. Farrar
Sep 21, 1800
Apr 29, 1886

Permelia M. Farrar
Apr 2, 1830
Feb 3, 1903

Nan Farrar
(no dates)

Elisha Eddy, son of
J. H. & M. A. Womack
Apr 10, 1875
Nov 25, 1875

Alfred Campbell
Apr 15, 1806
Jan 2, 1863

Sarah Campbell
Jan 14, 1811
Apr 10, 1869

Thomas J. Campbell
May 7, 1842
Jan 23, 1864

J. A., son of
Jno. N. & M. A. Harris
Aug 17, 1859
Aug 23, 1885

Carrie J., wife of
W. B. Lyon
Died Jun 10, 1888
aged: 22 yrs.

John N. Harris
Born May 17, 1829
married to Elizabeth Reagor
Jul 28, 1867
Died Jan 31, 1895
aged: 65y, 8m, 14d.

T. K. Gowen
Jan 28, 1863
Feb 17, 1893

Glenn Gowen
Sep 26, 1857
May 30, 1938

John Stephens
Nov 12, 1854
Oct 25, 1913

Mary Ann Stephens
Aug 23, 1864
Nov 27, 1885

Charley L. Stephens
Jun 10, 1882
Nov 26, 1903

M. A. Reaves
Dec 2, 1819
Feb 18, 1872

John Reaves
1854-1924

Elizabeth Reaves
Sep 27, 1852
Sep 22, 1879

J. M. Tillett
Jul 5, 1849
Jan 26, 1909

Ette Hannes, wife of
J. M. Tillett
Oct 22, 1857
Jul 17, 1896

Howard F. Kingree
Sep 24, 1880
Jul 27, 1896

Grace A. Kingree
Feb 7, 1879
Jul 14, 1896

Nora B. Kingree
Dec 25, 1881
Apr 18, 1890

John P. McManis
Jan 3, 1843
Nov 23, 1905
& wife:
Nancy Jane McManis
Mar 19, 1841
Dec 25, 1896

Elmo Finney
Sep 20, 1885
Jul 17, 1897

Sallie Floyd
Sep 1, 1799
Oct 18, 1891

Departed this life by
drowning in the Barren Fork
of Duck River near Normandy
May 1, 1859, Tarlton C. &
Virginia T., son & dau of
Thomas & Mary A. Newsom.
T.C.:aged 23y, 3m, 24d.
V.T.:aged 17y, 7m, 29d.

John A. Stanfield
Jul 16, 1853
Aug 3, 1869

Syrus, son of
A. M. & Mary A. Keith
Jul 13, 1869
Dec 28, 1891

Meeklee, son of
A. M. & Mary A. Keith
Jul 5, 1871
Oct 14, 1891

Delilah, wife of
Dillard Brooks
Jan 26, 1812
Aug 20, 1888

Elijah Floyd**
Feb 15, 1798
Sep 27, 1876
** Son of David Floyd, Sr.

No marker:**
David Floyd, Sr.
A Revolutionary Soldier, &
wife, who was a Norman, is
buried in this Cemetery.
(no dates)

Mary Ann, wife of
Elisha Bobo
May 18, 1812
Jan 30, 1877

J. C. (footmarker)

Herbert*, son of
J. W. & M. E. Frost
Died Nov 1, 1880
aged: 3y, 11m, 10d.
* Herbert, Born Nov 21, 1876
son of Joshua Wright &
Mary Ellen Reagor Frost.

John Ray, son of
J. W. & M. E. Frost
Died Aug 15, 1885
aged: 1y, 2m, 18d.

No marker:*
Caldonia Ann Reagor, wife
of Marion Hutson, & dau of
Abraham & Elizabeth Lacy
Reagor.
Born Mar 10, 1840
Married 1866
Died Feb 2, 1902

No marker:*
Martha Campbell Reagor
wife of Milton Alexander
Reagor & dau of Alfred &
Sarah Reeves Campbell
(no dates)

J. C.(foot marker)

Leander C. Clenney
Tennessee
Pvt 605 SVC Bn Engrs Corps
W. W. I
Sep 22, 1886
Aug 4, 1953

Charles J. McClenney
1861-1952
&
Finette M. McClenney
1867-1945

HALE CEMETERY

Infant Son of
Paul & Alice Hale
Nov 24, 1943

Roger Gowen Hale
Dec 7, 1937
Jul 7, 1939

W. Birnie Floyd
Jul 20, 1867
Jan 27, 1934
&
Etta Hale Floyd
Apr 12, 1866
Mar 16, 1950

Infant son of
Charles J. & Lizzie Hale
Dec 31, 1894
Jan 3, 1895

Lillis Hale
Apr 17, 1896
Apr 23, 1967

W. Joe Hale
1861-1934

Mary Cassie Hale
1907-1909

James M. Hale
1873-1936

Mamie Robinson Hale
1876-1939

Alfred H. Hale
Jan 15, 1859
Jan 10, 1921

Mary E. Hale
Oct 2, 1863
Aug 16, 1949

Ozelle, dau of Charles J. &
Lizzie Hale
Aug 26, 1889-Oct 19, 1893

Jno. F. Renegar
Feb 24, 1865
Oct 19, 1920
&
Nancy J. Renegar
Mar 13, 1868
Mar 10, 1919

D. D. Hix
Sep 13, 1855
Dec 26, 1934

Maud Hale Hix
Feb 1, 1856
Nov 29, 1923

Mary Edna Hix
Feb 8, 1881
Dec 21, 1969

Charles J. Hale   and
Feb 4, 1860
Oct 6, 1932

Clark M. Hale
Jun 21, 1902
May 28, 1903

Fannie May Hale
Mar 17, 1905
Aug 8, 1905

J. R. Hale
Jul 28, 1823
Jul 13, 1910
&
A. C. Hale
Aug 14, 1834
Oct 2, 1914

Jordan, son of
J. R. & Cassie Hale
Dec 14, 1870
Jun 16, 1897

Elizabeth Gowen Hale
Aug 21, 1866
Apr 19, 1933

Ardecy Alllona Nelms
Apr 1, 1858
Oct 29, 1876

* by Frost Family Records.

** Records of William Floyd.

Polly Nelms Sauls
May 25, 1838
Dec 20, 1876

Infant son of
John & Polly Sauls
1876

L. Logan
May 31, 1827
Nov 26, 1908

Mary A., wife of
J. L. Hutson & dau of
Watson & Ann Floyd
Nov 27, 1853
Mar 10, 1876

Infant Son of
J. L. & Mary A. Hutson
(no dates)

26 ROSEBANK CEMETERY   Map # 11
This Cemetery is located just South of Flat Creek, on New Herman Road.

Les Nelson
Jun 30, 1907
Aug 10, 1972

Henry L. Rutledge
Dec 30, 1895

&
Leila Porter Rutledge
Feb 24, 1903

Arthur D. Lightfoot, Jr.
1950-1968
&
Christopher D. Lightfoot
1959-1968
&
Stephen A. Lightfoot
1952-1968

Frances Wiggins, wife of
Lionel R. Barrett
Mar 24, 1909
Aug 14, 1966

Van Deering Snell
Dec 12, 1886
Sep 9, 1957
&
Lois McClenney Snell
Jan 11, 1896
Nov 23, 1965

Judge Miller Mac Farrar
Sep 14, 1911
Nov 23, 1970
&
Mabel Phillips Farrar
Mar 24, 1920

Clayton Farrar
1880-1941
&
Elizabeth Farrar
1883-1972

Clara Bob Farrar James
1910-1952

J. T. Davis
1878-1942
&
Edna Davis
1883-1953

Hugh Frank Womack
Sep 9, 1896
Jan 18, 1900

Carroll L. Martin
Mar 27, 1899

&
Eula Gilliland Martin
Sep 8, 1896
Jun 15, 1974

Dave H. Ashby
Mar 19, 1889
Jul 7, 1971
&
Clara W. Ashby
Dec 27, 1890
----
married Jun 27, 1908

Margaret S. Wiggins Reeves
Feb 1, 1886
Mar 5, 1975

Roscoe Shofner
Dec 9, 1887
Sep 11, 1965
&
Nell Davidson Shofner
Jul 12, 1888

&
Roscoe D. Shofner
Nov 1, 1922

John T. Hix
Sep 9, 1919

&
Mary E. Hix
Oct 26, 1925
Jun 8, 1963

J. T. Hix, Jr.
1961-1961
(Howell)

Barbara Hix
1956-1962
(McFarlin-Thompson)

Walter L. Hix
Aug 7, 1874
Sep 5, 1950

Eula May Hix
Aug 19, 1878
Apr 15, 1966

Bradford Earl Hix   and
Dec 9, 1881

Albert R. Clanton
Dec 1, 1938
Jul 15, 1972

Clara Anne,
Jan 9, 1971
Infant dau of
Phillip T. & Betty L. Farrar

Billy Dwight Ervin
Tennessee
Sp4 1Bn 98 Arty 2 armd Div
Jun 29, 1945
Dec 7, 1968

Horace C. Bartlett
May 10, 1891

&
Ezell Snell Cobb Bartlett
Jul 22, 1890
Jul 4, 1968

Albert Estin Bridges
Dec 23, 1893
Jul 15, 1972
&
Aline Noblitt Bridges
Oct 17, 1898

Allison M. Cook
May 28, 1928
Jun 15, 1968
&
Claytie R. Cook
Sep 11, 1929

Eugenia R. Cook
Mar 2, 1922
May 5, 1972

Verna A. Snell
Oct 24, 1889
Jul 27, 1929

Fannie Snell
Jun 6, 1861
Aug 18, 1934

Arnie H. Snell
Aug 27, 1897
Dec 26, 1932

Hester Watson Hix
Dec 13, 1884
Jan 1, 1967

Henry Hix
Apr 1, 1888
Mar 10, 1972

Effie S. Hix
1896-1973
(Howell)

Ernest Love Hix
Jul 30, 1921
Jul 20, 1974

Harold Snell
1920-1974
(Gowen-Smith)

W. William Bearden
Oct 3, 1906
Mar 19, 1967
&
Mabel S. Bearden
Jul 4, 1917

Isaac L. Travis
1879-1941
&
Sarah B. Travis
1885-1958

Joe B. Rosborough
Jun 24, 1896
Sep 23, 1966
&
Kathleen C. Rosborough
Jan 14, 1901
Nov 15, 1971

William Claude Hix
Jul 17, 1886
Apr 17, 1934
&
Louise Love Hix
Dec 28, 1897
Feb 18, 1974

William Claude Hix, Jr.
1917-1942

Sarah Vivian Hix
Oct 11, 1925
Feb 16, 1926
&
Infant Son of
W. C. & Louise Hix
Apr 5, 1916

W. J. Farrar
Nov 26, 1855
Apr 2, 1912

278

Richard P. Mullins
1876-1934
&
Luna V. Mullins
1877-1963

Monnie, dau of
W. J. & Eliza Farrar
Dec 10, 1879
Dec 10, 1902

Sallie, dau of
A. J. & Sarah E. Womack
Nov 23, 1880
Jun 18, 1900

Lucile, dau of
A. J. & Sarah E. Womack
Jan 10, 1888
Sep 1, 1901

Bertie, dau of
A. J. & Sarah E. Womack
Aug 2, 1882
Nov 2, 1901

Alpha Williams
Nov 2, 1873
Sep 3, 1901

Ollie H. Williams
Dec 1, 1876
Apr 27, 1903

W. A. Williams
May 12, 1852
Mar 30, 1912

Josie B. Williams
Mar 5, 1857
Jul 17, 1945

Tennessee, dau of
O. G. Steagall & wife of
W. A. Williams
Jul 2, 1851
Oct 17, 1898

Ura Bearden, wife of
Alpha Williams
1877-1957

Mike M. Womack
Sep 5, 1879
Feb 17, 1959
&
Elma Bearden Womack
Aug 19, 1880
Sep 19, 1966

Verna Floyd, Infant son of
Wilson & Mabel Bearden
Aug 10, 1947
Aug 14, 1947

Jarrell F. Gammill
Jan 13, 1872
May 3, 1906

Closs Gordon
1882-1940
&
Myrtle Gordon
1885-1973

James C. Bryant
Nov 25, 1870
Sep 1, 1912

John C. Bryant
Dec 10, 1843
Jun 29, 1929

Louise Bearden Bryant
Sep 11, 1848
Dec 30, 1901

Jesse L. Bryant
Jan 7, 1883
Sep 30, 1907

Edith Ione Reagor
Jan 26, 1906
Nov 18, 1908

Louis Pearson
May 31, 1869
May 8, 1899
&
Florence B. Pearson
Sep 8, 1871
Jun 18, 1957

William Bibb Pearson
1881-1937

Alberts Pearson
Jan 30, 1907
Jul 30, 1973

Floyd Bearden
1878-1940

Ada Reagor Bearden
1882-1958

Earl, Infant Son of
Floyd & Ada Bearden
1908-1909

James A. Bearden
Tennessee
Pvt Field Artillery, W.W.II
Jul 8, 1916
Oct 31, 1945

W. E. Bearden
1842-1923

Victoria Bearden
1851-1929

Henry C. Bearden
1860-1923

Bettie Bearden
1868-1951

Lottie H. Gammill
Dec 30, 1878
Oct 7, 1955

Margaret Gammill Wiseman
Mar 1, 1904
Nov 22, 1970

Ray Gowen
1898-1963
&
Ray Gowen, II
1937-1937
&
Hazel Gowen
1901-1937
&
Sara Jeanne Gowen
1934-1937

Finn Gowen
1870-1940
&
Kitty Gowen
1871-1954

Thurston Farrar
Jan 24, 1873
Sep 14, 1961
&
Clara Holt Farrar
Feb 25, 1881
Feb 7, 1967

Onie May, wife of
T. E. Harkin
Jul 9, 1879
Jul 13, 1900

"Mother"
Emily Reagor Bearden
1835-1911

Richard Calvin Bearden
Mar 4, 1835
Mar 26, 1893
age: 58y & 22d.
&
Emley C. Bearden(same as above)
Feb 28, 1835
Jul 17, 1911

Cecil M. Bearden
1892-1971
&
Alta Mai Bearden
1898-

Carl W. Frost
Feb 16, 1892
Feb 11, 1967

Ollie Lee Frost
Aug 25, 1881
Jan 20, 1964

Sam Bearden
1871-1947
&
Ida Bearden
1883-19

Infant Dau of
Mr & Mrs Sam Bearden
Jan 7, 1918

Nancy Hix Hudson
1883-1975
(Gowen-Smith)

Andrew Womack
Oct 29, 1839
Oct 29, 1904

Sarah E., wife of
A. J. Womack
Mar 19, 1847
Dec 8, 1898

Bettie T., dau of
A. J. & Sarah E. Womack
Nov 26, 1878
Aug 3, 1899

Maudy M., dau of
O. C. & Minnie Womack
Mar 7, 1898
Jan 25, 1899

Wynn Bearden
Oct 19, 1823
Mar 27, 1903
& wife:
Elizabeth J. Bearden
Jul 18, 1826
Jan 7, 1903

Malissa E., Consort of
W. G. Smiley
Oct 9, 1855
Jul 22, 1910

S. I. R.(footstone)

Betsy B. Lacy
1873-1936

Wayne B. Womack
1908-1933

T. J. Baxter
Feb 22, 1849
Feb 26, 1909

Mary Isabell Gowen
1874-1957

Nancy Waddle Dance
Feb 1, 1882
Mar 23, 1959

William Thomas Bicknell
Apr 27, 1958
Apr 28, 1958

Alvin E. Jackson
Jul 18, 1904
Aug 23, 1963

Thomas K. Pearson
1883-1921
&
Musa M. Pearson
1889-1965

J. L. Hutson
1852-1927

Nettie Hutson
1855-1932

Frankie Gammill Moore
Oct 21, 1906

Leland Bearden
1887-1909

Lonnie Bearden
1891-1971

Lillian F. Bearden
1894-1971

Henry L. Woodard
Jun 25, 1900
Feb 14, 1961
&
Olive B. Woodard
Oct 11, 1903

John B. Woodard
Dec 2, 1923
Jun 26, 1928

Mary Adams
May 7, 1846
Feb 8, 1929

Ollie Clyde Landers
Dec 18, 1905
Oct 22, 1971

Ruth Foster Landers
Aug 30, 1908
May 23, 1973

Virginia Parker Landers
1906-1942

Charles James Enochs
Jun 11, 1870
Apr 13, 1960
&
Annie Holt Enochs
Jul 27, 1876
Jun 18, 1957

Lola May Parker
Jan 12, 1883
Jan 12, 1962

Edmond Cooper Parker
Dec 5, 1873
Apr 11, 1961
&
Myrtle Enochs Parker
Feb 21, 1877
Aug 8, 1954

Dr. M. A. L. Enochs
Dec 19, 1843
Mar 17, 1918
&
Elizabeth A. Enochs
Apr 4, 1845
Jan 27, 1919

W. C. Enochs   and
Jan 15, 1874
Oct 13, 1919

Clarence A. Hart, Sr.
Jun 6, 1901
Oct 17 1965

Thomas Roy Hix
Sep 22, 1907
Oct 17, 1967

Knox M. Hart
Jan 7, 1905
Jun 16, 1953

William Ernest Snell
1882-1945

Pearl W. Snell
1890-1959

Capt. E. G. Fleming
   Co F
5th Tenn Cav.

James W. Robinson
Oct 19, 1907
Jan 12, 1972
&
Dolly M. Robinson
Sep 6, 1912

Alden M. Shofner
Nov 6, 1870
Feb 24, 1944

William Edgar Shofner
Oct 4, 1884
Dec 25, 1929

Elisha Cobb
Mar 17, 1887
Feb 25, 1970
&
Annie Lee Cobb
Nov 11, 1892
Aug 27, 1966

Pierre Parker Weatherly
Sep 17, 1887
May 27, 1933

Mollie C. Lacy
Feb 18, 1843
Jan 30, 1921

Charlie G. Willisma
1870-1926
&
Beulah S. Williams
1873-1940

Francis H. Williams
Jul 31, 1846
Oct 31, 1919

Martha A., wife of
F. H. Williams
Nov 18, 1845
Feb 2, 1906

Leila Reagor Enochs
Feb 25, 1885

Joe T. Williamson
1860-1941
&
Sallie E. Williamson
1865-1937

Mary R. Williamson
Apr 23, 1895
(no date)

Lucile Williamson
1903-1920

James Burrum
1865-1931
&
Thursa E.(Ellen) Burrum
Jul 13, 1869
Jul 26, 1920

Edward J. Hale
Feb 3, 1936
Jun 2, 1971

Alice H. Hale
Apr 11, 1902

Charles Paul Hale
Apr 2, 1899

Garry Benjamin Parker
1936-1942

Rosanah Parker
1845-1924

Grace Bobo Parker
Nov 20, 1880
May 19, 1970

Ben Parker
1873-1933

Walter E. Bearden
1875-1942

Zula Parker Bearden
1878-1961

Joseph Renegar
1823-1909
&
Sarah Renegar
Mar 30, 1836
Jul 21, 1909

J. H. Renegar
Mar 27, 1863
Sep 4, 1907
&
Libby Shofner Renegar
Feb 19, 1872
Apr 14, 1968

J. B. Parker
1848-1919
&
Ellen Cheshire Parker
1852-1934

William F. Parker
1885-1913

Mary C., wife of
T. H. Hutson
Nov 7, 1831
Aug 30, 1918

R. B. Hutson
Jun 1, 1868
Mar 29, 1936

Ethel O. Hutson
Jan 4, 1883
Aug 30, 1944

James Roy, son of
R. B. & Ethel Hutson
Feb 5, 1915
Dec 12, 1916

Robert S. Hutson
Oct 14, 1882
Feb 7, 1963

John Simmons
Apr 10, 1899
Oct 19, 1973

Alma W. Simmons
Aug 19, 1896
Dec 12, 1970

Infant Hix
1962-1962
(Gowen-Smith)

Ollie J. Renegar
Apr 25, 1893
Sep 5, 1960

Dollie M. Renegar
Aug 25, 1898
Mar 18, 1920

Duke Bowers Piper
Tennessee
Tec 5 789 Mil Police Bn
W. W. II
Aug 25, 1901
Sep 27, 1947
&
Hazelle E. Piper
1900-19

Jas. B. Shofner
Jun 14, 1849
Nov 19, 1911
&
C. E. Shofner
Apr 3, 1850
May 5, 1936

Ada Shofner
Apr 11, 1876
Oct 21, 1963

Alice Shofner
Jan 2, 1882
Aug 12, 1971

Elizabeth J. Payne
Jul 27, 1856
Jan 23, 1905

Addie C. McRory
Jan 21, 1878
May 27, 1964

J. W. Frost
Apr 26, 1854
Dec 31, 1931
&
M. E. Frost
Nov 8, 1854
Jul 2, 1911

Elizabeth Harris
Mar 18, 1834
Apr 10, 1913

"Father"
J. F. Pollock
Apr 1, 1844
Sep 8, 1903
&
"Mother"
F. E. Pollock
Apr 27, 1850
(no date)

Walter A. Johnson
1860-1936
&
Brunette Parker Johnson
1867-1941

Mary Ann Parker
Apr 8, 1843
Dec 2, 1919

Isiah Parker
Jun 5, 1830
Sep 8, 1904

Charles G. Parker
Dec 2, 1864
Aug 1, 1913

George W. Floyd
Born Mar 23, 1870
Died June 26, 1900
at Majay Jay,
Philippine Islands
37th Regt U.S.V.
Co G.

Dr. F. B. Reagor
1861-1917

Fannie Sullivan, wife of
F. B. Reagor, M.D.
1867-1894

Reuel S. Reagor
Mar 12, 1893
May 13, 1958

Infant Floyd Reagor
1894

Mary Jane, wife of
W. D. Blankinship
Mar 6, 1835
Nov 18, 1900

J. G. Parker, Sr.
1852-1928

Raus W. Bearden
Feb 4, 1910

&
Virginia H. Bearden
Jul 11, 1915
Feb 8, 1971

I. S. Reagor
Jun 17, 1858
Nov 1, 1908
&
Sallie R. Reagor
May 22, 1863
Oct 26, 1946

William E. Raney
1884-1944 (TM)

Carol Ann Peace
Jun 8, 1955
May 18, 1956

Mrs. L. P. Crigler
1866-1961
(Gowen-Smith)

Walter Lewis Crigler
1855-1938
&
Lizzie Dean Crigler
1862-1960

Willie Parker Pearson
Dec 23, 1884
Dec 29, 1955

William Amos Gammill
Mar 4, 1871
May 2, 1951

Lizzie P. Gammill
Dec 27, 1878
May 11, 1968

Mary Morris Gammill
May 18, 1903
Aug 1, 1904

James Emmet Reagor
Sep 13, 1863
Oct 31, 1944
&
Avie Jane Henderson Reagor
Jan 28, 1882
Jul 13, 1952

Infant of
J. E. & S. Reagor
Born Feb 15, 1892

Sallie Ingle, wife of
J. E. Reagor
Died Jul 2, 1894
aged: 24y & 16d.

Rilla A. Blankinship
Sep 27, 1861
Jul 3, 1909

Anna Parker
1861-1926

James R. Haithcote
Tennessee
Cpt. H.H.C. 1 Bn 50 Inf.
Vietnam, BSM & OLC ARCOM PH
Sep 25, 1944
Oct 16, 1972

Eardley W. Haithcote
1882-1964
&
Lula E. Haithcote
1888-1952

Eura Robinson Raney
Nov 22, 1892
Aug 29, 1952

Ollie Marsh Robinson
Sep 2, 1881
Feb 7, 1925
&
Nettie Alma Robinson
Sep 7, 1882
Jul 5, 1925

Elam Robinson
Oct 29, 1886
Jan 13, 1929
(picture)

John E. Haynes
Aug 25, 1888
Oct 15, 1970
&
Irene P. Haynes
Jul 22, 1900

Rebecca Frances Haynes
1937

Christine G. Gunn
May 25, 1899
Mar 7, 1972

Wilma G. Smoot
Apr 15, 1905
Jun 30, 1971

"Father"
W. H. Kingree
May 31, 1850
Sep 26, 1906
&
"Mother"
F. M. Kingree
Jan 19, 1851
Feb 5, 1911

Charles D. Hix
May 26, 1858
Jan 17, 1899

Ida Hix Shoffner
Feb 29, 1868
Feb 10, 1938

Albert Dillingham
1867-1902

Clark Parker
1899-1900

Albert Frierson Parker
1870-1943
&
Otha Stanfield Parker
1875-1906

Johnson Goodrich Parker
Jul 9, 1900
Jan 20, 1963

C. V. Bobo
1853-1925

Martha Leititia Bobo
1858-1940

Argie V. Bobo
Jan 18, 1883
Jul 22, 1969

E. C. Bobo
1898-1906

Andrew Womack
1880-1934

Georgia P. Womack
1881-1960

Price Womack, M.D.
1903-1947

Paul Womack
1905-1962

Horace Price Parker
Aug 25, 1902
Aug 10, 1904

Joseph G. Parker
Aug 21, 1876
Apr 7, 1960
&
Ermine P. Parker
Apr 4, 1876
Aug 24, 1964

Howard, son of
John & Nora Kingree
Jul 4, 1904
(date in gournd, deep)

Alford Lee, son of
John & Nora Kingree
Aug 20, 1905
(in ground) 1908

John A. Kingree
Mar 12, 1877
Jan 10, 1948

Nora Kingree
Mar 12, 1884
Sep 9, 1938

W. C. Dillingham
Jan 25, 1869-Apr 26, 1901

Gertie Dillingham Ray
Dec 31, 1875-Apr 6, 1951

James Oscar Shofner
May 10, 1886
Jul 15, 1963
&
Mary F. Cooper Shofner
Nov 8, 1893

Porter Shofner
1895-1975
(Gowen-Smith)

Margaret Elizabeth Shofner
1922-1930

Baby of
Porter & Sarah Shofner
1923

George F. Shofner
1854-1942
&
Mary L. Shofner
Jan 20, 1859
Sep 21, 1925

M. J. Throneberry
1861-19(no date)
&
Bettie Throneberry
1865-1937

Richard M. Snoddy
1865-1937
&
Dora Lee Snoddy

Robert Lacy Bearden
1865-1945

Susie H. Bearden
1865-1922

O. E. Bearden
1866-1932

Mabel H. Bearden
1894-1969
(Harrison)

Ray L. Mitchell
Tennessee
Pvt U.S.Army   W.W.I
Nov 11, 1895
Mar 20, 1873

E. A. Reagor
Dec 9, 1836
Jul 25, 1904

Martha Ann Reagor
Apr 7, 1839
Jul 16, 1919

Isaiah Parker, son of
Charles G. & Mollie R.
Parker
Mar 24, 1895
Jul 10, 1948

Doyle B. Parker
Sep 22, 1883
Aug 30, 1965
&
Lena H. Parker
Sep 26, 1889
Apr 18, 1959

Nell Hale
July 14, 1892
Mar 24, 1972
& "Sister"
Mary Cassie Hale
Jun 7, 1907
Oct 29, 1909
"Interred in Hale Cemetery"
(Old Flat Creek Cemetery)

J. Dennis Hale
May 18, 1902

&
Thelma D. Hale
Mar 20, 1904
Jan 24, 1951

W. Joe Hale
Oct 11, 1861
Nov 25, 1934
"Interred at Hale Cemetery"
(Old Flat Creek Cemetery)
&
Orrie B. Hale
May 30, 1871
Jun 15, 1964

Abidah Atwell
Co I
1st U.S. Inf.
Sharpshtrs

George C. Gowen
Tennessee
Cpl U.S.Marine Corps, Korea
Nov 17, 1933
Sep 7, 1961

John D. Floyd
1839-1919

Susan M., wife of
J. D. Floyd
1840-1919

Emma Floyd
1866-1919

Helen E. Conditt
Oct 11, 1919
Nov 1, 1920

Beulah Law Conditt
Jun 27, 1891
Dec 24, 1931

Caleb W. Halmontaller
Feb 23, 1909
Jan 17, 1975
&
Rose C. Halmontaller
Nov 7, 1914

Alice Parker Linch
Aug 19, 1890
Feb 15, 1974

Ozelle Floyd Martin
Dec 31, 1876
Sep 17, 1963

James W. Floyd
Nov 7, 1843
Jun 17, 1911
&
Mary A. Floyd
Jan 13, 1847
Jun 5, 1918

Nancy G. Cunningham
Jan 17, 1818
Apr 15, 1893

William R. Young
1883-1969
(Howell-Thompson)

Charlie Young
1877-1962
(Howell-Thompson)

Ray J. King
(no dates)
&
Dora L. Ray

John B. Ray
1874-1934
&
Argie L. Ray
1884-1941

Lena Gowen Hice
1905-1938

Peyton L. Williams
Feb 22, 1844
May 17, 1901
&
Sophronia A. Williams
Oct 9, 1847
Jun 13, 1925

Thomas A. Williams
1870-1951
&
Mary Lou Williams
1878-1961

John A. Hix
1878-1952
&
Joe Etta Hix
1882-1962

Mandanie Templeton
Jul 18, 1848
May 21, 1921
"Mother"

James E. Bryant
1878-1924
&
Seiota C. Bryant
1884-1934

James Franklin Womack
1867-1936
&
Tennie Kiser Womack
1870-1957

Robert B. Bradshaw
1869-1941
&
Eunice R. Bradshaw
1880-1949

George T. Reagor
Jun 14, 1894
Mar 14, 1972
&
Irene W. Reagor
Nov 18, 1896

J. W. Hitt
Jun 9, 1885
Apr 21, 1960
&
Dora Lee Hitt
Nov 9, 1887

David Franklin Shofner, Jr.
1918-1919

Sara Lynn Shofner
1933-1934

J. W. Snell
1858-1940

Thomas Edward Snell
1897-1954

Della Pauline Snell
1875-1954

James T. Williams
1824-1909
&
Elizabeth Williams
1832-1911

John A. Williams
1859-1925
&
Bettie May Williams
1870-1965

Jas. T. Williams, Jr.
Feb 15, 1863
Nov 26, 1896
aged: 33y, 9m, 11d.

Jas. F. Farrar
Oct 4, 1819
Mar 16, 1904
&
Sarah J. Farrar
Apr 15, 1839
Nov 14, 1921

Joe W. Farrar
Jul 20, 1866
Jan 7, 1950

Vester Coleman, son of
J. E. & S. F. Bryant
Jan 9, 1903
Jun 21, 1904

James D. Bryant
1847-1932

Mary Eglentine, wife of
J. D. Bryant
1846-1924

Rev. Ernest M. Bryant
Nov 4, 1881
Jan 22, 1970
&
Suda Hicks Bryant
Sep 4, 1883
May 22, 1918

Ernest M. Bryant, Jr.
Born & Died
Jul 31, 1909

R. Foster Farrar
1895-1971
(Howell)

James Samuel Farrar
Oct 15, 1857
Jul 21, 1928

Ella Warren Farrar
Jun 16, 1868
Jun 5, 1947

Henry Cecil Sutton
Tennessee
BM1 U.S.N.R. W.W.II
Aug 15, 1908
Feb 7, 1965
&
Elizabeth H. Sutton
Feb 25, 1918

Allen E. Bobo
1891-1945

Walter Gowen
Aug 29, 1884
Oct 3, 1906

Clara D. Gowen
Mar 11, 1881
May 8, 1909

Henry Lee Gowen
Oct 5, 1882
Jun 27, 1905

Benjamin Franklin Rudd
1852-1934
&
Elnora Josephine Rudd
1875-1934

Clyde Gardner
1888-1961

Floye Gardner Bomar
1889-1956

Frank Gardenr
1885-1931

Jeff Gardner
1861-1930

Cora Gardner
1862-1945

Kelly Gardner
1902-1956

Haskell Clenney
1905-1970
&
Jessie Fay Clenney
1915-

Thomas M. Farrar
1871-1948

Roy E. Womble
Sep 30, 1901
Mar 15, 1975
&
Aline B. Womble
Oct 2, 1903
Dec 13, 1964

Billy Clay Raney
Tennessee
Pfc U.S.Army
Korea
Oct 22, 1931
Aug 4, 1969

George Rufus Swing
1875-1948
&
Argie R. Swing
1883-1953

J. J. "Bud" Hix
1868-1951

Lois Parker Hix
1870-1941

Georgia Frost Driskill
Aug 29, 1875
Jul 8, 1959

Andrew Jackson Driskill
Aug 17, 1872
Apr 16, 1962

Harry R. Driskill
Tennessee
Pvt 329 Inf 83 Div W.W.I
Sep 24, 1896
Jun 19, 1947
&
Rosalie Broiles Driskill
Feb 1, 1904

Ethel P. Farrar
1878-1955

Joseph F. Gowen
Oct 22, 1854
Oct 17, 1914
&
Fannie E. Gowen
May 18, 1856
Jul 13, 1901

W. P. Mullins
Sep 26, 1883
May 11, 1943
&
Laylon Hice Mullins
Sep 11, 1887
Oct 17, 1961

Everette W. Mullins, Jr.
1947-

Mary Swing Mullins
1908-

Everette W. Mullins, Sr.
1906-1969

Jerman W. Ogle, Sr.
Jul 23, 1891
Feb 6, 1962

Leatha A. Ogle
Apr 12, 1886
Mar 13, 1962

Jerman W. Ogle, Jr.
May 11, 1925

Sara Reagor Ogle
Aug 10, 1926

Dorris L. Gardner
1923-1961

#27 SHOOK CEMETERY   Map # 11
This Cemetery is located about 1 mile South of Flat Creek, Tenn.

Thomas Edward Coleman
1863-1927

Jesse Coleman
Sep 17, 1818
Feb 22, 1891

William J. Coleman
May 17, 1854
Oct 29, 1881

Mary F. Coleman
Apr 18, 1854
Sep 1, 1892

Thurman, son of
John & Mattie Coleman
Jun 20, 1888
Feb 25, 1889

John Coleman
Dec 8, 1855
Jun 16, 1889

Joseph N. Coleman
Feb 11, 1861
Nov 25, 1881

Everline G. Coleman
Jan 8, 1882
Oct 26, 1882

Ellen G. Coleman
Feb 4, 1883
Aug 29, 1883

David E. Reagor*
Sep 24, 1828
Jul 17, 1858
* David Ekels Reagor
(stone in very bad condition)

Lucinda, dau of
Marion & Jane Guthrie
Jul 24, 1858
Feb 20, 1889

Infant of
W. H. & A. E. Williams
Jul 28, 1914

Nancy Caroline Dean
Jun 21, 1828
Nov 30, 1899

Mary R., wife of
Thomas H. Dance
Oct 9, 1862
Aug 25, 1881

W. S. Castleman*
1850-1923
* W. Scott Castleman

Andrew J. Driskill*
Feb 13, 1836
Apr 17, 1873
* Andrew Jackson Driskill
    mrd-Nov 21, 1869

Mary M. Driskill*
Jan 23, 1842
Jul 28, 1893
* Mary Margaret Driskill

Milton M., dau of
A. J. & M. N. Driskill
May 7, 1871
May 10, 1881

Ruth E. Farrar
Oct 9, 1865
Sep 21, 1879

John B. Reagor*
Feb 22, 1852
Dec 17, 1875
    & wife:
Mary C. Reagor*
Feb 9, 1854
Jan 9, 1876
*John Bell Reagor &
Mary Caldonia Reagor

J. M. Reagor*
*Jacob Newton Reagor
Dec 16, 1845
Jan 27, 1871
    &
I. N. Reagor*
*Isaac Newton Reagor
Dec 16, 1845
Aug 15, 1880
*Children of Abraham &
Elizabeth Lacy Reagor

George A. Reagor
May 20, 1830
Mar 18, 1862
"Burried with the Honors
of War"

Jane Coleman
Jan 16, 1831
Dec 10, 1880

Annie A., dau of
J. B. & E. V. Parker
Jan 21, 1878
Jan 22, 1878

Edgar, son of
J. B. & E. V. Parker
May 1, 1880
May 10, 1880

Rebeca Farrar
Nov 26, 1818
Nov 26, 1858

No marker:*
Abraham Shook
Born 1770
Died after 1850, census.

[Abraham Shook. Jr.
died in War of 1812]

Abm. Reagor
Oct 24, 1802
Feb 21, 1863
    &
Elizabeth Reagor
Nov 8, 1809
Jan 23, 1873

Mary R., wife of
S. L. Reagor, M.D.*
Nov 26, 1838
Aug 30, 1872
* Samuel Lacy Reagor

James B. Reagor*, Consort
of Elizabeth Reagor
Oct 22, 1800
May 12, 1863
* James Brock Reagor
  mrd-Sep 8, 1825

Elizabeth Covey, Born
Dec 27, 1806
Married to James B. Reagor
Sep 8, 1825
Died Dec 21, 1894
aged: 87y, 11m, 24d.

William J. Reagor
Mar 9, 1832
Oct 25, 1874

David Floyd**
Jun 19, 1786
Dec 18, 1856
aged: 70y & 6m.
** War of 1812

Mary Magdalene,**Consort of
David Floyd
Dec 9, 1793
Nov 22, 1856
aged: 62y, 11m, 13d.
** Mary Magdalene Floyd was
a Reagor, dau of Anthony
Reagor, SOR.

Several fieldstones, no insc.

Several unmarked graves.

No marker*
William Shook & wife:
Catherine Sears Shook

Rhoda Ellen, wife of
W. S. Castleman (page 283)
Oct 31, 1849
Aug 19, 1902

Clara E., dau of
W. S. & R. E. Castleman
Sep 16, 1875
Apr 25, 1876

John Benjamin Parker, Consort
of Rosanah M. Parker
Jul 1, 1837
Aug 12, 1873

Orrie P., dau of
J. F. & S. J. Farrar
Jan 9, 1870
Sep 9, 1870

Earnest W., son of
J. F. & M. Watson
May 22, 1875
Nov 25, 1876

Tom Luther Watson
Jun 14, 1882
Jan 31, 1883

James David Floyd
Aug 16, 1864
Jan 11, 1888

Ara L., dau of
James D. & Mary A. Floyd
Oct 26, 1887
Feb 2, 1888

Catharine Coleman
Mar 14, 1824
Jan 14, 1856

S. J. Godwin
  Co F
5th Tenn Cav.

M.----- ----an
(could be a Coleman)
(illegible)

* Records of Frost Family

** William Floyd Records.

George W. Floyd
Nov 20, 1832
Feb 14, 1870
age: 37y, 2m, 25d.
    &
Elizabeth T. Floyd*
Apr 11, 1838
Mar 25, 1881
age: 42y, 11m, 14d.
* Elizabeth Tabitha Floyd
  mrd-Jan 30, 1861

Edgar, son of
G. W. & E. Floyd
Dec 28, 1867
Jul 24, 1886

Mathew W., son of
J. F. & M. Watson
Sep 25, 1873
Nov 15, 1873

James J., son of
J. F. & M. Watson
Oct 9, 1869
Dec 13, 1875

Rebeca E., dau of
J. F. & M. Watson
Dec 2, 1871
Jan 7, 1876

James K. Floyd
Sep 11, 1832
Sep 2, 1871
    & wife:
Mary Jane Floyd
Dec 15, 1840
Aug 13, 1875

A. R.*
* Anthony Reagor, SOR.
1760-1824

M. R.*
* M. Reagor, wife to
Anthony Reagor, she was
a Shook.
1766-1838

28 PARKER CEMETERY   Map # 11
This Cemetery is located about 1½ miles Southwest of Flat Creek,
          on Goose Creek Road.

No markers.

29 NORMAN CEMETERY   Map # 11
This Cemetery is located near Flat Creek, on Goose Creek Road.

J. E. Norman   4 adult graves, no insc.
Jun 6, 1803
--- --, 1856   2 childs graves, no insc.

30 UNKNOWN CEMETERY   Map # 11
This Cemetery is located South of Flat Creek, on Goose Creek Road.

About 3 graves, no markers.

#·31 PLEASANT GARDEN CEMETERY   Map # 11
This Cemetery is located South of Flat Creek, on Goose Creek Road.

Calldenia Williams
nee Campbell
Jan 4, 1853
Jun 22, 1891

William Campbell
Mar 1, 1814
Mar 28, 1894

Letha B. Campbell
Jun 8, 1818
Jan 9, 1898

W. A. Patterson
Oct 18, 1840
Apr 17, 1908

Caledonia, wife of
W. A. Patterson
Apr 19, 1843
Nov 5, 1895
"She professed the Christian
Religion at abt the age of
14 yrs"

No marker:*
Pearl Casteel, dau of
Matilda Hasty
Died 1915/1916
age:(no age given)

Virge Burrow
Born Dec 18, 1848
Died (date gone)

B. A. Burrow
Born 1814
Died Mar 3, 1879

Jemima, wife of
B. A. Burrow
Jan 19, 1815
Mar 16, 1891

Charlie J. Warren
Mar 11, 1883
Mar 9, 1962

Minnie, wife of
Charlie Warren
Jan 22, 1892
Mar 20, 1927

No marker*
Matilda Hasty
Died Oct 1926
age: abt 65 yrs.

Ephraim Burrow
Died Aug 1, 1851
(no marker-Chancery Record)

L. C. Arnold
Jul 23, 1849
Mar 31, 1909

Elijah Benjamin Arnold
Jan 8, 1851
Dec 18, 1934

Victoria Arnold
Jun 20, 1869
May 13, 1925

L. B. Robinson
Jan 10, 1858
Mar 1, 1919
&
M. M. Robinson
May 24, 1848
Aug 22, 1898

Hattie, wife of
B. F. Rudd
May 12, 1873
Aug 12, 1899

No marker:*
Zade Hasty, son of
Matilda Hasty
(no dates)

J. S. Hasty
Jul 20, 1866
Aug 21, 1894
age: 34y, 1m, 1d.

Chris Heath
Jul 29, 1884
(no date)
&
Jessie Heath
Sep 20, 1889
Mar 4, 1920

Clay Raney
Jun 18, 1839
Jan 16, 1921

Victoria C. Raney
Feb 20, 1856
Oct 21, 1895

Infant of
W. E. & Willie Raney
(no dates)

Several unmarked graves.

Several fieldstones, no insc.

* Mrs. Charlie Warren

32 REAVES CEMETERY   Map # 11
This Cemetery is located about 3 miles Southwest of Flat Creek.

Archibald Reaves, who
departed this life
Sep 15, 1840
(no age given)

John Reaves, who
departed this life
Aug 22, 1836
aged: 21 yrs.

A. S. Reaves
Aug 14, 1820
Jul 8, 1875

George Reaves, who
departed this life
Sep 20, 1849
aged: 18 yrs.

Margaret, wife of
A. S. Reaves
Born June --, 1828
Died Oct 7, 1872

Huldy Ann Reaves,
departed this life
Jul 15, 1855
aged: 7 yrs & 22 days.

Several graves, no markers.

33 UNKNOWN CEMETERY   Map # 11
This Cemetery is located South of Flat Creek, on Crooked Run Road.

No markers.

34 HIX CEMETERY
This Cemetery is located about 1½ miles Southeast of Center Church,
                South of Wiggins Hill.

Mrs. Ellender, Consort of
J. C. Hix
Jan 20, 1813
Apr 29, 185-(gone)

Elizabeth M., dau of
J. C. & Ellender Hix
Apr 13, 1838
Jul 7, 1852

1 Adult grave marker
3 Children graves
1 grave, no inscriptions.

35 WORD CEMETERY   Map # 11
This Cemetery is located on Crooked Run Road, off Center Church Road.

J. C. Smiley
Apr 7, 1869
May 10, 1873

Sarah J., wife of
Robert Hastings
Dec 14, 1827
Apr 8, 1850

A. P. Smiley
May 27, 1877
May 15, 1906

Several graves, fieldstones.

Several unmarked graves.

T. S. Word
Jun 29, 1807
Aug 28, 1894
aged: 87y, 1m, 26d.

Thanks to:Mrs Caroline W. Pierce,
           Miss Lisa Pierce &
           Miss Marsha Westbrooks.

Nancy C., wife of
T. S. Word
Sep 18, 1805
Sep 20, 1880

36 HASTINGS CEMETERY   Map # 11
This Cemetery is located near Flat Creek, off Center Church Road.

Robert Hastings
Nov 11, 1820
Feb 19, 1903

Catharine Elizabeth Bryant,
wife of Robert Hastings, Jr.
Mar 16, 1839
Jun 13, 1872
age: 33y & 27d.

Robert E., son of
Robert & H. E. Hastings
May 17, 1882
Jun 24, 1882

Willis Hastings
Jun 21, 1807
Oct 15, 1836
age: 28y, 3m, 24d.

Robert Hastings, Sr.
Feb 7, 1785
May 20, 1834
age: 49y, 3m, 13d.

Jane Pitmon, wife of
R. Hastings, Sr.
Jun 12, 1785
Dec 15, 1871
age: 86y, 6m, 3d.

7 or 8 graves with
fieldstones, no insc.

37 FROST CEMETERY   Map # 11
This Cemetery is located on Center Church Road.

Several graves.

No markers.

38 CENTER CHURCH CEMETERY   Map # 11
(HOLT'S CAMP GROUND)
This Cemetery is located across the Road from Center Church,
on Center Church Road.

Sarah E. Wiggins
1848-1878

Jane H. Wiggins
1820-1880

B. F. Wiggins
1816-1884

Johnnie Elmo, Infant son
of B. F. & S. E. Wiggins
Apr 1, 1882
Sep 19, 1882

Henry M., son of
B. F. & S. E. Wiggins
Apr 11, 1889
Oct 30, 1897
age: 8y, 6m, 19d.

Sam Davis
Apr 7, 1841
Sep 29, 1889

Sarah Antnett Davis, wife of
J. T. Muse
Jan 10, 1858
Mar 3, 1894

Samie Davis
1890-(no date)
&
Vida Davis
1888-

John E. Davis
Mar 18, 1827
Feb 10, 1887

Rhoda Eveline, wife of
John E. Davis
Sep 15, 1829
Feb 11, 1903

John Davis
Mar 20, 1880
May 17, 1916

Polly Davis
1856-1943

Fannie B., wife of
R. W. Davis
Dec 26, 1868
Jun 6, 1896

Infant dau of
R. W. & F. B. Davis
Oct 3, 1894
Mar 6, 1894

Ity Adline Sutton, wife of
Stanford Sutton
Jul 11, 1832
Oct 15, 1894
aged: 62y, 3m, 4d.
NOTE: Another adult grave, no
marker, could be Stanford
Sutton.Iron fence around these
two graves.

Mandy Ross, wife of
John Ross
Jun 13, 1847
Jun 13, 1894
(An Iron fence around this
                     grave)

Miss Kate Haile, dau of
Rube Haile
Dec 1, 1850
Apr 14, 1909

James Simmons, Jr., son of
James & Clemmie Simmons
Feb 17, 1926
May 20, 1927

M. E. Frost Dunaway, dau of
J. N. Dunaway
Oct 8, 1862
Nov 22, 1894

Ellenor Edde Hastings
Dec 1, 1828
Jul 7, 1896
"Presented by her Sister
Nanny"
&
Nanny P. Edde
Born Aug 25, 1844 in
Shelbyville, Tenn.
Died (no date)

Dan Parker
May 3, 1856
Jun 4, 1926

Martha Dean, wife of
Dan Parker
May 15, 1864
Mar 8, 1948

Sarah E. Dunaway
Dec 28, 1831
Dec 30, 1904
age: 73y & 2d.

Jasper Newton Dunaway
Apr 20, 1828
Jul 31, 1885
age: 57y, 3m, 11d.

Pearl Dixon, dau of
James B. & S. M. Dixon
Apr 14, 1880
Apr 14, 1886
age: 6 yrs.

Lee W. Barrett
Mar 29, 1818
Apr 6, 1900

Lucy B., wife of
L. W. Barrett & dau of
Allen Knight
Died Mar 22, 1875
aged: 51 y & 2d.

G. B. Morgan
Feb 2, 1830
Jun 22, 1906

Alice Holt, wife of
G. B. Morgan
Nov 9, 1842
Mar 12, 1919

Margaret Elizabeth, dau of
G. B. & A. Morgan
May 5, 1868
Oct 30, 1887

Kate Nease Rutledge
Jul 1, 1864
Dec 8, 1934

Nease Rutledge
Feb 5, 1887
Dec 18, 1966

Daisy Rutledge
Apr 30, 1892
Apr 4, 1894

Joseph G. McEwen
1842-1909

Ann M. McEwen
1843-1910

John E. McEwen
1869-1899

Daniel F., son of
J. G. & A. M. McEwen
1884-1885

Infant son of
R. C. & M. V. McEwen
1904-1904

O. S. Dixon
Jun 17, 1870
Mar 21, 1901

Mrs. Cynthia Dixon
Oct 14, 1794
Feb 22, 1880
age: 85y, 4m, 8d.

G. Robert Dixon
1867-1935
&
Annie Y. Dixon
1867-1929

John Wilhoite
Oct 4, 1824
Jul 23, 1871
age: 46y, 9m, 19d.

Sarah E. Wilhoite
Mar 9, 1829
Mar 17, 1908
age: 79y, & 8d.

Ollie Sidney Himes
Jan 18, 1880
Jan 13, 1911

E. A. Himes
1877-1964

Myrtle Himes
Oct 1, 1874
May 28, 1915

George F. Himes
1852-1939

Eliza Alice, wife of
G. F. Himes
Jan 22, 1852
Oct 29, 1895

"Father"
John G. Frost
Oct 13, 1858
Dec 15, 1914

"Sister"
Lucy Nell Frost
Aug 7, 1896
Jan 20, 1915

Ida Myrtle Scales
May 23, 1882
Jan --, 1884

Mary Kathleen, dau of
T. & M. Puckett
Born & Died
Apr 17, 1917

Stoke Elliott
1864-1947
&
Viola Elliott
1875-1941

Helen Virginia Elliott
Aug 7, 1914
Apr 27, 1918

William Riggs Dixon
Feb 22, 1843
Aug 19, 1924

Sallie Elizabeth, wife of
W. R. Dixon
Jun 21, 1842
Aug 8, 1891

Lynn Y. Dixon
1894-1912

J. R. Wright
Co M
5th Tenn Cav.

Robert S. Dwiggins
Sep 18, 1808
Sep 3, 1875

Louisa Dwiggins
1826-1897

Joshua Wright, son of
J. C. & M. J. Frost
Oct 7, 1885
Nov 24, 1890

Ella, wife of
Horace Shearin
Aug 1, 1872
Feb 7, 1898

Nancy C. Wiggins
Dec 28, 1822
Aug 3, 1897
age: 74y, 7m, 5d.

Edwin Kimery
Jan 10, 1818
Oct 10, 1886 age: 68y & 9m.

Sidney T. Kimery
Jan 15, 1863
Apr 28, 1885

"Father"
Hiram H. Nease
Sep 5, 1824
Aug 6, 1893

"Mother"
Emily J. Nease
May 11, 1826
Jul 15, 1891

"Brother"
Sammie H. Nease
Jan 1, 1862
Sep 17, 1886

Dr. H. L. Nease
Mar 13, 1867
May 9, 1910

Hiram H. Nease, son of
Dr. H. L. & Mattie Nease
Jan 23, 1894
Jun 16, 1894

Edward S. Webster
Jan 17, 1915
Mar 28, 1918

George Castleman
1819-1890

Emily Hix
May 16, 1820
Apr 20, 1900
age: 79y, 11m, 4d.

Ben F. Wiggins
1858-1937
&
Bettie E. Wiggins
1858-1933

John Riggs, son of
R. B. & L. C. Dixon
Nov 12, 1875
Jan 23, 1877
age: 1y, 2m, 11d.

Nora Frost, dau of
R. B. & L. C. Dixon
Jan 3, 1871
Sep 18, 1877
age: 6y, 8m, 15d.

Bunyan Carter, son of
R. B. & L. C. Dixon
Apr 4, 1880
Dec 26, 1880
age: 8m & 12d.

Joshua Herbert, son of
R. B. & L. C. Dixon
Jan 5, 1889
Jul 8, 1890
age: 1y, 7m, 3d.

Jimmie D. Dixon
Aug 14, 1891
Sep 20, 1908
age: 17y, 1m, 6d.

Robert B. Dixon
May 10, 1848
Sep 26, 1891
age: 43y, 4m, 16d.

Louisa C. Dixon
May 6, 1852
Apr 22, 1920

Mitchell Dixon, Infant son
of --- S. E. Dixon
--- 14, 1860
Feb 28, ----
(Bad condition)

James H. Craig
Apr 1, 1889
Nov 21, 1930

Ada Harbin
1908-1936

Arlinda Bartlett
May 10, 1859
Jun 25, 1906

Daniel Bartlett
Oct 18, 1830
Jan 5, 1916

Adaline, wife of
Daniel Bartlett
Jun 27, 1833
Dec 24, 1903

Herburt Wiggins
Aug 16, 1883
Jul 10, 1914

A. F. Wiggins
Nov 9, 1874
Jun 18, 1913

J. Greer Wiggins
1842-1918
&
Emily Wiggins
1846-1922

H. Evans Wiggins
1882-1924

Alice Evans
1850-1930

Bessie Wiggins
1872-1946

A. L. Hastings
1884-1885

Jas. S. Newton
Aug 16, 1812
Feb 4, 1872

Edwin S. Newton
Dec 13, 1863
Aug 30, 1864
age: 8m & 12d.

Benjamin L. Newton
Oct 31, 1863
Jan 19, 1864
age: 8m & 12d.

Albert T. Newton
  Co U
5th Tenn
Apr 23, 1845, killed at
Mulberry, Tenn.
Jan 30, 1863

Thomas H. Newton
Feb 17, 1859
Sep 7, 1862
age: 3y, 6m, 7d.

Eugene Newton
Nov 16, 1867
May 2, 1868
age: 5m & 16d.

Sue M. Newton
May 17, 1841
Nov 4, 1862
age: 21y, 9m, 18d.

Sarah S., wife of
J. C. Holt
Jan 10, 1843
Jun 3, 1868
age: 19y, 11m, 28d.

Infant Children of
Isaac B. Holt
(no dates)

Isaac B. Holt
Oct 10, 1817
May 20, 1887

Louisa J. Holt
Nov 16, 1835
Dec 31, 1908

Mary J., wife of
J. F. Johnson
Jun 4, 1850
Apr 4, 1886

Hattie O., dau of
J. F. & M. J. Johnson
Nov 7, 1872
Oct 10, 1876

Annie L., dau of
J. F. & M. J. Johnson
Aug 13, 1874
Oct 15, 1876

Sam B. McLaughlin
Sep 18, 1893
May 13, 1932

Beulah Lee McLaughlin
1889-1947

Lucile McLaughlin
1915-1927

Michael Holt
Aug 1, 1790
Feb 1, 1854

Jane Holt
Jul 17, 1793
Sep 19, 1844

Henrietta Holt
Mar 18, 1844
Dec 29, 1862

Mary A. Barrett
Dec 28, 1844
Nov 5, 1852

Cynthia S. Thompson
Jun 19, 1818
Jun 21, 1851

Michael B. Holt, son of
Isaac Holt
aged: 9 yrs.
(no dates)

Bessie Stone
Aug 1, 1879
Jun 6, 1902

H. H. Holt
May 4, 1820
Sep 13, 1876
&
Mary C. Holt
Dec 27, 1831
Nov 27, 1878
age: 46y & 11m.

Mary E., wife of
H. H. Holt
Oct 25, 1820
Nov 16, 1862

John White, son of
H. H. & M. C. Holt
Died Jul 28, 1873
age: 4y, 7m, 7d.

George Smith
Died Aug 14, 1926
age: 66 yrs.

Sophia A. Smith
1830-1903

Harvey Crosslin
Died Nov 21, 1933
(no age given)

Mrs. Mary Crosslin
1871-1953

Mollie E. Casteel
1858-1929

Charles E. Casteel
Jan 3, 1937
Feb 15, 1937

Lillian Casteel
Oct 14, 1914
Sep 19, 1920

Ernest C. Casteel
Sep 15, 1885
Jun 29, 1941
&
Mary E. Casteel
Jan 24, 1890
(no date)

John Coy Casteel
1929-1958

Jacob Greer
Born Jan 17, 1777 in
Union District, So. Carolina
Died Jan 21, 1864
aged: 86y, 11m, 5d.
Jacob Greer
North Carolins 1st Sgt. N.C.
Det. Militia- War of 1812
Jan 17, 1777-Jan 21, 1864
  Military Stone:
Jacob Greer
  N.C.
1Sgt N.C.Det. Militia
War of 1812

Mary S. Greer, Born
Apr 2, 1784 in Orange Co.,
N. C., & Died Jun 6, 1863
aged: 79y, 3m, 24d.

Jackson M. Greer
Dec 12, 1826
Feb 24, 1865
aged: 38y, 2m, 12d.

Jordon C. Holt
Jul 28, 1794
Sep 11, 1853
age: 59y, 11m, 17d.

Margaret Holt
Nov 20, 1797
Jul 31, 1853
aged: 56y, 9m, 19d.

J. Earl Hastings
1889-1919

Mary A. Hastings
Oct 17, 1830
Jan 17, 1912

Joe M. Hastings
1859-1946
&
Bettie A. Hastings
1862-1937

Christine Delk
1905-1926

Nadean Delk
1917-1924

Pauline Delk
1907-1924

Robert Dixon
Jan 8, 1822
Jul 22, 1854

Clement C. Dixon
Jun 29, 1824
Dec 25, 1851
age: 27y, 5m, 27d.

Emily E. Mosley, wife of
Robert Mosley & dau of
James & Syntha Dixon
Oct 10, 1819
Dec 10, 1854

Susan Ann Wiggins
Aug 4, 1852
Oct 3, 1853
age: 1y, 1m, 20d.

Maggie Minter, wife of
Dr. P. W. McRee
Jul 29, 1856
Mar 3, 1887

Erastus Virgil McRee
Feb 12, 1885
Aug 4, 1885

Elizabeth P. Kingree
Oct 3, 1824
Oct 20, 1903

Joseph W., son of
W. H. & F. M. Kingree
Jul 15, 1872
Sep 14, 1884

Rhodie E., dau of
W. H. & F. M. Kingree
May 8, 1875
Nov 2, 1879

Jarrel B. Smith
Sep 23, 1818
Apr 22, 1862

Martha A., wife of
Jarrel B. Smith
Jun 3, 1821
Dec 9, 1852

Joshua Holt, Sen.
Born in Oragne Co., N.C.
Nov 3, 1768 & Died
Oct 20, 1839
age: 70y, 11m, 17d.

Elanor C. Holt
Apr 6, 1763
Dec 24, 1852
aged: 89y, 8m, 18d.

Infant dau of
A. D. & M. J. Hart
1854

William Kingree
Mar 24, 1815
Sep 10, 1857

Nancy W., dau of
William E. P. Kingree
Nov 7, 1844
Sep 13, 1859
age: 14y, 1m, 6d.

Worren P. Kingree
Sep 12, 1848
Mar 1, 1850

Margarette M. Kingree
Aug 8, 1846
Dec 11, 1847

A. H. Evans   and
Aug 27, 1814
Jul 1, 1880
age: 65y, 10m, 5d.

Nimrod B. Holt
May 22, 1799
Sep 20, 1823

Sally S. Holt
Oct 10, 1805
Aug 27, 1839

Infant of
Herrod G. & America Holt
(no dates)

Infant of Herrod G. &
America Holt
(no dates)

James Murry, Sr.
Jul 7, 1754
Sep 17, 1840
"A Soldier of the Revolution,
Born in Carolina County, Va.
7th July 1754, Emigrated to
Franklin County, No. Carolina
& departed this life 17th
Sep 1840. Aged: 86y & 10d.

Joshua C., son of
F. F. & M. A. Fonville
Nov 15, 1841
Dec 25, 1874
age: 33y, 1m, 9d.

Eleanor C. Evans
Apr 6, 1818
Jun 26, 1868
age: 50y, 2m, 20d.

Jacob Albright
Born in Orange Co., N.C.
Jan 4, 1784 & Died
Jan 25, 1845 at his
residence in Bedford Co.,
Tenn.

Sarah Albright
Nov 26, 1786
Dec 7, 1852

Nancy B., Consort of
George Waite
Nov 30, 179-(gone)
Dec 5, 1838

Mary Morgan, wife of
Daniel Morgan
Oct 7, 1820
Jul 7, 1853

Margaret Ann, wife of
F. F. Fonville
Feb 18, 1816
Feb 4, 1856

Marsee N., dau of
F. F. & M. A. Fonville
Jan 10, 1856
Jul 7, 1873
age: 22y, 5m, 27d.

Carson G. Evans
Aug 26, 1838
Jun 21, 1855

Candace Edde
Jun 10, 1808
Oct 24, 1851

Sarah Edde
Nov 15, 1849
Dec 5, 1849

Candace Edde
Oct 24, 1851
Oct 10, 1853

Cassa D. Edde
Apr 28, 1834
Apr 25, 1835

Virgil A., son of
J. H. & M. Reeves
Jan 1842
Apr 30, 1845

James Bird
Died Aug 1853
aged: 60 yrs.

Lucy, wife of
James Bird
Died Jul 1852
aged: 50 yrs.

many fieldstones, no
           inscriptions.

Many unmarked graves.

39 GILL CEMETERY   Map # 11
This Cemetery is located about 3/4 mile North of Hawthorn.

Winston W. Gill
Born in Adair Co., Ky.
Mar 10, 1809
Died Mar 10, 1902

Henrietta B., wife of
W. W. Gill
Sep 28, 1829
Jan 29, 1881

Winston W., son of
W. W. & S. A. Gill
Sep 5, 1853
Died while attending School
at the University of Va.
Mar 22, 1875

Martha Gill
Oct 8, 1848
Dec 17, 1849
age: 1y, 2m, 9d.
     &
Sallie Gill
Oct 13, 1851
Sep 18, 1862
age: 10y, 11m, 5d.
Children of W.W.& S.A.Gill

Alexander Gill
Oct 13, 1781
Sep 3, 1868
age: 86y, 10m, 21d.
     &
Mary, wife of
Alexander Gill
Jun 17, 1779
Dec 4, 1851
age: 72y, 5m, 17d.

John J. Gill
Son of W. W. & S. A. Gill
May 26, 1841
May 8, 1918
     &
Sue S., dau of
Rev. A. S. & S. H. Riggs
Dec 15, 1845 & Died in
Orlando, Fla.
Mar 17, 1912
married Feb 8, 1870

Sallie, Infant dau of
J. J. & S. R. Gill
Aug 29, 1872
Jan 7, 1874

Winston W., son of
John J. & Sue Riggs Gill
Apr 1, 1875
Feb 11, 1877

[This Cemetery is located on part
of the old James McKissick North
Carolina Grant that was later
purchased by George Waite, who
sold to W. W. Gill]

40 McCUISTION CEMETERY   Map # 11
This Cemetery is located about 1½ miles out Unionville Hwy,
South of Fairlane Estates.

John McCuistion
Born Jul 29, 1774 in Guil-
ford Co., NC, migrated to
Tenn. 1796, mrd in William-
son Co., TN
Died May 10, 1854

Margaret, wife of
John McCuistion
Born Jul 11, 1784
Died Aug 29, 1854

Mrs. Jane Robinson, wife of
Joseph Robinson
Born Jul 3, 1819
Died Dec 25, 1847 age: 28 yrs.

Claiborne McCuistion, born
Aug 5, 1821 in Bedford Co.
Died May 27, 1858 mrd Oct 31,
1853 to Frances M.Wynns Lane
May 30, 1832-Jun 17, 1915

1 PETER MILLER CEMETERY   Map # 12
This Cemetery is located on Fay Creek Road, near Butler Creek.

No marker: No marker:
Peter Miller   and   Dolly, wife of
(no dates)   Peter Miller
A Soldier of the Revolution. (no dates)

2 DICKERSON CEMETERY   Map # 12
This Cemetery is located on the Shelbyville-Wartrace Highway,
          about 1 mile South of Mt.Olivet Church.

William Dickerson
Born in Louisa Co., Va.
Apr 25, 1776, was married
to Easther Coots Mar 3, 1807
Died Jun 20, 1821
aged: 45y, 1m, 25d.

Easther Dickerson
was born in Gilford C.,N.C.
Dec 3, 1778
Died Mar 14, 1836
aged: 58y, 3m, 11d.
"Member of M.E.Church"

Rufus A. Burrow
Dec 23, 1868
Aug 1, 1873
age: 4y, 8m, 8d.

James W. Dickerson
Oct 18, 1815
married Nancy Young
Oct 27, 1840 & Died
Jun 26, 1893
   & wife:
Nancy Young Dickerson
Dec 27, 1822
Oct 12, 1871

G. W. Burrow
Dec 16, 1839
Feb 24, 1917

Ann Eliza Dickerson, wife of
G. W. Burrow
Jun 12, 1844
Dec 17, 1904

Thomas A. Dickerson
Apr 20, 1852
Mar 21, 1864

Raleigh M. Dickerson
Mar 21, 1857
Aug 19, 1864

Laura B. Dickerson
Aug 3, 1859
Sep 29, 1880

Nancy H. Dickerson
Jun 14, 1863
Apr 30, 1881

John W. Dickerson
May 14, 1849
Aug 15, 1897

James Shofner Dickerson
1900-1964
   &
Sarah J. Edwards Dickerson

Henry Clay Dickerson
Jun 13, 1854
Dec 20, 1938
   &
Mary Ellen Shofner Dickerson
Jan 1, 1860
May 11, 1924

Nannie, dau of
H. C. & M. E. Dickerson
Jan 7, 1888
Jun 28, 1894

3 KIMBRO CEMETERY   Map # 12
This Cemetery is located near Three-Fork Bridge.

George Kimbro, Born in N.C.
Apr 11, 1779 & Died in
Bedford Co., Tenn.
Jul 17, 1859
"Having consecrated his heart
to God, conected himself with
the Baptist Church in 1803 &
remained a consistent Member
until God called him home"

Rachel Kimbro
Dec   1775
Aug 3, 1857

George M. Hooser
Born Nov 4, 1832
Died Nov 2, 1876

Several other graves, no
              inscriptions.

4 HOOSER CEMETERY   Map # 12
This Cemetery is located near Three-Fork Church Cemetery.

Lester Hooser
1908-1917
   &
Fred Hooser
1905-1917

Mary Hooser
Jan 31, 1878
Feb 29, 1912

Edmond Cooper Hooser
Nov 2, 1872
Nov 18, 1898
age: 26y, & 16d.

Several graves with
fieldstones, no inscriptions.

William M. Hooser
Dec 18, 1840
Dec 15, 1907
age: 66y, 11m, 27d.
   &
Jane Hooser
1845-1929

Infant son of
William & S. J. Hooser
Born & Died
Oct 21, 1881

Infant son of
William & S. J. Hooser
Born & Died
Mar 29, 1869

Infant of
William & S. J. Hooser
Died Jul 12, 1871

Infant son of
William & S. J. Hooser
Born & Died
Jul 12, 1876

Mary Ann, dau of
Dan'l & Francis Hooser
Aug 20, 1831
Aug 12, 1856

A. Troxler
Dec 27, 1840
Mar 1, 1918
   &
Martha F. Troxler
Nov 12, 1842
Apr 13, 1924

Maggie Lee, dau of
A. G. & Etta Hooser
Sep 20, 1894
Sep 21, 1894

Francis Hooser
Jul 11, 1807
May 6, 1885
age: 77y, 9m, 25d.

Daniel Hooser
Jun 1, 1807
Apr 2, 1864
age: 56y & 10m.
"Lived a consistant Member
of the Methodist Church"

Infant dau of
A. G. & Etta Hooser
Mar 16, 1896
Mar 20, 1896

Infant dau of
A. G. & Etta Hooser
Feb 3, 1899
Feb 9, 1899

5 THREE-FORKS CHURCH CEMETERY   Map # 12

This Cemetery is located about 1½ miles Northwest of Roseville.

John W. Fuller
Jan 17, 1881
Nov 18, 1931

Jennie N. Fuller
Feb 16, 1886
May 21, 1960

Thomas W. Fuller
Nov 27, 1920
Nov 18, 1922

Here lies the body of
Ambro Timmens
Died July 30, 1815
age: 56 yrs.

Roena Shofner Webster
Nov 19, 1815
Aug 1, 1893

Albert Jenkins Shofner
Mar 21, 1829
Jul 27, 1863

Bettie Ayers
1845-1934
&
Rena Crandson Ayers
1875-1920
&
James Ayers
1900-1921

No marker:*
W. B. Bates
Died Jun 27, 1892
by hanging
(Hoskins-Nance FH)
*Shelbyville Gazette
June 30, 1892, Obit.

Scott Bates
---- - 1898

Infant son of
Odell & Beulah Talley
Apr 24, 1925

J. W. Rowe
(Infant)
1832

C. Knox Lawerence
Died Aug 7, 1879
aged: 33y, 3m, 26d.

John C. Lawrence
Died Jul 23, 1861
age: 8y & 4d.

Magie Lawrence
Died Sep 28, 1868
age: 24y, 8m, 14d.

Albert Wesley Webster
Jan 6, 1847
Jan 6, 1904

Ben S. Kimbro
1846-1915
&
Ellen Kimbro
1854-1888

Charles W. Kimbro
Georgia
Pvt 43 Co 20 Engineers W.W.I
Dec 15, 1888
Aug 29, 1961

In Memory of
Emily Koonce who was born
Feb 13th 1815 & Died
Oct 1st 1852.

Thomas H. Bernard
Jun 1, 1769
Jan 31, 1824
age: 40 yrs.

Jacob Coble
Dec 15, 1791
May 15, 1840
Professed religion
12 yrs old, joined the
C. P. Church.

Elizabeth R. Coble
Jan 18, 1840
Sep 22, 1842
age: 20 months & 4 days

Infant dau of
J. D. & Mary Coble
Born & Died
Apr 9, 1869

Martha Catharine Coble
Aug 26, 1836
Aug 24, 1882

Nicholas Coble
N. Carolina
Rev. War
1759-1838

John Daniel Coble
1828-1912
&
Mary Rebecca Coble
1835-1921

Many unmarked graves.

* See Addendum

Many fieldstones, no inscriptions.

William McGee*
Minister of the Gospel
departed this life the
Sep 20, 1817 in the
Truimphs of faith
aged: abt 50 yrs.

A. S. Lawrence
Died Oct 31, 1896
age: 92y, 9m, 8d.

Charlotte Lawrence
Died May 2, 1885
age: 71y, 2m, 7d.

Jacob Troxler
Feb 6, 1800
Sep 1, 1827

John F. McKaig
Nov 20, 1861
Sep 30, 1883
age: 21y, 10m, 10d.

Roean Ann McKaig
Jul 6, 1872
Sep 20, 1876

Neely Coble
Jan 17, 1802
Sep 30, 1866
& wife:
Martha Coble
Jan 10, 1803
Oct 26, 1836

Margaret Roberson
Born --- --, 1770 (broken)
Died May 12, 1855

6 HAILEY CEMETERY   Map # 12

This Cemetery is located about 1½ miles West of Roseville.

Blan Williams, son of
P. W. & Lucy Williams
Born 1850 - Died young
(marker now gone, 1985)

Allice Hailey
Born Mar --, 186-
Died Jul 19, 187-

-----------, dau of
E. W. -----------(Brown)
departed this life
--- --, 1845

Several unmarked graves.

Several fieldstones,
no inscriptions.

7 MAUPIN CEMETERY   Map # 12

This Cemetery is located about ½ mile Northwest of Roseville.

Gabriel Maupin   and
Sep 7, 1810
Mar 20, 1895

Sallie Maupin
Jan 2, 1820
Jul 27, 1884

G. M. (foot marker)

2 or 3 unmarked graves.

8 MAUPIN CEMETERY   Map # 12

This Cemetery is located about 1 mile South of Haley, on River.

Robert B. Maupin   and
Apr 17, 1800
Aug 20, 1867

Nancy W. Maupin
Oct 13, 1807
Apr 26, 1897

Blan T. Maupin
May 5, 1831
Apr 12, 1850

Sarah S. Caruthers
Jan 8, 1789
Sep 15, 1863

William D., son of
R. B. & N. W. Maupin
Sep 3, 1850
Nov 3, 1850

Gabriel A., son of
R. B. & N. W. Maupin
Jul 5, 1838
Jul 6, 1838

Many unmarked graves.

9 EASON CEMETERY   Map # 12
This Cemetery is located near Haley, Tenn.

Susan Nancy, wife of
W. M. Eason
Feb 21, 1845
Mar 25, 1898

James G., son of
W. H. & Nancy Eason
Mar 10, 1868
Oct 8, 1886

Willie E. Sanders
Jan 24, 1870
Jan 17, 1873

Nancy, dau of
Susan & W. M. Eason
Born Jul 28, 1871
age: 3y, 2m, 3d.

10 HOLT CEMETERY   Map #12
This Cemetery is located about 1 mile Southeast of Haley, Tenn.

SEE ADDENDUM

page 327

11 HALL-THOMPSON CEMETERY   Map # 12
This Cemetery is located about 1 mile East of Haley, Tenn.

J. M. Hall
Oct 3, 1846
Oct 18, 1906
&
Kate Snoddy Hall
Aug 5, 1848
Oct 14, 1886

John B., son of
J. M. & M. J. Hall
Feb 4, 1872
Dec 24, 1872

W. F. Thompson
Died Oct 24, 1865
age: 49y, 1m, 15d.

Emma Franklin, dau of
W. F. & M. C. Thompson
Aug 9, 1865
Feb 3, 1875

S. C. Davidson   and
Jun 15, 1805
Aug 28, 1888

William Meadows   and
Mar 13, 1810
Oct 8, 1873

Mary Jestania, dau of
J. M. & M. J. C. Hall
Apr 2, 1869
Aug --, 1875

Ada Matilda, dau of
J. M. & M. J. C. Hall
Oct 10, 1873
Aug 29, 1875

Kittie Ann Hall
Jun 5, 1883
Jul 20, 1883

S. M. Thompson
Died Apr 8, 1863
age: 17y, 5m, 18d.

H. P. Hall Thompson
Died May 10, 1850
age: 30 yrs.

D. V. Davidson   and
May 29, 1803
Nov 3, 1869

Martha A. Meadows
Feb 27, 1820
Jul 1, 1897

Jestiana Hall
Jun 8, 1813
Jul 13, 1882
age: 69y, 1m, 5d.

John Hall
May 1, 1810
Feb 5, 1868

Jas. Thompson
Died Sep 1847
age: 60 yrs.

Fergus Hall
Died May 17, 1845
age: 73y, 2m, 21d.

Mary Bell Hall
Died May 27, 1863
age: 84y, 10m, 12d.

M. M. Davidson   and
Jul 10, 1833
Jul 31, 1878

Attie Elenor, dau of
J. W. & H. A. Meadows
Jul 2, 1870
Oct 16, 1874

Lady Virginia Caldwell
Aug 27, 1857
Jun 18, 1898
&
Maggie Pearl Caldwell
Jan 11, 1889
Jun 29, 1889

Mrs. Hannah Yates
Sep 5, 1781
Aug 28, 1827

W. M. D.
(fieldstone, no dates)

M. A. D.
(fieldstone-No dates)

J. M. Davidson
Apr 1, 1855
Mar 5, 1875

Many graves with fieldstones
   no inscriptions.

Many unmarked graves.

12 RUSSELL CEMETERY   Map # 12
This Cemetery is located about ½ mile North of Dement Bridge,
at "Parrish Patch".   Copied by Jerry Wayne Cook.

Emmett E. Russell
Apr 15, 1880
May 6, 1951

Culley
(no dates)

Infant of
James & Nancy Russell
Feb 22, 1866
Feb 23, 1866

Albert D., son of
James L. & Nancy Russell
Nov 2, 1870
Jul 9, 1871

Zachariah Culley
Nov 3, 1803
Sep 6, 1887
age: 83y, 10m, 3d.

Sarah, wife of
Z. Culley
Feb 5, 1809
Oct 1, 1886
age: 77y, 7m, 26d.

In Memory of my Dear Mother,
by J. L. Payne.(all on stone)

J. M. Culley
(no dates)

Mary Throneberry
Feb 2, 1842
Oct 19, 1916

Harriet Culley Reed
Jan 3, 1831
Sep 25, 1869

John Z. Russell
Jul 5, 1857
Sep 8, 1857

Allen Knight
Jun 27, 1790
Sep 25, 1849
[First Allen Knight homeplace, then
Zachariah Culley, later James Russell]

James L., Husband of
Nancy Russell
Sep 15, 1828
Sep 18, 1890
age: 62y & 3d.

Nancy, wife of
James Russell
Apr 22, 1838
Apr 20, 1899
age: 60y, 11m, 28d.

Henry T. Russell
Apr 19, 1877
Nov 12, 1927

J. N. Russell
1860-1922

13 TROXLER CEMETERY   Map # 12
This Cemetery is located about 2 miles Northwest of Normandy, Tenn.

Ernest W. Nowlin
Jan 8, 1872
Oct 11, 1957
&
Sarah Ann Nowlin
Sep 26, 1876
TM-1973

Bryant W. Nowlin
Jan 18, 1904
Nov 4, 1963

"Mother"
Elizabeth S. Williams
Born Oct 6, 1837
married to Newton J. Kimbro
Jan 26, 1858
Died Jul 27, 1909

James Newton Kimbro
Aug 11, 1864
Jan 8, 1936
&
Panola Adaline Kimbro
Sep 21, 1865
May 8, 1948

Beulah, dau of
M. L. & L. M. Bond
(no dates)

Walter C. Troxler
1964-1968
(Gowen-Smith)

Joseph D. Troxler
1968-1968
(Gowen-Smith)

Elizabeth, wife of
Isaac Troxler
May 27, 1803
Jun 20, 1848

Nancy C. Troxler
Sep 21, 1851
Nov 16, 1851

Ewin Burks
Apr 8, 1898
Jun 12, 1973
&
Effie Burks
Jan 12, 1902
Feb 16, 1972
married Sep 21, 1924

Elizabeth Burks
1925-1943

Frank Nutt
Nov 12, 1851
Feb 12, 1921
&
Sarah Nutt
Sep 22, 1858
(no date)

H. W. McKaig
1860-1926
&
Susie McKaig
1861-1922

Shirley Houston McKaig
Jan 31, 1897
Aug 26, 1898

Forrest Williams
Oct 15, 1877
Jul 5, 1900
age: 22y, 8m, 20d.

M. L. Bond
1855-1929
&
Lucy M. Bond
1859-1930

Isaac Troxler
Sep 11, 1803
Mar 15, 1866
age: 62y, 6m, 4d.

John P. Martin
1869-1925
&
Martha E. Brixey Martin
1882-1963

Susan E. Bishop
Sep 12, 1911
Aug 5, 1916

F. R. Miller
Jul 3, 1837
Mar 22, 1920
&
Ann Miller
Feb 14, 1842
Oct 10, 1919

James H. Miller
May 25, 1915
May 23, 1919

Nancy Jane Williams
Born Jul 9, 1839
married to E. D. Brumfield
Jun 1, 1865 &
Died Oct 28, 1886

P. W. Williams
Apr 11, 1811
Oct 10, 1895

Lucinda Maupin
Born Dec 14, 1814
married to P. W. Williams
Oct 21, 1834 &
Died Mar 4, 1862

Mary J. Williams
Feb 14, 1834
May 15, 1911

Mary M., wife of
Isaac Troxler
Oct 29, 1817
Mar 11, 1888
age: 70y, 4m, 11d.

Adam D. Cawthron
1869-1935
&
Bettie E. Cawthron
1870-1943

Joe Edmon Edwards, Jr.
Aug 19, 1914
May 30, 1919

Carl R. Miller
Jan 4, 1881
Aug 17, 1965
&
Mittie N. Miller
Jul 28, 1882
Nov 27, 1970

W. H. Sparks
Dec 5, 1836
Feb 25, 1902

Nannie Maupin Sparks
Sep 5, 1846
Jan 8, 1917

Charles S. Sparks
Jan 2, 1806
Apr 28, 1896
&
Frances H. Sparks
May 7, 1810
Sep 2, 1870

Henry Odus Hensley
Dec 21, 1899
Feb 2, 1960

Doris Aline McConnell
1954-1954 (TM)

David Carl McConnell
1949-1949 (TM)

James A. McConnell
1948-1948 (TM)

Mary Ellen McConnell
1946-1946 (TM)

Virginia C. McConnell
1944-1944 (TM)

Lena Bell Hensley
1930-1930 (TM)

Arvie E. Hensley
1923-1924 (TM)

Infant dau of
Arnold & Frances Givens
1933

Sam Jordan
1872-1938
&
Eliza Jordan
1877-1913

Robert, son of
Sam & Eliza Jordan
1908 age: 1m & 15d.

Allen W. Kimbro   and
Aug 24, 1855
Apr 20, 1941

John Ezra Hitt
Apr 5, 1876
Jul 10, 1967
&
Eva Bond Hitt
Sep 16, 1881
May 8, 1963

Willie, dau of
J. E. & Eva Hitt
1906-1931

Judith Ann Kimbro
Nov 25, 1856
Oct 28, 1937

George W. Kimbro
Tennessee
Pvt 1928 SVC Comd Unit
W. W. II
Jan 5, 1916
Apr 12, 1969

T. L. Kimbro
Jul 22, 1878
Mar 8, 1942

Several unmarked graves.

14 CORTNER CEMETERY   Map # 12
This Cemetery is located near Cortner's Station, North of Normandy, Tn.

Johney, son of
W. E. & Marilla Blake
May 9, 1881
Aug 12, 1881

Emilley Cortner
Aug 5, 1810
Sep 5, 1893

Babe of
G. M. & Sallie Huffman
Born & Died
Nov 3, 1888

John M. Russel
Jan 10, 1842
May 20, 1857
age: 15y, 4m, 10d.

Mary M. Courtner
Feb 2, 1837
Aug 17, 1868
age: 31y, 6m, 15d.

Lucy Ann Courtner
Sep 28, 1838
Oct 6, 1866
age: 28y & 8d.

Daniel M. Cortner
Aug 18, 1844
Jan 17, 1846
age: 1y & 5m.

Hattie Cortner McNutt
1892-1932

Emilla Keck
Nov 5, 1795
Feb 22, 1836
aged: 40y, 3m, 17d.

Matthias Cortner, Born in
Guilford Co., N.Carolina
Jun 25, 1773 & Died Apr 22,
1854. aged: 80y, 9m, 29d.

Carbany Cortner
Oct 3, 1780
Jun 19, 1867
aged: 86y, 8m, 10d.

Nicolas Troxler
Jul 2, 1792
May 1, 1781
&
Amelia Troxler
Oct 23, 1795
May 29, 1835

Barbara Troxler
May 1, 1820
Jul 14, 1854

George Cortner
Nov 15, 1801
Oct 7, 1884
&
Delila Troxler Cortner
Oct 6, 1807
Jan 16, 1871

Elizabeth Cortner
Dec 10, 1841
Jul 14, 1865
age: 23y, 7m, 4d.

William P. Cortner
Nov 16, 1846
Sep 30, 1848
age: 1y, 10m, 15d.

Rev. John A. Troxler
1876-1928
&
May Prince Troxler
1876-1945

Henry Troxler
Oct 3, 1824
Jun 26, 1894

Jacob Troxler, who was born
in Orange Co., N.C. Oct 19,
1763 & departed this life
Dec 12, 1854.
aged: 91y, 1m, 23d.

Infant Son of
George & Delia Cortner
Born & Died
Oct 4, 1826

No marker:*
Mathew Cortner
Born abt 1831 & Died 1888

John Henry Cortner
Nov 15, 1854
Nov 21, 1857

Alexander Cortner
Dec 20, 1827
Sep 12, 1911
&
Mary E. Cortner
Dec 22, 1836
May 11, 1879

Sarah E., dau of
A. C. & M. E. Cortner
May 24, 1879
Jul 12, 1879

Anthony Troxler
Feb 16, 1802
Aug 11, 1843

Sarah, wife of
Anthony Troxler
Aug 5, 1810
Feb 6, 1886

William Troxler
Jan 8, 1870
Apr 7, 1900

Mary Marguerite Troxler
Jan 29, 1900
Sep 27, 1905

John C. Troxler
1840-1918

Margaret P. Troxler
1848-1915

Barbara Troxler, who was born
in Randolph Co., N.C. Sep 27,
1769 & Died Mar 20, 1820
aged: 50y, 5m, 22d.

James Isaac Newton
Jun 30, 1845
Jul 10, 1852
aged: 7y & 10d.

William T. Newton
Dec 12, 1846
Jul 23, 1852

Susan M. Loyd
Mar 23, 1854
Apr 4, 1878

Mary Lucy, dau of
Tom & Susan M. Loyd
Sep 19, 1877
May 3, 1878

Mattie L. Cortner
Jun 29, 1887
May 27, 1918

George R. Cortner
Mar 23, 1858
Jun 18, 1917

Roy E. Cortner
Oct 21, 1871
Mar 28, 1887

William F. Justice
Jan 19, 1835
Nov 13, 1874

Joseph A. Justice
Dec 26, 1868
May 18, 1871

Andrew A. Justice
Oct 15, 1872
Oct 11, 1877

Nannie A., wife of
W. A. Huffman
Feb 26, 1861
Feb 1, 1891

William, son of
Jacob & Eve Troxler
Oct 13, 1828
Sep 5, 1850

Mary Burrow
Oct 13, 1821
Jun 25, 1854

John H. Burrow
Dec 19, 1850
Jul 11, 1854

Hiram A. J. Burrow
Mar 14, 1845
Aug 30, 1854

No marker:*
John W. Gardner, son of
William Robert & Sarah
Troxler Gardner.,
Dec 31, 1906
Mar 14, 1908

* by- Jerry Wayne Cook.

Many unmarked graves.

Many fieldstones, no insc.

15 AUSTIN CEMETERY   Map # 12
This Cemetery is located about ½ mile North of Normandy, between
the Railroad Tracks & Duck River.

Son of
C. & T. Austin
Sep 26, 1881
Nov 11, 1881

Infant of
C. & T. Austin
Born & Died
Dec 25, 1883

Annie, dau of
C. & T. Austin
Mar 11, 1885
Jun 30, 1886

Edner E. Holt, dau of
I. L. & R. B. Holt
(no dates)

Temperance S., wife of
Eli Robertson
Jan 2, 1823
Aug 2, 1884

Samuel T. Cribbs
Jul 4, 1870
Sep 8, 1873

Lucy M., dau of
B. M. & E. Cribbs
Dec 11, 1868
Nov 7, 1870

Daniel J. Huffman
Feb 15, 1834
Sep 23, 1899
  & wife:
Mary J. Huffman
Apr 7, 1832
Jul 1, 1900

Many fieldstones, no insc.

Many unmarked graves.

16 GEORGE CEMETERY   Map # 12
This Cemetery is located about 1 mile West of Normandy, Tenn.

W. F. George
Mar 14, 1812
Jan 24, 1894

Bettie, wife of
W. F. George
Feb 23, 1817
Jun 30, 1899

17 HUFFMAN CEMETERY   Map # 12
This Cemetery is located about 2 miles Northeast of Normandy, Tenn.

Wright Huffman
Sep 16, 1872
May 24, 1874

Elijah Huffman
Aug 16, 1840
Jan 17, 1876

John Huffman
Oct 21, 1800
Jul 16, 1878

Thomas Jefferson Gambill
Dec 14, 1852
Oct 29, 1915

Napoleon Huffman
Oct 26, 1861
Oct 28, 1863

Eliz. A. Huffman
Sep 18, 1841
Nov 1, 1887

Polly Cortner, wife of
John Huffman
Mar 5, 1805
Feb 22, 1876

Lucy Templeton, wife of
T. J. Gambill
Dec 10, 1858
Aug 7, 1909

Lewis M. Huffman
Aug 20, 1860
Nov 23, 1863

Mattie J. Laurence, wife of
Elijah Huffman
Apr 19, 1850
Jun 12, 1876

Clarence Dale Huffman
Nov 2, 1901
Mar 22, 1918

Newton Templeton
Dec 20, 1823
Feb 11, 1883

Dora, wife of
Thomas L. Huffman
Nov 3, 1878
Nov 30, 1897

Della E. Huffman
Jun 11, 1875
Oct 11, 1876

John P. Templeton
1872-1909

Telitha Ann, wife of
Newton Templeton
Jan 3, 1834
Nov 21, 1879

18 WAITE CEMETERY   Map # 12
This Cemetery is located about 1½ miles North of Normandy, Tenn.
This Cemetery joines the McQuiddy Cemetery.

J. A. Bramblett
Aug 13, 1831
Jun 12, 1905
    & His wife:
C. Bramblett
Dec 5, 1834
Jun 25, 1903

Miss Della E. Bramblett
Nov 20, 1873
May 28, 1897

Gerhardt
(all on stone)

Walter T., son of
J. A. & L. C. Bramblett
Aug 15, 1870
Mar 17, 1905

I. O. B. Richardson
1847-1900
    &
Bettie Richardson
1856-1944
    &
Alvin Richardson
1882-1897

Malinda T., wife of
I. O. B. Richardson & dau of
F. M. & Juda Yell
Jul 8, 1857
married Aug 25, 1878 &
Died Mar 20, 1879

G. W. Richardson
Jun 17, 1842
May 9, 1880
another marker:
Corp'l George W. Richardson
        Co C
5 Tenn. Cav.

F. M. Yell
Nov 25, 1820
Jul 22, 1892
    &
Juda L. Yell
Jan 29, 1815
Dec 30, 1892

Francis M., son of
J. C. & J. A. Yell
Mar 23, 1886
Sep 27, 1886

Robert, son of
R. H. & D. D. Richardson
Oct 5, 1884
Oct 29, 1884

Baby Carman
1961-1961 (TM)

No marker:*
Thomas Holland, Husband of
Mary Elizabeth Holland
(no dates)

R. H. Richardson
Nov 7, 1846
Jul 12, 1909

Delilah D., wife of
R. H. Richardson
Mar 5, 1855
Jun 2, 1912

No marker:*
Jim H. McMillan, son of
Joseph & Betty McMillan
Born abt 1905
Died abt 1917

R. H., son of
R. H. & D. D. Richardson
Oct 30, 1889
Jun 16, 1891

Judah Marion, dau of
R. H. & D. D. Richardson
Sep 12, 1887
Jan 17, 1888

* by Jerry Wayne Cook.

Joseph Alexander Ayers
May 20, 1869
May 31, 1950
&
Betty K. Holland Ayers
Dec 15, 1872
Mar 2, 1956

Mary Elizabeth Holland
Jan 22, 1858
Nov 21, 1905

19 McQUIDDY CEMETERY   Map # 12
This Cemetery is located about 1½ miles North of Normandy, Tenn.

Jane, wife of
John V. Biddle
Mar 5, 1828
Jun 23, 1880
aged: 52y, 3m, 18d.

"Billy"
William Brandon, son of
V. C. & Alda McQuiddy
Sep 12, 1918
Nov 19, 1922

Virginia W., dau of
V. C. & Alda McQuiddy
Feb 27, 1912
Nov 20, 1912

Minnie Lee, dau of
John G. & Annie Bates
May 22, 1882
Jul 21, 1883

Robert K. Stephens
1858-1935
&
Jennie King Stephens
1865-1958

Little Babe of
Charley & Mamie King
Born & Died
Jun 30, 1880

Dennie, son of
R. J. & M. J. King
Oct 20, 1872
Nov 21, 1872
age: 1m & 1d.

Willie Wade, dau of
W. B. & C. W. McQuiddy
Jun 20, 1895
Jan 5, 1909

Lucile, dau of
W. B. & C. W. McQuiddy
Aug 21, 1893
Aug 23, 1893

Eva Pearl, dau of
J. W. & N. C. McQuiddy
Mar 20, 1880
Sep 6, 1881

Jane M. McQuiddy
Feb 11, 1828
Aug 30, 1864
aged: 36y, 6m, 19d.

Lila Cyrene McQuiddy
Mar 3, 1868
Nov 8, 1868
age: 8m & 5d.

C. B. King
Dec 18, 1808
Jun 14, 1892
aged: 83y, 5m, 26d.
&
M. C. King
Nov 3, 1823
Jun 24, 1871
age: 47y, 7m, 2d.

John McQuiddy
was born in Woodford Co., Ky.
Jun 12, 1790 & Died
Oct 10, 1863
aged: 73y, 3m, 28d.

Achsah McQuiddy
was born in Woodford Co., Ky.
Feb 20, 1793 & Died in
Bedford Co., Tenn.
Mar 7, 1881

James B. Thompson
Dec 5, 1873
Mar 15, 1943
&
Fannie Thompson
Jan 6, 1875
May 22, 1965

Joseph N. Huffman
Sep 26, 1875
Mar 30, 1876

Margaret J. Huffman, dau of
Adam & Sally Anthony & wife
of John P. Huffman
Feb 16, 1843
married Jan 3, 1867 & Died
(dates in ground)

J. F. Rippey
1859-1908

Sallie B. Rippey
1862-1903

Johnnie N. Rippey
Jan 31, 1897
Aug 24, 1901

T. C. Thompson
1843-1924
&
Achsah Thompson
1848-1882

Thomas E. Thompson
Jan 10, 1880
Mar 5, 1906

Bettie, dau of
T. C. & A. N. Thompson
Nov 15, 1875
Jul 15, 1879

George W., Jr., son of
G. W. & M. J. King
Died Jul 2, 1884
(no age given)
& Wife:
M. J., wife of
G. W. King
Died Nov 28, 1884
(no age given)

20 CULLEY-HOLT CEMETERY   Map # 12
This Cemetery is located about 2 miles North of Normandy, Tenn.

W. E. Bramblett
Jan 2, 1853
Sep 6, 1854

R. E. B. Bramblett
Aug 5, 1867
Sep 23, 1873

F. M., Son of
William Culley
Aug 31, 1832
Jul 5, 1854

William Culley
Died Dec 25, 1872
aged: 72y, 1m, 9d.

Mary, Consort of
William Culley & dau of
William S. Sitt
Dec 18, 1805
Aug 24, 1860

L. J., dau of
William Culley
Sep 25, 1844
Jun 26, 1859

Jane A., Consort of
J. W. Culley & dau of
L. Holt
Died Sep 1, 1857
(no age given)

Larkin Holt
Jul 22, 1805
Jul 17, 1840

Cemetery is in very bad
                     condition.

Many unmarked graves.

Elijah Holt
Aug 17, 1786
Sep 29, 1868

Jane Holt
May 18, 1787
Oct 27, 1853

Martha, dau of
W. J. & E. Smith
Nov 23, 1856
Dec 20, 1856

296

21 GREEN CEMETERY   Map # 12
This Cemetery is located near Lake Bedford.

David R. S. V. Green
Oct 16, 1853
Jun 25, 1854

1 Lt.
William M. Green
Co A
44 Tenn Inf C.S.A.
Dec 12, 1829
May 31, 1910

Mary A. Green
Feb 16, 1829
Nov 16, 1867

Robert W. Green
1869-1931

Zephaniah Roberts, Born in
Penleton District, S.C.
Nov 13, 1803
Nov 16, 1869
aged: 66y & 3d.

Rebecca Roberts
Born May 12, 1809
married Sep 1824
Died Oct 24, 1889
aged: 80y, 5m, 12d.

* by Miss Mary Bass.

Emily Floyd
1856-1941

Z. C. Roberts
Jan 25, 1844
Nov 4, 1891

Infant Son of
J. Y. & L. E. Roberts
Sep 13, 1884
Sep 30, 1884

Zephaniah J. B., son of
J. S. & S. E. Roberts
Mar 9, 1861
Oct 26, 1865

J. F., son of
Z. C. & E. E. Roberts
Born & Died
Dec 8, 1872

Rachel Roberts
Aug 4, 1839
Jul 1, 1898

No marker:*
James Green   and wife:
Oct 10, 1800 in N.C.
Nov 17, 1853

J. S. Roberts
Sep 22, 1836
Sep 3, 1926
   & wife:
Sarah E. Roberts
Sep 2, 1835
Nov 26, 1884
2nd marker:
Sarah E., wife of
J. S. Roberts
Oct 11, 1835
Nov 26, 1884
   & wife:
Sue F. Roberts
Jan 14, 1847
Jul 25, 1917

Mary P. Roberts
May 12, 1825
May 11, 1864
aged: 38y, 11m, 28d.

J. F. E., son of
Z. & Rebecca Roberts
Sep 30, 1849
Oct 16, 1854

No marker:*
Mary Smith Green
Mar 3, 1801 in Ga.
Aug 29, 1885

J. J. Smith
Dec 1, 1853
May 19, 1884
   &
Miss R. I. Smith
Oct 27, 1865
May 3, 1887

S. R. Smith
Jul 7, 1861
Sep 20, 1865
   &
J. W. Smith
Mar 15, 1858
Sep 11, 1865

W. B. Rhoton
Jan 14, 1866
Jun 27, 1939

Jennie (Green) Rhoton
(Marker face down)

Pearl L. Rhoton
Jul 20, 1897
May 27, 1909

No marker:*
Willis Green, father of
James Green

22 LEMING CEMETERY   Map # 12
"Old Prince Cemetery"
This Cemetery is located about ½ mile South of Normandy, Tenn.

-. W. Montgomery
Born Dec 8, 1845
Died (gone)

Mrs. Alzira Montgomery
Dec 10, 1811
Mar 11, 1881

Delinda E. Riggens
Feb 13, 1837
Sep 18, 1856
aged: 19 yrs.

John H. H. Glascow
Jan 14, 1875
Feb 26, 1906

Offit L. Bryant
1881-1930
   &
Pearl L. Bryant
1885-1942

Annie Maie, dau of
R. S. & Lula Spencer
Jan 17, 1898
Jul 25, 1903

Bedie Koonce Clayton
1882-1955

James & Dykes, Infant Sons
of James & Bedie Clayton
(no dates)

Samuel A. Wellborn, son of
Samuel & Mary Wellborn
Died in Bedford Co., Tenn.
Aug 31, 1821
aged: 21 yrs. Was a Native
      of Wilkes Co., Ga.

Minnie May Moore
Mar 2, 1890
Feb 7, 1919

George H. Huffman
Dec 22, 1802
Oct 2, 1884

Lucinda, wife of
G. H. Huffman
Oct 16, 1803
Jan 19, 1871

Loyd Dance
Apr 20, 1901
Dec 29, 1968
   &
Willie May Dance
Feb 2, 1904
Apr 9, 1971

Albert Marvin Koonce
Mar 12, 1913
Jan 26, 1970
   &
Elizabeth F. Koonce
Sep 22, 1911- ----------

J. H. Prince
Dec 14, 1859
Dec 25, 1883

Johnie, dau of
J. H. & Virginia Prince
Sep 1, 1883
Oct 16, 1883

H. Prince
Oct 2, 1823
Jul 15, 1887

Sallie H. Prince
Mar 2, 1825
Nov 13, 1880

William H. Leming
Jul 7, 1868
Aug 22, 1907
   &
Connie V. Leming
Mar 7, 1879
Mar 28, 1965

Argie Sue Pall, dau of
William H. & Connie V. Leming
Aug 16, 1907
Jan 26, 1908

Harry Clay Leming
Jan 5, 1902
Nov 29, 1902

Francis M. Prince
Jan 1, 1851
Sep 9, 1869
"Member of the M.E.Church"

Isaac B. Prince
Feb 25, 1847
Dec 18, 1866

James P. Prince
Jul 18, 1845
Dec 11, 1865

Henry C. Koonce
Sep 20, 1850
Dec 14, 1924
aged: 74 yrs.

Mary F., wife of
Henry C. Koonce
Sep 27, 1852
Oct 7, 1909

Argie Carr Koonce
Jan 22, 1889
Jan 20, 1908

W. T. Koonce
Jan 17, 1877
Oct 30, 1927

Mary E. Koonce
Oct 3, 1887
Feb 8, 1964

Hearnder Roy Koonce
Dec 19, 1898
Jan 26, 1905
age: 6y, 1m, 7d

Fannie V. Koonce
Apr 10, 1879
Sep 14, 1903
age: 24y, 5m, 4d.

Beulah Pauline Daniel
Jul 25, 1899
Aug 12, 1969
(picture)

J. W. Elkins
Aug 13, 1853
Mar 5, 1923

Sam B. Gibson
Dec 16, 1873
Sep 16, 1929

B. Throneberry
1880-1945
&
Sallie Throneberry
1882-1961

Charles L. Hickerson
Apr 17, 1865
(no date)
&
Mollie E. Hickerson
Dec 29, 1869
Mar 29, 1934

"Mother"
Sallie C., wife of
W. D. Hickerson
Apr 16, 1872
Aug 3, 1926

Clarence W. Roulett
May 1, 1899

&
Dellie E. Roulett
Dec 8, 1900
Jul 16, 1955

William C. Throneberry
New York
CMOMM U.S.Coast Guard RES
W. W. II
Sep 5, 1904
Sep 2, 1962

Merna S. Throneberry
Oct 10, 1911

William Ed. Throneberry
1879-1960
&
Blanche Throneberry
1881-1947

Minnie May Holland
Mar 2, 1890
Feb 7, 1919

John Meakin Lane
Sep 10, 1889
Jul 7, 1921

Ruby B. Lane
Oct 12, 1914
Jan 29, 1923

Robert W. White
1880-1944

Gracie D. White
1883-1972
(Daves-Culberson)

Emmett Wooten
Sep 18, 1886

&
Kate W. Wooten
May 30, 1880

Pompy Hyles
Born Feb --, 182-
Died --- --, ----(broken)

Katie, wife of
Pompy Hyles
Jan 7, 1823
Apr 28, 1883(broken)

D. R. Throneberry
Feb 1, 1839
Dec 11, 1923
&
Sarah Shelton Throneberry
Oct 19, 1840
Nov 14, 1914
age: 74y & 25d.

S. S. Throneberry
1859-1936
& Wife:
Nannie A. Throneberry
1859-1918

Stephen Lee Onie Moore
Jan 28, 1887
Nov 8, 1961
&
Hester Belle Rhoton Moore
Mar 18, 1899

James S. Arnold
Jun 10, 1850
Mar 28, 1928

Bettie Arnold
Mar 1, 1861
Jun 30, 1937

Isaac J. Keeling
1857-1921

Pauling Keeling
1918-1920

John Smith
Oct 18, 1869
Feb 23, 1928
&
Lula Smith
Dec 7, 1873
(no date)

Ella Knowles Roulett
1915-1957

No marker:*
Mrs. Jane Daniel

* by Jerry Wayne Cook.

Alpha E. Hitt
Oct 10, 1901

&
Laura E. Hitt
Jun 10, 1903
Jul 1, 1949

Thomas Gordon Sharrock
Aug 20, 1883
Jul 12, 1965
&
Bessie Iona Sharrock
Sep 20, 1883
Nov 2, 1949

Jake M. Moore
1861-1950
&
Pearlie A. Moore
1867-1953

Calvin C. Arnold
Jan 15, 1887
Mar 24, 1935

Dosia Gowen Arnold
Feb 15, 1887
Jun 22, 1922

Isaac Jesse McNutt
1875-1937
&
Anna McNutt
1877-(no date)

Infant Son of
Mr & Mrs H. E. Prince
1920

H. W. Roulett
1928-1933
(Tullahoma)

Aug Roulett
1935-1935
(Tullahoma)

Many unmarked graves.

---

23 WEAVER CEMETERY   Map # 12
This Cemetery is located about 1 mile South of Normandy, Tenn.

Cecil B., son of
J. F. & S. E. Weaver
Jan 10, 1900
Nov 21, 1900

Lillan P., dau of
J. F. & S. E. Weaver
Oct 10, 1901
Jul 11, 1903

No Marker:*
Green Weaver, son of
Z. Weaver
(no dates)

Copied by Jerry Wayne Cook.

* by Jerry W. Cook.

---

24 GREEN CEMETERY   Map # 12
This Cemetery is located about 1 mile South of Normandy, Tenn.,
on Carr Creek.

James A., son of   and
J. L. & S. E. Vincent
Mar 18, 1883
Sep 13, 1883

Sarah E., wife of
J. L. Vincent & dau of
J. C. & M. F. Leming
Feb 16, 1863
Mar 30, 1883

James C. Leming
Dec 6, 1839
Jun 21, 1901

N. E. Leming   and wife:
Aug 4, 1871
Aug 30, 1928

Mary F. Leming
Aug 23, 1838
May 21, 1904

Helen Bryant Leming
Feb 8, 1879
Feb 4, 1925

298

J. D. Jetton
Nov 21, 1857
May 18, 1915

Mary Ann Jetton
Feb 4, 1866
May 6, 1946

William A. Jetton
Sep 11, 1897
May 27, 1964

James E. Jetton
Jun 7, 1904
May 10, 1950

R. A. Schrimsher
May 11, 1829
Aug 6, 1909

A. J. Schrimsher
Jul 15, 1844
Apr 26, 1892

Elizabeth A. Sherrill
May 24, 1823
May 13, 1870

Fannie Huffman
Jul 27, 1832
Dec 14, 1907

Sarah A., wife of
J. A. Vincent
Oct 6, 1847
Oct 23, 1877

Sarah A., dau of
J. A. & S. A. Vincent
Dec 16, 1871
Apr 23, 1873

Mary E., dau of
J. A. & S. A. Vincent
Jan 27, 1870
Apr 19, 1873

Thomas B. Carr
Apr 3, 1815
Feb 2, 1893

Mary, wife of
T. B. Carr
Sep 1, 1819
Oct 6, 1887

John Sherrill
Jul 6, 1852
Aug 24, 1915

Laura Sherrill
Jun 11, 1865
Apr 5, 1949

Horace Sherrill
Jan 29, 1890
Nov 15, 1964

Thomas J. Scruggs
Nov 13, 1844
Sep 25, 1879

James K. Polk Leming
Mar 30, 1877
Apr 5, 1960
&
Mary Russell Leming
Nov 3, 1885
Nov 4, 1965

James P. Sutton
May 31, 1838
Oct 14, 1899

Ann Sutton
Apr 6, 1844
Aug 25, 1910

John T. Weaver, son of
Samuel & Sarah Weaver
Mar 3, 1830
May 25, 1863
age: 33y, 2m, 22d.

Medie L., wife of
J. R. Green
Dec 14, 1868
May 22, 1892

Thomas Clarence, son of
M. L. & J. R. Green
Apr 2, 1890
Mar 23, 1891

Johnie, son of
M. L. & J. R. Green
Dec 31, 1891
Jun 4, 1892

Wilson Anthony
Sep 8, 1827
Apr 27, 1861

Revolutionary Soldier
James Miller
departed this life
Mar 16, 1840
aged: 86 yrs.
"I have fought a good fight
and have gone home"

Elizabeth Miller
departed this life
Mar 13, 1830
aged: 70 yrs.
"Gone but not forgotten"

Elizabeth Phillips
1839-1923

"Mother"
Sarah A. Bomar
Jul 2, 1848
Mar 18, 1895

Cathrine Prince, wife of
J. R. Prince
Jan 18, 1842
Apr 4, 1889

This above Cemetery is separated from the
Green Cemetery.

John Sutton
Jan 26, 1870
Feb 23, 1870

William Sutton
Jan 3, 1872
Apr 3, 1872

Sarah C., wife of
Jacob Renegar
Apr 11, 1833
Oct 4, 1874

Martha J., dau of
Jacob & S. C. Renegar
Jul 28, 1871
Died 1872

George W. Sherrill
Sep 12, 1811
Mar 27, 1865

Lucretia F., wife of
George W. Sherrill
Jun 29, 1812
Oct 28, 1882

Sarah J., dau of
George & Fielder Sherrill
Jan 18, 1840
(no date-broken)

William Carr
Born Sep 30, 1766
departed this life
Sep 17, 1850
"Asleep in Jesus, that dear
friend in whom my hopes of
Heaven depend"

Rachel Carr
Born Feb 26, 1785
departed this life
Feb 22, 1818
"Sleep on dear Mother & take
thy rest--God called thee home
He thought it best"

Infant Babe of
J. F. & G. A. Phillips
Apr 15, to Apr 22, 1905

James F. Phillips   and
Apr 25, 1863
Jul 21, 1941

Henry P. Prince
Nov 11, 1876
Oct 29, 1880

N. A., dau of
J. D. & M. E. Carr
Dec 24, 1878
Sep 27, 1879
age: 9m & 3d.

Thomas W. Carr
Apr 8, 1842
Jun 9, 1880
age: 38y, 2m, -d.

John H. Carr
Jan 13, 1847
Oct 29, 1872

Elizabeth T., dau of
Z. & A. Weaver
Jan 24, 1832
Nov 4, 1834

Sarah A., dau of
Z. & A. Weaver
Nov 18, 1826
Oct 16, 1833

Joseph D., son of
Z. & A. Weaver
Apr 11, 1838
Sep 23, 1842

Monroe T., son of
Z. & A. Weaver
Nov 17, 1847
Jul 8, 1855

"Father"
Zephaniah Weaver
May 9, 1798
Jan 8, 1886
aged: 87y, 7m, 29d.

Annie, wife of
Zephaniah Weaver
Apr 12, 1805
Jan 20, 1878

Georgia A. Phillips
Jun 11, 1877
Jan 10, 1955

Thomas Fred, son of
T. J. & S. A. Scruggs
Oct 24, 1878
Sep 29, 1880

Lyndell E. Carr
1900-1967
(Daves)

J. D. Carr
Jan 11, 1855
Sep 17, 1907

Joseph B. Carr
May 24, 1887
Mar 19, 1917

James Ellis Ray
Jul 18, 1869
Apr 30, 1955
&
Mettie Carr Ray
Oct 2, 1880
Aug 26, 1908

Janice Lee Ray
Aug 25, 1925
Sep 16, 1925

Minnie Lee Ray
Oct 2, 1881
Jan 28, 1926

Ollie Lee Ray, son of
B. M. & M. L. Ray
Jul 13, 1905
Dec 22, 1907

* by Jerry Wayne Cook.

George W. Vibbart
1874-1952
&
Ada C. Vibbart
1875-1937

Davis Baby
(no dates)

B. W. Bond
Oct 11, 1857
May 5, 1899

Eliza A. Bond
1819-1892

Loddie L. Woodard
1900-1954
(Moore-Motlow)

Ettie B., dau of
W. R. & Inez Foster
Apr 9, 1900
Sep 5, 1917

Ernest Wesley, son of
Lee & Lizzie Stone
Dec 30, 1914
Nov 30, 1919

Jasper J. Davis
Born May 29, 1903
married to Clara B. Stone
Dec 24, 1921 & Died
Jan 13, 1923

No marker:*
Daisy Woodard
Born Nov 27, 1895
Died May 13, 1937

Charlie Parks
Aug 13, 1877
Nov 14, 1973

Minnie Etta Martin
1879-1959
(Daves-Culberson)

William L. Weaver
1828-1906
&
Sallie Weaver
1833-1883

Guy Stephen Short
Born & Died
Jun 30, 1953

John Lane
Co E
4 Tenn Cav.
C.S.A.

T. J. Grooms
Nov 7, 1901
Mar 11, 1904

"Wooden Cross"
T. G.
(no dates)

No marker:*
Sallie Fuller (no dates)
Lester Fuller (no dates)
Boss Shelton (no dates)
Dink Shelton (no dates)
Willie Woodard (no dates)
Clarence Woodard (no dates)

Many unmarked graves.

Zora Edde Carr
Apr 21, 1895
Oct 4, 1974

"Father"
Samuel A. Sherrill
Jul 24, 1872
Nov 27, 1950
&
"Mother"
Maggie Uselton Sherrill
Dec 31, 1873
Mar 26, 1960

Paul Alexander Sherrill
1901-1928
&
Gladys Gambill Sherrill
1906-

Carroll W. Davis
Aug 28, 1935
Aug 3, 1936

Paul R. Davis
Nov 26, 1931
Jul 25, 1932

Robert E. Fuller
Dec 31, 1899
Mar 12, 1917
age: 17y, 2m, 12d.

Sarah Fuller
Died May 17, 1945
aged: 96 yrs.
(Daves-Ramsey)

Many fieldstones, no
inscriptions.

25 RENEGAR CEMETERY   Map # 12
This Cemetery is located about 1 mile South of Normandy, Tenn.

Sarah C. Renegar
Aug 10, 1843
May 4, 1905

This is the only marker left.
Cemetery is now in Cow-pasture.

26 STONE CEMETERY   Map # 12
This Cemetery is near Moore County Line, on Carr Creek.

Ida Richards, wife of
James W. Richards & dau of
Andrew & Martha Stone
Jul 23, 1880
Jun 11, 1901
age: 20y, 11m, 19d.

Mattie Stone
Died 1939
(Thompson Service)

abt 20 or more graves, with fieldstones, no insc.

Mattie Jones
1886-1913

James Andrew Short
1871-1948
(Fred Davis Service)

27 VANCE CEMETERY   Map # 12
This Cemetery is located about 1 mile East of Roseville, Tenn.

Mary Ewell
Born in Augusta Co., Va.
Feb 11, 1750 & Died
May 10, 1841

[Located on John Ewell Grant]

Anne Vance
Born Aug 13, 1827
Died Jan 4, 1854

Lela, dau of
A. E. & Mittie J. Derham
Mar 30, 1867
Mar 21, 1871(broken)

Several unmarked graves.

28 NUTT CEMETERY   Map # 12
This Cemetery is located about ½ mile South of Roseville, Tenn.
Copied by Jerry Wayne Cook

[Located on the old Daniel Ship-
-man grant, probably started as
Shipman graveyard]

Jessie Nutt
Jun 21, 1805
May 15, 1883

3 or 4 wives of Jessie Nutt
are buried here.

Many unmarked graves

Lee Nutt, son of
Jessie Nutt
(no dates)

Edmond Cortner was buried here
1907- age about 7 years.

29 DANIEL CEMETERY   Map # 12
This Cemetery is located about 2 miles Southeast of Shofner Lutheran
Church, near the Trout Farm.

H. D. (Daniel)
(fieldstone)

Several fieldstones, no insc.

30 LANDIS CEMETERY   Map # 12
This Cemetery is located about 1 mile Southeast of Shofner Lutheran
Church, on Thompson Creek Road.

Phebe Angeline, third dau
of J. & M. Landis
Jun 27, 1830
Oct 11, 1839

Robert Wilson, second son
of J. & M. Landis
Dec 13, 1831
Oct 25, 1839

No marker:*
Haley Harrison, son of
Jake Harrison
Died abt 1910, at an
advanced age.

Absalom M. Landis, son of
Absalome & Nancy Landis
Apr 3, 1846
Sep 23, 1847

Emma, wife of
Dr. S. P. King
Died Nov 3, 1873
aged: 28y, 9m, 2d.

William, Infant son of
A. E. & Nancy Landis
Died Dec 16, 1873
aged: 6 days

Phoebe Lee Landis
Born Feb 26, 1774
Died   1841

John Landis
Apr 19, 1795
Jul 4, 1854

Mary Landis
Oct 14, 1796
Dec 14, 1868

---------, dau of
R. L. & Susan Landers
Born Sep 2, ----
Died Aug 2, 1839

Robert A., son of
R. L. & Susan Landers
Died in Bedford Co., Tenn
Born Nov 15, 1841
Died Mar 6, 1872

[Located on Christopher & Phoebe (Lee)
Landers old land grant]

Martha L. Troxler
Died Oct 11, 1868
age: 75 yrs.

Eran Shofner
Oct 15, 1826
Jun 21, 1869

William C. Shofner
1861-1881

Letitia Landers Boyers
Dec 20, 1843
Jun 18, 1867
Age: 29y, 5m, 23d.

Lavoy Penn, fourth son of
A. & N. Landis
Mar 9, 1854
Aug 9, 1868

Many unmarked graves.
Many fieldstones, no insc.

BRONZE PLAQUE
In Memory

Phoebe Lee Landis	1774-1841	William Shofner	1863-1881
John Landis	1795-1854	John Koonce	1854-1879
Mary Lowe Landis	1796-1868	Margaret L. Bennett	1839-1877
Phoebe Landis	1830-1839	Absalom Landis	1846-1847
Robert Landis	1832-1839	Melville Landis	1849-1914
Abel U. Landis	1837-1876	Leroy Penn Landis	1854-1868
John C. Landis	1845-19	Martha L. Troxler	1794-1868
Eran Landis Shofner	1826-1869	Albert Lowe	1827-1899

31 ANTHONY CEMETERY   Map # 12
This Cemetery is located about 2 miles Northeast of Raus, Tenn.

Daniel Anthony
   Co B
17 Reg. Tenn. Inf.
   C.S.A.

32 STONE CEMETERY   Map # 12
This Cemetery is located about 2 miles Northeast of Raus, Tenn.
Copied by Winston Roberts.

J. B. Stone
Jul 12, 1856
(no date)

Alonzo H. Carpenter   and
Jun 6, 1891

Della S. (Stone) Carpenter
Jan 30, 1881
Oct 29, 1943

This Cemetery is located about 1 mile Southeast of Singleton, Tenn.

Sarah Ann Holt, Consort of
J. H. Holt
Jan 30, 1824
Oct 30, 1852

Logan Mitchell
(no dates)

Henry Holt
Sep 22, 1820
Oct 30, 1854
aged: 33y, 11m, 8d.

Nannie Mitchell
(no dates)

Nancy Jane Ray, Consort of
G. M. Ray
Apr 17, 1823
Aug 18, 1852

Mary Mitchell
(No dates)

Green Holt
1845-1930
&
Martha Holt
1845-1929

Many unmarked graves.

34 POWELL CEMETERY   Map # 12
This Cemetery is located near Raus, Tenn.

Loddie Prince
May 18, 1888
Jan 3, 1959
(picture)
& Granddaughter:
Martha Ruth Reid
Mar 25, 1956
Apr 14, 1956

Opal Payne
Jan 8, 1915

George Earl Prince
Born & Died
Mar 19, 1948

Bobby Wayne Prince
Mar 2, 1949
Apr 2, 1949

C. R. Riddle
1857-1930
(Tullahoma)

Lizzie Riddle
Apr 20, 1857
Apr 29, 1914
"Mother"

Sarah E. Riddle
1888-1932
(Tullahoma)

Lewis T. Powell
1838-1918
&
Martha C. Powell
1847-1904

John O. Powell
1874-1948

John Powell
(no dates)

Naomi Powell
(no dates)

Charlie Pinkney Prince
Feb 17, 1882
Aug 15, 1956
&
Maggie Elizabeth Prince
Feb 21, 1887
Jan 15, 1960

C. W. Prince
1915-1975 (TM)

Dewey Evans
1920-1937(Tullahoma)

Louise Evans
1929-1930(Tullahoma)

Betty Evans
1942-1942
(Tullahoma)

Alvis G. Evans
1898-1943
(Motlow)

Laura Evans
1901-1972
(Tullahoma)

Mrs. Ella Gwynn Chipps
1926-1943 (TM)

Arthur L. Riddle
May 30, 1894
Jul 5, 1956
&
Myrtle V. Riddle
Jun 16, 1899
Aug 28, 1966

George Petersen
1873-1939
&
Rosa E. Petersen
1876-(no date)

Charles Powell
Apr 18, 1821
May 8, 1906

James F. Powell
Oct 26, 1872
Oct 10, 1899
age: 26y, 11m, 11d.

Infant Son of
J. & Sarah L. Smith
Oct 12, 1901
Oct 31, 1901

Sarah L., wife of
Joseph Smith
Jan 13, 1881
Oct 16, 1901

June E. Prince
Jul 10, 1942
Feb 1, 1970

Robert M. Curl
1927-1928

S. J. Curl
1885-1945

Ellen Ann Cashion
Jun 23, 1938

Harry Penn
Feb 9, 1852
Aug 19, 1887
&
Almeda Penn
May 2, 1857
Jul 21, 1945

Carley T. Penn
Sep 3, 1885
Sep 17, 1968
&
Tennie Penn
Jun 4, 1884
Oct 5, 1951

George Roy Jones
Nov 22, 1884
Jun 22, 1966
&
Josie D. Jones
Aug 6, 1887
TM-   1969

Thomas J. Laseter
Aug 17, 1870
Mar 1, 1942
&
Mary Jane Laseter
Mar 17, 1878

George T. Evans
Aug 6, 1878
Dec 27, 1925

Lillie D. Evans
Nov 6, 1884
May 9, 1926

Nannie Duckworth
Mar 11, 1881
Mar 7, 1956

Marie L. Carter
1900-1957
(Motlow)

Jack Brinkley
Apr 9, 1865
Apr 1, 1906

Mattie Brinkley
Jul 24, 1872
Feb 26, 1943

Raymond Cecil Penn
Tennessee
Pvt U.S.Army W.W.II
Dec 5, 1908
Mar 8, 1954

John W. Penn
May 13, 1883
Jan 27, 1975
&
Clara N. Penn
Sep 26, 1895
Dec 19, 1931

Oza L. Woodard
Tennessee
Cpl Co B 167 Inf W.W.I
Mar 11, 1893
Apr 12, 1969
&
Fannie R. Woodard
Feb 6, 1890
TM-   1972

J. J. Dial
Jul 3, 1845
Oct 7, 1920

Martha C. Dial
Feb 17, 1845
Feb 10, 1923

James R. Prince
Aug 6, 1851
Aug 3, 1945

James R. Prince
Oct 9, 1838
Apr 20, 1914

Ed Prince
Aug 26, 1879
Mar 1, 1928

Mollie A. Prince
1877-19(no date)
&
Ida I. Prince
1884-1947

Thomas Avery Himes
Mar 14, 1847
Feb 11, 1941
&
Martha A. Shofner Himes
Apr 7, 1849
Oct 9, 1925

Lenner Lue Eller, dau of
John & Willie Hitt
Feb 2, 1891

John M. Hitt
May 20, 1863
Mar 17, 1922
&
Willie M. Hitt
May 12, 1873
(no date)

Carolyn Richards
1858-1937

Mary M. Gunn
Jul 1, 1860
May 10, 1947

Sylvester, son of
A. H. & M. M. Gunn
Oct 17, 1886
Dec 5, 1887

Charles Ivy Bingham
Apr 3, 1885
Mar 21, 1967

Bonnie Bennett Bingham
Sep 3, 1889
May 14, 1937

Floyd Earl Prince
1940-1966
(Daves-Culberson)

Shelia Prince
1967-1967
(Motlow)

Ollie Sanders
Oct 3, 1893
Nov 15, 1959

Dr. W. J. Trott
Dec 23, 1861
Jun 28, 1914

Infant dau of
Dr. W. J. & V. C. Trott
Sep 24, 1894
Oct 26, 1894

Infant Son of
Dr. W. J. & V. C. Trott
Aug 8, 1895

John M. Bennett
Sep 22, 1862
Mar 27, 1924

Effie Bennett
1880-1928

Callie Weaver Ferrell
Apr 27, 1877
Feb 15, 1933

Chanie Marshall Weaver
Sep 16, 1884
Nov 26, 1926

Margorie Riddle
Sep 2, 1930
Dec 22, 1930

Roy N. Prince
1895-1969
(Tullahoma)

Walter Prince
1880-1963
(Motlow)

Minnie Prince
1890-1956
(motlow)

Infant Prince
1956-1956
(Daves-Culberson)

Herbert Sanders
1896-1971
(Tullahoma)

Aubry D., son of
Mr & Mrs T. Swing
(no dates)

Ettie Lou Reagor
1896-1931

Eliza J., wife of
J. W. Gunn
Aug 6, 1856
Dec 4, 1884

Susan Gunn
1847-1912

W. M. Brinkley
1861-1938

Margaret, wife of
W. M. Brinkley
1856-1927

Walter Smith
1884-1968
(Daves-Culberson)

Alice M. Vibbart
Nov 20, 1902
Jan 23, 1903

William H. Anderton
Jul 6, 1849
Oct 16, 1921
&
Sallie Anderton
Oct 29, 1850
(no date)

Sam Smotherman
1871-1940
&
Dessie Smotherman
1890-(no date)

Dot Sanders
Jan 29, 1903
Jan 31, 1909

Steven Dale Sanders
Nov 8, 1951
Sep 26, 1973

No marker:*
Mary Brinkley Lehr
Born abt 1820
mrd-John F. Lehr 1842
Died abt 1900

* by Mr. Brice Brinkley.

John Brinkley
Jan 1, 1817
May 23, 1900
aged: 83y, 4m, 22d.

Nancy, wife of
John Brinkley
May 11, 1824
May 13, 1887
aged: 63y, & 2d.

Peter C. Brinkley
Jan 4, 1845
Feb 21, 1903

Cassie Brinkley
Dec 11, 1849
Sep 14, 1923

John W. Taylor
Jun 18, 1848
Feb 20, 1906

Edward Prince
1914-1973
(Tullahoma)

Sam M. Sanders, Husband of
Helen S. Sanders
Born Sep 17, 1901
Died   1926

William Prince
1853-1936
&
Rosie Prince
1863-1938

Lillie Mae Smith
1911-1951

Over 100 graves with
fieldstones, no inscriptions

35 FERGURSON CEMETERY   Map # 12
This Cemetery is located about ½ mile North of Raus, on
Thompsons Creek.

Copied by Winston Roberts.

Rev. H. C. Fergurson* &
wife: Harriett C. Fergurson*
*1850 Census:
Henry C. Fergurson born in
N. C., died after 1850,
he was 49 in 1850 and wife
Harriett C. Fergurson, born
in Va., died after 1850, she
was 45 in 1850.

[Harriett Fergurson(Ferguson)
  Born Feb.18, 1804
  Died Jan. 3, 1892]

Dr. H.(Henry) P. Ferguson
Jul 11, 1831
Jan 2, 1882

No marker:
Margaret Ferguson [2]
Born 1774
Died after 1850

[2] Widow of John Ferguson

Fannie Ferguson
Aug 1, 1838
Dec 1, 1881

2 or 3 unmarked graves.

A.(Alexander) D. Ferguson
Sep 26, 1827
Jan 28, 1906

303

36 PARKER CEMETERY   Map # 12
This Cemetery is located at Raus, Tenn.

"Pinkney"
Daniel Parker
Jan 20, 1844
Jun 8, 1901

Jett Parker, son of
M. & E. Parker
May 17, 1850
Mar 28, 1864

James McGill
Born near Dublin, Ireland
1787-1860

Sallie McGill
Born Apr 10, 1791
Died Oct 27, 1884
aged: 93y, 5m, 17d.

Ollie B., son of
B.P. & Mary Prince
Jan 25, 1866
Aug 8, 1889
&
Homer, son of
B. B. & Mary Prince
Jan 4, ----
Feb 29, ----(in ground, deep)

Henry Grady Parker
1890-1890
&
Infant Sister
1884-1884
Children of
H. T. & E. M. Parker

Ruth S., dau of
H. T. & E. M. Parker
1893-1922

Dr. J. W. McGill
Jul 26, 1833
Jul 4, 1893
aged: 60y & 9d.

Elizabeth E. High
Feb 28, 1814
Aug 8, 1882

Captain Elijah Parker
1768-1853
"State of North Carolina,
To Elijah Parker, Greeting,
We repossing Special Trust
& Confedence in your Patriot-
ism, Valour, Conduct & abili-
ties, do, by these presents,
constitute & appoint you
Captain in the Duch District
witness Richard Dobbs Spaight,
Esquire, Our Governor, Captain-
General & Commander in Chief,
under his hand and seal which
he has caused to be here to
affixed, at New Bern on the
10th Day of Dec., A.D., 1791,
& in the 15th year of our
Independence.
    Rich'd Dobbs Spaight.

Henry T. Parker
Apr 27, 1856
May 29, 1939
&
May E. Parker
Jul 18, 1861
Aug 12, 1938

Susan Ella Parker
Sep 1, 1885

Daniel Parker
Sep 17, 1816
Feb 7, 1886
&
Susan Whitaker Grisard, wife
of Daniel Parker
1826-1893
&
Nancy Dean, wife of
D. Parker --------------------
1814-1852

Polly Dean
1818-1845 2nd marker:
Polly A., wife of
D. P. Parker
Mar 13, 1818
Sep 18, 1845

Daniel William Parker
Oct 29, 1887
Jan 22, 1972
&
Ella Tarpley Parker
Feb 28, 1895

Henry Douglas Parker
1895-1951
&
Hettye Mai Wallis Parker
1901-

James H., son of
D. P. & Polly A. Parker
Jul 12, 1847
Dec 22, 1859

2nd marker for:

Nancy P., wife of
D. P. Parker
Died Aug 27, 1852
aged: 38 yrs.

---

37 HORNADAY-PROBY CEMETERY   Map # 12
This Cemetery is located about 1 mile Northwest of Raus, Tenn.

Walter S., son of
Joseph A. & Selina K.
Hornaday
Born Mar 8, 1850
Died Aug 13, 1852
age: 2y, 4m, 5d.

Joseph A. Hornaday
Feb 25, 1818
Apr 24, 1885
aged: 67y, 1m, 29d.

Annie, wife of
J. W. McGill
May 7, 1850
Apr 28, 1899

Salina K. Hornaday
Sep 30, 1830
Jan 17, 1862

2 or 3 unmarked graves.

James W. Proby
Born Jun 8, 1812
Baptised into the Baptist
Church 1849
Died Oct 10, 1855

J. W. Proby
Nov 21, 1844
Dec 26, 1917

---

38 ROBERTS CEMETERY   Map # 12
This Cemetery is located about 1 mile North of Raus, on Thompson Creek Road.

Robert H. Glasgow
Jan 11, 1914
Oct 13, 1974
&
Inez Glasgow
Oct 28, 1930
----
married Aug 22, 1945

------ Daniel
(marker gone)

James F. Davis
Nov 11, 1863
Oct 22, 1956
&
Lucy M. Davis
May 1, 1867
Feb 27, 1947

Clabe Glascoe
1888-1947

John William Sons
Apr 12, 1877
Apr 26, 1950
&
Cynthia Leona Sons
Sep 17, 1892
Oct 26, 1966

Lucy S. Glascoe
1889-1955

Jeff D. Glascoe
Oct 8, 1861
Jan 31, 1934 (TM)

Mary Ann Short Glascoe
wife of J. D. Glascoe
(TM-No dates)

Dora B. Glascoe
1925-1925

Albert M. Glascoe
1901-1956
(Daves-Culberson)

Charles D. Glascoe, Sr.
1896-1974
(Daves-Culberson)

"Mother"
Plinie E. Glascoe
1899-1950
(TM-Plinie Ellen)

No markers:*
Thomas Roberts[2]
(no dates)

No marker:*
Elizabeth Roberts[3] wife of
Thomas Roberts (no dates)

Ed Springfield*
(no marker)

Bill Sons
(no dates)

Nan Cross Sons
(no dates)

T. L.(Thomas Lacy) Roberts
Dec 28, 1807
Aug 10, 1884
    & wife:
Priscilla Roberts
Aug 31, 1820
Jul 22, 1897

No marker:*
Betsey Lacy Roberts, wife
of Thomas Roberts(no dates)

Andy Glascoe
1965-1965
(Daves-Culberson)

Lindy Glascoe
Infant
(no dates)

Patsy Lee Glasgow
1949-1949
(Fred Daves FH)

Elizabeth Roberts
Aug 24, 1836
Jun   1852

Smith Family*
no markers

* by Winston Roberts

Columbus D. Roberts
Feb 6, 1856
Sep 28, 1895
    &
Fannie B. Roberts
Jun 17, 1867
Nov 1, 1952

Beuford, son of
C. D. & F. B. Roberts
May 28, 1892
Jun 3, 1892

Matthew Lacy Roberts
C.S.A.

[2]Native of Halifax Co., VA
[3]Dau of Matthew Lacy native of
 Halifax Co., VA

39 BOMAR CEMETERY   Map # 12
This Cemetery is located just Southwest of Raus, Tenn.

John M. Honeycutt
1875-1954
    &
Argie H. Honeycutt
1887-TM-1968

Everette Edde
Dec 28, 1897
Oct 1, 1919

Lonnie Edith Fuller
1904-1906

Ruthy Lorean Fuller
1912-1914

Henreta Lokey, wife of
H. R. Allmon
1850-1877

Weldon Cheshire
Mar 18, 1839
Apr 21, 1901
"Confederate Soldier"

Mary A. Cheshire
Apr 23, 1847
Apr 4, 1923

J. G. Tillett
Jul 21, 1840
Oct 27, 1909
    &
Delana Tillett
Nov 29, 1850
Jun 9, 1940

Arch E. Caruthers
1859-1902
    &
Mollie Caruthers
1865-1941

Mrs. Nancy Elizabeth
Caruthers Pearson
Jan 13, 1877
Jan 19, 1906

J. D. Hitt
Mar 10, 1840
Feb 16, 1913
    &
M. E. Hitt
Nov 15, 1860
(no date)

Offitt O. Hitt
1880-1935

Jery Holt
Nov 13, 1806
Mar 14, 1877

Katey, wife of
Jery Holt
Apr 13, 1814
Jan 1, 1859

Leander Holt
Mar 7, 1834
Oct   1852

Sarah E. Holt
Dec 7, 1851
May 3, 1873

Leland C. Tillett
Tennessee
S2 U.S.Navy   W.W.II
Sep 10, 1921
Oct 5, 1970

Eliza Mae A. Tillett
1884-1956
(McFarland-Thompson)

Mattie Tillett Davis
Mar 29, 1885
Aug 23, 1920
married Jan 7, 1913

William Edward Tillett
Jan 24, 1874
Dec 27, 1907

Aline Cates
Apr 7, 1917
Oct 5, 1920

Robert D. Cates
May 29, 1904
Apr 25, 1918

Mildred P. Cates
Mar 27, 1914
Jan 21, 1917

Thomas Fuller
Feb 3, 1852
Feb 27, 1923
    &
M. Jane Fuller
Jun 29, 1850
Sep 19, 1925

J. Lafatte Fuller
Jun 18, 1884
Aug 6, 1932
    &
M. Priscilla Fuller
Oct 17, 1888

Horace C. Richards
Sep 27, 1886
Dec 12, 1927

Joe T. Gunn
1858-1910
    &
Katie L. Gunn
1874-1960

Dora Gunn Bomar
1905-1928

William H. Kimbro
1834-1900
    &
Polly Ann Kimbro
1840-1906

Rev. John B. Byrom
Jul 15, 1809
Feb 2, 1863
    &
Mary Byrom
Apr 23, 1813
Jan 6, 1896

Richard Ensil Fuller
1914-1935

Offit Ensil Fuller
1877-1947

Mrs. Mamie Fuller
1884-1956
(Cothron-Thompson)

Amos G. Ray
1837-1902

Sallie E. Ray
1851-1936

Bonnie Lois, dau of
J. H. & J. C. Richards
Nov 19, 1896
Feb 7, 1899

Rufus B., son of
J. H. & J. C. Richards
Mar 10, 1880
Mar 14, 1902
aged: 22y & 4d.

Oscar, son of
J. H. & J. C. Richards
Oct 23, 1884
Jan 19, 1904
aged: 19y, 2m, 27d.

John Henry Richards
Jun 24, 1853
Apr 1, 1916
    &
Jane Catharine Richards
Jul 24, 1855
Mar 31, 1903

W. N. Carothers
May 31, 1863
Feb 2, 1899
&
N. A., wife of
James Carothers
Mar 25, 1832
Nov 27, 1899

Sarah Cross Sons
1851-1928

Edward Edwards
Tennessee
Pvt U.S.Army
Mar 19, 1941
Jul 4, 1973

Jesse Sharpe
May 22, 1807
Oct 29, 1880
age: 73y, 5m, 7d.
&
M. M. E. Dickert, dau of
J. R. & S. A. Sharpe
Sep 30, 1860
May 5, 1883
age: 22y, 7m, 5d.

J. R. Sharp
Feb 12, 1836
Apr 27, 1880

Sallie E., wife of
J. R. Sharp
Feb 28, 1849
May 1, 1918

Infant Son of
E. & Maggie Roberts
Died Oct 19, 1876
age: 4weeks

Elijah Roberts
Jul 22, 1850
Jan 23, 1911
&
Maggie Roberts
Jul 19, 1854
Oct 25, 1886

Lavoy Riddle
Mar 19, 1880
Dec 4, 1902

Ara B. Riddle
May 26, 1874
Oct 7, 1890
&
Dora F. Riddle
Mar 21, 1871
Feb 10, 1887
Daughters of John &
Caroline Riddle.

John N. Pearson
Jul 1, 1847
Dec 14, 1935

Kate Pearson
Nov 30, 1847
Nov 6, 1899

Walter L. Gambill
1876-TM-1969
&
Ola C. Gambill
1883-1922
&
Lula T. Gambill
1883-1963

Minnie Gambill Majors
1890-1954

Fannie Wiseman Stephens
Dec 5, 1867
Oct 14, 1896

Sallie Wiseman
1842-1926

Ella Hasty
1878-1934

Eliza Jane High, wife of
C. P. High
Aug 8, 1843
Mar 15, 1875
aged: 30y, 7m, 7d.

Feriba Ladd
Aug 21, 1821
Dec 16, 1892

Margaret Ladd
Sep 16, 1850
Nov 12, 1926

Eliza, wife of
G. M. Ray
1838-1870

S. C. Stone
Feb 28, 1839
Jun 9, 1910
"Mother"

John Riddle
Feb 22, 1822
Apr 10, 1888

Rebekah Riddle, Consort of
John Riddle & dau of
Hezekiah Ray
Sep 30, 1825
Aug 5, 1859

Arviller, son of
H. J. & L. E. Prince
Jun 3, 1881
Dec 16, 1889

Carrie Prince
Apr 13, 1884
Oct 25, 1888

Ella Pearson
Aug 17, 1869
Aug 14, 1870

Mollie M. Pearson
Jul 1, 1871
Oct 15, 1899

------ Daniel
1882-1954
(Moore-Motlow)

Lou Hill Daniel
1890-1957
(Cothran-Thompson)

Catharine Keller Shofner
1910-1937

Rev. Joe Byrom
1840-1914
&
Trissia Byrom
1842-1893

Mac E. Arnold
Oct 3, 1818
Aug 5, 1855
&
Catherine Wise Arnold
Apr 24, 1820
Dec 14, 1898

Sarah Ann Dean
Nov 25, 1846
Aug 30, 1847
&
Mary C. Dean
Apr 13, 1840
Nov 5, 1841

Austin Dean
Died May 31, 1891
aged: 65y, 3m, 27d.

Eliza, wife of
Austin Dean
Died Jan 3, 1903
aged: abt 79 yrs.

Bettie Dean
Oct 10, 1865
Feb 14, 1893

Sarah Ann, wife of
Alfred Prince & dau of
John & Polly Carpenter
Sep 2, 1839
Mar 14, 1864

Mary Jane Jolly
Aug 1, 1844
Mar 30, 1915

William Prince
Apr 11, 1812
Jan 20, 1867
age: 54y, 9m, 9d.

Sarah, wife of
William Prince
May 11, 1816
Apr 8, 1891

Lucy A. Ray
Mar 1, 1856
Mar 2, 1863

No marker:*
Martha Jane Davis
Born Dec 24, 1861/2
Died   1889

"Father"
James H. Frazier
Aug 20, 1916
Jul 11, 1965
& Daughter:
Mildred R. Frazier
Mar 7, 1949
May 1, 1950

Cecil T. Wiggs
1914-1951
(Daves)

Susie McAfee
1923-1952
(Harrison)

Martha E., wife of
W. M. Holt
Jul 3, 1856
Aug 13, 1904
&
W. M. Holt
Jan 20, 1838
May 15, 1921
&
Catharine, wife of
W. M. Holt
Apr 29, 1844
Jun 16, 1874

John Dean, Sr.
Mar 19, 1791
Jan 17, 1871
age: 80y, 3m, 28d.

Sarah, Consort of
John Dean, Sr.
Dec 14, 1796
Apr 6, 1869
aged: 72y, 3m, 22d.

John A. Dean, son of
John & Sarah Dean
Feb 28, 1818
Jun 27, 1864
aged: 46y, 3m, 27d.

John Haithcoat
Apr 12, 1810
Jun 22, 1898
&
Margaret Haithcoat
Jun 18, 1821
Jun 22, 1901

Manuel Ray
Jul 4, 1818
Sep 10, 1901
&
Sarah Ann Ray
Feb 14, 1827
Dec 29, 1910

Hezekiah Ray
Died Jun 4, 1870
aged: 90 yrs.

Patsy Ray
Died Jan 2, 1863
aged: 70 yrs.

Tolton F. Mitchell
Jul 24, 1808
Sep 8, 1887
age: 79y, 1m, 14d.

John Allen Haithcoat
Apr 29, 1852
Oct 31, 1889

Millie A., dau of
John & Margaret Haithcoat
Jan *2, 1854
Apr 2, 1876

Infant Son of
J. A. & Josie Haithcoat
(no dates)

Turlie E., dau of
John & Margaret Haithcoat
(no dates)

Enoch Grant Haithcoat
Oct 26, 1860
Oct 12, 1935
&
Mary Josephine Haithcoat
Oct 2, 1858
Mar 12, 1943

John Almer Haithcoat
Apr 20, 1881
Nov 16, 1959
&
Nancy Alice Haithcoat
Feb 6, 1881
Sep 14, 1935

Baliss Davis
May 20, 1819
Aug 6, 1885
&
Katie Davis
Nov 18, 1820
May 19, 1885

Austin Trimble
May 1, 1872
Apr 30, 1909

Alford Prince
1857-1888
& wife:
Diva Prince Brinkley
1860-1937

Laura C. Edmondson
Jan 6, 1858
Nov 26, 1914

Alice Smith
Dec 28, 1860
Sep 5, 1890

Joseph Brinkley
Mar 15, 1822
Oct 14, 1890

Cordelia Frances Brinkley
Dec 7, 1855
Apr 2, 1906

McLin Lavoy, son of
F. J. & E. F. Davis
Sep 25, 1875
Jan 12, 1880
age: 4y, 3m, 17d.

Martha Jane Davis
Aug 9, 1832
Sep 30, 1867

Polly, dau of
M. C. & M. J. Davis
(no dates)

James Henry Haithcoat
1858-1943

Mary C., wife of
J. H. Haithcoat
Feb 28, 1863
Jun 1, 1910

Eld. B. J. Byrom
1847-1926
& wife:
Dora Price Byrom
1859-1922
& wife:
Sarah Wiseman Byrom
1851-1883

Infant dau of
D. J. & Dora Byrom
Jan 29, 1886

Joseph P. Hornaday
1852-1899
&
Laura A. Hornaday
1858-1927

Mrs. Letitia C. Davis, the
devoted companion and much
beloved wife of James B.
Davis & daughter of Thompson
& Bettie Anthony. Born Feb 7,
1858 Married Jan 29, 1883
Titia's own words the day of
her death, Shout Jim, Shout,
We are gaining ground, there
is nothing between me and God.
Died Dec 13, 1887.

"Father"
Robert Henry Brinkley
Jun 4, 1861
May 3, 1945
& Son:
Lestell H. Brinkley
Mar 17, 1892
Jun 27, 1946

Alice Brinkley
Sep 4, 1859
Jan 1, 1939

L. J., wife of
J. D. Cates
Nov 5, 1858
Apr 5, 1897

Sarah Carline Anthony
Nov 23, 1833
Jul 17, 1913

D. Carpenter
(no dates)

R. M. Carpenter
(no dates)

Hewey, Infant Son of
A. G. & S. E. Ray
(no dates)

Ligie, son of
Larkin & Martha Johnson
Died Dec 2, 1883
aged: 2y, 3m, 19d.

Sallia, wife of
Newman Stewart
May 21, 1864
Nov 20, 1892

William Hammond
Mar 18, 1843
Dec 31, 1883
age: 40y, 9m, 13d.

Jas. W. Brinkley
1854-1919

Josia, wife of
J. W. Brinkley & dau of
Joe & Prissa Byrom
Died Jul 2, 1889
aged: 21y, 6m, 2d.

James L. Bomar, Sr.
1890-1943
&
Aetna Hix Bomar
1891-1958

Morgan Bomar
Apr 27, 1862
Mar 9, 1941
&
Etta Angeline Holt Bomar
May 26, 1864
married Oct 25, 1884
Died Mar 3, 1915

Elva May, dau of
Elijah & Ella Floyd
Dec 21, 1913
Dec 4, 1920

Elijah Floyd
1879-1970
&
Ella Luvata Floyd
1885-1950

Moses J. Trimble
Apr 18, 1847
Jul 29, 1899
&
Lou T. Trimble
Sep 11, 1855
Dec 11, 1926

Jennie Bomar
1854-1922

Harvey Bomar
1884-1901

Scott Prince
1866-1963
&
Mollie Prince
(no dates)

Ollie F. Prince
1894-1924

Infant Timothy Hice
1962-1962
(Gowen-Smith)

"Brother"
Hubert Hice
1928-1941
&
"Sister"
Dollie Dimple Hice
Died 1936
age: 10m.

"Father"
G. P. Woosley
Oct 7, 1845
Feb 4, 1933
&
"Mother"
R. J. Woosley
Sep 30, 1851
May 27, 1943
& Son:
O. L. Woosley
Aug 11, 1874
Oct 5, 1880

William J. Bomar
May 13, 1828
Dec 9, 1890

Mary R., wife of
W. J. Bomar & dau of
Hezekiah & Martha Ray
Born Jan 6, 1828
married Sep 12, 1846
Died Apr 12, 1884

James C., son of
W. J. & Mary Bomar
Aug 12, 1854
Dec 27, 1889

Doyle Lamont, son of
D. E. & Lois Cates
1921

Jay Julius Cates
1930-1935

James H. Ray
Nov 20, 1837
May 10, 1933
&
Caroline Byrom Ray
Jan 30, 1844
Nov 26, 1887

T. B., son of
W. J. & Mary J. Bomar
Born Dec 2, 1847
married Jun 1, 1870
Died Feb 6, 1885

Ella R., wife of
R. H. Brinkley
Apr 3, 1873
Sep 14, 1894
age: 21y, 5m, 11d.

J. W. C. Mitchell
1842-1928

Catherine, wife of
J. W. C. Mitchell
Apr 10, 1852
Aug 21, 1900
age: 48y, 4m, 11d.

Bessie, dau of
J. W. C. & C. Mitchell
Oct 27, 1884
Mar 24, 1903

James Walter, son of
J. W. C. & C. Mitchell
Aug 27, 1877
Jan 27, 1916

Macklin Davis
1826-1910

George T., son of
T. S. & T. J. Davis
May 3, 1882
Oct 28, 1889

Jim Gambill
1871-1961
&
Addie Gambill
1873-1939

Amos Milton Stephens
1869-1941
&
Eliza Byrom Stephens
1877-1964

William Ray, Husband of
M. A. Ray
Mar 1, 1853
Apr 28, 1892

Mary A. Ray
Jul 24, 1853
Nov 2, 1903

Pinkney Prince
1845-1926
"A Confederate Soldier"
&
Mollie J. Prince
1855-1936

Orpha Manuel Prince
Mar 14, 1886
Feb 22, 1965
&
Emma Phillips Prince
Mar 14, 1887
Oct 15, 1914

W. M. Prince
1847-1913
&
Mary E. Prince
1850-1923

Warner Mitchell
1886-1918

H. Boyd Mitchell
1904-1950

Infant Mitchell
1900

Owen L. Mitchell
1906-1926

Oscar L. Mitchell
1874-1947
&
Gertie Mitchell
1875-19(no date)

Janie Hutson
Dec 24, 1861
Nov 30, 1888

Margaret Riddle
Died 1920
age: 137 days
&
Millard Riddle
Died 1920
age: 157 days

Eldie, son of
J. H. & Mary Riddle
Jan 14, 1890
Apr 4, 1891

John H. Riddle
1859-1917
&
Mary A. Riddle
1862-1939

Olie M., wife of
L. M. Anthony
Mar 18, 1879
Mar 25, 1905

Nannie Lee, dau of
L. M. & Olie M. Anthony
Jul 11, 1897
Sep 20, 1900

Mariah, wife of
Anderson Anthony
Aug 4, 1832
Sep 26, 1910

William Burgess
1892-1930
&
Jessie M. Burgess
1895-1935

John R. Prince
Apr 17, 1879
Oct 20, 1954
&
Birdie R. Prince
Oct 7, 1882
Jul 30, 1954

Eustace J. Prince   and
Jul 11, 1873
Jul 12, 1967

Eldridge L. Bomar
Jun 17, 1884
Dec 27, 1953
&
Laurabet H. Bomar
Jul 7, 1889

Newt Bomar
1859-1945
&
Lora Bomar
1870-1941

Shirley, son of
M. N. & Lora Bomar
Feb 23, 1904
Jan 15, 1905

Infant son of
M. N. & Lorah Bomar
Nov 12, 1894
Nov 28, 1894

D. Edgar Cates
Nov 9, 1892
Feb 1, 1966
Tennessee
Pvt Co E. 168 Inf W.W.I
&
Lois S. Cates
Aug 2, 1894

James E. Byrom
Nov 25, 1869
Apr 17, 1914
&
Florella P. Byrom
Jan 31, 1875
Jul 17, 1867

James Guy, son of
J. E. & Florella Byrom
Dec 18, 1902
Jan 18, 1906

Wayne, son of
Joe & Allie Tillett
Jun 22, 1919
Nov 23, 1922

John W. Mullins
1862-1926
&
Dosia W. Mullins
1874-1951

W. N."Jack" Brown
1889-1947
&
Ruby P. Brown
1894-1966

Prince Brown
Mar 24, 1920
&
Margie Brown
Oct 15, 1918

Orrie Hix Prince
Feb 18, 1878
Aug 14, 1940

"Father"
J. H. Lokey
Sep 27, 1830
Apr 5, 1913
&
"Mother"
A. E. Lokey
Feb 28, 1836
Nov 23, 1917

Fannie, dau of
J. & A. Lokey, wife of
M. N. Bomar
Nov 5, 1864
Nov 4, 1886

Infant Son of
M. N. & Lorah Bomar
Jan 6, 1891
Feb 6, 1891

Infant son of
M. N. & Lorah Bomar
Born & Died
Jul 3, 1892

John Washington Pitts
1872-1942

Annie C. Prince, wife of
J. T. Anderton
Jun 3, 1886
Jul 30, 1917

Herbert E. Prince
Dec 29, 1889
Dec 25, 1974
&
Nellie McKaig Prince
Sep 3, 1891
----
married Feb 12, 1914

Elijah Wiseman
Sep 12, 1842
Jul 3, 1914
&
Martha Ann Wiseman
Sep 15, 1848
May 30, 1902

James E. Wiseman
1867-1933
&
Idona E. Wiseman
1873-1911

Vera T. Wiseman
Jul 1910
Feb 1911

John R. Wiseman
1871-1955

Edna Prince, wife of
John R. Wiseman
1878-1945

James Paul Wiseman, D.C.
Aug 13, 1899
Sep 19, 1955

Horace M. Prince
1901-1924

Thomas Wiley Prince
1852-1929
&
Emily Wiseman Prince
1855-1941

Josie Holt Arnette
Sep 9, 1886

Ela Riddle Hitt
1890-1965

Ethel Brinkley Davis
Dec 16, 1893
(no date)

Daphne Glover Brinkley
Apr 17, 1925
Oct 11, 1953

Paul Robin Prince
1909-1971
&
Eldora Cates Prince

Will Bomar
Sep 26, 1886
Mar 7, 1973
&
Eula Bomar
Nov 25, 1887

Eulan B. Bomar
Dec 3, 1888
Mar 10, 1957

Oscar Anthony
Aug 1, 1902
Oct 25, 1947
&
Grace Anthony
May 2, 1904

Newt Anthony
1866-1946
&
Cora Anthony
1881-1946

Franklin Anthony
1882-1932
&
Della Anthony
1880-19(no date)

Oscar H. Bryant
1889-1952
&
Eunice R. Bryant
1897-19

Oliver H. Bryant, Jr.
Tennessee
Pfc U.S.Marine Corps W.W.II
Oct 6, 1918
Dec 17, 1972

Samuel Joe Wright
Oct 29, 1939
Oct 3, 1959

James William Wright
Dec 1, 1958
Jan 29, 1975

Carl G. Aulabaugh
Illinois
Pvt 1 Co Development Bn W.W.I
Jul 8, 1888
Jun 28, 1962

Edgar Stephens
1872-1961

Carl L. Tims
1902-1970
&
Leola W. Tims
1904-

Rev. Allen Roscoe Fuller
Nov 18, 1917
Mar 24, 1969
&
Mildred Louise Fuller
Oct 27, 1924
----
married Feb 28, 1942

* by Mrs. A. G. McBee.

"Father"
W. A. Pitts
May 2, 1848
Jun 18, 1915
&
"Mother"
M. J. Pitts
Oct 25, 1847
Jan 1, 1930

Lucy Elizabeth Pitts
1872-1935

Roy C. Prince
1891-1949
&
Ruby Prince
1904-19

Gorman E. Boney
1898-1958

Addie B. Wise
1883-1968

William D. Wise
1880-1945

Lizzie Wise
1880-1974

John D. Cates
1858-1945
&
Mollie R. Cates
1868-1946

Horace Wiseman
Jul 28, 1897

&
Aileen T. Wiseman
Sep 17, 1905
Oct 21, 1973

Robert M. Sons
Sep 24, 1894
TM-   1974
(Tullahoma)
&
Jewell S. Sons
Aug 6, 1912
Apr 15, 1970

Glenn D. Riddle
Apr 29, 1901
May 4, 1960
&
Lucile Riddle
Nov 1, 1903

Bryce Riddle
1905-1932

Albert H. Riddle
1873-1918
&
Addie Riddle Harrison
1883-1952

Manuel Riddle
Jan 1, 1847
Oct 18, 1913
& wife:
Sydney J. Riddle
Aug 20, 1844
Aug 31, 1913

Martin L. Riddle
Jan 24, 1877
Nov 7, 1967
&
Nannie F. Brown Riddle
Mar 2, 1879
Dec 21, 1966

Claude H. Tillett
1889-1974
&
Ethel B. Tillett
1892-

Dock J. Shofner
1867-1963
&
Julia B. Shofner
1874-1957

Burnie E. Evans
Sep 24, 1907
May 9, 1974
&
Olive M. Evans
Dec 19, 1916
----
married Nov 14, 1942

40 TERRY CEMETERY   Map # 12
This Cemetery is located about 2 miles South of Singleton,
            on Bottle Hollow Road.

R. H. Terry   and   E. R. Bobo, wife of
Aug 11, 1816   R. H. Terry   This Cemetery is in very
Mar 9, 1874   Aug 22, 1821   bad condition.
                               Dec 3, 1891

41 ELKINS CEMETERY   Map # 12
This Cemetery is located South of Singleton on Bottle Hollow Road.

Matilda E. Elkins   Asa W. Elkins   Lafayette Elkins   Cheshire Baby
Feb 2, 1826   Jul 10, 1821   Feb 17, 1862   (no dates)
Jan 26, 1894   Mar 24, 1893   May 19, 1885
                                 &   &   Prince Baby
Several fieldstones, no insc. Angeline Elkins   Nancy V. Elkins   (no dates)
Several unmarked graves.   Aug 12, 1828-Apr 12, 1911 Aug 30, 1851-Jun 12, 1875

309

42 KIMZEY CEMETERY   Map # 12
This Cemetery is located near Raus and Bottle Hollow Road.

James Kimzey
was born
Oct 22, 1805
Died Sep 7, 1827   3 or 4 other unmarked graves.

43 YOUNG CEMETERY   Map # 12
This Cemetery is located about 1½ miles Southeast of Singleton, Tenn.

Memel Matterson
Aug 16, 1896
Aug 16, 1897

Newell Matterson
Aug 16, 1896
Aug 16, 1897

Mark M. Young
Apr 30, 1830
Feb 25, 1904

Malindie E., wife of
M. M. Young
Oct 13, 1838
Aug 25, 1923

Burnice, wife of
J. M. Young
Sep 24, 1872
Dec 9, 1900

Ethel Young
Feb 2, 1887
Mar 16, 1906

Gracy B.
Oct 8, 1898
Mar 17, 1899
(footmarker has G. B.)

44 HORNADAY-MILES CEMETERY   Map # 12
This Cemetery is located about 1½ miles East of Singleton, Tenn.

Henrietta Hornaday
Jul 26, 1814
Oct 12, 1886
aged: 72y, 2m, 17d.

James H. Miles
Mar 30, 1816
Dec 8, 1851

6 with Hewn Rock Vaults.
Many unmarked graves.
Many fieldstones, no insc.

45 KEY CEMETERY   Map # 12
This Cemetery is located just West of Midway, Thompson Creek Road.

No markers:*   * by Brice Brinkley.
Mr & Mrs. ----- Key
(only rock slabs)

46 SHOFNER CEMETERY   Map # 12
This Cemetery is located behind the Shofner Lutheran Church, on Hill.

Catharine Shoffner
Aug 21, 1827
Aug 8, 1852

Parnella Jane Dunaway
Died Sep 15, 1847
aged: 1y & 15d.

Charles M., son of
John & Nancy Brinkley
Apr 19, 1852
Aug 14, 1853
age: 13m & 26d.

Mary F., dau of
John & Nancy Brinkley
Dec 10, 1842
Jul 31, 1852
aged: 9y, 7m, 20d.

Joseph Brinkley
Feb 20, 1815
Nov 8, 1864
aged: 49y, 8m, 18d.

"Exit in 1832
Little Charlotte Shofner"

Emily M. Shofner, Consort of
Loton S. Shofner
& dau of Shadrach Brown
Exit Aug 10, 1839 Age: 20 yrs.

Mary E. Euless, dau of
M. & C. D. Euless
Dec 16, 1846
Sep 27, 1847

Eli S., son of
M. & C. D. Euless
Jan 5, 1845
Oct 15, 1849

E. E.
(fieldstone)

Sarah, wife of
M. D. Shofner
Mar 8, 1827
Sep 3, 1899

Adam Euliss
Nov 22, 1778
Dec 29, 1843
aged: 65y, 1m, 7d.

Labon Shofner
Jan 3, 1816
Oct 20, 1824

Exit   1841
Sophronia Ann Haseltine,
youngest child of John &
Amelia Shofner.

Harriet Angeline, Consort of
M. E. W. Dunaway
Jun 21, 1826
Jul 21, 1848
aged: 24y & 1m.

Infant Son of
M. E. W. & H. A. Dunaway
Died Jul 19, 1848
(no age given)

Mattie Morgan
May 7, 1885
Sep 3, 1888

Bular & Lula Morgan
Born & Died
Feb 25, 1887

James Ella Daniel
Born Mar 18, 1866
Married to J. T. Morgan
Jul 13, 1881
Died Nov 17, 1897

Lular Clarence, dau of
J. T. & J. E. (Daniel)
1897-Apr 27, 1898

[This is site of 1st Church built on
land donated by Shofner & Gilbert]

Cornelia L. Anthony
Aug 8, 1840
Mar 28, 1866

Sarah Jane Kimbro
Feb 18, 1860
Jul 20, 1869

Margaret Kimbro
Mar 6, 1810
Aug 29, 1894
"Farewell Mother"

Margret H., wife of
W. A. Groomes
Nov 20, 1853
Jan 18, 1887

Rebecca Shofner
Apr 21, 1798
Oct 10, 18--(living in 1850)

Austin Shofner
Aug 16, 1801
Oct 18, 1852
aged: 51y, 2m, 2d.

Phebe C. Shofner
Mar 20, 1825
Oct 8, 1826

David D. Low
Feb 17, 1851
Nov 28, 1871

Sarah J. Low
Mar 22, 1852
Nov 28, 1852

Many unmarked graves.

Iredell H. Low
Feb 13, 1815
Jul 13, 1851

Many graves with fieldstones, no inscriptions.

Sarah K. Bowers
Apr 9, 1823
Feb 25, 1870

No marker:*
Margaret Brinkley Mitchell
Born (no date)
married to Tarlton Mitchell,
who is buried in Bomar Cem.,
Dec 26, 1832
Died (no date)

No marker:*
Sarah Brinkley Shofner
Born Mar 8, 1827
Married Mitchell Davidson
             Shofner,
Sep 27, 1846 & Died
Mar 9, 1899

No marker:*
Mitchell D. Shofner is buried
at the National Military
Cemetery in Atlanta, Ga., in
1863.

* by Brice Brinkley

No markers:**
Nathaniel Cheshire, son of
James & Elizabeth Brumfield
Cheshire, and his wife:
Synthia Ann Cross Cheshire
(no dates)
** by Mr. John Lane.

47 SHOFNER LUTHERAN CHURCH CEMETERY   Map # 12
This Cemetery is located at Shofner Lutheran Church, on the
New Tullahoma Highway.

In Memory of MARTIN SHOFNER
was born December the 3 day
1758. Departed this life
September the 30 day 1838

MARTIN SHOFNER
1758-1838
Son of Michael an immigrant
from Frankfurt on Main, Germany in 1760, migrated by
covered wagon, horseback &
afoot from North Carolina
in 1808 with his family and
settled this tract of land
on Thompsons Creek. This
land was granted to him by
the Continental Congress for
Military Service rendered
his Country during the Revolutionary War as a cavalry-
man in a N.C. Regiment under
Gen Green. Near this place
in a log cabin, the first
Lutheran Church in Middle
Tenn. founded in 1808, and
in 1871 the present Shofner
Lutheran Church building was
erected on land donated by
his son, Austin Shofner,
Pioneer Settler of Bedford
Co., Patriarch of Lutheran-
ism and his wife Catherine
Cook Shofner lie buried under these stones. This Memorial, a gift from W. O.
Jenkins of Puebla, Mexico
and designed by G. Edwin
Shofner, descendants of
Martin Shofner...1961.

Revolutionary Soldier
MARTIN SHOFNER
1758-1838
Placed by: Shelby Chapter
DAR

N. A. E. Parks, wife of
J. R. Nutt
Sep 15, 1854
Apr 14, 1909

Floy Smith
May 26, 1892
Jul 12, 1896

In Memory of
Catherine Shofner
was born May 27 day 1762.
Joined in wedlock to Martin
Shofner July 7 day 1780. Was
the mother of ten children,
deceased June 14 day 1823.

Everett C. Jenkins
Jun 17, 1864
Jul 18, 1908

Calvin E. Jenkins
Oct 14, 1831
Feb 19, 1906
&
Sidey Jenkins
May 21, 1839
Feb 11, 1913

Monroe Shofner
Sep 16, 1833
May 2, 1913
& wife:
Mattie Shofner
Feb 6, 1868
Jun 3, 1946

Austin W. Shofner
Jul 13, 1888
Dec 12, 1969
&
Rachel C. Shofner
Jan 12, 1892

Emory M. Shofner
Tennessee
Lt Col U.S. Air Force
W. W. II C.R.
Aug 15, 1912
Nov 4, 1965

Clyde E. Davis
1901-1972
&
Bessie D. Davis
1896-TM-1974
married Dec 22, 1924

Hubert Y. Shoffner
Dec 30, 1898
Apr 30, 1951

Martin Euless
Nov 30, 1819
Apr 1, 1900
&
Cassie Euless
Dec 10, 1825
Apr 11, 1910

Thomas P. Ayers
Nov 26, 1888
Dec 6, 1941
&
Delsie J. Ayers
Jul 1, 1888
Feb 7, 1940

Clarence Payne Meadows
Jan 13, 1888
Jan 10, 1962
&
Joella Kimbro Meadows
Mar 7, 1890
Aug 26, 1968

George R. Cortner
Feb 16, 1901

&
Sadie K. Cortner
Jul 18, 1909
Aug 30, 1967
married Nov 26, 1930

A. Sidney Sparks
Dec 18, 1871
Mar 7, 1970
&
Ida Cruse Sparks
Mar 20, 1886

Ruby Snyder Weller
Nov 23, 1885
Aug 3, 1970

David F. Shoffner
Oct 6, 1892

&
Wilsie H. Shoffner
Mar 7, 1892
Oct 17, 1966

Sam Houston Johnson
Mar 15, 1849
Jan 17, 1926

Lula Euless Johnson
Jul 17, 1862
Jan 5, 1945

Aubrey Young Johnson
Nov 18, 1885
Apr 11, 1901

Brown Johnson
Feb 20, 1890
Aug 23, 1956

Martwill Johnson Johnson
Oct 7, 1895
Jun 21, 1969

Mary June Wooten
Jul 1, 1932
Dec 8, 1932

Robert T. Murchison
Jan 30, 1877
Apr 8, 1951
&
Clara Shofner Murchison
Mar 6, 1879
Aug 1, 1965

C. H. "Bill" Murchison
May 19, 1914

&
Ruth K. Murchison
Sep 19, 1913
Jun 13, 1966

Reba Shofner McLain
1894-1971
(Daves-Culbertson)

Flossie B., dau of
Mr & Mrs W. R. Martin
1905-1919

Terry Bryan Cortner
Sep 14, 1967

Macon Brown, wife of
Orpha M. Prince
Jul 31, 1889
Sep 21, 1971

Jake L. Nutt
Jul 17, 1897
Apr 13, 1903

Annie L. Nutt
Aug 17, 1898
Sep 26, 1898

Ike Moore Murchinson
1910-1928

Mary E. Nutt
Nov 14, 1875
Feb 13, 1915

Horace Nutt
Mar 29, 1880
Feb 5, 1923

A. F. Shoffner
Oct 24, 1854
Jan 19, 1913

Sarah W. Shoffner
1862-1941

James Henderson Shoffner
Aug 20, 1884
Feb 11, 1899
age: 14y, 5m, 21d.

Martin Lee Bond
Jan 16, 1882
Jan 19, 1965

Argie Shoffner, wife of
M. L. Bond
Aug 7, 1881
Mar 7, 1920

George F. Slater
Jul 12, 1832
May 12, 1913
&
Mary E. Slater
Jul 18, 1836
Jan 3, 1906

G. Elmer Slater
Mar 19, 1863
May 18, 1931

Lily M. Slater
Jul 13, 1867
Apr 1, 1905

Mary K. Slater
Jun 2, 1901
Jul 21, 1901

Dorothy M. Slater
Jul 22, 1899
Aug 16, 1899

John Shofner
Mar 19, 1829
Feb 7, 1882
age: 52y, 10m, 18d.

Fannie, wife of
Henry W. McKaig
Jan 27, 1859
Nov 25, 1884

Thomas F. Wooten
Feb 15, 1847
Jul 11, 1912
&
Hannah A. Wooten
Jul 25, 1850
(no date)

Charlie Wooten
1893-1966
(Daves-Culbertson)

Sallie Wooten
Jun 18, 1881
Dec 30, 1896

Offie Wooten
1896-1970
(Daves-Culbertson)

Joseph E. Hornaday
Sep 23, 1885
Dec 23, 1964
&
Mary Allie Hornaday
Jun 18, 1890
Aug 25, 1960

Infant son of
Joe & Mary Hornaday
Jul 14, 1926

William Thomas Hornaday
May 18, 1847
Oct 3, 1925

Nancy Catherine Hornaday
Apr 28, 1861
Jul 12, 1908

Allen Low Shoffner
1887-1943

Rufus Smith
Aug 10, 1818
Mar 15, 1899
age: 80y, 6m, 27d.

Joe Thomas Shofner
1863-1947
&
Annie Slater Shofner
1868-1937

Mose Cruse
1854-1906
&
Bettie Cruse
1862-1943

William M. Cruse
Oct 27, 1895
Jul 24, 1961

Herbert B. Cruse
Jun 5, 1899
Jan 10, 1931

Lucy Cruse
1888-1891

Beulah Cruse
1893-1893

Howard Bentley Shofner
Tennessee
Major 4 AM TN 4 Div
Oct 4, 1886
Apr 14, 1941
&
Kate Jenkins Shofner
May 4, 1889
Mar 21, 1972

Chris H. Shofner
1851-1919
&
Vinnie Shofner
1857-1920

Joe Biddle Landis
Sep 2, 1890
Dec 4, 1890
&
Lauren Landis
Sep 3, 1886
Oct 30, 1887

Major A. L. Landis
Born in Bedford Co., Tenn.
Aug 31, 1823 & Died in
Nashville, Tenn
Jun 5, 1896
&
Nancy C. Landis
Mar 20, 1826
Feb 6, 1901
"Erected in loving Memory by
his Sons John & Lulan"

Gabe Sparks
1874-1950
&
Effie Sparks
1873-1940

Polly, wife of
A. M. Dement
Jan 26, 1869
May 21, 1903

Wilson Roscoe Dement
Dec 16, 1894
Sep 24, 1896

Thornton P. Maupin
Dec 25, 1861
Apr 23, 1917

May Dora, wife of
T. P. Maupin
Feb 22, 1865
Feb 15, 1910

Dora Alice, dau of
T. P. & Dora Maupin
1887

Infant Son of
T. P. & Dora Maupin
1900

James Oscar Cruse
Jul 21, 1890
Jun 28, 1972

Thomas Ervin, son of
W. T. & Mary L. Keller
Jan 31, 1887
Oct 20, 1889

Albert Lyndall Troxler, Sr.
Tennessee
Pvt U.S.Army   W. W. I
Sep 16, 1894
Aug 9, 1973
&
Kate Huffman Troxler
Jul 31, 1898

James Huffman Troxler
Mar 6, 1925
Jun 1, 1925

Joe D. Troxler
1866-1934
&
Blanche Troxler
1874-1937

Little Fred, son of
Smith & Minnie Lawrence
Jun 7, 1890
Aug 1, 1891
age: 14 months.

Paul Edwin Nash
1954-1958
&
Ray Charles Nash
1958

James C. Jenkins
Pfc U.S.Army W.W.II
Apr 13, 1915
Aug 3, 1966

Eva Dean Jenkins
1893-1955
(Thompson)

J. A. M. (Stone)
(no other info)

Mary M., wife of
G. D. Searcy
Dec 19, 1846
Sep 8, 1900

Anderson Anthony
Feb 26, 1830
Apr 30, 1892

W. B. Brown
1868-1941

Bettie, wife of
W. B. Brown
Oct 5, 1870
Oct 19, 1895

Eula, dau of
W. B. & Bettie Brown
Mar 18, 1893
Dec 19, 1895

Roy Koonce
May 27, 1875
Jun 18, 1903

S. E. Anthony, dau of
Levi & Margaret Kimbro &
wife of Rev. E. M. Anthony
Dec 2, 1840
Jun 24, 1881

Ellen, wife of
Rev. E. M. Anthony
Jun 26, 1865
Apr 24, 1894
"Erected by the W.H.& F.M.
Society of Shofner's Church"

Adam Anthony
1795-1878

Sarah Anthony
1797-1884

Polly Anthony
1825-1887

Frances S. Bramblett
Nov 10, 1881
Jul 23, 1960
"Wife of W. D. Bramblett,
who was interred in Keller
Cemetery"

Haskell Shofner
1856-1931
&
Cassie Shofner
1861-1929

Ernest P. Shofner
Jun 13, 1880
Dec 6, 1957

R. W. Shofner
Feb 2, 1839
May 28, 1901

Haskell Milton Shofner
1920-1922

Maggie, wife of
H. J. Miller
Jul 28, 1857
Feb 7, 1886
age: 28y, 6m, 9d.

Lena Roseborough
Nov 17, 1880
Jul 20, 1899

George Barnes
Died May 27, 1883
Aged: 33y, 6m, 26d.

William F. Slater
Oct 19, 1856
Dec 31, 1930
& wife:
Claudia Haniley Slater
Died Jun 15, 1899
aged: 36y, 2m, 21d.

Thomas W. Hickerson
Jun 12, 1893
Aug 11, 1926

W. O. Renegar
Nov 6, 1890-Jul 3, 1897

Peter S. Anthony
Sep 13, 1840
Sep 9, 1911

Beula Anthony
Oct 9, 1876
Feb 6, 1956

Ruthie E., dau of
P. S. & S. J. Anthony
Aug 14, 1884
Jan 14, 1888

John Edward Moore
Dec 20, 1876
Nov 5, 1954

James O. Davis
Jun 22, 1887
Dec 6, 1953
&
Martha J. Davis
Oct 24, 1880
Jan 18, 1974

James H. Cheshire
Apr 22, 1853
Sep 6, 1837
age: 34y, 4m, 15d.

William J. Shofner
Sep 10, 1887
Nov 19, 1970

Arzalena Shofner
1897-1930

Jacob Harrison
Jun 17, 1810
Oct 7, 1874
aged: 64y, 3m, 20d.

Bula, dau of
C. E. & R. A. S. Jenkins
Apr 17, 1873
Oct 13, 1876

Perry, son of
E. C. & M. M. Jenkins
Nov 10, 1890
Dec 24, 1891

Will Earl, son of
W. F. & C. H. Slater
Feb 25, 1891
Jun 11, 1891

Lizzie H., wife of
G. E. Slater
Oct 20, 1865
Jan 4, 1893
aged: 27y, 2m, 14d.
&
Boyd, son of
G. E. & L. H. Slater
Jul 10, 1891
Jul 18, 1891
age: 8 days.

Morris E. Wilson
Aug 25, 1932
Feb 3, 1934
Son of Mr & Mrs Jim Wilson

Robert Williams Jenkins
Nov 1, 1867
Sep 24, 1954
&
Margaret Emma Jenkins
Oct 19, 1868
Jan 3, 1959

Bobbie, dau of
R. W. & M. E. Jenkins
Dec 5, 1892
Sep 11, 1893
&
Clifford Jenkins
Dec 24, 1897
Sep 23, 1902

Daniel M. Jenkins
Dec 10, 1838
Mar 20, 1896

Martha E. Jenkins
Oct 18, 1841
Sep 17, 1912

Peter Graves
Oct 18, 1782
Mar 21, 1869
aged: 86y, 5m, 3d.

Margret Graves
Nov 30, 1789
Feb 29, 1872
aged: 82y & 3m.

Rev. William Jenkins
Mar 24, 1802
Oct 27, 1877
aged: 75y, 7m, 3d.
"He spent his life in the
service of God as a Ministry
of 55 yrs."

Mary Jenkins, wife of
Rev. W. Jenkins
Died Nov 15, 1876
aged: 67y, 5m, 15d.

Benie, dau of
John W. & Bettie Jenkins
Jun 26, 1886
Jul 4, 1886

Little Boy Bebe of
J. W. & S. E. Jenkins
Born & Died
May 15, 1876

Mrs. L. M. Wilson
Jan 18, 1875
Jan 10, 1933

Sarah Aline Wilson
Mar 11, 1904
Jul 9, 1942

Infant of
R. W. & L. M. Wilson
(no dates)

Frank Wilson
1896

John W. Jenkins
Sep 2, 1852
Jan 4, 1935

Bettie, wife of
John W. Jenkins
Sep 18, 1857
Sep 27, 1899

Roscoe Jenkins
May 28, 1873
Feb 10, 1895
age: 21y, 8m, 12d.

Mary Belle Jenkins
Oct 24, 1880
May 2, 1908

Ruth Jenkins
Oct 20, 1892
Nov 5, 1972

Claude J. Jenkins
1871-1951
&
Emma Burrow Jenkins
1876-1940

Martha J. Gordon
Nov 7, 1834
Jul 16, 1914

Babe
Born & Died Sept.
(all on stone)

Rosa B. Gordon
1875-1946

William R. Jenkins
1861-1938

Martin L. Jenkins
Died Aug 11, 1868
aged: 38y, 9m, 6d.

Medora May Jenkins
Died Feb 22, 1866
aged: 8y & 3d.

William Emmett, son of
W. A. & A. M. Jenkins
Died Aug 10, 1880
aged: 1y, 4m, 5d.

W. A. Jenkins
Jan 15, 1850
Jun 26, 1885
aged: 35y, 5m, 11d.

M. H."Bud" Brinkley
Jul 16, 1857
Mar 20, 1933

Ella H. Brinkley
Nov 17, 1862
Nov 16, 1953

Ocie K. Brinkley
Jan 16, 1891
Jan 23, 1968

James K. Polk Lloyd
Jan 22, 1845
Oct 19, 1931
&
Catherine Harrison Lloyd
Mar 20, 1853
Apr 6, 1939

Homer Harrison Lloyd
Apr 6, 1888
Nov 25, 1910

Wallace Monroe Lloyd
Jun 23, 1881
May 2, 1913
&
Florence Hollis Lloyd
Oct 30, 1880
Nov 16, 1956

J. Walter Lloyd
Feb 22, 1876
Jul 11, 1962

James Ozroe Lloyd
Oct 17, 1878
Feb 28, 1881
&
Birdie Minnie Lloyd
Feb 5, 1873
Oct 7, 1875
&
Girl Baby
Apr 11, 1871
Children of
J. K. & Katherine Lloyd.

Sarah Elizabeth Lloyd
Oct 15, 1823
Oct 5, 1915

Clarence H. Shofner
Dec 22, 1830
Aug 13, 1959
&
Kate Shofner
Feb 18, 1885
Mar 10, 1920

Emma E., dau of
C. H. & Kate Shofner
Oct 2, 1918
Nov 30, 1918

Mary Alice Shofner
May 7, 1933
Feb 20, 1934
dau of W. J. & Ruth Shofner

Jeptha B. Shofner
Mar 20, 1847
Sep 5, 1916

Maggie B., wife of
J. B. Shoffner
Jun 6, 1858
Mar 24, 1889

Allie Shofner
Mar 22, 1833
Nov 19, 1899

Chanie, dau of
W. P. & L. F. Brown
Jun 23, 1892
Oct 17, 1896

Howard, son of
W. P. & L. F. Brown
Feb 8, 1888
Mar 25, 1889

Benjamin K. Coble
Died Mar 26, 1865
aged: 36y, 1m, 19d.

Mary L. Jenkins
1877-1942

Hosea Cheshire
Sep 30, 1827
Jan 17, 1901
&
Mary A. Cheshire
May 22, 1827
Sep 9, 1884

Mary Lou Cheshire
May 6, 1885
Jan 14, 1972

L. H. Montgomery
Dec 26, 1823
May 4, 1872

A. J. Montgomery
May 7, 1864
Mar 14, 1865

Lula C. Montgomery
Nov 28, 1866
Mar 30, 1882

Esther, wife of
J. E. Roberts
Oct 2, 1884
Sep 4, 1906

Nathaniel Martin
1859-1920
& wife:
Nancy Martin
1855-1932

Gerda, dau of
C. H. & Lavinia C. Shofner
Dec 24, 1876
Oct 26, 1882

Newton McQuiddy, son of
W. J. & R. Shofner
Feb 1, 1868
Sep 16, 1871

Albert, son of
W. J. & Rhoda Shofner
Jun 17, 1859
Nov 10, 1861

Keddar Shofner
Apr 25, 1873
Nov 15, 1878
age: 5y, 6m, 20d.

Frederick L. Shofner
1858-1933

Plummer L. Shofner
Mar 20, 1811
Mar 8, 1888
&
Elizabeth Shofner
Oct 6, 1813
Jan 14, 1888

Robert N., son of
C. H. & Kate Shofner
Mar 6, 1920
Sep 2, 1920

Joseph E. Stephens
Oct 4, 1831
Nov 29, 1873

Purlina Stephens
Jan 11, 1831
May 19, 1901

John A., son of
J. H. & A. E. Lokey
Dec 2, 1858
Jan 10, 1860

Sarah A., dau of
J. H. & A. E. Lokey
Nov 15, 1862
Jan 4, 1864

William C. Gordon
1819-1903

Sarah Gordon
1820-1869

Julia Gordon
1843-1880

Jas. A. Gordon
1850-1870

Muse H. Lokey
Oct 1, 1825
Nov 12, 1876
age: 51y, 1m, 11d.

William J. Shofner
May 3, 1819
Feb 25, 1907
& wife:
Rhoda Shofner
May 29, 1828
Jan 9, 1887
age: 58y, 7m, 20d.

Loton D. Shoffner
1833-1883
&
Susanna Shoffner
1838-1932

Jammie, dau of
L. D. & Sue Shoffner
Jul 16, 1857
Oct 22, 1861
age: 4y, 3m, 6d.

Martha, wife of
J. W. Proby
Jun 5, 1844
May 24, 1907

George W. Williams
Jan 28, 1850
Apr 1, 1880

Sallie C. Tilford Williams
Feb 5, 1856
May 15, 1892

Richard J. Williams
Died Mar 27, 1865
aged: 68y, 3m, 4d.

Eliza Jane, wife of
William M. Wilhoite
Mar 12, 1826
Feb 1, 1864

Margaret Kimsey
Mar 21, 1807
Dec 31, 1831

Benjamin A. Kimsey
Jan 9, 1844
Feb 13, 1868

William Kimsey
Jan 22, 1829
Aug 11, 1853

John Lawrence Roseborough
Jun 7, 1820
May 24, 1871

Sallie A. Smith Roseborough
Sep 15, 1822
Apr 9, 1911

Sarah Francis Roseborough
Sep 14, 1847
Aug 7, 1872

Leonard Napoleon
            Roseborough
Jul 30, 1850
Sep 19, 1881

Nettie Oneita Roseborough
Apr 14, 1869
Jan 13, 1953

William Lawrence Roseborough
Mar 26, 1862
Mar 14, 1882

White Ulyses Roseborough
May 13, 1864
Nov 16, 1943

Joseph Hiles
Feb 23, 1796
Jan 23, 1868

Alfred Hiles
Mar 11, 1828
Aug 17, 1852
age: 24y, 5m, 6d.

Roanna M. Hiles
Jan 23, 1841
Mar 27, 1847
age: 6y, 2m, 4d.

R. M. Heard
Sep 15, 1851
Sep 12, 1852

M. K.(foot marker)

L. J. Anthony
Dec 1, 1826
Jan --, 188-
(broken)

Doror C., dau of
L. J. Anthony
May 9, 1870
Dec 6, 1893

L. M., wife of
L. J. Anthony
Jan 4, 1830
May 15, 1899

Olpha Kimbro
Mar 19, 1880
Oct 25, 1882

Henderson Shofner
Apr 1, 1825
Jun 24, 1913
&
Margaret A. Shofner
Feb 27, 1828
Mar 29, 1917

H. P. Shofner, son of
Henderson & M. A. Shofner
Feb 27, 1863
Jun 19, 1885
aged: 22y, 3m, 20d.

Argie Euless, dau of
G. S. & Emma Saunders
Oct 13, 1882
Sep 21, 1883

Martin L. Gordon
Jan 25, 1851
Sep 19, 1876
    & "Brother"
Amzy C. Gordon
Jul 3, 1844
Sep 25, 1863
"Was a Member of Co F
5 Tenn U.S.Cav.
"Brothers"

Adam Euless
Nov 22, 1778
Dec 29, 1843
    &
Turley Euless
Feb 2, 1783
Mar 28, 1871

Barbery A., wife of
A. Marchbank
Died Feb 17, 1877
aged: 49 yrs.

Infant of
D. B. & S. Holt
Oct 1, 1852
Oct 7, 1852

C. P. Holt
Aug 5, 1853
Jul 28, 1857

Austin Brinkley
1825-1873

Peggy J. Brinkley
May 5, 1831
Jun 18, 1890

J. W. "Babe" Brinkley
Jun 27, 1859
Sep 26, 1937

David Cecil, son of
Cecil & Mary Lee Gibson
    1934

Infant dau of
Sewell & Helen Gibson
Dec 15, 1939

Sam S. Wilson
Feb 22, 1894
Dec 16, 1918
"Soldier"

David Low
Sep 15, 1780
Mar 21, 1872
aged: 91y, 6m, 6d.

Elender Low
Nov 28, 1792
Oct 20, 1873
aged: 80y, 10m, 22d.

D. A. Low
Dec 29, 1818
Feb 5, 1897
aged: 78y, 1m, 6d.

Mary L., dau of
Frank & Mattie Euless
Dec 16, 1875
Oct 13, 1876

Johnie, dau of
Johnie M. & Bettie Euless
Oct 25, 1874
Feb 28, 1875

John M. Euless
Dec 18, 1852
Oct 9, 1874

Ella Jane, dau of
Martin & C. D. M. Euless
Dec 11, 1857
Jan 21, 1861

Eva, dau of
T. A. & J. B. Gattis & wife
of Rev. W. A. McCullough
Jan 21, 1856
Sep 22, 1886

P. W. Shofner
Jan 23, 1821
Mar 27, 1910
    &
Nancy Conwell Shofner
Apr 23, 1827
Nov 6, 1919

T. A. Shofner
Mar 12, 1849
May 14, 1934
    &
Anna V. Shofner
Jul 23, 1853
Feb 9, 1920

Willis M. Shofner
Dec 3, 1883
Jan 19, 1925

William L. Cortner
1866-1947
    &
Katherine E. Cortner
1876-1957

Victoria A. Hitt
1849-1916
    &
Cordelia P. Hitt
1847-1923
"Sisters"

John J. Hitt
1839-1912

Luther J. Hitt
1852-1920
    &
Nannie M. Hitt
1853-1906

Aubry Robert, son of
L. J. & N. N. Hitt
Sep 10, 1882
Sep 3, 1884

John R. Hitt
Feb 1, 1815
Feb 7, 1900

Mariah Hitt
Aug 1, 1808
Sep 17, 1879

Infant dau of
H. & M. A. Shofner
Born & Died
Apr 27, 1859

Child of
H. & M. A. Shofner
Born & Died
Jan 30, 1858

Infant son of
H. & M. A. Shofner
Born & Died
Mar 10, 1857

Infant son of
H. & M. A. Shofner
Born & Died
Jul 3, 1856

James W., son of
Minerva S. & Wilburn Hiles
May 10, 1875
Jul 25, 1876

Infant dau of
F. E. & Rebecca Lacy
(no dates)

Sarah Ellen, dau of
F. E. & Rebecca Lacy
Jan 1, 1858
Mar 13, 1870

Laura, dau of
F. E. & Rebecca Lacy
Aug 29, 1855
Sep 5, 1877

F. E. Lacy
Sep 16, 1830
Oct 9, 1899
"A Preacher of the Gospel
of the Lord Jesus Christ"

Rebecca, wife of
F. E. Lacy
Nov 18, 1836
Sep 26, 1835

William P. Hitt
Aug 3, 1844
Sep 19, 1922
aged: 78y, 1m, 16d.
    &
Mary E. Low Hitt
Jul 29, 1844
Aug 19, 1926

George F., son of
W. P. & M. E. Hitt
Apr 23, 1871
Apr 22, 1873

Ira J. Hitt
1884-1935

H. M. J., wife of
W. L. Smith
Apr 26, 1844
Dec 1, 1877
aged: 33y, 7m, 6d.

Mary E., dau of
H. & M. A. Shofner
Nov 10, 1852
Nov 24, 1854

Marion Alexander, son of
P. W. & Nancy Shoffner
Oct 18, 1853
Nov 25, 1854
aged: 1y, 1m, 7d.

Henderson, son of
P. W. & Nancy Shoffner
May 1, 1851
Dec 1, 1854
aged: 2y, & 7m.

Blanch Elizabeth Harmon
Apr 23, 1909
May 10, 1909

Albert N., son of
T. J. & Julia Koonce
Apr 11, 1876
Nov 3, 1876
age: 6m & 23d.

Lydia T., dau of
T. J. & Julia Koonce
Dec 13, 1873
Jan 17, 1875
aged: 2y, 1m, 5d.

No marker:
Thurs Aug 17, 1899,
Shelbyville Gazette:
Mrs. Martha Dyer, widow of
the late W. H. Dyer, died
Tues. Aug 15, 1899
aged: 70 yrs. (Obit)

T. J. Koonce
Feb 18, 1845
Dec 13, 1905

Elizabeth, wife of
T. J. Koonce
Apr 25, 1863
Oct 7, 1906

Julia, wife of
T. J. Koonce
Jun 9, 1851
Dec 5, 1882
aged: 31y, 5m, 26d.

[This Cemetery is located on part
of Clement Cannon Grant #33,
purchased by Martin Shofner of
Cannon in 1812]

B. Koonce
Jan 6, 1815
May 21, 1891
& wife:
Lydia Koonce
Aug 23, 1818
May 12, 1871

Virginia, dau of
B. Koonce
Jan 13, 1859
Mar 17, 1871

Little Elmo, son of
J. C. & M. J. Couch
May 22, 1871
Jul 11, 1873

Clara Blanche Koonce
Dec 28, 1885
Dec 13, 1906

Ida Bates, dau of
T. J. Koonce
May 26, 1870
Jun 24, 1892

Harvey T. Bates
Tennessee
Pvt 16 Inf 1 Div
Jan 23, 1940

Martha J., Consort of
J. C. Couch
Dec 29, 1853
May 22, 1872

48 EDMONSON CEMETERY   Map # 12
This Cemetery is located near Singleton, Tenn.

[Located on the old Peter Singleton
Estate]

James W. Edmonson
Jul 14, 1842
Jun 3, 1875

Susan, wife of
Thomas Terry
Died Oct 24, 1832
aged: 26 yrs.

Several fieldstones, no insc.

Several unmarked graves.

1 MT. HERMON CEMETERY (OLD CEMETERY) Map # 13
This Cemetery is located at Mt. Hermon.

Samuel Winsted
Sep 20, 1801
Oct 6, 1861

Fanny Ann, wife of
Samuel Winsted
Jan 26, 1801
Apr 3, 1871
aged: 70y, 2m, 10d.

E. H. Granville
Feb 25, 1803
Mar 15, 1857

Presley Petty
Jun 26, 1811
Jan 9, 1866

Mary Petty
Died Jan 8, 1866
aged: abt 50 yrs.

Fannie D. Petty
Died Nov 22, 1887
aged: abt 41 yrs.

Robert Askins
(no dates)

Askins Baby
(no dates)

R. E. Askins, Jr.
(no dates)

Ruby Earnestine Askins
1892-1956
(Cothran-Thompson)

Maud Rozer
Oct. 5, 1850
Feb. 2, 1851 (no marker)

Pharaby Ann Bedwell, wife of
J. B. Bedwell
Died Aug 27, 1857
aged: 31 yrs.

Granville L. Rees
Born 1849
Died 1850
aged: 1 yr.

Sarah Reese
Died Dec 21, 1854
aged: 89 yrs.

W. Smith
(fieldstone, no dates)

-. Smith
(fieldstone, no dates)

William Henry Smith
1882-1959
(Gowen-Smith)

D. W. Thompson
(fieldstone, no dates)

James Davis
1869-1942

Annis -----(broken away)
Died Sep 16, 1883
aged: 64y, 5m, 12d.

E. M. C.(foot marker)

Alvira -------s
Apr 18, 1851
Aug 21, 1852

Henry Hart
Dec 25, 1783
Oct 23, 1857

C. A. Womble
Apr 9, 1825
Dec 5, 1887

No marker:*
Mary H. "Polly" Bennett Womble
2nd wife of C. A. Womble
Born abt 1821
Died between 1909/1911

Henry C. Pierce
1875-1953

F. S. Rees
Jul 10, 1836
Jul 1, 1900

Luretha A. Phelps
Jan 8, 1836
Jan 10, 1901

Rufus W. Rees
Feb 17, 1847
Jun 17, 1907
&
Coanza Rees
Aug 28, 1854
Jun 28, 1927

William Woodard
Died Nov 28, 1873
aged: abt 88 yrs.

Sam G. Gammill
Jun 6, 1882
Jul 5, 1882

G. M. Conwell
Nov 16, 1838
May 20, 1865

John Bennett
Apr 11, 1815
Dec 2, 1888

Granville Sharp
Died July 1886
aged: abt 30 yrs.

John Gilliland
1850-1939
&
Laura F. Gilliland
1849-1932

Infant dau of
J. W. & L. F. Gilliland
Born & Died
Sep 4, 1884

William T. Gilliland
Dec 1, 1888
May 22, 1906

Jessie Turpen
Nov 9, 1828
May 1, 1906
&
Matilda A. Turpen
Dec 14, 1838
Aug 2, 1904

Jack Eaton
Jul 25, 1904
Mar 1, 1958

William Henry Gilliland
1882-1959 (no marker)

J. L. Burrow
Co M
5th Tenn Cav.

Lousetty L., dau of
W. M. & Joanna Burrow
Dec 5, 1878
Apr 8, 1881

David W. Rozar
May 21, 1854
May. 22, 1854

Amandy J. Rozar
Oct 5, 1850
Feb 2, 1851

Joshua, son of
W. M. & Eliza A. Gammill
Jan 18, 1873
Oct 14, 1875

James E. Gammill
Feb 28, 1862
Jul 10, 1891

E. H. Gammill
Feb 25, 1802
Mar 15, 1887

No marker:*
Addie Lou, dau of Harrison &
Charity Burrow McLaughlin
Born abt 1897, died small

Johnnie Eaton
Died Nov 4, 1953
age: 63 yrs.
(Spry, Alabama)

Lige Eaton
Died 1956
age:(gone)
(Spry)

Derrel B. Heart(Hart), son of
J. F. & M. M. Heart(Hart)
Aug 26, 1882
Sep 15, 1882

Eliza Ann Gammill
Apr 12, 1843
Jul 1, 1876

W. M. Gammill
Apr 12, 1837
Sep 11, 1906
&
Sarah A. Gammill [2]
Aug 16, 1852
(no date)

No marker:*
Emma, dau of Harrison &
Charity Burrow McLaughlin
Born abt 1888, died when
small

* by Mrs. R. L. Patterson.

Thursey E., dau of
Samuel & Rachel Hart
Feb 20, 1884
Oct 1, 1885

Bell, wife of
A. F. Nelms
Jul 31, 1852
Oct 1, 1891
aged: 39y, 2m, 1d.

Oscar F., son of
E. B. & S. M. Parks
Jan 4, 1884
Sep 13, 1888

Scott Gammill
1879-1941
&
Ola R. Gammill
1884-1945

Virginia Burns
Apr 18, 1928
Apr 23, 1928

No marker:*
Payton, son of Harrison &
Charity Burrow McLaughlin
Born abt 1881, died as a
small child

Many unmarked graves.

Derrel Hart
Jun 5, 1818
Oct 9, 1876
&
Rachel Hart
Mar 10, 1819
Mar 26, 1914

W. G. Reid
Jul 2, 1852
Jan 19, 1934

S. E., wife of
W. G. Reid
Nov 22, 1852
Nov 30, 1913

Sarah J. Reid
Jul 22, 1853
May 23, 1891

No marker:*
Daniel Freeman , son of
Harrison & Charity Burrow
McLaughlin
Born abt 1871
Died at age 1 month

No marker:*
Zora, dau of
Harrison & Charity Burrow
McLaughlin
Born abt 1879, died in
infancy

2 MT. HERMON CEMETERY (NEW CEMETERY)   Map # 13
This Cemetery is located at Mt Hermon.

Jimmie Casteel
1902-1941

Evie Ruban Warren
1901-1972(TM)

Jerry Dan Wilhoite
1962-1962

Dewey Bingham
1931-1931
&
Virginia Arlen Bingham
1918-1918

Jessie L. Bingham
1888-
&
Essie Lee Bingham
1895-1958

Andy Bingham
May 19, 1854
Sep 19, 1910
&
Nancie Bingham
Feb 20, 1860
Feb 19, 1910

Raymond L. Moore
Tennessee
Pfc MP Plot 34 Inf Div W.W.II
Oct 7, 1916
May 12, 1971

William O. Howard
1906-1968
&
Clara W. Howard
1906-

Howard Twins
William A. & John T.
1929

Blanch P. Howard
1926-1928

Margaret Simmons
Oct 15, 1847
Dec 7, 1913

J. D. Moore
1861-1916

Mrs. Mary Ann Moore
1869-1950

Jeff Shelton Moore
1909-1966

D. E. Moore
1897-1968

Sally Jane Moore
1896-1973
(Gowen-Smith)

[2] [Died Oct. 27, 1930
brd. in Willowmount]

Daniel Joseph Mason
1940-1941

Virgie Alma Mason
1915-1969
(Gowen)

Infant Moulder
1965-1965
(Gowen)

Infant Moulder
1963-1963
(Gowen)

No marker:*
Will Redd
Died 1935

Bell Redd
Mar 1, 1877
Apr 21, 1908

C. A. Womble
1860-1941
&
Elizabeth Womble
1867-1949

Hattie F., dau of
C. A. & M. E. Womble
Feb 4, 1901
Oct 19, 1902

Albert Smith
1877-1935
&
Georgie Smith
1882-1944

Lee Roy Smith
Jul 24, 1926
Jun 20, 1961

W. J. Murray
Aug 5, 1856
May 30, 1921

Fannie Bartlett
Oct 8, 1882
Apr 27, 1909

Isaac Bartlett
Jun 25, 1855
Sep 28, 1921
&
Margaret Bartlett
Oct 5, 1858
Jul 21, 1924

Thomas Guy Prosser
1896-1952
&
Julia W. Prosser
1898-

Maggie Hale
Feb 28, 1844-Sep 12, 1918

Dollie A. Moore
1925-1972

No marker:*
Neal Womble
Died 1941

John William Womble
Apr 26, 1884
Apr 13, 1975
&
Delsy McLaughlin Womble
Jun 18, 1890
----
married Nov 19, 1911

Lige Woodard**
age: 59 yrs (no dates)
** Died 1931

Mittie Burrow
1891-1948
(Raby)

M. L. Burrow
1837-1947
(Raby)

Cad C. Burrow
Apr 23, 1861
Dec 6, 1935
&
Nannie L. Burrow
Mar 3, 1871
Jun 29, 1925

Rev. Artie Roberts
1906-
&
Lou Annie Roberts
1908-1946

Ola B. Jones
Sep 7, 1906
Jun 6, 1934

Thomas M. Turpen
1866-1947
&
Susan E. Turpen
1864-1942

Mollie Woodard
1866-1947
&
J. B. Woodard
1858-1932
&
Cyntha Woodard
1862-1899

Peyton B. Woodard
1905-1968
&
Effie H. Woodard
1905-1940

Ewing R. Woodard
Born Oct 20, 1906
Died ------------

Wilma M. Wilhoit(e)
Jun 20, 1923
Aug 18, 1968

William P. Thomas
May 14, 1825
Aug 20, 1893
&
Elizabeth O. Thomas
May 5, 1837
May 16, 1892

E. E. Jones
May 22, 1883
Mar 7, 1911

Neal Bartlett
May 25, 1871
Mar 26, 1909

No marker:**
Sallie Bartlett
(no dates)

Mrs. John Delk**
189- -1930
(broken)
** Pearl W. Delk

John Delk
Feb 12, 1888
Apr 4, 1963

Annie Woodard
1915-1943
(Raby)

No marker:**
Woodard Baby
(no dates)

Dave Bledsoe
Jun 16, 1861
Jul 2, 1966
&
Willie Bledsoe
May 20, 1885

Rex Bonner Murray
Jun 18, 1913
Sep 4, 1970
&
Irene W. Murray
Jun 15, 1920

George Edward Murray
Dec 19, 1875
Apr 20, 1947
&
Dillie A. Murray
Aug 15, 1883
Oct 20, 1933

No marker:*
Cora Murray Evans
(no dates)

William A. Murray
Jul 4, 1850
Mar 7, 1930
&
Mary J. Murray
Jun 22, 1851
Sep 14, 1928

T. B. Petty
Jan 10, 1841
Feb 27, 1916
&
Classie J. Petty
Mar 14, 1859
Mar 29, 1936

Dewey C. Petty
Jun 28, 1900
Dec 11, 1962

Travis F. Petty
Nov 14, 1888
Jun 29, 1972
&
Edna M. Petty
Mar 1, 1894

No marker:*
Petty Baby
Died 1918

No marker:*
Petty Baby
(no dates)

Henry C. Craig
Pvt Co G
1 Tenn Inf
Spanish Am. War
Nov 11, 1872
Jun 25, 1937

James Clark McGee
1903-1955
&
Laster McGee
1908-1972

No marker**
Lettie McGee
Died 1934

Thomas Walter Murray
1888-1968
(Gowen)

Maggie Murray
1895-1930

Miss Frances Murray
1859-1941
(Thompson)

Sarah F. Murray
1882-1920

John A. Murray
1880-1920

John Lee, son of
J. A. & S. F. Murray
May 20, 1905
Aug 9, 1905

W. O. "Butch" Murray
1880-1966

Gracie, Infant dau of
Peyton & Effie Woodard
Jan 29, 1932

W. R. Clifford
Mar 23, 1859
May 21, 1931

Mary E., wife of
W. R. Clifford
Mar 13, 1861
Mar 29, 1900

No marker:**
Clifford Baby
(no dates)

Clyde Lee Woodard
1900-1971
&
Ethel Woodard
1903-1970

Mary M. Woodard
1873-1958
(McFarlin-Thompson)

Gilford D. Freeman
Oct 13, 1889
Dec 20, 1934
&
Minnie R. Freeman
Jan 16, 1889
IM- 1967

"Father"
D. F. Freeman**
(no dates)
** Died 1927

Mrs. Susan Freeman
1869-1942
(Thompson)

Necil E. Broadrick
Dec 3, 1922
Jul 17, 1967
Tennessee
Pfc 904 FA Bn 79 Inf Div
&
Virginia E. Broadrick
Feb 19, 1927

T. B. Wilkes
Apr 30, 1871
Jan 3, 1923

Leonard C. Wilkes
Apr 26, 1882
Apr 23, 1900

W. P. Wilkes
Jul 6, 1832
Jun 30, 1899
&
Sarah L. Wilkes
Jan 22, 1840
Jun 30, 1899

Jesse Pierce
1884-1957
&
Myrtle Pierce
1891-1934

William Ollie Woodard
Nov 16, 1884
Nov 17, 1966
&
Allie Birtie Woodard
Nov 9, 1887
Nov 24, 1968

Dan Madison
Sep 3, 1879
May 16, 1959

W. M. Burrow
May 24, 1854
Apr 2, 1930

Joannie Burrow
1849-1932

Faylene Wilhoit
1945-1947

Peggy Ann Wilhoit
1941-1943

Orville Reaves
1909-1938

Agnes Jane Reaves
Mar 23, 1872
Jan 26, 1956

Albert Reeves
Tennessee
Pvt Co F 57 Pioneer Inf W.W.I
Sep 24, 1896
Apr 22, 1970

George C. "Son" Reeves
Jul 14, 1929
Dec 3, 1955

James Harold Roberson
Nov 7, 1890
Sep 30, 1948
&
Jennye Roberson
Aug 8, 1895
TM-   1975

R. O. Petty
Apr 10, 1842
Mar 26, 1912
&
M. J. Petty
May 27, 1862
May 14, 1906

Susie M. Petty
Jun 19, 1893
Sep 23, 1893

William F. Steed
1872-1945
&
Fannie J. Steed
1880-1935

Maggie Jordan
Jul 8, 1864
Nov 17, 1952

Belle Burrow
Jul 12, 1884
Jul 12, 1972

Margaret Burrow
Nov 2, 1876
Mar 8, 1959

James A. Wilhoit
Sep 10, 1882
Jul 23, 1962
&
Narcie A. Wilhoit
Nov 24, 1880
Jul 30, 1961

Frank Wilhoit
Apr 26, 1874
Aug 26, 1945

No marker:**
Jim Burrow
(no dates)

M. J., wife of
J. M. Burrow
Aug 6, 1875
Mar 6, 1897

Virgil H. Ballinger
Jul 18, 1888
Jun 22, 1951
&
Kizzie Ballinger
Sep 23, 1886
1968

Joan Carol Ballinger
Feb 22, 1956
Jul 25, 1956

Billie Bartlett
May 7, 1857
May 20, 1956
&
Cynthia J. Bartlett
Jun 22, 1862
May 31, 1937

Ernest Bartlett
Dec 4, 1890
May 9, 1910

Perry Bartlett
May 6, 1888
1972
&
Susie M. Bartlett
Sep 12, 1894

Lillie M. Patterson, wife of
W. M. Bates
May 11, 1890
Jan 2, 1911

W. M. Bates
Sep 12, 1884
Apr 17, 1951

Archie Hart
Sep 25, 1878
Apr 4, 1906

Ruthie Mae Wilson
1926-1946

Leon, son of
E. B. & C. M. Wilhoit
1932   age: 12 days

John Wilhoit
Apr 3, 1924
Mar 23, 1925

Pierce Wilhoit
1845-1932

Susie Wilhoit
1850-1924

Jacob Wilhoit
Dec 25, 1819
Mar 12, 1894

Finetta Wilhoit
Mar 2, 1868
Jun 9, 1927

Sam Mullins
1870-1934
& wife:
Lillie Cashion Mullins Hart
1878-1958

R. G. Mullins
Dec 24, 1837
Feb 9, 1912
&
M. A. Mullins
Aug 29, 1841
Dec 2, 1931

William F. Smith
Jan 7, 1904
Aug 25, 1950
&
Jessie L. Smith
Jan 14, 1909
Apr 5, 1940

Fulton Smith
1954-1954
(Gowen)

Lee J. Patterson
Nov 14, 1888

&
Ocie Ola Patterson
May 1, 1888
Feb 8, 1952
(picture of both)

Banks M. Patterson
Mar 28, 1866
Feb 15, 1952
&
Mary C. Patterson
Sep 20, 1866
Sep 7, 1942

Janie L. Patterson
Oct 15, 1893
Mar 24, 1911

Avery L. Vann
1927-1929

Luna N. Petty
Apr 18, 1899
Jul 13, 1909

Willie Petty
1885-1952
(picture)

No marker:
Charlie Mitchell Petty
Aug 18, 1881
Jul 26, 1937
Obit: Newspaper

No marker:
Ollie Mitchell Petty
Died Mar 17, 1938
age:abt 30 yrs.
Obit: Newspaper

Joseph P. Petty
Jan 10, 1844
Jan 2, 1912
&
Annie J. Petty
Oct 14, 1859
Jun 19, 1938

J. E. Wilhoit
Apr 21, 1891
Jul 5, 1962
&
Ruth H. Wilhoit
Jun 7, 1914

"Mother"
Addie F. Reid
Oct 13, 1897

& "Son":
Raymond Reid
Feb 14, 1918
Apr 25, 1963

Sallie Ruth Holder
1900-1952
(Gowen)

Sam Hart
May 10, 1845
Oct 27, 1918
&
Rachel L. Hart
May 18, 1846
Jul 6, 1938

Sarah E., dau of
Samuel & Rachel Hart
Jul 5, 1873
Nov 25, 1896

Exie Odel Hart
1899-1967
(Gowen)

David Samuel Hart
1898-1949
(Thompson)

Ruth Morris Womack
May 24, 1850
Mar 5, 1941

J. Dillard Cooper
Jul 5, 1905
Nov 15, 1946
&
Clarice W. Cooper
Jan 23, 1906

Pete C. Cooper
1884-1941
(Thompson)

Lucian C. Wise
Tennessee
Pvt Co B. 127 Inf W. W. I
Jan 4, 1894
Jul 15, 1955

Will H. Hart
Jul 9, 1875
Apr 5, 1939
&
L. Ellen Hart
Jul 22, 1875
Mar 1, 1940

Dr. J. R. Hart
Sep 28, 1877
Mar 13, 1921

John S. Hart
Feb 25, 1879
Jan 5, 1951
&
Lizzie E. Hart
Nov 3, 1878
(no date)

Melba Hart, Infant dau of
John & Lizzie Hart
1915

Jesse L. Hart
Sep 9, 1909
Oct 18, 1971
&
Addie W. Hart
Jun 27, 1912

W. R. Bartlett
1872-1939

Nora Alma Womack, wife of
D. C. Bennett
Sep 12, 1875
Oct 28, 1895

Isaac Asberry Allen
Sep 16, 1872
Dec 1, 1949
&
Myrtle Arnold Allen
Apr 18, 1877
Dec 29, 1951

Lala N. Allen
Oct 4, 1879
May 11, 1937

William J. Solomon
Sep 7, 1869
Nov 21, 1953
&
Sallie M. Solomon
Jan 3, 1882
Apr 15, 1961

James Everette Solomon
Tennessee
Pvt 132 ORD Med. Maint. Co
W. W. II
Feb 2, 1907
May 18, 1969

Bennie Solomon Thomas
May 30, 1940
Mar 26, 1959

Virgie Smith Askins
1927-1969
(Howell-Thompson)

Rev. J. F. Hart
Jul 24, 1854
Apr 10, 1936
&
Mattie M. Hart
Dec 20, 1858
May 20, 1906

George Earl Hart
1913-1969
(Gowen)

Claud S. Hart
1903-1950
&
Annie Lee Hart**
1905-(no date)
** Annie Lee Hart Ward
Died 1972.

Elizabeth A. Sharp
1915-1969

Thomas Brown
Feb 14, 1853
Jul 25, 1940
&
F. L. Brown
Mar 21, 1858
Aug 28, 1908

Mary Ann, wife of
A. Cluverius
Jun 2, 1829
Apr 3, 1911

James Farris Allen
Mar 21, 1837
Mar 12, 1900
&
Mahalah Ellen Allen
Nov 15, 1839
Apr 23, 1905

George B. Wilks
1874-1932
&
Ione F. Wilks
1874-1949

James A. Womble
Sep 30, 1887
Apr 25, 1967
&
Cornelia I. Womble
Oct 8, 1883

Irene Woodard
May 30, 1909
Aug 18, 1967

T. G. Hart
1882-1939
&
Sallie B. Hart
1878-1962

Willie Edd Warren
1878-1955
(Thompson)

Mary E. Warren
1884-1969
(Gowen)

Floy May Pope
1907-1934

J. E. Clifford
1884-1944

Lorena Clifford
1907-1912

Pauline Reid
1908-1911

T. A. Bledsoe
Sep 27, 1841
Nov 27, 1911
&
H. M. Bledsoe
Jul 14, 1849
Feb 10, 1919

Oscar Lee Wrather
1885-1967
(Gowen)

Ada Pierce Wrather
1888-1965
(Howell-Thompson)

May Cashion
Jul 24, 1885
Jan 17, 1913

No marker:*
John Cashion & wife:
Lena Cashion (no dates)

Fred W. Cashion
Jul 28, 1916
Jul 31, 1916

V. Lorina Raby
Sep 21, 1899
Aug 28, 1963
&
W. Shofner Raby
Nov 27, 1898

James T. Craig
Jun 9, 1923

&
Olga Morrison Craig
Aug 7, 1922
May 13, 1964

Sandra Ann Craig
Jan 1, 1950
Jan 4, 1950

Samuel A. Craig
Oct 30, 1884
Feb 21, 1961
&
Effie R. Craig
May 22, 1888

W. Alford Smith
Oct 26, 1907
Apr 29, 1966
&
Robbie T. Smith
Sep 17, 1901

Claude E. Bingham
Apr 2, 1893
Jun 5, 1967
&
Edna C. Bingham*
Mar 24, 1895
(no date)
* Edna Casteel Bingham
Died Aug 4, 1975.

John Earl Bonner
May 6, 1915
Aug 18, 1969
&
Clara W. Bonner
Oct 8, 1915

George W. Bonner
1917-1933

Infant dau of
Mr & Mrs Earl Bonner
1943

Luther Hendrix Bonner
Apr 15, 1881
Feb 26, 1969
&
Pearl W. Bonner
Oct 23, 1894
Jan 21, 1967

Walter W. Bonner
1879-1950

Arcie Anna Bonner
Jun 26, 1906
Nov 9, 1914

George Cannon Murray
Mar 10, 1907
Aug 20, 1972
&
Maude L. Murray
Aug 3, 1911- ----------

Paul Avon Murray
1917-1975
(Gowen-Smith)

No marker:*
John Euless Redd
1902-1974

No marker:*
Moody Lee Burrow
Oct 27, 1887
Apr 21, 1947
&
Mittie Burrow
Apr 10, 1891
Jul 19, 1948

William Neal Potts
Sep 25, 1951
Apr 22, 1973
(color picture)

No marker:*
Clyde L. Woodard
1900-1971
&
Ethel Woodard
1903-1970

No marker:*
John Delk
Feb 22, 1888
Apr 4, 1963

William Dee Warren
Born 1910
Died Aug 18, 1975

No marker:*
Loucillis "Cillis" Dodson
1905-1933

No marker:*
A Son of Cillis &
Louella Dodson
(no dates)

No marker:*
Annie May Woodard
1915-1943

No marker:*
Mamie McNatt Porch
Born (no date)
Died abt 1942
married 1st Will Holt
married 2nd Jim Dick Warren
married 3rd ----- Porch

No marker:*
Jack Holt, son of
Will & Mamie McNatt Holt
Died abt 1929

No marker:
W. O. "Ollie" Murray
Died Aug 9, 1966
(Newspaper Obit.)

The following list was kept by Mr Graham & given by
Mrs. R. L. Patterson.

No markers:
Jones Baby, 1st to be buried
in this Cemetery
Died abt 1865

Newton Leathers
Katie Leathers
(no dates)

Simmons
Simmons
Simmons
Simmons
Simmons (fieldstones, no insc.

No markers:
O'Neal Baby (no dates)

Joe Bennett
Maggie Bennett
(no dates)

Mr. Bonnie Reese
(no dates)

Bell Burrow
(no dates)

Rubin Warren
Died 1972

No markers:
Everett Murray
(no dates)

T. B. "Tom" Murray, died 1919
Margret Murray, died 1901
W. A. Murray, Sr., died-
Ruth Murray, died 1878
Miles Murray, died 1907
Elizabeth Murray, died-
G. W. "Wash" Murray, died 1920
Nan B. Murray, died 1918
Parthenia Murray, died 1930
John William Womble,
Died Apr 13, 1975

No markers:
Buford Woodard
(no dates)
Sophia Reese (no dates)
Mrs. --- Armstrong (no dates)
Andrew Wilhoit (no dates)
Holder Baby (no dates)
Frame Baby (no dates)
Will Warren (no dates)
Willie Marion "Jack" Holt
(no dates)
Mamie Holt McNatt Warden
(no dates)
Lucy B. Pierce (no dates)

3 STACY CEMETERY   Map # 13
This Cemetery is located in Possumtrott Hollow.

Jennie, wife of
W. B. Stacy
Feb 14, 1858
Apr 12, 1882

6 Adult graves
2 Children graves
no inscriptions.

4 PARKER CEMETERY   Map # 13
This Cemetery is located about 1 mile West of New Herman.

Rosannah B. Parker
Born Mar 28, 1785
Died Dec 7, 1875

copied by Winston Roberts.

5 NEW HERMAN CEMETERY   Map # 13
This Cemetery is located at New Herman, Tenn.

John S. Woodard
Apr 5, 1872
Sep 27, 1951
&
Jennie Adams Woodard
Jan 21, 1873
Dec 7, 1956

Laura Gardner
1854-1940

James W. Hart
Mar 17, 1843
Nov 3, 1933

Edd Morris
1872-1928

Boise F. Hart
1882-1943
&
Daisy W. Hart
1875-1932

Allie Hart
Dec 16, 1873
Jan 2, 1893
age: 19y & 17d.
&
Mary C. Hart
Jan 25, 1836
May 5, 1901

Horace Williams
1891-1923
&
Arlene Williams
1892-1957

Infant of W. M. &
Virginia Mullins
Dec 26, 1913

Andrew J. Monette
1865-1948
&
Mattie H. Monette
1872-1965

James Mullins
Mar 4, 1844
Dec 9, 1910
&
Parthenia Mullins
Sep 8, 1849
(no date)
married Mar 8, 1864

W. M. Mullins
Nov 26, 1860
(no date)
&
Virgie C. Mullins
Sep 19, 1874
Feb 13, 1939

Nettie Pearson, wife of
David Mullins
Dec 22, 1832
Nov 29, 1907

Infant of
J. W. & M. L. Hart
Feb 22, 1906
Mar 1, 1906

Annie Miller, dau of
J. W. & Lena Hart
Feb 19, 1911
Jun 22, 1914

Samuel King Bicknell
Feb 8, 1879
Oct 3, 1958
&
Mary Myrtle Bicknell
Dec 10, 1882
Dec 14, 1961

E. C. Conwell
Apr 25, 1828
Apr 28, 1891
&
W. K. Conwell
May 8, 1823
Jan 5, 1898

Ellis Pierce
Dec 18, 1876
Mar 29, 1932

Eva E. Pierce
Aug 5, 1902
Jan 29, 1964

Bessie M. Woodard
Jul 29, 1891
May 28, 1968
&
George W. Woodard
Jun 8, 1876
Aug 24, 1951
&
Mittie J. Woodard
Jul 22, 1881
Apr 21, 1906

J. J. Woodard
Dec 25, 1849
Aug 26, 1911

G. W. Woodard, Jr.
Aug 22, 1914
Jul 7, 1948

Effie Snell
Mar 25, 1892
Sep 20, 1918

Herman, son of
V. D. & E. F. Snell
Jan 18, 1914
Dec 15, 1915

Died Mar 3, 1908
aged: about 80 yrs.

K. J. Reagor
1865-1959
&
Laura Morris Reagor
1881-1915

Thomas B. Morris
Jun 23, 1846
Apr 19, 1928
&
Nancy Morris
Nov 6, 1840
May 9, 1920

William H. Morris
1876-1956
&
Bettie Morris
1877-1959

Cassie Dean Morris
1856-1952

J. Earl Armstrong
1897-1926

J. Florence Armstrong
1901-1926

John Noblitt
age about 61 yrs.
(no dates)

"Mother"
Mayme Wilhoit
Dec 17, 1902

"Father"
Joe B. Wilhoit
Jul 4, 1903
May 8, 1969

"Mother"
Elma Wilhoit
1907-1935

Mary M. Clark
May 21, 1855
Feb 8, 1929

J. H. Eaton
Mar 3, 1857
Oct 7, 1904

Infant son of
R. S. & Laura Bedford
Feb 21, 1911

Peyton S. Dean
Nov 25, 1830
Jan 13, 1894
age: 63y, 1m, 18d.
&
Nancy P. Dean
Nov 19, 1833
Sep 16, 1895
age: 61y, 9m, 27d.

William C. Morris
1891-1973
(Howell)

Ott Gilliland
1886-1939

Arthur C. Pierce
1883-1968
(Howell-Thompson)

Bessie Noblitt Pierce
Nov 17, 1892
Jul 9, 1928

Leonidas T. Thompson
1873-1913
&
Frances E. Thompson
1874-1943

James Earl Thompson
1900-1913

Infant Son (Thompson)
Jan 20, 1903

Myrtle Kerby
1875-1954

Polly Dean
Jan 20, 1809
Aug 9, 1888

J. R. Rees
May 26, 1826
Jul 24, 1906

Elizabeth Rees
Feb 27, 1826
(no date)

Martha Carline Mullins
Mar 20, 1860
Jun 30, 1927

Patricia Lynn Foster
Died Jan 18, 1943
age: 10 days

John B. Stacy
1857-1923

Mrs. Sidney Stacy
1858-1942
(Thompson)

Bettie Stacy
May 15, 1884
Feb 15, 1906

William Mullens, Husband of
Mary Ann Mullens
Dec 15, 1831
Apr 12, 1904

Mary Ann, wife of
William Mullens
Mar 18, 1833
Nov 14, 1900

Charles L. Bartlett
1881-1926
& wife:
Ada Bartlett
1887-1910

Alberta Lurena, dau of
R. A. & P. T. Musgrave
Nov 1, 1884
Mar 27, 1893

Charles W. Womack
Sep 9, 1816
Aug 4, 1888

Sophia E., dau of
C. W. & Elizabeth Womack
Mar 22, 1859
Jan 27, 1885

Corene Womack
1871-1946
(Gowen-Smith)

Will Wiley Womack
1880-1959
(Thompson)

Etta Maria Randolph
1874-1884

J. C. Baker
1872-1922

Ethel Baker, Mother of
Jannie Lee Baker
Aug 6, 1881
Jan 7, 1915

Jannie Lee, dau of
J. C. & Ethel Baker
Sep 28, 1913
Jan 19, 1918

Joshua Pierce
Feb 20, 1836
Jan 30, 1914

Caroline, wife of
Joshua M. Pierce
Died Mar 6, 1896
aged: 73 yrs.

James M. Gilliland
1859-1934
&
Kate M. Gilliland
1862-1936

Susan Caroline, wife of
T. P. Noblitt
Aug 26, 1856
Jul 28, 1909

Jasper Noblitt
Aug 26, 1897
Apr 4, 1913

Josh Pinknie Noblitt
Oct 3, 1867
Sep 14, 1917

G. W. Noblitt
1879-1928

Ella Noblitt
1886-1943

John W. Noblitt
Oct 3, 1867
Feb 15, 1944
&
Mary Etta Noblitt
Apr 4, 1869
May 1, 1942

Thomas J. Waggoner
1874-1955
&
Itys Sullivan Waggoner
1877-1970

Isaac Williams
Nov 23, 1852
Nov 18, 1938
&
Tennie Davis Williams
Sep 27, 1862
Nov 29, 1928

Nannie Birtie, dau of
J. C. & F. M. Williams
Mar 20, 1887
Jun 26, 1887
&
Frances M., wife of
J. C. Williams & dau of
J. & P. F. Stone
May 12, 1846
Mar 26, 1887

W. G. McAdams
1874-1948

Maggie McAdams
1872-1937

Joshua K. Speer
Died May 27, 1859
aged: 64 yrs.

Margaret Dixon, Consort of
Joshua K. Speer
Died Jul 11, 1885
aged: 73 yrs.

Lottus Reagor, son of
Mr & Mrs G. W. Wadkins
Oct 1, 1915
Oct 4, 1915
age: 4 days

Elijah Stone Morris
Apr 10, 1871
Feb 23, 1956
&
S. Finetta Bartlett Morris
Feb 17, 1871
Mar 15, 1951

James Morris
Sep 2, 1931
Sep 2, 1931
&
Mary Felicia Morris
Jun 10, 1919
Dec 15, 1921
Children of Clarence &
Myrtle Morris.

J. W. Martin
Jul 19, 1849
Jun 24, 1920
&
Sarah E. Martin
Jul 29, 1851
Mar 25, 1905

J. T. Martin
Nov 4, 1856
Nov 26, 1902
&
S. T., wife of
J. T. Martin
Sep 8, 1863
Apr 29, 1925

Early Martin
Dec 13, 1890
Jan 5, 1909

Charles W. Stephens, Jr.
1942-1945

Emmett C. Stephens
Jun 9, 1889
Feb 1, 1939
&
Gwynn Stephens
Oct 10, 1888

Edward E. Dean
1855-1913

Lou Dean, wife of
E. E. Dean & dau of
J. W. & S. J. Reagor
Dec 21, 1858
Jan 29, 1884
aged: 25y, 1m, 8d.

Edward E. Dean
1892-1963
&
Minnie L. Dean
1891-1941

John I. Cobb
1880-1951
&
Jessie W. Cobb
1894-19

Lois W. Bobo
Jul 27, 1885
Dec 29, 1970
&
Lanna F. Bobo
Apr 13, 1883
May 3, 1947

David Tolbert Noblitt
1839-1930
&
Tappie Lipscomb Noblitt
1846-1915

Deloris Noblitt, dau of
J. B. & Cora Noblitt
Sep 7, 1899
Nov 21, 1916

Banks Harris
Oct 14, 1876
Apr 8, 1921
&
Sallie Harris
Apr 4, 1879
(no date)
TM- Mrs. Sallie Chapman
1879-1960

Henry Dennis Harris
Jun 13, 1894
Nov 8, 1960

Claude M. Harris
Jul 1, 1898
Apr 16, 1968

Ruby Hunt
Jan 15, 1896
Oct 5, 1916

Katy Morris
Nov 12, 1824
Mar 18, 1905

John W. Reagor
Feb 14, 1834
May 22, 1887

Sidney Jane Pearson, wife of
Jno. W. Reagor
1839-1920

Etta, dau of
J. W. & S. J. Reagor
Feb 7, 1861
May 19, 1880
aged: 19y, 3m, 12d.

J. P. (foot marker)

2 fieldstones, illegible

Horace Gene Bobo
Jul 17, 1922
Oct 4, 1933

Ronnie Gale Allen
Feb 17, 1952

Andrew J. Woodard
Nov 7, 1867
Sep 15, 1953
&
Bettie Woodard
Apr 8, 1873
Aug 31, 1962

Fannie Day, wife of
T. M. Robinson
Mar 27, 1866
Sep 17, 1899
aged: 33 yrs.

James M. Mullins
1854-1925
&
Nannie B. White Mullins
1858-1928

James E. Mullins
1886-1901

J. N. Sullivan
Nov 2, 1838
Jun 17, 1925

Bettie Logan, wife of
J. N. Sullivan
married Mar 1, 1865
Died Nov 4, 1891
aged: 46 yrs.

B. F. Sullivan
Nov 20, 1879
Apr 20, 1894
&
E. H. Sullivan
Mar 29, 1888
Dec 26, 1906

Thomas H. Wiggins
Nov 13, 1858
Feb 25, 1943
&
Nannie Logan Wiggins
Sep 9, 1860
Jul 1, 1921

Fannie Ella (Wiggins)
1886-1912

Mollie Bet (Wiggins)
1892-1919

Robert Carroll (Wiggins)
1895-1923

John D. (Wiggins)
1901-1926

Sterling Levoy (Wiggins)
1882-1910

Logan B. Wiggins
Apr 30, 1881
Apr 26, 1917

William David Mullins
1867-1947
&
Lettie F. Mullins
1869-1931

Florence Mullins
1891-1931

Edwin E. Hart
Jul 28, 1869
Jul 22, 1937
&
Hester F. Hart
Aug 6, 1872
May 4, 1964

Erle T. Hart
Jan 29, 1902
May 21, 1916

Mannon Mullins
Jun 8, 1860
Oct 7, 1940
&
Martha L. Pierce Mullins
Mar 20, 1869
Jan 28, 1927

S. I. Driskill
May 4, 1839
Jan 16, 1901
&
C. G. Driskill
Apr 19, 1842
(no date)

Joseph Broughton
Born Dec 2, 1833
married to E. J. Felps
Aug 2, 1866
Died Oct 12, 1892

Rufus M. Allen
Oct 10, 1848
Nov 9, 1922
&
Nannie Williams Allen
Nov 26, 1854
Dec 12, 1927

Willie A. Baker
1901-1971
(Howell)

Archie Lee Baker
1935-1935 (TM)

Martha Ann Baker
1937-1947
(Thompson)

Mary E., wife of
L. W. Gowen
Dec 5, 1848
Jul 20, 1921

Julie Ann Harris
Jan 27, 1861
Aug 15, 1884

J. R. Reese
May 26, 1826
Jul 24, 1906

Elizabeth Reese
Feb 27, 1826
(no date)

"Grand Father"   and
Genrel Watkins
Feb 2, 1876
Jun 12, 1949

W. V. Mullins
1838-1927
&
Margaret Mullins
1839-1905

John Allen
Mar 10, 1881
Mar 14, 1902

Infant son of
B. F. & S. J. Harris
Jul 10, 1897

Amanda M. Harris
Jul 28, 1866
Apr 19, 1885

John D. Harris
Mar 24, 1841
(no date)
&
Malinda A. Harris
Mar 28, 1846
Jul 27, 1903

Mrs. Sallie L., wife of
W. J. S. Adkinson
Jan 28, 1842
Sep 29, 1891

Frances, dau of
Harvey & Bessie Word
Jul 11, 1911
Apr 21, 1923

James David Chilton, Jr.
Sep 15, 1955
Jun 28, 1959

Kate Hart
Aug 24, 1882
Jan 18, 1969

Joe L. Hart
Jul 23, 1900
Feb 8, 1967

"Dad"
Thomas B. Watkins
Jan 2, 1900
Oct 10, 1961
& "Grand Mother"
Pink Watkins
Jan 28, 1875
May 16, 1929

Mannon G. Noblitt
1851-1928
&
Maggie M. Noblitt
1872-1951

Jerry Levon Noblitt, son of
Felix & Wilma Noblitt
Feb 10, 1941

A. E. Bridges, Jr.
Jul 19, 1926

Sam Andrew Harris
Jul 29, 1885
Apr 19, 1895

J. B. Harris
Nov 3, 1894
Mar 14, 1899

Stella, dau of
Richard & Essie Williams
Nov 28, 1898
Aug 3, 1899

Infant of
E. L. & M. B. Williams
(no dates)

Judith Ann Williams
1940-1940

O. E. Williams
1881-1948

William Hart
1851-1936
&
Fannie Hart
1859-1901
&
Bayard Hart
1879-1903

Etta, dau of
William & Fannie Hart
Jan 27, 1881
Aug 15, 1885

Several unmarked fieldstones.
Several unmarked graves.

Tolbert Wilson Noblitt
Feb 23, 1904
Jul 14, 1956

Mattie B., dau of
M. G. & Maggie Noblitt
Dec 21, 1901
Dec 7, 1933

Felix Massey Noblitt
Aug 25, 1939
Feb 5, 1941

Isaac Williams, Sr.
Jun 19, 1808
Nov 16, 1887
aged: 81y, 5m, 27d.

Susan Williams
Nov 1, 1826
Mar 28, 1896

Essie Williams, wife of
Richard Williams
Sep 16, 1866
Sep 19, 1899

Richard Williams
Jun 9, 1862
Jun 20, 1934

Drucilla Bean Williams
Jan 8, 1872
Mar 14, 1963

Dorthy Ruth Wilhoite
1944-1946

James Mannon Noblitt
1877-1958
(McFarlin-Thompson)

Martha Noblitt
1881-1971
(Howell)

Robert I. Eaton
Jul 3, 1887
Oct 29, 1957

Georgia M. Eaton
Mar 9, 1912

W. D. Eaton
Died Dec 10, 1900
aged: 24y, 5m, 10d.

6 LYON CEMETERY   Map # 13
This Cemetery is located about 2 miles North of New Herman, Tenn.

G. K. Lyon
Nov 1, 1828
Aug 24, 1856
aged: 28y, 9m, 24d.

1 grave with marker broken & gone.
Maybe 2 other graves.

7 FLOYD CEMETERY   Map # 13
This Cemetery is located about 1½ miles Southwest of Flat Creek, Tenn.

W. M. Floyd
Born Oct 4, 1850
Died Jul 13, 1851 aged: 20m & 9d.

Several unmarked graves.

8 BOONE CEMETERY   Map # 13
This Cemetery is located about 1½ miles South of Flat Creek, Tenn.

Henry Boone   4 Rock Slab Vaults, no insc.
Jun 11, 1855
Jul 9, 1885

9 MORRIS CEMETERY   Map # 13
This Cemetery is located on Wiseman Road.

Samuel M. Morris Nov 12, 1784 Feb 25, 1852	Charlie W., son of C. W. & E. A. Womack Dec 17, 1862 Dec 16, 1863	Reuben F. Darnaby, son of Reuben & Catharine Darnaby Aug 21, 1836 Nov 2, 1883	Sarah E., wife of Lemuel Broadaway Oct 11, 1806 Sep 12, 1897
Several unmarked graves.	Many fieldstones, no insc.		Lemuel Broadaway, son of John & Agness Broadaway Nov 30, 1793 Jun 28, 1873

10 MORRIS CEMETERY   Map # 13
This Cemetery is located near Ward's Cave.

Francis M. Morris Mar 25, 1828 Aug 31, 1902 & Mary, wife of F. M. Morris Jun 2, 1830 May 3, 1914	Samuel Morris Dec 20, 1815 Oct 11, 1883 & Nancy Morris Mar 14, 1816 Jan 27, 1862	James B. Morris Sep 10, 1813 Dec 2, 1886 aged: 73y, 2m, 22d.	James H. Morris Mar 5, 1848 Jun 10, 1901
W. R. Woodard Oct 31, 1842 Nov 29, 1913	Finetta Morris 1847-1930	Elizabeth Morris Aug 5, 1820 Jun 6, 1896	James C. Morris Mar 17, 1855 Jan 13, 1890
	F. P. Jones Died Sep 18, 1909 (no age given)	Lemuel Morris 1847-1930	Mary Morris 1851-1936
		About 25 graves marked with fieldstones, no insc.	Infant Dau of C. W. & E. A. Womack.B&D-May 8, 1855

11 PEARSON CEMETERY   Map # 13
This Cemetery is located just off Lynchburg Highway, about
2½ miles Southeast of Flat Creek.

Rollo, son of Jessie & M. A. Neece Jun 22, 1881 Jul 16, 1897	E. G. Montgomery Feb 8, 1848 Apr 5, 1926	Kindred Pearson May 29, 1798 Sep 10, 1871	John D., son of T. I. & M. A. Hix Feb 17, 1880 Sep 14, 1901
William C. Hix May 20, 1818 May 23, 1877 & Rosanah Hix Sep 26, 1821 Feb 13, 1895	Sallie E. Montgomery Jan 7, 1850 Apr 11, 1900	Sidney Pearson Oct 4, 1801 Mar 3, 1870	Edgar, son of T. I. & M. A. Hix Mar 7, 1895 Mar 3, 1895
	Ruth Noblitt May 6, 1894 Oct 6, 1915	William Bibb Pearson Dec 17, 1823 Aug 30, 1849	Lou T., dau of A. J. & S. E. Womack Oct 10, 1873 Jun 10, 1874
K. J. Pearson Lieut. Co C 23rd Battalion Tenn Inf C.S.A. 1862-1865 Apr 23, 1835 Jul 26, 1909 & Liza Pearson Oct 16, 1842 Dec 23, 1915	Elise Patton Dec 23, 1907 Jul 13, 1909	Horace Pearson Oct 15, 1870 Sep 8, 1902 & Eugene Pearson May 4, 1866 Jul 3, 1889	Len Stone Moore Jul 22, 1898 Aug 10, 1898 & Glenara Moore Jul 22, 1898 Nov 21, 1898 "Twins of E. D. & S. F. Moore"
	James, son of Fred & Stella Pearson Apr 4, 1911 Jul 9, 1911	J. C. Moore Mar 19, 1836 Sep 2, 1866 aged: 30y, 6m, 13d.	
Pheeby A. Bobo, Consort of John A. Bobo Dec 2, 1835 May 6, 1861	Buford Grady, son of Louis & Florence Pearson Jul 19, 1893 Apr 15, 1896	Julia E. Bobo Aug 14, 1859 Apr 11, 1861	Cathleen Moore Nov 27, 1896 Jan 28, 1897
	Mary Francis Bobo Sep 2, 1844 Oct 8, 1854		

Joseph A., son of
W. P. & C. E. Bobo
Aug 26, 1851
Jul 16, 1852

Hester C., dau of
W. P. & C. E. Bobo
Jul 4, 1853
Mar 23, 1854

Sarah Bobo
was born
Mar 7, 1793 & died
Mar 22, 1849
(fieldstone)

* from Records of
    William Floyd.

Mary Frances, dau of
J. E. & Pheeby A. Bobo
Oct 15, 1856
Apr 17, 1863

Infant Son of
John & Pheeby A. Bobo
(no dates)

Sarah L. Bobo
Mar 25, 1837
Jun 29, 1852

Elijah P. Bobo
Nov 16, 1846
May 18, 1870

2 Infant graves, unmarked.

No marker:*
John Watson of Union District,
S. C., a cripple.

M. W. Watson
Jun 26, 1820
May 25, 1891

Rebekah, wife of
M. W. Watson
Jan 18, 1816
Dec 14, 1908

Many old graves with Rock Walls, no insc.

Many fieldstones, no inscriptions.

Rosa Couch, dau of
M. W. & Rebecca Watson
Mar 12, 1851
Dec 4, 1876
"Remember friends, as you
pass by, as you are now,
so once was I, as I am now,
So you must be, prepare
for death & follow me."

Mary Myrtle, Infant dau of
Z. & N. H. Motlow
Jan 15, 1873
Sep 7, 1873

1 BRYANT CEMETERY   Map # 14
This Cemetery is located at Hilltop.

W. N. Bryant   and wife: Mary Ellen Bryant and Dau: Myrtle Bryant
1855-1932   1864-1911   1883-1898

                             Several unmarked graves.

Robert N. Smith
Sep 7, 1850
Sep 17, 1887

2 HIX CEMETERY   Map # 14
This Cemetery is located South of Flat Creek, Tenn., on
                       Farrar's Branch.

W. P. Hix
May 20, 1811
Jun 16, 1893
aged: 82y & 27d.

Manerva, wife of
W. P. Hix
Jul 8, 1812
Mar 2, 1895
aged: 82y, 7m, 24d.
"Confined to her bed 54 yrs."

John W., son of
W. P. & Manerva Hix
Born Jun 8, 1834
Died (no date)

James M., son of
W. P. & Manerva Hix
Born Feb 7, 1844
aged: 11 yrs.

3 RUSSELL CEMETERY   Map # 14
This Cemetery is located near Hilltop.

William H. Russell
Born in Wilks Co., N.C.
Oct 15, 1805
Sep 8, 1879

Eliza Russell
Sep 20, 1805
Oct 25, 1877
aged: 72y, 1m, 5d.

1 grave with fieldstone,
    no inscription.

ADDENDUM

33 MOON CEMETERY   Map # 6   (page 71)

R. M. Thomson
Oct 1, 1878
Oct 3, 1899

Alexander J., son of
William H. & S. J. Moon
Died Aug 28, 1857
age: 1 yr & 1 mo

Joel Alexander, son of
Robert & Susan Wallis
Oct 17, 1860
Dec 19, 1863

Indiana Rhio, wife of
W. H. Moon
Oct 17, 1848
Jan 15, 1909

George Allen, son of
W. H. & Sarah J. Moon
Mar 16, 1870
Apr 14, 1903

R. M. Thomson
Mar 21, 1900
Apr 5, 1903

Albert F. Moon
Oct 22, 1848
Nob 6, 1854

Sue, daughter of
Robert F. & Susan Wallis
Born & Died July 20, 1858

William H. Moon
May 1, 1830
Feb 12, 1906

Sarah J., wife of
W. H. Moon
Sep 20, 1836
Sep 1, 1884

Bettie L. Hopkins, dau of
W. H. & Sarah Moon
May 28, 1859
Jan 26, 1899

Alexander D. Moon
Apr 11, 1801
Sep 14, 1856

Robert Ripley Moon
22 Jun 1828
7 Aug 1839

Infant Son of
A. S. & R. C. Jeffress
Oct 14, 1906
Oct 31, 1906

Rauleigh C. Jeffress
Aug 2, 1837
Feb 7, 1847

William H., son of
James D. & Frances A. Jeffress
Oct 26, 1872
Oct 9, 1873

Nancy, wife of
A. B. Moon
Feb 26, 1810
Feb 14, 1900

Elizabeth J. Moon
Apr 19, 1851
Mar 27, 1868

Nancy W. Jeffress
Sep 22, 1830
Sep 19, 1903

Thomas B. Jeffress
Mar 26, 1805
Nov 29, 1876

Polly H., wife of
T. B. Jeffress
Mar 2, 1808
Dec 9, 1853

11 POWELL CEMETERY   Map # 3
This Cemetery is located about ½ mile west of 231 North, on
County Line Road. [Now Squire Hall Road]

Thomas -. ------ [P. Powell]
Born in the State of -- [VA]
Died the 8th ----------
aged: 50

About 3 or 4 graves, no markers.

46 MARBURY CEMETERY   Map # 7
This Cemetery is located about 1 mile North West of Vannatta.

Mrs. J. P. Marbury
Feb 26, 1838
Apr 11, 1896
age: 58 Yrs, 1 mo, 16 days

Luella J., daughter of
H. L. & J. P. Marbury
Apr 15, 1863
Sep 3, 1864

Several unmarked graves.

10 HOLT CEMETERY   Map # 12   page 292

Annie Stewart Holt
Aug 4, 1882
Nov 26, 1909

George Smith
1860-1924

Sallie J., wife of
J. A. Smith
Jan 25, 1868
Aug 14, 1896

Stephens F. Roberts
Jan 11, 1841
Apr 29, 1919
"A Confederate Soldier"

Emily Leever Roberts
1878-1958
(Cothron-Thompson)

William V. Harris
Apr 15, 1901
Aug 29, 1956
&
(footmarker) E.E.H.

Joseph Holt
Sept 1787
Sept 17, 1856
aged: 65 yrs.

Catharine Holt
Aug 18, 1797
Sep 2, 1852
age: 55 yrs, & 14 days

R. Sular Roberts
Oct 28, 1871
Mar 30, 1902
age: 30y, 5m, 2d.

Hubert Bennett
1885-19(no date)
&
Myrtle Bennett
1891-1938

Dr. D. C. Bennett
Jul 12, 1836
Dec 24, 1904

Roena B., wife of
D. C. Bennett
Jul 26, 1858
May 4, 1882

Belinda, wife of
R. W. Couch
Oct 10, 1835
Oct 9, 1895

Joseph Alexander Couch
Jan 31, 1862-Jan 9, 1919

William J. Brown
1879-1956

Mai J. Brown
1881-1933

Elizabeth A. Brown
1863-1937
(Cothron-Thompson)

Mary A. Culley
May 14, 1826
Jun 18, 1906

Mamie V., daughter of
Reubin & Belinda Couch
Jan 10, 1864
Dec 18 1889

Williamson Mackey Couch
Aug 22, 1873
Jun 2, 1907

John Green Nash
Apr 18, 1869
Dec 4, 1918

Emma B. Nash
Aug 9, 1871
Oct 26, 1954

Emily C. Green
Nov 18, 1828
Jul 30, 1912

Harriet Virginia, wife of
G. M. Hooser
Mar 31, 1843
Jan 28, 1891

G. B. Kimbro
1847-1913

Frances Kimbro
1847-1923

F. M. Keller
Feb 2, 1844
Dec 23, 1900

Lucinda Keller
Dec 5, 1841
Jun 11, 1909

Jerry D., son of
Lane & Ellen Keller
Nov 21, 1892
Oct 19, 1897

Robert T. Kimbro
Jan 30, 1874
May 26, 1920

James A. Throneberry
1876-1955
&
Almeada B. Throneberry
1883-1963

L. W. Blackman
(dates gone)

Burrell Blackman
Mar 25, 1811
Apr 2, 1897

Frances, wife of
Burrell Blackman
Mar 15, 1824
Sep 16, 1905

Bessie W. Smith
Oct 1, 1891
Nov 30, 1908

Kittie B., wife of
R. E. Barton
May 19, 1872
Jun 29, 1899

Infants of
R. E. & Kittie Barton
Born & Died Jun 21, 1899

James M. Isom
Aug 1820
Apr 12, 1884
aged: 64 yrs.

Louisa Holt Isom
Sep 26, 1820
Aug 15, 1901

Robert E. Holt
Jan 31, 1866
Mar 2, 1936

Mary C., wife of
R. E. Holt
Jul 20, 1871
Feb 14, 1900

Rufus L. Holt
Aug 8, 1856
Jan 17, 1892
aged: 36y, 4m, 17d.

Jonie Dalby Holt
Jun 25, 1876
Mar 1, 1963

John L. Ayers
Aug 3, 1813
Aug 17, 1863

Sarrah, wife of
John L. Ayers
Aug 16, 1816
Oct 27, 1875
aged: 59y, 2m, 11d.

Jasper Newton Ayers
Dec 31, 1842
Nov 22, 1871
aged: 28y, 10m, 21d.

James P. Ayers
Mar 26, 1845
Oct 24, 1919

Joseph M. Holt
Jun 6, 1837
Jun 22, 1896

Margaret C. Holt
Sep 15, 1842
Jul 24, 1898

Elias C. Holt
Jun 2, 1830
Feb 21, 1897

Nancy Holt
Jan 6, 1838
Nov 30, 1903

F. M. Yates
Nov 15, 1835
Feb 9, 1897

W. T. Yates
Dec 30, 1847
Jun 24, 1902

J. W., son of
G. C. & E. J. Yell
Jul 5, 1872
Jul 14, 1888

Elijah Holt
Oct 30, 1831
Sep 28, 1893

Elizabeth M., wife of
Elijah Holt
May 4, 1833
Oct 19, 1883
aged: 50y, 5m, 15d.

Sarah Catherine Holt
Oct 8, 1867
May 24, 1918

R. E. Ayers
1853-1919
&
Jane S. Ayers
1862-(no date)

J. K. Ayers
1851-1919

Emma Phillips Ayers
Mar 16, 1865
Jun 16, 1931

Mary E. Ayers
Dec 23, 1858
Jun 26, 1887

William C. Ayers
1856-1915
&
Emma Ayers
1856-1936

Joe Lane, son of
W. C. & Emma Ayers
Jul 6, 1881
Jun 13, 1896

W. H. Isom
Oct 10, 1840
Jul 7, 1908
"Member of Co. B, 17 Regt
Tenn. Vol. C.S.A."

Emma Isom
May 31, 1851
Feb 3, 1930

James T. Isom
Dec 21, 1917
Mar 10, 1919

Babies of J. G. & M. A. Isom
Oct 12, 1921

W. Horton Isom
1912-1932

Mabel Ann Isom
1923-1936

Nora I. Justice
1878-1934

James D. Stephens
1852-1901
&
Jennie Stephens
1854-1934

"Little" J. D., son of
J. D. & Jennie Stephens
Sep 3, 1885
Nov 13, 1885

Daughter of
J. D. & Jennie Stephens
Oct 1, 1879

Joe R. Black
Jan 10, 1879
Feb 18, 1919
&
Luella, daughter of
Joe R. & Mollie Black
Apr 16, 1907
Aug 20, 1920

Jerry K. Ayers, Jr.
Apr 14, 1887
Aug 3, 1887

Oscar M. Ayers
Dec 28, 1883
Jun 15, 1966
&
Virgie M. Ayers
Sep 2, 1887
Sep 9, 1964

Lizzie Ayers
1882-1940

Bertie Hickerson
1880-1951

Marvin, son of
R. L. & Olive Smith
Oct 12, 1905
Oct 8, 1909

Sarrah Sehons(e)
Jul 18, 1853
Feb 28, 1885

"Husband and Father"
Joe B. Isom
Jul 25, 1842
Dec 26, 1903

Mollie E. Isom
Feb 19, 1854
Mar 2, 1933

"Son"
Ira B. Isom
Mar 21, 1880
Jun 5, 1904

James G. Isom
1880-1940

Mabel J. Isom
1890-1955

R. F., son of
J. R. & M. A. Ensey
Nov 8, 1876
Feb 17, 1898
age: 21y, 3m, 9d.

James P. Taylor, Jr.
Sep 14, 1895
Sep 18, 1901

Josie, wife of
J. J. Roberts
Dec 23, 1878
Oct 25, 1924

Joseph J. Roberts
Mar 27, 1846
Apr 28, 1928

Sallie, wife of
J. J. Roberts
Dec 5, 1836
Jan 21, 1911

J. W. Meadows
Mar 29, 1837
Jul 12, 1900

James E. Holt
1861-1936
&
Annie M. Holt
1875-1953

Albert A. Caldwell
Mar 9, 1844
Apr 7, 1908
& wife
Rilla Caldwell
Apr 27, 1866
(no date)

Calvin Ayers
Jan 11, 1828
May 9, 187_
(broken in 3 pieces)

T. H. Ayers
Dec 16, 1834
Feb 28, 1912
&
Telitha Ayers
Dec 5, 1842
Jul 12, 1927

Elender E., daughter of
T. H. & Telitha Ayers
(dates in ground)

Meady Ayers
Jul 9, 1873
May 5, 1943

Louise Ayers Harris
Nov 25, 1861
Oct 5, 1949

William B. Ferrell
Jan 12, 1815
Aug 9, 1886

Eliza B., wife of
William B. Ferrell
Feb 1, 1823
Mar 30, 1896

J. C., wife of
B. L. THroneberry
May 14, 1875
Mar 3, 1899

B. P., son of
B. L. & J. C. Throneberry
Oct 3, 1898
Jul 13, 1899

J. P. Throneberry
Apr 11, 1840
Mar 5, 1916
&
Amandaville Throneberry
Feb 25, 1842
Apr 11, 1918

James Alford Throneberry
1905-1923

R. A. Sims
Jul 27, 1821
Jun 13, 1888
aged: 66y, 10m, --days.
(broken)

Margret, wife of
R. A. Sims
Jun 1, 1820
Jun 8, 1894

Mary R. Kimbro
Oct 31, 1905
Nov 28, 1905

Elizabeth Kimbro Brown
Sep 23, 1902
Dec 25, 1927

Walter C. Kimbro
Jan 22, 1875
Oct 7, 1934
&
Rebecca Jane Kimbro
Jun 26, 1880
Aug 17, 1957

S. D. Kimbro
Aug 1, 1870
Aug 18, 1937

Susie, wife of
B. M. Hill
Dec 25, 1863
Apr 6, 1910

Alice Marie, daughter of
H. M. & Reitta Hill
Jul 29, 1922
Jul 9, 1923

J. W. Minnis SNoddy
Jan 23, 1844
Mar 1, 1912

Almedia Snoddy
Mar 21, 1849
Jan 22, 1902

W. M. Ayers
Aug 10, 1794
Nov 11, 1878

Nellie Ayers
May 10, 1802
Oct 11, 1885

Thomas H. Maupin
(no dates)

Lillie Ada Maupin
1871-1953
(Thompson)

NOTE: There are 2 children
graves, no inscriptions

Dorothy Talley
1933-1938

-------- Shofner
Born (dates gone)
Died July 16, 1881

Mrs. Sallie Shofner
May 30, 1822
Mar 23, 1894

Mary A., daughter of
V. A. & J. W. Shofner
Oct 6, 1881
Oct 29, 1881

Ada Lou Burton
Jan 28, 1896
Dec 11, 1896

Willis Taylor, son of
S. W. & Kate Burton
Sep 4, 1888
May 2, 1907

Elias P. Meadows
Dec 21, 1852
Dec 18, 1919
&
Eliza C. Meadows
Dec 29, 1859
Mar 31, 1937

Alice P. Meadows
May 12, 1899
Nov 19, 1912

Infant daughter of
H. N. & Lettie Meadows
1920

Edward B. Snoddy
Oct 25, 1808
Sep 25, 1877

Mary Kathrine Snoddy
Jun 25, 1807
Jul 3, 1894

Barnett Luster
Mar 5, 1813
Jun 4, 1898

Charlotte H. Luster
Nov 27, 1825
Aug 25, 1881
aged: 55y, 8m, 28d.

D. M. Luster
Mar 25, 1864
Apr 19, 1886
aged: 22y & 24d.

W. Paul Brown
Dec 29, 1910
Jan 5, 1970
&
Margaret Isom Brown
Nov 20, 1915

Lt. Samuel William Gibbs, Jr.
Mar 16, 1917
Killed Aug 11, 1966
"Member of Tennessee Highway
Patrol"

Samuel Yates
May 10, 1812
May 25, 1884
age: 72y & 15d.
(marker broken)

E.(Eldridge) L. Yates
Jan 8, 1841
Feb 8, 1894

Willie Yates Baker
Aug 16, 1861
Dec 24, 1933

S. F. Holland
Jul 7, 1874
Dec 25, 1905

Mattie, wife of
J. J. Phillips
Mar 17, 1882
Jul 19, 1923 "Mother"

Myrtle Rigney
Oct 4, 1890
May 18, 1913

Nellie Mai, wife of
H. N. Meadows
Aug 18, 1895
Mar 12, 1917

45   DAVIDSON CEMETERY   Map 8

Located 3½ miles east-south-east of Wartrace, on Union
Ridge, site of the old Union Meeting House, on upper
side of a large black graveyard. Located by Jerry
Wayne Cook, 1983, copied by Marsh, April 1985.

In Memory of
John Davidson, Sr. (SOR)
who was born in the State of
North Carolina on the 26th
Oct 1764 & died the 29th Nov
1845, age 81 yrs, 1 mon, &
3 days.

Martha Davidson
Consort of John Davidson
Aged 63 years, ---- 1842.

Angeline J., daughter of
J. E. & E. J. Hough
Died Jun 18, 1852
Aged: 2y, 4m, 15days.

H. L. Brittain
Nov 20, 1837
Aug 1, 1854

In Memory of Hugh Davidson
who departed this life Sept
19th, 1841 in the 73 year of
his age

Jane Davidson
Nov 30, 1777
Jan 12, 1858

Samuel A., son of
John Q. & Susan S. Davidson
Died Nov 4, 1843
Aged: 2y, 11m, 11days.

James M., son of
John Q. & Susan S. Davidson
Died Mar 17, 1851
Aged: 2y, 6m, 11 days

W. C. D. (footstone)
(In same enclosure as
Samuel A. Davidson)

W. A. H. Bradshaw, son of
Rev. A. & H. Bradshaw
Dec 5, 1826
Jan 31, 1846

Narcissa D., daughter of
H. & A. Morgan
Aug 28, 1847
Feb 21, 1848

Angeline Morgan, late wife of
Harwood Morgan & daughter of
Hugh & Jane Davidson
Jul 26, 1806
Aug 16, 1848

[William P. Campbell married
Permelia Hord, dau of Edmund
& Mary Hord]

William P. Campbell
Aug 3, 1802
Jun 7, 1841

_____ Campbell
Born Jan --, ----(broken)
Died Aug 24, 1840

William H. Campbell
Nov 1, 1834
Jul 25, 1839

_____y S. Campbell
Born Mar 22, 1837
Died Aug --, 1852 (broken)

[All the old vaults are broke
and scattered. Abandoned lon
ago]

---

10   DOZIER CEMETERY   Map 3

Located three quarter mile west of 231 North, on Big Spring
Road. 2 miles north northwest of Deason.

Zachariah Dozier
Feb 12, 1800
Feb 20, 1870

Cynthia Ann Dozier
Dec 21, 1818
Jul 5, 1885

Walter Dozier
Feb 7, 1881
Aug 29, 1886

[No markers found, this was
once the Dozier farm]

---

50   UNKNOWN CEMETERY   Map # 10   Page 193

Located one mile northwest of Richmond, Tennessee.

DAVID REAVIS, 1758-1852, born in Northampton County, North Carolina, served in the Revolution under Francis Marion. He
came to Bedford County, Tennessee in ca 1817. Settled on land where this graveyard is located, near Branchville, and
died here. Reavis families of Bedford, Lincoln, Moore and Marshall descend from David and Patience Reavis.

---

8   GUY CEMETERY   Map # 3   Page 42

MAJOR WILLIAM GUY settled here in ca 1814-15 on the north east corner of the Matthew Locke North Carolina 5000 acre
Grant. He lived first west of the present location near the old Middleton or Murfreesboro Road, moving to the present
site in 1837 where he erected a spacious brick house on the turnpike. He had one known child, Eliza, who married
Dr. Preston Frazier son of Hugh and Jane Frazier. They continued to live here after Major Guy's death. The property
descended to the wife of Rev. T. S. McFerrin, a Methodist Minister who later retired to raising thoroughbred horses
there at Roseland. Mrs. Frazier caused a Methodist Church to be built a short distance north of the house. Part of
the Army of the Cumberland camped here in the winter of 1862. Rev. J. B. McFerrin often called the father of Method-
ism in middle Tennessee, later to head the Methodist Publishing House in Nashville, wintered with the troops here in
the capacity of Chaplain. Many grave markers once here were destroyed, only those noted on page 42 remain today.

---

24   PISGAH CEMETERY   Map # 6   Page 67

This graveyard was used first by the John Sanders family
who were Pioneer Settlers here. Sometime after the graveyard was copied by the Compilers, the following marker was
dug out of the ground by Buck Claxton of Shelbyville.

Sallie, wife of
John Claxton
Jun 10, 1802
Jul 24, 1835
"Mother"

This cemetery is located on land once owned by Moses and Jane Yell, early settlers in the area, who are probably buried here in unmarked graves. They were living nearby when they died. This is an old graveyard and has many unmarked graves. The Old Mr. Moriah Methodist Episcopal Church stood on the lower side of the graveyard. Also buried here in unmarked graves are Thomas N. and Frances (Moore) Stokes. This cemetery is located on part of a 5000 acre North Carolina Grant patented to John G. and Thomas Blount and later purchased by General Andrew Jackson.

5   THREE FORKS CHURCH CEMETERY   Map # 12   Page 291

This graveyard grew around the Three Forks Meeting House, a Cumberland Presbyterian Church, that was started as a Camp Ground by Reverends Samuel King and William McGee, Co-founders of the Cumberland Presbyterian Denomination in 1810. They jointly owned and erected the Mills at Three Forks near by. Rev. McGee died in 1817, members of his family moved to Missouri in the 1820s. Rev. King also made the westward move about the same time. The Old Church stood to the rear of the graveyard by the lane that ran down to the river to Rev. McGee's house.

42   PORTER-CORTNER CEMETERY   Map # 10   Page 291

In 1812, Nathaniel Porter purchased 1088 acres of the George Doherty 5000 acre North Carolina Grant. Sinking Creek ran through this tract, where he erected Porter's Mill. Porter died in 1813. The land changed hands many times after the Porter family disposed of it, later it was home of Meredith Gentry, one time Politation and Orator of some note.

12   MARSH CEMETERY   Map # 10   Page 177

In 1975, all markers were standing and graves intact. Later after the Sub-division of this farm once owned by the Jordan and Marsh families, events were set in motion that has resulted in the demise of this graveyard. Little is left of the original today. A Memorial Marker has been placed by descendants in the Churchyard at New Bethel Baptist Church nearby, which was built on part of the Marsh land, once owned by Michael and Elizabeth (Landing) Marsh, natives of Hertford and Gates Counties, North Carolina. Members of the Zachariah Jordan family are buried in this graveyard in graves once marked by native field stones.

10   NEW BETHEL CEMETERY   Map # 10   Page 171

Memorial to
MARSH

Michael   Elizabeth
1800-1859   1800-1875

They owned this land that was conveyed by Deed to the Trustees of the New Bethel Baptist Church on December 18, 1883. They along with three children, George, Elizabeth and Caladonia are buried in the family graveyard approximately 1800 feet south-southeast.

EDITOR'S NOTE

We have been asked from time to time why we did not copy the New Section of Willow Mount, that lies to the south and west of the older Section, also, the Memorial Gardens. The reasons are twofold, first, by copying all the newer graves, the book would have been so large that publishing and printing problems would have been encountered. Secondly, the primary purpose of copying and publishing cemetery records is to "publish" and preserve older graveyards and gravestone records for genealogical and family research. "It is a book of records", that cannot be found elsewhere. Information on newer burials can be readily obtained from newspapers, funeral homes, and vital state statistics. Naturally in all other graveyards the new were copied with the old.

44   MT. LEBANON CEMETERY   Map # 6

J. C. J. Paschal	&	Rachel, his wife	&	J. H. Paschal	&	Mary R. Paschal
Sep 28, 1841		May 17, 1844		Jul 18, 1879		Feb 6, 1885
Mar 28, 1920		Mar 8, 1910		Apr 7, 1889		Aug 15, 1885
&				&		
E. B. Paschal	&	Zilpha J. Paschal	&	H. J. Muse		
Sep 2, 1867		Sep 24, 1876		Mar 18, 1843		
Dec 7, 1883		Jan 9, 1899		Mar 10, 1908		

333

339